1495

A Class of Their Own

A CLASS OF THEIR OWN

Black Teachers in the
Segregated South

ADAM FAIRCLOUGH

THE BELKNAP PRESS OF
HARVARD UNIVERSITY PRESS
Cambridge, Massachusetts
London, England
2007

Library of Congress Cataloging-in-Publication Data

Fairclough, Adam, 1952–
A class of their own : black teachers in the
segregated south / Adam Fairclough.
p.   cm.
Includes bibliographical references and index.
ISBN 13: 978-0-674-02307-9 (alk. paper)
ISBN 10: 0-674-02307-2 (alk. paper)
1. African American teachers—Southern states—History.
2. African Americans—Education—Southern states—History.
3. Segregation in education—United States.
4. African American educators—Southern states—History.
5. Southern states—Race relations.
I. Title.

LC2802.S9 F35   2006
371.10089/96073 22   2006049874

Designed by Gwen Nefsky Frankfeldt

To the memory of
Siabreen Fairclough
(1958–2004)

Contents

Abbreviations

ABHMS	American Baptist Home Missionary Society
ACSSN	Association of Colleges and Secondary Schools for Negroes
AFSC	American Friends Service Committee
AFT	American Federation of Teachers
AMA	American Missionary Association
AME Church	African Methodist Episcopal Church
AMEZ Church	African Methodist Episcopal Zion Church
ASNLH	Association for the Study of Negro Life and History
ASTA	Alabama State Teachers Association
ATA	American Teachers Association
CIC	Commission on Interracial Cooperation
CME Church	Colored Methodist Episcopal Church
CORE	Congress of Racial Equality
FEPC	Fair Employment Practices Committee
GEB	General Education Board
GTEA	Georgia Teachers and Education Association
HBCUs	historically black colleges and universities
LCTA	Louisiana Colored Teachers Association
LDF	NAACP Legal Defense and Educational Fund
LEA	Louisiana Education Association
MEC	Methodist Episcopal Church
NAACP	National Association for the Advancement of Colored People
NACW	National Association of Colored Women
NATCS	National Association of Teachers in Colored Schools
NBC	National Baptist Convention
NCOSTA	National Conference of State Teachers Associations
NCSTA	North Carolina State Teachers Association
NEA	National Education Association
SCLC	Southern Christian Leadership Conference
SNCC	Student Nonviolent Coordinating Committee
VTA	Virginia Teachers Association

There is more fascination and interest in this work of Negro education than there is in hunting for gold mines.

Booker T. Washington, 1913

The Odyssey of Black Teachers

Yesteryear many decisions were made which seemed undesirable and spineless. As we have grown older . . . we can see why these things were done and at what a high cost to the individuals who were noble and strong enough to make them.

Brice F. Taylor, 1960

Pleasant Green School, Marlinton, Pocahontas County, West Virginia.

Lewis Hine Collection, Library of Congress,
Prints and Photographs Division

In 1933 a white anthropologist watched in amazement as Lillian P. Rogers, a black teacher whom she knew to be "a strong, self-respecting person," entered the office of the schools superintendent of Sunflower County, Mississippi. In the presence of this white official, Rogers's "vibrant personality" disappeared. "She was the essence of meekness: eyes downcast, accepting with a smile being called 'Annie' by white people . . . [and] waiting patiently to speak to Mr. Smith, who saw all whites first regardless of the time of their arrival, and who remained seated when, standing, she finally talked with him." Afterward, with a cynical chuckle, Rogers explained that submissiveness was the best way to get better buildings, textbooks, and equipment for black schools.

As a "Jeanes teacher"—a supervisor of other black teachers in the county—Lillian Rogers possessed more influence than most. Yet the techniques she employed were typical of black teachers during the age of segregation. When dealing with whites, black teachers could not demand; they could only request, persuade, and manipulate. Black communities acknowledged these limitations, and they supported and respected black teachers as long as the latter displayed integrity and commitment. Lillian Rogers was not only the most influential African American in Sunflower County, she was also "admired and liked by all the Negroes."[1]

Being a black teacher during the age of white supremacy demanded faith in the future when the present often seemed hopeless. It asked for patience and self-possession when interactions with white people entailed ritual humiliation. For many it also meant not-so-genteel poverty. Until the 1940s, black teachers received the equivalent of a laborer's pay but had to dress like ladies and gentlemen, buy books and teaching supplies, and spend part of their salaries attending summer schools. To survive, they also farmed, preached, dug ditches, and washed clothes. Many would rather have been lawyers, journalists, businesspeople, or government workers—anything but teachers—had they not been so restricted by discrimination. But others regarded teaching as a missionary calling and devoted their lives to unselfish service.

To the chief architect of integration, the National Association for the Advancement of Colored People (NAACP), the abolition of segregated black schools was a price worth paying in order to secure a better education for all black children. It considered these schools irredeemably second-rate. Besides, the South's schools were segregated by laws that had been passed by white people. These laws codified and systematized racism. They symbolized a refusal by whites to associate with blacks on the basis of equality. They implied that African Americans were inferior people and turned them into inferior citizens. They discriminated *against* blacks. Segregated schools were part of a broad system of white supremacy—commonly known as Jim Crow—that oppressed blacks in virtually every sphere of their lives. They were just as much a part of that system as were sharecropping, job discrimination, denial of the right to vote, all-white juries, and lynching.

Yet it was not so much racial "separateness" that vexed black southerners as the principle of legal segregation, and the misallocation of resources that accompanied it. The primary aim of integration was to secure better schools, not to mix with whites. This produced a paradox. Blacks liked the sense of community and solidarity that segregated schools fostered. But they disliked segregation by law, on white terms, and the denial of equal opportunity. When the late 1960s finally brought wholesale school integration to the South, black pupils, parents, and teachers felt deeply ambivalent. They welcomed the passing of Jim Crow but also mourned the loss of institutions that boasted long histories and proud traditions. Alongside the church, the school had been the institutional and emotional anchor of black life under segregation. When he learned that integration would mean the closure of his high school in Franklin, Tennessee, Harvey Chrisman "just broke down and cried." Across the South, black students experienced similar feelings as they transferred to formerly white schools. Shock, sadness, and anger muted any sense of elation over a long-delayed civil rights victory.[2]

No group of people felt the closure of black schools more keenly than black teachers—even though many accepted the desirability of integration. The discontinuation of segregated black schools drastically altered the teacher's position in the community. For about one hundred years, from 1870 to 1970, black teachers instructed the vast majority of black children inside all-black schools. Segregation—sometimes voluntary, sometimes imposed by whites—had nurtured black solidarity and black leadership. Ever since Reconstruction, black teachers had acted as community leaders, interracial diplomats, and builders of black institutions. Integration undermined those functions and diminished the relative status of black teachers. For some black teachers, integration brought demotion or dismissal.

The abolition of segregated black schools weakened the strong sense of educational mission that had characterized the work of black teachers. To a far greater extent than their white counterparts, black teachers had identified with their schools. Although Jim Crow schools had labored under grave handicaps—they rarely matched in material terms what white schools offered—segregation fostered a special sense of commitment among black teachers that helped to compensate for poor buildings, scanty equipment, and lack of books. Many black schools owed their existence and growth to the vision and dedication of black teachers. Hence some teachers interpreted the closure of their schools as a personal rebuff, a negative verdict on their professional competence. "We were in shock, we were hurt, we were disappointed," recalled Robert Reynolds of Booker T. Washington High School in Columbia, South Carolina. "We felt betrayed."[3]

When the Supreme Court decided in 1954 that segregated public schools were unconstitutional, it mortally wounded the South's system of white supremacy and helped spark the civil rights movement. It was a brave and necessary decision. However, the failure of integrated schools to live up to their promise has led to a belated recognition that many segregated black schools of the pre-*Brown* era had been successful institutions. A few were as academically successful as the best white schools. Moreover, the central assertion of the *Brown* decision—that segregated schools generated feelings of inferiority in the black children who attended them—has never been proven. In fact, the more we learn about those segregated schools, the more dubious that assertion seems. Black teachers inspired and motivated generations of African American children, instilling values and knowledge that nourished racial pride and a desire for equality. Indeed, as Robert H. Jackson noted in a private memorandum to his fellow Supreme Court justices, it was the very success of segregated schools in raising educational standards among blacks that made integration feasible.[4]

THIS study is neither a panegyric for Jim Crow schools nor an encomium for black teachers. Rather, it analyzes what the men and women who taught in the segregated schools, colleges, and universities of the South actually did. Although that story has been told in part, no book provides us with an overview of what African American teachers attempted and achieved. There are biographies aplenty and numerous histories of schools and colleges. Studies of school integration would fill a small library. A few ambitious books chart the contours of black education since emancipation. But nobody has written the history of black teachers as a group, tracking that history over a hundred years. Yet a study of black teachers is indispensable for understanding how blacks and whites interacted and coexisted after the abolition of slavery. It illuminates how black communities came into being and coped with the challenges of freedom and oppression.

Chronicling the odyssey of black teachers from emancipation in 1865 to integration one hundred years later is a challenging undertaking. To write about African American teachers over a period of a century, and to define as a teacher *anyone* engaged in education, might appear impossibly ambitious. On the face of it, the thousands of women who toiled in the little schoolhouses of the rural South had little in common with the eighty or so men who presided over black colleges and universities. How can one usefully compare Charles S. Johnson, the world-renowned sociologist and president of Fisk University, with Priscilla T. Mainer, who taught in a one-room public school in Bulloch County, Georgia? Moreover, the changes that affected every aspect of education since the end of the Civil War—from the way teachers were trained to the textbooks they use—make the compression of a hundred years into a single volume a risky endeavor. The age of the computer and the Internet makes the era of the slate, the dunce's cap, and the blue-back speller seem impossibly remote.

Yet the era of segregation was a distinct historical epoch with a beginning, middle, and end. Its history is best understood if it is told in full. Black ambivalence over school integration makes no sense unless one investigates the origins of black public schools and the emergence in the late nineteenth century of an all-black teaching force. The distinctiveness of the segregation era also allows us to include black teachers of every description: the forces of white supremacy acted upon them all. Although segregated schools were not wholly the creation of white racism—many blacks preferred to be taught by and among their own kind—antiblack prejudice molded the system of separate schools and stunted black education. For most of this period whites dominated and exploited the black minority, and they believed it was essential to limit black education. One way they attempted to do this was to restrict the education of black teachers. It is a truism that all education is political. In the American South, where the race issue was raw and often violent, the link between education and politics was brutally clear. Black teachers were on the front line in battles over education.

The issue of leadership reinforced black teachers' sense of common identity. Teachers shared a belief that education would liberate the black masses from ignorance, degradation, and poverty. They insisted that the colored race would sink or swim according to the education they received. A people impoverished by slavery and benighted by enforced ignorance urgently required lessons in freedom. Whether their classrooms were in redbrick, Gothic-towered universities or ram-

— 7 —

shackle schoolhouses of rough-sawn planks, teachers saw themselves as leaders of the race and considered themselves, to use modern parlance, role models. "If it is true that the salvation of the Negro lies in his being educated," affirmed Arthur St. George Richardson, a native of the Bermudas who taught in Georgia and Florida, "then to the Negro teacher must be attributed the greater portion of his salvation."[5]

Black teachers accompanied their faith in the power of education with a strong sense of historical mission. Following the disorganization of civil war and emancipation, African Americans reconstituted stable communities. Despite smatterings of racial integration during Reconstruction, it quickly became clear that blacks and whites would live apart for the foreseeable future. Teachers were strategically placed to influence emergent black communities at a time when they were fluid and malleable. Many believed that God had called them to perform a particular work of redemption. The presidential address of Rev. G. M. Elliott to the Alabama State Teachers Association, delivered in Selma in 1888, typified a thousand such clarion calls: "Teachers, you are the shapers of thought and the molders of sentiment, not of this age and of this generation alone, but of ages and generations to come. You are making history by those you teach. You are the few that are molding the masses."[6]

African Americans were not the only teachers, of course, who saw themselves as bearers of progress and civilization. Advocates of mass education in the nineteenth century, black and white alike, shared a fervent belief in the power of schools to improve society. In the South, which lagged decades behind the North in the development of public schools, and where evangelical religion exerted a particularly strong influence, this missionary impulse persisted well into the twentieth century.[7] Even after the First World War, when education became increasingly bureaucratic, professional, and secular, many black teachers still thought of teaching as a religious duty and continued to invest education with an almost mystical power. In the middle of the Great Depression—which for some blacks exposed a fallacy in believing that education could build a better world—Ambrose Caliver, the highest-ranking black official in the U.S. Office of Education, wrote, "In the hands of the Negro teacher rests the destiny of the race." Black teachers, he insisted, "must be dominated by a passion for service, motivated by a love for humanity, and guided by the ideals of the Master Teacher."[8]

In many respects, the experiences of black teachers were similar to those of white teachers, particularly in rural schools of the nineteenth and early twentieth centuries. Reading the memoirs of a country teacher—the crowded one-room schoolhouse, the barefooted children, the erratic attendance, the rough discipline—one would be hard put to tell the author's race. The most obvious difference between white and black schools was that the latter had less of everything. To put it crudely, if the white schools were bad, the black ones were worse. But a history of black education that focused solely upon the material disparities between white and black schools—a subject that has been exhaustively explored already—would fail to reveal how black teachers acted as leaders in their communities.

Teachers made up the backbone of the black middle class, and were, along with ministers, the most important source of black leadership. Literacy was so scarce among the freedmen that those who possessed it quickly attained influence. The literate few furnished the first black teachers, as well as many of the politicians and preachers. In practice, these categories overlapped: Black preachers taught; teachers and preachers engaged in politics. Indeed, blacks who aspired to political position, if they possessed any degree of literacy, often turned to teaching as a means of building political constituencies. The ambitions of these teacher-politicians sometimes brought them into sharp conflict with the white missionaries from the North, who provided most of the teachers in the first freedmen's schools after the Civil War.[9]

When the white missionaries returned North and Reconstruction ended, black teachers pushed for the expansion of public school systems and organized themselves as a profession. State by state, they formed associations that opposed Democratic efforts to deny tax money to black public schools, and which lobbied for the establishment of state-funded normal schools and universities. As the lines of racial segregation hardened, black teachers campaigned to replace the white teachers who monopolized the best positions in the black public schools. They also pressed the northern missionary associations active in the South to employ black teachers in their white-staffed colleges and universities.[10]

Black teachers argued vigorously and sometimes bitterly about politics and education. Loss of the franchise, and the tightening of racial segregation, intensified those arguments. The failure of Reconstruction prompted many teachers to question the value of political activity. Disenfranchisement and the decline in black political officeholding caused teachers to seek nonpolitical strategies for strengthening black schools. Some, like Booker T. Washington, argued that politics was an irrelevant distraction from moral and economic improvement. Others believed that accepting anything less than Constitutional equality would be the height of folly—tantamount to a betrayal of the race. Nevertheless, ideological differences never prevented teachers from regarding themselves as a leadership class or recognizing that they shared many basic values, especially a belief in the liberating potential of education.

Disenfranchisement eliminated officeholding by blacks, leaving teachers and ministers as the main representatives of the black community. There was tension between the two groups, who sometimes operated as rivals. Still, the continuing overlap of religion and education sustained a missionary vision among black teachers. At the same time, segregation encouraged a drive toward racial autonomy in both church and school. "The providence of God," claimed teacher-minister G. M. Elliott, made black teachers responsible for deciding "what the Negro in America is to be, what the Negro in Africa is to be, and in short what the Negro in the world is to be."[11]

Racial discrimination and abject poverty compelled black teachers to act as community leaders. Teachers had to create and sustain schools. They struggled to attract and retain patrons; to procure buildings, furniture, and equipment; to ensure regular sources of income; to neutralize white hostility and cultivate white support. Teachers were institution builders, on both a small and a large scale. They founded schools and colleges and often devoted their lives to them.

Teachers did not work alone, of course. Blacks, and sometimes whites, donated land and lumber. Black farmers gave their labor to erect school buildings. Black parents paid tuition fees to augment the teacher's pay. Even when black schools were adopted by local school boards, the public subsidy provided little more than a teacher's salary for perhaps four months of the year. Black trustees boarded the teachers, provided fuel in winter, and kept the schoolhouse in repair. Parent-teacher associations raised money for supplies and improvements. Black private schools secured gifts from wealthy whites, and the cultivation of northern benefactors demanded months of bone-wearying travel by principals, teachers, and singing quartets. Hundreds of private schools founded between 1880 and 1920 depended almost entirely upon black support. Local Baptist associations, for example, sustained dozens of elementary and secondary schools in Louisiana, Virginia, and other states.

For their own leadership, teachers looked most often to the black universities, colleges, and normal schools. These institutions trained an influential minority of black teachers and reached a far larger number of public school teachers—many of whom had never got beyond secondary or even elementary school—by providing annual summer schools. The presidents of black colleges were articulate advocates for black education. They represented schoolteachers by heading their professional associations, dealt with white politicians and public officials, lobbied the federal government, and negotiated with philanthropic foundations. Some of them—Booker T. Washington, Charles S. Johnson, Mary McLeod Bethune—became nationally prominent figures.

The black colleges loom large in a history of black teachers. For most of this period the distance between the college and the elementary school was not great. "Higher education" for blacks often existed in name only. Black "universities" started out as elementary schools, concentrated for many years on the secondary grades, and only in the 1920s became institutions devoted entirely to college-level education. Similarly, most of the pupils who attended the innumerable "academies," "institutes," and "colleges" that flourished between the 1880s and the 1920s studied at the elementary and secondary levels. In other words, scarcity of resources, and the historical circumstances that compelled black education to start virtually from scratch, made black educators continually aware of how much they had in common. Lest they forget those common interests, white attacks upon higher education for blacks provided repeated reminders. Whoever controlled black higher education could influence the overall quality of the thousands of ordinary schoolteachers. College teachers and schoolteachers swam or sank together.

When the civil rights movement questioned the value of segregated schools and elevated loud protest over quiet diplomacy, black teachers were largely displaced as community leaders. Moreover, integration rendered the long history of black educational initiative, spearheaded by black teachers, virtually invisible. Many of the black public high schools created between the 1930s and the 1950s originated in private schools founded by black teachers decades earlier. In the 1960s and 1970s they became casualties of integration: phased out, downgraded, their names changed. Virtually nothing remains of what were the most common type of black school from Reconstruction to the 1950s—the myriad one- and two-room schoolhouses that once dotted the rural South. Even the five thousand or so "Rosenwald schools" that were built between 1917 and 1932—model schoolhouses for their time—became redundant; some of these wooden structures stand, but they are no longer in service as schools. A few of the private schools founded by black teachers in the late nineteenth and early twentieth centuries survive as today's "HBCUs" (historically black colleges and universities). Some, like Grambling State University in Louisiana and Albany State University in Georgia, were absorbed into state higher education systems. Others, like Huston-Tillotson College in Austin, Texas, and Bethune-Cookman College in Daytona, Florida, hang on as private institutions.

The disappearance of the black high schools owed much to political malice and bureaucratic vandalism by southern white school boards. But their disappearance also stemmed from indifference and insensitivity on the part of supporters of integration. To integrationists, blacks as well as whites, the history of segregated black schools was less a past to be celebrated than a record of failure to be erased.

When the early promise of school integration turned sour, black communities lamented the loss of these institutions and tried to recover their histories. Alumni associations now faithfully guard the memory of long-defunct high schools. Historians, amateur and academic, craft loving accounts of their birth, life, and death. In hundreds of oral histories, retired teachers and former pupils have bequeathed to posterity their memories of these schools. The belief that Jim Crow schools were terminally second-rate—purveyors of academic under-achievement and perpetuators of second-class citizenship—is being challenged and even supplanted. Dozens of institutional histories portray the segregated black high schools as centers of scholarly excellence that were populated by dedicated and caring teachers, principals of almost superhuman industry and wisdom, and pupils who repaid their teachers' devotion with respect and hard work. According to these accounts, such schools involved parents, served as neighborhood centers, and were objects of pride for the black community. Their loss constituted a historical tragedy.[12]

Yet a praiseworthy desire to rescue segregated schools from oblivion runs the danger of producing a hagiographic history that is as one-sided as the integrationist critique of segregated schools. We can acknowledge that segregated schools, despite their inadequacies, possessed certain strengths. But we should not be blinded to their failings by the shortcomings of today's integrated schools—which are partly shortcomings of present-day schools in general. Segregated schools did not symbolize a golden era of community stability and educational progress. Uncritical celebration of segregated black schools obscures the extent to which white supremacy blighted black education. Segregation institutionalized the denial of equal opportunity. It meant that separate could hardly ever be equal.

Historians of black education place great stress on the importance of black initiative, and blacks' desire to control their own institutions. "The history of black education is a study in black self-help," asserts one. Yet blacks were far too impecunious to sustain a system of universal education through self-help alone. According to the survey undertaken by Thomas Jesse Jones on behalf of the U.S. Bureau of Education, the 625 private schools for blacks that existed in 1916 taught fewer than 1 percent of the 1,175,000 black pupils attending elementary schools. Of the 24,189 black children enrolled in secondary grades, private schools taught the majority. But that enrollment represented less than 2 percent of black children aged fifteen to nineteen years. Moreover, less than half of these private schools were owned and taught by blacks. As Jones noted in his survey, "Inadequacy and poverty are the outstanding characteristics of every type and grade of education for Negroes."[13]

What this meant, in blunt terms, was that blacks had to seek financial assistance from whites if they were to furnish even rudimentary schooling for most black children. When African Americans voted, black teachers could wield political influence to back up their calls for an equitable share of state funds. Even after Reconstruction, black leaders traded votes with white politicians in return for schools and teaching jobs. Disenfranchisement, however, radically altered the position of black teachers. They had no black politicians to represent their cause, and no political pressure to exert upon the all-powerful, all-white Democratic Party. The survival, let alone the improvement, of black schools became overwhelmingly dependent upon the goodwill of whites. In the age of segregation, black teachers approached whites as powerless supplicants.

The northern philanthropic foundations formed in the early twentieth century—the General Education Board, the Anna T. Jeanes Foundation, the Julius Rosenwald Fund, and the Phelps-Stokes Fund—provided a modicum of support for black education. By the 1920s that aid was substantial. These foundations provided black teachers with powerful allies, cushioning them against the extremes of southern racism. For black teachers, however, philanthropic support entailed yet another form of dependency. White philanthropists not only pulled the purse strings but also looked to native white southerners, not blacks, to advise them how to spend their money. In addition, the success of the foundations' efforts to expand public education further limited the independence of black teachers. The multiplication of black public schools—first elementary schools, then high schools—meant that a growing percentage of the overall funding devoted to black education fell under the control of white politicians. Then came the Great Depression, which caused most of the private black schools to either close their doors or throw themselves on the mercy of local school boards, tightening white control yet again. Ironically, as black schooling improved, black autonomy in education declined.

This condition of dependency rendered the leadership role of teachers highly ambiguous. Between the 1890s and the 1950s, the classic era of segregation, most black teachers resorted to accommodationism in one form or another. Accommodationism meant accepting the political reality of white supremacy and abandoning, for the moment at least, the Reconstruction project of civil and political equality. It could also mean criticizing the shortcomings of black people rather than attacking the prejudice of whites. It often entailed employing deference and flattery to plead for, rather then demand, concessions from whites. Only a few black teachers, mainly the dwindling group of men and women who headed private institutions, enjoyed enough independence to risk being assertive and outspoken.

Dependency made teachers vulnerable to manipulation by whites. Politicians expected black teachers to discourage militancy or radicalism. They called upon teachers to "represent" the black community in the expectation that they would toe the line. They asked teachers to be their eyes and ears within the black community, even to act as spies and informers. While teachers could argue that their cautious tactics secured tangible benefits for black schools, and that accommodationism represented constructive racial diplomacy, a growing number of black critics—including not a few teachers—questioned whether the game was worth the candle. Glacial progress hardly justified submissiveness when the gap between black and white widened. The "goodwill" and "racial cooperation" that black teachers constantly invoked appeared to do little to weaken white supremacy. The recognition that whites accorded colored "professors" and "doctors" symbolized condescension, not respect. Teachers often acted as if they spoke for the black community, but many suspected them of looking out for their own self-interest.

The vehement opposition that Booker T. Washington evoked among blacks exemplified the controversial nature of accommodationism. Teachers faced continual criticism that they were selling the race short and even betraying it. Withering portrayals of corrupt, dictatorial college presidents, which reached their apogee in Saunders Redding's

Stranger and Alone (1950) and Ralph Ellison's *Invisible Man* (1952), vented widespread cynicism about black educators. These novels presented villainous caricatures that gleefully punctured the sanctimonious image of the black teacher as a heroic builder, selfless servant, and wise leader. Like the equally one-sided literature of racial uplift, exemplified by Washington's autobiography *Up from Slavery* (1901), they depicted, in an exaggerated form, one face of black education. It would be a gross error to treat Ellison's Dr. Bledsoe as a realistic or representative figure. "You laid it on a bit thick," complained Horace Mann Bond, himself a college president, to Ellison. But although overdone, this literature of betrayal is a salutary reminder of the flimsy and double-edged character of southern black leadership in the era of white supremacy. It is a theme that resonates in many of the best historical studies of black education.[14]

The relationship of black teachers to the black community was like that of the black minister, only more tenuous. Indeed, a comparison of teachers and ministers discloses important differences in the ways these groups functioned as leaders. Because Christianity was already well established under slavery, black preachers used their knowledge of the Bible and their ability to move people through the spoken word to quickly establish themselves as leaders of the freed people. They strengthened their authority by countering the proselytizing efforts of the white churches. They organized congregations, acquired or erected church buildings, and set up separate denominations. Ministers thus became powerful figures—often rated the *most* powerful—among African Americans. The fact that blacks owned their own church buildings, that ministers were independent of whites, and that religion provided emotional solace for all, regardless of education, made the church the strongest black institution. It was the most direct expression, physically and spiritually, of individual black communities.

Teachers were a part of, but also apart from, the larger black population. The fact that public school teachers were appointed by white superintendents and paid by white school boards distinguished them from ministers. However, their economic dependence probably mattered less to ordinary blacks—most of whom were also dependent upon white employers—than their role as bearers of a different kind of culture. While blacks understood the value of education, many found the language of education strange and forbidding. Ministers attuned their language to their church members, who were poorly educated, often illiterate, and responsive to eloquence rather than erudition. Teachers, by contrast, communicated in an entirely different way. They sought to *change* the way blacks spoke, thought, and behaved—to raise blacks to their level and encourage them to adopt different values. Whereas the church emphasized the unity between the minister and his congregation—exemplified by the "call and response" pattern of the preacher's sermon—the school stressed the separation of the teacher from the community.

The very process of education set up tensions between teachers, children, and parents. One kind of tension estranged the teacher from the community. The mere fact of being educated fostered feelings of alienation in teachers. Aware that their skills, values, and interests differed from those of the masses, they acquired a consciousness of difference and even superiority. "Numbers of us," warned an early graduate of Hampton Institute, "seem to allow our ideas to soar so loftily while we are away improving ourselves until it is difficult to stoop to the lower grades of our people." Even if they guarded against snobbery, it was hard not to think in terms of higher and lower, inferior and superior. Teachers everywhere bemoaned the "ignorance" and "superstition" that they saw all around them. Those who prized books often felt painfully isolated, unable to discuss ideas and literature. Moreover, unless teachers reverted to black vernacular, which many of them had never picked up, their "correct" English made everyday communication a trial. In 1875 Charles W. Chesnutt, then teaching in rural North Carolina, complained, "The people don't know words enough for a fellow to carry on a conversation with them. He must reduce his phraseology several degrees lower than that of the first reader." Speech became a key indicator of class difference.[15]

Another kind of tension, the resistance of unlettered blacks to the values of education, produced a different form of alienation between teacher and community. Virtually all studies of black schooling, from the reports of the Freedmen's Bureau to studies by historians today, stress black enthusiasm for education. Only rarely do they mention skepticism, indifference, and hostility. Yet the letters of black teachers were full of complaints about how difficult it was to persuade parents to support schools. Simple poverty meant that many parents could not afford tuition fees. Even when offered free schools, parents often refused to send their children. Black farmers depended upon family labor: the more hands the better. The demands of cotton and tobacco meant that, as under slavery, all but the smallest children worked. Many parents, especially fathers, believed that keeping children home was an economic necessity. Black autobiographies and oral histories offer bitter memories of fathers and stepfathers who angrily insisted that children work rather than go to school. The value of education was not at all clear to sharecroppers whose primary goal was the acquisition of land. Blacks in the rural South often questioned the notion that education was the main route, let alone the sole route, out of poverty and dependency.[16]

Even when public elementary schools became well established, and attendance was the rule rather than the exception, children often disliked their experience of the classroom. Based on his studies of rural schools in the 1930s, sociologist Charles S. Johnson concluded that the values of black teachers often conflicted with those of their patrons. Caught up in a "desperate struggle for existence," many sharecroppers and laborers failed to see the practical value of education beyond the rudiments of the "three R's." For the poorest children, in particular, school was a place of bewilderment and failure, "a serious and disturbing emotional adventure." As one would expect, people who were skeptical about schools did little to encourage their own children to persevere. In this respect, blacks differed little from whites, many of whom also hated the classroom for many of the same reasons. Indeed, the cultural conflict between middle-class teachers and working-class pupils is a major theme of recent work on the history of public education. Not surprisingly, some blacks directed their hostility to schooling against the teachers themselves. "They don't like to see anyone of their rank get above them," complained a Virginia teacher in 1876. "They say I am stuck up, because I don't stand on the corner of streets and in store doors with them."[17]

Racial chauvinism reinforced class resentment. Educated blacks sometimes attracted derision for emulating the speech and mannerisms of white people. Recalling his childhood in late nineteenth-century Georgia, Richard R. Wright Jr. wrote, "When one spoke correctly, he was sometimes ridiculed and called 'proper' or 'white folksy.'" An instinctive desire to seek security within the group, and a corresponding fear that to become educated was to risk isolation from the group, fed distrust of education. This anti-intellectualism prevented large numbers of African Americans from fulfilling their academic potential.[18]

It would be false, then, to depict teachers as community leaders who enjoyed unalloyed support from parents and pupils. Indeed, it was a source of frustration to many teachers that ministers commanded greater prestige and influence within black communities. The fact that so many ill-educated ministers taught school—and often failed to observe the strict personal morality expected of other teachers—increased that resentment. Graduates of the black colleges and normal schools looked askance at the semiliterate "preacher-teachers." As the patchwork of public schools developed into a proper system, secular and religious values in education came into conflict. Booker T. Washington, for example, castigated the majority of black ministers for being ill-trained and dissolute, and accused the church of fostering an intolerant sectarianism that impeded the work of education, especially efforts to improve public schools. Few teachers could afford to be so outspoken, knowing that an influential minister could make or break a school. However, many silently deplored sectarianism and obscurantism, seeking to work around, rather than against, black ministers.

THE most trenchant analysis of black teachers as leaders came from the acid pen of Carter G. Woodson, the indefatigable promoter of Negro history. In *The Mis-Education of the Negro* (1933), Woodson singled out teachers for letting the race down. Far from facilitating the liberation of the Negro from poverty and oppression, he argued, teachers failed to encourage the kind of race pride that nurtured group strength. Class distinctions explained part of this failure. Like middle-class people everywhere, educated blacks tended to look down upon the lower classes. But educated blacks seemed to have contempt for their own race, Woodson asserted. He attributed this disdain to the education that black teachers had received at the hands of white missionary teachers from the North. Unlike both Washington and Du Bois, who lauded the missionaries for their Christlike sincerity of purpose, Woodson excoriated these whites for treating the freedmen as if they were primitives to be civilized. With the arrogance of colonialists, they had made little effort to understand black culture and simply assumed the superiority of their own. With "more enthusiasm than knowledge," they sought to "transform the Negroes, not develop them." They passed on that attitude to the black teachers they trained.[19]

Black schools and colleges, according to Woodson, perpetuated contempt for black culture even after their white teachers had left the South. The traditional curriculum, with its heavy diet of the classics, taught blacks "to admire the Hebrew, the Greek, the Latin and the Teuton and to despise the African." The Victorian middle-class morality of the white missionaries influenced generation after generation of black teachers. What black schools taught black children therefore derived almost entirely from white models and values: a curriculum that "did not take the Negro into consideration except to condemn or pity him." The Eurocentric culture of black schools crippled their efforts to elevate their largely Afrocentric clientele. The causes of black educational failure should therefore be sought in the teachers, Woodson concluded, not the children. "Most of those [teachers] with whom we are afflicted today know nothing about the children whom they teach or about their parents . . . When a boy comes to school without knowing his lesson he should be studied instead of being punished."[20]

Like most polemics, *The Mis-Education of the Negro* was overheated. Among its many contradictions, one stands out. In deploring the enduring influence of the white missionary teachers, Woodson assumed the existence of an autonomous "Negro" culture that was basically African. This supposition not only minimized the extent to which European culture had already influenced blacks under slavery but also wrongly implied that African American culture was a sufficient basis for black advancement. It was one thing to foster racial pride through, for example, the teaching of Negro history and the cultivation of African cultural survivals. It was quite another to assume that Negro culture, however defined, could sustain an adequate program of education for blacks. When it came to literacy and other academic skills, European models were the only ones available. The contradictory nature of Woodson's analysis came out most blatantly in his analysis of the black church. In *Mis-Education,* Woodson caricatured the institution as an unthinking imitation of white Christianity that attracted "incompetents and undesirables" whose principal aim was "the exploitation of the people." Yet in his earlier work, *The History of the Negro Church,* published in 1921, he had depicted the black church as a creative fusion of African and American culture that represented the greatest asset of the race.[21]

A similar contradiction bedeviled Woodson's treatment of Yankee efforts to change the moral habits of the freedmen. Accusing the white missionaries and their black protégés of disdaining the folk culture of the masses, Woodson himself looked askance at the behavior of many lower-class blacks. He deplored "howling, crying, singing, dancing, and groveling on the floor in answer to the emotional appeal of an insane or depraved preacher." Holding to an idealized image of Africa, he insisted that the emotionalism of black ministers reflected white, not African, influence. He even contended that jazz, which he also disliked, grew out of European music.

The Mis-Education of the Negro would merit less attention had it not been so influential. Several generations of black students—the book has never been out of print—have imbibed its racial militancy. Moreover, Woodson's denunciation of white influence over black education finds strong echoes in recent studies of southern black schooling that lament the missionary teachers' emphasis upon middle-class morality. Convinced that slavery had made the freedmen improvident and morally lax, white teachers believed they had to mold black habits according to their own precepts of thrift and sobriety. This emphasis upon character reform, some argue, failed to address the economic and political causes of black oppression. As perpetuated by schools such as Hampton Institute and Tuskegee Institute, this philosophy of self-help and moral discipline played into the hands of white racists by ascribing African American backwardness to blacks themselves.

It is doubtful, however, that the tenets of the white missionaries were as alien to southern black culture, or as harmful to the advancement of the group, as Woodson and others have claimed. The fact that so many free Negroes in the antebellum era discovered the transformative power of moral uplift for themselves—as did many of the freedmen—suggests that New England's "puritan" values were both more potent and more universal than modern critics suppose. The ethos of strict morality and temperance practiced by Elijah P. Marrs, a former slave who became a teacher and preacher, strikingly resembled that of the Yankee missionaries. Yet Marrs was largely self-taught, and, like many black Baptists, he espoused denominational independence from the white church. Because uplift had worked for himself, comments one historian, Marrs "sought to uplift others." It is a telling irony that Woodson's own life exemplified the middle-class virtues preached by the Yankee schoolteachers he criticized, namely thrift, sobriety, moral purpose, hard work, and a passion for education—only the Christian piety was absent.[22]

It would be simplistic to depict black teachers as purveyors of enlightenment and progress, and leave it at that. Black schooling constituted a major area of disagreement not only between blacks and whites, but within each group. Arguments about curriculum, funding, staffing, and control all stemmed from the central question: What were the likely *effects* of educating blacks in a particular way? And this issue admitted of no easy resolution. Conflicts over black education took place within wider debates over the form, content, and purpose of public education. And as happens so often in the sphere of education, no sooner is one debate resolved than the same question reappears in a different guise. Dissatisfaction with schools (and, by implication, teachers) has been the rule, not the exception.

In the case of black teachers, sheer poverty of resources shrouded bitter controversies over content and pedagogy with a miasma of unreality. For example, the conflict between advocates of "industrial education" and supporters of "classical education"—an issue that obsessed black educators for a quarter of a century—remained for the most part an abstraction. It "developed into a sort of battle of minds," commented Woodson, "for in spite of all they said and did the majority of Negroes . . . did not actually receive either the industrial or the classical education." It was a cruel irony that underfunding and discrimination intensified the vehemence with which blacks conducted arguments about education. An educated elite, denied opportunities commensurate with their talents and training, fought over crumbs.

An air of futility often surrounded the best efforts of black teachers. Despite islands of excellence and much-touted evidence of progress, the condition of most rural schools was about the same in 1940 as it had been in 1870. Black teachers campaigned, lobbied, argued, and pleaded for better buildings, more training, higher salaries, and an equitable share of public funds. No matter how valiantly they struggled, however, the gap between black and white schools persisted. Only in the 1940s, when whites faced the imminent threat of federally enforced integration, did the gap start to narrow. The history of black education "seems not so much an evolving linear narrative as a sociology of oppression in which debates over means recur within a common context of victimization."[23]

Inflated estimates of what education could achieve for blacks, on top of rank discrimination, imposed a double cruelty upon black teachers. The northern philanthropic foundations, for example, piled expectation upon expectation onto the shoulders of black teachers: fundraising, school beautification, public health, agricultural extension work, parent-teacher associations, interracial committees, and summer schools to improve their own education. In fact, the foundations treated teachers as if they were the *primary* agents of community improvement. Many teachers responded heroically to these exhortations, which tapped into the missionary fervor that blacks had always brought to teaching. The reports of Jeanes teachers like Lillian Rogers provide moving insights into the Herculean efforts of black teachers. However, teachers could not possibly fulfill the demands of the foundations and the expectations of parents. Underneath the mask of optimism that black teachers habitually donned, lurked resignation and despair.[24]

Failure and even betrayal can be found in this history, but they are not its dominant notes. For all the ambiguities and limitations of their work, black teachers played a crucial part in building black communities after the Civil War. During the most oppressive years of Jim Crow, teachers skillfully cultivated white support for black schools and adroitly minimized opposition to them. They displayed integrity and commitment; their tactics were subtle and tenacious.

To what extent did black teachers help topple white supremacy? Some argue that the civil rights movement of the 1950s and 1960s was the progressive fulfillment of education's promise. Others contend that black teachers were too limited by institutional constraints, and too wedded to their privileged status, to challenge segregation. Certainly, the well-known tension between black teachers and the civil rights movement makes it hard to establish a direct link between education and black insurgency. Yet the dismissive view of black teachers held by many civil rights activists, who often characterized black teachers as conservative "Uncle Toms," was misguided. Despite their compromises and evasions, black teachers kept the goal of equality in sight. Although education was not inherently progressive or automatically liberating, teachers insisted that it was a necessary condition for challenging and overturning white supremacy. Constantly battling poverty and prejudice, walking a precarious line between two communities, the wonder is that black teachers achieved so much. In the 1950s and 1960s, boycotts and demonstrations achieved dramatic breakthroughs; the heroes and martyrs of those struggles became household names. Compared to the headline battles of the civil rights movement, the struggles of black teachers are not well known. But they were, in their own way, just as dramatic and equally important.

CHAPTER ONE

Freedom's First Generation

Captain Gallaspy said if I came to the polls the next day he would blow my brains out . . . I know of nothing they have against me, except that I taught a colored school, and that I read the radical papers to the colored people, and tried to enlighten them as much as I could. . . . I have heard them say they didn't want a black teacher in town.

Sworn statement of Abraham Jackson of Catahoula Parish,
Louisiana, 17 November 1868

Teacher holding up a sphere during object teaching, *Harper's Weekly,* 26 Feb. 1870.

Schomburg Center for Research in Black Culture,
Photographs and Prints Division

THE FIRST GENERATION of southern black teachers was forged in the furnaces of slavery, the Civil War, and Reconstruction. During this violent, disordered period of America's history, black teachers faced difficulties of staggering magnitude. Although some black teachers had taught before, either in public schools in the North or in "secret schools" in the South, most black teachers lacked any experience of the classroom. Many were barely literate. As a consequence, black teachers suffered the condescension of white schoolteachers and missionaries from the North who deemed them ignorant and incompetent. Worse, they had to contend against the opposition—often expressed in threats and sometimes in acts of violence—of southern whites who feared the education of blacks. They could not rely upon the federal government to protect them against arson, intimidation, and physical harm. Even the limited federal financial support for freedmen's schools came to an abrupt end in 1870.

Yet the former slaves and freeborn blacks who taught freedmen's schools were buoyed by idealism, ambition, religious zeal, and the enthusiasm of a people who hungered and thirsted for literacy. As Union armies occupied rebel territory, emancipating slaves along their path, black southerners clamored for education. In the words of Booker T. Washington, a young boy in Virginia at the time, "it was a whole race going to school." For blacks, the association between education and freedom was so powerful that teachers at once became inspirers, preachers, community builders, and political leaders. That same association made southern whites regard black teachers with suspicion, and freedmen's schools were established in the teeth of white hostility. Reconstruction embedded black schools in state systems of public education, but at the same time it pitched black teachers into a raging conflict between Democrats and Republicans. Black schools survived the defeat of the Republican Party and the unraveling of Reconstruction, but their future was uncertain. Reconstruction's failure ushered in an era of white supremacy during which black teachers had little power, limited means, and few white friends. Nevertheless, they continued to seek better schools and to oppose the ideology of racism.[1]

THE value of literacy was so obvious to the freed people that black teachers felt little need to explain their enthusiasm for learning. The mere fact that the master class had gone to such lengths to discourage slaves from acquiring knowledge of books was reason enough to seek it. "They have seen the power and influence among white people always coupled with *learning*," noted John W. Alvord, the inspector of schools for the Freedmen's Bureau. "Very early in life I took up the idea that I wanted to learn to read and write," recorded Elijah P. Marrs, one of Kentucky's first black teachers. "I was convinced that there could be something for me to do in the future that I could not accomplish by remaining in ignorance." A thirst for religious knowledge often underpinned this desire for literacy. Charles O. Boothe, a teacher and Baptist minister—he was the first pastor of Dexter Avenue Baptist Church in Montgomery, Alabama, which was later led by Martin Luther King Jr.—explained, "Listening to the reading of the Bible, I was drawn toward it, and began to read it for myself."[2]

In their impatience to acquire literacy, black southerners organized their own schools and pressed any literate person—anyone with the merest smattering of literacy—into service. Booker T. Washington's first teacher was William Davis, a "young colored man from Ohio, who had been a soldier." Other black teachers were southerners, former free Negroes and even recent slaves, who by hook or by crook had acquired some literacy. J. W. Alvord conveyed the flavor of these "native schools." Typically, he wrote, he encountered "a group, perhaps, of all ages, *trying to learn*. Some young man, some woman, or old preacher, in cellar, or shed, or corner of a negro meeting-house, with the alphabet in hand, or a torn spelling-book, is their teacher."[3]

Blacks supported these "private schools" or "native schools" through churches and community associations, and parents paid tuition fees. In Marietta, Georgia, a small town near Atlanta, ninety-five blacks subscribed fifty cents a month to an educational association that employed three teachers. Farther south, in Macon, where thousands of refugees from Georgia's countryside swelled the black population, ten blacks and two whites were teaching freedmen's school in the summer of 1865. Freedmen's Bureau officials could only guess at the number of "native schools" in the South's vast hinterland. Because they were supported wholly by blacks, they failed to figure in official statistics. After a four-thousand-mile trip through the South, J. W. Alvord estimated that in addition to the 740 schools supported by the Freedmen's Bureau and the various northern aid societies, there were five hundred "native" or "self-sustaining schools."[4]

Even more numerous were the "Sabbath schools" or "Sunday schools" organized by black churches. Compared to the Sunday schools of white churches, they paid greater attention to teaching literacy, sometimes meeting in the afternoon so that adults could attend them after morning worship. "They had been having a Sunday school throughout the summer, taught by the preacher's daughter, but very differently to what I had seen it taught," wrote Mary C. Robinson, a black teacher in Bedford County, Virginia. "They all had their spelling books the same as when they went to the day school, excepting five, who had testaments. They had a little singing, after which they said the Lord's Prayer, then they said their lessons. After their lessons were said they repeated the 23rd Psalm." How much did blacks learn in these Sabbath schools? All we can say with certainty is that they transmitted basic literacy to some blacks, most of whom never attended freedmen's schools.[5]

Northern white teachers were astonished at the level of literacy among the South's black population. One of the most widely believed charges in the abolitionist indictment of slavery was that bondage kept slaves in enforced ignorance. Yet northerners encountered far more literate blacks than abolitionist propaganda had led them to expect. According to one estimate, about 10 percent of African Americans in the South, at least four hundred thousand people, possessed some degree of literacy in 1865. The presence of so many black teachers—whatever their limitations as teachers—so soon after the Civil War showed that black literacy had taken root under the very noses of the slavemasters.[6]

In practice, antebellum efforts to deny blacks literacy were never entirely effective. Despite laws banning the teaching of slaves, many bondsmen had learned to read. Slaves who lived in towns and cities had ample opportunity to see and acquire reading matter. Many were hired out by their masters, escaping the strict supervision experienced by plantation slaves. J. E. Jones, who later taught Greek and homiletics at Richmond Theological Seminary, worked in a Lynchburg tobacco factory from the age of six, and received his first lessons from another slave at the insistence of his mother. Other urban slaves attended clandestine schools. Susie King Taylor, born in 1848 and brought up by a grandmother in Savannah, attended a secret school kept by a free woman and her daughter. About two dozen children attended. There were even clandestine schools taught by white people. "Some aged impecunious white lady would agree to teach the children of free colored people and the children of such slaves as had hired their time," recorded Richard R. Wright, one of Georgia's pioneer black teachers.[7]

On the large plantations of the lower South, the risks and difficulties of teaching and learning were far greater. Wright estimated that in Georgia, outside the largest towns, "almost unbroken and unrelieved illiteracy and ignorance . . . reigned," with "not a dozen colored people able to read and write." Nevertheless, the New Orleans Creole Jean-Baptiste Roudanez recalled that some degree of literacy penetrated the slave quarters. "Generally upon every plantation there was at least one man who had learned to read a little, and in secret learned to read to the others." Of the 3,428 former slaves who were interviewed during the 1930s by the Works Progress Administration, 179, about 5 percent, had become literate before emancipation.[8]

Whites themselves taught slaves by inadvertence. Slaves were expert at appealing to the vanity and paternalistic feelings of their masters, prizing knowledge from whites through subtle manipulation. As they smiled and laughed, they also watched, listened, and asked seemingly innocent questions. Early childhood, when slave children often played alongside white children, provided particularly good opportunities for acquiring forbidden knowledge. Robert R. Moton, who succeeded Booker T. Washington as president of Tuskegee Institute, recalled that one of his uncles "learned to read and write from his young master, picking up snatches of information while they played and worked together, ofttimes without the young master's realizing the gravity of his actions." That uncle taught a night school in Amelia County, Virginia, before any official freedmen's school had been established.[9]

Remarkably, many of the South's first black teachers had been taught to read by their owners. Henry B. Delaney, born of a free father and a slave mother, owed his earliest education "to the Christian woman, whose property we were. . . . My mistress herself taught my eldest sister to read and write, in order that she might carry on a school secretly in the upper rooms of the house for the benefit of the other children of my family." The first black instructor at St. Augustine's College in Raleigh, North Carolina, and later a bishop in the Episcopalian Church, Delaney headed a family of teachers, two of whom, daughters Sadie and Bessie, became famous for their long and exemplary lives.[10] Slaveholders who favored the education of slaves petitioned state legislatures for the repeal of laws against slave literacy. Nothing came of these requests. But the law, community disapproval, and occasional intimidation failed to prevent slaveholders from teaching slaves if they so desired. As Governor Hayne of South Carolina told Benjamin Morgan Palmer: "Well, Doctor, we are not afraid that you will teach them anything bad. Do as you please, but keep it to yourself."[11]

Why did slaveholders teach slaves to read and write, or allow them to acquire literacy on their own? Personal affection for certain house servants was one reason. Mulatto slaves were sometimes pampered by their white fathers. Blanche K. Bruce's master-father gave him a private tutor. Taken by his master from Virginia to Missouri, he "studied the printing trade, and later dealt in books and papers." Even when slaves received no direct instruction from whites, they sometimes enjoyed such a close relationship with their masters that the pursuit of knowledge became easy. Slaveholders had practical reasons, too, for encouraging certain slaves to become literate. Absent from their plantations for much of the year, large slaveholders relied upon "key slaves" to act as stewards. Brothers Jefferson and Joseph Davis placed the management of their plantation at Davis Bend, Mississippi, in the hands of Benjamin Montgomery. In towns, businessmen turned trusted slaves into clerks and secretaries. As one southern congressman explained, he required his slave to "know the titles of books, superscription of letter, and other things in performing errands or receiving written instructions."[12]

Slaveholders also flouted the ban on slave literacy because it clashed with their Christian faith. They believed that slaves should be furnished proper religious instruction. The law permitted slaves to learn catechisms through oral instruction, but it denied them the most basic source of Protestant Christianity. "When we reflect, as Christians, how can we justify it, that a slave is not permitted to read the Bible?" asked John Belton O'Neall, a South Carolina Baptist, in 1853. In Virginia, where the law still allowed individual slaveowners to educate their bondsmen, pious Christians like Thomas J. Jackson—"Stonewall Jackson" of Civil War fame—taught Sunday schools for slaves and encouraged Bible reading. Elsewhere, masters and mistresses simply ignored the law. Slaveholders tried to supervise the religious lives of their slaves, but they often compromised on the question of control. Whites not only permitted independent black churches among the free blacks but also allowed black preachers among the slaves. White ministers sometimes taught slave preachers. One black preacher recalled that "when de white preacher foun' I could read some, he use' to take me nights an teach me to read de hymes an' de church 'scipline." It was useful for the white minister to have a black assistant who could "lead de prayer-meetin's, an' to preach when he war away."[13]

The laws designed to suppress literacy among the 261,000 free Negroes of the antebellum South—whom whites always found difficult to control—were almost wholly ineffective. In Richmond, Petersburg, Charleston, Savannah, Mobile, and New Orleans, free blacks forged resilient communities that enjoyed a good deal of autonomy, especially in their religious life. True, whites reacted harshly when the northern-based black African Methodist Episcopal (AME) denomination attempted to organize churches in the South. But in most of the South's cities, whites allowed blacks to establish their own Baptist churches—by 1860 there were at least 130 of them. Although subjected to varying degrees of oversight by suspicious whites, these independent churches functioned as incubators of black literacy.[14]

By the time southern legislatures attempted to suppress black schools, literacy had already taken root in the free black population. Until the 1830s whites had placed virtually no restrictions on the efforts of free blacks to organize schools. Such schools were especially numerous in North Carolina. Indeed, some of North Carolina's free black teachers were so respected that whites sought their services. John Chavis of Raleigh, a "full-blooded Negro of dark-brown color" and a licensed preacher of the Presbyterian Church, taught a day school for whites and a night school for blacks.[15]

Most southern states banned all black schools after the Nat Turner rebellion of 1831. However, a few continued to allow them. In New Orleans, the free people of color, French-speaking Creoles, founded the Catholic Institute for Indigent Orphans which provided a six-year course of instruction for about two hundred pupils. It received a state charter and even a state subsidy. Schools for free blacks could also be found, operating openly, in Opelousas, Baton Rouge, and Point Coupée Parish. Kentucky, like Louisiana, never made schools for free blacks illegal. Missouri did not get around to prohibiting black schools until 1847. In North Carolina, which never banned the private education of free Negroes, 43 percent of the free Negroes were literate by 1850.[16]

Elsewhere, laws against free black schools were rarely invoked.

Charleston quietly disregarded an 1835 law: private schools for wealthier free blacks, and more humble schools operated by benevolent associations, went unmolested by the authorities. In Savannah, free blacks were able to operate schools as long as they did so discreetly: Jane Deveaux ran one for almost thirty years. References to secret schools are scattered throughout black biographies and memoirs. In states like Virginia, where the authorities were vigilant in suppressing black schools, free blacks could still teach each other within the home. Everywhere, free blacks had access to newspapers, books, and religious publications. Literary societies flourished. All these non-school activities remained legal.[17]

Free blacks picked up literacy haphazardly, exploiting whatever opportunities came their way. South Carolina native Henry McNeal Turner learned the rudiments of spelling from a white playmate. For a while—until white disapproval ended them—he received lessons from a white woman hired by his mother. When he went to work in a law office in the town of Abbeville, Turner found himself surrounded by books, letters, papers, and rhetoric. Encouraged by the young attorneys, he learned "arithmetic, astronomy, geography, history, law, and theology." In 1853 the southern Methodist Episcopal Church (MEC, South) licensed him to preach. Turner became a fluent writer, an erratic speller, and a spellbinding orator.[18]

The Civil War prompted a clampdown on black churches and schools. However, it strained and then broke established mechanisms for controlling the black population. Resourceful slaves turned the disruptions of war to their advantage. Some whites now agreed to tutor slaves because, in their straightened circumstances, they needed what their pupils could pay. In Lynchburg, Virginia, J. E. Jones gave food to a "sick Confederate soldier" in return for lessons. As Union armies invaded the Confederacy, northern missionaries and teachers followed. At first the schools they opened were confined to patches of coast seized early in the war: Hampton and Norfolk, Virginia; New Bern, North Carolina; the sea islands of Port Royal, South Carolina. By the end of the war they were also operating in inland areas that covered large black populations. Under General John Eaton, more than one hundred instructors taught in fifty-one freedmen's schools in the cities of Memphis, Vicksburg, Little Rock, and Pine Bluff, as well as in plantation areas such as Davis Bend, Mississippi. The largest and best-organized system of freedmen's schools could be found in New Orleans, the largest city in the South, captured by Union forces in April 1862. For the 180,000 blacks who joined the Union army and navy, many of them former slaves, military encampments doubled as schools. General Samuel Chapman Armstrong, founder of Hampton Institute, reckoned that a quarter of all black soldiers learned to read while in the army.[19]

In the dying months of the war and the first days of freedom, blacks with a smattering of letters scrambled to extend their literacy. In 1865 William Heard, a fifteen-year-old in Elberton, Georgia, could already "repeat whole Psalms and chapter after chapter in the Shorter Catechism." Armed with a copy of Webster's "blue-back" spelling book, he paid a poor white boy ten cents a lesson. After "laying by" the cotton crop in June, he attended six weeks of a school taught by George H. Washington of Augusta. By the end of the session he could spell words of five and six syllables, compose a letter, and do simple arithmetic. Working as a laborer, Heard persuaded his white employer to give him "a lesson a night" on top of his wages and board. After breaking his contract, he attended a "regular school" while working mornings and evenings at his father's wheelwright shop. In the fall of 1866 he organized his own school, charging pupils a dollar a month. Meanwhile, he took private lessons in grammar, mathematics, and history from a white man. "When I learnt the parts of speech in Smith's grammar . . . it was a revelation to me."[20]

CRITICISMS of black teachers, however, pepper the records of the Freedmen's Bureau and the northern aid societies. Northern whites doubted the abilities of these teachers and mistrusted the assertion of black autonomy that the native schools seemed to represent. In the eyes of northern missionaries and Freedmen's Bureau officials, most black teachers were practically useless. What little knowledge they possessed could be imparted in a few weeks; after that, they held their pupils back. Colored teachers "were limited to the merest rudiments of knowledge," complained an official in Arkansas. The Bureau's man in Albany, Georgia, considered "none of them competent to teach, even reading and writing." Some of the native teachers, northerners charged, were little more than parasites. "They are taking advantage of the ignorance of these people, and of their great eagerness to learn," complained an American Missionary Association (AMA) official in Tennessee. Writing from Lauderdale, Mississippi, AMA missionary J. P. Bardwell described "a colored school here now, taught by a man who can barely read and write, and I am not sure he can write at all." This teacher charged his thirty-eight students two dollars a month.[21]

Complaints about preacher-teachers abounded. As blacks left the white churches and formed their own congregations, their preachers often doubled as teachers. But the education of these men rarely matched their eloquence. Black Baptist ministers were a byword for ignorance, and some candidly admitted that they merited that reputation. In 1865, for example, Alabama could claim "but one Baptist preacher who could, with any degree of honesty, claim to be an educated black preacher." Yet men who had been slave preachers, and now headed churches, not only insisted that they could teach but also sometimes opposed better-trained white teachers who might threaten their influence. A minister in Opelousas, Louisiana, refused to rent his church building to the Freedmen's Bureau, "giving as his reason that the colored people would own their own schools and appoint their own Teachers." One Bureau official, writing from Liberty, Texas, suspected that the black preachers, "*not one* of whom can read or write," wanted ignorance to prevail lest the freedmen discover for themselves "what nonsense has been preached to them as religion."[22]

Northerners believed in the inferiority of southern society. In seeking to impose northern models on the ex-Confederacy, they expected black southerners to defer to their superior knowledge and leadership. Black autonomy, whether in religion or education, threatened that leadership. Native teachers, especially the preacher-teachers, impeded northern efforts to mold the freedmen according to the missionaries' designs.

The AMA's hostility to the black-run Savannah Education Association (SEA) exemplified this assumption of northern superiority. Within days of Savannah's liberation in December 1865, the SEA organized four schools, commissioned fifteen teachers, and enrolled five hundred children. Eleven of the SEA's founding members had been free before the Civil War; its superintendent, James D. Porter, had taught a secret school. An agent of the Freedmen's Bureau had nothing but praise for the SEA's schools. "The teachers . . . are intelligent, assiduous, and well qualified," he reported. "The children are neat in their appearance, exceedingly well behaved . . . and passed a better examination, as I am informed by the late Superintendent of Schools, than any white school in the city." However, the AMA considered the SEA "radically defective" and rated its teachers "deficient in education." It criticized the SEA for racial "exclusiveness" and condemned as "preposterous" its suggestion that white northern teachers act as classroom assistants to the blacks. It did its best to undermine the SEA, and eventually the AMA gained control of Savannah's black schools. "A good northern teacher can do more for fifty [pupils] than a southern born colored teacher for thirty," claimed Rev. E. A. Cooley, head of the AMA in Savannah.[23]

Arrogance and condescension tinged such criticism. Yet the fact that black northerners also disdained native black teachers suggests that a belief in the superiority of Yankee culture, rather than racial prejudice, may have been the most salient issue. Francis Cardozo, the colored superintendent of AMA schools in Charleston, South Carolina, preferred to appoint northern teachers, black or white. Ohio-educated Robert Harris, writing from Fayetteville, North Carolina, bluntly cautioned the AMA against commissioning southern blacks: "These native teachers are not competent to manage a class, or to give proper instruction to those who are beyond the alphabet. We can only use them as assistants, and they are poor at that." The Freedmen's Bureau and the northern aid societies therefore had good reason to oppose the proliferation of "native schools" and to be cautious about appointing freedmen as teachers. Outside the towns and cities, the scale of illiteracy among blacks was overwhelming. In Alabama, for example, the prewar free blacks had accounted for a mere 0.6 percent of the state's total black population. Even if one assumed that all the free blacks had been literate, and added a generous estimate of slave literacy, the proportion of blacks who were literate must have been much less than the figure of 5 to 10 percent that is usually cited as the average for the South.[24]

Literacy, however, was only part of the problem. The freedmen's aid societies shared a belief that mere literacy did not equip a person to be a teacher. Teachers should ideally possess "normal training," that is, training in pedagogy of the kind taught in the "normal schools" of the North. Teaching was still a young profession in 1860, but the professional expertise had been developed in the North. Massachusetts had pioneered public education in the form of "common schools" for the masses, and other northern states had followed. Although the South was not the morass of ignorance it was often made out to be—New Orleans and North Carolina, for example, had developed fairly extensive public school systems before the Civil War—in most of the South there were few common schools. Where they did exist, whites often disdained them as "pauper schools." Of the twenty normal schools in existence by 1861, all but two could be found in the North.[25]

Hence, to northern educators, the establishment of freedmen's schools in the South involved more than appointing teachers. It also entailed building a system—a northern system—that incorporated up-to-date pedagogical methods. Teachers could not simply stand in front of a class and teach. They needed to know how to "grade" children according to age and ability; how to divide classes into small groups and organize "recitations"; how to employ student monitors; how to manage pupils without corporal punishment; and how to use modern teaching methods of the kind advocated by Herbart, Pestalozzi, and other theorists. Few southern blacks possessed these skills.

Still, northerners recognized effective teaching when they saw it. "The teachers are not as efficient as desired," a Bureau agent reported from Fort Valley, Georgia, "yet the children seem to be learning in the lower grades very well." From Navasota, Texas, a Bureau officer praised a freedman named Reinhard. "He teaches very well indeed. I have spent several hours at the school, and was surprised at the rapid progress, many of the children have made in a few months."[26]

The school in Greenville, South Carolina, established by ex-slave Charles Hopkins, perfectly illustrated the importance of native teachers and community effort. Freedmen's Bureau agent John W. De

Forest, who admired and helped him, described Hopkins as "a full-blooded black" who had gathered his education "in the chance opportunities of fifty years." Formerly a slave preacher, Hopkins quickly emerged as a leader of the freedmen. In 1866, obtaining a room in a deserted hotel that the army had commandeered, he began teaching spelling and reading. When the government restored the hotel to its previous owner, Hopkins bought an old storehouse and leased a plot of land nearby. "A mass meeting of freedmen tore the building to pieces, moved it nearly two miles, and set it up on the new site. Then came much labor of carpenters, masons, and plasterers, and much expense for new materials." De Forest estimated that Greenville's freedmen, helped by local whites, raised more than five hundred dollars to pay for the building and the land. Ordained by the northern Methodist church, Hopkins secured financial support from the Methodist missionary society. Two white teachers arrived to teach higher classes. Hopkins continued to teach basic literacy. "He was a meek, amiable, judicious, virtuous, godly man," wrote De Forest, "zealous for the good of the freedmen, yet . . . thoroughly trusted by the whites."

Native teachers like Hopkins often acknowledged their deficiencies. "Though I don't stile myself a Schollar or as competent to Teach School, you can judge for yourself," Macon resident R. W. Mitchell informed the Freedmen's Bureau. "Yet I thought I could do some good to teach among the People of my color." Such teachers usually welcomed the arrival of white teachers from the northern aid societies. They then stepped down or agreed to continue as assistant teachers. Conflict ensued, however, when native black teachers refused to withdraw in favor of white teachers, or competed with them by setting up rival schools. Moreover, some black communities—often egged on by black preachers—insisted upon black teachers.[27]

The establishment of native schools, however, did not reflect a straightforward desire for black autonomy. Their material and cultural poverty trammeled the freedmen's desire for racial independence and for control of their own schools. Black southerners looked to the North to supply trained teachers and to the Union army to provide better school buildings. A desire for racial solidarity and community control pulled in one direction. Suspicion of racial segregation, and recognition of white expertise, pulled in another. Money, or usually the lack of it, pulled in both directions, often in complicated ways. In short, the challenge of securing effective teachers and establishing good schools strained black solidarity.

The southern black population, moreover, did not constitute a unified community. Despite a shared history of oppression and the continuing weight of racial discrimination, the black society that emerged from slavery exhibited differences of class, color, origin, culture, religion, and politics. The departure of blacks from the South's white churches was a strong assertion of racial independence, but the rivalry between black Methodist denominations and the more numerous black Baptist churches divided many communities. Dark-complexioned blacks often resented mulattos; mulattos frequently looked down upon blacks. The distinction between "freedmen" and "freeborn"—those who gained freedom as a result of the Civil War and those who had been free before the war—contributed to a black class system. Hence black teachers from the North, whose attitudes often mirrored those of northern white teachers, sometimes clashed with semiliterate "preacher-teachers."[28]

ALTHOUGH nearly all of them were better educated than their southern counterparts, black teachers from the North formed a disparate group. Some were regional hybrids—free Negroes who had left the South in the 1850s. John Wesley Cromwell, one of the first black teachers in Virginia, was a native of Portsmouth, Virginia, the youngest of twelve children, who moved to Philadelphia at the age of five when his slave father gained his freedom. Cromwell attended public schools in Philadelphia and then the Institute for Colored Youth, a Quaker school chartered in 1842 that educated dozens of freedmen's teachers. A remarkable group of teachers from Fayetteville, North Carolina, returned south by way of Ohio. The parents of William, Robert, and Cicero Harris left the South in 1850, eventually settling in Cleveland. In 1864 Robert and William Harris, plasterers by trade, received appointments from the AMA to teach in Virginia. After the war, Robert and Cicero Harris opened a school in Fayetteville that the

Freedmen's Bureau rated one of the best in North Carolina. It provided the foundation for what is today Fayetteville State University.[29]

Some returning southerners had been born into slavery. Hardy Mobley, for example, was a slave in Augusta, Georgia. His letters to the American Colonization Society, in which he expressed interest in emigration to Liberia, show that he could already write, albeit crudely, by 1851. Two years later he spent three thousand dollars to purchase his own and his family's freedom. After living in Brooklyn, Mobley returned to the South in 1865 as an AMA-sponsored teacher and a missionary of the Congregational Church. His wife and four daughters also taught in freedmen's schools.[30]

Northern-born black teachers made up an even more disparate group. The best known, although not necessarily the most representative, were the teachers who became prominent politicians. George T. Ruby, born in New York City and raised in Maine, arrived in Union-occupied New Orleans in 1864 as a correspondent for William Lloyd Garrison's *Anti-Slavery Standard.* He taught in government schools in Louisiana for two years, worked for the Freedmen's Bureau as a traveling agent, and then moved to Texas, where he became a leader of the Republican Party. New Orleans superintendent of schools Mortimer A. Warren praised Ruby's work. As principal of Frederick Douglass School, he faced pupils whom Warren described as "Creole French, plantation negroes and wild men," who spoke an "abominable 'gumbo' talk." Ruby was "fast getting them civilized," Warren reported. "I do not know of any school, which considering the material to be wrought upon, shows better skill in management, or more improvement."[31]

Delaware native Robert Fitzgerald was more typical of the native northerners in that he did not use teaching as a stepping stone to political office. Born in 1840, the oldest of twelve children born of a manumitted slave, Fitzgerald attended a Quaker school for blacks in Wilmington and then, after his family moved to Pennsylvania, spent two years at Philadelphia's Institute for Colored Youth. From there he went to Ashmun Institute, a college for blacks founded by the Presbyterian Church in 1854. On the outbreak of the Civil War he found employment with the Quartermaster's Department as a teamster. When

President Lincoln authorized black troops, he joined the navy and then the army. Discharged in 1864 owing to poor eyesight, he returned to Lincoln University (formerly Ashmun Institute). Like other Lincoln students, he passed his summers teaching in the South, at first assisting an army chaplain who taught a freedmen's school in Amelia County, Virginia. In 1868 the Friends Freedmen's Association of Philadelphia assigned him to a school in Hillsboro, North Carolina, and he settled in that state. When his freedmen's school lost northern funding, he taught in the new public schools until blindness forced him to stop.[32]

A study of New York State offers an interesting sample of the black teachers from the North. Ronald Butchart identified fifty-one black New Yorkers (some of them southern-born) who taught in freedmen's schools during Reconstruction. With an average age of thirty-one, they taught an average of three school terms in the South. Of the twenty-nine teachers whose occupations could be traced, nineteen had prior teaching experience that averaged seven years. About two-thirds of the teachers were women. Butchart suggests that the black teachers had a stronger sense of commitment to the freedmen's cause than the more numerous white teachers. They stayed in the South longer and included a greater proportion of abolitionists. Although blacks constituted only 1.2 percent of New York's population, they contributed 14 percent of the freedmen's teachers from the Empire State.[33]

The northern teachers brought a strong sense of commitment to their duties, a fact reflected in their length of service in the South. Black Oberlinites taught in freedmen's schools for an average of six years, whereas a typical northern white teacher stayed only two. Racial pride obviously fueled that sense of devotion. Black northerners believed that they could divine the feelings and aspirations of the former slaves in a way that white teachers could not. Blacks like themselves, they implied, were best suited to teach the freedmen and their children. "My reasons for seeking to engage in instructing the Freed people of the South are few and simple," explained Sarah G. Stanley. "I am myself a colored woman, bound to that ignorant, degraded, long enslaved race, by the ties of love and consanguinity; they are socially, and politically, 'my people.'" A majority of the black teachers from the

North were single women like Stanley. They were a well-educated group, for the freedmen's aid societies followed rigorous selection procedures. And as their letters attest, they were not merely literate but also eloquent.[34]

Claims to racial solidarity aside, northern black teachers approached their work very much like the white Yankee teachers. They used the same pedagogy. They regarded themselves as missionaries as well as teachers. They, too, found the culture of the freed people disquieting, disliked the emotional excesses of southern black religion, and regarded many preachers as ignorant and unscrupulous. Like their white co-workers, they believed that northern institutions had to be imposed upon a backward South. If the government would "dot this Barbaric corner of Virginia with schoolhouses," wrote John Oliver in 1862, "there would spring up here a race of thinkers, who with God's blessing would soon redeem the land which has so long been cursed by the slavery of their race." Without schools and churches, warned Louisiana teacher P. B. Randolph, blacks would "fall back into a careless, heedless, barbarous, and vicious state."[35]

Some black northerners found the freedmen profoundly disappointing. Having expected to encounter a kind of noble savage, with boundless enthusiasm for learning, Sarah Stanley recoiled from the real-life children she found in Louisville, Kentucky—"hundreds of filthy, squalid, untaught children . . . apparently indifferent to their wretched condition." When she smilingly inquired if they wished to go to school, they responded only with blank stares and a mumbled "Dunno Misses." Only the "brutalizing influence of slavery," she believed, could account for "such a desert mentally and morally, such a dead waste, . . . such inertia in humanity as the Freedmen congregated in this town present." Stanley's missionary fervor waned. Physically exhausted by each day's "laborious and exhausting" work, she often felt tempted to quit. But duty battled against disillusionment. "There is no alternative, the work must be done and there are none to do it." As often happened when teachers felt discouraged, Stanley's mood brightened when she saw her pupils improve. After two months she had classified them into primary, secondary, and intermediate grades. Bursting with pride, she reported that some prominent former Confederates had visited her school, professing themselves "surprised at the order, decorum, and general proficiency of the pupils." Sometimes, however, teachers lost all confidence. "I am quite willing to do what I can," wrote Mary J. R. Richards from St. Mary, Georgia, "but I fear that in the end it will not prove much. The colored people here are not of the best type of freedmen."[36]

BLACK teachers, like all freedmen's teachers, faced a battery of obstacles. The first challenge was to find a building that could serve as a schoolhouse. Churches provided a common location, but the freedmen were still in the process of erecting or acquiring church buildings, and this entailed a struggle of its own. Whites often voluntarily relinquished control of churches that blacks had customarily used under slavery, and in many instances helped blacks build new churches. However, when blacks separated from white congregations, disputes over church property frequently ensued. Moreover, even when whites helped blacks acquire churches, they often opposed their use as schools. Buildings of any kind were difficult to come by. A large number of the South's structures had suffered war damage. Whites who owned serviceable buildings often refused to rent rooms to freedmen's teachers. A Freedman's Bureau official in Texas described the problem: "We do not possess in the entire State a school-house with two rooms, or the facilities for grading pupils, while in many promising localities it is impossible to rent even a cabin."[37]

Money was a perpetual headache. Black communities made prodigious efforts to raise funds to build and support schools, but they could rarely sustain them solely on the basis of voluntary effort. Many communities were too poor to support a teacher. Others started schools but quickly ran into financial difficulties. The nub of the problem was that black families could not afford monthly tuition fees, which averaged $1.50 even for school terms that lasted only a few months. Under the emerging sharecropping system, black farmers rented land in return for a portion of the crop, but they saw little return until the cotton was harvested. Floods, droughts, and crop failures added to their woes. Grinding poverty not only undermined blacks' ability to pay tuition fees but also placed them under great pressure to put all their children to work. For both reasons, school attendance declined. Teachers, dependent upon the tuition fees, suffered desperate privation and sometimes gave up. "The enthusiasm of the people for Schools is great and intense but very short-lived," observed one Freedmen's Bureau agent, "especially when the money question is involved."[38]

Help from the Freedmen's Bureau, and the arrival of teachers from the North, transformed this dire situation. In theory, the Bureau was not permitted to pay salaries or build schoolhouses. In practice, however, it did both. The Bureau requisitioned buildings that had been abandoned or confiscated. Loosely interpreting its power to rent and repair buildings, it often paid the lion's share of the construction costs of new buildings. By March 1869 it had helped build or repair 630 schoolhouses, spending $1.7 million under the heading of "rents and repairs." The Bureau also allowed "rent" money to be applied to salaries—a subsidy amounting to $10 per teacher—and helped teachers secure books and other supplies. It paid the cost of transporting northern teachers to the South, helped them find accommodation, and tried to protect them. Bureau agents visited and inspected freedmen's schools, and sometimes taught in them. All told, the Bureau spent about $13 million on black schools during its five-year existence. Working closely with the northern aid societies, which between them spent an equivalent sum, it facilitated the work of about ten thousand northern teachers and several thousand southern black ones.[39]

The Freedmen's Bureau also helped black communities overcome their reluctance to organize schools for fear of white reprisals. At meetings in churches or in the open air, agents informed freed people of their rights, described the benefits of education, and explained how to organize a school. Freedmen needed this help. Between emancipation and the passage of the Fourteenth Amendment in 1867, their legal status was unclear. Even such an elementary right as the right to own property needed confirmation. A black teacher in Monticello, Georgia, for example, informed the Bureau that blacks wished to buy land for a school, but whites had told them that "according to their law" they could not hold land. "I would be extremely grateful if you will tell us if we have not the right to hold land that we buy." Bureau agents tried to guarantee the future of freedmen's schools by insisting that black trustees owned the land on which they stood. They also negotiated with local whites in an attempt to prevent crippling opposition.[40]

The black agents appointed by the Bureau were especially effective in stimulating the freedmen's efforts. In Missouri, John Milton Turner, an Oberlin-educated former slave with a reputation as a "fiery orator," traveled eight thousand miles in 1869–70 and helped found thirty-two schools. The Freedmen's Bureau in Georgia employed William Jefferson White, a Baptist minister and political leader in Augusta. The bearded, beetle-browed White had the appearance of a white man, but he identified completely with the freedmen. William H. Heard, the seventeen-year-old teacher who later became a bishop in the AME Church, heard White address a meeting in Elberton. It was a "political speech," he recalled. "He was the first colored man I had ever seen who was so well educated, and who could use the King's English readily, accurately, and convincingly. He very much influenced me and I determined from that night to be a MAN, and to fill an important place in life's arena."[41]

George T. Ruby, the black Bureau agent in Louisiana who was the former principal of Frederick Douglass School in New Orleans and a highly regarded teacher, in 1866 crisscrossed ten parishes, assessing where it would be feasible to establish schools. The white attitudes he encountered ran the gamut. In Terrebonne Parish, he reported, planters "are generally unwilling to tolerate freedmen's schools, and have told me plainly that they wish as little to do with the Bureau as possible." On the other hand, the mayor of Jackson, East Feliciana Parish, possessed "tolerably right feelings on the subject." At a meeting of freedmen in the same parish, two dozen poor whites created a shiver of fear by entering the church. Ruby refused to be intimidated. "I calmly got up and stated to the freedmen the purpose of my coming among them—spoke of the advantages of education, [and] alluded to the fact of their freedom giving them to understand that if they could sustain a school no person could molest them." The white "Chivalry . . . slunk gradually away leaving the meeting to the freedmen."[42]

Radical Reconstruction, which Congress imposed on the South in 1867 after repudiating the Reconstruction plan of President Andrew

Johnson, encouraged black teachers to become political leaders because freedmen now became voters. Yet partisan politics exposed black teachers to fresh dangers. The struggle between Republicans and Democrats for political control of the South intensified white violence when the Ku Klux Klan targeted Republican activists. Kentucky teacher Elijah P. Marrs, a former slave and veteran of the Union army, felt like a marked man. "For three years," he recalled, "I slept with a pistol under my head, an Enfield rifle at my side, and a corn-knife at the door." Teachers who became Republican leaders had good reason to fear that every day might be their last. In 1870 Richard Burke, a teacher-preacher in Sumter County, Alabama, and a member of the state legislature, was gunned down in his home. His former owner described Burke as "a quiet man" who had "made himself obnoxious to a certain class of young men by having been a leader in the Loyal League and by having acquired a great influence over people of his color." The Ku Klux Klan destroyed school buildings. "They were school-houses in which colored pupils were taught by Republican teachers," explained Dr. N. B. Cloud, Alabama's superintendent of education. That freedmen often used schoolhouses as community halls made them doubly attractive as targets.[43]

Although Radical Reconstruction ended disastrously for blacks in the South, the Republican Party had meant well. President Andrew Johnson had inherited both the White House and a conciliatory Reconstruction policy from Abraham Lincoln. However, his political ineptitude and crude racism alienated the Republican Party and discredited the policy of leniency. In 1867, incensed by white southerners' mistreatment of blacks and white Unionists, the Republican-controlled Congress seized control of Reconstruction policy from the president. It returned the southern states to military rule and imposed stringent conditions for the restoration of their rights as full-fledged members of the Union. Striking down state laws that discriminated against blacks, Congress passed the Fourteenth Amendment to the Constitution, thereby creating a uniform definition of national citizenship that placed the former slaves on an equal legal footing with whites. Congress also insisted upon new state constitutions that enfranchised adult black males. At the same time, it barred most of the South's former leaders from holding public office.

Congressional Reconstruction—better known as Radical Reconstruction—brought about a political revolution in the South. It made the ex-slaves suddenly more powerful than their old masters: black votes enabled the Republican Party to control almost every southern state for a time. Indeed, Radical Reconstruction *demanded* the political participation of black southerners. Instead of making Reconstruction an administrative matter—by continuing military rule, for example—Congress quickly restored the ex-Confederate states to equal membership in the Union. Hence the fortunes of the freed people were linked to the electoral success of the Republican Party. In lieu of military protection, Radical Reconstruction gave freedmen the vote. The fortunes of the freed people were tied to the ability of the Republicans to control both the federal government and state governments in the South. Blacks therefore rallied to politics as a means of self-defense. As North Carolina teacher William D. Harris put it, "Unless we curtail the political power of the Rebels and increase the power of the loyal people by giving the negro the ballot, the South may yet succeed in ruining our great Republic."[44]

As bearers of literacy in a population that was 95 percent illiterate, black teachers were a natural source of leadership. Lest they be criticized for sullying education with politics, we must remember the intensely partisan culture of the nineteenth century. The notion of teachers as nonpolitical public employees was alien to that age. Teaching was not, in any case, a clearly defined profession but rather an occasional or part-time occupation. Teachers moved in and out of the classroom; they were also lawyers, planters, farmers, sharecroppers, newspaper editors, and ministers. In the broad process of community formation, blacks did not regard education as a distinct category. As a white Democrat from Louisiana noted, the freedmen "mix up in their churches religion, school, and politics."[45]

Plunging into politics, black teachers made a vital contribution to building the southern Republican Party. They served as voter registrars and election supervisors. They headed Union Leagues and Republican clubs, drilled the freedmen on the mechanics of voting, and distributed ballot papers. They conveyed information from newspapers, political tracts, and official documents to the overwhelmingly illiterate masses. Of the approximately fifteen hundred blacks who held public office during Reconstruction, 11 percent of them, 176 people, had taught in schools. Every state had its complement of teacher-politicians. Only ministers, 243 of whom held political office, 16 percent of the total, furnished a greater number of black political leaders.[46]

BLACK teachers had a particular stake in the political success of the Republican Party: they believed that the education of black southerners depended upon it. This is not to say that southern whites were overwhelmingly hostile to black schools. Many agreed that the freedmen needed literacy. White southerners helped blacks build churches and schoolhouses. Many taught in freedmen's schools.[47] However, the argument of historian Walter L. Fleming that southern whites supported black schools in the immediate aftermath of the Civil War, before Radical Reconstruction soured them, is misleading. Schoolhouses were being lost to arson, and black teachers threatened and even killed, long before Radical Reconstruction.[48] Freedmen's Bureau agents described the wider picture. From Georgia, General Davis Tillson complained, "In almost every case . . . the withdrawal of troops has been followed by outrages on the freed people; their school-houses have been burned, [and] their teachers driven off or threatened with death." In Louisiana, the school system virtually collapsed in the summer of 1866 when a wave of political violence engulfed the state. "Many acts of personal violence and insult were committed on the teachers," reported General Sheridan.[49] It would be wrong, of course, to tar all white southerners with the brush of violence. Although common, incendiary attacks upon schools and violence against freedmen's teachers were the exception, not the rule.[50] Most southern whites seem to have been passively hostile or coldly indifferent toward black schools.[51]

Perhaps the most accurate measure of white attitudes toward the education of blacks was the failure of white southerners, when they controlled state governments between 1865 and 1867, to make any public provision for black schools. This neglect did not reflect opposition to the principle of public education—several states had already inaugurated public schools systems before the Civil War. But the state with the most advanced system, North Carolina, abolished its public schools after the war because, explained Governor Jonathan Worth, it wished to "avoid this question of educating negroes." In Mississippi, writes historian Vernon Lane Wharton, "from press and pulpit came the call for action," but "the movement [to establish schools for blacks] was almost completely without results."[52]

The creation of public school systems that included *both* races was the single most enduring achievement of Radical Reconstruction. Unfortunately those systems were financially and administratively weak. Many Republicans believed the time was ripe to establish a national school system, with compulsory school attendance, compulsory integration, and a dominant role for the federal government. Indeed, some blacks looked to Prussia for their model rather than New England, attributing Prussia's stunning victory over Austria in 1866 to the excellence of its education system as much as to military might. Instead of a building a national education system, however, Congress left it to the individual states to construct public school systems upon traditional, locally based lines. In doing so, southern Republicans opted for voluntary attendance rather than Prussian-style compulsion.[53] Moreover, rather than invite a mass boycott by southern whites by insisting upon integration, blacks permitted the public schools to be organized along racially separate lines. South Carolina's Republicans provided that all public schools, colleges, and universities should be "free and open to all," but permitted single-race schools, knowing full well that virtually all the public schools would be either black or white. Still, the Republicans were careful to specify that black schools and white schools should receive public funding on an equal basis.[54]

Racial segregation enabled the public schools to enroll a substantial number of white children. Nevertheless, many whites bitterly resented paying taxes to support the education of blacks. As one white educator put it, "The free schools were generally regarded by the white man as part and parcel of that system which sought to . . . place him under the domination of his former slaves and their abolition friends."[55] The situation in Weakley County, Tennessee, illustrated the extreme form that white opposition to public schools sometimes took. Archelaus M. Hughes, the superintendent of schools, organized forty-three schools for whites before daring to establish a black school. After some difficulty he found a property owner who was prepared to offer some land. He then secured aid from the Freedmen's Bureau to build a schoolhouse, and appointed a black teacher, a student from Fisk University. The school flourished, and Hughes felt confident that other schools for black children could soon be started. But then disaster struck. "The Ku-Klux or at least men in disguise broke up the colored school at Dresden Thursday night by taking out the teacher—a colored man named Wells—and whipping him severely and ordering him to leave town on the first train."[56]

In Mississippi, the passage of a public school law in 1870 precipitated a wave of Klan violence in the northeastern section of the State. Parties of Klansmen ordered teachers to quit, forced school directors to resign, and ordered county superintendents to step down. Teachers and officials were threatened and beaten. The raiders shot into schoolhouses and set them ablaze. In one county, the Klan made a bonfire of the scrip issued by the state to pay teachers. Those whom the Klan "dealt with" included southerners and northerners, whites and blacks, Democrats and Republicans, men and women. Resentment against a "Radical" tax that maintained schools for blacks fueled the violence. As the Klansmen who whipped Cornelius McBride, a young Irish-born teacher, explained, "the people" would not pay taxes to keep "lazy niggers in school." The Klan destroyed at least twenty-five schools, including half a dozen church buildings. Hundreds of blacks, and a few whites, were whipped. About fifty blacks were killed.[57]

ALTHOUGH the level of violence against black schools and their teachers declined, Radical Reconstruction backfired disastrously. In the words of North Carolina carpetbagger Albion W. Tourgee, it pitted "a race unskilled in public affairs, poor to a degree hardly to be matched in the civilized world, and so ignorant that not five out a hundred of its voters could read their own ballots" against "the wealth, the intelligence, the organizing skill, the pride, and the hate of a people it had taken four years to conquer." In mobilizing the freedmen as voters and politicians against a white population that had been bloodied, impoverished, and politically decapitated, the Republicans miscalculated. The majority of southern whites rejected Radical Reconstruction and set about destroying it. White opposition ranged from sullen noncooperation to organized terrorism. It gained in force as the federal government scaled down its military presence in the South and the national Republican Party showed irresolution, disunity, and waning interest in black rights. Blacks resisted the Democratic counterattack, but they either lacked the numbers to prevail, or, if they did possess the numbers, succumbed to the paramilitary skill and ruthlessness of well-armed Confederate veterans.[58]

Alfred Raford Blunt, a former slave and a Republican leader in Natchitoches Parish, Louisiana, typified the kind of teacher-politician whom white Democrats were bent on silencing. Thirty years old when the Civil War ended, Blunt quickly emerged as the most influential black leader in northwestern Louisiana. In 1869 he organized the First Baptist Church in Natchitoches, which soon boasted five hundred members. The following year he became president of the Twelfth District Baptist Association, which embraced twenty-eight black churches. Blunt also acquired property, owning two houses, several town lots, 120 acres of land, and a newspaper, the *Natchitoches Republican.* A popular politician, he served six years in the state legislature. As secretary of the parish school board, he was instrumental in setting up the public schools in Natchitoches, and he taught one of them himself.

White Democrats loathed Blunt's passionate appeals to race solidarity. They accused him of abusing his position as a minister in order to enforce Republican loyalty. He urged the party faithful to ostracize any blacks who voted the Democratic ticket; he allegedly told wives to "consider the marriage-bond dissolved" if their husbands deserted the Republican Party. Such was Blunt's influence that many dubbed him a "bishop," although Baptists, of course, recognized no such title.[59]

When the Republican Party organized Natchitoches Parish, black teachers enrolled and drilled the freedmen. This exposed them to threats and violence. Schoolteacher R. L. Faulkner received a nighttime visitation from a group of disguised men. "I was taken out and blindfolded and questioned." Berating Faulkner for distributing Republican tickets, the masked men destroyed his ballot papers, burnt his schoolbooks, and "beat him near to death." The whites warned him to stay out of politics or "they would hang him." Notwithstanding such intimidation, the Republicans won the 1868 election handily, gaining control of both the town and the parish. Natchitoches provided the key to Republican control of Louisiana's Fourth Congressional District, which consisted of four majority-black parishes.[60]

In the confused election of 1872 the Democrats changed tactics. Abandoning their party label, they supported a "fusion" ticket consisting of Democrats and disillusioned Republicans. In Natchitoches, Democrat E. L. Pierson ran for the state legislature as a "liberal Republican." To ease his election, Governor Henry C. Warmoth, who had bolted the Republican Party, appointed Pierson the supervisor of elections and decreed that Natchitoches Parish could be treated as a single precinct. On election day, Pierson set up only four ballot boxes for the entire parish, which four, in his own words, "the whites took possession of." He also deputized virtually all the white men in the town of Natchitoches as "special policemen." Black teacher John G. Lewis tried to observe the count as a federal election supervisor, but Pierson's officials barred his way. Lewis did not force the issue: "I did not wish to imperil my person by going in." Across the state, both the Republicans and the "fusion party" claimed victory. Louisiana had two rival governments until federal troops restored Republican control of the statehouse.[61] In order to avoid the kind of bloodshed that occurred in neighboring Grant Parish—where a pitched battle for possession of the courthouse in Colfax left 108 people dead, all but three of them blacks—party leaders in Natchitoches agreed to divide the parish offices between Democrats and Republicans.[62]

The truce lasted about a year. In 1874 Louisiana Democrats organized the White League, with the goal of "cleansing" the state of Republican rule. In Natchitoches the White League disguised itself as the "Tax-Payers' Association," which ratcheted up the pressure by holding a series of mass meetings in the summer of 1874. Its propaganda, published in James H. Cosgrove's *Natchitoches Vindicator,* harped on the onerous taxation levied by Republican officials and alleged that the public school system was riddled with corruption. The Tax-Payers' Association demanded the resignation of Republican officials on the grounds that they were "ignorant and corrupt." If they quit, the Association pledged, "no violence would be offered . . . and no harm done by the people." The Republican officials resigned. Some also fled.[63]

The White League also targeted teachers of black schools. The *Natchitoches Vindicator* accused a white teacher from Vermont, a "fiend in human shape," of inciting blacks to "murder and rapine." In Bienville Parish a party of armed men beat one teacher and ordered another, a former Confederate soldier, to leave. A band of White Leaguers ordered a black teacher from Pennsylvania to quit the parish within ten hours. He did so.[64]

On August 30, 1874, the White League seized six white Republican officials in the town of Coushatta. While the prisoners were being escorted out of Red River Parish, a band of whites from De Soto Parish, led by a man who styled himself "Captain Jack," murdered them. The "Coushatta Massacre" sent tremors of fear through the Republican Party of Natchitoches. Blunt hid in the woods, eventually emerging to plead for his life. He told the White Leaguers that he would quit politics, "promising to attend to my own business." The Democratic leaders ordered him to withdraw from the campaign and "quiet the tone" of his paper, the *Natchitoches Republican.* Blunt spent much of September looking over his shoulder. He never slept in his house at night. "I had friends who would secrete me in places where I would not likely be found."

But the Republicans of Natchitoches stubbornly refused to give up the ghost. After the "Coushatta Massacre," a federal posse rounded up and arrested twenty-five leading Democrats, including Cosgrave, the editor of the *Natchitoches Vindicator.* The arrests bucked up the Republicans. In the 1874 election, the black vote in Natchitoches actually *increased* over 1872. Moreover, Republican state election officials, after weighing evidence of fraud and intimidation in adjoining parishes, awarded the state senate seat to Raford Blunt. Intimidation reduced the Republican vote in 1876, but black voters still refused to cave in. Once again, the state election board set aside the results in two rural precincts and declared Blunt the elected senator. The Republicans in

Natchitoches were dangerously isolated, however. Although he represented four parishes, Blunt rarely ventured outside Natchitoches.

The Compromise of 1877 gave Louisiana's Democrats control over the state government. In permitting Republican candidate Rutherford B. Hayes to enter the White House, thereby resolving a bitterly disputed election, the Democratic Party compelled the Republican Party to concede defeat in Florida, South Carolina, and Louisiana. The Democrats in Natchitoches moved in for the kill. In the run-up to the 1878 elections, Democratic leaders claimed that the Republicans, led by Blunt, planned an armed insurrection. In response to this spurious threat, the Democrats occupied Natchitoches with hundreds of armed men. Blunt took two pistols and a Winchester rifle and barricaded himself in the garret of his house. Friends, armed with double-barrel shotguns, took up vantage points. Armed whites, perhaps two hundred strong, converged on Blunt's home and shouted for Blunt to surrender. They took him to jail. M. J. Cunningham, the district attorney, demanded that Blunt "say to the niggers to desist from politics at once." When his prisoner caviled, Cunningham exploded. "By God, Blunt, we ain't going to let you dictate now; we are going to dictate, and you must comply." His captors escorted Blunt out of town and told him to leave Natchitoches Parish. He made his way to New Orleans. In the November election the Democrats carried Natchitoches Parish by 2,811 to 0.[65]

RECONSTRUCTION ended in a crushing defeat for black southerners. Yet after the dust of the political war had settled, black schools were an accomplished fact. Ironically, the demise of Republican rule in some ways diminished white opposition to them. The "redemption" of each southern state from Republican control, the failure of the 1875 Civil Rights Bill to outlaw segregated public schools, and the final collapse of Radical Reconstruction in 1877 made black schools seem less threatening to white southerners. Moreover, now that the Democrats controlled every state government in the former Confederacy, they could weaken the links between the public schools and the Republican Party.

Black schools also survived because the freedmen, in effect, wore down white opposition through sheer tenacity. In the tight labor market wrought by emancipation, white landlords had to compete for black workers. Just as blacks insisted upon sharecropping rather than gang labor, so too sharecroppers often demanded schools as a condition of employment. Hence a significant number of white landlords allowed blacks to establish public schools upon their property and disapproved of Ku Klux Klan attacks on them. Pearson J. Glover, a planter in Marengo County, Alabama, employed a nineteen-year-old white man to teach "the colored school on my place." When Klan members whipped the unfortunate teacher, Glover attributed the attack to "jealousy among the lower classes for the negro." Partly because of the influence of the large planters, violence against black schools had already subsided by the time Reconstruction ended.[66]

The "Redeemers"—Democrats who "redeemed" the South by ending Republican rule—did not suppress black schools. They were wary of provoking further federal intervention. They also wished to attract black support, for blacks continued to vote in large numbers. Incoming Democratic governors of Mississippi, South Carolina, and Louisiana therefore pledged to support the public schools and administer them without discrimination. Moreover, every state in the South could produce prominent Democrats and former Confederates—men like Gustavus Orr of Georgia, William H. Ruffner of Virginia, and Jabez L. M. Curry of Alabama—who worked to strengthen public schools and dispel the stigma of their being associated with Radical Reconstruction. They even supported proposals for federal aid to public schools.[67]

Still, the collapse of Radical Reconstruction had damaging consequences for black education. In the minds of many white southerners, teachers had encouraged the former slaves to hate their old masters and to follow northern leadership. Freedmen's schools became synonymous with a Yankee-led effort to mold blacks into a political bloc that the Republican Party manipulated. They were part and parcel of a policy designed to oppress and humiliate the white South. The public schools also suffered from being associated with financial malfeasance. Shady accounting, the use of teaching posts as political patronage, speculation in the vouchers or warrants that were issued to pay teachers, and outright stealing of school funds were all too common. It was Radical Reconstruction, argued Alabama-born historian Walter L. Fleming, not hostility to black education per se, that caused so many white southerners to resent the freedmen's schools. The politicization of black schools, first by the intervention of white northern teachers and then by the direct involvement of black teachers in Republican Party politics, embittered southern whites. Although Fleming's argument was flawed—black schools had received little encouragement from southern whites before Congress took over Reconstruction—it was not wholly wrong. The close association of black teachers with Radical Reconstruction fueled white distrust of the public school systems inaugurated by Republican governments.[68]

White hostility to black schools stubbornly persisted. Many planters believed that schools weakened their ability to retain blacks as sharecroppers and laborers. White southerners continued to be suspicious of black teachers, and of educated blacks in general, especially if they refused to abjure their loyalty to the Republican Party. Whites everywhere believed that they were massively subsidizing black schools, and they strongly supported proposals to divide taxes by race—on the premise that black schools would wither away if they depended upon black property owners alone. Although the Redeemers did not abolish the public schools, therefore, they slashed expenditures on public education. They also sought to blunt the influence of black teachers by limiting their numbers, training, and pay. The same motive drove them to discourage the efforts of northern white educators to promote the "higher education" of black southerners.[69]

Some blacks sought an accommodation with the South's new political rulers. Discouraged by the unraveling of Reconstruction, they lost faith in the Republican Party and debated the wisdom of retreating from politics in an effort to remove education from the partisan battlefield. Others, although shocked by the Democratic triumph, were determined to remain active Republicans. Either way, black communities still looked to teachers to provide inspiration and leadership. With integration outside the realm of possibility, the building and strengthening of black institutions provided a basis for common action for black southerners, a means of salvaging small victories from the larger defeat of Reconstruction. The notion that schools for black children should be run by black teachers, and black teachers only, was not a new one. After 1877, however, it became an unstoppable movement.

CHAPTER TWO

Black Teachers for Black Children

The future educators of the blacks both in
America and Africa, are the blacks.

Joseph C. Price, diary entry, 1877

Miss Hardie Martin, teacher in public
school, Montgomery, Alabama.

New York Public Library

Bꜱʜᴏᴘ Jᴀᴍᴇꜱ Wᴀʟᴋᴇʀ Hᴏᴏᴅ believed that black children should be taught by black teachers. "It is impossible for white teachers, educated as they necessarily are in this country, to enter into the feelings of colored pupils as the colored teacher does," he told North Carolina's constitutional convention in 1869. "I do not think that it is good for our children to eat and drink daily the sentiment that they are naturally inferior to the whites, which they do in three-fourths of all the schools where they have white teachers." A native of Pennsylvania, Hood was instrumental in planting the AME Zion (AMEZ) Church in North Carolina, and he quickly established himself as an influential Republican leader there. He adamantly opposed requiring racial segregation by law, arguing that any legal distinction between white and black schools would open the door to discrimination. As a practical reality, however, he favored racially separate schools.[1]

By 1900 Hood's wish had come true. In virtually all of the rural public schools, and in most of the urban ones as well, black teachers had replaced whites. Whites still taught in a few public schools for black children—mainly in Charleston, New Orleans, and Richmond—but they constituted only a tiny fraction of the teaching force. By the 1920s hardly any white teachers could be found in black schools.

In an obvious sense, the emergence of a racially segregated teaching force was the logical consequence of a racially segregated school system. Yet it was not as straightforward and inevitable as it seemed. After all, white southerners had tried to suppress black literacy under slavery, deplored the political activities of black teachers during Reconstruction, and continued to be deeply suspicious of black schools. Why, then, did they allow black teachers to monopolize the classroom? The most effective way of policing black education, and of reducing its potential to contest white supremacy, would have been to install southern-born white teachers, preferably reliable Democrats, in black schools. Yet the Redeemers made no systematic attempt to do this; on the contrary, they acquiesced in the replacement of native white teachers with blacks.

The position of the "Yankee schoolmarms" added a further complication. Of all the whites in America, the northerners who taught in freedmen's schools were the ones most dedicated to black uplift and equality. Many stayed beyond the customary year or two and devoted their lives to this cause. Some founded colleges and universities for blacks. Indeed, northern white teachers provided the main lever for raising the standard of black education. Yet they, too, found themselves under pressure to step down in favor of black teachers. Campaigns to replace white teachers exuded a racial chauvinism that questioned the wisdom of allowing *any* whites to instruct black children. The movement to oust white teachers therefore produced strange alliances between black and white southerners who shared a desire to replace white northerners.

But if the replacement of white teachers with blacks represented a rough kind of compromise between white and black southerners, the latter got the worst of the deal. White supremacists acceded to the demand for black teachers as a way to weaken black education. Eliminating the "Yankee schoolmarms" lowered the educational ceiling and deprived blacks of influential northern allies. Replacing white teachers with blacks reinforced racial segregation and made it easier for whites to neglect black schools as black political influence declined and then vanished.

The freedmen's aid societies never believed that the North could supply enough white teachers to sustain a system of mass education for black southerners. By the end of 1865, northern churches and freedmen's aid societies supported 1,314 teachers in the South, of whom 90 percent were whites. But the freedmen's schools reached, at most, 10 percent of the black school-age population. The freedmen's aid societies could not possibly finance a universal school system in the South; moreover, most of the white teachers they sponsored did not intend to stay in the South for long. The northern churches therefore founded "universities" such as Fisk and Atlanta, as well as secondary or "normal" schools, whose principal function was the production of black teachers. The abolition of the Freedmen's Bureau in 1870 and declining white interest in the problems of the freed people hastened the shift to black teachers. Northern whites soldiered on, however, in many of the black private schools. Moreover, they continued to dominate black higher education.[2]

Security also favored the employment of black teachers. White teachers from the North were so hated by white southerners that the Freedmen's Bureau often feared for their safety. Said army chaplain George Hovey, writing from the relative security of Galveston, Texas, "Not one of them could remain here *24 hours* if the Military were to be removed." However, the army, now a skeleton force of less than twenty thousand men, could not possibly safeguard every freedmen's school. Therefore, argued Edwin Wheelock, it was prudent to locate freedmen's schools in the towns, "where there are troops, and an agent of the Bureau to protect the teachers." For reasons of safety, therefore, as well as for reasons of economy, most northern white teachers were assigned to urban areas. This meant that vast stretches of the rural South—where the bulk of the black population resided—had no freedmen's schools. Bureau officials like Wheelock believed that southern-born black teachers would be more readily tolerated by the white population. "Native teachers will arouse less opposition than any other, will penetrate where a white instructor dare not, and will live where he would starve."[3]

Blacks themselves sometimes requested teachers of their own race. In some cases the same concern for safety influenced their preference. The trustees of a freedmen's school in Fayetteville, Tennessee, told the Bureau that a white teacher had been unable to find lodging with a white family, and that the schoolhouse had gone up in flames. A colored teacher, they hoped, would meet the approval of local whites. Most often, however, the freed people preferred black teachers because they objected to white southerners instructing their children. "Prefer Colored [teachers] if they can be procured," requested a freedman in Greensboro, Georgia, explaining that "several White men . . . want to get the School but they are Bitter rebs. We don't want them to have it."[4]

Why did so many former Confederates wish to teach in freedmen's schools? In many cases, sheer grinding poverty persuaded native whites to ignore the stigma attached to teaching black children. In 1867, reporting from Georgia, G. L. Eberhart of the Freedmen's Bureau described with a touch of *Schadenfreude* the pathetic desperation with which former Confederates sought teaching commissions. "Preachers, doctors—white men and women—within the last month continuously besieging me to teach colored schools!" Native-born whites quickly supplied a substantial portion, and sometimes a majority, of the teachers in black schools during Reconstruction. In the cities of the South, the proportion of white teachers was often much higher. Indeed, school boards in Montgomery, Richmond, Nashville, Charleston, Raleigh, and elsewhere refused to appoint any black teachers at all.[5]

Blacks appear to have disliked most of these native whites. White teachers failed to associate with the freed people on a plane of equality, complained P. B. Randolph of the Freedmen's Bureau. Blacks "object to paying persons who continually insult them, called them 'Niggers,' rap their children over the head with heavy sticks, and totally neglect everything connected with their vocation except the collection of the salary." Of the Bureau's black agents, Randolph may have been the most outspoken in advocating race as a factor in the appointment of teachers. "The Freed people open their hearts to me because I am colored," he claimed. "[They] everywhere ask for [black teachers.]"[6]

But other Bureau agents feared that bowing to racial considerations might saddle the freed people with incompetents. A Tennessee official complained that many blacks had no idea what made a good teacher: "The colored people . . . are often 'mighty proud' of would-be teachers who can scarcely read." When popular but incompetent native black teachers kept children away from more rigorous, predominantly white, northern-trained teachers, the effects were doubly damaging. In Tennessee, Assistant Commissioner D. Burt rejected requests for colored teachers. "I know of none to be had." In Louisiana, George T. Ruby usually approved the freedmen's own choice of teacher, but then tried to find a more competent instructor.[7]

Bureau officials also worried that racial chauvinism would play into the hands of white southerners unsympathetic to black education. After the southern states passed public school laws, the appointment of teachers shifted from the Freedmen's Bureau and the freedmen's aid societies to local school boards. As Republican power receded, white Democrats gained control of these school boards. Having lost the battle to prevent the establishment of schools for blacks, some Democrats sought to cripple those schools by appointing semiliterate teachers. In Tipton, Missouri, for example, the school board proposed to employ, in the words of Bureau agent J. Milton Turner, "an incompetent and very ignorant Negro man." Turner, himself black, persuaded the board to employ "a very good teacher and a white man." If neither side could agree on a competent teacher, Turner sometimes withheld Bureau funding. "In many localities positive objections are raised by both white and colored inhabitants to the appointment of white teachers in colored schools. Whenever practical I have respected this prejudice but owing to the scarcity of efficient teachers of my own color . . . the establishment of schools has been considerably hindered."[8]

Still, the number of black teachers steadily increased. The proportion varied from state to state. In North Carolina, Georgia, Virginia, and Tennessee, where the freedmen's aid societies invested heavily of their resources, blacks at first constituted only a small percentage. Where the societies were less active, black teachers soon outnumbered whites. In Kentucky, which received relatively little attention from the freedmen's aid societies, black teachers were a majority from the outset. Across the South as a whole, by 1868 more than half of the eight thousand freedmen's schoolteachers were black.[9]

SOUTHERN whites rejoiced at the departure of northern white schoolteachers. Alabama educator J. L. M. Curry described them as "fanatical men and women ignorant of negro peculiarities, inexperienced as to methods of teaching, full of self-conceit, and possessed of a fatal facility of rubbing fur the wrong way." Many believed that if native-born whites—loyal Democrats—replaced them, black children could be taught to accept a subordinate position in the new social order. As the editor of the *Daily Mississippi Standard* put it, native whites would teach black children "Southern ideas of the relative social relations, rights and duties of the races."[10]

But the Redeemer vision of molding the freed people through the agency of conservative white teachers failed to endure. The Redeemers lacked a strong commitment to public education: lukewarm in their support for white public schools, they spent even less on black ones. As black schools languished, the job of teaching in black schools became increasingly unattractive. When the South's economy revived, and when more jobs became available at the expanding white public schools, southern white teachers—most of whom had been driven to teach black children by near-starvation, rather than by any missionary impulse or political conviction—left black schools. After the demise of Reconstruction, the number of white people teaching black children declined precipitously. From time to time, whites debated the merits of placing native white teachers in black schools. But such a policy had no chance of widespread implementation without public funding and support.

The replacement of white teachers with blacks occurred first in rural schools, then in the urban ones. The situation in the two areas differed considerably. In the rural South, whites generally did not resist the appointment of black teachers because the job was so poorly paid. In the South's cities, on the other hand, school boards made a systematic effort to place white teachers over black children. They succeeded for a time because longer terms, better schoolhouses, and higher pay made city schools fairly attractive places to teach in. Moreover, there was no substantial difference between what white and black teachers earned. Hence whites taught in black city schools long after they had all but disappeared from black rural schools.

Yet the same economic and political logic that produced an all-black teaching force in rural public schools eventually produced the same result in the cities. School boards realized that they could appoint black teachers without losing control of black schools, and at the same time they could save money by paying black teachers less. By the First World War only Charleston, South Carolina, continued to staff its black public schools with white teachers. In the rest of the South, it was a settled principle that blacks, not whites, taught black children.

To many African Americans, demanding black teachers for black schools was a Faustian pact. It was the best bargain they could strike under an unjust system of racial segregation—not an endorsement of that system or a recognition of any claims to racial superiority or inferiority. "The line of demarkation on the school question . . . was not drawn by us," black leaders in Petersburg, Virginia, pointed out. However, if blacks were forced to submit to that color line, "let the submissiveness be *in toto* i.e. colored pupils, colored teachers."[11]

OTHER blacks regarded segregation in a more positive light. The parallel is not perfect, but the desire for black teachers resembled the widespread preference for black ministers. By 1870 most black southerners had quit white churches, organized their own congregations, and selected preachers of their own race. They did this partly to escape the racism of the white southern denominations that had defended slavery with such vigor. But ethnocentrism—a desire for self-direction—also spurred the formation of black churches. Hence even the egalitarian churches of northern-based white denominations such as the Congregationalists and the Methodists attracted relatively few black members. Schools, like churches, were pillars of emerging black communities. Underpinning the demand for black teachers was a desire for black leadership and cultural autonomy.

To be sure, many blacks felt that southern white teachers were prejudiced or incompetent, and often both. They complained that school boards forced black schools to accept "poor white teachers who are not allowed to teach in the white schools." And they asserted that even the better-educated white teachers often displayed a lack of interest in, and even a dislike of, their black pupils. The fact that most of the native whites were Democrats made them even more objectionable. Although the Freedmen's Bureau favored southern white teachers

from Unionist backgrounds, it also appointed innumerable former
Confederates, many of whom made little pretense of hiding their belief in black inferiority. Black schools tended to attract destitute and
crippled whites—war widows, deserted wives, limbless ex-Confeder-
ates—who looked upon teaching black children as a last resort. A
Democrat from St. James Parish, Louisiana, expressed a widespread
prejudice when he referred to such teachers as "ward bummers,"
"men of dissipated habits," and "brigadier generals of the confederate
army, majors, captains, and so forth."[12]

Yet some southern white teachers were conscientious and fair-
minded. Robert R. Moton attended a public school in Prince Edward
County, Virginia, taught by John Morisette, a former Confederate officer. He remembered Morisette as "kind and thoughtful and very
patient." College president Nathan B. Young, who grew up in Tuscaloosa, Alabama, described his first teacher, a southern-born white
Baptist minister, as a "philosopher, guide, and friend." He responded
warmly to this man's relaxed attitude to discipline, democratic approach, and enthusiasm for the classics. His white teacher's stories
from Greek and Roman mythology transfixed Young, inspiring him to
master Latin and Greek. Rev. James H. Eason, a Baptist preacher from
Sumter County, Alabama, recalled that his first teacher, a white man
named Poe, encouraged him through praise: "You will be a smart man
one of these days."[13]

A few white southerners emulated the dedication of the northern
missionaries. Major Giles B. Cooke, for example, who had served on
the staff of Robert E. Lee during the Civil War, was a driving force
behind the establishment of black schools in Petersburg, Virginia.
In 1868 he served as principal of Number One Colored Elementary
School and the associated Colored Public High School—the first in
the South—whose curriculum included "the higher math, the classics,
and the sciences." In 1873, after ordination as an Episcopalian minister, Cooke became rector of St. Stephen's Parish, a black congregation,
and organized a church school. St. Stephen's School maintained primary, intermediate, and higher education departments, the last functioning as a "normal school" that prepared pupils to teach in Virginia's
rural schools. One of Cooke's pupils, Rev. James Solomon Russell,

founded a successful private school in Lawrenceville that survives to this day. Cooke and Russell became lifelong friends: the pair agreed that whoever died first, the other would officiate at his funeral.[14]

In 1869, however, blacks in Petersburg petitioned the school board to replace white teachers with black ones. The petitioners argued that white teachers, however well intentioned, were incapable of overcoming their deeply rooted racial prejudice. They charged that the white teacher—"unless an abolitionist of the deepest dye"—failed to instill ambition in black pupils and refused to associate with blacks outside the schoolhouse "from a dread of social equality." If white teachers were strangers to black parents and black communities, they could not be effective teachers of black children. "We do not want our children to be trained to think or feel that they are inferior." Spurned by the school board, blacks petitioned again in 1875 and 1881.[15]

Behind the petitions lay a fundamental question: Who should lead the black community? Southern white teachers like Giles B. Cooke adapted the tradition of slaveholder paternalism to postwar conditions. They still believed that blacks required moral, religious, and political guidance from whites, and were convinced that they, the former slaveholders, were best qualified to provide such guidance. They profoundly distrusted black preachers, who, according to Bishop Atkinson of North Carolina, were leading the freed people "into the wildest excesses of delusion and fanaticism." Above all, these southern white teachers had no sympathy at all for the political aspirations of the freedmen, whose ignorance, they complained, made them vulnerable to the blandishments of the Republican Party and the "fanatical and political preaching" of their religious allies.[16]

In Petersburg, the religious paternalism of Giles B. Cooke clashed with the assertive race consciousness of the black church. Cooke accused black preachers of seeking to undermine St. Stephen's School. "These so-called spiritual pastors . . . instead of preaching the blessed Gospel of love and peace, substitute thereof, the teaching of enmity and strife between the races." The colored preachers, he complained, had told their congregations "that there is no religion in the Episcopal Church." They had even threatened to exclude any of their members who attended St. Stephen's Sunday school. But Cooke insisted upon giving his pupils religious instruction on the Sabbath because, in his view, blacks were in a "woeful spiritual condition." Repelled by a millenarian frenzy that had gripped blacks in Petersburg, Cooke denounced "wild religious feeling" as "blasphemous and heathenish." Even the most respected Baptist church in Petersburg, he alleged, discouraged its members from reading the Bible, arguing that religion came from the heart, not "out of a book." Cooke complained that blacks regarded conversion and baptism as the be-all and end-all of Christianity. "There might not be so much objection if they were improved by it," he concluded, "But . . . the majority of them become worthless." Not surprisingly, members of Gillfield Baptist Church led by Reverend Henry Williams—the church Cooke singled out for criticism—took the lead in demanding that black teachers replace whites.[17]

The evangelical goals of northern white missionaries also conflicted with the freed people's desire for autonomy. J. Brinton Smith, a minister from New Jersey, founded St. Augustine's Normal and Collegiate Institute in 1867. Blacks in Raleigh welcomed the school but resented Smith's courting of southern whites. Smith appointed a board of trustees that consisted only of conservative white southerners—no blacks, northerners, or Republicans. Determined to insulate St. Augustine from any association with Radical Reconstruction, he boasted that his was "the only school in Raleigh whose teachers are not active politicians." He admitted that his nonpolitical stance had caused the school to "suffer in the estimation of many of the colored people." Nevertheless, Smith insisted that St. Augustine's could survive only by gaining the acceptance of southern whites.

This was a dangerous position to adopt in the heated political context of the time. It aligned Smith, if only by default, with the conservative opponents of Radical Reconstruction. Testifying before a congressional committee investigating the Ku Klux Klan, Smith denied the existence of any organized conspiracy on the part of white southerners to deprive blacks of their rights. He made the preposterous assertion that the only organization known as the Ku Klux Klan of which he was aware consisted of "colored people [who] band together, wearing disguises calling themselves Ku-Klux . . . [and] whipping persons of their own race." A year after claiming that the Klan was got up by blacks, Smith suddenly died. The cause of his cause of death was never determined. Rumor had it that he was poisoned.[18]

Giles B. Cooke and J. Brinton Smith represented a denomination that aroused black suspicion. The Episcopalian Church had been favored by the slaveholding elite. Indeed, it bred so few critics of slavery that it was the only major church that failed to split along North–South lines before the Civil War. It was unique, too, in refusing to accord its black congregations any form of independent status after the Civil War. Moreover, its efforts to further the education of the freedmen were slight when compared with those of other denominations. The Episcopalian Church—sometimes disparaged as "the white man's church"—had fewer black members than any other denomination.[19]

Yet the experience of Henry M. Tupper, a Baptist, showed that the more egalitarian churches—those churches that did most to educate the freed people—also evoked black opposition. Tupper was a Union soldier and missionary who founded Shaw University, Raleigh's second black normal school, in 1870. The school was initially housed in the Second Baptist Church, which Tupper erected in 1866 with the help of his black congregation. However, Tupper's combined role of teacher, missionary, and political leader led to bitter dissension among the members of his church, some of whom wanted to replace him with a black preacher.

Matters came to a head in 1872 when Tupper declared his intention to bolt the Republican Party and vote for Horace Greeley, who was seeking to defeat President U. S. Grant with the backing of both the Liberal Republicans and the Democrats. A church meeting on September 25 descended into uncontrollable acrimony. Tupper tried to silence his critics, but the latter shouted him down and called for a vote. Abram Nichols, the leading dissident, "in a very excited manner said all that want a Black man for preacher come out on this side." Amid uproar, the dissidents claimed to have won the vote 54 to 13. Tupper conceded the pastorate to Rev. A. Shepard, an African American loyal to him, but continued to serve as assistant pastor. This arrangement did nothing to mollify his opponents, who declared that Tupper had "made himself odious to a majority of the church." The dissident faction held meetings in a private home and, claiming to be the legitimate congregation, sued for possession of the church building. A city judge ruled for the plaintiffs, and Tupper was kicked out of his church and school. In 1874 he regained possession, but the dispute dragged through the courts for another four years.[20]

This was primarily a dispute over a church. Yet religion and education were thoroughly entangled. The northern aid societies that did most to organize schools for blacks—the AMA, the Freedmen's Aid Society of the Methodist Episcopal Church, the American Baptist Home Missionary Society—were evangelical. They believed that the freedmen were ignorant of Christian doctrine and in desperate need of religious instruction. Their work among the freedmen was therefore as much about saving souls as overcoming illiteracy. Their teachers began the school day with prayers and hymns. They distributed Bibles and tracts. They organized Sunday schools and formed temperance societies. Along with white teachers came white missionaries, their aim to recruit blacks to their northern-based denominations and to inculcate "calmer and better habits of worship." Men like Henry M. Tupper were both missionaries and teachers. Tupper founded Shaw University with the dual purpose of combating the "ignorance and folly of the colored people" and opposing the "Congregational influence" of an AMA-supported freedmen's school. "May the day come when all the colored Baptists in North Carolina shall be Baptists."[21]

Their fervent evangelicalism brought the white teacher-missionaries not only into fierce competition with each other but also into direct conflict with black preachers. Religious education was an integral part of nineteenth-century schooling, and the use of churches as schoolhouses reinforced this connection. Churches naturally assumed that teachers could sway the denominational allegiance of both pupils and parents. Black preachers bent upon promoting black-controlled churches regarded white teachers from the North, however well intentioned, as being just as much a threat to their religious ambitions as openly prejudiced southern whites. Black and white ministers fought over the allegiance of black Christians, and they regarded schools as crucial weapons in their struggle.

The most uncompromising advocates of black independence, in

both religion and education, were the black-controlled Methodist denominations and the hundreds—eventually thousands—of independent Baptist churches. Arriving in the South in the wake of the Union armies, black missionaries like Henry McNeal Turner, Richard H. Cain, Theophilus G. Steward (AME), and James Walker Hood (AMEZ) proclaimed that they were the natural leaders of the freedmen. Although disavowing any spirit of caste, and condemning race prejudice, they nonetheless insisted that providence and blood tied them to the ex-slaves. "We come to seek those who are our brethren by virtue of race," explained Steward, "not because we care anything for races or nations, but because they have been and are yet in great measure our brethren in affliction." No matter how sincere, argued R. H. Cain, whites could never fully understand "our poor down-trodden brethren."[22]

The AME insisted that blacks and blacks alone should teach and minister to the freedmen. Northern whites could not be trusted. The white teachers in Wilmington, reported one black missionary, "are full of pro-slavery notions." Richard H. Cain, who worked as an AME missionary in South Carolina, was more charitable but made essentially the same point. "Other teachers and preachers have feelings, but not as we feel for our kindred." The AME Church denied that it was racially exclusive, and occasionally debated whether to drop the word *African*. But its appeal was plainly based upon racial identity: "Blood is always more potent than money." Only in a church of their own, argued Bishop Daniel Payne, the black Methodist, could blacks attain their "heaven-created manhood."[23]

As the AME and AMEZ missionaries left the Atlantic ports and fanned out into the hinterlands of Georgia and the Carolinas, they organized schools and churches together. New Jersey–born Theophilus G. Steward was a typical missionary-teacher. In 1866 he led blacks in Marion, South Carolina, out of the MEC, South, and built an AME church that doubled as a schoolhouse. "When I assembled nearly one hundred children of school age," he recalled, "I found only two who knew the alphabet. . . . At the close of the school in June, practically all of the one hundred children could read and many could write." The next year, 1867, saw him in Lumpkin, Georgia, organizing another AME congregation. "Beside carrying on church and Sunday school, my wife and I conducted a day school, which we called Union School." During his first three years in the South, Steward traveled eight thousand miles, received thousands of blacks into the AME Church, and taught four different schools.[24]

Black Baptists also saw schools as adjuncts of their churches. Charles Octavius Boothe was an eminent but otherwise typical Baptist preacher-teacher. Baptized in 1866 at the age of twenty-one, this former slave taught a Freedmen's Bureau school in Alabama, then various public schools, and served as the pastor of churches in Mississippi and Alabama, including Dexter Avenue Baptist Church. By organizing schools, Baptist preachers bound their congregations to them more tightly.[25]

The competition between white and black missionaries developed into a free-for-all. It pitted northern white denominations against southern white denominations, some northern white churches against other northern white churches, black Baptists against black Methodists, and the two black Methodist denominations against each other. A foretaste of the battle came in New Bern, the North Carolina port captured by Union forces in 1862. Here the northern Methodists, the Congregationalists, the AME Church, and the AME Zion Church vied for control of Andrew's Chapel, formerly owned by the MEC, South. Two years of squabbling and politicking ended with the AME Zionites occupying the church.

Some of the bitterest clashes pitted the AME against the MEC, North. Of all the white denominations, the northern Methodists had the greatest success in winning black converts, amassing a southern membership of a hundred thousand by 1890. The northern MEC was also (unlike the Congregationalists) quite deliberate in its use of schools to proselytize. Bishop Richard H. Cain accused the northern white Methodists of bribing the freedmen to desert the AME Church—even branding one white missionary a "Judas." Both churches resorted to unprincipled tactics. The MEC, North, licensed illiterate black preachers. The AME Church retaliated by making a tactical alliance with the MEC, South, to gain possession of church properties. The northern white missionaries were infuriated by this unholy marriage between blacks and former slaveholders. "The Affricans [*sic*] turned me and my congregation out of their house," reported Rev. A. H. Caldwell from Rome, Georgia. "We are compelled to hold our meetings and our Sunday School in the open air." [26]

With the advent of Radical Reconstruction, in which the AME Church played a major role in mobilizing black voters, the MEC, South, had second thoughts about assisting the northern black Methodists. Ditching its alliance with the AME, the MEC, South, created an affiliated black denomination, the Colored Methodist Episcopal Church (CME), in an effort to limit the influence of both the northern black and the northern white Methodists. The tactic worked. The organization of the CME Church slowed the growth of both the AME and the MEC, North. Some AME congregations suffered splits. In Macon, Georgia, for example, the MEC, South, sued AME minister Theophilus G. Steward for the return of his church building, hoping to install the leader of a dissident faction as a CME minister. When Steward fought the lawsuit, the church burned to the ground. The AME denounced the CME as the "Rebel Church," the "Democratic Church," and the "old slavery Church."[27]

THE fact that northern whites could be as scathing about black religion as southern whites helps explain why so many black preachers distrusted white teachers in general. Yankee Christians regarded southern black worship, unfettered by white spiritual guidance, with disdain. In contrast to the services of the New England church, where congregations listened in silence to sermons, and expressed themselves in hymn and prayer in a suitably restrained manner, and only when called upon to do so, black worship seemed anarchic and emotional. "A more melancholy misnomer than that of the Christian religion, as applied to the heathenish utterances of the plantation blacks, cannot be conceived," wrote Charles Stearns. Their "insane yellings, and violent contortions of the body, totally disconnected with any idea," constituted a travesty of Christianity. Moreover, whites were often disturbed by the sexual overtones they detected in black notions of spirituality. AMA missionary Henry Blake was certain that no "Spirit of God" caused the "wild excitement which leads them to dance, shout, wail, and go into convulsions, and which is unquestionably demoralizing and licentious."[28]

White missionaries and teachers blamed "noisy, ignorant and uncultivated" black preachers for corrupting the Christian gospel. Yankee Protestants complained that they mangled the English language, betrayed ignorance of the Bible, and preached for emotional effect— "joyful exhilaration" and a "condition of catalepsy"—rather the instruction of blacks in the Ten Commandments. They regarded many back preachers as scoundrels, drunkards, adulterers, and thieves. Not every northern teacher or missionary condemned the freedmen's religion so emphatically. Many praised the sincerity of their faith and recognized the eloquence of their preachers. But there was near-universal agreement that the current crop of preachers was inadequate, and that black churches had to be either reformed or replaced.[29]

Not surprisingly, many black ministers regarded northern white teachers with ill-disguised hostility. Connecticut-born John Scott encountered opposition from the moment he opened an AMA school in a black Baptist church in Staunton, Virginia, in 1868. "[Rev. Lewis] is a man of much pomp and some arrogance," Scott reported, "who charged me with incivility in not informing them of my intended arrival." Scott and Lewis soon locked horns over the use of the church building. Confined to a "damp smoky basement," Scott complained that the minister not only refused him use of the main part of the church but also held noisy "protracted meetings" that disrupted his night school. He charged Lewis with stirring up opposition to him "by preaching the doctrine that now the colored people are free they should become independent of northern aid." When Scott appointed a white assistant, Lewis objected. "You don't need any Northern teachers," he told his congregation, "let your own people teach you." Matters came to a head when Scott, his basement school bursting at the seams, moved one of his assistant teachers to the body of the church. Lewis thereupon "turned the school and teachers out of doors." After teaching in a kitchen, and then outdoors, a humiliated Scott was allowed back into the basement. "There is no equal to this minister," he ruefully conceded. "His ingenious and persistent opposition to every plan for the education of these children is a favorable comment on the ability of the negro."[30]

Even when white teachers made no effort to organize churches, their Sunday schools evoked the distrust of many black preachers. Instructing the freedmen in Bible study and encouraging restrained worship, these Sunday schools implicitly criticized black preachers. Sarah W. Stansbury, an AMA teacher in Cuthbert, Georgia, taught a Sunday school in a black Methodist church. But the minister told her to stop teaching a Sunday afternoon Bible class on the grounds that it deterred young people from attending church services. Judging by Stansbury's reports to the AMA, the preacher was probably right to see this white teacher as a threat to his authority. "I think the services made up of savage exhortations, shouting and long prayers, and that without so much as the reading of the Scriptures, less edifying than a Bible Class," wrote Stansbury. "I ache to see an educated ministry free from tobacco and whiskey."

Sectarian rivalry between blacks fueled hostility to northern white teachers. When Sarah Stansbury taught in the Methodist church, the Baptists objected. When she moved her Sabbath school into a new schoolhouse, both churches complained. At a public meeting in 1871 Ruben Richards, a prominent black landowner and merchant, denounced Stansbury for "never coming among them to church" anymore. Vigorously defending her nonsectarian teaching, Stansbury argued that "a Sabbath School in the School building would be in the interests of both churches and against neither." She had no intention "to build up or pull down their churches." Although she received a rising vote of confidence from the people at the meeting, Stansbury failed to dissuade the Baptists and Methodists from setting up schools in their own churches. "I am thoroughly disgusted with some of them," she told the AMA.[31]

The proliferation of private schools taught by poorly trained black teachers annoyed and perplexed white teachers from the North. "The freedmen will send their children to ignorant colored teachers, occupying uncomfortable school-rooms," said one puzzled AMA official, complaining that they did this in preference to schools with "excellent white teachers and convenient school-houses." White teachers regarded these black-taught "petty schools" with contempt. John Scott thought they "stand in the way of education rather than act as an aid to it." Sarah Stansbury described an "opposition school" in Cuthbert in words dripping with sarcasm: "The teacher is so learned I cannot understand the language he used." Whites complained that blacks who set up private schools were more interested in making money through the collection of tuition fees—sometimes charging extortionate rates—than in educating children. They considered ministers, many of whom taught schools in their churches, the worst offenders.[32]

As to why blacks patronized poorly taught schools, whites kept returning to the insidious influence of black ministers. "By their bombastic and vociferous preaching," complained a Freedmen's Bureau official in Natchez, Mississippi, black men "who think they have a greater amount of knowledge than they really possess . . . create great excitement and gain an influence over the great mass and become the ruling minds of this people." These preachers then turned blacks against the white teachers and missionaries "who would teach them the more perfect way." Edward P. Smith, who oversaw the AMA's schools in the South, concluded that black preachers feared that well-taught schools would enable their followers, currently illiterate, to see through their "absurdity, ignorance and immorality." Afraid of having their ignorance thus exposed, they formed "the greatest opposition now to our schools."[33]

The most damning assessment of black preachers came from John Scott, who offered a composite portrait, in his "Uncle Cato," of the "ignorant bigots" who had obstructed his work. Uncle Cato was a "Hard-Shell Baptist," a whisky-swigging, leather-lunged, quick-witted, iron-willed preacher whose sermons ran up to eight hours long and who possessed the authority, in the eyes of his people, of an Old Testament prophet. Uncle Cato feared and hated the freedmen's school and its white teacher because, like the Catholic Church in medieval times, he claimed sole authority to interpret the divine word, and realized that people who could read the Bible for themselves would dispute him. Charismatic and despotic, his power rested upon verbal pyrotechnics and conjured emotion. Uncle Cato obstinately resisted "the progress of religion and true education."[34]

Many of these Baptist and Methodist ministers, however, had been slave preachers; they had already established a claim to leadership. For the former slaves, the decision to form religious communities— withdrawing from the southern white churches, rejecting the overtures of the northern white churches, and selecting their own preachers—was a logical consequence of emancipation. Their consciousness of being a people, a race, had been formed in slavery. By founding churches under black leadership, independent of white control, they affirmed their sense of peoplehood. White missionaries could only see ignorant men drawing the color line in a demagogic way. But their own proselytizing efforts, in challenging black preachers, contradicted this powerful movement for religious autonomy. The desire to create a community, not simply ignorance and emotionalism, fostered the freed people's preference for black preachers and black teachers.

The success of the northern black denominations in planting churches among the freedmen adds force to this argument. In their theology, liturgy, and class attitudes, the missionaries of the AME and AMEZ churches closely resembled their white northern counterparts. They, too, disdained the unlettered preachers, unrestrained worship, and paganlike rituals they encountered in the South. They, too, viewed the freedmen as improvident and licentious. And black Methodists from the North likewise incurred opposition from the "Uncle Catos" of the South. Unlike the white churches, however, the AME and the AMEZ churches made hundreds of thousands of converts, gaining the allegiance of almost a third of the freedmen. Their appeal to consanguinity—to racial solidarity and racial destiny—gave them a decisive advantage over the wealthier and more numerous white missionaries.[35]

Although whites bemoaned the power of black preachers, they recognized its reality. The freedmen considered black preachers superior, admitted John Scott, and they considered any white missionary "an invader of their territory." After struggling to establish a Congregational church in Macon, its white pastor urged the AMA to appoint a black successor. "The prejudice against a white man as pastor of any colored church . . . is very strong . . . It is also increasing." The northern Methodists quickly recognized that they could recruit and retain a substantial black membership only if they ordained black ministers. The fact that so many of the freedmen formed Baptist churches—by 1890 over half of black Christians were Baptists—stemmed from both the democratic nature of that church and the fact that it offered freedom from white control.[36]

Black ministers were therefore in the forefront of campaigns to replace white teachers with blacks. Rev. Henry Williams, pastor of Gillfield Baptist Church, led the petition drives in Petersburg. In Atlanta, too, black ministers demanded black teachers. That some of these preachers wished to blunt the influence of the northern churches by dismissing northern white teachers seems clear. By the 1870s, relations between the black churches and the northern white missionaries had deteriorated to the point that AME minister Francis Peck could charge that the AMA "had declared the intention of destroying the AME Church in the South." When Peck and a group of AME ministers in Atlanta demanded the employment of black teachers, they were motivated, at least in part, by fear that the AMA's Storrs School—the best in the city—might lure its pupils into the Congregational Church.[37]

The AMA was entirely in accord with the idea that local school boards should take control of most of its schools. But the Association was appalled that some black leaders—in the spirit of the AME's pact with the southern white Methodists to exclude the MEC, North—colluded with the southern Democrats to replace northern white teachers with blacks. Sarah Stansbury complained that the appointment of a black teacher to the new public school in Cuthbert, Georgia, was a ploy by local Democrats to substitute a poorly taught school that ran only three months of the year for the far superior AMA school. Stansbury claimed that a prominent Democrat, a local lawyer, had coached the black teacher so that he could pass the county examination. "He is ignoramus enough to suit the 'Southern Idea' of education for the Colored people."

The AMA tried to protect the jobs of at least some white teachers when it negotiated the transfer of its school properties to local school boards. But once the AMA's schools had been absorbed into public school systems, pressure to dismiss the northern whites mounted. In Raleigh, North Carolina, Louise Dorr reported, "An attempt [is being] made by certain of the colored people to throw out all the northern teachers from my school . . . and to put all colored teachers in." In Pensacola, Florida, a white teacher complained that "fanatical men who belong to the so-called Equal Rights League" had drawn the "color line" against northern whites.[38]

Many northern white teachers were hurt and confused by the speed with which many blacks came to view them as redundant. Although the northern aid societies claimed to be training black leaders with a view to making the freedmen self-reliant, they believed that the former slaves needed a long period of white tutelage: "The colored people are yet children, and need to be taught everything," averred a white Methodist in 1874. The northern whites doubted the competence of black teachers, apart from those they had trained themselves, and questioned whether the mass of freedmen possessed the capacity for independent leadership. "Can the colored people—so very few of whom can read and write and own a home of their own—cut loose from all the ties of sympathy and charity that have befriended them thus far?" asked the AMA in 1875. Its plaintive question invited a negative reply.[39]

For many African Americans, however, the answer to that question was yes. They harbored mixed feelings—resentment as well as gratitude—about the northern teachers. By the standards of the time, organizations like the AMA were paragons of racial equality. Yet they occasionally breached their high ideals. The black teachers employed by the AMA, for example, sometimes found that they were not housed with the white teachers. In Wilmington, North Carolina, AMA superintendent Samuel. S. Ashley insisted that this kind of segregation was necessary in order to mitigate southern white hostility. Ashley forbade white teachers from fraternizing with blacks outside school and church. But opposition to "social equality" also reflected the views of many white teachers. The AMA's schools in wartime Virginia, for example, were wracked by racial tensions. Black women teachers in

Norfolk complained about "exhibitions of prejudice" by their white co-workers. Indeed, one black minister working for the AMA wondered why any white person would come South "to Teach as a Christian Missionary to these freedmen" when they had "hearts full of prejudice" that stopped them "identifying with those they come to teach."[40]

Blacks who failed to meet the aid societies' stringent conditions for employment often resented their rejection. The most influential society, the AMA, commissioned relatively few black teachers. In addition to barring women with children, it screened out anybody who failed to measure up to its strict standards of piety and morality. Use of alcohol and tobacco rendered people unemployable. Failure to demonstrate religious belief aroused deep suspicion. John Wesley Cromwell, who was otherwise well qualified, struggled to overcome the AMA's misgivings about his lack of church membership. He explained that religious instruction, in his view, belonged in the Sunday school, not the day school. Although owning up to being "weak and sinful," he claimed the ability to teach "moral principles, thus preparing the way for religious impressions." The AMA considered Cromwell a man of dubious morality who might "expose our ladies to much needless gossip." Ten years later, as president of the Virginia Educational and Historical Association, Cromwell campaigned to replace the white teachers in Richmond with black ones.[41]

By the 1870s many blacks had become cynical about white paternalism. Booker T. Washington, W. E. B. Du Bois, and other black memoirists lauded the missionary teachers for their self-sacrificing altruism. But these men were writing long after Reconstruction had ended, at a time when southern whites were trying to persuade the nation that the northern white teachers had been misguided zealots. During Reconstruction itself, blacks had not been starry-eyed about the white northerners. Many bristled at the arrogant self-righteousness of the missionary teachers, who regarded blacks as children and continually harped upon their deficiencies. In 1875 Frederick Douglass complained, "We have been more injured than benefitted by the efforts of the so-called benevolent societies." Nine years later, black journalist and author T. Thomas Fortune sarcastically wondered "whether the black man has any manhood left, after the missionaries and religious enthusiasts had done picturing, or rather caricaturing, his debased moral and mental condition." Scorning the romantic image of the missionary teachers as "pampered children of fortune, laboring simply for god and humanity," Fortune endorsed the call for black teachers.[42]

Teaching was gainful employment. Literate blacks therefore had little sympathy for the view that whites should monopolize the field, or that the northern aid societies should dictate when and where black teachers should be employed. Many simply organized their own private schools and charged tuition fees. Although the aid societies criticized these schools as inferior, and sometimes viewed them as hostile efforts to undermine their own schools, the black-taught schools represented natural competition in what was, in effect, a free market. Moreover, the fact that black parents often preferred schools taught by members of their own race underlined a belief shared by many black teachers that they, not whites, were best suited to instruct black children. "I am not opposed to white teachers," wrote Sarah Thompson, a black teacher in Memphis. "But I think where colored teachers can be found equally competent they should have a preference in the colored schools. . . . I am aware that in an educational way, we have received a great deal from the whites. But are we always to be led by them? Are we never to 'go it alone'?"[43]

When the normal schools and universities had produced a cohort of educated African Americans willing and able to teach, the argument for replacing white teachers became compelling. "There can be no doubt of competent colored teachers being found," insisted the black petitioners of Petersburg. Moreover, blacks who wanted to escape farming and laboring had few careers available to them other than preaching and teaching. Petition campaigns seized upon the issue of separate schools—which whites insisted upon—to demand black teachers in black schools. It was a logical extension of the principle of racial segregation. Pointing out that blacks were barred from the white schools, the campaigners asked for reciprocity, astutely demanding an end to all "mixing" in the public schools.[44]

As Reconstruction came to an end, blacks traded votes with Redeemer politicians, exchanging their political support for black schools and jobs for black teachers. Sometimes these bargains seemed like opportunistic ploys by ambitious individuals. In 1874, for example, Alabama schoolteacher William H. Councill threw his support to the Democratic candidate for governor, who, after redeeming the state from Republican control, appointed him head of the new Normal and Industrial School in Huntsville. Although many blacks excoriated Councill as a political apostate, dealing with the Democrats became common. The founding of Tuskegee Institute—which became the best-known black school in America, even in the world, under the direction of Booker T. Washington—was a classic example of this kind of horse trading. In return for supporting two Democratic candidates for the Alabama legislature in the 1880 elections, Lewis Adams, a black storekeeper and Republican leader, asked the white men to establish a normal school for the training of black teachers. The Democratic politicians kept their promise. They steered a bill through the legislature that granted two thousand dollars a year to Tuskegee Normal and Industrial Institute.[45]

When the Democratic Party split, and a seceding faction sought their votes, blacks could gain substantial concessions. In Virginia, for example, blacks profited handsomely from their support of the Readjuster Party, led by General William Mahone, which governed the state from 1879 to 1883. Alfred W. Harris, a black state legislator from Petersburg, gained Mahone's support for a bill establishing Virginia Normal and Industrial Institute in Petersburg. This law authorized not only a normal school for the training of black teachers but also "professional departments . . . for the higher education of colored persons." When the Petersburg school board once again rebuffed demands to employ black teachers, Mahone dismissed the old board and appointed a new one. A quarter of the city's white teachers lost their jobs, to be replaced by blacks. By the end of 1882, writes historian Jane Dailey, "black teachers had been substituted for whites in the black schools of Lynchburg, Norfolk, Hampton, Danville, and Charlottesville." In Richmond, too, black teachers displaced white ones. Although many of the city schools retained white principals, by 1900 African Americans accounted for 93 percent of the teachers in Virginia's black schools. In the rest of the South, the proportion of black teachers was even greater. In the rural areas, white teachers deserted the black schools en masse when pay deteriorated. Of the main cities, only Charleston, South Carolina, which did not employ black instructors until 1919, resisted the trend toward the wholesale replacement of whites.[46]

Race alone, however, did not guarantee a black teacher's acceptance by a black community. African Americans tended to favor teachers who supported their political aims, respected their moral codes, and adapted to their religious preferences. If teachers or ministers appeared to work against the community rather than with it—or if they were too closely identified with a white-controlled church—blacks sometimes closed ranks against them.

Take, for example, the starkly contrasting experiences of Hardy Mobley and Robert Harris, black teachers who founded schools during Reconstruction. The two men came from similar backgrounds. Both were native southerners, both had been free blacks, and both had migrated with their families to the North in the 1850s. Mobley took his family from Augusta, Georgia, to Brooklyn, New York. Harris moved from Fayetteville, North Carolina, to Cleveland, Ohio, when still a young boy. After the Civil War, both men returned to the South as AMA teachers. But while Harris earned the respect of his patrons and bequeathed an enduring legacy, Mobley alienated his community and left scarcely a trace.

Hardy Mobley took over St. Paul's Church in New Iberia, Louisiana, in the summer of 1873. Helped by his wife and four daughters, he organized a school. Within two years, however, the members of St. Paul's voted Mobley out of office and refused to let him continue his school in the church building. The problems encountered by Mobley were strikingly similar to those experienced by white AMA teachers like John Scott and Sarah Stansbury. Mobley aroused the jealousy of local blacks who fancied themselves religious leaders. One man in particular, "who was once the preacher in this church, and thinks he ought to be now," resented being supplanted by an educated outsider. Then again, Mobley's brand of religion, Congregationalism, did not sit well with some of his church members, who included former Baptists. When a successful revival meeting netted forty converts, many of the new church members clamored for the full-immersion form of baptism practiced by Baptist churches. Mobley adamantly refused. "This Church is not the place for emotion," he admonished them. The only mode of baptism permitted in St. Paul's would be "pouring the water."[47]

Politics intensified the differences between Mobley and his church members. When he arrived in New Iberia, Mobley worked hard to disarm the suspicions of local whites who feared that that he might be "preaching Radical doctrines." To this end he abstained from politics, conspicuously refusing to campaign for the Republican Party in the 1874 elections. Such neutrality angered local Republican candidates. One of Mobley's daughters, Laura, recorded that when two of Mobley's own church members, a trustee and a deacon, went down to defeat, they "told the people that Pa and his family were White Leaguers and that he used his influence for the Democrats." According to Laura Mobley, she and her father believed that blacks paid too high a price for their support of the Republican Party, suffering evictions, intimidation, and even murder. Fearful that the political warfare between whites and blacks would "finally ruin the state," they considered black defections to the Democratic Party "a wise move."[48]

Tensions between Mobley and his congregation went from bad to worse when, in the middle of a church service, one of Mobley's daughters confiscated a note that a young man was passing to a young woman. Laura Mobley read out loud the contents of the note. Her father then lectured the younger members of the congregation for neglecting their education. "I fear that you boys and girls think more of courting, and getting married, than of learning how to take care of a family." When his comments were greeted with embarrassed laughter, Mobley delivered a stinging rebuke. The episode caused great offense. The AMA received angry complaints about Laura Mobley's "unladylike conduct" and Hardy Mobley's "unbecoming manner."

Matters came to a head when the *American Missionary* published two letters from Laura Mobley that included frank but impolitic complaints about the moral deficiencies of the freed people. Shocked by the "wickedness" that produced "little fatherless waifs" and "colored families that have two or three sets of children in them," Laura Mobley lamented the "immorality and degradation" that surrounded her in New Iberia. "What it is to be a pure Christian, very few of these people understand. They profess to be religious, yet the Ten Commandments are a dead letter to them." Her strictures outraged the members of St. Paul's Church. One comment—"The women in this place are very immoral"—caused particular scandal. As far as the ladies of St. Paul's were concerned, Laura Mobley had branded them whores. But Mobley refused to retract her statement.[49]

By the beginning of 1875, relations between the Mobley family and the congregation of St. Paul's had broken down irretrievably. Family members and church members exchanged insults on the streets of New Iberia. Most of the congregation left. A majority of the members ejected Mobley and barred him from setting foot in the church. Mobley threatened to drag the insurgent deacons through the courts in order to regain possession. Meanwhile, he continued his school in rented rooms. His effort to build a new church, however, quickly foundered. The deacons of St. Paul's threatened to disaffiliate from the AMA, complaining, "We have had trouble with all of ministers that we ever had, since we have been with your Society." Rather than lose St. Paul's, the AMA withdrew its support from Mobley and sent a new minister.[50]

Robert Harris, who began teaching in Fayetteville, North Carolina, in 1867, won the respect of the black community despite his Yankee-flavored evangelism. He also achieved the support of local whites without compromising his Republican politics. In 1869 Harris moved his school into a new building, named after O. O. Howard. In 1877 the state legislature selected the Howard School to be State Colored Normal School, the first publicly funded institution for the training of black teachers in North Carolina. Steering the school between the rocks of partisan politics, Harris died in 1880, mourned by black and white alike. His school survived—it is now Fayetteville State University—and trained many of the black teachers of eastern North Carolina.[51]

Harris, it is true, had one distinct advantage over Hardy Mobley.

Whereas Mobley entered a community that was strange to him, where many regarded him with suspicion as a "foreign teacher," Harris returned to the town of his birth, where his family was known and respected. Yet his success in gaining acceptance had a deeper explanation. In many respects, Harris was a typical northern missionary-teacher. Sharing the AMA's belief that the work of "elevating and evangelizing" went hand in hand, he distributed tracts, taught Sunday school, organized a Band of Hope, and delighted in reporting that "large numbers are seeking Jesus." Yet Harris adapted his Christian beliefs to the religious values of Fayetteville's native-born blacks. Crucially, he did not look down upon the freedmen. Despite lamenting the ubiquity of sin, the indifference of parents to temperance, and "the almost universal use of tobacco among all classes," Harris did not engage in the kind of moral strictures that had caused such offense to blacks in New Iberia. He possessed a basic respect for the community he served.[52]

Most important of all, Harris refused to promote the sectarian interests of the AMA. He rejoiced in the religious revival conducted by the AMEZ Church in 1867—"Truly the Lord is pouring his spirit upon us"—and boasted that one hundred former pupils had been converted. Instead of disparaging the ignorance and emotionalism of black preachers, Harris praised their eloquence. He rated Bishop James Walker Hood, for example, "a man of extraordinary ability," and called one of Hood's sermons "the most impassioned . . . which has been delivered in this place for a generation at least." Brimming with pride, Harris exulted that "the whites are opening their eyes to the fact that colored men are possessed of talent and ability as well as whites." Rejecting Congregationalism, Robert Harris joined the AMEZ Church. So did his brother and fellow teacher Cicero, who explained, "The majority of our people are Methodists or inclined in that way . . . 'If the mountain will not come to Mahomet, Mahomet will go to the mountain.'"[53]

There was nothing calculated in the Harris brothers' decision to affiliate with the AMEZ Church. It seemed to them a perfectly natural choice. Yet they knew full well that Congregationalism would have hampered their work. By joining a church of the masses, they found a position at the center of the black community. They quickly became influential leaders. "We are so connected to the educational, religious, social and industrial affairs of our people," Robert Harris told the AMA, that they hated to leave Fayetteville, even for a summer visit to Ohio. So high was Robert Harris's standing among blacks in Fayetteville that even his acceptance of state funding in 1877 did not seriously damage his reputation. By maintaining his Republican loyalties he succeeded in consolidating black support for State Colored Normal, despite charges that the legislature established it as a "Democratic School" for the training of "Democratic canvassers."[54]

It was even possible for a black teacher to attain great influence while remaining loyal to the Congregational Church. Richard R. Wright, for example, the first graduate of Atlanta University, became the most prominent black teacher in Georgia in the 1880s. Yet Wright was the exception that proved the rule. Although a deeply religious man, he carefully downplayed his religious affiliation when he took charge of Howard School at Cuthbert, Georgia, in 1876. Devoting his energies to teaching, he did not pastor a church. Making no effort to proselytize, he worshipped at the Methodist and Baptist churches on alternate Sundays and taught Sabbath schools in both. "Notwithstanding what a few superstitious fools may say," reported Wright, his school enjoyed "the undivided support of both Baptists and Methodists."[55]

If some black teachers failed to win the support of their patrons, it seemed clear nonetheless that race was assuming a compelling importance in the selection of public schoolteachers. Richard Wright succeeded in Cuthbert where, only five years earlier, Sarah Stansbury had confronted debilitating opposition. Wright himself, although a product of white teachers, eventually came to the conclusion that whites were not well suited to teaching black children. Blacks possessed distinctive "mental, moral and physical constitutions" that rendered teaching methods devised for white children less effective. "The environments of the American Negro" made the education of blacks "the peculiar work of colored teachers only." According to this view, even prejudice-free northern whites ought to give way to blacks.[56]

The demand for black teachers troubled some African Americans.

Many disliked endorsing racial segregation, or discriminating against whites solely by reason of color. Despite heading an AME school that had an all-black faculty, D. J. Jordan warned against "any unnecessary drawing of the color line," lest it "close our mouths against making protest or complaint on account of our being discriminated against."

The fact that a few white teachers participated in mixed but overwhelmingly black professional organizations underlined the sensitive nature of the issue. In Alabama, for example, a white man, William B. Paterson, headed the State Normal School in Montgomery and played a leading role in the Alabama State Teachers Association (ASTA). Paterson bitterly resented black appeals to racial solidarity, and he accused men like William H. Councill of "drawing the color line" against him in jockeying for funds and influence. Black teachers usually addressed these issues by resolving, in the words of the ASTA, that when the law required separate schools, "where colored teachers, equally competent with whites can be found, the colored teacher should be put in control of the colored school."[57]

George A. Goodwin, a teacher and Baptist minister, dismissed the notion that black teachers possessed some kind of innate advantage when it came to instructing black children. Teachers were effective according to how much training they had received: "color is not a qualification." To insist otherwise, some feared, would be to trade good teachers for bad ones. As Rev. S. R. Hughes of Maryland put it, "We don't want teachers with no brains." Communities were not united, therefore, in the campaigns for the replacement of white teachers. In Atlanta, for example, the school board received counter-petitions demanding the retention of northern whites. According to one historian, clergymen, alumni, and younger people usually desired black teachers because of their own ambitions or their belief in race pride. Parents of school-age children generally favored white teachers, whom they considered more intelligent, more experienced, and better disciplinarians."[58]

The issue was further complicated by the fact that white mission boards provided blacks with practically all of their educational opportunities above the elementary level—the AMA alone controlled four colleges, four theological schools, and twenty-nine secondary schools.

These private educational institutions controlled their own appointments, and, if they saw fit, could resist pressure to recruit black teachers. It was one thing to appoint an all-black teaching force in the public schools, quite another to appoint all-black faculties in private secondary schools, colleges, and universities. Many blacks admitted the distinction. "There are not enough really educated men fully equipped to manage the colleges such as we have, not to say anything of those that we ought to have," argued Nathan B. Young. "The race is not yet far enough removed from slavery to have that intellectual and moral background necessary to the bringing out of college professors and college presidents." According to D. J. Jordan, blacks would be cutting their own throats if they insisted on the wholesale replacement of white faculties, or a transfer of administrative control to black trustees—blacks could not sustain these schools without white funding, and they "should have to close the majority of them at once."[59]

In public, the white mission boards insisted that appointments would not be influenced by color. In private they admitted the need to mollify black opinion by appointing black teachers but continued to harbor deep reservations about them. "It is [not] wrong for them to aspire to teach their own schools and manage their own concerns," wrote L. M. Dunton, the white president of Claflin University, "but unfortunately for them not one in 1,000 has enough executive ability to manage his own household successfully."

Such attitudes help explain why, even as they appointed black faculty members, white-controlled colleges were wracked by racial tensions in the 1880s and 1890s. Claflin itself, a South Carolina school under the control of the northern Methodists, witnessed an ugly dispute between a black teacher and a white teacher that degenerated into physical violence. In Bishop College, Texas, a feud between the white president and a black teacher got so out of hand that the American Baptist Home Missionary Society (ABHMS) forced both men to resign. Some racially tinged disputes drew in students. At Roger Williams University in Nashville, the students accused a white teacher of a variety of offenses, including "using abusive language . . . such as liars, fools, stabbers, mobers [sic] and worse than the heathen in Africa." Student protests virtually paralyzed Roger Williams University in 1886–87.[60]

At differing tempi, and with varying degrees of enthusiasm, the white mission boards appointed black teachers to their colleges and secondary schools. There seemed to be no obvious pattern. The most conservative denomination, the Episcopalians, appointed black teachers at St. Augustine College as early as 1885. Biddle University, in nearby Charlotte, a school controlled by the northern Presbyterians, appointed its first black professor in 1886. By 1891 seven of Biddle's eight teachers were black, and the school had a black president as well. In the schools controlled by the northern Methodists—far more numerous than Episcopalian and Presbyterian institutions—the racial makeup of faculties had changed drastically by 1895, when almost half of the teachers were blacks. Schools sponsored by the ABHMS underwent a similar transformation, with black teachers outnumbering whites by end of the nineteenth century.

The AMA, however, bucked the trend, remaining reluctant to appoint black teachers. In 1895, all but 16 of the Association's 251 teachers were white. The AMA commissioned many more black teachers over the following decade, but it still lagged behind the other mission boards. The reluctance of white teachers to retire caused seething frustration. "Young Negro men fresh from Northern postgraduate study . . . found the dedication of elderly whites quite a bore," recalled AMA official Lura Beam. Wrote one: "If that old bitch from Massachusetts would ever die or get through here, I could begin to live."[61]

THE demand for black teachers echoed a powerful surge of race consciousness. By the 1880s the AME's argument that black instructors were the best people to educate black children had become widely accepted by African American teachers. Some developed the argument along pedagogical lines. Others emphasized that blacks had to cease relying upon whites if they were to develop racial pride and acquire the ability to stand on their own two feet. "We need more of an independent, self-reliant air," proclaimed North Carolina teacher E. A. Johnson, who wrote one of the first school texts on Negro history. "Away with fawning, away with humility, away [with] grinners when white men speak."[62]

Black churches continued to propel the movement away from white leadership. Baptist and Methodist ministers expounded a theology that placed black Americans at the center of a providential history. Bishop Henry McNeal Turner, for example, reasoned that God had allowed Africans to be transported to America as slaves in order to subject the Negro to "moral and intellectual culture." Turner further believed that whites had violated God's trust by degrading the Negro and seeking to make slavery perpetual. Having received the word of God, the slaves became instruments of a divine plan for the destruction of slavery and the redemption of Africa. Bishop James Walker Hood likened the shackling of slaves in the white churches to the plight of the Israelites in Egypt.

> We see the Egyptians oppressing Israel; that was God's way to get Israel out of Egypt and into the wilderness, where he could form them into a people for himself—that he might, through them, make himself known to the nations of the earth. Likewise we see the black man oppressed and fettered in the white church, his life made bitter and his condition rendered intolerable; that was God's way to get him out of the white church and into an organization of his own, that he might have a field for development untrammeled.

This divine plan provided a crucial role for African American Christians in "evangelization of the world."[63]

The conviction that a divine will shaped the destiny of the race became a commonplace among black religious leaders. Its appeal was many-sided. It accorded with the folk religion that had developed under slavery, which drew heavily upon the Book of Exodus. It expressed the Christian churches' common interest in preaching to the Africans. It even reflected some of the pseudoscientific notions of racial difference that abounded in the late nineteenth century. "Every individual race and age contributes to the well-meaning and happiness of mankind by the due performance of peculiar and specified work," explained Joseph C. Price. A freeborn North Carolinian who became president of Livingstone College and head of the North Carolina State Teachers Association, Price believed that God's plan for "Americanized Africans" was to be realized through black teachers and leaders.[64]

As the nation repudiated the ideal of racial equality, hostility toward all white people tinged black ministers' calls for race solidarity. Among black Baptists, suspicion of whites grew so intense that it threatened to end all cooperation with the white church. Attending a conference in the South in 1883, a white Baptist from the North was disturbed by the rhetoric employed by blacks. "Nearly every speaker announced himself as a 'race man' and avowed his determination to 'stand by his race.'" Within a few years, white representatives of the American Baptist Home Mission Society found themselves all but shouted down when they met with black Baptists. Black Baptists disliked having to buy their religious literature from the white Baptists' publishing houses, especially when the latter employed few, if any, blacks. They also they resented white control of the Baptist colleges sponsored by the ABHMS. When black Baptists formed a national organization, the National Baptist Convention (NBC), they set up their own publishing house. They also pressed the ABHMS to appoint more black trustees at its colleges.[65]

The white churches went out of their way to reassure black ministers that they were not bent upon stealing their congregations. The Baptists had in any case always encouraged blacks to organize upon congregational lines, making no attempt to impose white ministers. The other denominations resigned themselves to the fact that they must content themselves with small black memberships. They abandoned their efforts to proselytize en masse. The white-controlled colleges downplayed their denominational character and accepted all faiths. St. Augustine's College even accommodated to the Baptist inclinations of its students by installing a baptism pool in the school chapel—possibly the only Episcopalian church in America that provided for baptism by immersion.[66]

Some black religious leaders refused to be mollified, however. They spurned any cooperation with whites. The "separatist" faction of the black Baptists, for example, rejected all financial and educational aid from the ABHMS. Rev. E. K. Love, the pastor of Savannah's First African Baptist Church, condemned white teachers in uncompromising terms. Whites could not know their pupils socially; they were "incompetent to teach the Negroes civil rights, equity and justice;" they taught that "all the heroes and heroines were white;" they educated blacks away from their cultural roots, estranging them from the masses. Love frankly admitted that their sufferings had prejudiced blacks against all whites. "Our race battles must be fought by Negroes alone. Negroes must lead and teach Negroes." In Georgia, Virginia, Texas, and elsewhere, the dispute over cooperation divided black Baptists into warring camps. Advocates of noncooperation with whites formed separate state conventions and founded their own schools, colleges, and seminaries.[67]

The departure of white teachers from the South's black public schools represented a momentous change, and the consequences for blacks were both positive and negative. It ended the effort by southern whites to directly police black schools, but inaugurated a system of indirect white control. It diminished the influence of northern white educators, but also reduced the scope of interracial cooperation between southern blacks and northern whites. It provided tens of thousands of jobs for black teachers, but also entrenched racial segregation—making it easier for school boards to discriminate against black schools and to appoint poorly trained teachers. It consolidated the power of the black church, but did not eliminate sectarian divisions among African Americans. It cast black teachers in the role of community leaders, but placed severe limits upon what they could achieve. It nurtured a sense of racial solidarity, but solved few of the difficulties that faced teachers in black schools. The majority of black teachers continued to suffer poverty and isolation in one-room schoolhouses across the rural South.

CHAPTER THREE

Missionaries to the Dark South

Yesterday four pupils entered school who were perfect wonders. . . . They have never in their lives heard the word Bible. . . . They do not know who made them! Ever since their arrival I have been saying over and over, "Surely we have Africa at our very door." . . . The responsibility is so great that it makes me tremble.

Anna W. Richardson, 1889

Normal class, Roger Williams University, Nashville, 1899.

Library of Congress, Prints and Photographs Division

THE BLACK TEACHERS who set out from the normal schools and universities of the South brimmed with the enthusiasm of the Yankee schoolmarms of Reconstruction legend. Education was no mere profession. Being a teacher meant observing a way of life that pervaded every waking hour. It was a vocation that required moral strength and mental discipline. The ideal teacher should be a sincere Christian who worshipped modestly and lived soberly. That person should be a moral exemplar, molding the character of a people who, it was commonly believed, had been degraded by immorality and deceived by superstition. The teacher should uplift communities through his or her example.

New teachers confronted this challenge with a flash of recognition, a rush of excitement, and a solemn sense of duty. They now understood what their own teachers had felt—what it meant to be a teacher. Laura Mason, writing from Greensboro, Georgia, in 1876, described her "great experience" to Professor Thomas N. Chase of Atlanta University.

> Never in my life before have I thought so much of a teacher's responsibilities troubles and trials as I do now. When I was at school I couldn't see why one or two imperfect recitations and all those petty things (as we thought) that we did could discourage the teachers so much, but now I see. . . . It is my whole soul's desire to do all the good I can in the line of

teaching, and I ask your prayers that I *may* do much good toward the building of His kingdom and the elevation of this poor race.

Such teachers saw themselves as missionaries. The dead weight of illiteracy they encountered underlined the awesome challenge that confronted them. After praying to become "a man and a Christian," sixteen-year-old teacher Charles W. Chesnutt confided to his diary that the man he was boarding with could not even recite the Lord's Prayer without getting it wrong. "Schools are certainly needed here. The people are deplorably ignorant."[1]

In the one-room schoolhouses of the rural South, a region of scattered farms and hamlets, teachers faced an uphill struggle. They worked in rickety schoolhouses, lacked furniture and equipment, were paid a pittance, and taught for only three or four months a year. Most black children still did not attend school. Those who did show up were often hungry, ill clad, and sickly. Books were scarce, and most teachers also possessed few of them. Before 1940 most black teachers worked in isolation, the only instructor in a one-room schoolhouse that enrolled both toddlers and young adults. They received little supervision or professional guidance, and they were cut off from the amenities and amusements of urban life.

Teachers met resistance from the very people whom they sought to educate and improve. Many ex-slaves did not take kindly to having their folkways criticized. Teachers' campaigns for temperance evoked apathy or opposition. Their calls for restraint in religious worship produced indifference or resentment. Rural black communities, on the other hand, often subjected *them* to moral scrutiny of a religious and sectarian nature. The need to disarm white hostility, and to secure white support, further complicated teachers' relationship to their communities.

The white northern teachers of the Reconstruction era had experienced similar difficulties. But the context in which they worked had been quite different. Most of the Yankee teachers stayed in the South only a year or two, taught school terms of eight months, and visited their northern homes regularly. Moreover, they did their work during a period that was, for all its dangers, an exciting experiment in democracy and freedom. Black teachers, by contrast, did not enjoy the luxury of a safe haven in the North, and they were starting their careers when Reconstruction had either failed or was about to fail. They lacked institutional support, and their white paymasters generally cared little about them or their schools. "There are a great many unpleasant features in the work, of which we teachers never speak" noted one, "because we feel that there is no true glory in any work like ours, unless some sacrifice and self-denial is made performing it." For many teachers, idealism gave way to discouragement, disillusionment, or a kind of weary stoicism.[2]

BLACK teachers in the rural South faced daunting challenges. Their first was deceptively simple: they had to organize schools. The schools of the Freedmen's Bureau and the northern aid societies had reached, at most, 10 percent of the black school-age population. Thanks to Reconstruction, every state had established a system of public schools. But the ability of that fledgling system to enroll more black children depended upon black initiative. It fell largely upon individual teachers to establish public schools where none existed. In the parlance of the time, they had to "get up a school." And for this they needed community backing, for as often as not the black patrons of the school, not the white county superintendent, "elected" the teacher. In short, teachers must first set up a school, then ask the county to pay their salary.

Teachers met with every kind of response, ranging from enthusiasm to indifference. Many parents displayed eagerness and determination in the quest to educate their children. The very proliferation of public schools testified to that fact. Some parents even moved, or boarded their children with relatives in towns and cities, so that their children could attend private schools or better public schools.

But enthusiasm for education was not universal. Richard R. Wright Jr., the son of one of the first black public school teachers in Georgia, recalled, "The mass of Negro-Americans was practically untouched by education. They did not understand what it was all about, and many still under the influence of slavery did not think this innovation would help them." Teachers often complained that parents were skeptical about schooling. "The majority of the people are ignorant," wrote North Carolina teacher J. C. Price, "and therefore a popular interest is not manifested in educational matters. . . . The older ones are quite indifferent." The irregularity of the few public schools that existed—many were short-lived and ephemeral—dulled interest in them. In many counties, fear still inhibited blacks from asking for public schools. "The people in general are too 'weak-kneed,'" Price complained. "They know their rights but fail to demand them."[3]

A teacher who succeeded in gaining a community's backing still had to persuade the county board of education, or a local district committee, to furnish a salary. In many localities, blacks sat on these school committees or operated as school trustees underneath them. But whites invariably controlled the county school boards and held the purse strings. With so little money available for public schools, white school officials tended to be miserly. They could also be capricious.

Teachers often spent weeks and sometimes months searching for an appointment, making long, uncomfortable journeys that left them weary, hungry, and penniless. Charles W. Chesnutt thought he had found a school near Charlotte, North Carolina, only to learn from the white committeeman that "there was no money for that school." William H. Johnson, a former slave who graduated from Hampton Institute in 1878, "walked the roadways and hillsides of Amelia, Prince George, and Chesterfield Counties, counting railroad ties, measuring the dust of the earth, pressing tree leaves, and scanning tree tops, encountering discouragements and disappointments." After five months on the road, he finally began teaching a night school in Surry County, boarding with a church deacon.[4]

The third challenge facing the teacher was to obtain a teaching certificate. This entailed passing an "examination" to the satisfaction of the county superintendent of education, who was nearly always a white man. The examinations followed no uniform pattern. When William H. Johnson journeyed to the Amelia County courthouse to apply for a certificate, the superintendent conversed with him for two hours and then said, "All right, you get a first grade certificate." The exam had consisted of the conversation. Oral examinations could be more searching, however. James S. Russell received a second-grade certificate from Warren County, North Carolina, on the basis of answering the questions that the other candidate, a white man, got wrong. But in Robeson County, also in North Carolina, Charles N. Hunter was flabbergasted when after a "stiff examination" conducted by three "scholars of the old school" he received only a third-grade certificate. In Spartanburg, South Carolina, Charles Chesnutt gained a "splendid" first-grade certificate after sitting a two-day written examination.

Because the grade of certificate usually determined the salary—the higher the grade, with the first grade being the highest, the higher the pay—black teachers often suspected that examiners were unduly harsh in assessing them. Yet some admitted that they found the examinations quite difficult. After sitting three written exams, which tested him on the art of teaching, orthography, penmanship, English grammar, geography, mathematics, history, and reading, James A. Fields found it hard to agree with the superintendent that "they were not hard." Although he "came off tolerably well," this Hampton graduate conceded that his result was "nothing to brag about."[5]

There was, in fact, a complete lack of consistency in the standards applied to candidates for teaching positions, whether the hopefuls were blacks or whites. The lack of a proper examination system, and a culture of amateurism, partisanship, and even corruption at the county level, meant that the individual superintendent decided who to pass and what grade of certificate to award. Only the need to procure a certain number of teachers, and the efforts of school board members, school trustees, planters, and others to influence appointments, limited his discretion. Alabama state superintendent John W. Abercrombie noted that his state operated on a different standard in each of its sixty-six counties. "In some counties the examinations were rigid; in some they were mild; in some they amounted to nothing. In some counties the examinations were written; in some they were oral; in some they were sold." When states attempted to impose uniform standards, they proved impossible to enforce. The test devised by North Carolina in 1890, which covered spelling, geography, arithmetic, state history, U.S. history, grammar, physiology and hygiene, and the theory and practice of teaching, drew horrified gasps from county officials. If applied by the book, protested one, none of the colored applicants would pass. In practice, many superintendents applied their own "rule of thumb" standards. The following was typical: "Give a first grade certificate to any one who had completed the seventh grade; a second grade certificate to anyone who could read and write intelligently; and a third grade certificate to any one who could read and write, but not necessarily intelligently."[6]

Political acceptability sometimes was an informal element of the selection process. Some county school superintendents did not wish to employ teachers whom they regarded as overeducated, tainted by "northern" attitudes, and likely to be politically troublesome. In rural Georgia, for example, students from Atlanta University—sometimes dubbed the "Nigger College"—were especially suspect. "I could not get a public school because I am from Atlanta University," reported Edward Johnson. White hostility to Senator Charles Sumner's Civil Rights Bill, which became law in 1875, fueled such antagonism. "In this county if a colored person wants to teach in the public school system he must not advocate 'civil rights' or have much to say about it— if he do they dump him on the spot," complained another Atlanta University student, writing from Bolingbroke, Georgia. The school commissioner in Savannah, according to an official of the AMA, questioned teachers "about their feeling toward white southerners" and asked if they "talked politics." In some Black Belt counties, prospective teachers were asked to pledge their support for the Democratic Party. When the Democrats gained control of Madison County, Mississippi, in the election of 1883, they replaced all the teachers who had supported their political opponents.[7]

Political tests were rarely this explicit, and black public school teachers continued to engage in Republican politics. More usually, applicants received a broad hint that they should defer to whites and not rock the boat. John W. Collins reported a bizarre but revealing examination that he and two other blacks underwent in Charlottesville, Virginia. The superintendent and the school trustees, who were white, orally examined the candidates in a group, blacks and whites together. "The examination began with a debate upon how to teach Orthography." The superintendent then asked "a few questions in Arithmetic, Geography, and Grammar. The questions were answered promptly and correctly and the Superintendent said that he was satisfied." One of the trustees then congratulated the blacks for not acting "as if we thought we *knew* it *all*," and proceeded to lecture them on how to conduct themselves as teachers. "Just as long as we manifested such an interest, they, the trustees and the white teachers, were ready and willing to give us any aid in our work they could; but just as soon as we got to a point where we thought we could not be taught anything, and just as soon as we thought it our duty to teach Baptist, or any Sectarianism, or politics in our schools, that they had no further use for us as teachers." At the conclusion of the examination, the trustee asked Collins to sing, for the benefit of the superintendent, "O, Bear Me Away on Your Snowy Wings to My Immortal Home."[8]

Blacks routinely questioned prospective teachers about their religious beliefs. This was an age of intense sectarianism. Although the freed people exhibited a strong sense of racial independence in rejecting white-controlled churches, the various black denominations eyed each other with suspicion and outright hostility. The principal division separated the Baptists from the Methodists. As W. E. B. Du Bois once noted, with little exaggeration, "the differences between the Methodists and the Baptists overshadow the differences between heaven and hell." However, the two black Methodist churches, the AME and the AMEZ, were also bitter rivals.[9]

In the rural South, where churches rather than villages brought people together, denominational loyalties created tightly knit, inward-looking religious communities that prized conformity. This was especially true among black Baptists, whose independence from any ecclesiastical hierarchy made their control of the local church democratic but absolute. Robert R. Moton recalled how he absorbed, as a child, the denominational prejudices of a "strongly Baptist community" in Prince Edward County, Virginia. He once rejected an invitation to attend Stillman Institute by proudly stating that he "preferred being an ignorant Baptist than an educated Presbyterian"—an expression of sectarian devotion that "never failed to bring forth much approval and applause from the colored people of the community." Another college president, Jacob L. Reddix, grew up among Baptists in Vancleave, Mississippi. "Religious dogma was so strong in our community that a person belonging to any other than the Baptist denomination was 'looked down on.'"[10]

The fact that public schools were organized around church communities, and held their classes in church buildings, made the religious affiliation of the teacher a matter of crucial importance to trustees and patrons. In selecting teachers they favored people of their own denomination, and they expected their teachers to attend church. A student of Hampton Institute complained in 1876 that Baptists stuck together: "If you say, I am a Methodist, or a Congregationalist, or some other denomination, you stand a very poor chance for a school." The custom of boarding the teacher with a local family—often headed by a school trustee or a church deacon—reinforced the pressure to conform. Sectarianism was less obtrusive in city schools, which had larger enrollments and mixed children of different denominations. Ignoring the religious affiliation of the teacher, however, could still create difficulties. In Raleigh, North Carolina, black school trustee Charles N. Otey inadvertently favored Methodists and Episcopalians when appointing teachers in the 1870s. Recalled Otey, "The other denominations spared me not for two years, . . . [giving a] good deal of abuse."[11]

Teachers responded to sectarian pressures in different ways. When the teacher's denomination corresponded with that of the school community, no difficulty arose. When it did not, teachers faced a dilemma. In general, teachers learned to play down their denominational loyalties, although the extent to which their consciences allowed them to trim varied. A letter from a firm Baptist to an open-minded Episcopalian, both of them public school teachers in North Carolina, reflected the different approaches. "You have the advantage of me," James A. Whitted told Charles N. Hunter, "in being of such a flexible nature as to be able to adjust your religion to local [conditions], according to convictions and circumstances. I am so narrowly constructed that I cannot embrace all the 'isms,' as true worshippers, who in modern times profess Christianity. I am such an old fogey that I still believe in the plain teaching of the Bible—One God, one faith, and one baptism."[12]

When teachers and patrons failed to submerge their religious differences, schools sometimes "broke up." Patrons either dismissed the teacher or withdrew from the school. In many counties, school boards bowed to the strength of sectarian feeling by dividing the funds between the Baptists and the Methodists, allowing them to operate the public schools virtually as church schools. Denominational rivalry thus multiplied the number of black schools just as it did black churches. Teachers who belonged to the predominantly white denominations sometimes failed completely, their schools shunned by Methodists and Baptists alike.[13]

HAVING steered between the Scylla of politics and the Charybdis of religion, teachers could get down to teaching. Irregular attendance was their constant headache. Pupils missed, on average, between a third and a half of the school term, short as it was. "Goodness, they had every type of reason for not coming," recalled Mamie Garvin Fields, a teacher on St. John's Island, South Carolina. Children stayed home because of illness, inclement weather, lack of adequate clothing, and the need to look after smaller children. Religious activities also kept them from school. Revival meetings took up much of August. "All the public schools cooperated with the churches," remembered Richard R. Wright Jr., "and there was little time for lessons." In some parts of the South, the month of March saw children praying all night and roaming the woods, a process of joining the church known as "travelling through the wilderness" or "seeking." Teachers complained about it, but preachers defended the custom as "an old habit of slavery."[14]

Much of the nonattendance could be attributed to the demands of farm life in the South, the intensity of which fluctuated according to the day of the week and the seasons of the year. Black farmers depended upon the labor of their children. "The parents . . . are very poor," explained William Wilkins, a teacher in Bedford County, Virginia, "and at times they are compelled to keep their children at home to work, and to help them about the farm." Attendance declined as children grew older and their value as laborers increased. "Some of the larger scholars have to stay from school two and very often three days a week to sustain themselves the rest of the time," complained one teacher. Throughout the year, mothers often kept children home to help with chores. Monday was washday; on Friday the family prepared for the trip to town on Saturday. If the mother worked, an older child looked after babies and toddlers.

Seasons of intensive work pulled children out of the classroom—often at the insistence of the landlord as much as the parents—for days and weeks at a time. "Some 'can't come no more right now, till we finish layin' by [the crops],'" reported Charles Chesnutt in July 1875. "I suppose they will return when they get through pulling fodder," wrote a teacher in Flat Shoals, Georgia, a few weeks later. But slack times on the farm were rare. Depending upon geographical latitude, cotton picking started as early as August and ended as late as December. This was a time for families to maximize their income by putting all able-bodied members to work: picking required dexterity rather than strength, and children could be as productive as adults. Moreover, in addition to picking their own crop, families could hire themselves out by the day to other farmers. Corn also had to be harvested. In November farmers dug up sweet potatoes and made syrup. Christmas and New Year's festivities dominated December. Plowing and planting consumed March and April. When the warmer weather arrived, cotton had to be hoed and corn replanted. "Then we would use all of the children for a few days, girls and boys," recalled John Wilson of Washington Parish, Louisiana. The demands of other staples—tobacco, rice, sugar—varied, but they also took priority over schooling.[15]

A constantly changing school population made it hard for teachers to make headway. The emergence of sharecropping as the dominant form of farming among blacks discouraged families from staying put. Frustrated by their inability to realize a decent profit after the annual "settlement" with the landlord—in many cases finding themselves once more in debt—families migrated from plantation to plantation. Every year, January witnessed a general upheaval as hosts of sharecroppers, having fulfilled their yearlong contract, exchanged one landlord for another in the hope of improving their lot. The constant goal of his Mississippi sharecropper parents, recalled John M. Gandy—who eventually became a college president in Virginia—was "a better bargain, or one that would permit them to come out at a profit when 'settling-up-time' came around." William Pickens, the son of South Carolina sharecroppers who migrated to Arkansas, reckoned that his parents moved twenty times in eighteen years. A third of all families moved each year, and in some areas the turnover was still higher. Teachers who had gotten to know their pupils suddenly noticed missing faces and a batch of new ones.[16]

Nonattendance put teachers in a dilemma. Given the paucity of teachers, class sizes would have been enormous, and unmanageable, if all the pupils who enrolled attended every day. Yet teachers knew that irregular attendance undermined the effectiveness of their teaching. The experience of Virginia L. Adams, a teacher in Tallassee, Alabama, illustrated the problem. When she opened her school after Christmas, one hundred children enrolled—"more than I can well manage alone." By May, the planting season, the number had dropped to twenty-five. "It is one of the most difficult things that I have to contend with to get the people to keep their children in school long enough to do them some good."[17]

Discipline, one of the challenges that all new teachers confront, was usually the least of the teacher's problems. Although some were at first intimidated by the larger boys, their matter-of-fact references to "the rod" and "the switch" indicate that teachers—regardless of what they may have learned in normal school—relied upon corporal punishment. "Persuasion to study and good deportment," recalled William Pickens, from the perspective of a pupil, "consisted of a hickory switch, a cone-shaped paper 'dunce's cap' and a stool on which the offender must stand on one foot for an enormous length of time." Richard R. Wright Jr. retained a vivid memory of "abundant switches, straps, and paddles" in the public schools of Augusta. But corporal punishment could occasionally backfire. John Gandy once whipped a boy who was considered unteachable, eliciting a message from the boy's father "that he was going to kill me if I did not let the boy alone." Another teacher, from Hampton Institute, was threatened by "two, big rough men" after whipping a female pupil. Most parents, however, thoroughly approved of corporal punishment, which they frequently administered to their children at home.[18]

Isolation was another problem that black teachers shared with whites. The one-room schoolhouse was the standard type of school in rural America in the nineteenth century. A lone instructor had to cope with a group of children, numbering anywhere from twenty to one hundred, whose ages typically ranged from seven to fifteen. Age, however, was not a reliable guide to ability or knowledge. "I found that more than half of my scholars to be larger than I was," reported one teacher. "Five could read words of one syllable, six knew the alphabet, the remainder knew nothing; three could count a hundred, and five could not tell their names." William H. Johnson's first class included "young men and maidens, old men and elderly women, boys and girls of all sizes, and of all conditions of mentality."[19]

Standard practice called for teachers to divide their pupils into groups according to age and ability, teaching each group in turn, and sometimes using student monitors to help with the other groups. It proved impractical for a teacher to handle more than four groups or five groups, and most of the pupils were concentrated in the equivalent of grades one and two, with smaller groups in grades three and four. Moreover, because school terms were so short, many teachers kept pupils at the first-grade level for two years. This bunching of children in grades one and two discouraged the older children from staying in school. Hence few pupils received more than the equivalent of a fourth-grade education. Their ability to advance any farther was handicapped by both the lack of time that teachers could devote to them and the restricted training of the teachers themselves—most of whom had never proceeded beyond the same kind of one-teacher school.[20]

Teaching methods were simple. "The method used was that of rote-learning," recalled John Gandy, "that is learning to read by learning the abc's and as the students progressed the memory method, committing to memory the contents of grammar and history." Teachers drilled their pupils by means of "recitations," whereby the children chanted their answers in unison. In William Pickens's Arkansas school, the teacher tested ability to spell by forming the pupils in line, the strongest at the "head" and the weakest at the "foot." As the children spelled or misspelled words, they moved up or down the line. Recalling the curriculum, many simply described it as the "three R's." Gandy, elaborating a little, cited "Robinson's complete arithmetic,

Swinton's Word Study, Physiology, Grammar, United States History, and the like." Most teachers provided religious instruction, starting each day with a prayer, verses from the Bible, and hymns. James Russell, later ordained in the Episcopal Church, "also had them recite the Apostle's Creed every Friday afternoon." Fridays, in general, saw a relaxation of the normal school routine. "We have rhetorical exercises every Friday afternoon which consist of dialogues, declarations, readings from different writers, and music" reported C. D. Johnson of Hampton's Lincoln School.[21]

Even under the best conditions the "ungraded" rural school presented a formidable challenge, but the typical rural schoolhouse made the teacher's job even more difficult. "I found a little log house, plastered inside with mud," wrote a Virginia teacher. "It had no desk, a few planks, with holes bored in each end, and two sticks put in, formed the seats." Indeed, desks were virtually unknown outside city schools: students sat on backless, rough-hewn benches, the legs of the younger pupils dangling in the air. "Writing was done by the children while upon their knees, the copy books lying open on the benches," recalled William Johnson. "We manufactured a blackboard." Few schools had any water supply other than a jug filled from a nearby spring or well. Washing facilities did not exist and even outdoor privies were rare. School boards set no minimum standards for schoolhouses. As the superintendent of Clarke County, Georgia explained, "We say to the people . . . that the schoolhouse they furnish must be good enough to winter a cow."[22]

The absence of glass windows, and the cracks often evident between the roughly dressed floorboards, made rural schools notoriously difficult to heat and light. Iron stoves were a luxury; open fires were far more common. In one of the Mississippi schools that John Gandy attended, an open fire burned on a pile of dirt in the middle of the floor, with "no arrangement to take the smoke away." A school taught by Charles Hunter in Wake County, North Carolina, boasted a chimney made of sticks and dirt that "frequently caught fire." Lest all the heat escape, the sole source of light, a large flap held open by sticks, had to be closed, leaving fire's flames, and the cracks between the logs, the sole sources of illumination. Churches, although sometimes lighter and more airy, were even more difficult to heat. Charles Chesnutt described one in Jonesville, North Carolina:

> The church . . . was a very dilapidated log structure, without a window; but there was no need of one, for the cracks between the logs furnished a plentiful supply. . . . The interior was rougher than the outside; ten or a dozen "slabs" with legs made of oak saplings. An awful looking pulpit on the side of the room, and a lamp without a chimney suspended to the joists by a string. The chimney had been made for a fireplace but I pity the deluded being who imagines a fire would burn in it.

During the months of winter, schoolhouses like this chilled pupils and teachers alike. "My schoolhouse is given very much to exposure which caused me to take very much cold," complained I. H. Tazewell of Southampton County, Virginia. William Johnson remembered one year when he suffered "a dumb chill, or one that would speak through a hard ague," each and every day between September and February.[23]

The life of many teachers was peripatetic. Because the school terms were so short and the schools themselves so impermanent—their number and location shifted from year to year—teachers moved often. Robert Fitzgerald of Orange County, North Carolina, was an "itinerant teacher," recalled his granddaughter. "Before a school term opened, he'd walk miles across the country, find an empty township house most centrally located and take possession of it for his school. If enrollment was poor he'd have to move to another locality." Charles Hunter combined teaching a four-month term in a Robeson County school with teaching split terms—two months in the summer and two in winter—in Wake County schools.[24]

Teachers commonly boarded with local families for the two, three, or four months they held school. They were variously amazed and appalled by the crudity of their rural dwelling places. "I would advise everyone who comes into the country to teach to bring a few things with them," wrote Ellen Garrison Jackson, "such as a Knife and fork, spoon, cup and saucer etc. They will be needed." With all the members of a family often occupying one room, few enjoyed much privacy. Charles Chesnutt, who slept in a shed with the youngest of his landlord's six children, did relatively well. The family boarding James

Weldon Johnson had created two rooms by employing a partition, but the partition stopped several feet short of the principal room's ceiling. Asked to share one side of the partition with a fourteen-year-old boy, Johnson declined, determined to hang on to "the narrow margin of my privacy." Charles Hunter endured the embarrassment of undressing in a one-room house, with only a curtain separating him from the rest of the family and its occasional house visitor, a "comely young lady." He soon got used to it. Virginia teacher Della Irving Hayden, however, could not face the prospect of sharing "one room about 20 by 24 feet" with a married couple and two daughters. After collapsing in tears on her first night, she persuaded the school's patrons to build an addition to the house if she supplied the nails. Most teachers were at least well fed, although the standard country fare of fried chicken, cornbread, pork, and greens could soon jade even the heartiest appetite.[25]

White opposition remained a problem, especially in areas that had never before seen black schools or black teachers. In March 1872 Edward Bowman, teaching in Kempville, Virginia, escaped through the schoolhouse window, followed by his pupils, when "a low class of rowdies" equipped with "guns and pistols" tried to catch him. The destruction of schools by arson—simple, effective, difficult to prevent, and impossible to prove—still occurred from time to time. "As I went to my schoolhouse yesterday I found it in ashes, burned by some incendiary," wrote one teacher in 1873. "I left it Friday about four o'clock, and about one o'clock in the night, the Rev. Israel Cross saw the light, and when he got there it was falling in."

More frequently, teachers experienced minor harassment. Whites refused to let children cross their land to get to school, forcing them to take circuitous detours; "Rebels won't let the colored people board any teacher on their land." Teachers found themselves evicted for nonpayment of rent, or shut out of the schoolhouse by a landowner who "nailed up the doors." As black political power declined, however, even harassment diminished. One Hampton graduate reported with evident relief that he had been "treated with respect," even though "some of the whites are very much opposed to free schools and colored teachers." Another even claimed, "The white citizens have encouraged me a great deal."[26]

The "school-closing exercise" or "exhibition" enabled teachers to cultivate the support of both black patrons and white neighbors. Black schools adopted the practice soon after the Civil War and it quickly became a universal custom. An annual celebration of the pupils' achievements—and the teacher's—it featured a program of songs, poems, recitations, and dramatic dialogues. White notables—school committee members, ministers, editors, politicians—were routinely invited, and some invariably did attend. The 1880 exhibition at Fayetteville Normal School lasted more than three hours, and "was quite a success" judging by the fact that "very few of the audience left during the exercises." Writing in old age of memories from the 1890s, Charles N. Hunter fondly recalled the excitement that these events occasioned:

> With the children it was one great thrill. They all wanted to have a part in the Exhibition and Concert. They wanted to speak their pieces. They wanted to sing their songs. They wanted to say their dialogues. They wanted a part in the beautiful drills. . . . We were kept busy afternoons and evenings in rehearsals. The work was not irksome. No one tires of it. When the eventful night rolled around there was always a crowd of people. . . . On each occasion they were surprised. They were pleased. They paid us the highest compliments. And the children, their parents, and their teachers, were very happy.

In some counties, teachers organized a common closing exercise, or commencement, in which all the schools in the area took part. In New Hanover County, North Carolina, people from miles around gathered for a public dinner. Indeed, the school-closing exercise was one of the few occasions on which blacks and whites might eat together. Bridging, for once, the denominational division between Baptists and Methodists, it became "the gala social event of the year" in many rural communities.[27]

Having established their schools, black teachers faced the more intractable problem of keeping them in operation long enough. School terms of four months were too short to provide pupils with much more than basic literacy, especially if pupils were absent half the time. In some years and in some counties, terms were as short as three or even two months. Split terms, with two months of school in midwinter and two months in high summer—the coldest and hottest times of the year—exacerbated the problem. Designed to accommodate landlords who did not wish schooling to impinge upon the planting and cotton-picking seasons, they made the job of the teacher a task of Sisyphus. "The children have hardly got a good understanding of what they have gone over before the term closes," complained one teacher. School terms of such brevity also, of course, failed to provide teachers with a living wage.

Teachers tried to address these problems by extending the school term, asking parents to contribute tuition fees of about one dollar a month for each child. Some cash-poor communities paid in cotton, each bale raising enough money to cover a month's salary. But both tuition fees and public funding were unpredictable. Many parents agreed to pay for extra schooling, but as one teacher noted, "unlooked for events often require that monies religiously laid aside for educational purposes be paid out for other things." Even in good times black farmers saw little cash. Agricultural wages varied from five dollars to fifteen dollars a month; sharecroppers might see a year-end profit of thirty-eight dollars, or they might make nothing at all. In lean years parents simply could not afford to subsidize the schools directly. "You want us to pay you thirty or forty dollars a month for sitting in the shade," a black farmer told Charles Chesnutt, "and that is as much as we can make in two or three months." When the young teacher replied that education soon paid for itself—preaching the middle-class faith that knowledge and material prosperity went hand in hand—the farmer remained dubious. "We all of [us] work on other people's, white people's, land, and sometimes get cheated out of all we make; we can't get the money."[28]

Public pay was also unreliable. The Redeemers cut spending to the bone, and they doled out money with erratic parsimony. Blacks rarely knew how many schools would be approved, and for how long, in any given year. Teachers often found themselves in a kind of cat-and-mouse game with the school committees, which opened and closed schools at whim. It was only after a week of teaching in the summer of 1875 that Charles Chesnutt found out that his school near Spartanburg "would probably run but two months." In Wilson, North Carolina, the school committee allowed J. C. Price to continue his subscription school as a free public school, but after three weeks ordered him to close it. After the patrons registered a protest, the committee allowed a one-week extension. By the end of the summer Price had taught for three months, but the county had paid him for just one. Price thought that the Democrats wanted him out of the county. "They think the negroes are advancing too far for them. Too many of them are meriting and demanding higher grades." But the whim of local committee members could sometimes be benign. John Gandy expected to teach for only three months in Tiptonville, Tennessee, but he ended up teaching six.[29]

Extracting money from school boards, even after they had agreed upon a salary, often proved vexatious. Teachers usually had to travel to the county courthouse each month to receive a pay warrant from the school superintendent. But counties often failed to pay on time, or paid only after the schools had closed. "The schools are taught before the taxes are collected," a Mississippi official explained, "and the warrants are sold." Teachers could rarely obtain the face value of their warrants, however, if selling them to speculators. One Virginia teacher complained that he lost the equivalent of a month's salary through selling his pay warrants at a discount of five dollars each. In some cases, the public officials of the county, or their relatives, were the people doing the speculating. When taxes arrived in dribs and drabs, teachers were paid when money became available. William Johnson recalled following the treasurer of Chesterfield County from to town to town in order to get his warrants cashed. Public schools were on such a tenuous financial basis that school boards sometimes failed to pay their teachers at all. In 1901 the state of Georgia was sixteen months behind in its payments to teachers.[30]

As rural schools stagnated in their poverty and inadequacy, the initial idealism of many black teachers gave way to disillusionment. High hopes ebbed away. W. H. Lee, writing from Nansemond County, Virginia, in 1874, vented his own frustration. "The public schools here don't encourage competent teachers to stay. They don't pay enough;

they don't carry on the schools long enough, only three months a year; and the teacher has sometimes to wait nine months for his pay."[31]

Teaching under these conditions required extraordinary dedication. Teachers often had long walks—a five-mile journey was common—to and from their schoolhouses. They visited the homes of parents, attended church, prepared lessons, and often taught in the evenings and on Sundays. They could usually enjoy community support—local residents boarded them, sometimes passing the teacher from house to house each week, and school trustees maintained the schoolhouse. But when trustees proved unreliable, teachers themselves dressed lumber, made benches, replaced shingles, and gathered fuel. And at any time, teachers could be called upon to act as scribe or amanuensis. "I am in school every day until after four," explained Julia A. Rutledge, a Virginia teacher, "then I either have a letter to write or read for some one; and as I have evening school from seven to ten, it leaves very little chance for writing."[32]

RELIGIOUS faith enabled many teachers to endure hardships that might otherwise have defeated them. "I am back in the woods but I have faith in God with me just the same as when I was in school," wrote an Atlanta University student who was teaching near Statesboro, Georgia. "He is with me in every time of need." Their commitment to racial uplift also sustained them. Those who received any kind of advanced training absorbed the missionary spirit of northern Protestantism. "There is a great deal of Christian work to be done in every direction," a Virginia teacher affirmed. "Here are minds to be cultivated and aspirations to be raised above the common standard that is now prevalent among our people."[33]

Teachers also tried to bring Christianity—of the right kind—to their rural patrons. Like their middle-class mentors, they were appalled by rural preachers' ignorance of the Bible, repelled by the "noise" and "superstition" of vernacular religion, and disgusted by the addiction of country folk to whiskey and tobacco. They abhorred the squalor of rural homes and deplored the frequency of sexual immorality. Hence they taught Sunday schools, organized temperance societies, advocated thrift, and preached that cleanliness was next to godliness. Beneath the Victorian moralizing lay an equally Victorian conception of service. "We were never allowed to entertain any thought of being educated as 'go-getters,'" James Weldon Johnson recalled of his years at Atlanta University. "Most of us knew that we were being educated for life work as underpaid teachers. The ideal constantly held up to us was education as a means of living, not of making a living."[34]

This missionary desire to bring civilization and true Christianity to the rural masses ran up against cultural resistance. Like the white teachers of the AMA, they found that blacks all too often laughed at their temperance sermons and were bemused by their strictures against the "filthy weed." And the religious practices that offended northern whites proved equally impervious to criticism from educated southern blacks. Just as General Samuel Chapman Armstrong, the founder of Hampton Institute, inveighed against "preachers who are blind leaders of the blind," so his protégé Booker T. Washington condemned "three-quarters of the Baptist ministers and two-thirds of the Methodists" as "unfit, either mentally or morally, or both, to preach the gospel to anyone." But when teacher and minister contended for religious influence in rural communities, the preacher had the advantage. "Most of the colored race have these strange ideas about Christianity," complained one frustrated Sunday school teacher. "If you don't make a great noise, they don't enjoy your teaching of the Bible." Others acknowledged the power of the minister and tried to enlist his cooperation. "Our people can be better reached from the pulpit than any other place," avowed a contributor to the *Southern Workman*. "They will go to church if nowhere else, and in most cases whatever is said from the sacred stands is law and gospel."[35]

Their commitment to correct speech could also distance well-trained teachers from the rural communities they served. In their diaries from the 1870s, two North Carolina teachers, J. C. Price, the future bishop, and Charles W. Chesnutt, the future novelist, revealed their concern to teach standard American English. "Grammar is the vehicle of thought and expression," wrote Price, "and if we could speak and write well we must give untiring attention to the peculiarities of the vehicle." Chesnutt complained about the uncouth speech and elongated vowels of his pupils, and vowed to "unteach" their rural brogue. In seeking to replace dialect with the language of the educated middle class, they were simply doing their jobs as teachers. Moreover, not all blacks resented or resisted such instruction; many, in fact, expected it. But in reacting against the patois of the freedmen—partly because it was an object of such ridicule and amusement to white people—teachers sometimes overreacted. So much so, believed Richard Wright Jr., that teachers, and educated blacks generally, alienated a portion of the lower classes. They failed to appreciate the "vivacious and sometimes elegant and eloquent speech" of the uneducated. Their sometimes exaggerated enunciation was often scorned by the latter as "proper" or "white folksy." This was, of course, an issue of class. In the flattened social pyramid of the black population, where the distance between base and apex was short, education alone indicated middle-class status.[36]

Intellectual isolation accompanied social distance. Men like Charles Chesnutt and James Weldon Johnson, both possessed of a keen talent for social observation, could write lyrically about the rural communities where they taught. "Life here is simple and pleasant," Chesnutt noted in his diary. "I rise at six, read till breakfast, if it is not ready; eat, read till school time, half past eight. Go to school, let out at about three o'clock, come home and read until dark. Then I can sit and sing, and recite pieces I have learned, think over what I have read." Johnson regarded the "three months I spent in the backwoods of Georgia" as the most important part of his "education for life." The relentlessly self-improving Chesnutt—in his spare hours cramming Latin and German, and devouring the classics—soon felt frustrated by his inability to discuss ideas and literature. His fascination with the rural characters that peopled his neck of the woods alternated with irritation. "Well! uneducated people, are the most bigoted, superstitious, hardest headed people in the world!" For the urbane, multitalented Johnson, who passed his lunch hour reading *Don Quixote* in the original Spanish, the rural school was a vacation job that helped to defray his expenses at Atlanta University.[37]

Chesnutt and Johnson were hardly typical teachers. But they illustrated in an extreme form the paradox of education. Ambitious blacks saw education as a means of leaving behind the poverty and isolation of the countryside. The more education they acquired, the better their prospects for leaving the farm and moving to the city. The best-educated blacks, the students who completed normal and college courses, were not, by and large, destined for rural schools. They taught in the country during their summer vacations while students, but they were not disposed to molder away in rural poverty. Most settled in the towns and cities, which offered greater scope for leadership, a richer intellectual life, a less oppressive atmosphere, and better schools—longer terms, better facilities, higher salaries. The urban origins of many students encouraged this concentration in the cities. The best of the freedmen's schools, and most of the northern white teachers, had been located in urban areas; these schools furnished the universities with a disproportionate number of their students. "Most of the pupils at Atlanta University come from the cities and small towns of the South," explained president Edward T. Ware. "It is natural, therefore, that most of the graduates . . . should become teachers in the city public schools."[38]

H AMPTON Institute, founded by the American Missionary Association and developed by former Union general Samuel Chapman Armstrong, devised an alternative method of training black teachers, one specifically designed to produce teachers of rural schools. Unlike Fisk or Atlanta, or the twenty or so other institutions bearing the name *university* or *college,* Hampton did not aspire to higher education: it was a secondary school and a normal school. Moreover, instead of imitating the classical curriculum of the New England academies or the private white academies of the South, Hampton eschewed Latin, Greek, and foreign languages. Instead it focused on the "three R's," supplemented by history, geography, and elementary science. Hampton also insisted that all its students undertake "manual training." Apart from enabling students to earn money toward their board and tuition—an opportunity that black colleges also provided—manual training performed two other functions that were, in Armstrong's eyes, more important. The first was to impart skills. Trades like bricklaying and farming enabled students to supplement their meager pay when they taught in rural schools. The second was to instill the habits of self-discipline, which, according to Armstrong, slavery had discouraged. Manual training became known as "industrial education" because it aimed to teach blacks to be industrious, not because it equipped them with the skills adapted to modern industry.

From the start, Hampton Institute was criticized by blacks for providing a substandard education that overemphasized manual training and discouraged black aspirations to equality. It was not so much the fact that Armstrong compelled students to work that made his methods controversial. Rather, it was the amount of manual training he required and the conservative political philosophy that underpinned his institution. Hampton students initially spent half of their days working and only half in the classroom. By 1879, with the establishment of the night school, in which pupils studied for two hours after having labored for ten, Hampton raised the proportion of the school year devoted to manual training to something like two-thirds. Moreover, Armstrong frankly strove to produce teachers who would return to the countryside, abstain from politics, accept racial segregation, and defer to the southern Democrats rather than the northern Republicans.[39]

If Hampton's influence had been proportionate to its size, critics would not have been so concerned. However, white opponents of black equality, both southerners and northerners, singled out Hampton Institute for praise and support in a calculated attempt to reduce the influence of the black universities, and to prescribe a limited and narrow curriculum for black schools. The Hampton model—imitated by Booker T. Washington at Tuskegee Institute—became an ideological force of enormous influence, far greater than Hampton's size alone would have merited. Many historians have decried that influence. They contend that the Hampton model expressed racist assumptions about black moral deficiency, trained blacks for a subordinate role in the South's workforce, and encouraged blacks to adjust to white supremacy. Such criticisms have particular force for the period after 1900, when northern philanthropic foundations such as the General

Education Board used Hampton as a conservative counterweight to the private universities and sought to extend Hampton's influence throughout the public school system.[40]

During its early years, however, Hampton Institute served a real need in rural education. Although it did not train students exclusively for rural schools—many Hampton graduates taught in Virginia's towns and some went on to attend college—it sent people to rural schools who were more likely to stay in them. Hampton also expected teachers to become leaders in rural communities. By restricting Hampton's curriculum to the equivalent of a secondary school education, and a limited one at that, Armstrong tried to avoid producing teachers who were vastly "overeducated" for the typical rural school. By no means did all Hampton students share Armstrong's conservative political philosophy, which advised blacks to "let politics severely alone." Nevertheless, Hampton's imprimatur made teachers more acceptable to white school superintendents in Virginia and elsewhere. Hampton softened white opposition to black public schools.[41]

Armstrong described Hampton students as "dull plodders." Yet Hampton produced teachers who were, within their limits, well trained. Admission requirements included "sound health and good character" as well as "ability to read and write, and knowledge of Arithmetic through Long Division." Pupils between the ages of fourteen and twenty-five were eligible for admission. Once at Hampton, they were subjected to rigorous pruning: about a fifth of the them did not survive their first year. By 1893, when most students entered the night school, only a quarter stayed the course. "Many must be dropped," explained Armstrong, "as poor material, morally, mentally, or physically." However, those who graduated and became teachers were well treated by their alma mater. "Hampton Institute established an elaborate system of correspondence and support for its former students," writes historian Robert Engs. The Hampton staff connected black schools to northern charitable groups, helped individuals in need, and supplied teachers with clothes, toys, and books.[42]

Hampton graduates also received a subscription to *Southern Workman.* This monthly newspaper contained state, national, and foreign news, as well as much else. Feature articles were lavishly illustrated with engravings donated by northern magazines. Vigorously argued editorials were nothing if not stimulating. An agricultural column dispensed advice on topics like "preserving eggs in winter." There was a children's page with stories and nursery rhymes, and a letters page. The paper also included material designed specifically to help teachers. A page of Bible stories gave teachers ready-made Sunday school lessons. A column entitled "The Teacher's Table" offered practical tips that incorporated the latest thinking in pedagogy: how to secure the attention of pupils, how to teach using the object lesson method, how to manage a classroom without resorting to corporal punishment. A letters page documented the teaching experiences, good and bad, of Hampton graduates, encouraging the exchange of information and ideas.[43]

Tuskegee Institute, headed by Armstrong's protégé Booker T. Washington, imitated Hampton's educational philosophy. However, Tuskegee and Hampton differed in two important ways. First, Tuskegee had a black principal and a black faculty. Given the antipathy of white southerners to white northern teachers, Tuskegee's all-black faculty provided a degree of political protection. It was also a racial manifesto. Tuskegee told the world, by demonstration rather than rhetoric, that blacks had the capacity to teach themselves, manage complex institutions, and elevate themselves through their own efforts. It proclaimed that blacks could furnish their own leaders. "The colored people do not need charity scattered among them," Washington told an audience of New York Congregationalists, "but they do need to be led, to be guided, to be stimulated until they get on their own feet."[44]

In the second place, Tuskegee set its entry requirements at a lower level than Hampton Institute. The superiority of the black schools in Virginia explained the difference. Virginia boasted more secondary schools for blacks, both public and private, and its public schools had longer terms—117 days in 1890 as opposed to Alabama's 72. Indeed, the public schools of Alabama were the worst in the nation with the exception of Louisiana. If Tuskegee's students routinely "murdered the King's English in their letters back to the school," as one of Washington's biographers has complained, their academic deficiencies could be explained by the appalling inadequacies of the public schools whence they came and Tuskegee's generous admissions policy. Any student who was over fourteen, possessed the ten dollar admission fee, had a modicum of schooling, and showed sufficient determination would be admitted. "Anybody who had any ability *at all* could get into Tuskegee Institute," claimed one of its teachers.[45]

Tuskegee's complicated program catered to all, including the near-destitute and the near-illiterate. Taking a leaf from Hampton Institute, its night school enabled penniless students to earn their board and part of the following year's tuition by working ten hours a day at a trade followed by two hours of study. "They would work on the farm during the day to raise vegetables for the day school students—and in the chicken department, the dairy department, and all over," recalled Francis Mary Albrier, who grew up on campus. "It took them two years to make one grade." Students in the day school devoted four days a week to academic study and one day, plus alternate Saturdays, to "industrial classes." The possibility of switching back and forth between the night school and the day school, and the existence of seven academic levels in an ostensibly four-year program, provided a variety of routes, traveled at different speeds, to the senior class. If they stayed the course, students gained a diploma that entitled them teach in Alabama's public schools without taking a county examination.[46]

Located in the heart of Alabama's Black Belt, Tuskegee Institute, even more than Hampton Institute, geared its program to rural life. Convinced that blacks were better off staying on the farm, Washington described cities as forbidding, alien places where blacks were rootless, friendless, and in constant danger of corruption. His ideal citizens were those of traditional American republicanism: the yeoman farmer and the small-town mechanic.

In pursuit of his Jeffersonian dream, Washington adapted the training of black teachers to a single, overriding goal: the transformation of the debt-ridden sharecroppers of the South into a prosperous class of independent landowners. Convinced that the classical curriculum of the black universities was largely irrelevant to the rural masses, and worried that too many black schools were making half-baked efforts to imitate that curriculum, Washington rigorously excluded Latin, Greek, and modern languages from the subjects taught at Tuskegee. He also inculcated his rural ideals through the work program—most students came from farms, and they were quickly disabused of the idea that education meant abandoning rural life. Washington tried as far as possible to relate the academic subjects to trades. "Everything was geared to that vocation." said a former student, "I remember I asked why I had to learn how many shingles it takes to go on a trapezoid roof. The boys would say, 'Why do I have to learn how many cubic inches in a cake pan?'" Abhorring the flowery, pretentious speech of the intellectual, and with little appreciation for art or literature, Washington insisted on "correlating" or "dovetailing" the literary and industrial subjects. For example, "The students in their composition work can go to the brick yard and write compositions about the manner of making bricks or harnessing horses."[47]

Washington expected Tuskegee-trained teachers to act as agents of rural progress. "You can revolutionize the communities where you go," he insisted. "In a few months you see results; the people brightening up; . . . they dress their children better, save their money, get homes, add to the school term." Above all, teachers should show farmers how to beat the crop-lien system, whereby sharecroppers paid a third of their cotton crop to the landlord as rent, but saw their own portion of the crop claimed by the merchant who had advanced them food and other supplies at exorbitant rates of interest. The ideal teacher, Washington argued, could tell black farmers "in a plain, simple, common-sense manner how to keep out of debt, how to stop mortgaging; . . . what to buy and what not to buy, how to sacrifice—to live on bread and water if necessary until they could . . . begin the buying of a home of their own."[48]

This was not an easy life, Washington warned his students. The paltry sums that school boards doled out could not sustain a teacher for anything like a year. Teachers had to appeal to patrons directly, asking them for money to build a decent schoolhouse and to double, even triple, the school term. To overcome the suspicion of rural folk, they needed to become part of their community. They must get to know the people, visit their homes, and talk to them in simple language without "big words and high flowing sentences." They should also enlist the cooperation of the local minister, however morally objectionable that individual might be. It might take two or three years to win the people's confidence, and during that time teachers must be ready to suffer. "You are going to have a hard time," he predicted. "You cannot get hold of large salaries at first. If you can get your board and some clothes for the first year you are being paid pretty well." If they were dedicated and sincere, however, communities would rally around them. And such a life brought deeper rewards. "There is a kind of satisfaction in doing such work in the South that you can get in no other way."[49]

BLACK teachers in the South's rural public schools, however, faced the harsh reality that conditions were getting worse, not better. Self-sacrificing individuals, and communities that responded to them, worked educational wonders. But the inexorable decline in teachers' salaries meant that local success stories could only mitigate, not halt, overall retrogression.

During Reconstruction, many black teachers had earned $40 or $50 a month. A few earned $100, $125, or even $150 a month. During the early years of the public school system, the salaries of black teachers and white teachers had been about equal. But as the system expanded and the number of public schools multiplied, salaries fell and a gap opened up between what white and black teachers earned. Black teachers in Mississippi averaged $53 a month in 1875, only $4 less than the average salary of white teachers. But in 1890 they were earning only $23, which was $10 less than the white average. In Alabama, black teachers had earned *more* than white teachers in 1875. Even in 1886, after twelve years of Democratic rule, the average monthly pay of a white teacher, $23.76, was only $1 more than what a black teacher earned. By 1900, however, black teachers earned only $17.66 a month, $7 less than the salary of white teachers.[50]

White officials denied that paying black teachers less than whites was an injustice, arguing that black teachers were invariably inferior. Allegations of incompetence were not wholly motivated by racial prejudice. Some county superintendents made honest efforts to certify teachers fairly and weed out the most unfit. When J. H. Shepherd, the inspector of schools for Shreveport, Louisiana, made teachers take a written examination, he found that scarcely any of the blacks could pass, "easy as it was." One applicant, already teaching in a rural school, "could not set down a sum in simple arithmetic"; others could "hardly read at all." The superintendent of Greene County, Alabama, complained to Booker T. Washington that a graduate of Tusgekee Institute could not parse the sentence *John killed a rabbit* and exhibited similar ignorance when quizzed on hygiene and arithmetic. This white official admitted to having no particular interest in black schools beyond that of "any other Christian man." But he wished to carry out his duties conscientiously: "I do not wish to be compelled to fill our schools with incompetent teachers."[51]

In many cases, however, a superintendent's opinion of black teachers was a function of his interest, or lack thereof, in the education of blacks. Those who complained loudest about incompetent black teachers tended to be the very people who were most willing to appoint them. "Most of the colored teachers are lazy devils of men, who want the money, and who hire somebody for $5 a month to cultivate a little crop for them," complained Alexander Yerger of Bolivar County, Mississippi. "I have letters from people wanting to be appointed teachers who do not seem to be able to spell three words in the English language correctly." Yerger, however, also thought that blacks "do not care much" about education—"the negro has big ideas but very little energy." The superintendent of Concordia Parish, Louisiana, complained that black children were making "little or no advance" because of "incompetent colored teachers." His own interest in black schools could be inferred from his belief that "each race should educate its own children." White officials also reasoned that black teachers had fewer social needs and could live more cheaply than white teachers. If they practiced "rigid economy," claimed a Mississippi superintendent, they could "live upon the salary now fixed."[52]

The poor training of many black teachers is not in doubt. It did not, however, account for the growing difference in pay for black and white teachers. After all, white teachers were, as a group, only slightly better educated. For example, when North Carolina made its first serious effort to apply a uniform standard of certification, about 40 percent of the white teachers, and about 75 percent of the black ones, failed to reach the lowest standard, the third-grade certificate. Yet under the old system, two-thirds of the state's white teachers had held first-grade certificates, compared with about one-third of the black teachers.[53]

Such figures suggest discrimination but do not prove it. Occasionally, however, white officials let the cat out of the bag. "We got teachers of colored schools for one-half or even one-third of what we paid teachers of white schools," admitted Henry B. Whitfield, a member of the Lowndes County, Mississippi, school board. "Besides, the houses used for the colored schools were very inexpensive. . . . We did not buy a dollar's worth of furniture for the colored schools in our county." This testimony from 1871 shows that in some counties the habit of treating black and white schools differently was as old as the public school system itself.

Over the next thirty years whites searched for a way to formalize such discrimination. State courts ruled that dividing tax money by race was unconstitutional. But school boards simply used the discretion granted to them by state legislatures to reduce per capita spending on black children. The simplest way to do that was to pay black teachers less. "None, of the colored teachers deserve as large a salary as the white teachers," explained the superintendent of Sampson County, North Carolina. A school board could therefore "so adjust teachers' wages as to give both races schools of the same length, and yet the white race gets more of the school fund to which they are entitled."[54]

By depressing the salaries of black teachers, white officials created a vicious cycle. Low pay deterred the best-educated blacks from staying in teaching, and as the good teachers left for better-paid employment, the less qualified and the semiliterate took their places. A high annual turnover of teachers ensured that much experience went to waste and made it difficult for teaching to become a stable profession. Corruption in the appointment of teachers made matters worse. Undercutting rival applicants by offering to teach for less money became a common practice. So did kickbacks to superintendents, school board members, and black trustees.[55]

More-enlightened whites—those who cared anything at all about the education of blacks—conceded that pay amounting to a dollar a day, and sometimes less, could not possibly attract and retain good teachers. "Many of the best teachers have quit the business," reported one county superintendent. "I know of one good teacher who gets only $13 per month and boards herself." The state superintendent of Alabama admitted that a black teacher earned less than a teamster, a porter, a washerwoman, or a cook. Teachers, moreover, had to buy suitable clothes, spent part of their own salaries on school supplies, and frequently paid for their board. But county superintendents often *preferred* to appoint poorly trained teachers, either because they did not wish to pay more, or because, as white officials in South Carolina later admitted, they feared that "the more educated the Negro was, the greater the possibility that he would stir up trouble in the community." The widespread desire to place a low ceiling upon black education led naturally to the appointment of incompetent teachers.[56]

Nobody could support themselves on $60, $80, or even $100 a year. A man could easily earn $200 to $400 a year as a preacher. A man who worked for the post office as a letter carrier earned $14 a week, a clerk $16. Both occupations carried more job security than that of teacher. An able-bodied man might even make more money as a day laborer. A person could earn from $1.50 to $3 a day picking cotton. A master cooper could earn $4 a day making beer barrels.[57]

The only way to survive as a rural public school teacher was by combining teaching with another occupation. Many teachers were also preachers; others farmed; some even labored by the day. A few did all three. "For twenty-two years I have been a preacher," reported a graduate of Hampton Institute in 1893, "but I have also been a teacher, a carpenter, a painter and a whitewasher." Robert Fitzgerald of Orange County, North Carolina, supported himself with farming, brick making, and road building. During the months he taught, he rose at dawn to attend to the farm, walked several miles to the schoolhouse, taught for six hours, and then walked five miles home to face additional chores. But many other farmer-teachers were simply amateurs. "If they had a good farm year they quit teaching and went to farming," recalled Kenneth B. Young of Tuskegee, Alabama. "The crops started to failing, they'd put that [plow] down and get his teacher's books and teach school." Remembering his childhood in Barnwell County, South Carolina, Lewis K. McMillan described a black minister sitting "drowsily by a flaming wood stove in the midst of his listless, greasy-faced charges a few hours daily, when rain and cold weather made field work impossible." Such men were preachers first, teachers second; McMillan did not even dignify such settings as "schools."[58]

By the end of the nineteenth century, the spirit of self-sacrifice was wearing thin. When Washington chaired a meeting of Hampton Institute alumni in 1893, the discussions revealed a clear division between those who appealed to missionary altruism and those who complained about atrocious pay. "To be a good teacher you must be preacher, housekeeper and carpenter and farmer," announced Rebecca Wright of Surry County, Virginia. "My husband bought a place in the woods. . . . I went to the homes within reach and asked the people to send their children to my little house and I would have a school. If you want one, tell your people as I did, to give what they can—eggs or butter etc., and have a festival and buy lumber and soon you'll get them interested and they'll build their own school house and then the Supt. will send you a teacher and let you pick out such as you want." This rousing statement of the Hampton-Tuskegee philosophy of self-help brought the house down.

But others insisted that the way to get better teachers—and teachers who would stay put—was to pay them more. A. B. Roberts could not have put the matter more bluntly.

> When I entered Hampton, I signed an agreement to teach for three years, I taught fourteen. I often went hungry. I walked hundreds of miles . . . to take examinations and to my school. . . . I was once threatened with violence if I didn't leave the district. I found one door of my school house nailed up. I stayed. I armed myself with a pistol and my boys with razors and taught the term out. There is enough money in the South to support the schools and pay decent salaries, but it goes into politics instead. Mr Washington said he'd rather teach for $10 a month than work for money at $100. I wouldn't. Mr. Washington is a great man, I am not a great man. I am in the minority perhaps, but if you want me to teach you must show me the money.

Roberts was no longer a teacher. Thousands of other male teachers also quit. Some left the countryside to teach in city schools, or in the numerous private schools that came into being after 1890. Others left teaching altogether.[59]

B LACK public schools were in a state of crisis. They had never been secure. Now they bore the brunt of a broad-ranged attack upon the rights of black southerners that rolled back the gains of Reconstruction and widened the gap between black schools and white schools. In 1890, Mississippi disenfranchised its black citizens; South Carolina did so in 1895, Louisiana in 1898. Over the next decade the remaining southern states followed suit. Blacks disappeared from Congress, state legislatures, county commissions, city councils, police forces, and juries. Slandered by a new wave of demagogic politicians, blacks were subjected to increasingly pervasive and strict segregation laws, the most humiliating of which assigned blacks to separate railway carriages and to the rear sections of streetcars. Blacks suffered a wave of lynchings and a series of race riots.

Having stripped blacks of political power and undermined their civil rights, white southerners debated how they might use education to cement white supremacy. Many argued that controlling what blacks thought meant controlling what they were taught. That, in turn, meant securing the right kind of teachers, trained in the correct way. As whites attempted to degrade black education, black teachers confronted new difficulties of staggering complexity.

CHAPTER FOUR

White Supremacy and Black Teachers

His education must be industrial, technical and moral, rather than literary, professional and cultural. . . . We may not go into his schools and
instruct his children; but, without doing violence to custom or tradition,
might we not train the teachers who are to conduct his schools?

Professor John W. Abercrombie, presidential address,
Southern Educational Association,
December 11, 1911

Senator Ben Tillman.

Library of Congress, Prints and
Photographs Division

Benjamin Ryan Tillman, a one-eyed politician from South Carolina, personified the white supremacy movement and its deep antipathy to black education. Governor of his state in the 1890s and then a U.S. senator until his death in 1918, Tillman was the South's best-known Negrophobe. He defended and even applauded lynching. He saw to it that blacks in South Carolina were stripped of the right to vote. And he argued that the "little smattering of education" blacks received had destroyed their "original virtues" as a race. "When you educate a negro," he explained, "you educate a candidate for the penitentiary or spoil a good field hand." He singled out "the teachings of northern fanatics" for encouraging blacks to hate white people. "The Northern millions which have gone . . . into negro colleges," he charged, aimed to "build up an African domination."[1]

Harbison College in Abbeville, South Carolina, was precisely the kind of institution that Tillman feared. It was typical of the two hundred or so private schools in the South that offered blacks something better than a public school education. Founded in 1885 by Rev. and Mrs. Emory W. Williams, black Presbyterians from New Jersey, it started life as an elementary school. After a fire destroyed the half-completed building in 1890, the northern Presbyterian Church assumed control of the school. When Rev. Williams defected to the southern Presbyterians and set up a rival school, the northern Presbyterians installed a new principal, Rev. Thomas H. Amos. A graduate of Lincoln University and the child of black Presbyterian missionaries—he was born in Monrovia, Liberia, in 1866—Amos spent fourteen years building up the institution. Speaking and lecturing across the country, he raised forty-five thousand dollars. In 1901 the school changed its name to Harbison College in honor of a northern benefactor. New buildings went up. The school added "Normal" and "College" departments. It boasted three hundred students, a third of whom boarded.[2]

In 1906, however, whites in Abbeville decided that the presence of Harbison College had become intolerable. They charged Amos with dabbling in politics by criticizing gubernatorial candidate Cole Blease, a man who bluntly opposed public education for blacks. They further claimed that Amos boasted about putting white women to work in the college kitchen and laundry. They blamed labor unrest among black agricultural laborers, who were demanding higher wages, on the influence of the college. They accused Harbison students of fomenting a "disturbance" in the town square, when shots were fired during the unveiling of a Confederate monument. A committee composed of Abbeville's leading white citizens demanded that Amos explain himself. Protesting his innocence, Amos denied that the college exerted a malign influence. "We have always closed our school on the first Monday of May to allow the boys and girls to reach home in time to make the crop." His interrogators were not convinced. Shortly thereafter a white physician who served as the college's doctor warned Amos that his life was in danger. He put Amos, his wife, and their eight children in a wagon and drove them to Greenville. He then put them on a train to Philadelphia. By encouraging "false ideas of what is called 'social equality' of the negro," explained the *Abbeville Press and Banner,* Amos had made himself "objectionable to some of our people."

Harbison College stayed closed during the autumn of 1906. The Presbyterian Church's board of home missions appointed a new president, Rev. C. M. Young, a former slave and South Carolinian. This southern black man "seems to be acceptable to a majority of our people," reported the *Press and Banner.* A few days before its scheduled reopening, however, the college's main building and two dormitories went up in flames. Whites advised Rev. Young to keep the college closed until things calmed down. The college opened again in 1907, having lost an entire academic year. But contrary to the *Press and Banner*'s advice, Young did not place more emphasis on farming and less on literary subjects. Indeed, the college reassured students that "care will be taken not to let [industrial work] conflict with the student's studies." In 1910 another fire at the college killed three students. Although some whites wanted the college to stay, the Presbyterian Church concluded that Abbeville was too hostile. The college acquired a large tract of land in Irmo, near Columbia, and turned itself into a boys-only school that emphasized agriculture.[3]

The crisis that bore down upon black teachers at the juncture of the nineteenth and twentieth centuries arose out of a relentless drive by white southerners to establish their racial supremacy beyond question or challenge. An upsurge in racial violence, the entrenchment of racial segregation, and the mass disenfranchisement of black voters destroyed any semblance of racial equality. Black teachers, members of a political leadership that whites were bent on destroying, suffered repeated humiliations. And their schools—the most visible and successful symbols of Reconstruction—came under a renewed wave of political and sometimes physical attack.

However, this assault on black education, although damaging, ultimately failed. White southerners complained that black teachers were overeducated and impractical, but they neglected to provide an alternative system of training them. They weakened and degraded state-controlled schools for blacks, but the private mission schools continued to produce well-educated teachers. White supremacists wanted to control and limit black education, but they never solved the problem of how to do it. They never succeeded in completely subordinating black schools to their political ends. Indeed, education remained one of the principal arenas of resistance to white supremacy.

To understand the white supremacist assault on black education, and the reason for its ultimate failure, one must examine how black teachers were educated. An enormous gulf existed between the majority who were educated exclusively in public schools and the minority who attended private schools for all or part of their education. The first group of teachers—with the exception of a few dedicated souls who supplemented their schooling with private study—were almost wholly untrained. Many were barely literate. The second group embraced almost all the teachers who satisfied some standard of professional competence.

The job of training black teachers had fallen by default to the private schools founded by the freedmen's aid societies of northern churches. From the start, the northern missionary boards intended their best southern schools to become "normal schools." By training a corps of professional teachers for the public schools, they hoped to raise educational standards across the board. Hence, although most of the northern teachers had left the South by the mid-1870s, the northern aid societies perpetuated their influence by building up schools of secondary level and higher. From Reconstruction through the beginning of the twentieth century, they founded new private schools—variously called universities, colleges, academies, high schools, institutes, and normal schools—that became dynamos of educational advance. In 1915 the northern mission societies maintained 354 private schools in the South, about half of which offered education above the elementary level. Throughout vast tracts of the South, these schools supplied blacks with their only means of progressing beyond the limited and often appalling public schools. Boasted Albert Salisbury of the AMA, "The missionary schools became more clearly than ever the educators of the freed race." Without them, black schools would have regressed under the tutelage of semiliterate teachers who had never attended a modern primary school, let alone a good secondary school or a college of higher education. As Salisbury put it, "I can count on my fingers all the [public] schools in the South . . . in which a colored man can get anything above a common school training."[4]

Nevertheless, during the years between Reconstruction and the end of the nineteenth century, white hostility to the education of blacks waned. The persistence of black voting, fear of federal intervention, and a desire for calm after the turmoil of Reconstruction discouraged southern whites from attacking black education too blatantly. The frozen hostility and occasional violence that had greeted the northern-run mission schools abated, allowing these institutions to take root and grow.

The mission schools themselves helped disarm white opposition. As much as Armstrong's Hampton or Washington's Tuskegee had, the private colleges stressed the development of moral character. By training teachers to be good citizens—churchgoing, property-owning, and virtuous—they claimed to be strengthening society, not threatening it. "Although they are reformers in the best sense of the word," Atlanta University claimed, "they are an eminently conservative social element." The mission schools went to great lengths to cultivate southern whites. They invited local worthies to attend their public examinations and closing ceremonies, and were delighted when native whites uttered words of praise. Atlanta University was thrilled when, in 1871, former Confederate governor Joseph E. Brown commended the examinations he witnessed, admitting that they disproved the idea that "members of the African race are not capable of a high grade of intellectual culture." The 1882 closing exercises of Avery Institute moved the *Charleston News and Courier* to praise the "neat rhetoric and obvious originality" of the student essays. Southern education officials even began to cooperate with the mission schools. In Tennessee, South Carolina and elsewhere, state superintendents of education located summer schools for black teachers on the campuses of black colleges.[5]

The mission schools reassured southern whites that they taught practical skills that would benefit the economy. Assisted by grants from the John F. Slater Fund, a charitable foundation established in New York, they incorporated "manual training" or "industrial education" into their curricula. Tougaloo University operated a plantation. At Shaw University, wrote Henry M. Tupper, the men took carpentry or joinery while the women cooked, served food, and sewed: "The practical side is steadily kept in view, guarding against what has been sometimes affirmed that the education of the colored people has proved a failure, that in some instances the education received has rendered them helpless, indolent and unpractical, and not fitted even to grapple with the ordinary and every day duties of life." Atlanta University taught housekeeping, sewing, cookery, carpentry, metalwork, and printing; in 1885 it opened the Knowles Industrial Building. By

1890 all the black colleges and universities in the South taught some form of industrial education.[6]

Their efforts to propitiate southern whites sometimes went too far. At Talladega College's 1877 commencement ceremony, president Edward P. Land seated the white visitors in a separate section, and then ejected a black man who sat on a "reserved" seat. Blacks boycotted the 1878 commencement. Usually, however, college heads tried to mollify southern whites without violating their commitment to racial equality. Edmund Asa Ware, for example, told the librarian of Atlanta University to remove books about the Civil War, including a history of Georgia's notorious Andersonville prison, that offended former Confederates. But when the legislature threatened to terminate its state subsidy unless the university ceased to teach members of both races—which would have compelled the white teachers to exclude their own children—Horace Bumstead, Ware's successor, refused to comply. Atlanta University lost its state funding.[7]

Still, there is little evidence that blacks educated by northern mission schools had much difficulty finding employment in the South's public schools. In Georgia, graduates of Atlanta University furnished most of the teachers in Atlanta's black schools. Claflin University trained most of the black teachers in and around Orangeburg, South Carolina. Charleston's Avery Institute sent its graduates all over the state. Gregory Normal Institute provided black teachers for the public schools of Wilmington, North Carolina, and its rural hinterland. Southern whites may have found the mission schools irksome, but education officials tacitly recognized they had become an essential support for the South's public school system.[8]

During this period of what C. Vann Woodward termed "forgotten alternatives" in race relations—a time when southern whites were politically dominant but not politically absolute—a certain amount of negotiation and compromise took place.[9] When the Redeemers came to power in the 1870s, they faced the fact that several publicly funded black colleges had already been established. In addition, a few private institutions were in receipt of state subsidies. Honoring election pledges, the Redeemers for the most part left these arrangements undisturbed. They also founded new institutions for the purpose of training black teachers. Alabama's Democrats established State Normal School in Huntsville in 1874 and Tuskegee Institute in 1881. Democrats in North Carolina funded a normal school in Fayetteville in 1877. Texas established Prairie View Normal School two years later. Louisiana created Southern University in 1881. Virginia's Readjuster Party founded Virginia Normal and Collegiate Institute in 1882. Four years later, Democrats in Kentucky and Florida created black normal schools.[10]

Blacks also pressed for state-funded "higher education." They wanted black universities on a par with the University of Virginia, the University of Georgia, and the University of North Carolina. "We do not desire simply to become a race of teachers," explained Alfred W. Harris, a black Republican from Petersburg, Virginia. "I want a place where our . . . girls and boys may go and drink from the fountain of knowledge until their ambition is satiated." Southern whites resisted such pleas. Dignifying a black school with the title of "college" or "university" smacked too much of social equality. However, state schools created by Virginia, Alabama, and Louisiana included a collegiate level. Elsewhere, taking advantage of federal subsidies offered by the Morrill Act of 1890, states established "A&M" or "land grant" colleges that offered something by way of higher education but stopped short of being universities. By 1912 every southern and border state was using Morrill Act money to support a state school for blacks.[11]

Whites gave these institutions very little money, and they often located them well away from centers of black population in order to minimize their influence. One story, perhaps apocryphal, recounts the argument put forward by a member of the Alabama legislature when the question of a colored land-grant college was being considered. "Since we have to have this institution, I move that we put [William H.] Councill's school up there in the mountains at Huntsville, where it will do the Negroes least good." Benign neglect had its benefits, however. Whites controlled these institutions, but, lacking much interest in them, left the teachers more or less alone. As a result, many of the state-funded normal schools and land-grant colleges mirrored the organization and curriculum of the northern-inspired private colleges. At State Colored Normal School in Fayetteville, for example, pupils attended a nine-month session consisting of three twelve-week terms. The school taught three preparatory grades and a three-year normal course. Pupils studied a wide variety of literary and scientific subjects. In their last two years, they took algebra, philosophy, ancient history, rhetoric, and Latin. The "Preparatory Department" functioned as a practice school for the normal students. Some of the state schools added college courses and began to award degrees.[12]

BY 1900, however, the laissez-faire policy of the states toward the training of black teachers—providing a small amount of state aid, but leaving the job mostly to the mission schools—was coming under fire. White progressives understood that the South needed a thoroughgoing reform of its patchwork, underfunded public school system. But white antipathy to the education of blacks presented a major obstacle to such reform. The perception by whites that they were massively subsidizing black schools, and that the education of blacks harmed their interests, fueled widespread opposition to higher school taxes. As the schools superintendent in one of Louisiana's majority-black cotton parishes put it, "A little learning with the negro is a dangerous thing. Why should the white race be forced to aid and abet *a dangerous thing?*"[13]

A growing chorus of influential whites declared that black education was a failure, and they pinned the blame on "higher education." They argued that the public school system was fundamentally flawed because it had been constructed on the principle that blacks should receive the same kind of education that whites received. That basic error stemmed from the discredited policy of Radical Reconstruction, with its misconceived belief in racial equality. Although Reconstruction itself had ended long ago, its spirit lived on in the private missionary schools that stubbornly survived, even prospered, in the New South. By offering blacks "higher education," these institutions kept the doctrine of equality alive and impeded the establishment of white supremacy. They were outposts of Yankee fanaticism that produced, said North Carolina superintendent of education J. Y. Joyner, "a multitude of pretentious, half-taught, bigoted preachers and school-teachers constituting themselves leaders of their race and filling the negroes . . . with all sorts of false notions."[14]

The root of the issue was the same as ever: white control over black labor. Planters and landlords worried that education diminished their supply of cheap labor by drawing blacks from the country to the city, away from tenancy, sharecropping, and day labor. They argued that black farmers did not need much schooling, and complained that what schooling blacks did receive weakened their value. "To give him any education at all takes him out of the field and he is not worth anything to the farmer," a white North Carolinian explained. "When they learn to spell dog and cat they throw away the hoe," complained a Virginia newspaper. Leading politicians took up this theme. "Whenever the nigger learns his [hic], haec, hoc," joked Georgia Democrat Clark Howell, "he right away forgets all about his gee-whoa-buck!"[15]

In the towns and cities, middle-class whites complained that education hampered their ability to secure and command domestic servants. They contrasted the "faithful old cook who came up under the slave regime" with the modern house servant who stole, answered back, and failed to show up for work. In the towns and cities, they moaned, there were too many well-dressed black men and women with no obvious means of support. Teach blacks "higher mathematics and composition," declared one Georgia man, "and they become the 'dudes' and vagabonds of the town." Throughout the South, whites of every class—rich and poor, illiterate and erudite—argued that education unfitted blacks for manual labor. In the words of North Carolina governor Robert B. Glenn, it "rendered them indolent and thriftless." Once again, Clark Howell, editor of the *Atlanta Constitution,* summed up this popular prejudice: "It is an easy enough matter to go out and get a Greek or Latin graduate, but they do not want domestic work."[16]

Whites feared that they were losing control over the black population. The old paternalism that had bound masters and slaves in personal relationships survived emancipation, albeit in a weakened form. Many former slaveholders took a personal interest in their former bondsmen, and the freedmen often looked to their erstwhile masters for help and protection. By the 1890s, however, the Civil War generation was dying. Blacks looked within their own race for leadership—to politicians, ministers, and teachers—not to landlords, employers, or former masters. The new generation of whites continually criticized the younger generation of blacks for lacking the amiability and subservience of the "old time darky." Harping upon black idleness, sexual promiscuity, insolence, and criminality, they blamed education for encouraging what North Carolina newspaper editor Josephus Daniels called "a vicious attitude."[17]

If, as white reformers believed, blacks were the biggest obstacle to the cause of education in the South, then they somehow had to remove that obstacle. Some whites proposed dividing school taxes by race. "I would recommend that the [school] districts be allowed to tax themselves," suggested the schools superintendent of Ponder County, North Carolina, "as this does away with the negro bugaboo—of helping the negro." But attempts to divide taxes in this way—which would have destroyed black public schools—fell afoul of the courts, which ruled that they violated the Fourteenth Amendment. These decisions ensured the continuation of a modicum of state funding for black schools, but they reinforced white reluctance to vote for the higher taxes needed to place ragged and inadequate public school systems on a sound footing. Whites would vote for local school taxes, reported Georgia's commissioner of education, but only if convinced that public schools could be expanded "without so much of the money raised . . . going to educate the negro." Reformers believed that they might overcome opposition to higher taxes if black teachers could be subordinated and northern influences erased.[18]

An atmosphere of political crisis underlined the basic inconsistency between black education and white supremacy. The Democratic Party had defeated the Populist threat of the 1890s—a revolt of white farmers, sometimes in alliance with black Republicans—by resorting to fraud, violence, and alarmist warnings of black domination. In depicting blacks as a threat to white safety, the Democrats promised to curb black ambition. Campaigns to disenfranchise black voters whipped up hostility to black education. But preventing blacks from voting did not relieve the economic distress of the poorer whites or make up for their loss of social status in the industrializing South. A new breed of white politician—sometimes called the "demagogues"—encouraged lower-class whites to believe that blacks were out of control and were prospering at their expense. Educating blacks, they argued, was positively dangerous. "What the North is sending down is not money but dynamite," ranted James K. Vardaman, the governor of Mississippi. "This education is ruining our negroes. They're demanding equality."[19]

Southern politics became a vicious racist circle in which candidates vied to outflank, or "out-nigger," their rivals. In Georgia in 1906, for example, gubernatorial candidates Clark Howell and Hoke Smith—both of them educated men who enjoyed reputations as racial moderates—each claimed to be more hostile to black education than the other. In the pages of the *Atlanta Constitution,* which he owned and edited, Howell published letter after letter criticizing the effects of education upon blacks. "The educated negro and the quasi-educated negro who have been inspired by a hope that can never be fulfilled . . . hate the ground the white man walks on," wrote the scion of a prominent slaveholding family. "We have tried for forty years to make something of the negro by educating him, and we have failed. . . . [T]he only use we have for the negro is as a laborer." Howell's editorials were no less virulent. The education of blacks, he warned, was "galvanizing into life a race of frankensteins." Hoke Smith quickly demonstrated his own disdain for black education. "These people are descended from ancestors who a little more than a century ago were savages in Africa. . . . Mere instruction from books will accomplish almost nothing for him."[20]

Other whites had a much more constructive view of black education. Some former slaveholders acknowledged an obligation to give blacks "generous and helpful treatment." They recognized that slaves had created their family wealth; they spoke of their affection for the "black Mammies" who had raised them, and of their gratitude to the loyal house servants who had guarded their "white folks" during the Civil War. A few appealed to republican principles, warning that the formation of a permanent underclass of ignorant and diseased blacks would threaten society's health, safety, and stability. Perhaps the strongest argument in favor of black education was economic. The most successful economies of the late nineteenth century—Germany, Britain, the northern states—had developed strong public schools that turned out educated workforces. Illiteracy was a major factor in the South's poor economic performance. The iron masters of Birmingham, Alabama, acknowledged this argument by supporting some of the best black public schools in the South. Southern "schoolmen"— white education reformers—tried to persuade white planters that they, too, would benefit if rural blacks were better schooled. Educated farmers were more productive farmers. Moreover, it was not the presence of decent schools that induced blacks to leave farming, claimed the reformers; rather, the lack of school facilities in the country fueled black migration to the towns.[21]

But the white schoolmen met their opponents halfway. Indeed, they shared many of the assumptions of those whites who were bitterly hostile to black schools. "History demonstrates that the Caucasian must rule," agreed J. L. M. Curry, perhaps the most influential white advocate of black education. Hence the reformers scorned any hint of "social equality." They refused, for example, to associate with black teachers as professional equals. The annual conference of the National Education Association occasionally included distinguished black speakers like Booker T. Washington, but the Southern Educational Association was a whites-only affair.

The reformers above all echoed the widespread complaint that the education of blacks had been directed "along improper or impractical lines." Black schools that were carbon copies of white schools caused blacks to aspire to the economic and social status that whites enjoyed. Like the outright opponents of black education, these progressives heaped scorn upon the missionary schools for providing the wrong template for black education. Thanks to the northern white teachers—Curry called them "fanatical men and women ignorant of negro peculiarities"—blacks had been misled. The missionary teachers' "radical and hurtful attempts at social equality," claimed George T. Winston, president of the University of North Carolina, caused blacks to associate education with "escaping labor."[22]

Instead of abandoning black schools, therefore, the reformers proposed taking charge of them. "We have turned the negro over to himself and to outside influences," warned Congressmen John W. Abercrombie, one of the South's most respected educators, "and for more than a generation he has been drifting away from us." White southerners had little knowledge of what blacks were being taught, Abercrombie noted, and the displacement of white teachers by blacks was now a fait accompli. The solution was to ensure that the right kind of black teachers were appointed to the black public schools. J. H. Phillips of Birmingham agreed. "The negro teacher must be sympathetically and helpfully directed by the skill and wisdom of the superior race." As North Carolina's J. Y. Joyner put it, the blind should not be permitted to lead the blind.[23]

WHAT kind of black teacher did the reformers envisage? Tellingly, they invoked the example of slavery as a model for the kind of status and schooling blacks needed. It had become a truism among white southerners that blacks had benefited from slavery because bondage had provided training, both industrial and moral, under white direction. These elements were lacking in the New South's black schools. The freedom from restraint that accompanied emancipation was proving ruinous to blacks, argued George T. Winston; it pointed them toward "gradual decay and extinction" or, at best, a "condition more degrading than slavery." Industrial education, taught in the black public schools "from top to bottom," would supply the discipline that blacks desperately needed. According to Walter B. Hill, chancellor of the University of Georgia, whites should devise for blacks "not so much a reversal of that education which began under slavery as a system [to] supplement it."[24]

When the reformers proposed to make black schools teach "industrial education," they praised Booker T. Washington. But the southern schoolmen gave industrial education a white-supremacist twist. Instead of viewing it as an evolutionary process—the beginning of black education rather than the end of it—they treated industrial education as a be-all and end-all. Whereas Washington saw it as a means of helping blacks become landowners, artisans, and small business owners, white southerners wanted better-trained sharecroppers, laborers, and domestic servants. Washington strove to promote black independence, but the schoolmen wished to reimpose white control.

"The negro school should be made an instrument for the elevation of the negro laborer, by training him for the immediate work of the shop, the field, and the household," argued J. H. Phillips. There would be few books in this kind of school. Their lessons would be practical rather than academic, dispensing "training"—the preferred term— rather than education. In the rural South, Phillips pointed out, the "purely academic negro school" was superfluous. Even in the cities, he went on, book learning too left blacks with a "chaotic jumble of incoherent knowledge . . . and a woeful distaste for any useful service." Black schools should emphasize hygiene, home sanitation, and domestic service for the girls; agriculture and woodworking for the boys. Such training should begin in the kindergarten, at an age when black children were especially impressionable. Some academic subjects would be taught, but "the technical and abstract portions of grammar, arithmetic and other topics should be eliminated." City schools should teach agriculture, argued J. R. Guy of Charleston, because "the country is unquestionably the best place for the Negroes." Walter B. Hill wanted black schools to produce the kind of field hand "to whom I can send a written inquiry or direction and who can return to me in writing an intelligent response."[25]

White reformers also believed that blacks needed lessons in morality and obedience. "It is through training that the negro is to attain thrift and clean living, love of social order and social progress," thought Professor S. C. Mitchell of Richmond. Paul Barringer of the University of Virginia recommended that black schools dispense "primarily a Sunday-school training." County school superintendents throughout the South joined in the refrain. "Teach him honesty, industry, and obedience to law and order," urged Cone of Bulloch County, Georgia. "The great lesson to teach these children is not a written one," agreed E. S. Richardson of Webster Parish, Louisiana. What blacks needed most were lessons in "clean, wholesome living" and "one's lawful place in the community." If blacks could also learn that "their only true friends are in the South," thought Richardson, "we need have no fear for white supremacy."[26]

There was little role in this educational scheme for the black colleges and universities. White educators and school officials shared the popular distaste for what they termed the "higher education" of blacks. The teaching of Latin and Greek, in particular, irritated and even obsessed them. When he traveled in the South by train, wrote Harvard historian Alfred Bushnell Hart, "the intelligent man on the cars will tell you that the negro college graduates with their Greek and Latin are spoiling the whole race." Whites quipped, "No man can be a fool until he has learned Latin," and "You can't go shooting in Virginia without shooting a Professor." A wisecrack that enjoyed decades of popularity—one raggedly clad black asking of another, "Mandy, is yo' did yo' Greek yit?"—served as proof positive of the absurdity of giving blacks higher education.[27]

Black college students certainly received a heavy dose of the classics. At St. Augustine's College in Raleigh, for example, they took beginners' Latin in their first year, added Greek in their second year, and in their third year read Caesar, Virgil, and Xenophon. Final-year students studied Homer, Plato, Horace, and Cicero. In 1895 Atlanta University devoted half its entire college course to Latin, Greek, and ancient history. The balance of college study consisted mainly of modern languages, mathematics, philosophy, and science. English often came last. Lower-level institutions also taught the classics. For example, Avery Institute, an AMA normal school in Charleston, South Carolina, offered a four-year "college preparatory" course that required three years of Latin and two of Greek.[28]

But the South was in little danger of being overrun by black college graduates "chanting Homer and engaging in Aristotelian dialectic." By 1900 a mere 2,331 blacks had earned the degree of A.B. or B.S. This represented one college graduate for every 3,600 blacks—0.027 percent of the black population. True, about one hundred black institutions called themselves "college" or "university." However, most of them had no college-level students—they were glorified elementary and secondary schools. Even the thirty or so institutions with bona fide college students, which had a total enrollment of approximately thirteen thousand students, enrolled 90 percent of their pupils in precollegiate grades. In 1901 the American Missionary Association counted only 180 college students among its 13,203 pupils. Whites were six times more likely than blacks to earn a college degree, and four times as likely to receive a high school education. As for teaching Latin and Greek, the colleges pleaded for a sense of proportion. The South need not fear "that the foundations of society would be shattered," wrote Horace Bumstead, the president of Atlanta University, "if a few hundred out of 7 million colored people should be taught Latin."[29]

The issue of classics, however, was not really about numbers. The study of Latin and Greek symbolized something much bigger—black ambition, a determination to share in the highest culture that America had to offer. It demonstrated that some blacks could be the intellectual equals, even superiors, of white people. J. C. Price, the North Carolina teacher and bishop, recalled hearing as a small boy that Senator John C. Calhoun had once defended slavery by asserting that blacks were incapable of learning Greek. "If he were living today," Price boasted, "he would come across scores of Negroes not only versed in Greek syntax, but [also] . . . some learned professors, one the author of a new Greek grammar."[30]

The teaching of classics in black colleges—which reflected the curriculum of white colleges—symbolized the idea that blacks should be thoroughly assimilated into American culture. The examples of Greece and Rome had shaped the early American republic and continued to influence political thought, education, art, and architecture. Knowledge of the classics was still regarded as the mark of an educated person, especially in the South. True, educational thinkers were questioning the value of the classics in a system of mass education; many advocated vocational education for white and black alike. But the traditional curriculum had influential defenders. William T. Harris, the U.S. commissioner of education, argued that only through knowledge of Greek and Latin could persons attain individual consciousness and analyze, rather than simply experience, the world around them. If blacks were to emancipate their minds, rather than simply train their hands, they needed "a liberal education by the same means that the white youth reaches it." In 1895 Harris exhorted students at Atlanta University to carry on studying the classics. "You have the same mind that white people have."[31]

The emancipating effects of a classical education were precisely what southern whites, including the school reformers, objected to. They knew full well that the education blacks received in the private colleges flatly contradicted their belief that blacks should belong to a fixed, subordinate position. They loathed the black colleges as humiliating reminders of Reconstruction, irritating outposts of Yankee influence. These mission schools challenged the principle, and flouted the practice, of white supremacy. True, they produced black leaders. But southern whites did not want black leaders who answered back. Hence they tended to see educated blacks in the same light as their forbears had seen the antebellum free Negroes. They could not be trusted because they could not be controlled. They were an unsettling influence. To many whites, admitted an Alabama educator, a highly literate black man was "a firebrand among the more ignorant of his race, [who] uses his acquired talents in stirring up hatred and strife between the races." As a governor of Georgia once put it, "I do not believe in the higher education of the darky. . . . [H]e gets educated above his caste and it makes him unhappy."[32]

In 1906, therefore, the Southern Educational Association resolved that all black schools—private as well as public—should be regulated by the states, and that "their methods be adjusted to the civilization in which they exist." It also proposed putting white instructors into the black normal schools. The mission schools, J. H. Phillips explained, were failing to produce teachers prepared to "co-ordinate their lives with the social and industrial requirements of their civilization." They were "out of touch, if not at positive variance with" the views of white southerners. They impeded the substitution of "training" for "book learning," and hampered the adjustment of black children to white supremacy.[33]

School officials at the county level were clear about the kind of black teachers they preferred. They wanted native southerners who were untainted by northern influences and amenable to the direction of southern whites. "If a negro teacher is to go out in his community and array himself against the white race," warned Captain C. W. Vawter, a white school principal in Charlottesville, Virginia, "he will be a curse." The schools superintendent of Lafourche Parish, Louisiana, held out a man called G. G. Bryan as the ideal black teacher. "He lives a wholesome, model life and knows his place, never presuming to be anything but a colored man. . . . He has never aspired to leadership and has never gone into politics." For many superintendents, a teacher's attitude and conduct outweighed his educational attainment. "A cornfield negro" who taught "honesty and purity," thought one, was dispensing "the sort of education it pays to give the negro."[34]

THE most salient characteristic of the mission schools was, in fact, their vast superiority over the public schools. Although they began their lives in makeshift buildings of extreme inadequacy—Atlanta University taught its first classes in a railroad boxcar—by the 1890s they boasted large buildings and spacious campuses. But the difference between the mission schools and the public schools went beyond physical appearances. The private schools offered terms of eight to ten months, graded classes, well-equipped classrooms (even laboratories), and a broad curriculum. Above all, they employed well-trained teachers, including graduates of the best northern colleges, universities, and normal schools. Moreover, the private schools cast their nets widely. To attract good students from farther afield, including rural areas, they built dormitories. They charged fees, but offered pupils some paid work under the guise of "manual" or "industrial" training. By the end of the nineteenth century the mission schools had evolved into a differentiated system in which private elementary schools acted as feeders for high schools and normal schools, which in turn fed colleges and universities. In 1900, for example, the AMA alone operated seventy-seven schools in the South, including forty-three secondary schools and five universities.[35]

The colleges and universities, the capstone of the missionary education system, offered blacks a course of study that was literary, academic, and classical—the kind of education that the northern white teachers had themselves received. But they adapted the New England model of the liberal arts college to a people who had a 90 percent illiteracy rate. In theory, the colleges expected entrants to demonstrate basic literacy and numeracy so that they could progress swiftly to the "grammar," "normal," and "college" courses. Students entering Fisk University, for example, "must be able to write a letter and punctuate it correctly, have completed elementary geography, [and] have a thorough knowledge of both common and decimal fractions." In practice, few public schools could teach to this level, and the private schools, insisting upon New England standards, had to start virtually from scratch. They also had to assist rural students, most of whom came from homes that lacked the basic rudiments of modern life, in making an enormous cultural adjustment. When thirteen-year-old Mary McLeod Bethune entered Scotia Seminary in 1888, she had never been on a train before, had never seen the inside of a brick building, had never climbed a staircase, and never eaten with a knife and fork. "Pupils come to us heavily handicapped by a lack of proper training . . . in early childhood," explained Horace Bumstead of Atlanta University.[36]

For their first three decades, therefore, the private universities, colleges, and normal schools enrolled the bulk of their pupils in lower grades. Claflin University in Orangeburg, South Carolina, did not graduate anyone from its normal department during the first ten years of its existence; it took thirteen years to produce a college graduate. Even Atlanta University, the flagship of black higher education, placed most of its students in elementary or grammar grades until 1895. By 1900 only three black colleges—Atlanta University, Shaw University, and Biddle University—had stopped teaching primary students. Elsewhere, entry standards remained low.[37]

Typically, a college divided itself into three "departments," which roughly corresponded to the elementary, secondary, and college grades. The courses in each department varied in length, sometimes overlapped, were constantly chopped and changed, and were known by a confusing variety of names. The overall trend, however, was for the total number of grades to increase. By the 1870s most colleges offered twelve years of education. In the "preparatory department"— sometimes subdivided into "primary" and "grammar" as the course lengthened to seven or eight grades—students received instruction in the "three R's," with a little geography. In the "normal" or "college preparatory" department, where the course lasted two to five years, their studies broadened to include algebra, natural philosophy, geometry, trigonometry, physiology, rhetoric, and history (U.S. and state). "College departments" offered four years of study leading to the award of a degree.

In the postbellum South the term *normal school* applied to virtually any institution where pupils, graded by age and ability, and instructed by halfway competent teachers, went out to teach. In the 1880s and 1890s, however, the normal schools of the North—exemplified by Oswego Normal School in western New York—defined teaching as a skill, even a science, that had to be studied. They introduced American teachers to the educational philosophies of European reformers such as Pestalozzi, Froebel, and Herbart. Northern teachers now imparted those philosophies to their southern black students. Normal training included specific courses in pedagogy and, in the twentieth century, psychology and sociology.

In the late nineteenth century the key influence was Johann Heinrich Pestalozzi, who fostered most of the basic ideas of modern education: learning through active inquiry rather than passive memorizing; learning by doing rather than learning by rote; relating knowledge to pupils' experience of their everyday world; using concrete examples, or "object lessons," instead of relying upon abstract concepts. Pestalozzi's child-centered approach implied a movement away from authoritarian teaching methods in which the teacher demanded blind obedience and ruled with an iron rod. In its place, it developed a pedagogy based upon the cultivation of moral values in the pupil. The modern approach to classroom discipline discouraged coercion, especially corporal punishment, in favor of encouraging self-restraint. The teacher exerted moral authority and gained respect and attention by inculcating proper values in the pupil. Through conscience and guilt, by learning to distinguish right from wrong, the pupil acquired self-discipline. The teacher sought to be "an object of affection and sentimental veneration" rather than a stern disciplinarian. Teachers should motivate their pupils through praise rather than fear of punishment. "I know of no more potent or effectual way of securing the student's attention," stated a typical piece of advice, "than by giving him full credit for whatever talent he may display or possess, thus raising his aspirations."

Trainee teachers learned that the classroom should be a space that combined order, cleanliness, and beauty. An example from Scotland, reprinted for the benefit of Hampton Institute's students, offered an almost rhapsodic picture of the ideal schoolroom: "The walls are hung with maps, coloured pictures, good prints, and illuminated sayings of the good and the great tastefully arranged. Festoons of leaves mingled with flowers hang gracefully on the walls . . . The desks are free from littered books and bonnets. The books are placed on shelves below. . . . The children are clean in hands, faces, and dress, their hair is neatly combed, and their boots will show the morning polish." To the black students who had spent their summers teaching in rural schools, such advice must have seemed absurdly utopian. Most black schools lacked desks. Many pupils had no boots to polish. Books were scarce, and teachers could hardly afford to buy pictures and maps. But even in the most primitive conditions, black teachers could use their ingenuity and improvise. "Cleanliness, order, leaves, and wild flowers cost only time, patience and taste."[38]

Practice teaching took much the same form that it does today: observing experienced teachers at work, followed by practice in front of a "critic teacher." Many colleges used their own primary grades, which sometimes functioned as the local elementary school, for practice teaching. When colleges eventually sloughed off their primary grades, they arranged for local school boards to maintain them at public expense as practice or "laboratory" schools. Sometimes students taught in various public or private elementary schools nearby. To bolster their students' confidence before standing at the front of a classroom, teachers at Atlanta University made their students give recitations as if they were lessons, "with each pupil . . . subject to the criticism of his classmates and instructors." Some colleges possessed no facilities for practice teaching, simply assuming that some version of a secondary education qualified a person to teach. However, virtually all students had the opportunity to teach in rural schools during the summer. Indeed, many depended upon the income from summer teaching to see them through college.

"We learned exactly what to expect in our schools," recalled South Carolina teacher Mamie Garvin Fields of her classes in pedagogy at Claflin University. Her instructors, knowing that students would be teaching in rural schools among impoverished people, dispensed severely practical advice. "What to do with 125 children, by yourself, in a one-room school, for example; how to divide that crowd into groups and supervise all at one time." Discipline, students were told, should flow from confidence, effective teaching, and knowledge of their pupils. They were told not to forget that pupils may be tired, cold, or hungry; that many had to walk miles to school; that they missed school often because their parents needed them on the farm, not because they played truant. The regimentation of a city school should not be applied to rural children. Disobedient children should be faced down, shamed, but never beaten. "It should never be necessary to raise your voice or lose your calm." If teachers inculcated the right spirit in the classroom, awkward characters would be dealt with by their own peers. If not, then the parents would punish them. Indeed, students were told that visiting parents was one of the most effective ways of guaranteeing children's behavior.[39]

Perhaps the most important lessons imparted by the black colleges were moral ones. Northern white teachers saw themselves as missionaries who were redeeming a race from poverty, ignorance, and vice. They believed that freedmen wanted for thrift, sobriety, self-discipline, sexual morality, and sincere religion. The colleges planned to reach the Negro masses—"weak, degraded, untutored, semi-barbarous"—through their students. Black teachers would "shape and guide the people from serfdom to an intelligent, Christian citizenship." But the students were themselves handicapped by the legacy of slavery. They could not be of service to their people before the northern missionaries shaped them in their own image. Atlanta University, explained Rev. C. W. Francis, separated its students "from all old associations and habits, . . . subjecting them for months to a long and watchful discipline . . . surrounding them with the most earnest and aggressive religious influences, [and] giving them the best mental training." If students were to resist the evils and temptations of the outside world, "they need to be thoroughly fixed and set in character before leaving school."[40]

The colleges inculcated the Protestant work ethic with a rigorous daily routine that began when a "rising bell" awakened students between 5 and 6 a.m. They then had half an hour to wash, dress, and tidy up before a matron inspected their rooms. An hour of private study followed breakfast and morning prayers, then four hours of classes, or "recitations," with a twenty-minute midmorning recess. Nearly all colleges required students to perform an hour or two of work about the campus—sometimes dignified by the term "manual training"—usually performed after lunch. Late afternoon gave students two hours of recreational time, followed by evening prayer, supper, and private study. Lights went out by 10 p.m., and the colleges had strict curfews.[41]

This program of character transformation involved insulating the students from outside influences and imposing a stern code of conduct. Movements to and from campus were strictly regulated. Near the gates of Claflin University stood the "checkhouse," recalled Mamie Garvin Fields. "Someone always stood guard . . . You had to have a 'ticket' to go out." Students walking through the college gates entered a self-contained world in which rules and regulations governed their every waking hour. The colleges strictly forbade alcohol, tobacco, and card playing. They did not permit dancing or profane, disrespectful, or even loud talk. "No frivolous or useless conversation," instructed Shaw University, "or attention to trivial and unimportant matters, or visiting each other's rooms, or lounging upon beds or loitering upon the grounds." The colleges frowned upon "extravagance in dress" and specified what students could and could not wear. For girls at St. Augustine's Normal School, dresses had to be dark blue, shirts either dark blue or white, hats dark blue or black. Large hats, "white sailor hats," and hats with feathers or flowers were not permitted. Male students wore dark suits; a few colleges clad them in uniforms and made them do military-style drill.

The colleges discouraged romantic relationships and forbade any contact between the sexes except under close supervision. Shaw University's regulations were typical: "No young man shall be allowed to converse or in any way communicate with any young lady, either passing through the halls, or upon the grounds, with the exception of the first fifteen minutes after school in which the young ladies and young gentlemen will be allowed to converse with each other." Rules also applied to off-campus contact. Visits to the city required presidential permission. Incoming letters could be scrutinized, withheld, or forbidden. Female students were allowed out on Saturday afternoons, but only if accompanied by a female teacher, and only to do shopping. The protection of female students' chastity was the college's overriding concern. "There was no offense in the Atlanta University calendar that more perturbed the authorities than approaching a girl," recalled James Weldon Johnson of the 1880s. "A boy could see a girl upon a written application with the girl's name filled in, signed by herself and, if granted, countersigned by the president or dean." The time and place of the venue, twenty minutes in the North Hall parlor, further restricted the opportunities for making love—even in the milder Victorian sense of that term.

A system of incentives and punishments enforced the rule book. St. Augustine's College awarded merits for "studies, punctuality and deportment," leading to inclusion in a "Roll of Honor." An accumulation of demerits led to the humiliation of seeing one's name "stricken from the roll" or a public reprimand in chapel. For many miscreants, an interview with a matron, dean, or president was punishment enough. The chilling effects of being summoned before the stern patriarchs who headed the private colleges were heightened by the startling white beards that framed their Victorian visages. More serious infractions of the rules carried work punishments, confinements, suspensions, or dismissal.[42]

Religion suffused campus life. "The first schools were mission stations," recalled Charles F. Meserve, president of Shaw University, "and the object of the founders was to train leaders and workers for church and Sunday School." Whether they were Baptist, Methodist, Congregationalist, Presbyterian, or Episcopalian, all the colleges prescribed Bible study and Christian worship. Students attended daily chapel or recited daily, sometimes twice-daily, prayers. On the Sabbath they went to church in the morning, attended Sunday school in the afternoon, and took part in a prayer meeting at night. Additional religious activities were voluntary—midweek prayer meetings, the YMCA and YWCA, temperance societies, foreign mission societies, the White Cross Society for "social purity"—but students felt moral pressure to join. "Students who were religiously observant . . . enjoyed certain preferences," remembered James Weldon Johnson. When they taught during their summer breaks, students were expected to organize Sunday schools and act as temperance recruits. They were greeted at summer's end as "returning missionaries."

This intense religious activity meant that even the most pious, wilting under the strain, suffered pangs of conscience. "This is missionary night, but I did not feel like going," a young black teacher at Scotia Seminary confided to her diary. "I am so wicked at times. . . . Some people think it no trouble for me to do right always, but if they could only see and know the contents of my heart." Whenever the colleges' piety showed signs of cooling, periodic religious revivals heated things up again. "I have never seen the school so stirred," came a report from Straight University in New Orleans. "Every girl boarding in Stone Hall is profoundly converted, and there are not more than eight or ten boys who are not in the same good way." Even allowing for exaggeration, revivals had an effect. During one revival at Fisk, recalled John M. Gandy, "most of the non-church members made professions of religion."[43]

For nearly all black teachers, the quest for a decent education was a desperate struggle. Gaining admission to a private school, normal school, or college was only half the battle; staying there often posed insuperable difficulties. The low educational attainment of students entering colleges and normal schools made the challenge of graduating a daunting one. Pupils coming from the public schools in Mississippi were "without any foundation whatever," reported an inspector of Methodist schools in 1908. When they entered higher institutions they found themselves "crowded into more advanced studies while they were ignorant of the essentials." No wonder that instructors like Charles Chesnutt, principal of North Carolina's State Colored Normal, found themselves "compelled to give the greater portion of the time to systematic drill in the rudiments." Twenty years later, in 1901, a professor of education from the University of North Carolina found many pupil teachers "unable to write correctly a page of every day English." For students of mature age, forced to begin again at the elementary level, many years of full-time education stretched in front of them before they even reached the normal or collegiate level.[44]

Private education imposed an enormous financial burden upon the students and their families. They had to find money to pay for tuition fees, boarding costs, train fares, textbooks, and decent clothes. Moreover, the absence of an older son or daughter for nine or ten months of the year depleted the labor force of a farming family, making the financial sacrifice even greater. For all but a privileged few, the earning of a college degree was a near miracle. As the president of Straight University explained, "Many of our brightest young men . . . feel constrained by filial and brotherly affection to go out and earn money to support aged and dependent parents and give their younger brothers and sisters the same blessed educational advantages."[45]

Irregular attendance and a high attrition rate plagued black colleges and normal schools. Students arrived late because they did not finish bringing in the harvest until mid or late October. They quit early to attend to spring planting. They left at any time in between if their families needed them or if finances required them to work. "A large proportion of our students are self-supporting," explained Charles Chesnutt in 1880. "They teach in the country and work on the farm . . . and come into school for one, two, or three terms a year, as their means will permit." More than a quarter of a century later, Chesnutt's successor, E. E. Smith, reported an identical situation. Upon enrollment in October 1908, a third of the students left after the first day "to assist in gathering and housing the crops." During the course of the month, half the students asked for permission to leave. For his first two years as a student at South Carolina State College for Negroes, Benjamin Mays was called home by his father at the end of February to work on the family farm. "I was nineteen and not once in my life had I been able to remain in school more than four months in any year."[46]

Broken attendance hampered the progress of students and made teaching them frustratingly difficult. "Where students leave and return at any time during the session," complained the president of Shaw University, "a proper classification is rendered much more difficult." Maintaining continuity of teaching when students had to be continually reshuffled taxed even the most experienced instructor. Large class sizes, even in the black colleges, added yet another difficulty. In 1907, one teacher at Clark University in Atlanta instructed one hundred pupils, classified in three different grades, in a single room.[47]

Few students stayed the course. During the 1890s, Branch Normal College in Pine Bluff, Arkansas, enrolled about two hundred students a year, of whom only nine completed the normal course. St. Augustine's College in Raleigh, North Carolina, enrolled twenty-six normal students in 1892–93 and graduated one. The figures for 1905–06 illustrated the persistent pattern: twenty-one students entered the "first year normal," twelve made it to the "second year normal," and a handful graduated. Atlanta University produced about a dozen "normal trained" teachers a year in the 1880s and 1890s, but sometimes—in times of economic depression—the number fell as low as six. Everywhere, the number of nongraduates vastly outnumbered those who completed teacher training.[48]

The ease with which students could find teaching positions in rural schools presented a constant temptation to drop out. In 1880 Charles Chesnutt complained that preparatory students at his normal school, whom he deemed incompetent to teach, were being certified by county examiners. At St. Augustine's College, many entering students possessed the equivalent of a fifth-grade education but left after a year or even a semester to become teachers. Twenty years later, standards had not improved. "There is such a demand for teachers," reported the principal of Ballard Normal School in Macon, Georgia, "that pupils often go out from our intermediate grades even, and secure schools without recommendations from us." As long as county school superintendents appointed underqualified teachers, students had little incentive to see their studies through to completion. In general, only the city schools and private schools—which provided relatively few jobs—insisted upon higher qualifications.[49]

CARTER G. Woodson famously charged the northern missionary teachers with "mis-educating" the Negro. According to Woodson, the mission schools taught that black culture had little intrinsic merit, criticized the freedmen as immoral and superstitious, and implied that everything of value in religion and culture came from white people. Thus indoctrinated, college-educated blacks learned to despise their own people, admiring every culture but the African. A few modern historians have echoed and amplified Woodson's critique. They castigate the missionary teachers for their religious dogmatism and sectarianism. Intolerant of Catholics, worried about Mormons, opposed to alcohol, censorious of tobacco, northern whites thrust the values and the bigotry of evangelical Protestantism upon African Americans. The colleges' rigid notions of morality, rigidly enforced, bred habits of submissiveness that ill-served their students. South Carolina's black colleges rendered a "major service to white supremacy" by teaching their students to obey authority so unquestioningly.[50]

Perhaps the colleges' biggest failing, according to critics, was their single-minded belief in the potency of "character." Northern teachers taught an ethos of individualism that embodied Yankee values of education, hard work, thrift, chastity, and temperance. This message benefited a small minority of middle-class strivers but had little relevance to the mass of sharecroppers and laborers, who were oppressed by a racist system that exploited and impoverished them. By encouraging bourgeois values, patriarchal authority, and the adoption of white cultural forms, the colleges sought deliberately to distance their students from those masses. Frankly elitist in their mission to foster black leaders—the concept of the "talented tenth" originated with white Baptist missionary Henry L. Morehouse, not W. E. B. Du Bois—the colleges sought to undermine racist stereotypes, and to win acceptance for blacks, by turning out people who were culturally indistinguishable from educated whites. As one AMA official put it, the missionary-educated students "have proven the ability of the industry, frugality, intelligence and character that can overcome caste prejudice. When a black man ceases to be brutal, licentious, and becomes a man, his color is no more an offense than that of a resident of Seville or Lombardy." But this was a flawed strategy—white southerners were impressed by power, not character.[51]

That so many black college students accepted the assimilationist thinking of their white mentors was, critics believe, unfortunate. For behind it lay an assumption that the putative weaknesses of the black masses—crime, immorality, fecklessness—sustained white prejudice. By stressing their own superiority over the black lower classes—often referring to themselves as "the best men" and "the best women" who comprised the "better class of blacks"—the college-educated elite inadvertently played into the hands of white racists. Although committed to the "uplift" of the race by means of their own leadership and example, middle-class blacks criticized the masses in terms that, although shorn of racism, resembled the arguments of the white supremacists. By dwelling on the moral failings of the black masses and underlining their own virtues, writes one of their modern critics, educated blacks "replicated the dehumanizing logic of racism." The achievement of the northern white teachers in creating a black middle class that adopted their values was, in the words of another historian, "a mixed blessing."[52]

These criticisms overlook the obvious point that the black community did not emerge fully formed and fully sufficient, like Athena from the head of Zeus, at the moment of emancipation. African Americans knew that slavery had not prepared them for freedom. They lacked land, capital, literacy, adequate housing, sanitation, access to medical care, and experience of urban civilization. And while stable families had been much more common under slavery than white and black moralists believed, the obstacles to family stability remained formidable. The missionaries' recipe of Christian morality, self-help, education, and middle-class discipline was not the complete answer to the freedmen's predicament. However, it was not irrelevant or detrimental. The values promoted by the northern white teachers were so deeply rooted in northern American culture that the black-run colleges of the AME, AMEZ, and Baptist churches dispensed almost identical moral lessons. They, too, abhorred the ignorance and moral laxity that the slave regime had encouraged. They, also, believed that education and strength of character, bolstered by moral discipline and Christian piety, could offset the handicaps of poverty, illiteracy, and racism. When the odds were stacked so heavily against black success, the stern discipline of the mission schools proved to be of inestimable value.[53]

It is a fallacy to assume that black students were blank pages upon which the northern missionaries inscribed their own values. To do so overlooks the influence of parents, communities, previous schooling, and past experiences on these students. The example of John M. Gandy illustrates the point. The fifth of fourteen children, Gandy attended a succession of one-room schoolhouses because his parents, Mississippi sharecroppers, were constantly on the move. He was a precocious learner, and his parents encouraged his schooling. Between the ages of fifteen and twenty, he taught in the summer and worked at different jobs during the rest of the year. When his family moved to Arkansas in 1890, Gandy collected enough money from friends and relatives to enter Jackson College, Mississippi, a Baptist school, where he studied for two years. Rejoining his family in Arkansas, he taught school and worked in a cotton gin mill. Then, inspired by Bishop Henry McNeal Turner's back-to-Africa movement, he and a group of others moved to New York with the aim of emigrating to Liberia. It proved a disastrous mistake. Only one member of the group made it to Liberia, where he died. Stranded in New York, penniless, Gandy found work in a saloon, a doctor's office, and a brickyard. In 1892 he enrolled at Oberlin College, only to leave after two years when he ran out of money. He applied to Colgate University, which rejected him. Fisk University accepted him. Raising his train fare from friends, the twenty-four-year-old Gandy arrived in Nashville in 1894 with fifty cents to his name. Graduating in 1898, he spent the next forty-five years at Virginia State College, serving as the school's president between 1914 and 1943.[54]

Here, indeed, was one of the "Black Puritans" whom sociologist E. Franklin Frazier described as typical of the black middle class. Such people took from their white teachers values that were consonant with their own. The mission schools, notwithstanding their evangelicalism, did not demand conformity of belief. The white missionaries of the AMA constantly lamented their failure to attract black students to the Congregational Church. Moreover, many students resisted the religious fervor of their teachers. As Henry Tupper of Shaw University complained, too many students "are not Christians and yet are seeking a higher education." Certainly, the religious skepticism of Johnson and Du Bois survived—was heightened by—the Christianity of Atlanta and Fisk. In practice, the religious orthodoxy of the mission schools belied the fact that they were ecumenical in their recruitment policies, and that students could get by with an outward show of conformity. Similarly, the colleges accompanied their authoritarian organizational structure with an educational philosophy that was fundamentally democratic. Students were encouraged to think for themselves. The fact that they periodically criticized and occasionally rebelled against their white teachers—even Booker T. Washington signed a petition challenging one of Samuel Chapman Armstrong's decisions—shows that they did so.[55]

Had the white missionaries taught only elitism and class consciousness, then their influence upon black teachers might be deplored. But they never let their students forget that privilege carries a heavy responsibility. They were being educated for a purpose: not for themselves alone, but for the benefit of their race. "If a college makes the man despise the people rather than the bad *conditions*," affirmed a Fisk graduate, "then it is falling far short of the purpose for which it was founded." Christian service was the guiding principle. Teachers must be dedicated, loving, unselfish, inured to hardship, and self-sacrificing. The future of the race depended upon them.[56]

For all their sometimes heavy-handed paternalism, the mission schools sought to create a black leadership that would provide direction for the entire race. "The welfare of the masses demands that we train up leaders of intelligence and principle," wrote Horace Bumstead. And whatever their private doubts about the capacity of blacks to lead themselves, the colleges told their students that the future of the race lay in their hands, not those of their mentors. For Du Bois, the years at Fisk University constituted a turning point in his consciousness. "I replaced my hitherto egocentric world by a world centering and whirling about my race . . . Through the leadership of men like myself, we were going to have these enslaved Israelites out of . . . bondage in short order."

The missionaries encouraged a racial pride that eschewed racism, and a racial independence that allowed for cooperation with whites. The pioneers and supporters of the black history movement—Edward A. Johnson, Carter G. Woodson. Richard R. Wright, John M. Gandy— were educated at white mission schools. They did not learn racial self-hatred there. As William H. Councill explained, the results of giving blacks the same kind of education that whites received could easily be predicted. "The educated Negro will feel that there is no disgrace attached to physical features or to his previous condition; hence, he will more and more love and honor his race." A graduate of Virginia Union University recalled his own experience: "The rather orthodox value system that Union imposed . . . was selectively internalized, but the more fundamental belief was embraced in full. It was the doctrine that the Negro college was to develop the leadership for the emancipation of the Negro American."[57]

No matter how hard they tried to palliate southern whites, therefore, the private colleges could only plead guilty to the charge that they rejected white supremacy. Their own statements of principle spoke for themselves, and they never really changed. The mission schools denied the alleged racial inferiority of the colored race. "They are as well endowed by their Creator as any people in the world." They rejected the view that "the place of the negro is definitely known and that it is one which . . . allows a very limited range of intellectual power and requires the exercise of his muscles chiefly." The mission schools insisted that blacks were entitled to precisely the same educational opportunities that whites enjoyed. Education must always aim for "the highest perfection of intellectual capacity," the AMA affirmed in 1901. "Anything in education which restricts the growth of aptitude or narrows the opportunities of the intellect does violence to this law."

The northern teachers' continual references to "manhood" and "womanhood" as qualities to be cultivated in their students amplified this humanistic—they called it democratic and Christian—concept of education. Faced with the rushing tide of white supremacy, the mission schools denounced race riots and lynching. Insisting that "the Negro is a man and is entitled to be treated as a man," they confessed that "a college education worthy of the name" would make every student "fully aware of the discriminations and injustices that fall to his lot because he is a Negro and lives in America." According to Edward T. Ware, president of Atlanta University, college students were bound to claim full citizenship rights, including the right to vote and unrestricted educational opportunities. "What educated American citizen would demand less?"[58]

The influence of the mission schools extended far beyond the relatively small numbers who graduated with normal certificates or college degrees. More than half of those who gained formal qualifications became teachers, and most found employment in the larger and better public schools, and in the private schools of higher grade. A calculation by Du Bois may have exaggerated a little, but it made the point nicely: 550 teachers who had graduated from black colleges "have taught about 300,000 children in primary grades and 200,000 in secondary grades." The many thousands of teachers who had attended colleges or normal school without ever graduating diffused the influence of the mission schools even farther, projecting their values well into the rural areas. "These teachers possessed a poise which carried over into the behavior of their pupils," noted one observer. "[They] are by far the best teachers in the rural schools."[59]

THE resilient idealism of the mission schools ensured that the grandiose plan of school reformers like J. H. Phillips and John W. Abercrombie—that whites should take charge of black schools by training black teachers—came to little. In 1900 the black public schools of the South needed about 7,000 new teachers a year, but fewer than 2,100 blacks completed any kind of education above the elementary level. And the states themselves produced only 156 trained teachers—graduates of normal schools—that year. The situation in Texas illustrated the problem. Of the 2,551 black teachers in the state's public schools, only 159, or 6.2 percent, had graduated from the state normal school at Prairie View. The record of Texas in training black teachers was better than most. Mississippi, Louisiana, Florida, Georgia, South Carolina, and Tennessee did not support black normal schools at all. The goal of having cities and states train black teachers, thus wresting teacher training away from the mission schools, would have required an enormous public investment. The South declined to make that investment. It preferred to expand public education for whites at the expense of black schools.[60]

What white politicians and school officials could do—and cheaply—was degrade the curriculum of the black state colleges, discipline the men who headed them, and get rid of Latin. The downgrading of Virginia Normal and Collegiate Institute (VNCI) provides a typical example. Between 1886 and 1900, VNCI trained 222 teachers and granted forty-nine degrees. However, Democrats disliked its collegiate features and political associations. In 1887 the governor ousted VNCI's principal, prominent black Republican John Mercer Langston, and reduced its funding. Three years later the state replaced the biracial board of trustees with an all-white board. One board member complained that black students were "learning, or pretending to learn," Latin, Greek and chemistry. "I think it is time for that sort of nonsense to stop." The board's chairman, Captain C. W. Vawter, an ardent advocate of "manual training," pressed the Institute to introduce cooking, sewing, and other "industrial courses." Principal James Hugo Johnston resisted, explaining that he could not afford to buy the requisite equipment or pay the kind of salaries that would attract capable instructors. But in 1903—after Virginia had disenfranchised its black voters—the legislature forced Johnston to introduce the new curriculum and abolished the Institute's college department to help pay for it. "I was allowed to remodel the entire curriculum," Vawter boasted. "We took out all that Latin, Greek, and Hebrew." The state deleted the word *College* from the school's name, renaming the school Virginia Normal and Industrial Institute. All students were required to take either manual training or domestic science. The institution became the equivalent of a three-year high school.[61]

An incident in 1907 illustrates the personal humiliation that such reforms entailed. Otis Ashmore, the superintendent of schools in Savannah, Georgia, entered a classroom at Savannah State Industrial

College to find the principal, Richard R. Wright, teaching Virgil. Outraged, Ashmore ordered Wright to "cut this Latin out and teach these boys to farm." When Wright demurred, Ashmore lost his temper and threatened to have him dismissed. Wright, a former slave, a teacher of thirty years' experience—one of the first blacks to receive a degree from Atlanta University—kept his job by the skin of his teeth. But he curtailed his political activities. Moreover, the governing board of Savannah State Industrial College lopped off the college's upper-division courses and forbade the teaching of Latin and Greek. For five years the college awarded no degrees. After a two-year boycott that denuded the college of students, the board reluctantly reinstated college-level work. However, only about twenty of the five thousand students who attended the college between 1910 and 1920 earned degrees. In effect, the state of Georgia reduced Savannah State Industrial College to the level of an elementary and secondary school.[62]

Across the South, blacks who headed publicly funded colleges were bullied, dressed down, and subjected to a style of micromanagement that underlined their lack of authority. Unable to spend more than a few dollars without written authorization, in some cases they could not even leave campus without higher authority. They found their ability to hire, fire, and discipline employees circumvented by staff members who appealed directly to white trustees. Joseph C. Corbin, the titular head of Branch Normal College in Pine Bluff, Arkansas, watched in impotent fury as the trustees accorded a white teacher—the head of the school's "industrial department"—the power to admit students, collect fees, and report to the board. Attempts to resist attacks upon their authority often cost school heads their jobs. Three successive principals of Prairie View Normal School in Texas, for example, were dismissed for assertions of independence. One lost his temper when a trustee disparaged Negro rights, another backed a Prohibitionist candidate for governor, and a third refused to surrender his authority to discipline faculty members, only to be "fired like some irresponsible miscreant—turned out like a janitor."[63]

By 1916 the twenty-six state-funded institutions that were styled normal schools or land-grant colleges had just twelve college-level students among them. In some cases, state legislatures abolished existing college courses; in others, they prevented black institutions from developing upward.[64]

The most drastic transformation of a state-funded institution took place in Louisiana. In 1915 the legislature changed the name of Southern University to "Southern Agricultural and Mechanical College," stripped the institution of its degree-granting powers, and relocated it from New Orleans to a site outside Baton Rouge. There, on the outskirts of the state capital, Southern A&M was insulated from the politically conscious blacks of the Crescent City. Formerly staffed by a racially mixed faculty, the new incarnation of Southern had no white teachers. Southern did not regain its college department until 1924.[65]

The degradation of black state colleges fostered decadence, corruption, and even violence. At Alcorn University in Mississippi, black president Edward H. Triplett, a Baptist minister, was shot and wounded by the secretary-treasurer. A poorly educated man, Triplett had alienated most of his faculty members, who were college-educated teachers, by promoting industrial education. He was later implicated in a scandal involving the sale of teaching certificates. Dennis H. Anderson, the principal of West Kentucky Industrial College, tried to silence one of his critics by framing him on a charge of statutory rape. At Florida A&M, the ouster of Nathan B. Young, who resisted the expansion of vocational education, prompted students to boycott classes. Two buildings went up in flames.[66]

The states made no real effort to train more black teachers. In Mississippi, the situation actually deteriorated. The state withdrew its subsidy to Tougaloo University's normal department, and in 1904 James K. Vardaman, the newly elected governor, vetoed the annual appropriation to Holly Springs State Normal School. The result was a "decided retrogression" in the quality of black teachers. Between 1900 and 1910 the proportion of white teachers holding the lowest grade of teaching certificate declined from 4.9 percent to 1.4 percent while the proportion of black teachers holding this qualification increased from 39 percent to 51 percent. In the 1920s Alcorn A&M, together with five private colleges, produced only one hundred trained teachers a year. The black schools of the state needed a thousand.[67]

Elsewhere, despite some modest expenditures for capital improvements, the states allowed black institutions to stagnate. Before 1905, for example, the black normal schools in North Carolina possessed no buildings of their own. In 1915 Virginia allocated 95 percent of its spending on colleges and normal schools to white institutions. Georgia's gesture toward higher education for blacks—half of the state's population—amounted to 1.3 percent of what it spent on white colleges. Typically what passed for a college library at a black college consisted of "little more than a reading room with a few periodicals . . . [and] a few shelves of dusty old books and government reports." Black colleges in Pine Bluff and Savannah had no libraries at all. In 1922, six of the state colleges spent no money on books. Four state institutions that were supposed to be training teachers had no facilities for practice teaching.[68]

The South's failure to develop black high schools underlined its lack of commitment to training black teachers. In 1910 the nation boasted 141 public high schools for blacks, of which the southern and border states accounted for 123. Outside Texas and Missouri, which had 57 between them, black public high schools were rare. Secondary education for whites was expanding at such a fast pace that during a two-year period the number of new white high schools in Virginia exceeded the total number of black high schools in the entire country. The white high schools of Virginia enrolled more pupils than the black high schools of all sixteen southern and border states. Augusta, Georgia, closed its black high school. New Orleans, the South's largest city, not only refused to build a black high school but in 1904 restricted the black public schools to the first five grades—abolishing grades six, seven, and eight. By 1922 it was estimated that the South needed to recruit 8,000 black teachers a year. That year, state colleges and normal schools graduated only 387 trained black teachers.[69]

Aꜰᴛᴇʀ the end of Reconstruction, many black teachers had pinned their faith on an alliance between "our good white people" and "the better element of our race." By emphasizing education and moral character rather than politics and civil rights—a strategy urged by Booker

T. Washington and widely supported among the black middle class—
they hoped to secure respect and protection from the South's rulers.
Many acknowledged, in the words of teacher Charles N. Hunter, the
"superior intelligence, wisdom and governing ability of the white people" and recommended "docility on the part of the Negro." They publicly regretted that Reconstruction had enfranchised blacks en masse,
and they agreed that voting should be made dependent upon literacy.
Accepting racial segregation, they promised not to encroach upon the
"social and private life" of white people. But they clung to the hope
that whites would not close "the door of opportunity . . . to those who
prove worthy to ascend." When the Democratic party unveiled proposals to disenfranchise all black voters regardless of character, property, or education, they were shocked. "We cannot well retain our self-
respect nor the respect of our nation if we sit quietly by and make no
protest," advised a teacher at Livingstone College. But protests proved
unavailing. The "'right-thinking' element of the whites," who fellow
North Carolinian Simon G. Atkins had hoped "will stand up for us,"
slammed the door in their faces.[70]

The hardening of white supremacy left black teachers feeling confused, depressed, and vulnerable. Outbreaks of violence such as the
Wilmington and Atlanta riots underlined the fact that the new system made no distinction between "deserving" blacks and "undeserving" blacks. Indeed, in some instances racial violence singled out the
prosperous and the well-to-do. Rushing back to his hometown of Wilmington after the riot of 1898, James B. Dudley, president of North
Carolina A&M College, was shocked to see about a thousand soldiers
drumming four black men from the city. "They were not the indolent
drones or paupers; they represented between thirty and fifty thousand
dollars worth of property." Having rendered even wealthy and educated blacks powerless, whites now demanded deference and outright servility from them. The elimination of Latin from state-funded
schools was on a par with the racial etiquette that forbade a white person from ever addressing a black person as "Mr." or "Mrs." "We are in
an awful state of affairs," admitted Simon Atkins. "Some of us who
have been conservative and hopeful are almost getting ready to throw

in the sponge." Atkins even wondered, in his gloomiest moments, "whether God is dead."[71]

The indifference of whites in the North to the suppression of black rights heightened the isolation of southern black educators. In blatantly destroying the centerpiece of Reconstruction, black voting, white southerners no longer felt any need to placate northern public opinion. They believed that they had won the propaganda battle, forging a national consensus regarding the basic inferiority of African Americans. They even claimed that other white nations looked to the South for guidance in dealing with darker races. The traditional allies of southern blacks—the missionary schools and their northern white teachers—were still there, but their influence was waning. The new sources of northern support for southern education, philanthropic foundations like the General Education Board (GEB), regarded racial equality as a sentimental fallacy. They wanted to help black schools, but only with the consent of white southerners. Scared of the potential for racist violence, the GEB quickly decided to make the improvement of white public schools its first priority. And the GEB, like all the foundations, tailored its efforts toward stabilizing, rather than threatening, the new system of white supremacy. As T. Thomas Fortune mordantly pointed out to Charles N. Hunter, "The deuce of the matter is that the Southern white men have educated the Northern white men so that they have no faith whatever in black men."[72]

Yet white southerners failed to turn black schools into engines for the reproduction of white supremacy. They neglected to create the kind of administrative machinery essential to such a system. The whites' refusal to take charge of black education stemmed, in part, from sheer financial meanness. Instead of "educating the Negroes to become faithful helots," argued Gunnar Myrdal, whites "merely kept Negro education poor and bad." But it also, in Myrdal's view, reflected white ambivalence toward racial discrimination. Enough white southerners believed in republican ideals of education to ensure that efforts to create a "caste education" for blacks remained "half-hearted." Even their efforts to suppress the classics quickly ran out of steam. All of this meant that black teachers could still find room to maneuver. The

mission schools kept alive the ideal of racial equality and trained another generation of teachers. Northern philanthropic foundations offered new opportunities for support. And there were many white
southerners whose sympathetic actions spoke louder than their white
supremacist words. Most important of all, perhaps, the consolidation
of white supremacy stimulated black self-help. Hundreds of black
teachers decided to found their own schools.[73]

CHAPTER FIVE

The Founders

I found the school in wonderful condition, with
the exception of there being no money.

Mary McLeod Bethune

Simon G. Atkins, founder of Winston-Salem
State University.

New York Public Library

THE WORK WAS HARD AND DIRTY," recalled Booker T. Washington. He and his fellow teachers, along with their students, stood in an Alabama field up to their knees in mud, trying to make bricks. After laboriously molding twenty-five thousand bricks of clay, they saw their handiwork perish when their homemade kiln misfired. A second kiln also failed. A third kiln caved in. Without a dollar to his name, and with his colleagues urging him to abandon the brick-making effort, Washington pawned his watch for fifteen dollars and "rallied our . . . demoralized and discouraged forces." The fourth kiln worked. Now Washington could replace the flimsy wooden shacks of Tuskegee Institute with buildings of solid red brick. By 1900 his school boasted forty brick structures, all but four of them erected by the students themselves.[1]

Washington's parable of "making bricks without straw" is rich in metaphorical meanings. But the most obvious meaning is the most important one. Through sheer determination and force of leadership, Washington overcame poverty and repeated failure to build a school. That school, moreover, outclassed anything that the public schools of Alabama could offer to black people.[2]

Hundreds of other black teachers also founded schools between 1880 and 1920. Scattered throughout the South, these private schools could be found in cities and towns, as well as in the piedmont, piney

woods, and Black Belt of the rural hinterland. Almost every one represented Herculean effort and selfless dedication on the part of an individual teacher. Booker T. Washington was the best known, and others
drew inspiration from his example. But private schools came in every
shape and size, and a variety of motives, both religious and secular,
drove the men and women who created them. However, the founders shared a common vision. Forced to live within the political constraints of white supremacy, they sought a future for black children
that would transcend poverty and prejudice. Dissatisfied with broken-
backed, white-controlled systems of public education, they did what
the states were signally failing to do.

Not many of these private schools remain. Many disappeared during the 1920s and 1930s, taken over by local school boards or killed off
by the Great Depression. The ones that survived the Second World
War eventually succumbed to fires, better public schools, and integration. By 1970 most of them had vanished. Even at their height, around
the time of the First World War, the private schools founded and
taught by black teachers probably enrolled fewer than 5 percent of
black children.

Yet between 1890 and 1920, black-run private schools assumed an
importance that was out of all proportion to their numbers. At a time
when public schools enrolled barely half of the South's black children, and when they usually stopped at the fifth grade, private schools
provided rare opportunities for higher education, secondary education, and decent elementary education. The mission schools run by
white teachers did this too, of course. But as the number of northern
white teachers declined, black teachers assumed an increasing burden. Moreover, black-run private schools helped sustain the mission
schools by furnishing them with students and providing employment
to their graduates.

Private schools nurtured African American leaders. With so many
fields of endeavor—politics, big business, the professions—entirely or
largely closed to them, education provided blacks with a way to apply
their talent and ambition to the building of large institutions. It attracted hard-driving, enterprising people. The field was so competi-
tive, in fact, that a kind of Darwinian law favored the most deter-

mined and resourceful. Hence the men and women who led private schools often acted as community leaders as well. Education being the main site of interracial cooperation, teachers became the principal interlocutors between whites and blacks. During the era of white supremacy, roughly 1890 to 1950, private schools supplied many of the South's best-known African American spokespeople, including Booker T. Washington, Robert R. Moton, John Hope, and Charles S. Johnson. The private schools produced female leaders as well. The highest positions in public education—head of a state college and principal of a city high school—were restricted to men. Teachers like Charlotte Hawkins Brown and Mary McLeod Bethune avoided this "glass ceiling" by founding their own schools.

Black teachers did not constitute a unified leadership, present a common front in race relations, or share the same approach to education. The arguments between supporters and opponents of Booker T. Washington produced bitter divisions. Poverty, sectarianism, and color consciousness fueled other conflicts. The continual necessity of raising money, especially the need to solicit funds in the North, promoted fierce and sometimes cutthroat competition. Religion promoted denominational rivalry, as well as tensions between teachers in church schools and those who, like Washington, advocated nonsectarian education. Color consciousness rarely caused open conflict, but it often lurked below the surface, causing resentments and complicating other divisions.

However, the harsh, inescapable facts of southern conditions tended to mute hostility and competition. Southern black teachers were all in the same boat: powerless and vulnerable. They understood that differences between public schools and private schools, between the city and the country, and between the Deep South and the Upper South conditioned what teachers could do and say. Rivalry did not preclude a sense of fellowship among black teachers, and a feeling that they shared a common interest.

Like the white-taught mission schools, black private schools impeded the construction of a racial caste system. Even as they accommodated to white supremacy, they exerted constant upward pressure against the ceiling that whites tried to impose upon blacks. Moreover, although poverty and lack of political influence limited their independence, black teachers in private schools preserved a degree of autonomy. Maneuvering between white mission boards, northern benefactors, educational foundations, state officials, local white elites, and their own black constituencies, they were often canny diplomats.

Two schools that survive, Winston-Salem State University and Bethune-Cookman College, provide insights into the resourcefulness and contrasting strategies employed by black founders. The former originated in 1893 as Slater Industrial Academy, founded by Simon G. Atkins; the latter started life in 1904 as Daytona Educational and Industrial Training School for Negro Girls, founded by Mary McLeod Bethune. Both Atkins and Bethune depended upon white support, but they pursued different strategies for securing it. Both schools included the word *Industrial* in their names, but it meant something different in each case. The fact that these schools endure is partly a matter of chance, but it also owes something to the determination and resourcefulness of their founders

Simon Green Atkins began facing up to the political realities of the New South well before the final blow of disenfranchisement fell. Born into slavery in 1863, Atkins grew up on a North Carolina farm rented from his former master. While attending school one summer he had the luck to encounter Anna Julia Cooper, a student at St. Augustine's College and the future author of *A Voice from the South* (1892), who was one of the most articulate and accomplished women of her generation. Cooper took Atkins under her wing and encouraged his thirst for education. By age seventeen Atkins was teaching in a rural public school. After graduating from St. Augustine College in 1884, he quickly became one of the leading black educators in North Carolina. By his mid-twenties Atkins was teaching at Livingstone College, editing a magazine called *The Southland,* and conducting summer teachers' institutes. He also helped organize the North Carolina State Teachers Association. Atkins and the NCSTA were staunch advocates of civil rights and equality of educational opportunity. They protested against politically biased school textbooks, opposed a bill that would divide education taxes by race, and pressed the state legislature not to pass Jim Crow legislation.[3]

In the 1890s, however, after he moved to the industrial town of Winston and became principal of Depot Street Colored Graded School, the emphasis of Atkins's work shifted. Working in a public school robbed him of the relative independence he had enjoyed at Livingstone College. It also brought home the fact that the main educational problem confronting most blacks was lack of money. The controversy over the appropriate curriculum for black schools—industrial education versus literary education—tended to obscure the fact that any education was better than none. Regardless of the kind of education they received, blacks needed more years of schooling. Determined to found an advanced school in Winston, Atkins organized Slater Industrial Academy. Two years later, in 1895, he became its principal.

Atkins confronted the hard question of resources. The black community was too poor to sustain the kind of school he had in mind. The white authorities showed no disposition to fund black high schools or colleges. The budgets of the northern missionary societies were stretched to the limit. That left two other sources of support: northern philanthropists and southern whites. Cultivating northern benefactors was a straightforward if bone-wearying task. From the outset, however, Atkins hoped to secure the future of his school by attracting state funding. He therefore modified his commitment to classical and literary education and tilted toward industrial education.

The name of his school was deliberately ambiguous, even misleading. "Slater Industrial Academy" implied that it received backing from the John F. Slater Fund, which, under its agent J. L. M. Curry, vigorously promoted industrial education for blacks. Yet the name represented only the hope of Slater funding, for the school received none at the time. In any case, a name combining *Slater* with *Industrial* made a clear statement that the school was not modeled on the classical curriculum of the mission schools, thereby facilitating Atkins's efforts to cultivate the support of local whites. After Booker T. Washington shot to national fame after his Atlanta Exposition address of 1895, Atkins never missed an opportunity to associate his school with the educational philosophy of Tuskegee Institute. In 1897 he dropped the word *Academy* and substituted *School.* He visited Hampton Institute and recruited a man to teach shoe-making. "You will be pleased, Mr. Mebane, to note the excellent spirit with which our students go about their industrial work," he informed the state superintendent of education. Slater's curriculum limited "literary work" to one session per day. The intention of a glossy brochure that Slater put out in 1900 could not have been plainer in its title: *Industrial Education in the South: The Negro Problem Being Solved: Hampton, Tuskegee, Slater.*[4]

Atkins's strategy paid off handsomely. His school received numerous donations from wealthy northerners. Appealing to civic boosterism, it also won support from local whites. In 1899, for example, Winston tobacco manufacturer R. J. Reynolds offered Slater five thousand dollars toward a nurses' training school. The political backing of Winston's white leaders—whom Atkins recruited to Slater's board of trustees—proved even more important. Having lost out to Greensboro in the competition for North Carolina's land-grant college, Winston's civic elite backed Atkins's plans to site a state normal school in their city. Henry E. Fries, a local industrialist, chaired Slater's board and consistently championed its interests. In June 1903 Fries lobbied for Slater to receive state funding as a normal school. So did Winston's mayor, chief of police, board of education, and Chamber of Commerce.

Atkins needed all the political support he could muster in competing against other black teachers for public funding. The decision of the North Carolina legislature to prune the number of black normal schools intensified that competition. Atkins succeeded: in 1905 Slater became one of five normal schools to receive state funding. In 1916 it became one of three. Nine years later, with Atkins still at the helm, Slater shed the words *Slater, Industrial,* and *School* to became Winston-Salem Teachers College. Now a state university, it stands as a monument to Atkins's vision and political skill.[5]

Was Atkins ever really committed to "industrial education"? It seems unlikely. Slater's "industrial" features were superficial; Atkins never seriously attempted to emulate Tuskegee or Hampton. Apart from the fact that students did two hours of "industrial work" each day instead of one, its curriculum resembled that of the private colleges. Slater's preparatory department took students to the fifth grade, its four-year normal department took them through the first two years of high school, and its two-year academic course (which included Latin) was equivalent to the last two years of high school. This already took Slater's students—those who persisted—above the academic ceilings of Hampton and Tuskegee. Moreover, Atkins never hid his ambition to convert Slater into a college of higher education. He struggled to shed the school's preparatory grades, and by 1919 he had turned Slater into a standard four-year high school. By 1925 it could offer four years of college work—although Atkins admitted it was "hard sledding" to attract enough students of college caliber.

Despite his endorsement of industrial education, Atkins rejected the idea that blacks should receive an education different from that of whites. "It is presented in certain catchy and specious phrases such as the necessity of beginning at the bottom rather than at the top, the necessity of giving to the colored American a kind of colored education . . . [and] of making his civilization earthbound and breadwinning rather than heavenbound and soul-satisfying." In this not-so-veiled criticism of Washington, Atkins stated the time-honored argument in favor of a liberal, literary, and classical curriculum. "Education is not a question of mechanics; it is rather a question of ethics and morality. Education is primarily an effort to realize in man his possibilities as a thinking and feeling being." By defining Slater's chief function as the training of elementary school teachers, and obtaining state support for his institution, Atkins disseminated the humanistic philosophy of education that he first acquired from Anna Julia Cooper and the other teachers at St. Augustine College.

In order to pursue the long-term goal of equality, Atkins accepted the short-term necessity of accommodating to white supremacy. He recognized the need to cultivate whites who regarded disenfranchisement and segregation as essential elements of southern race relations. Longtime white supporter H. E. Fries praised his "wise conservative leadership." After Atkins died in 1934 at the age of seventy-one, Fries described him as "singularly modest and self-effacing."[6]

Nobody applied such words to Mary McLeod Bethune. A forceful, eloquent, and supremely self-confident woman, Bethune turned her life into a metaphor for black success in much the same way that Booker T. Washington did. Indeed, the similarities between the two educators are striking. Like Washington, Bethune built an independent school that symbolized black autonomy and achievement. Both preached a message of racial reconciliation and cooperation; both built bridges between black and white America. Like Washington, Bethune took personal rebuffs and humiliations philosophically, secure in her moral superiority. "When hate has been projected toward me, I have known that the persons who extended it lacked spiritual understanding. I have had great pity and compassion for them." Washington reassured whites rather than threatened them; Bethune sought their help rather than castigated them. An astute racial diplomat, she came as close to the center of political power as Washington had.[7]

The fifteenth of seventeen children, Bethune was born on a plantation near Mayesville, South Carolina, in 1875. Her family made its living through sharecropping, laboring, and domestic service. Neither of her parents could read. But the northern Presbyterian Church had made South Carolina one if its foci, and its mission schools there launched the careers of an extraordinary number of distinguished black educators. Bethune had the good fortune to attend one of them. She then entered Scotia Seminary for Negro Girls, a Presbyterian school in Concord, North Carolina, taught by northern-educated women and headed by a white man. Scotia left an indelible imprint upon her. Its religious atmosphere reinforced her piety. The dedication of its teachers nurtured her desire for missionary work. Its rules and regimentation, although strict, created a safe, family-like environment that she later reproduced in her own school. Scotia's interracial staff brought her into close contact with white people for the first time; said Bethune of this experience, "[It] clinched my confidence in the interest, and wholeheartedness of white people in Negroes." Of the school's black teachers, well educated and ladylike, she said, "[They] gave me my very first vision of the culture and ability of Negro women . . . and made me feel that if they could do it, I could do it, too."[8]

The road that took Bethune to Daytona Beach, Florida, led from Scotia Seminary by way of Moody Bible Institute in Chicago and Haines Institute in Augusta, Georgia. The Bible school, founded by renowned evangelist Dwight L. Moody, encouraged her to think of missionary work in the Dark Continent. "I just had a yearning to go to Africa," she recalled. Failing to find sponsorship, however, she redirected her missionary zeal toward the Deep South, and toward the education of black girls in particular. She returned to Mayesville to teach at her old school. Through her Presbyterian connections, she then found a position at Haines Institute.[9]

Her year at Haines provided Bethune with a blueprint. Here was a school created from scratch through the skill and will of Lucy Craft Laney, a dark-skinned African American woman who inspired countless black women teachers. Through gifts from wealthy northerners, affiliation with the northern Presbyterian Church, and grants from educational foundations, Laney built a private school that became a byword for good teaching, community service, and sturdy independence. Laney "demonstrated to me that it could be done," Bethune remembered. "I studied her, watched her every move and gave myself fully to the cause she represented."[10]

Despite her mission school education, Bethune also idolized Booker T. Washington. She visited Tuskegee Institute in 1896—at the zenith of Washington's fame—and was awed by its size and ambition. Here was another model. Bethune's consuming ambition became "the building of an institution." Years later, she recalled a vivid dream that sustained her when she began this venture. In this dream, she was sitting by a bank of the Halifax River, praying for help, when she saw a man "galloping down the street on a beautiful horse."

> He was dressed in a uniform suit, and when he got near me he jumped off his horse and said, "What are you sitting here for?" I said to him, "I am just trying to see my way clear to build a school." He said, "I am Booker T. Washington," and he placed his hand back in his hip pocket and pulled out a parcel in a seemingly soiled handkerchief—a soiled handkerchief that had evidently been used for mopping off the perspiration—and out

of this handkerchief he gave me a large diamond and said, "Here, take this and build your school." And . . . he remounted his horse and galloped away.

The diamond did not represent money, Bethune believed, but the qualities that had created Tuskegee—"confidence, will power, stick-to-it-iveness, work, suffering, friends, doubt, wisdom, common sense."[11]

Bethune needed those qualities in abundance during the five years she struggled to establish a school in Florida. Her first effort, in Palatka, failed. The community was too small and too poor. Having a husband and caring for a baby, moreover, proved a distraction. In 1904 Bethune moved to Daytona Beach and founded the Daytona Educational and Industrial Training School for Negro Girls. Her marriage suffered and her husband left her. Bethune also saw less and less of her son, to her later regret, as she devoted her energies to the school.[12]

Legend has it—and Bethune was always the source of such legends—that she started the school with just $1.50 in her purse. Local blacks rendered such assistance as they could. "I begged dry goods boxes and made benches and stools; begged a basin and other things I needed." The churches tried to help. A black landlord trusted her to find the rent on a small house. When it came to money, however, blacks "had little to offer."[13]

Bethune's selection of Daytona Beach seems to have been carefully calculated, however. Founded mainly by northerners, some of whom came from abolitionist backgrounds, the town had become a fashionable winter resort for northern millionaires. It was awash with Yankee dollars. Carefully scanning the local newspaper for the comings and goings of "society," she invited prominent whites to visit the school. She set her sights on James Gamble, the soap king, Thomas White, a manufacturer of sewing machines, and the philanthropically minded women of the Palmetto Club. Once exposed to her missionary enthusiasm, they could rarely keep their wallets closed. When Gamble first visited Bethune's school and saw a cabin, a few dry-goods boxes, and five pupils, he asked her, "What do you want me to be trustee of?" When Bethune had finished telling him her vision of her dream school, he agreed to chair the board.[14]

Subjected to rigorous discipline, the girls at Daytona learned the "three R's," studied the Bible, and received instruction in homemaking and domestic science. Bethune's commitment to industrial education, unlike Atkins's, was thoroughgoing. In a curriculum that Booker T. Washington heartily endorsed—he visited the school in 1912—teachers showed girls how to cook, clean, sew, weave rugs, make brooms, cane chairs, and raise poultry. Education must root itself "in the life and needs of the people," Bethune insisted. The training her girls received helped them, when they became mothers, to keep their families healthy, well clad, and adequately fed. It equipped them to earn a living in a society that barred women from virtually all jobs except domestic service and teaching. And it imparted moral virtues—temperance, chastity, race pride, and a desire to serve others—that endowed women with self-respect and earned them the respect of others. Her school, said Bethune, helped "bring order" out of the surrounding "chaos." Growing by leaps and bounds, it acquired a farm, built a hospital, and added a high school. By 1914 it was training black girls to be nurses and teachers as well as mothers and domestic servants.[15]

A former pupil, Lucy Miller Mitchell, recalled the imprint of Bethune's domineering presence and "boundless energy" upon the school. Her insistence upon rules, routine, order, and thoroughness profoundly impressed the young pupils. The embodiment of the work ethic—her days started before dawn and rarely ended before midnight—Bethune peppered her conversation with clichés that exalted the dignity of labor: "Any work is honest, however humble." The girls were amazed at her ability to interpret their behavior and sense when things were bothering them. Although they held her in awe, "she was the person to whom the students always turned with their troubles." Starting each day with a prayer, and gathering her pupils in the chapel for daily talks, Bethune "wove into the warp and woof of our personality and character her philosophy of life, her inspiration, [and] her deep religious fervor . . . And she gave to us a feeling that through God's power all things are possible."[16]

To raise money, Bethune employed all the techniques refined by southern school founders since the heyday of Booker T. Washington. She crisscrossed the country. She emitted a ceaseless flow of letters and appeals. She treated visitors to the campus royally—making sure, especially when giving southern whites the tour, to show off the basketry, dressmaking, and cooking. The school's singing quartet raised money in churches and other venues. Alumni formed fundraising clubs. Sixty wealthy or well-known women served on an advisory board, the main purpose of which was to stimulate giving. Associations of women supporters raised money in New York and New England. Bethune employed an agent to organize fundraising drives in northern cities. She drove him hard. "You have your ministers' organizations, the sororities, fraternities, the schools, and other organizations," she instructed, "so get it going." Every donation, however small, received a personal acknowledgement. A woman who sent one dollar would learn that "this gift filled a real need in our budget."[17]

Despite her phenomenal success as a fundraiser, however, Bethune's ability to secure donations never kept pace with the school's growing budget. This was the paradox of educational success: increasing enrollments and bigger buildings made independence an unaffordable luxury. Determined to preserve her school's autonomy, Bethune rejected state funding. But she did accept an affiliation with the Methodist Episcopal Church, North, that changed the character of her school. It ended her policy of nondenominationalism and subjected her to a church board that limited her freedom of action. It also entailed a merger with a Methodist boys' school that turned her school for girls into the coeducational Bethune-Cookman College. And in a reorientation forced by improvements in the public schools, Bethune's school dropped its lower grades and added two higher ones. It became a high school and junior college.

These changes made Bethune the first black woman to head a black college in the South. The affiliation with the Methodists did not, however, end the school's financial problems. The collapse of the Florida land boom pushed its deficit to twenty-two thousand dollars. Then came the Wall Street crash and the Great Depression. However, with support from the General Education Board, and donations from staff, students, alumni, black teachers, Methodist churches, and northern supporters—even the French ambassador sent ten dollars in response to an "S.O.S." appeal—the college survived.[18]

In founding their schools, Bethune and Atkins employed different strategies. The cautious Atkins began his work with community backing from both blacks and whites. Bethune started with practically nothing, trusting to faith in God and belief in herself. Atkins made his school part of the South's system of public education, anchoring it in the twentieth century, whereas Bethune's school harked back to the mission schools of the nineteenth century. In turning his school into a state institution, however, Atkins had to compromise his freedom of speech and action. Bethune doggedly preserved her independence, first by acquiring funds from northern donors and then, when forced to do so, by affiliating with a northern church. Despite Slater's nod toward industrial education, its organization and curriculum resembled that of the mission school, St. Augustine College, that had molded Atkins. Bethune borrowed heavily and sincerely from Washington's ideas about industrial education. But she also copied many of the features of Scotia Seminary—its single-sex organization, religious atmosphere, and training of girls to be homemakers—and ended up creating something very like a mission school.

THE confusing nomenclature of black schools—*institute, academy, college, university, seminary, training school, normal school, industrial school, normal* and *industrial school*—reflected something of their diversity. But they sometimes offered few clues as to their individual character. Indeed, they could be downright misleading. A few teachers made direct attempts to implement the educational philosophy of Booker T. Washington. Elizabeth E. Wright, William J. Edwards, Charles P. Adams, and other graduates of Tuskegee Institute founded schools in the Black Belt oriented toward agriculture. These "little Tuskegees," which always contained the word *Industrial* in their name, were among the best-known schools of their time.

Private schools of a conventional academic bent, however, outnumbered the "little Tuskegees." Many of them were denominational schools. Black graduates of the mission schools founded institutions that they affiliated with mainly white churches such as the Presbyterians, Congregationalists, and northern Methodists. Other denominational schools projected the racial independence of the AME and AMEZ churches. These schools accepted white support but jealously guarded their autonomy. Baptist schools—perhaps a majority of all the denominational schools—were rooted in independent black churches, but usually cooperated with, and were helped by, white Baptists. CME schools embodied a similar mixture of denominational autonomy and interracial cooperation. Only the schools established by "separatist" Baptists eschewed white assistance altogether, in principle if not always in practice.

Black teachers also founded a large number of private, nondenominational schools that attracted white and black support in varying proportions. Like the "little Tuskegees," many of them also included the word *Industrial* in their names, but they were not uniform in their commitment to industrial education.

Schools affiliated with black Baptist churches were long regarded as academically weak. Booker T. Washington periodically castigated "preacher-teachers" for hampering the educational progress of the race. He knew whereof he spoke. Ministers who could barely read commonly taught school in their churches and got school boards to pay them salaries. The educational caliber of such men can be inferred from a single example, one that could be multiplied many times over. The Rev. Jacobs Rivers Barnett, born in Dougherty County, Georgia, in 1857, taught in Mississippi for six years, holding a second-grade certificate, yet "all the school days of Rev. Barnett's life amounted to twenty-four months and three weeks, and he was twelve years getting that."[19]

Baptists were painfully aware of their educational deficiencies. "For years the Negro Baptists . . . have been held up to the ridicule of other denominations," admitted E. C. Morris, president of the National Baptist Convention, in 1894. "Their ministers have been classed as the most ignorant of their race." Struggling to overcome the limitations of their public school education, black Baptists founded dozens of private schools that aspired to something better. By 1910 they were supporting more than eighty—the largest single network of black private schools in the South—with strong concentrations in Virginia, the Carolinas, and Louisiana.[20]

Baptist schools labored under many handicaps. The Baptist Church embraced the largest and the poorest portion of the South's black population. It raised less money for education, per capita, than other black denominations. Moreover, the money was spread thinly, for the congregational character of the Baptist Church encouraged a large number of small schools. In the Piedmont region of South Carolina, for example, district Baptist associations established ten private schools but could not adequately support or find competent teachers for so many. Baptist schools also suffered from interfering trustee boards dominated by autocratic ministers and poorly educated laymen. As North Carolina teacher J. A. Whitted complained, instead of leaving the management of their schools to the faculty, trustees often "stood in the way of . . . progress and improvement." Finally, disputes over religious doctrine sometimes encroached upon Baptist schools, threatening free inquiry with intolerant dogmatism. In Kentucky, for example, Simmons University came under repeated criticism for employing Jews, non-Baptist Christians, and a president who allegedly believed in infant baptism.[21]

The tendency of Baptist churches toward schism exacerbated their problems. Denominational rivalry already fostered what leading black educator W. T. B. Williams called "useless and unreasonable duplication," producing schools that fulfilled a religious goal but fell woefully short of their educational one. When Baptist churches or district associations split, intradenominational strife weakened existing schools and spawned more weak ones.[22] Dissension among Baptists in eastern North Carolina, for example, caused endless difficulties for their efforts to found a strong private school. When members of the Kenansville Eastern Association failed to agree on a site for their school, the association divided. The Baptist churches of Duplin County established a school in Faison, those of Sampson County sponsored one in Clinton. The Clinton school "was not what it might have been" and went through several ineffective principals. The Faison school prospered under a strong principal, J. N. Bennett, and was sustained by county funds for four months and by private subscriptions for seven more. But when the board of trustees questioned the handling of monies, Bennett quit. Taking the other teachers with him, he began a rival school, moved it to the public schoolhouse, and kept the county subsidy. The Baptist ministers, left with an empty school-house, fought back. They built a new dormitory and pressed for the return of the county funds. The situation was thoroughly muddled, reported W. T. B. Williams. "Only one school can do good work here."[23]

For all that, Baptist schools became vital to black education. If the high-sounding name of the typical Baptist school—*College* or *Academy*—belied the fact that the bulk of its pupils worked at the elementary level, the fact remained that this school was often the only alternative to the wretched one-teacher public school that met only three or four months of the year. Moreover, the Baptist schools did not exist in isolation. They formed an educational system, supported by the white Baptists of the North. At the head of this system stood mission schools like Virginia Union University in Richmond and Leland University in New Orleans, which exerted a constant upward pull on the Baptist schools by taking their best pupils, educating them, and sending them back as teachers. Over time, this process pulled some of the lower schools up to the high school level. When the states finally started building public high schools for blacks, many of their teachers came from these Baptist schools. Indeed, the Baptist schools spawned family dynasties that provided educational leadership over two or three generations.

In Louisiana, for example, the state's 130,000 Baptists supported a network of fifteen academies "to do for their children what the state has felt unable to do." Leland University, a coeducational school supported by the ABHMS and staffed by a predominantly white faculty, directed this network. Leland's president named the principals of the affiliated schools and approved their curriculum. Each year the affiliated schools sent students to New Orleans, where Leland offered them high school, normal, and college education. In 1904 Leland's president, Ralph W. Perkins, was teaching education, ethics, civics, sociology, economics, "and everything else that is necessary." His wife taught English and history. A man who was formerly a missionary in India taught theology to black ministers. The school's atmosphere was "religious, quiet, earnest, and moral." The General Education Board considered Leland "over-bookish," but conceded that it furnished effective leadership to a "strongly organized system."[24]

The Baptist academies, the base of the system, were built and largely sustained by ordinary church members. Pupils paid tuition fees, and churches, organized into district associations, took collections. The little donations of sharecroppers, small farmers, laborers, and domestic servants added up. Referring to Coleman College, a Baptist school in Bienville Parish that raised fourteen hundred dollars a year from local sources, a white woman from Boston wrote, in amazement, "I cannot understand how such poor people could raise so much money."[25]

Oliver Lewis Coleman founded the school bearing his name in 1887. A native of Mississippi, he did not have much formal education—study at Alcorn University and summers at Chautauqua Institute—but it was enough to make him realize that he could not bear to teach in the miserable public schools of the day. When he found a northern businessman prepared to donate ten acres of timber land, he began building his own school near Gibsland, a railroad junction in an area of north Louisiana where most black children did not attend schools of any description. Teaching under a brush arbor in dry weather, and in Palestine Baptist Church when it rained, he started his school with five students. Local churches formed the Springfield Baptist Association to support him. Farmers donated crops and made lumber. Volunteer laborers erected three dormitories, a principal's home, and a two-story chapel. "The chapel building fell down two or three times before they could get it to stand." Through depression, drought, and fire, Coleman kept going. Local Baptists came to venerate him as a saint. They pointed to the "Praying Tree" where he sought God's intercession and where, legend had it, during the parched summer of 1896 a spring gushed from the tree's roots. A few years later, however, the school's wooden buildings burned down. Utterly worn out, Coleman spent a summer in Maine at the invitation of the Women's Missionary Society of Boston. Upon his return, he rebuilt the school in bricks molded and fired by the students themselves, made from local clay.

By 1918 Coleman College enrolled four hundred students, over half of them boarders, and had a faculty of sixteen teachers. As it expanded, however, the contributions of black Baptists could not keep pace. In addition to long-standing support from white Baptists in New

York and New England, it began to receive money from the northern foundations as well as a subsidy from the Bienville Parish School Board. When Louisiana reformed its wholly ineffective system of teacher certification—introducing certificates based upon college qualifications rather than exams administered by local schools superintendents—Coleman struggled to meet the new standard. He beefed up the curriculum by recruiting "nine college graduates who have been taught by white teachers." After much pleading, he convinced state officials to give his graduates first-grade teaching certificates even though Coleman College did not grant degrees. In 1927 Coleman died in a car crash. His son took over, but the college closed during the Depression.[26]

During its forty-year life, Coleman College provided a pathway for hundreds of black teachers in northern Louisiana. The education of these teachers might have been limited, especially in the college's early years. But without Coleman College the teachers could have only been worse, because before 1915 the state government did nothing to train black teachers. "We have made more teachers . . . directly and indirectly than any other school for Negroes in the state," Coleman pointed out, "and it has cost the state nothing." Coleman took particular pride in the fact that some of the leading black teachers in Louisiana "got their first inspiration of manhood, push and work from here."

Joseph S. Clark, one of Coleman College's earliest students, was born on a Bienville Parish plantation and came to Gibsland at the age of nineteen after hearing Coleman speak about his school in a local church. After four years at Coleman—supporting himself by teaching each summer and working at the college as "part-time janitor, barber, and student assistant"—Clark entered Leland University, earning a degree in 1901. That year he became principal of Baton Rouge Academy, another Baptist school, and in 1915 the state appointed him the first black president of Southern University. J. S. Jones, another Coleman graduate, followed a similar path, teaching at Baton Rouge Academy, then becoming a dean at Southern University. Long after its demise, the influence of Coleman College endured through these men. J. S. Jones's son, Ralph Waldo Emerson Jones, became president of Grambling State College in 1936, eventually retiring in 1977. J. S. Clark's son, Felton Grandison Clark, inherited the presidency of Southern University in 1938, a position he held until 1968.[27]

Baptist institutions like Coleman College, like the better known and more polished mission schools, produced an educational "ripple effect." Many of their graduates founded schools of their own. R. E. Jacobs, who organized Sabine Normal and Industrial Institute, provides a classic example. Born in 1877 on a plantation near Shreveport, Jacobs attended a rough country school taught by his father, a sharecropper, and entered Coleman College at the age of nineteen. After six years at the college, Jacobs founded a school near the village of Converse, Sabine Parish. Rev. W. B. Purvis, a preacher-teacher-farmer whom he had met at Coleman College, helped him. Having tried to found a school and failed, Purvis urged local farmers to back Jacobs. A man of indefatigable energy, Jacobs traveled up and down the Kansas City Southern Railroad each spring, stopping at every mill to solicit subscriptions and donations from the owners and foremen. He won grants from the Slater Fund, and persuaded the Sabine Parish School Board to subsidize teachers' salaries for four and a half months—the length of the public school term—enabling Sabine Institute to offer a nine-month school year. When he died in 1917, his school had a faculty of seven teachers, a farm, girls' and boys' dormitories, a dining hall, a laundry, a workshop, and sanitary toilets.[28]

Two South Carolinians, Alexander Bettis and J. J. Starks, personified different qualities of leadership displayed by men who founded Baptist schools. Bettis, born a slave, was an architect of the Baptist Church during the early years of freedom. A rugged, unlettered man, he commanded authority through sheer faith and force of personality. Starks, who came of age during the 1890s, was a graduate of Benedict College and Morehouse College; his commitment to missionary uplift melded with personal ambition and a nose for church politics.

Alexander Bettis embodied many of the characteristics that white southerners prized in a slave, and his owner, "Widow Jones," exemplified the paternalism that defenders of the "peculiar institution" attributed to slaveholders in general. Jones taught Bettis to read, treated him with kindness, and placed her sawmills and plantations under his management. The pastor of Edgefield's First Baptist Church licensed him to preach. Hardworking and loyal, "Honest Aleck" stayed on the Jones plantation after emancipation. But he also led the secession of black Baptists from the white churches of Edgefield and Aiken counties. He organized more than forty churches, became pastor of four, and helped set up the South Carolina State Baptist Convention. Unlike A. R. Blunt, his counterpart in Louisiana, Bettis avoided politics. He also scorned "whangdoodle preachers"—although his own church services attracted thousands. He commanded such respect that he could, with impunity, take a buggy whip to any "obstreperous Negro" who misbehaved during his services.

Bettis never learned to write. He could not even sign his own name. But he organized Mt. Canaan Educational Union, and over the opposition of fellow preachers—who wanted to use any money raised to further their own education—he insisted upon buying land for a school. He asked local churches to help him select two young men he could send away to be educated. Hampton Mathias and Joseph W. Nicholson thus became the first principals of Bettis Academy, which opened in 1882. One attended Schofield Normal and Industrial Institute, and then Atlanta University, while the other ran the school. Bettis served as the school's president until his death in 1895 at the age of fifty-nine. An arch accommodationist, by nature as well as design, Bettis earned political protection for his school in an area of South Carolina where whites, heavily outnumbered, had engaged in violence and terrorism to defeat Reconstruction. Even that raging Negrophobe Ben Tillman could not find fault with him.[29]

The Rev. John J. Starks personified the next generation of Baptist school leader. His was a twentieth-century career, long past the pioneering days of Bettis. A fellow black Carolinian, Lewis K. McMillan, described him as "dynamic, resourceful, vain, and ambitious." With the benefit of a college education, Starks took advantage of a Baptist organization that by 1900 was solidly established. He founded one school, Seneca Institute, in 1899, for which the groundwork had been laid by local Baptists. Then he took over Morris College. He ended his career as the first black president of Benedict College, a mission school founded by the ABHMS. Starks combined school, church, and business interests, becoming a wealthy man and a powerful leader. He may have lacked the spiritual authority of a Bettis, but he had other ways of commanding loyalty. Starks always had cash on hand, explained McMillan, and most of the other influential preachers were perpetually "broke." "Dr. Starks tied all of these men to him through little insignificant emergency loans. All of the Baptist big shots owed Starks money."

Starks also possessed executive ability and practical sense. In setting up Seneca Institute, for example, he resisted pressure to house the school in an old building situated "in the yard of the Baptist Church." Methodists would refuse to patronize it, he explained, and "the Methodists were stronger than the Baptists in Seneca." Instead he waited a year and opened the school—which he described as "Christian rather than denominational"—in a new brick building some distance from the Baptist church. It was an immediate success. By its second year its pupils numbered two hundred, half of them boarders. Supported by a pliant board of trustees and leaving the day-to-day running of the school to his wife and other assistants, Starks turned Seneca Institute into a popular and self-supporting school that was "fast assuming the proportions of a real high school." All the while, Starks held the pastorship of several churches, ran two farms, and accumulated property in town. In 1912 he moved to the presidency of Morris College, a school founded in 1908—partly to offset white-controlled Benedict College—by the state convention of black Baptists. Here, too, Starks was an indefatigable promoter and fundraiser, wining support from the Jeanes Fund and the Southern Baptist Convention. When he assumed the presidency of Benedict College, Starks persuaded South Carolina's white Baptists to fund a seminary named in his honor.

Critics regarded schools like Bettis Academy, Seneca Institute, and Morris College as pretentious, puffed up, self-important, and grandiloquent. Lewis McMillan, who knew them well, lamented the fact that they rarely lived up to their impressive buildings and ambitious catalogues. Affecting the mannerisms, nomenclature, and academic rigmarole of the college, they were basically elementary schools that slowly dragged themselves up to high school level. Then they became "teacher training mills," adding slipshod "normal" courses that lacked both academic rigor and practical content.

Yet these Baptist schools served a desperate need. Seneca Institute, for example, was the only school between Columbia and Atlanta that offered blacks something better than an eighth-grade education. When it eventually graduated its first high school class, in 1914, twelve of the thirteen students went on to gain college degrees. Some went much further. Otto Hill attended Benedict College, Boston College, and Meharry medical school, and then practiced medicine in New Jersey. Elected to the state legislature, he drafted a fair employment bill and steered it into the statute book—only the second such law in the country. His brother, Horatio Hill, also a graduate of Seneca and Benedict, earned a Ph.D. from Yale University. These stellar successes should not obscure the larger work that Seneca did in educating thousands of rural blacks. "These country boys and girls achieved literacy in the truest sense of the word," admitted McMillan. "They learned the Latin and Greek classics, and appropriated to themselves what smattering of the sciences and what gems of American and English literature their far too inadequate instruction and exposure made available to them."[30]

Baptist schools geared their curricula toward the academic courses of the Baptist universities, and the ABHMS was fundamentally opposed to the notion that industrial education should be the basis of black schooling. Edward C. Mitchell, president of Leland University, argued that industrial education was wasteful, expensive, and ineffective. As a philosophy, he went on, it represented "class education" that promoted the "European idea that the child will follow the calling of his father." More fundamentally, Mitchell concluded, industrial education "divert[ed] attention away from the real aim and end of education, which is manhood."[31]

WHEN disciples of Booker T. Washington imitated his example by founding "Little Tuskegees," they often encountered stiff opposition from Baptist ministers. Poorly educated "preacher-teachers" regarded the nonsectarianism of the industrial schools as a threat to their own church schools; they also feared displacement and loss of influence. And many blacks disliked industrial education per se. The founders of industrial schools therefore struggled to win black support, some more successfully than others. The work of Elizabeth Wright, William J. Edwards, and Charles P. Adams illustrates the range of experiences encountered by Washington's followers.

Of all the men and women who founded "Little Tuskegees," Elizabeth Evelyn Wright probably encountered the least opposition from other blacks. Perhaps her gender made her appear less threatening to male preachers than a man would have been. Perhaps the absence of a rival church school—or even a rival public school—helped her. Perhaps the sheer depth of white opposition rallied blacks to her cause.

"A poor, sickly, friendless, Georgia peasant," Lizzie Wright entered Tuskegee Institute at the age of fifteen. Although physically frail, continually ill, and easily moved to tears, she possessed spirit and determination. When barely seventeen years old, she joined five others in interceding with Washington on behalf of a fellow student who had been suspended, asking him to take pity on the miscreant and set aside his punishment. She so impressed her teachers that Olivia Davidson Washington, the principal's second wife, recommended her to some of Tuskegee's northern white supporters. One of them, Judge George W. Kelley of Massachusetts, agreed to pay her school expenses. Another, Almira S. Steele, also of Massachusetts, invited her to teach at a school she had founded in McNeill's, a sawmill town in Hampton County, South Carolina, when ill health prevented Wright from starting her senior year. Upon graduating from Tuskegee in 1894, Wright returned to South Carolina to take over Mrs. Steele's school. Judge Kelley agreed to back her.[32]

But whites in Hampton County proved distinctly inhospitable. Almira Steele's schoolhouse burned down in April 1893. When Judge Kelley bought lumber for a new schoolhouse, the wood went up in flames. Kelley located an alternative site with usable buildings on it, but by the following day the buildings had turned to ashes. Wright was about to buy a third site when the owner felled all the trees and carted them off. After being insulted by a white man in the streets of Hampton, she decided to look elsewhere.[33]

In the town of Denmark, in the newly created county of Bamberg, Wright found a white man who could provide political protection. Stanwix G. Mayfield, a lawyer and state senator, was a political ally of Ben Tillman. When Wright offered to buy from him a two-hundred-acre tract that contained serviceable buildings, Mayfield demurred. But his devout and formidable mother-in-law, Ellen Kennerly, urged him to swallow his misgivings and give Wright a chance. Mayfield not only agreed to sell the land but also helped Wright set up the school. Needing two hundred dollars for a down payment, Wright quickly raised the money from sixty-six local black churches, which donated sums ranging from eight dollars to fifty cents.[34]

Despite evidence of widespread black support, however, Wright's staunch nondenominationalism provoked an unexpected attack from Rev. R. D. Rice, a Baptist minister who had initially befriended her. One of Wright's co-workers was a Seventh-Day Adventist whom she had met at the sanitarium in Battle Creek, Michigan, which she occasionally visited when her health failed her. The founder of this famous institution, Dr. John Harvey Kellogg, was a supporter of Wright's school and a Seventh-Day Adventist himself. Rice announced to his startled congregation that Wright was a sinner, an irreligious woman who did not observe the Sabbath. The denunciation caused temporary confusion but failed to deflect Wright. She even secured Rice's church—the deacons overruling their pastor—for her school's closing exercises. "I do not believe in denominational schools," she affirmed. When wealthy Dr. Kellogg offered her financial support on the condition that she affiliate her school with his church, she declined.[35]

Having begun Denmark Industrial School on the first floor of a grocery store owned by a sympathetic German woman, Wright moved it onto the Mayfield tract. In 1898 she managed an eight-month term— "the longest a school has ever [been] know[n] to run in these parts"— and made eager plans for improving her work. The school farm, she told Washington, would yield "enough . . . cotton to pay the salaries of two teachers for another term and sufficient food to keep five teachers and four students." Wright spent the summer canning fruit, despite a recurrent fever brought on by the notoriously unhealthy low-country climate. "As I do not get a salary and my means are none, I will have to remain and trust God for whatever may come." By tapping into Tuskegee's network of northern white contributors, and by mobilizing local support, mainly from blacks, Wright paid the balance on Mayfield's land and expanded her school. By 1900 it enrolled over three hundred pupils and employed five teachers. Ralph Voorhees, a New Jersey businessman, subsequently endowed it with four hundred additional acres of land and financed the construction of dormitories, a hospital, and other buildings. When Wright died in 1906, Voorhees Normal and Industrial School was flourishing.[36]

In cultivating state senator Mayfield, Wright followed the advice of Washington's "Atlanta Compromise" to the letter. Virtually all the founders of industrial schools recruited a southern white man—preferably a planter and prominent Democrat—to vouch for and support them. Mayfield, wrote Washington, was a "high-toned, clean, unselfish and liberal Southern white man."[37]

In the eyes of Washington's critics, however, the readiness of avowed white supremacists to support schools like Voorhees showed that "industrial education" played into the hands of the Negro's enemies by furnishing blacks with second-class education designed to keep them in economic and political subjection. It was certainly the case that southern whites sometimes backed "little Tuskegees" in order to weaken the influence of northern-controlled mission schools. South Carolina's superintendent of schools praised Voorhees as "the best Negro school in the state" but termed Schofield Normal and Industrial School in Aiken—headed by a northern white woman and sponsored by Pennsylvania Quakers—as a "curse to the state."[38]

At a time when the missionary impulse was waning, however, and when northern philanthropists were telling blacks to accept disenfranchisement and segregation, the founders of independent schools had little option but to seek the endorsement of powerful southern whites. Their strategy of aligning with the ruling Democrats often entailed, in the words of W. T. B. Williams, "humility and subserviency," and it always angered some portion of the black community. Yet men like Mayfield enabled black schools to survive in areas of intense white hostility to black education. To dismiss them as mere white supremacists is to misread the politics of the time and does them a disservice. Mayfield not only furnished Voorhees with political cover, he even provided physical protection. On more than one occasion, hearing rumors of an impending attack upon the school, Mayfield sat up all night with a friend, guns at the ready. Violating the racial etiquette of the times, Mayfield taught his sons to address the Voorhees principal as "Miss Wright." The main alternative to the sympathetic paternalism of a Mayfield was the hostile racism of a Cole Blease, who in his inaugural address as governor of South Carolina opined that when "the people of this country began to educate the Negro they made a serious and grave mistake."[39]

In a sense, the clear superiority of the "Little Tuskegees" over the rural public schools made the debate over industrial education academic. The mere fact of being a graded school with proper teaching facilities made Voorhees better than any one- or two-teacher elementary school. Moreover, Voorhees was the only school in Bamberg County where blacks could progress beyond the eighth grade—a situation that obtained into the 1950s—and its boarding facilities enabled children from many miles away to attend. "Voorhees reached down into the Allendale swamps and backwoods," testified Lewis K. McMillan, "and rescued me at the age of 11 from the primitive life to which my community, my county, and my section had damned me."[40]

William J. Edwards, who founded Snow Hill Normal and Industrial Institute in Wilcox County, Alabama, "in an old dilapidated room with one teacher and three students," discovered a white patron on the very plantation where his parents had labored as slaves and where he had spent much of his childhood. Like nearly all the founders of "little Tuskegees," the overcoming of early hardships endowed Edwards with formidable determination. He lost his mother before his first birthday and his father abandoned the family. A grandmother then raised him, but died when Edwards was ten. Taken in by an aunt, he was stricken with scrofula, which made him lame, and underwent a series of painful operations. On his first attempt to reach Tuskegee Institute, he walked fifty miles but then became discouraged and turned back. A second effort failed when his family persuaded him to donate his savings—all of three dollars—toward the purchase of a clock. After picking cotton to recover his squandered savings, Edwards finally reached Tuskegee in 1889. He stayed for four years. Shortly before graduating, he prevailed upon his former landlord, R. O. Simpson, to lend him the money to buy a suit.[41]

Thoroughly converted to Washington's ideas, Edwards returned to Wilcox County in 1893 and began teaching in a public school. He also repaid R. O. Simpson, who was so impressed by the change Tuskegee had wrought in Edwards that he invited the young teacher to open a school on his plantation, donating land and furnishing a schoolhouse. Over the years Simpson, a wealthy Black Belt planter, worked closely with Edwards to make the school succeed. He gave it more land, chaired its board of trustees, and generally championed the cause of black education. A mixture of religious humanitarianism and business acumen seems to have guided Simpson. He admitted to the exploitative nature of sharecropping, from which he personally benefited, and he wished to discourage black migration. "But I have been interested in the [Negro] race ever since I became a Christian. . . . The white people should make up their minds to live in peace with them and do away with race prejudices." Booker T. Washington was delighted with Edwards's success in cultivating this white-bearded Confederate veteran. "We must encourage such men as Mr. Simpson wherever we can find them in the South."[42]

The support of Snow Hill's blacks enabled Edwards to sustain and expand his school. Women "gave suppers, fairs, and picnics . . . to raise money" for the school. Local men turned out for a "house-raising" whenever a new building had to be constructed. Edwards himself supplied much of the lumber, spending his first summers working in a sawmill and receiving his pay in kind. His own extended family supplied many of the school's first pupils.[43]

But some blacks opposed Edwards. When Snow Hill first opened, many parents forbade Edwards to "work" their children, "stating as their objection that their children had been working all their lives and that they did not mean to send them to school to learn to work." Edwards attributed the opposition to "illiterate preachers and incompetent teachers." A loyal member of the AME Church, Edwards resisted pressure to affiliate his school with any denomination. Moreover, Edwards, like Washington, regarded the emotional excesses whipped up by Baptist and Methodist preachers as degrading, enervating, and time wasting. He once witnessed a "union meeting of two churches" at which six ministers each preached for an hour, prolonging the service until two in the morning. He found it difficult to decide what offended him more, the verbosity of the preachers or their ignorance. "Their texts were as often taken from the blue-back speller as from the Bible, and sometimes this would be held upside down."[44]

Edwards answered his critics by his actions. He created a school "thoroughly religious in spirit" but "free from . . . 'isms.'" In addition to industrial training, Snow Hill offered sound teaching in academic subjects. Edwards founded a Black Belt Improvement Society to help sharecroppers buy their own land, and the school purchased half of Simpson's plantation, twenty-four hundred acres of land, to further this project. To help meet the school's spiraling costs—eleven thousand dollars a year by 1900—Edwards spent summers in the North, raising money while he attended summer school at Harvard. By 1915, Snow Hill Institute embraced twenty-four buildings, a thousand acres of land, four hundred students, and twenty-two staff. It boasted the first, and for many years the only, brick schoolhouse in Wilcox County.[45]

A third Washington disciple, Charles P. Adams, had the misfortune to run afoul of black Baptists while lacking a strong white patron such as S. G. Mayfield or Randall O. Simpson. Indeed, he evoked such antipathy from blacks that only with the utmost difficulty did his school survive. Born in 1873 on a plantation in West Baton Rouge Parish, Louisiana, Adams, like Edwards, suffered early misfortunes that a grandmother helped him overcome. When Adams lost his mother and younger brother to fire, his grandmother—who had borne eight children by her master—took him in. This resourceful woman was a successful farmer and taught Adams how to grow crops. Turning into a giant of a man—he stood six feet ten inches tall and weighed three hundred pounds—Adams made money farming and, with an uncle, bought a hundred acres of prime delta land. However, he wanted to become a lawyer, and—perhaps misunderstanding Washington's educational mission—entered Tuskegee Institute in 1896. Five years later, Washington talked him out of going to Howard University Law School and sent him instead to Lincoln Parish, Louisiana, where a group of black farmers had clubbed together as the Farmers Relief Association to buy twenty-four acres of land and put up a school building. They wrote to Tuskegee for a teacher. "The race needs your service right here in the South," Washington told Adams. In 1901 Adams started teaching at the Allen Greene Normal and Industrial Institute. A second teacher taught agriculture, a third domestic science.

Within two years, however, Adams had fallen out with his board of trustees. Local Baptist ministers wanted a denominational school, independent of white control, that emphasized religious training and academic subjects. But they saw Adams creating a "little Tuskegee," and then organizing a new board of directors composed mainly of white people. There ensued a rancorous and long-running dispute. The original directors of the Farmers Relief Association sued Adams to regain control of the school. Adams won in the courts but his victory availed nothing; his opponents still owned the school and were determined to oust him. During one of his absences they forcibly removed the acting principal at gunpoint. In 1905 Adams started again on a new site, founding the North Louisiana Agricultural and Industrial Institute. He won a small subsidy from the Lincoln Parish School Board, and a wealthy California woman, Fidelia Jewett, gave regular donations. Slowly a small village, called Grambling, grew up around the school.

But Adams faced unrelenting opposition in a bitterly divided community. Although the Allen Greene school was "dirty and low in its standards," complained an officer of the Phelps-Stokes Fund, it commanded support among blacks "because it is of the prevailing denomination . . . and also because its principal is a shrewd and crafty manipulator of public affairs." Situated less than three miles apart, both schools suffered. A proposal to merge them fell victim to the old quarrel. "It seems almost impossible for Adams to overcome the prejudice that exists against him in the community," reported a state education official. His school, although superior to its rival, failed to prosper. In 1915 it consisted of a poorly built wooden structure of two stories, two "very small buildings used for a shop and a boys' dormitory," and two hundred acres of land. Six thousand dollars could have bought the lot. Visiting the school a year later, a northern visitor reported that the farm was idle because the mules and cows had all died through carelessness.[46]

Even if they silenced doubters and overcame denominational opposition, the founders of "little Tuskegees" faced the intractable problem of money. The needs of industrial schools—for land and for equipment—were far larger than those of purely academic schools. Moreover, unlike the world of business, success in education did not pay. The more an independent school grew, the greater its expenses. If it adhered to the principle of nonsectarianism, moreover, an industrial school had no churches or mission boards to support it. Student tuition fees could offset only a fraction of overall running costs. Industrial schools therefore became increasingly dependent upon private donations from the North, and they had to devote enormous amounts of time and energy to soliciting funds. Every year they sent out thousands of standardized appeal letters, often accompanied by lavishly illustrated newsletters. Founders also kept up a ceaseless personal correspondence with wealthy and well-known Americans, appealing for money, public endorsements, or service on a board of trustees. Every summer, schools sent singing quartets, modeled after the Fisk Jubilee Singers, to tour northern cities and vacation resorts. And founders or professional fundraisers spent month after month in travel, mainly in New York and New England, speaking at churches, hotels, meeting halls, and private homes—anywhere they might encounter wealthy northerners.

It was an uphill struggle. The smaller industrial schools competed not only among themselves but also against two older and bigger institutions, Hampton and Tuskegee, that dominated the field of industrial education and received the lion's share of philanthropic support. Moreover, many whites who had given in the past became increasingly cynical about the endless appeals from the South. Impatience with southern inefficiency, and ire over the fraudulent fundraising activities of a small number of confidence men, contributed to a feeling that much of the money that flowed South was wasted. Visiting some of the industrial schools in 1916, and talking to their founders, a professor of rural economics at the University of Chicago expressed his exasperation: "[T]hey are so courteous and such flatterers that one needs a different experience from any I have had to deal with them. I think they bluff and work with us Northerners in a way to get back a part of what the Southerners have worked out of them. I have not found an institution supported by Northern money that seems to get good value for the money expended." To make matters worse, the pot of private philanthropy was shrinking. As the Progressive Era unfolded, other worthy causes competed for the generosity of public-spirited northerners. Then the First World War brought a sharp decline in contributions and fueled inflation. The "little Tuskegees" faced financial disaster. The philanthropic foundations, despite approving of industrial education, were reluctant to rescue them.[47]

In an age when education was rapidly evolving, private schools had to adapt or die. By 1920 the "Tuskegee Idea" was becoming obsolete. State education departments now required public school teachers to measure up to higher academic standards. Blacks themselves wanted schools to teach the full range of subjects that white schools offered. And the big foundations like the General Education Board focused on the development of public schools, teacher training, and higher education. For most private schools, adapting to change simply meant adding grades, adding subjects, and shedding expensive industrial classes. They could evolve into high schools, normal schools, and "junior colleges." Tuskegee and Hampton—their massive endowments made them virtually invulnerable—could become colleges.

Change proved much more difficult, however, for the "Little Tuskegees." Their fixed costs inexorably mounted at precisely the time that industrial education was losing its popularity and utility. Some, like Voorhees, survived by compromising their nondenominational status and affiliating with a mission board. Others, like Grambling, won state funding and eventually became state colleges. Many, like Snow Hill, ended up becoming public schools—losing their independence, missionary spirit, and sense of identity.[48]

For some of the founders, the results were tragic. Snow Hill Institute, for example, was "hopelessly mired in debt" by 1920, and its founder, William J. Edwards, became embittered and desperate. His behavior betrayed symptoms of paranoia, and in 1924 he suffered a nervous breakdown. After a two-year struggle to regain his health, he resigned—was forced out—as principal of the school he founded. He bequeathed to his successor debts of twenty thousand dollars. Jackson Davis of the General Education Board reckoned Snow Hill beyond redemption: "There is a kind of 'jinx' about all these industrial schools. They pattern each other after Tuskegee and Hampton in the matter of size and scope . . . This leads to unfortunate mistakes . . . and to extravagance in that their whole efforts are so scattered and spread that too much of the money is spent for the expense of collecting and administering and too little for teaching." The founder's wife, Susie Edwards, wrote to Mrs. Anson Phelps Stokes in a pathetic request for financial assistance. On the advice of Thomas Jesse Jones, chief agent of the Phelps-Stokes Fund, she spurned Mrs. Edwards's plea. In a terrible irony, those most fully committed to Washington's educational ideals often proved the least able to survive change.[49]

For many founders of "Normal and Industrial" schools, however, industrial education was a flexible concept. Most of them came from mission schools and were never indoctrinated into the "Tuskegee Idea." Some, like Simon G. Atkins, used it to cloak their goal of promoting higher education. Others, like Mary McLeod Bethune, pursued the Washingtonian philosophy with greater conviction, but moved with the times, adapted their curricula, and devised a strategy for survival. Many of these hardened veterans allied guile and diplomacy to sheer determination. Some went to extraordinary lengths to preserve their independence—sometimes losing sight of their original educational mission and transforming their schools beyond recognition.

Few founders proved as adaptable or astute as Rev. James Solomon Russell, who in 1888 founded St. Paul's Normal and Industrial School in Lawrenceville, Virginia. An Episcopalian minister—friend and protégé of Giles B. Cooke—Russell emphasized industrial education because it was politically and financially advantageous to do so. By 1915 St. Paul's was a thriving school with fifteen teachers and four hundred pupils. Like Hampton Institute, it placed its boys under military-style discipline. The Jones report pronounced its industrial work "well done." However, at St. Paul's the commitment to industrial education, unlike at so many "N&I" schools, was not merely cosmetic.

Russell found a way of making it pay, and pay handsomely, by having his students do contract work for local employers. Indeed, this work became so profitable that the school paid taxes of a thousand dollars a year on the earnings of its industrial department. The American Church Institute for Negroes (ACIN), the Episcopalian body that sponsored the school, criticized Russell and his family for waxing fat off student labor, condemning St. Paul's' version of "industrial education" as educationally worthless. But with the support of local whites, Russell survived, "shrewdly shifting his public posture from accommodationist to race leader as it suited his purposes." Retiring in 1929, he handed the school to his son. A grandson took over in 1971. Now St. Paul's College, the school is flourishing.[50]

Emmanuel M. McDuffie showed a similar knack for survival. The school that he founded in North Carolina, Laurinburg Normal and Industrial Institute, seemed like a typical "Little Tuskegee." McDuffie kept it alive through craft, persistence, and luck, and passed control to a son. In the process of survival, however, the school underwent a metamorphosis.

McDuffie's early life resembled that of his mentor, William J. Edwards. He grew up in Wilcox County, Alabama, in what he called "the most adverse conditions." He lost his father when he was barely six months old, his mother when he was ten. He and six siblings were taken under the wing of their grandmother, "Aunt Polly," a sturdy farmer who put them to work in the fields. After five years, however, the grandmother died, "leaving a house full of children to shift for themselves." With only the clothes on his back, McDuffie entered Snow Hill Institute. William Edwards, like Booker T. Washington, used Sunday evening chapel to preach the gospels of Christian service and industrial education, "admonishing his students to . . . start their life's work among the lowly in the rural districts." In 1904 Edwards received a request from a black businessman and former politician, Walter P. Evans, to send a teacher who could build an "industrial school" in Laurinburg, in North Carolina's Black Belt. Edwards sent McDuffie.[51]

Having just come through a period of exhilarating political triumph and shattering political defeat, blacks in Laurinburg were rudderless.

Many treated McDuffie with suspicion. They resented his abjuration of politics and the way he cultivated the town's leading Democrats. Like Edwards in Alabama, McDuffie encountered opposition to industrial education. When he started his school, only seven children showed up. "The people had no confidence in me." In time, however, he built a black constituency. Under McDuffie's leadership, blacks defied their poverty to erect a substantial school building, largely through their own voluntary labor. In 1906 McDuffie incorporated the school and, "in spite of some devious methods and questionable practices," made it an effective institution. Although nearly all the work was at elementary level, the school was a graded one, and its term ran to nine months. Moreover, its boarding school offered students in outlying farms the chance of a better education. In 1914 the school boasted thirteen teachers and 110 pupils. It also operated a hospital. Local whites expressed their approval by giving McDuffie's school a small subsidy, $750 a year at first, to educate the town's four hundred black children.

This act of apparent generosity, however, masked fundamental problems with the school. Rather than provide a public school for blacks, the town of Laurinburg chose to subsidize McDuffie's school. In the 1900s, when public schools offered a school term of only four months, and when whites refused to build black high schools, this arrangement might have been attractive to blacks. But as public education in North Carolina improved, Laurinburg's subsidy to McDuffie's school looked increasingly meager. Whites in Laurinburg seemed to regard the payment as the "portion" of local school taxes paid by blacks. This assumption ignored other taxes paid by blacks and overlooked the contribution of black labor to white wealth. Besides, the division of taxes by race was illegal under state and federal law. By 1926 the town of Laurinburg allocated McDuffie's school two thousand dollars a year, far less than the sums expended by other communities to support public schools for blacks. At a time when other counties were building black "training schools" (quasi high schools), blacks in Laurinburg became increasingly unhappy with the McDuffie school. Several, including W. P. Evans, complained to the state department of education.

McDuffie's management of Laurinburg N&I deepened their concerns. Every year the school mailed appeals and newsletters to the North. Critics charged them with making exaggerated and even fictitious claims. Others objected to having their children represented as charity cases. Worse, there was no public scrutiny of the school's financial accounts. McDuffie assembled a board of trustees, but it appeared to consist of poorly educated black farmers and "a few persons from the North, who seem to know very little about the affairs of the school." This rubber-stamp board fueled suspicion that McDuffie ran the school as a moneymaking venture for the benefit of his family. He was rumored to be siphoning off money to buy farmland in North Carolina and real estate in Chicago. By the mid-1920s, black dissatisfaction with McDuffie's school, and with the lack of a public school, was rife.

Yet McDuffie could count upon influential whites. Indeed, those with long political memories heard echoes of their 1890s nightmare, the Republican-Populist Fusion government, in the opposition to McDuffie's school. Lawyer and former schools superintendent Maxcy L. John attributed black dissension to W. P. Evans, formerly a powerful black politician, who had served as a magistrate in Laurinburg when the Fusionists controlled Richmond County. In 1899 John wrote a bill that consolidated Democratic control in Laurinburg by making it the seat of a new political entity, Scotland County. Damning Evans as an "ever present and continuing agitator," John praised McDuffie as a political and economic realist. "He believes in work for the laboring man and tries to make the boys and girls see that the most of them must go to work and work hard at difficult and often dirty work." Above all, McDuffie knew how to get along with white people. "He is a quiet, capable man, says enough but is never talkative. He knows the race and understands the necessity for contacts that must be without friction."

Fending off criticisms from blacks—he did have his black supporters—McDuffie continued to receive public subsidies. By the 1930s Laurinburg and Scotland County were supporting, maintaining, and improving the school property. The state began subsidizing teachers' salaries and providing bus transportation for pupils. Slowly waking up to its duty toward blacks, however, the school board negotiated to rent or buy Laurinburg Institute for the purpose of converting it into a public school. The discussions dragged on from the late 1930s to the late 1940s, with no agreement reached. Meanwhile, the annual subsidy to McDuffie's school ballooned to sixty-seven thousand dollars. The school also acquired a hefty sum from the Duke Endowment Fund. Finally, in 1952–53, Laurinburg opened four black public schools. Overnight, the enrollment at Laurinburg Institute, previously eleven hundred children, all but vanished. Now in the charge of Frank H. McDuffie, the founder's son, the school found itself employing fourteen teachers—seven of them McDuffie family members—to teach eighty-seven fee-paying children. An official of the General Education Board described the school as a relic of a bygone era, facing "a present which is pathetic and a future in which I see little promise."[52]

Logically, McDuffie's school ought to have suffered the fate of hundreds of other black private schools, withering and dying. Yet Laurinburg Normal and Industrial Institute clung stubbornly to life. It reinvented itself as a private preparatory boarding school for boys and girls. The fact that that jazz trumpeter and "bebop" pioneer "Dizzy" Gillespie attended the school in the 1930s proved a boon. As Gillespie rose to international stardom as one of the all-time jazz greats, the school featured him ever more prominently in its literature. Moreover, although he spent only three years there, Gillespie gave generously to the school. The school also developed a rich tradition in basketball, producing prizewinning teams and star players, and instituting an additional year of school to coach athletes for college admission. Enrollment remained erratic, however, and in the 1990s the school appeared to be once again tottering toward the grave. Nevertheless, in 2004 Laurinburg Institute celebrated its centenary under Frank H. "Bishop" McDuffie, the founder's grandson. Enrolling 135 students, who pay fees of fourteen thousand dollars a year, it is one of only four historically black boarding schools in the United States. Having survived the Depression, resisted absorption into the public schools, and weathered the civil rights movement, it is the only school of its kind in the South.[53]

No "Normal and Industrial Institute" underwent a more dizzying transformation than Palmer Memorial Institute. The creation of Charlotte Hawkins Brown, it lasted for almost seventy years, closing in 1971. It might have endured longer but for the fact that Brown was a woman. Private schools like St. Paul's and Laurinburg survived partly because their founders had sons and grandsons to continue their work. Even state colleges—Southern University, for example—produced father-son dynasties. But the women who founded schools could rarely combine their educational work with marriage and motherhood. They either remained single or had brief, unhappy marriages. Brown married twice, but both unions were short-lived. She had no children. Her school became so dependent upon Brown's domineering leadership that it survived her death by only ten years.

Brown was born in Henderson, North Carolina, in 1883, the illegitimate child of Carrie Hawkins. Her mother, although born free in 1865, was raised in the "big house" by her white aunt, Jane Hawkins, whose brother was Carrie's white father, Charlotte's grandfather. Although very dark-complexioned, Brown's white ancestry was a source of lifelong pride to her—she claimed descent from the Elizabethan navigator and slave trader John Hawkins. And because her mother and grandmother remained so close to the white Hawkinses, and were helped by them in freedom, Brown bore no ill will toward the whites who had owned her family. She heard no "horrible stories about slavery." Rather, she associated bondage with the refined culture and patrician behavior of "one of the finest white families in the south." She described her blue-eyed grandmother as "an aristocrat to the manor born."[54]

Yet when she started teaching in 1901, Brown did not know the South well. Carrie Hawkins had taken Charlotte to live in Cambridge, Massachusetts, when she was five years old. There, Brown received the benefit of what may have been the best public school system in America. Sailing through grammar school, she graduated from high school with flying colors at the age of seventeen. She wanted to attend Radcliffe, but her mother regarded four years of private college as a luxury, so instead she went to Massachusetts State Normal School in Salem. She received encouragement and financial help from Alice Freeman Palmer, the president of Wellesley College, whose interest in Brown had been piqued by the sight of a black girl engrossed in Virgil while pushing a baby carriage. The American Missionary Association offered Brown a teaching position at Bethany Institute, an elementary school in North Carolina, near the hamlet of Sedalia. She curtailed her studies and returned to the South, carrying with her a piece of cautionary advice from her mother: "Try to make friends of these southern white people, for they can make or break you."[55]

Brown took those words to heart. She was moving from the freest part of America to a state where blacks were still in shock from the Wilmington riot, the white supremacy election, and the disenfranchisement of black voters. Growing up in Cambridge, Brown had been blissfully unaware of racial discrimination. She lived in a city where a "beautiful brown-skinned woman," Maria Baldwin, headed a public school attended by white children and taught by white teachers. That would be inconceivable in the South and impermissible even in New York. Brown later claimed—conceding "it is hard to believe"— that not one gesture or word ever made her feel "any different from anybody else." And if she ever encountered the color discrimination that African Americans sometimes practiced among themselves, she never referred to it. Any lingering suspicion that her own dark skin might prove a handicap was dispelled when she attended a public lecture on "The Progress of the Negro in America" at which the speaker showed pictures of the southern teachers Lucy Laney and J. C. Price, both of them very dark.[56]

Brown was appalled to find that Bethany Institute, despite being an AMA school, was housed in an unpainted, weather-beaten church building, with several broken windows, standing in a weed-infested yard. She was even more shocked when, after she had spent a year grading the students, creating dormitories for them, and moving the school out of the church, the AMA ended its financial support. Her prickly attitude, in addition, made a cross for her own back. Bristling at whites who addressed her by her first name, "I was constantly being insulting and insulted." Locals called her the "Yankee Huzzy."[57]

But Brown wielded her formidable determination to create a bigger and better school of which she would be the principal. In 1902 she returned to New England where, drawing upon her slight acquaintance-ship with Alice Freeman Palmer—who died that very year—she contacted potential benefactors and supporters. She also drew upon her mother's advice about white southerners. In nearby Greensboro, she unveiled her plans for "Palmer Memorial Institute" to Lula McIver, the wife of Charles D. McIver, the first president of the State Normal and Industrial School for Girls and current president of the Southern Educational Association. Impressed by Brown's enthusiasm, McIver "kept her for more than an hour, offering advice on the best way to win friends." With the endorsement of Lula McIver—and, after a determined courtship by Brown, that of Charles McIver—other whites came on board. Greensboro lawyer Frank Hobgood chaired a board of trustees and incorporated the school. County school superintendent Thomas Foust secured a small public subsidy. This vote of confidence from local whites was essential to securing northern support. A group of northern women formed a fundraising committee, the Sedalia Club, to raise money throughout New England. Endorsements from nationally known leaders—Seth Low, Charles W. Elliott, Sara Roosevelt—were gold dust. By 1914, contributions from the North accounted for half of the school's total income. In 1915 Booker T. Washington gave the most valuable endorsement of all: "You have one of the best and most useful of the smaller schools in the South."[58]

It has been suggested that Brown duped Washington into thinking that she had created an industrial school when in fact Palmer's primary emphasis was academic—that Brown, like Simon G. Atkins, used Washingtonian rhetoric as a smoke screen. This seems unlikely, for Washington was well informed about Palmer's work. To be sure, Brown may have been responding, in a purely pragmatic way, to northern supporters who gave money for the specific purpose of promoting industrial education. Yet her admiration for Washington seems to have been sincere. Brown's flattery apart, Palmer had several things to commend itself to Washington. It was the product of black initiative, had no church affiliation, offered industrial training, and operated a productive home farm.[59]

By then Palmer Memorial Institute consisted of seven well-trained teachers, 143 pupils, a handful of wooden buildings, and 350 acres of land. It was an excellent elementary school that also offered four years of high school. Of those who graduated—seven a year on average—

the women became housekeepers or teachers, the men artisans, farmers, and school principals. After the First World War, Brown replaced its wooden buildings with elegant brick ones and Palmer became an accredited high school.

But North Carolina was rapidly improving its public schools, and Palmer could not stand still for long. It needed a new educational role. Adding a junior college level, it tried to carve out a distinctive identity in the increasingly crowded higher education market by teaching "culture" to affluent black students. In the late 1930s, Brown gave Palmer another makeover. Battered by the Depression and failing to recruit enough junior college students, it reverted to being a high school. But it then lost most of its students when Guilford County opened a public high school for blacks. Abandoning the last vestiges of industrial education—paying full-time workers, rather than students, to run the school plant and farm—Brown tried to persuade North Carolina to adopt Palmer as a state women's college. Rebuffed, she converted it into an elite boarding school, "The School of Personal Charm," restricting its enrollment to 150 pupils and charging steep fees.

Brown's emphasis upon—obsession with—culture defined the new-look Palmer Memorial Institute. Culture meant an appreciation of music, literature, the fine arts, and, above all, manners. Brown combined New England education with southern charm: "a cultural program to prepare Negro youth to fit into human society with the rough edges removed." Upon their arrival, girls received the leaflet "The Earmarks of a Lady," boys "The Earmarks of a Gentleman." In 1940 Brown gained national fame when she spoke of "The Negro and the Social Graces" on national radio. The following year she published a best-selling booklet, *The Correct Thing to Do, to Say, to Wear.* It became Palmer's bible. "The little courtesies, the gentle voice, correct grooming, a knowledge of when to sit, stand, open and close a door, the correct attitude to persons in authority; good manners in public places . . . will go a long way in securing that recognition of ability needed to cope with human society, and will remove some of the commonest objections to our presence in large numbers."[60]

Brown's commitment to educating the black elite was a complete reversal of her original mission. Instead of teaching the barefoot children of Guilford County farmers, Brown's school picked students from "the very best families" and sent most of them to college. In 1940 Palmer enrolled students from twenty-one states, the District of Columbia, and the Canal Zone. By 1950, one student recalled, "Graduation exercises looked like a General Motors reunion—there were mostly Cadillacs with black suited chauffeurs. . . . We represented the collective efforts of the world's richest black bourgeoisie." When Palmer students wanted to see a movie, "rather than sit in the segregated section, we would rent the movie-theater for the day." A far cry indeed from Booker T. Washington's commitment to uplifting the masses.[61]

ACCORDING to a study published by the U.S. Bureau of Education in 1917, many of the black-taught private schools were poorly managed, badly taught, and "enslaved to ancient languages." Moreover, the schools that enjoyed the most independence from white control—especially those run by the black churches—often betrayed the most glaring weaknesses. White officials of the education foundations, who were attempting to modernize and systematize public education in the South, saw black private schools as nuisances, obstacles to the development of a proper public school system. "Let most of them die," urged James H. Dillard, director of the Slater Fund, in 1915. "They do not deserve help and I would not give them a cent."[62]

These criticisms were overwrought. Whatever their shortcomings, the private schools were rarely as bad as the public schools and many were much better. Moreover, the argument that the private schools impeded the improvement of public schools betrayed a lack of political understanding. The relationship of the private schools to the public schools was complex. The South's parsimony and poverty fostered a hybrid system of public education that mixed public and private funding. When school boards provided only a teacher's salary, with blacks themselves building and equipping the schoolhouse, as well as paying for a longer school term, the resulting school was part public, part private. An awkward but accurate description would be "quasi-public." In a similar fashion, private schools sometimes attracted a degree of public support that made them "quasi-private." Throughout much of the rural South, county school boards gave subsidies to black private schools rather than build public high schools. When white school boards eventually abandoned their opposition to black secondary education, they often bought private schools for a pittance and converted them into public schools. Thus the private schools functioned as institutional bridges between the establishment of black common schools and the creation of black high schools.

The white officials of the General Education Board saw things rather differently. They lamented the fact that black private schools reached only a small proportion of black children but virtually monopolized northern philanthropic efforts for blacks. They complained, too, that the existence of private schools provided a ready excuse for the southern states to neglect public education for blacks, especially the provision of secondary schools and colleges. In Augusta, Georgia, for example, the school board argued that the city's three private schools for blacks allowed it to abolish the black public high school without engaging in illegal discrimination. The U.S. Supreme Court agreed. In New Orleans, according to James H. Dillard, the existence of "four so-called universities . . . was the cause of the city's neglecting anything for the Negro children . . . above the fifth and sixth grades." And the situation in Chester, South Carolina, could be found in many parts of the rural South: the existence of a private school, Brainerd Institute, gave the school board an excuse to decline funding *any* public schools for blacks.[63]

It is impossible to prove or disprove the contention that southern whites would have done more for black public schools in the absence of black private schools. But the weight of evidence suggests that, take away the private schools, they still would have done very little. Knowing what we do about opposition to black education—especially "higher education," defined as anything above the elementary level— it seems unlikely that black private schools inhibited the establishment of equivalent public schools. Moreover, there was no geographical correlation between the presence of black private schools and the absence or presence of decent public schools for blacks. Whites who were more sympathetic to the education of blacks established relatively good public schools; whites who were less sympathetic did not.

Having black private schools nearby made little difference. The fact that southern states began to spend much less on black schools relative to white schools after 1900 can hardly be explained by the presence of back private schools. It had everything to do with the disenfranchisement of black voters.

The GEB's skeptical assessment of black private schools, moreover, was not free of racial bias. It mirrored the view of most white southerners that blacks should receive an elementary school education based upon "industrial education." In their eagerness to appease southern racism, the northern-born officials of the GEB allowed themselves to be misled by white southerners' own explanations for their neglect of black schools. And a lack of faith in independent black leadership colored the GEB's assessment of the private schools. Whites, it believed, should determine the character of the education blacks received.

The blacks who founded private schools believed that, far from damaging public education, they were trying to remedy the defects of public education. White hostility to the education of blacks, and white indifference to public education as a whole, created the need for private schools. But for the existence of private schools, there would have been no decent schools at all in much of the South. This was equally true after 1900, when blacks could no longer vote, and when improvements in black schools always lagged twenty years behind improvements in white schools. Even Wallace Buttrick of the GEB acknowledged that the "pressure of northern public sentiment"—which mainly expressed itself in support for private schools—stimulated public support for black education.

The history of institutions like Slater Industrial Academy shows that many state colleges for blacks originated in private initiatives by blacks. The same was true of many public high schools. Southern whites "rarely if ever originate such institutions," an AMA official noted in 1880. "I know of no instance when they have erected such school buildings as they erect for their own race." In founding private schools, therefore, black teachers made a substantial and pioneering contribution to the development of the South's public schools and state universities.[64]

The example of Palmer Memorial Institute, however, revealed a paradox of the private school movement. Private schools represented a creative response to black ambition when the public schools ranged from bad to nonexistent. Yet they also sowed the seeds of class inequality. In charging tuition fees, they gave an advantage to black families who could afford to pay for schooling. Most black families could not or would not. Moreover, educational advantage translated into economic advantage. In dispensing an education that was usually better than that provided by the public schools, private schools widened the distance between the two groups. Most members of the black middle class of teachers, preachers, small businessmen, postal workers, and Pullman Car porters received a least part of their education in private schools. And although the middle class justified their relatively privileged position by espousing an ideology of racial uplift, private schooling also appealed to rank self-interest. "I have never sent one of my children to a public school . . . in my life," boasted black congressman George H. White of North Carolina. Like whites who had money, he explained, many prosperous blacks did "not care to have their children go into the public school and be mixed up with the kind of pupils that are there."[65]

Despite their political naiveté and bias against black private schools, the officials of the General Education Board got one point right. The private schools would never reach more than a small minority of black children. In order to end mass illiteracy and improve education for the vast majority, there had to be more and better public schools. Such improvements would depend, overwhelmingly, upon black women.

CHAPTER SIX

The Faith of Women

Sometimes the prejudice is so great I feel that I can't stand it a day longer but then I look into their innocent faces and realize their needs and determine to stick to it whatever the cost.

Charlotte Hawkins Brown

Mrs. Nesmith, Jeanes teacher, Berkeley County, South Carolina, 1925.

*Papers of Jackson Davis, MSS3072, Special Collections
Library, University of Virginia*

In 1926 SARAH WEBB, a nervous teenager, stood before "fifteen pupils, all different grades, in one room." The schoolhouse was a Baptist church on a low hill outside Eufala, Alabama. Like many girls who chose teaching, Sarah was guided by her mother, Lizzie, who had completed nine grades at a good school in Columbus, Georgia, with the encouragement of her employers, a white doctor and his wife. After marrying an AME minister, Lizzie Webb took in washing, helped run the family farm, and taught school. Lizzie gave up teaching when her husband's death gave her enough insurance money to buy land of her own. Her daughter took over the little church school. A few months later Sarah passed the state teachers' examination. Appointed to a public school at the age of only seventeen—she had lied about her age—Sarah faced "big, husky country boys and girls" who towered over her. "I didn't have any teacher training or anything to work with but what I made up myself."[1]

In 1930 nine-tenths of the region's 53,812 black public school teachers taught in elementary schools, and 86 percent of those teachers were women. The training of public school teachers improved markedly in the 1920s. Most teachers attended annual summer schools, and thanks to the expansion of higher education, an increasing proportion of new teachers had attended college. In North Carolina the percentage of teachers who had earned college degrees rose from 2.5

to 12.1 percent. Across the South, about 9 percent of black teachers held degrees. By 1930, 42 percent of the South's black teachers had attended college for two years or more. The best-trained elementary school teachers were often products of the women-only missionary schools like Spelman College in Atlanta and Hartshorn Memorial College in Richmond. But many of the state colleges and normal schools were rapidly improving.

Most black teachers, however, were like Sarah Webb: they had a limited education and little or no professional training. The worst educated were to be found in the one- and two-teacher schoolhouses of the rural South. Dotting the countryside, these little schoolhouses accounted for 82 percent of the South's black schools and employed half of all the elementary teachers. In 1930 only about a third of those teachers had gone beyond high school. The median level of black teachers' education in Arkansas, Florida, Georgia, and Mississippi was less than a year above high school. Across the South, more than half of all black rural teachers had failed to complete high school. Two-fifths had studied at high school for only two years. About a quarter had attended for one year or less. Fully two-thirds of the elementary school teachers had never undertaken practice teaching before starting their jobs. Tests administered in the 1930s assessed half of Mississippi's black teachers at the seventh-grade level or below. In 1950 the state agent for Negro schools complained that "some of these teachers cannot even read very well." Nevertheless, for all their educational shortcomings, the women who staffed the South's public schools represented the best-educated portion of the black population.[2]

The men who built America's public school systems had long regarded women teachers, employed at low wages, as the mainstay of mass education. The feminization of teaching cut across color lines. Well before the Civil War, white women outnumbered white men in the public schools of the North. The South was the only region in the country where, after 1865, men made up a majority of the public school teachers. By 1900, however, women outnumbered men in every southern state except for Arkansas and Tennessee. Ten years later, men constituted only a quarter of the teaching force, not far from the national average of one-fifth.[3]

From the outset, the white missionaries who planted universities and secondary schools in the South implemented the New England model of training women to be teachers. They generally steered women into the "normal" departments and selected men to be the favored few who received college training. The mission schools' interest in training black ministers strengthened the bias of their collegiate programs toward men. Atlanta University, the flagship, exemplified the pattern. Of the 485 students who graduated from its normal department between 1873 and 1910, women accounted for 96 percent. Of the 171 students who received college degrees, 78 percent were men.[4]

Educated black women, like their white counterparts, gravitated toward teaching because their opportunities for paid employment were so restricted. Professional occupations such as law and medicine were virtually closed to them. Other occupations prized by educated blacks—Pullman porter, letter carrier, railway mail clerk—were entirely closed. Men all but monopolized a large swathe of unskilled occupations, such as factory work, portering, and general laboring, that often paid more than teaching. One study from the 1930s indicated that the most highly educated black women, college graduates, had access to only half as many occupations as black men. Even in the field of teaching, women stood on the lower rungs of the occupational ladder. The vast majority of high school principals and college teachers were men; women made up the bulk of the far more numerous and much worse paid elementary school teachers.[5]

The rates at which black men and white men left teaching varied from state to state, but the overall pattern was clear. In Alabama in 1875, 38 percent of the white teachers and 23 percent of the black teachers were women; by 1911 women accounted for 65 percent of the white teachers and 69 percent of the black teachers. In Georgia, the proportion of white teachers who were women increased from 45 percent in 1893 to 73 percent in 1910; for black teachers the proportion increased from 51 percent to 82 percent. In the entire state, only 710 black men could be found teaching in 1910, half as many as twenty years earlier. Women were filling most of the new teaching posts and men were leaving the profession.[6]

By the twentieth century, education had become the special province of African American women. But women became the mainstay of black schooling at a time when racial discrimination was intensifying. Indeed, the abysmally low salaries paid to black women teachers provided clear evidence of how the disenfranchisement of black voters widened the disparity between white and black schools. In 1900 a black teacher earned about 60 percent of what a white teacher earned. By 1930 that teacher received only 45 percent of the white teacher's salary. The gap varied from state to state. It was largest, as one would expect, in the Deep South. South Carolina paid its black teachers less than a third of what it paid whites. But in absolute terms the lowest-paid teachers—of both races—hailed from Mississippi. There, black teachers earned an average of $175 a year, 41 percent of what a white Mississippi teacher earned, and a paltry 18 percent of the white southern average.[7]

The displacement of black men by black women was both cause and consequence of these low salaries. Poor pay drove men out of teaching, and the recruitment of women then furnished a pretext to drive wages down more. In 1900, for example, a black female teacher in Louisiana earned 85 percent of the black male average, 57 percent of the white female rate, and 44 percent of a white male teacher's pay. By 1920 she received only 43 percent of what a white female earned, and a scant 32 percent of the white male average. The First World War exacerbated the problem. The war-generated economic boom lured male teachers into better-paid occupations, and then fueled an inflation that further eroded teachers' salaries. The teacher shortage was so acute in 1919–20 that many schools had to close.[8]

Black women teachers therefore labored under a double disadvantage. Enduring the racial discrimination meted out to blacks, they also suffered from the prejudice that placed women behind men. They confronted a gap between black and white schools that was getting wider, they lagged farther and farther behind white teachers in pay, and they faced an educational bureaucracy of white men who generally ignored, belittled, or patronized them. Even in their own professional organizations, women teachers found that men occupied most positions of leadership. "No white woman has ever been called upon to bear what the Negro woman has borne," insisted Charlotte Hawkins Brown, "for added to the struggle of womanhood . . . to gain recognition in the affairs of state in America, the Negro woman has the handicap of color, prejudice, unjust discrimination, and lack of respect for her personality."[9]

Still, as they battled to gain professional recognition and improve their schools, black women teachers drew upon a number of social resources. Because gender roles were less blatantly unequal within the black community, it was easier for women teachers to assume positions of leadership. They could not be preachers in the mainstream churches, but the position of teacher ran a close second in terms of prestige and influence. Black women teachers could take advantage of the lingering paternalism that made white southerners—many of whom waxed lyrical over their "black Mammies"—more tolerant of assertiveness when it came from women. Hence, although there were strong parallels between the feminization of teaching in black schools and white schools, black women teachers influenced the education of African Americans in distinctive ways. Perhaps the most important was the passion and dedication they brought to their jobs. Dorothy Redus Robinson, who taught in Texas from 1928 until the early 1970s, frankly acknowledged that low salaries, limited education, inadequate schoolhouses, and official neglect handicapped and sometimes crippled black teachers. Nevertheless, "many of those teachers taught with a zeal and commitment . . . as though they felt a personal mandate to compensate for the areas of lack in the lives of their students."[10]

To be sure, the memories of retired teachers can be self-serving, and their recollections of black schools are much brighter than the grim assessments proffered by social scientists in the 1930s. Doubtless, as well, there were plenty of teachers who, like the one observed by anthropologist Hortense Powdermaker, were "not particularly interested in teaching." Nevertheless, the deep commitment displayed by many women teachers was not a fiction of nostalgic memoirists. It stemmed in large part from black women's strong belief in the value of education. Among the black middle and lower classes, women were usually more encouraging of schooling than men were. "It is the mothers who are most ambitious for their children," noted Powdermaker in her study of Sunflower County, Mississippi. "Almost every mother is ardent in her wish that her child should receive more education than she did, and thus gain the prospect of an easier and a happier life." By the twentieth century, daughters, who were more likely to inherit that enthusiasm, were better educated than their brothers.[11]

It is striking how prominently mothers figure in the memories of black teachers. James Solomon Russell, born a slave in Mecklenberg County, Virginia, recalled, "My mother often told me that she named me Solomon . . . because she had hoped and prayed that somehow I could be as wise as the Solomon of the Bible about whom she had heard the white minister preach and the Negro lay-reader exhort." Before there were any schools for blacks, she found whites to tutor Solomon. Then a freedmen's school opened. Said Russell, "My mother sent me every day, to learn my alphabet, and little more, at the hands of a teacher who had gone no further than the second grade. But I was going to school, and that is what counted most with my mother and me."[12]

Teachers often attributed their own faith in education to their mothers' resolve—a steely determination informed by religious faith—that at least some of their children would lead better lives. Mary McLeod Bethune described her mother, Patsy, as "one of those grand educated persons that did not have letters" but who possessed "a great vision, a great understanding of human nature." This former slave, the mother of seventeen children, cooked for her old master in Mayesville, South Carolina, until she saved enough money to buy five acres for a family home. Her mother's prayers, uttered in "lonely vigils when she thought everyone in the house was asleep," strengthened Bethune's own religious beliefs, shaping her conviction that education was a form of Christian service. Charlotte Hawkins Brown, the founder of Palmer Memorial Institute, recorded an almost identical memory: "hearing mother pray in the chamber above me that God might fulfill in my life what she wanted to do and could not."[13]

Tear-misted memories of praying, self-sacrificing mothers seem shot through with Victorian sentimentality and conventional piety. But there is no reason to doubt that many black teachers owed their careers, in the words of James Weldon Johnson, "to the type of mothers whose love completely surrounds their children and is all-pervading; mothers for whom sacrifice for the child means only an extension of love." Mary Holly Jones raised her children in a two-room rented shack in Greensboro, North Carolina, where the sweet fumes of tobacco factories melded with the smell of whisky from nearby saloons. "For her to breathe was to pray, and to pray was then to plan and to act," recalled her son Robert Elijah. "The intenseness of her zeal for her children's education was consuming, unceasing."[14]

The image of the African American mother washing and ironing white people's clothes so that her children could attend school is a cliché, but only because real-life examples were so common. School-teacher Edith Polk, born in 1894 in New Iberia, Louisiana, had just such a mother. Determined that her own offspring would not have to work in white kitchens, she took in washing from four families to put her children though the local Catholic school. "My mother always said that an education is better than anything else in the world." Countless other teachers have told similar stories. "My mother's constant talk and ambition was to get an opportunity to 'school the children,'" wrote William Pickens, the son of sharecroppers who attended Yale University and taught at Talladega University before joining the staff of the National Association for the Advancement of Colored People (NAACP).[15]

Why did mothers appear to value education more highly than fathers? Perhaps it had something to do with the position of the mother within the black family. The lesser economic value of girls' labor to farm families, which enabled parents to allow daughters to acquire more years of schooling, also played a part. And because girls became better educated than boys, they were more likely to encourage their own children to become educated. Anthropologist Hortense Powdermaker speculated that women who invested their hopes for the future in their children found it easier to be buoyant amid adversity and oppression, and were better able to believe that education would be a worthwhile long-term investment. William Pickens, guided by his own experience, was convinced that "one of the chief causes of the rapid advancement of the Negro race since the Civil War has been the ambition of emancipated black mothers for the education of their children."

The position of the mother in the black family owed much to the legacy of slavery. The law of slavery had given no formal recognition to slave marriages, encouraging nonmarital childbearing and diminishing the authority of slave husbands. When husbands lived on a different plantation—the common arrangement of "abroad marriage"—mothers had sole charge of children for most of the time. When owners divided slave families through sale or inheritance, the father, not the mother, would be separated from the children.

There were endless other ways in which slavery disrupted family life, leaving mothers alone with children. Richard R. Wright's slave father, "a half breed Cherokee Indian," disappeared shortly after the boy's birth in 1855 following a row with his owner. His mother, Harriet Lynch, fended for her children without a husband during the turmoil of the Civil War. After emancipation she enrolled her two boys in a school in Cuthbert, Georgia, taught by a Union soldier. When that school closed, she took her sons on a 230-mile journey to Atlanta to place them in a school being taught by a northern missionary. Many fathers were absent, or unacknowledged, because they were white men. Booker T. Washington, for example, had a white father, whose identity was unknown to him and who played no role whatever in his life.[16]

After emancipation, marriages were solemnized in law and black families acquired more stability. Some 80 percent of black households included both a husband and a wife—about the same proportion as in white households. Black families became more patriarchal. Many freedmen regarded undisputed dominion over their wives as an essential attribute of freedom. They considered their wives as a kind of property. The Freedmen's Bureau encouraged this attitude, telling husbands to sign labor contracts for their wives on the assumption that husbands should compel wives to work in the fields. Blacks' entry into the public sphere also fostered male dominance. Only men could vote and hold political office; only men could serve as preachers and ministers.

But while a gendered division of labor appeared within the black family and the wider black community, black women engaged in a variety of tasks and shouldered multiple responsibilities. "As the persons responsible for child nurture and social welfare," writes Jacqueline Jones, "freedwomen cared not only for members of their nuclear families but also for dependent relatives and others in need." That they also worked in the fields and augmented the household income through domestic service made their economic contribution vital. Women attended church in larger numbers than men and soon formed their own auxiliary organizations. Although disenfranchised, many attended public meetings and sought to influence their husbands' political choices. They commonly resisted the kind of female submissiveness that husbands preferred.[17]

Higher morbidity among black men underlined women's parental responsibilities. A study from 1933 reported that 27 percent of black college students had fathers who were no longer living, while only 16 percent had lost their mothers. In times of emergency, when death or economic crisis threatened family stability, mothers most often saved the families from disintegration. "My mother's will power and drive . . . held our household together," recalled Mary McLeod Bethune. When mothers died, aunts and grandmothers often took young children into their homes.[18]

In their day-to-day reality, therefore, black families were often far from patriarchal. The concept of separate male and female spheres within the context of male dominance was always a middle-class ideal rather than a universal reality. It never accurately described the lives of the poor and was almost wholly irrelevant to slave families. After emancipation, the poverty of the freed people, the exclusion of black men from politics, and the systematic attempt by whites to deny black manhood—in its most extreme form by lynching—all militated against patriarchy. In the 1930s, social scientists, both white and black, depicted the lower-class black family as a matriarchy in the sense of the woman enjoying an equal or superior status to that of the man. This was not so much a carryover from slavery, thought sociologist Charles S. Johnson, as a reflection of the black woman's earning power. Domestic servants may have been poorly paid, "but they bring in more money than the odd jobs upon which the man must frequently depend." Even within the black middle class, whose families exhibited greater stability, women often exercised an authority equal to that of their husbands. When E. Franklin Frazier collected family histories from his students at Howard University—many of them the children of teachers, and many destined to become teachers themselves—only a small minority described their families in patriarchal terms.[19]

In the constant tug-of-war between their need to put children to work and their desire to educate them, mothers and fathers often pulled in opposite directions. In the rural South, children were a valuable economic asset. Sharecroppers set their children to working in the fields at an early age, and during the busiest seasons—planting and harvesting—their labor could not be spared. In the towns and cities, too, parents put children to work in order to bring in extra cash. When disputes over schooling occurred, fathers, who contracted with landlords and headed the family labor force, were usually more insistent that the children stay home and work. "The mothers of the children are more interested in school attendance than the fathers," noted G. T. Bludworth, the white official who supervised black public schools in Texas.[20]

In contrast to their tributes to self-sacrificing mothers, black teachers often recalled—sometimes bitterly—selfish or shortsighted fathers who opposed their efforts to gain an education. Benjamin Mays, the future president of Morehouse College, recalled his farmer father storming against him in 1900 when he was only six years old: "Weren't there only two honest occupations for Negro men—preaching and farming? My father must have repeated this dictum a thousand times. What did schooling have to do with farming? Would reading all the books in the world teach a man how to plow, to plant cotton and corn, gather the grain, and harvest the crop? . . . It was equally superfluous for the ministry. God 'called' men to preach; and when He called them, He would tell them what to say!" Enrolling in South Carolina State College "without father's blessing but with my mother's prayers," Mays obeyed his father's injunction to return home at the end of February, after only four months of schooling. In his third year, however, he refused to come home. "The break with my father came and it was final."[21]

Stepfathers could be especially obdurate. Washington Ferguson refused to allow his stepson, Booker T. Washington, to attend school, insisting that he labor at the saltworks. When the mother of Richard R. Wright remarried, her husband made his stepson leave school and get a job. Their mothers' intercession enabled Washington and Wright to go back to school. John O. Crosby, on the other hand, decided to leave home when his stepfather, over his mother's objections, forbade him to attend school, claiming that books were "spilin' all the boys on the place."[22]

Even when fathers were favorably disposed toward education— and of course many were—the economics of the family farm meant that girls usually received more schooling than boys. "Boys are more needed on the farm than girls," explained a female student at Howard University. "My father stressed education more than any other issue," recalled another student. "It was especially pointed out to the girls." Less valuable as farm laborers, girls were allowed to attend school more regularly. Although statistics from this period are notoriously unreliable, they all indicate that by the late nineteenth century a small but consistent disparity had opened up between the attendance rates of boys and girls. Whereas the enrollments of white schools showed a rough equality between the sexes, black schools invariably enrolled more girls. This was true, moreover, of city schools as well. At Howard School in Columbia, South Carolina, in 1892, for example, 58 percent of attendees were girls, on average.[23]

Partly because the value of their labor increased as boys became larger and stronger, the educational gender gap widened as children grew older. When the South began building secondary schools for blacks, they enrolled far more girls than boys. In 1921–22, for example, 48 percent of the children in elementary schools were boys but only 42 percent of the secondary school pupils were boys. "As the grades increase," noted sociologist Charles S. Johnson, "the proportion of girls to boys increases." In Kentucky's black high schools, girls made up 54 percent of the eighth-grade enrollment in 1938. By the twelfth grade they accounted for 64 percent of the pupils. In Louisiana in 1940, fully two-thirds of the girls stayed in school from grades eight through eleven. Less than a third of the boys did.[24]

Black colleges disclosed a similar imbalance. By the 1930s, female students made up 56 percent of all black college students in the southern and border states. In the public colleges, which emphasized the production of teachers even more than the private colleges, the proportion of females reached 60 percent. As one might expect, the mothers of black college students were usually better educated than the fathers. Moreover, female students generally achieved better grades than male students. The facts that teaching itself was the main occupation for better-educated blacks and that teaching had become a predominantly female profession meant that girls had a greater incentive to remain in school. Mothers encouraged them. Indeed, mothers commonly singled out individual daughters for careers as teachers—working themselves so the chosen daughter could stay in school.[25]

For many women, teaching became a kind of sacred calling, rather like that of the celibate priest. Many never married. Others subordinated husbands and children to their driving commitment as teachers. Frequently their marriages and families suffered. Either way, they acted as if God had called them to teach and expected their husbands to either help them or not interfere.

The model—the pioneer who inspired Charlotte Hawkins Brown, Mary McLeod Bethune, and many others—was Lucy Craft Laney. Born in Macon, Georgia, in 1854, Laney was the daughter of a free Negro father, David Laney, who was a carpenter and Presbyterian minister, and a slave mother, Louisa. She learned to read and write from her mother's mistress, whose father was a college professor. The young white woman encouraged Laney to attend the American Missionary Association's Lewis High School and, in 1869, to enter Atlanta University. After graduating from the university's normal department in 1873—she and three other women were the first graduates—she taught in public schools for ten years. In 1883, at the invitation of William Jefferson White, she organized a private school in Augusta, Georgia, that became known as Haines Normal and Industrial Institute, named for a white benefactor. By 1914 Laney's school had 860 pupils and twenty-two teachers, all of them African Americans. Although it never became as famous as Tuskegee Institute—its traditional academic curriculum, which included Latin and Greek, did not appeal to southern whites or northern foundations—Haines Institute established a far-reaching reputation as an example of what black teachers could achieve. Northern visitors sang Laney's praises. President William Howard Taft praised her "commitment and self-sacrifice." Carl Schurz, the veteran Republican politician and former Union general, considered Laney as eloquent a speaker as Booker T. Washington.[26]

For almost fifty years, Laney impressed her forceful personality upon Haines Institute. One former pupil, Richard R. Wright Jr., left this vivid portrait of her.

> In a time when authority of black leadership was too often challenged, she stood out as one who would "stand no foolishness." If you went to school it was to get an education, and if you stayed there she saw that you got an education. She believed in, and practiced, corporal punishment, and did not hesitate to take a young man of eighteen years of age down into the basement, throw him across a barrel and paddle him until he could feel it. Yet, she always taught us that only animals need to be beaten, and that she had to whip those who insisted upon behaving like animals, rather than conducting themselves like men of thought and reason. Miss Laney awakened in me a real love for study.

Another pupil, John Hope, the first black president of Morehouse College, recalled the mental discipline he learned from Haines's teachers. "Miss Georgia [Swift] would send me to the blackboard to multiply, and I always had to begin by saying, 'I'm required to prove,' before demonstrating, for example, that 12×12 is 144. Ever since those school days, all my life, I've been saying to myself, 'I'm required to prove, I'm required to prove.'"[27]

Imbued with the missionary idealism of her AMA teachers, Laney preached the Yankee gospel of education, thrift, and sobriety. She criticized overemotional religion, deplored the disruption caused by revivals, and denounced the wild, sacrilegious celebration of New Year's known as "Egypt Walking." She was an ardent supporter of the

Women's Christian Temperance Union. Committed to uplifting the masses according to her own precepts, she turned Haines into an institution that served the community. When the hospital burned down, Haines Institute gave temporary shelter to its patients. The school established Augusta's first kindergarten and turned out its first trained nurses. Although her description of motherhood as "the crown of womanhood" reflected conventional thinking about women's duties, Laney's maternalist vision went beyond the domestic sphere. Childless and unmarried, she exercised public leadership, projecting women's moral authority from the home to the community. She also personified an emerging belief that educated black women had a particular responsibility to uplift the masses and defend the good name of the race.[28]

The colored women's club movement gave organizational form to this belief. Composed mainly of teachers and the wives of businessmen and professionals, it drew upon feminism and maternalism, but interpreted those ideologies according to specific ideas about the position of black women in America, particularly in the South. Anna Julia Cooper, a teacher in North Carolina and Washington, D.C., made the earliest and most cogent public case for black women's leadership. Her 1892 book, *A Voice from the South,* was not only a manifesto for the equality of women but also an extended analysis of how race and gender affected black women. Cooper deplored the "sixteenth century logic" to which otherwise up-to-date men resorted when they discussed the role of women. She ridiculed the kind of genteel education—"the three R's, a little music and a good deal of dancing"— that fitted women "for worshipping masculinity" by training them in charm and tact. Arguing that black women were as deserving of higher education as black men, she recalled her exclusion from Greek lessons at St. Augustine's College on the grounds that the class had been designed for men going into the ministry. Complaining that black women had been misrepresented and maligned, she made the bold assertion that "the fundamental agency under God in the regeneration, the re-training of the race, as well as the grand work and starting point of the progress upward, must be the *black women.*" Even the conservative *Southern Workman,* published by Hampton Institute, hailed Cooper's book as an intellectual tour de force, stating that *A Voice from the South* revealed the "cultivated and refined colored woman" as a "new factor . . . in our complex civilization."[29]

Educated black women were ready to act as a distinct group with a special claim to leadership. Many had acquired organizational skills through participation in secret societies and churches. They would soon constitute a majority of the black public school teachers. In 1894 hundreds of local women's clubs banded together to form the National Association of Colored Women (NACW). The NACW echoed the public activism of middle-class white women. Sharing a belief that women were the natural moral guardians of society, female reformers of both races campaigned for temperance, the suppression of vice, and the protection of children. But black club women had their own distinct concerns. Although relatively privileged, they were acutely aware of suffering a double burden of sex discrimination and race discrimination. As Chicago's Fannie Barrier Williams put it, they belonged to "the most ill favored-class of women in this country." And although wealthier than the mass of sharecroppers, laborers, and domestic servants, their prosperity was usually modest and often precarious. The economic distance between the black middle class and the black working class was not great. Racial solidarity and self-interest promoted club women's sense of middle-class *noblesse oblige* toward the black poor. "We have more to do than other women," proclaimed Mary Church Terrell of Memphis. "Those of us fortunate enough to have an education must share it with the less fortunate of our race. We must go into our communities and improve them; we must go out into the nation and change it."[30]

The NACW was, in sense, a bid for the leadership of the black community—or a large share of that leadership—at a time when black politicians were passing from the scene and when most black ministers were ill-equipped or uninterested in addressing the problems of the black poor. Hence, although black club women were regular churchgoers, they echoed Booker T. Washington's complaint that preachers were talkers rather than doers, and that far too many of them were morally and intellectually wanting. The club women's movement was not only an assertion of female autonomy but also, at times, a claim to female superiority, at least in moral terms. "The Negro woman has been the motive power in whatever has been accomplished by the race," asserted one member. "It is to the Afro-American woman that the world looks for the solution of the race problem," claimed another.[31]

Black women teachers sought to substantiate their claim to community leadership by cultivating moral respectability. Whites of all classes, northerners and southerners, still associated African Americans with unbridled sexuality. "Neither the women nor the men as a mass look upon lasciviousness as impurity," claimed Virginia writer Philip A. Bruce in 1889. Northern missionary A. D. Mayo was hardly less complimentary: he praised the gentle bearing and "womanly charms" of the educated few, only to criticize the "slough of unchastity in which, as a race, they still flounder." Black women carried the additional stigma of being the object of white men's illicit sexual desires. Although abolitionist propaganda had exaggerated the sexual exploitation of slave women by white men, the notion of the slave plantation as a site of unbridled fornication persisted. "American slavery almost universally debauched slave women," wrote Arthur W. Calhoun, pioneer historian of the American family. "The master's right of rape wiped out female honor." The fact that southern white men continued to have sexual relationships with black women after emancipation encouraged, in the words of Du Bois, "utter disregard of a black women's virtue and self respect." In 1895 the president of the Missouri Press Association responded to British criticism of lynching with the intemperate comment that "[Negro] women are prostitutes and all are natural liars and thieves." The slander outraged educated black women and was a major stimulus for the formation of the NACW.[32]

Through sober and pious behavior, female teachers defined themselves as respectable members of the black middle class, fortified themselves against sexual predators, and combated degrading racist stereotypes. "Our people, as a whole, are charged with immorality and vice," wrote Memphis teacher Ida B. Wells, "[and] it depends upon the woman of today to refute such charges by her stainless life." A ladylike appearance was part of a teacher's moral armor, as well as a badge of middle-class status. "Their dress code was very strict," recalled one former teacher. "Plain cotton style dress, with polished shoes. You could tell a teacher from other parents by their shoes and well fitted clothes." Styles changed radically after the First World War, but teachers still had to dress like middle-class professionals.

In her demand for respect and recognition as a middle-class professional, Charlotte Hawkins Brown was the most outspoken woman teacher of her generation. When white people addressed them by their given names, black teachers usually bit their tongues and swallowed the insult. Not Brown. After 1920 she refused to let it pass. "I've had to close my eyes to many things that hurt my heart," she told a northern friend. "There are some men who occupy high places who feel that no Negro woman whether she be cook, criminal or principal of a school should ever be addressed as *Mrs.* I know how trivial that sounds to you, but there is a great principle back of it in the South, and I have always resented it." It was bad enough when white southerners withheld courtesy titles; when white northerners—including some of her own patrons— did it, her blood boiled. In indignant letters and speeches, Brown demanded that whites accord black women "respectful recognition of their womanhood" by showing them the "ordinary acts of courtesy and politeness due anybody in public places."[33]

Because she was the principal of a private school she had founded herself, Brown enjoyed the kind of independence that only a handful of women teachers in the South—Mary McLeod Bethune was another—possessed. Relishing her freedom, but aware of her privileged position, Brown used her voice to represent teachers and women. As president of the North Carolina Federation of Colored Women's Clubs, a position she held for twenty years, she enlisted white women in the cause of social justice and became a leader of the movement for interracial cooperation that flowered in the South after 1919. As president of the North Carolina Negro State Teachers Association in the mid-1930s, she propounded the case for equal salaries to white officials. As a national celebrity famous for her eloquence, she crisscrossed America addressing black and white audiences. The year 1938 saw her speaking to the North Philadelphia Civic Club, the New York Urban League, the Southern Negro Youth Conference in Richmond, the NAACP in Lynchburg, the Cooperative Women's Civic League in Baltimore, and the YWCA in Belmont. Negro History Week took her to Texas, where she spoke at half a dozen black colleges. These engagements covered only two months. Brown was indefatigable.[34]

She was also forthright to the point of bluntness. Indeed, some of Brown's statements might have caused violent retaliation had they been uttered by a black man. Whites were obsessed with miscegenation, she complained, but the "variegated shades of brown and mulatto" had been created by white masters forcing their lusts upon slave women. Brown was not interested in making white "friends of the Negro" feel good. "The unvarnished truth," she told one audience of southern moderates, was that their efforts to improve race relations—exemplified by the worthy but ineffective Commission on Interracial Cooperation—had advanced the Negro's cause scarcely a jot. "When it comes to recognition of [the Negro's] citizenship rights or when it comes to respect for him as a thinking man or woman," blacks had nothing to celebrate. Segregated railway carriages were "just as repulsive as they were twenty-five years ago." When blacks could still be burned at the stake, "the idea of simple justice . . . has not permeated into the heart of one individual out of a thousand." Northern whites had no cause to feel superior. "This malicious, malignant disease, prejudice, is taking a great hold in the North." Brown described her own miserable experience at New York's Biltmore Hotel, where the elevator operators refused to let her ride, to illustrate the point.[35]

Brown's was a high-wire balancing act. When she argued that educated, "respectable" blacks, especially women teachers, merited fair treatment from whites, she accentuated the difference between the black middle class and the black lower class. Too many white people, she complained, based their ideas about Negroes—and how much they should be paid—upon the domestic servants, their "Mary" and "John," who cooked and cleaned for them. "We are entitled to a new evaluation, different from that formally given by you to Mary and John." Yet if late Victorian conceptions of the "black better class" influenced her thinking, she resisted the conclusion that the poor, the ignorant, and even the criminal should be written off as undeserving: "I represent . . . the lowly Negro woman on the farms of Alabama, Georgia, and Florida . . . the Negro woman in domestic service in the north, the south, the east and the west . . . the thousands of Negro laundry workers . . . [and] the small and large Negro housekeepers. . . . Until women in our group, on the lowest rung of the ladder economically and morally, are unshackled from fear, are unfettered in their attempt to breathe in an atmosphere of freedom, all Negro women are slaves." She ended up running a finishing school for children of the black bourgeoisie. Nevertheless, Brown never forgot that her own family had been forerunners of the southern migrants to the North who, in the 1920s and 1930s, were despised as shiftless and ignorant.[36]

Her balancing act entailed tremendous emotional tension. "Mrs. Brown lives, all the time, between two fires," explained a northern sympathizer, "and we wonder how she manages to hold her own with two groups of people so diametrically opposed in their attitude toward the Negro race." She suffered depressions and physical breakdowns. Two marriages failed. Her short fuse and explosive temper—"an endless stream of words, accompanied by flashing eyes and a steady pacing of the floor"—left friends and colleagues bruised. But to the thousands of black public school teachers of North Carolina, Brown was a fighter. She said things to white people that ordinary black teachers dared not utter.[37]

Women teachers were continually exhorted to act as community leaders, and in many cases they did. In the rural South, the teacher enjoyed social standing purely by virtue of her position and education. "In the smaller towns . . . you were everything," explained one Alabama teacher. "Everything centered around the school and churches. Well, if you didn't have a program you had no community, nothing." Visiting parents' homes, attending church, organizing fundraising drives, and mounting elaborate school-closing exercises were all part of the job. Teachers acted as the first port of call for people with legal problems, difficulties with a landlord, letters that needed writing, and forms that needed filling in. "I was asked to teach Sunday school, write orders to Sears and Roebuck . . . and figure up weekly wages," recalled Dorothy Redus Robinson. "It never occurred to me to refuse their varied requests. . . . [E]veryone referred to me as 'our teacher.'"[38]

Teachers did not automatically become community leaders. They had to earn their patrons' respect and cooperation. For college-educated teachers, life in "the rural" demanded a cultural adjustment of the first order. Many were repelled by the primitive, unsanitary state of rural homes and by the ignorance and credulousness of their occupants. "I cried and cried for two whole weeks," recalled one teacher who came from Fayetteville State College to teach in Burke County, Georgia. However, if teachers betrayed disgust or condescension, rural blacks were quick to detect and resent it. "You better be careful what you say," an older teacher warned Irene Monroe, who came from Bessemer, Alabama, to teach in the country. "You know, people in the rural, they [might] think you're making fun of them or something." Monroe recalled eating with one family and feeling sick when the old lady of the house dipped snuff and spat on the floor throughout the meal. She said nothing.[39]

"Attending church with them is the real key to teacher-community relationships," concluded a group of Louisiana teachers in 1942. Sectarianism had declined by the 1930s, but teachers still had to be careful not to offend religious sensibilities. "Do not discuss [the] preacher's ability," Tennessee teachers were instructed. "Do not fight faiths. Work with all." Some teachers attended all the local churches, Methodist and Baptist alike, a practice facilitated by the fact that rural ministers rotated their Sunday services among three or four different churches. Faced with sectarian pressure, however, some teachers took the easy way out. "The family in which I lived were Baptists," reported an Alabama teacher. "My Methodism became quickly adjusted to the hospitable home, and I went regularly to the Baptist church and Sunday school." Teachers also needed to respect Baptist prohibitions against card playing, dancing, and other amusements that citified teachers might regard as entirely harmless. When teachers in Donaldsonville, Louisiana, held an Emancipation Day dance, Baptist ministers criticized them. The row contributed to the collapse of the local PTA.[40]

Teachers also had to be respectful of school trustees. The primary function of these men was to maintain and repair the schoolhouse. Although trustees were often poorly educated and illiterate, an Alabama teacher reported, they were usually "earnest and sincere," taking "much pride in attending to the affairs of the school." Indeed, school trustees often invested this relatively minor position with exaggerated weight. One teacher was surprised that a simple matter such as deciding which families should board her occasioned an earnest debate that lasted far into the night. "It was not so much a difference of opinion," she observed, "as a love for discussion."[41]

The trustees often wielded influence over the teacher. They possessed no independent power, being creatures of the school boards. However, white officials who had little interest in black schools— sometimes not even knowing where they were located—often permitted trustees to elect the teacher. Moreover, like church deacons, trustees exercised moral oversight. "A teacher had to be a certain thing," recalled Mississippi teacher Julia Taylor. "You couldn't go here, you couldn't do that." Male teachers, particularly, resented efforts to police their behavior, especially when moral surveillance entailed snooping and tittle-tattle. Trustee boards tried to keep him "in line," charged one former principal, "to see that he attended church services regularly . . . did not drink a lot of whiskey, gamble, or even smoke." Trustees "felt that they owned the school, and you too." It was here that the trustees' lack of education proved damaging. Often incapable of recognizing good teaching, they applied their own capricious standards. If the trustees took a dislike to you, recalled one teacher, "they could get you removed." Often trustees were less concerned with qualifications and experience than with "character," a Georgia teacher complained, "and they had their own definition of 'character.'" The influence of trustees added to teachers' job insecurity. In some schools the trustees changed teachers every year.[42]

For better-educated rural teachers, the most oppressive aspect of their job was the lack of contact with other educated people—the intellectual as well as the physical isolation. If they could manage it, therefore, teachers often boarded during the week and returned to urban homes at the weekend. Other teachers commuted daily from city to country. Patrons sometimes grumbled that these "suitcase teachers" took no interest in rural life and had little contact with the communities they served. In many parts of the rural South, therefore, the relationship between teachers and local communities was remote or even bad. In Goochland County, Virginia, for example, the PTA accused teachers, nearly all of whom lived in Richmond, of spending no time with parents, failing to attend church, and "taking part in illicit liquor handling."[43]

It is misleading, in any case, to speak as if "communities" were always characterized by solidarity and shared values. Teachers encountered divided communities, apathetic communities, and ones that lacked any sense of common interest or purpose. In the coal-mining towns of eastern Kentucky, for example, the bitter rivalry between the CIO and the AFL split black families. Elsewhere, teachers' efforts to exert leadership, or to impose their own educational values, provoked opposition from some parents. "When I first came out here to work some of the people tried to bully me," related A. C. Facen, a Tuskegee graduate who developed his school as the focal point of Mineral Springs, Ouchita Parish, Louisiana. When his wife "whipped one of the boys around the leg with a little switch . . . I began to receive threatening, anonymous notes." Community support, when he needed it, was not forthcoming. Facen therefore mentioned his predicament to the mail rider, a "mean white man," who sorted out the problem. As this example suggests, teachers' use of corporal punishment did not go unchallenged. In one Kentucky county, teachers were hauled into court five times in a single year by parents who objected to it.[44]

The longer a teacher stayed in a community, the greater her chance of exerting influence. However, poor pay and short school terms meant that teaching was slow to stabilize as a profession. About a quarter of black teachers had nine or more years of experience, but most teaching careers were much shorter. Turnover was greatest where the schools were worst: rural teachers changed schools more frequently than city teachers, and they quit teaching sooner. In 1930 about half of the South's black teachers had taught for four years or less. The average experience of Louisiana's rural teachers, at the end of the 1930s, was about three years. More than half of all black teachers in the rural South changed their schools every other year. Hence many teachers failed to acquire influence in their communities because of the simple fact that they did not stay in place long enough.[45]

Nevertheless, the concept of the rural teacher as a community leader died hard. The northern missionaries had viewed teachers as bearers of religion and morality. Booker T. Washington saw them as agents of economic progress. Now, in the twentieth century, the reforming spirit of the Progressive Era injected new vitality into the notion of community service. In addition to their traditional role as educational evangelists, teachers were called upon to be public health workers, teachers of agriculture, social workers, adult literacy teachers, and organizers of 4-H Clubs, Mothers' Clubs, and PTAs. "If you want to teach Negro welfare quickly and effectively," argued John Hope of Morehouse College, "do it through the teacher and the school. . . . The influence of the Negro teacher reaches out into the homes of the pupils, and often makes the difference between a good and a bad community."[46]

THE ideal of the teacher as an agent of rural improvement found its fullest expression in the Jeanes Teacher program. In the early twentieth century, when northern philanthropists and southern progressives formed an alliance to defend and extend public education, they believed that the Hampton-Tuskegee model of industrial education was the key to both improving black public schools and persuading southern whites to support them. And they found in one particular woman, Virginia Estelle Randolph, a model of how a black teacher could implement that kind of program within a broader vision of community leadership.

The career of Virginia Randolph, the original Jeanes teacher, provides a classic illustration of how women teachers influenced and manipulated programs that were funded and administered by whites. In 1892 Randolph was an eighteen-year-old graduate of Hampton Institute who had just started teaching at the Mountain Road School in Henrico County, Virginia. Like most black teachers, she received little supervision or guidance. All the school board expected from her was a monthly attendance report. The young teacher found a typical rural schoolhouse, a wooden structure consisting of one room, surrounded by mud. The situation dismayed her. Visiting pupils' homes, she found squalor and sickness. These rural folk needed help. She found herself ministering to the sick and burying the dead. In the absence of a church, she taught a Sunday school. Randolph set about improving the schoolhouse and its surroundings. Knowing it would be futile to ask the school board for more money, she began the work herself and enlisted the help of pupils and parents.

Community effort of this kind was nothing new—patrons often contributed land, lumber, and labor to erect schoolhouses. But Randolph departed from tradition in two respects. First, she put pupils to work on the schoolhouse and the school grounds, manual labor that got their hands dirty. Second, she taught them simple crafts like sewing, basket weaving, and making mats out of corn shucks. Thus far this kind of program—"industrial education" or "manual training"—had been confined largely to black private schools, notably the "little Tuskegees." Its introduction into public schools was an innovation. Randolph ran into the same kind of opposition that William J. Edwards was encountering at Snow Hill, Alabama. Parents protested. "The people said I was teaching a kind of work that they could teach their children at home, and got up a petition with eighty names signed to put me out." Some parents kept their children out of school. A minister criticized her from the pulpit.

Drawing upon her own faith, Randolph dug ditches, hauled gravel, and laid walks. She raised money from entertainments. Sympathetic whites helped her. Her efforts soon yielded visible results: a freshly painted and weatherproofed schoolhouse; grounds made attractive by landscaping and tree planting; additional classrooms, more teachers, a larger enrollment, and better attendance. "All the way along," she later recalled, "I could see, through faith, God's smiling face and my mother on bended knees." Her tact and devotion won over the school's patrons. In 1905 the newly appointed superintendent of schools, Jackson Davis, came across Virginia Randolph's work. He was impressed.

Jackson Davis personified a new breed of southern white educator. Proudly styling themselves "schoolmen," they were reformers who sought to replace the South's patchwork of cash-starved, politics-ridden public schools with a properly funded, comprehensive system, to be taught and administered by professionals. Holding a bachelor's degree from William and Mary College, Davis also boasted an M.A. from Teachers College of Columbia University, the nation's fountainhead of educational modernism. He had five years' experience as the principal of a black school in Richmond. Davis's approach to black education blended a concern for rural reform, an acceptance of white supremacy, and new ideas about the curriculum. Curriculum reformers were arguing that many of the traditional school subjects—algebra, foreign languages, the classics—suited a college-bound minority but were wasted on most children, who needed a more practical education. Such ideas fit snugly into Hampton and Tuskegee's "industrial education" model, with its emphasis on the elementary, the vocational, and the rural. Davis hit upon the idea of copying Virginia Randolph's methods in order to "put new life" into the other black schools of Henrico County. In 1908 he appointed Randolph "county supervisor of Negro rural schools."

Randolph's immediate goal was to introduce "manual training" or "industrial arts" into every classroom. In practice, however, her program went much farther. Randolph wanted teachers to stimulate popular support for school improvements by making the curriculum more relevant to the everyday needs of rural people. Children could apply the skills they learned at school—cooking, sewing, carpentry, hygiene—to the improvement of their own homes. And by beautifying the schoolhouse and the schoolyard, the teacher would make the school what it had long aspired to be but rarely ever had been: an object of pride, a community center. Setting out at the crack of dawn from her home in Richmond, Randolph made 190 school visits during her first year. Her annual report for 1908–09 claimed that manual training was being taught in all twenty-two schools. It also listed, school by school, the amount of money raised by the teachers and the sums expended on improvements—hedges set out, trees planted, walks graveled, and yards fenced. In total, the black teachers of Henrico County—all of them women—had collected $331 and spent $108. That was no small achievement. As Booker T. Washington enthused to white school man James H. Dillard, "You seem to have discovered a gold mine in Miss Virginia Randolph."[47]

Dillard was a patrician Virginian and former classics professor who presided over the Jeanes Fund, a new philanthropic foundation that subsidized Randolph's post and sought to spread her example. By 1909–10, after three years of operation, the Fund was sponsoring 129 "Jeanes teachers" in thirteen southern and border states. It was the first foundation devoted wholly to black schools. Moreover, thanks to Washington's cultivation of its benefactress, Anna T. Jeanes, an elderly Quaker from Philadelphia, the board of the Jeanes Fund included several black members, including Washington himself.[48]

The General Education Board, the biggest of the new philanthropic foundations, also found Randolph's methods worthy of support. Founded in 1903 with the aim of strengthening and systematizing the South's public school system, the GEB had neglected black schools. Between 1902 and 1918 it allocated only $2.4 million to black education, less than a tenth of what it spent on white schools. In its first solid gesture toward Negro education, however, the GEB began paying southern states to create the new position of "state agent of Negro rural schools." Jackson Davis, appointed by Virginia in 1910, was the first. By 1919 all the other southern states had followed Virginia's example. The state agents, white southerners all, received marching orders from the GEB to introduce the Hampton-Tuskegee model of industrial education into all the black public schools. The state agents envisaged the Jeanes teachers as their primary means of doing this.[49]

The state agents disseminated the new curriculum even more widely through the annual summer schools that many states required black teachers to attend. In 1913, for example, Alabama enrolled eighteen hundred people, about three-quarters of the state's black public school teachers, in thirty-seven "colored teachers' institutes." In addition to the usual academic subjects, the five-day program included farming, gardening, sewing, cooking, sanitation, and the organization of corn clubs and canning clubs. Even city teachers were force-fed industrial education. During a six-week summer school in Shelby County, Tennessee, "every man teacher was required to take a course in Manual Training . . . and every woman was required to take a course in Home Economics." In 1916 the GEB began directly subsidizing summer schools. By 1925 more than half the South's black teachers attended them.[50]

The state agents approached their task with the zeal of missionaries spreading the gospel. A state agent was never so happy as when a "Jeanes Industrial Teacher" induced the "regular teachers" to adopt "practical work." Reporting on the Foreman School in Baton Rouge, Louisiana, Leo M. Favrot offered glowing praise for the way the teacher "correlates the industry with language:" "We heard a group of pupils recite in succession on such subjects as the following: 1. How to clean a kitchen; 2. How to set a table (here the action suited the word); 3. How to clean a bedroom; 4. How to make a shuck hat, accompanied by a demonstration; 5. How to make a palmetto hat in a similar manner; 6. How to make a palmetto basket, by one of the boys." This was pure Booker T. Washington, even down to the stress upon "correlation."[51]

Every black teacher who introduced industrial education was another soul saved. Every school that dropped Latin was enemy territory conquered. Samuel L. Smith, Tennessee's state agent, offered one black principal five hundred dollars to add industrial education. By the following year, a miraculous transformation had occurred. "We just have not had time to take up Latin this year," the principal told Smith. "The children are so crazy about this new work . . . that they would stop school if I would suggest the dropping of this work to take up Latin." Smith's most edifying story was his experience in Dyersburg, where the president of the school board, a white physician, defended the traditional curriculum on the grounds that blacks needed Latin, Greek, and higher mathematics if they were to become lawyers and doctors. After hearing an inspirational speech from Smith, however, the burgers of Dyersburg offered to equip the black school with a kitchen so as to "better prepare the girls to do cooking for the white people of the town."[52]

But the introduction of "industrial education" into public schools evoked strong black opposition. Du Bois headed the attack by claiming that it degraded the academic curriculum. He disclaimed any hostility to manual training as such, but argued that given the shortness of the black school term, industrial education—not to mention setting children to work on decorating schoolhouses and beautifying school-yards—came "at the expense of teaching children to read and write and cipher well." In addition, too great a stress upon "industrial education" encouraged white officials to appoint black teachers according to their ability to cook and sew rather than their academic training. These very officials, Du Bois noted, were often the first to complain that black teachers lacked education and culture.[53]

Resentment of the new curriculum went far beyond Du Bois. When Jackson Davis addressed a national teachers' meeting in St. Louis, his plea for more industrial education met a frosty reception. The teachers doubted that the Jeanes teachers would improve schools' academic work. "They are jealous of the cultural and fear the industrial," thought Davis. From Arkansas, state agent Leo M. Favrot complained that black teachers showed no interest in industrial education. Month after month, he reported that the Jeanes teachers were failing to influence the regular teachers. "A Jeanes teacher frequently visits a rural school, and has each pupil to work for an hour or two one day in a week and comes back two weeks later and finds that no work of this kind has been done by the pupils during her absence."[54]

Yet black teachers were reluctant to reject industrial education in toto. They were deeply frustrated that white schools improved while black schools stagnated. Philanthropic money, however unfairly apportioned, was a new source of funding. Even if help came with strings attached, blacks could not afford to spurn it. Teachers therefore accepted the money but sought to untie the strings. They manipulated the progressive agenda to their own ends. The concept of "industrial education" was sufficiently vague to permit blacks and whites to work at cross-purposes while apparently agreeing upon common goals. Historian William A. Link explained this paradox by pointing out that whereas southern whites viewed industrial education as a bulwark of racial segregation—and often as a natural reflection of white supremacy—blacks could "accept it as a vehicle of autonomy and improvement" but simultaneously reject "any assumption of racial inferiority."[55]

The Jeanes teachers responded to black opposition by bending their work toward community improvement. "Industrial education" became a lever for raising living standards. It is easy to forget the extent to which poor diet, inadequate clothing, and unsanitary conditions wreaked havoc upon the health of African Americans. Lessons in sewing, cookery, hygiene, and the preservation of foods taught children how to dress more sturdily, eat nutritious and well-prepared food, and avoid dirt and disease. Even a simple shuck mat could help reduce the amount of dirt tracked from the field into the home. "Canning clubs" enabled rural folk to enjoy fruit and vegetables during the winter. Individual drinking cups discouraged the spread of germs when school-children shared water.

The career of Virginia Randolph illustrated the malleable character of northern philanthropy. The sewing, cookery, and shuck work that Randolph introduced into rural schools represented the starting-point of an unceasing effort to improve black education. In practice, her work emphasized school improvement as much as manual training. Through fundraising efforts led by teachers, black communities did for themselves what white school boards were failing to do for them. In 1912–13, for example, Virginia's twenty-three Jeanes "supervising industrial teachers" helped raise $22,655. With that money, 189 schools could extend their five-month terms to six months. Twenty schools erected new schoolhouses, 102 constructed outhouses, and 127 covered their buildings in whitewash or paint.[56]

Randolph's modus operandi rested upon the belief that if blacks pooled their money to improve their schools, whites would be shamed into matching their efforts. She never waited for the Henrico County School Board to grant a request: she always initiated the improvement herself. When she approached the school board she had already raised money from the black community and enlisted the support of sympathetic whites. Her case was by then all but irresistible.

Randolph's campaign for a black high school exhibited all the hallmarks of her style: persistence, tact, and a prodigious talent for fundraising. Early in 1911 she held a "quilt contest" among Henrico

County's twenty-three black schools. She organized it in such a way that the event provided a variety of opportunities to raise money—not a simple competition but a cumulative fundraising process.

> Each school, out of their own League treasury, has bought five yards of black cotton and five spools of red cotton at a cost of not over sixty cents. The quilts are not to have less than forty-eight squares to each one. These squares are distributed in each community among scholars and friends. Those that take squares are to work their names in the middle at a cost of ten cents. Then you are supposed to get nine additional names at ten cents each, making each one bring in one dollar. I have a set time for each to come in, and then they are joined together at each school. Then sold in raffle, at five cents a ticket. Prizes to school raising the most money and individual making the most squares.

The prize-giving ceremony itself provided another occasion for raising money. From the dimes of rural African Americans and sympathetic whites, Randolph collected eight hundred dollars. Later in the year, she organized a "George Washington Campaign" with the aim of raising a thousand dollars in ninety days. It actually raised two thousand. Randolph then bought a "lovely park in the country" for the school grounds. "We made a cash payment . . . and didn't owe another penny. Didn't have to ask the Board for five cents." When presented with this fait accompli, Arthur D. Wright, who succeeded Jackson Davis as superintendent of schools, was "agreeably surprised." The laying of the cornerstone in June 1912, another elaborate ceremony, netted five hundred dollars more.[57]

Having created the first public school for blacks that offered education above the seventh grade, Randolph wished to make it accessible to all the children of Henrico County. When the school board rebuffed her request for bus transportation, she laid plans to build a dormitory, so that children from afar could attend school during the week. Bypassing the school board and turning to the black community and "our good white friends," she raised the money, bought the land, and dedicated a girls' dormitory in 1924, ten years after first broaching the idea. Three years later, having bought two acres of land and gifted it to the school board, she opened a boys' dormitory. When the Great Depression made running the dormitories impractical—the school board refused to maintain them any longer—Randolph again requested bus transportation. Once again, the school board turned her down. In one of her last acts before retirement, Randolph raised enough money to purchase a bus. The "industrial and high school" was now "Virginia Randolph Training High School," and it offered four grades instead of the original two.[58]

These struggles took their toll on Randolph. Every step of the way, she faced indifference or opposition from the superintendent of schools, the school board, and the state supervisor of Negro schools. She resented the fact that white schools financed their improvements from public taxation while black schools had to raise the money from children and parents. In her letters to James H. Dillard, president of the Jeanes Fund, Randolph vented her frustrations. In 1926 she complained that the school board had spent four thousand dollars on a water system for the white high school, "but they haven't any money for us. Recently they took over one thousand dollars I had raised to pay the teachers. Anything we want to do we have to raise the money to get it." Even putting a coat of paint on the high school dormitories forced her to go out and beg for the money. When the Community Fund allocated money to various agencies but gave nothing to black schools, she seethed.[59]

Randolph knew she was being exploited. All her travel expenses came out of her own pocket. For the first few years she traveled around Henrico County on streetcar and on foot. In 1914 she begged the Jeanes Fund to pay for a horse and buggy. Six years later she requested "a little Ford car" as "I am getting old now [and] cannot walk like I used to." Randolph was the first person to contribute to her own multifarious fundraising activities. Not a month passed, she reminded Dillard, "that a part of my salary has not gone for something in regards to the work." And although she received national recognition, she still remained a poorly paid teacher while the whites who capitalized upon her work went on to become top foundation executives. Her former boss became head of the General Education Board. "Look at Mr. [Jackson] Davis 1907–08 and look now. Then look at poor little me." Bitterness and self-pity colored her later years. "I cannot tell half of the misery I have gone through."[60]

Still, in the state agents and the Jeanes teachers, black schools finally gained full-time advocates within an administrative system otherwise hostile or indifferent to black education. From one perspective, it is true, the self-help efforts of black communities represented an unfair system of "double taxation," for blacks were raising money that ought to have been provided by school boards. Advocates of self-help, on the other hand, believed that black-led campaigns for school improvements had a beneficial effect upon white attitudes. Fundraising efforts accompanied by diplomatic appeals to elite whites made education officials more, not less, sympathetic to black needs. The entire thrust of the new northern philanthropy was to encourage the South's white leaders to incorporate black children into the public school system in a full and fair way. It was this aspect of the foundations' work that Booker T. Washington found so alluring. As he advised Dillard during the formation of the Jeanes Fund, money itself was less important than "the opportunity to make and lead public sentiment. . . . There never was a time when there was a greater need for a strong sane influence to combat the present tendency to decry, discourage, and hamper Negro education." As Dillard himself told an early meeting of Jeanes teachers, "If we can make these rural schools more what they ought to be, we will stand a better chance of getting more money from these white school officials."[61]

Nearly all of the Jeanes teachers were women. That made sense: they were working alongside an overwhelming female teaching force. But the selection of women also reflected historical patterns of interracial contact, as well as white male assumptions about race and gender. The men who composed the ruling class of the South felt uncomfortable with assertive black men. Indeed, white supremacists depicted black males as sexually threatening and criminally inclined. If the white missionaries had stressed the importance of building black "manhood," the white supremacy movement set out to destroy that manhood. Whites defended lynching on the grounds that the male victims were beasts, not men; lynching often involved castration. Disenfranchisement destroyed male political leadership. The "etiquette" of race relations enforced by whites reduced black men to the status of children by denying them the title "Mr." and referring to them by first name only, or simply calling them "boy."

Elite whites rarely felt threatened by black women, however. Indeed, many of them had been raised by black nurses. The lachrymose references to "black mammies" that studded the speeches of southern white men were so stereotypical, and so often sugar-coated white supremacist arguments, that one is tempted to dismiss them as fiction. Yet they reflected close relationships that actually existed, both during and after slavery, between white families and black domestic servants. "To an extent not always recognized," a 1942 study of black women teachers asserted, "the Negro woman has been an instrument through which the thinking and feeling of the black world have played upon the white world." White men of the middle and upper classes felt comfortable with black women and even tolerated a degree of assertiveness from them. Black women could also approach white women without any of the sexual tension, and potentially lethal misunderstanding, that contact between a white woman and a black man entailed. If education officials had to delegate authority to a black official, and to work alongside that person, let her be a woman.[62]

The state agents of Negro schools were racial moderates and liberals. But they made it a cardinal principle never directly to challenge white supremacy. The officials with whom the Jeanes teachers had the closest contact—the county superintendents—reflected the attitudes of white voters who elected them. Many were deeply prejudiced against blacks. In selecting a Jeanes teacher, the most important qualification was what Alabama's state agent called "a satisfactory personality." Jeanes teachers nevertheless wielded considerable influence. Outside of the twenty or so presidents of black state colleges, all of whom were men, and the principals of black high schools in the South's cities, who were also men, they became the most powerful black public servants. In the rural areas where they did their work—counties that contained two-thirds of the black population and 85 percent of the black schools—they had more authority than any other black teacher.[63]

Jeanes teachers brought tremendous energy to their work and engaged in an astonishing range of activities. The annual report of Virginia L. Miller, who worked in Buckingham County, Virginia, near the foothills of the Blue Ridge mountains, provides a yardstick. Miller was responsible for overseeing thirty-seven schools and fifty teachers. She visited each school every month, held monthly teachers' meetings, weighed and measured two thousand children, organized Red Cross and tuberculosis drives, got the school board to donate books to indigent children, collected food and clothing from welfare agencies and distributed them to needy children, visited 118 homes, looked in on sick teachers and took some to the hospital, organized a "National History Week" and a "National Health and Clean-Up Week," and conducted a survey of school dropouts for the National Youth Administration. She also attended local, state, regional, and national meetings—about sixty in all—and took a college extension course. She reported with pride that 1939–40 was the first year the county's black schools had operated for as long as nine months. Although her travel expenses came out of her salary and she did much of her work "between midnight and day," she vowed to "go forward in the name of that great leader Jesus . . . giving to others the best that I have and being supremely happy to live a life of service."[64]

Her position within the state education bureaucracy gave the Jeanes teacher a great deal of autonomy and influence. She represented the interests of black education at the county level, and she had direct access to the county superintendent, her immediate superior. She also answered to the state agent of Negro schools, who selected her, and to the Jeanes Foundation, which subsidized her salary. The state agents gave the Jeanes teachers constant encouragement, using their influence with state and county officials to help them secure resources. The foundation officials organized summer schools at Hampton or Tuskegee, where the Jeanes teachers developed an esprit de corps and absorbed the latest trends in educational thinking. Contact with higher officials and outside agencies gave the Jeanes teacher a confidence in dealing with local whites that ordinary teachers—less educated and more isolated—usually lacked. The latitude accorded them by the foundations increased that confidence. From the start, the Jeanes Fund conceived of its work as experimental and innovative. It did not burden the Jeanes teachers with rules or targets, allowing them to adapt their activities to local conditions—the South, after all, had as many different education systems as it had cities and counties—and discover what worked. As long as they exercised "tact and discretion," they could devise their own strategies for improving black schools.[65]

Jeanes teachers exerted community pressure in ways that did not threaten white authority. They organized Parent-Teacher Associations and county teachers associations. In the 1920s they spearheaded fundraising drives to build Rosenwald schools. In the 1930s they raised money toward high schools. In East Feliciana Parish, Louisiana, for example, Mrs. M. E. Williams organized a "Negro School Board"— wholly unofficial, of course—that worked up sentiment and collected money. Within a few years Williams went to the white school board with seven thousand dollars. With a matching grant from the Works Progress Administration and the support of the school board, which contributed twenty-five hundred dollars, the high school was built. Everywhere, Jeanes teachers assisted the routine fundraising upon which black schools had always depended. In Fayette, Tennessee, Cattrell Collier reported, "We have to raise all of our money for playground equipment, maps, globes, and for all physical improvements. . . . Sometimes we have to raise money to complete buildings."[66]

Another way to improve schools was to increase enrollments. County superintendents made little effort to encourage attendance, let alone enforce compulsory attendance laws. School boards often had no idea how many black school-age children resided in their counties and made no effort to find out. Black parents often refused to cooperate with white census takers. "When the white folks would come around, they'd hide the children, thought they were trying to send them to a war," recalled Alabama teacher Irene Monroe. "They'd hide them under the bed. . . . 'I ain't got but two children.' Sometimes they had about seven or eight." When Monroe did the rounds with the Jeanes teacher, it was a different story. "Miss Todd told them what they'd get. 'You don't have but five months of school and you ought to get nine months . . . You've got to turn these children in.'" Confronting school boards with the true size of the school-age population—invariably much larger than supposed—Jeanes teachers could make a more effective case for better schools. And the better the schools, the bigger the attendance. The provision of school meals also worked wonders. "This called for many trips and much explanation," reported a Jeanes teacher from Carroll County, Tennessee, but the effort proved worthwhile. "Nothing has done so much to increase attendance as the hot lunch program."[67]

Black teachers could not demand, they could only request. Cultivating influential whites was part of their stock-in-trade. Black schools had always used the annual school-closing or commencement exercise to impress white trustees, school board members, and assorted dignitaries. Jeanes teachers encouraged this tradition. In some states they helped organize county-wide commencements that attracted thousands of people. These daylong celebrations involved parades, speeches, and entertainment, as well as the all-important "industrial exhibit" displaying sewing, embroidery, cooking, baskets, mats, woodwork, fruit, and vegetables. Over the years the industrial displays became smaller and fewer, but the commencement exercise, and the banquet honoring the superintendent and county school board, remained annual fixtures.[68]

Her relationship with the superintendent of schools could make or break a Jeanes teacher. In practice, her white boss often treated her like a senior assistant. County superintendents usually paid little attention to black schools, rarely visited them, and had few contacts with pupils or parents. Their contact with black teachers, outside of job interviews, would be limited to a handful of monthly meetings to discuss teaching methods. Politically, the superintendent had no incentive to devote much time to black schools, especially if he answered to a school board that was hostile to black education. Even conscientious officials—an increasing number of superintendents were professionally trained educators—found it hard to keep up with the paperwork spawned by state administrators and federal programs. In many cases, therefore, the superintendent charged the Jeanes teacher with supervising and administering the black schools. As Louis Cayer of Avoyelles Parish put it, "I just turn the colored schools over to Martha and she does the best she can with them."[69]

The fact that a superintendent delegated in this way was no guarantee that the Jeanes teacher could obtain additional resources. "The members of the school board don't want a nickel spent on Negro schools," complained one. "We have a hard time getting supplies for them—or anything else for that matter." In this situation there was little she could do. "We've got to live with these people, and we have got to get along with them even if we can't convince them about the right thing to do with regard to Negro schools."[70]

Yet many Jeanes teachers achieved a good deal, even with bosses who were not especially sympathetic to black education. One reason superintendents neglected black schools was that blacks did not submit requests. They were afraid to, or considered it futile. Blacks would readily communicate their needs through a Jeanes teacher, however. Superintendents sometimes told them not to organize Parent-Teacher Associations because they did not want to be bothered by black requests. "The white PTA is trouble enough," explained one. But the persistence of a Jeanes teacher could wear a superintendent down. In Davidson County, Tennessee, Georgia Cash moved her superintendent from flatly prohibiting PTAs to merely disliking them. "We have local PTAs in 50% of the schools and a countywide council by keeping doggedly at it." Some Jeanes teachers became legendary for their ability to procure books, money, and equipment. In Coweta County, Georgia, "you just went to Lillian Williams . . . and it was done."[71]

In Ouchita Parish, Louisiana, Gertrude Ammons virtually rebuilt the black public schools by securing Rosenwald buildings and by establishing schools where none had previously existed. The school in Mineral Springs, for example, was started by Anthony C. Facen, a former student of hers whom she persuaded to move to Ouchita Parish after graduating from Tuskegee Institute. Ammons organized teachers into a parish-wide association, and held monthly teachers' meetings. She dealt with the "constant stream of people" bearing complaints and requests "in a kind and sympathetic manner." Ammons transacted most of her business with the superintendent, T. O. Brown, over the telephone. When she met Brown in person, she endured lectures on the need to "keep your head and feet on the ground." If blacks attempted to vote, there would be "very serious trouble," he warned.

"There are some people fool enough to talk about race equality, but that will never be." Yet Brown, an elderly man who had held his job for thirty years, accorded Ammons respect and authority. He gave her power to hire and fire teachers, and cautiously supported her work to improve black schools. Ammons was grateful that Brown had never propositioned her—good behavior she considered "a bit unusual for superintendents in that section."[72]

When Jeanes teachers encountered apathy, divided communities, or outright opposition, they needed diplomatic skills of a high order, sometimes mixed with cunning. In Wilkinson County, Georgia, Tommie C. Calhoun wanted to build a decent schoolhouse in the town of Gordon, the site of a kaolin mine that employed about 150 blacks. Superintendent Julian Bloodworth promised her eight hundred dollars, but told her to first raise four hundred from local blacks. The head of the mine allowed her to solicit donations from the miners, but the men were not interested. "One told me he wasn't going to give me a damn thing on a school." She prevailed upon the white foreman to apply pressure, and six weeks later she had the money. When Bloodworth reneged on his promise, saying the school board had no money, Calhoun secured a donation of twenty-five hundred dollars from the head of the mining company. Bloodworth then suggested equipping the school with homemade wooden benches—calling Calhoun "too high-minded" for wanting proper desks—prompting her to raise the money herself. Told by the superintendent that she would not be able to order school furniture without his signature, she persuaded a prominent white citizen to place the order and organized a group of teachers, white and black, to raise a thousand dollars to pay for it.[73]

Securing better teachers taxed the Jeanes teachers' diplomatic skills to the limit, for it involved challenging long-established customs among both blacks and whites. Black teachers, often wholly untrained, had never received proper supervision. They did not make lesson plans, they used old-fashioned rote-learning methods, and they relied on corporal punishment. Many could not even fill in an attendance register. Their only exposure to modern ideas and methods came at the annual summer schools that many were obliged to attend in order to renew their certificates. Through school visits and monthly group meetings, Jeanes teachers could help some teachers to improve. But many were beyond improvement and needed replacing. Unless she enjoyed blanket authority to hire and fire, though—and many did not—the Jeanes teacher ran into all manner of obstacles in ousting incompetent teachers. The appointment of teachers was still amateurish, occasionally corrupt, and frequently influenced by personal relationships that amounted to a kind of patronage system. Black trustees tried to get wives, daughters, and church members appointed. Whites deferred to the black trustees' preferences or practiced their own kind of favoritism. In one Louisiana parish, Horace Mann Bond encountered six members of a single family, none of them remotely qualified, teaching in the public schools. He discovered that the family was still being rewarded for its support of the Democratic Party during Reconstruction.[74]

The experience of Ella A. Tackwood in finding a replacement for a beloved and effective principal of a three-teacher school in Jasper County, Georgia, illustrates some of the problems. Tackwood recommended a male teacher from Atlanta, whom the superintendent interviewed and hired. However, she discovered that the school's trustees had made their own appointment, choosing the daughter of the man who chaired the trustee board. When confronted with Tackwood's choice, the trustees refused to accept him. "We done 'lected," said one, "and we ain't gonna 'lect no more." Faced with this dispute, the superintendent advised Tackwood not to press the issue. "It is better to let folks have their way sometimes," he explained, "have your way maybe next time." As things turned out, the Jeanes teacher got her man, but only because the parents rebelled against the trustees' choice.[75]

Hence the Jeanes teacher's efforts sometimes caused ill feeling. In one Louisiana Parish, the teachers lived "in constant fear" of her. In another parish, the Jeanes teacher, a rare man, made himself thoroughly unpopular by treating the teachers "as though they are children." Most Jeanes teachers exercised great tact, knowing that without the cooperation of parents and teachers they would find it impossible to carry out fundraising activities. But no matter how considerate she was of others' feelings, the mere fact that she exercised authority over ordinary teachers—authority derived from the white power structure—caused resentment. Weaker teachers disliked having their methods criticized and felt insecure.[76]

Male teachers, particularly the principals of larger schools, found it galling to have a black woman as a superior. The principal felt that the Jeanes teacher weakened his authority over his own teachers, especially when she worked from an office in his school. He found it humiliating to depend upon the Jeanes teacher for textbooks and other supplies. "You danced to her music and if she didn't like you, move on somewhere else," recalled the former principal of Ocila High School in Irwinton, Georgia. Another principal routinely returned the paychecks that the Jeanes teacher delivered to his school once a month. Rather than acknowledge her power, he collected the checks from the school board office himself.[77]

By the 1930s the original goal of having Jeanes teachers spread the gospel of industrial education had been tacitly abandoned. The foundation officials periodically lamented a decline in missionary spirit and complained of a "degradation" in the Jeanes work. But the Jeanes Fund's field agent, veteran black educator W. T. B. Williams, argued that the role of the Jeanes teachers in promoting public health, school building, fundraising, and better teaching far outweighed any losses. "They cannot make exhibits of the better trained children as effectively as they used to make of aprons, dresses, cakes, and vegetables," he conceded, but what they now did was "vitally necessary, helpful, and valuable." The most serious threat to the work came when superintendents overloaded the Jeanes teachers with routine administration while doing nothing to help them improve black schools, and when school boards, during the Great Depression, assigned Jeanes teachers to regular classroom teaching.[78]

The Jeanes teacher was, in Gunnar Myrdal's phrase, "a remarkable and pathetic figure in the history of Negro education." Her work was creative, wide-ranging, and admirable, but all the impressive gains that could be attributed to her could only mitigate a problem that required drastic remedies. The basic conundrum of black southerners— how to advance within a system designed by white people to stop them from advancing—applied as forcefully to the Jeanes teachers as to any other black teachers. And it was an unpalatable fact that instead of narrowing, the inequalities between black schools and white schools widened in the 1920s and 1930s. Black schools improved but white schools improved more. Every educational innovation had to be first started in the white schools; a decade or two then went by before whites considered extending it to black schools. Every year, total spending on public schools increased, but the black schools did not catch up. The faith of women teachers sustained black schools and strengthened black communities at a time when white supremacy could not be directly challenged. But it would require organization, as well as faith, to bring about equality.[79]

CHAPTER SEVEN

The City and the Country

Get on board this noble vessel
She has landed many a thousand
It will take you home to glory
Get on board
Get on board.

Assembly song,
Fairfield Industrial
High School

Dunbar High School, Lynchburg, Virginia, 1924.

Papers of Jackson Davis, MSS3072,
Special Collections Library,
University of Virginia

On a January morning in 1888, Arthur Harold Parker found himself standing before a class of second-graders in the newly built Slater School in Birmingham, Alabama. It was a moment of profound satisfaction. "Right at the very first I became fascinated with the work of teaching," he recalled years later, "and as much so with the prestige that such a position carried among my people." Attired in a brand new Prince Albert coat, a plug hat atop his head as he traveled to and from school, the eighteen-year-old looked and felt like a member of the new black middle class, one of the "logical leaders of people." When he started teaching, Parker was only the thirteenth black instructor to be appointed to the public schools of Birmingham. Fifty years later the school he headed, Industrial High School for Negroes, employed ninety teachers and enrolled three thousand pupils. Parker High School—as the school board named it upon Parker's death in 1939—was the largest and most famous black school in the South. With a modern plant and well-equipped classrooms, it exemplified how much black teachers could achieve, even under white supremacy, in the cities of the South. It was a world away from the one-room shacks that still served as schools in rural areas just a few miles away.[1]

Building black high schools within the South's segregated public education system, at a time when blacks lacked any political voice, called for ambition, dedication, executive ability, and a knack for improvisation. It demanded, above all, diplomatic skills of a high order—the ability to command the confidence of, and win support from, both blacks and whites.

Parker possessed these qualities in abundance. He was the kind of man who could turn his hand to practically anything. Born in Springfield, Ohio, Parker never attended college but had the benefit of a northern high school education. He also acquired a profitable skill from his barber father, a resourceful man who had escaped from an Alabama plantation at the age of twelve. During his early years as a teacher, Parker augmented his income by barbering at county fairs. When Slater School bought an organ, he taught himself to play. He then turned his musical proficiency into extra income—he preferred playing the organ to barbering because of the "better class of people" he met. Parker also got himself a job with Rev. W. R. Pettiford, pastor of Birmingham's Sixteenth Street Baptist Church and founder of a savings bank. Using the typing, shorthand, and bookkeeping skills he had learned at a northern business college, Parker served as Pettiford's financial secretary. When in 1900 the school board agreed to create a public high school for blacks, superintendent J. H. Phillips appointed Parker to head it. "To this day I do not know why he selected me," Parker wrote thirty years later. The fact that Pettiford led the campaign for the high school and Parker was Pettiford's right-hand man—financial secretary, Sunday School superintendent, choirmaster—may have had something to with it. Parker promised Phillips that the enrollment would be sufficiently high to cover the high school's costs, each pupil paying $1.50 a month in tuition fees. The first class recruited eighteen pupils. It met on the second floor of Cameron elementary school.[2]

As enrollment snowballed and the high school outgrew its space, there was no question of the school board paying for a new building. So Parker found makeshifts, improvising his high school on the cheap. In 1910 he moved the school, which now enrolled two hundred pupils, to an old wooden frame building. When that structure was condemned as unsafe, he acquired an abandoned Presbyterian church that came with a small schoolhouse. He also bought fourteen shanties, "of the most ordinary and inexpensive southern type," that occupied an adjoining block. The pupils themselves converted the buildings into classrooms. As each one became vacant, boys moved in to take out the partitions, truss the roofs, and paint the interiors. "Then girls would come along with brooms, mops, scouring powder, tubs and pans." A wooden walkway connected all the cottages, so that pupils' feet did not wade through mud. The church steeple was cannibalized to build a toilet. Visitors marveled at the ingenuity of the transformation. But the school was soon bursting at the seams again. At one point Parker housed two classes in a large tent.[3]

In his quest for greater funding, Parker assiduously courted Birmingham's white leaders. By the 1900s, middle-class campaigns for honest, efficient, and stronger government—the political tendency known as "progressivism" or the "progressive movement"—were taking place in every region of the United States, including the South. Southern progressives combined their desire for reform with a firm belief in white supremacy, as notoriously personified by Georgia's Hoke Smith, who won the 1906 gubernatorial election after a viciously anti-Negro campaign. But blacks could sometimes make effective appeals to the progressives' commitment to economic efficiency and better public services. Birmingham progressive John Herbert Phillips, the superintendent of schools, became Parker's key ally. A native of Kentucky who was educated in Ohio, Phillips was an energetic and effective administrator who, like many of Birmingham's civic boosters, argued that an educated black population was necessary for social stability and economic growth. Although Phillips was also a convinced white supremacist who believed that the "Negro brain" stopped developing at the time of adolescence and that schooling for blacks after the age of fourteen was wasted, he still supported the black high school. Parker overcame Phillips's reservations by cultivating a close personal relationship with the man and by incorporating industrial education—one of the superintendent's enthusiasms—into the school's curriculum. From the outset, all students took either sewing or carpentry.

Parker also played upon the "Old South" nostalgia that, together with "Lost Cause" mythology, had become a kind of civic religion for many white southerners. Even in a bastion of the New South like Birmingham—an industrial city that had not existed before the Civil

War—nothing softened up a white audience, even a hardheaded administrator like John Herbert Phillips, better than a Negro choir singing "old plantation songs." Serenading white audiences with songs of the Old South was, of course, a time-honored fundraising ploy. After the Jubilee Singers saved Fisk University from bankruptcy in the 1870s, dozens—hundreds even— of black schools got in on the act. Parker played the game to perfection, exhibiting his choir on every conceivable public occasion. "The singing of 'Old Folks at Home' by upward of 65 voices was superb," enthused the *Birmingham News* in 1903. "What the Negro High School needs more than anything else are larger quarters and better equipment." Phillips was as sentimental as anyone. "You will get an instructor of orchestra on one condition," he told the 1914 commencement class, "and that is that you will always sing these old songs." In 1924, three years after Phillips's death, Industrial High School moved into a new brick building.[4]

Lauded by white leaders and revered by the black middle class, Parker was the most respected African American in Birmingham. But his racial diplomacy exemplified some of the costs that black educators paid, and some of the restrictions they accepted, in building institutions. Parker confessed that his constant recourse to plantation songs evoked "some unfavorable comment" among blacks. More generally, Parker, like Booker T. Washington, projected a cheery optimism and steadfast conservatism that reflected an image of blacks that white people wanted to see, not what blacks really thought and felt. Parker's autobiography, published in the school's magazine, is *Up from Slavery* warmed over, but without a trace of the subtle irony that made Washington's narrative a not-so-veiled critique of racism. Parker treated racial discrimination as if it did not exist. He made no reference to disenfranchisement or lynching. He made no mention of the Great Depression save for condemning the radicalism—"wild prophecies, meaningless isms, and ephemeral chimeras"—that it encouraged. Given his complete dependency upon white politicians and officials, one might argue that such political self-effacement was unavoidable. By the time of his death, however, the kind of institution-building strategy he exemplified seemed increasingly inadequate. "He was a very fine man," opined one former teacher, "but he kept himself in the

field of education and thought very little of the affairs of the Negro politically. . . . He did not act from a selfish point of view; but . . . his vision was so narrow."[5]

No black leader, let alone a public servant like Parker, could change
the web of racial discrimination, official and customary, that restricted
black lives in a city like Birmingham. Political activism was out of the
question for him. Challenging racial segregation—even if he wished
to—would have been futile. Nor was there much that Parker could do
about the job discrimination that was squeezing blacks out of traditional occupations and consigning them to the lower rungs of industrial work. Although Parker's school took "industrial education" more
seriously than most—pupils devoted fully a third of their time to it—
the skills children learned, while useful, were less and less relevant to
earning a living. The demand for carpenters, painters, bricklayers, and
tailors was declining. Moreover, Parker's efforts to update industrial
education by offering "vocational skills" adapted to the modern labor
market ran into stiff opposition from white workers. The school board
dropped plans to introduce plumbing, steam fitting, and electrical engineering. Even millinery evoked white objections, forcing Parker to
quietly obtain the necessary equipment from New York. The depth of
white hostility to black education—mainly from elements of the white
working class—meant that every improvement to black schools ran a
gauntlet of political opposition from white labor leaders. When the
city proposed a bond issue to build schoolhouses for blacks, including
a new Industrial High School, superintendent Charles B. Glenn received direct threats from the Ku Klux Klan.[6]

In this context, Parker's achievement was substantial. At a time
when other states in the Deep South—Georgia, Louisiana, Mississippi, South Carolina—did not fund a single public high school for
blacks, he and other black leaders created an outstandingly successful
one. Industrial High School helped to shape a black middle class of
teachers, nurses, businessmen, and professionals, who repaid it with
loyalty and affection. The school also helped to produce a strong black
working class by giving thousands of its pupils a high level of literacy.
Fostering an esprit de corps through its concerts, clubs, and other extracurricular activities, the school became a cultural anchor of Bir-

mingham's black community. If it accommodated to racial segregation, it also tried to instill racial pride. Spirituals, Parker insisted, "are
part of our life and history as a race . . . They are evidences of our
power to create a music of our own, based on our experiences and re-
flecting our ideals." Shortly before he died, he introduced Negro history into the curriculum, despite "keen opposition."[7]

URBAN public schools were, virtually by definition, better than rural schools. The scattered settlement pattern of the South's countryside made the one-room schoolhouse the rural norm. The concentrated populations of large towns and cities favored the multiteacher,
graded school. Moreover, whites in the cities—those who dominated
economic and political life—did not usually exhibit the kind of deep
hostility to black education that whites in the plantation counties often displayed. True, the black urban presence aroused mixed feelings
among whites. Alarmed by the post–Civil War influx of freedmen
from the plantations, they constantly complained about vice, crime,
and pauperism among city blacks. Yet the white middle and upper
classes depended upon blacks for domestic servants, manual laborers,
and industrial workers. Once they recognized the futility of trying to
keep blacks out of cities, white civic leaders endeavored to more effectively control and manage them. Disenfranchisement and racial segregation represented the more coercive aspect of that strategy; education was the more benevolent part. Urban schools taught blacks to a
higher standard because city life demanded a higher level of literacy.
"Merchants wanted Negroes to be able to read their advertisements,"
writes Louis Harlan. Employers needed their workers to read instructions that were often quite complex. Moreover, whites in the cities
had less cause to actively discourage black schooling. Unlike planters,
who depended upon children's nimble fingers to gather in the crop,
city employees had far less use for black child labor. Longer school
sessions did not weaken their ability to command black workers.[8]

This is not to say that white elites were generous or evenhanded.
Everywhere city school boards spent relatively less on black schools;
and the replacement of white teachers with black ones, followed by
the disenfranchisement of black voters, made the discrimination

worse. In Nashville, for example, black teachers experienced a relative decline in pay and an absolute increase in their teaching loads. And when the school board implemented a building program in 1905, it "overwhelmingly favored whites." Having enjoyed near parity in 1870, by 1915 blacks received only half the per capita spending allocated to whites.[9]

Rates of discrimination varied between cities. The relative size of the black population, the nature of the urban economy, and the relationship between white and black leaders all influenced the level of support that black schools received. In states with relatively small black populations—Texas, Virginia, Tennessee, Arkansas, Kentucky, Missouri—black city schools fared better than those in Deep South states. By 1911, for example, Texas and Missouri accounted for nearly half of all black public high schools in the southern and border states. In Texas, where the rural schools for blacks were as bad as any in the South, urban blacks enjoyed unparalleled access to secondary education. Every city with a population of more than twenty thousand established a colored high school. Galveston started one in 1885—forty years before Atlanta—and in 1893 moved it to a new stone building that boasted "steam heat, oak woodwork, indoor lavatories, and floors of wide pine board." In the Deep South, on the other hand, city school boards spent less on black schools and were reluctant to fund anything beyond the elementary grades. Older cities that depended upon the plantation economy tended to do the least. At about the time that Birmingham established Industrial High School, Augusta closed its only black public high school and New Orleans reduced public education for blacks from seven grades to five.[10]

Even the sympathetic white superintendents had a hard time securing resources for black schools. J. H. Phillips, for example, continually drew the attention of his board of education to the deplorable state of Birmingham's black schools. The main problems—common to nearly all southern cities—were severe overcrowding and inadequate buildings. In 1908 Phillips complained, "No new school building has been erected for the negroes during the last fifteen years." Pupils from a school that burned down in 1895 still met in a church basement that flooded after every heavy rainfall. "I shall not attempt to describe the congested condition of some of the negro schools," Phillips despaired. "These conditions must be seen . . . to be fully appreciated." The size of the average class reached seventy-seven pupils. Frame school-houses had been repaired so many times that only the patches held them together. Continuing black migration to the city, and an urban population that moved frequently, accentuated these problems. As a result, many children went completely unschooled. Phillips reckoned that Birmingham's public schools enrolled as few as 42 percent of black school-age children. In nearby Anniston, another industrial city, the situation was even worse: two black schools accounted for less than 20 percent of the black school-age population. A few children attended private and church schools, reported James L. Sibley, the state agent of Negro education, but "a large proportion of the Negro children do not attend any school at all."[11]

Still, few black teachers would have exchanged city schools for country schools. City teachers taught longer terms and earned twice as much. While rural teachers had to farm, preach, barber, nurse, and launder to eke out an existence, urban teachers could make their primary living from teaching school. The rural teacher worked in physical isolation, lacked intellectual stimulation, and commanded little standing as a professional. The only real opportunity to develop her limited skills came through the annual summer school that she was virtually compelled to attend in order to renew her teaching certificate. The city teacher belonged to a distinct, tightly knit group that formed the backbone of the black middle class. She not only enjoyed a varied cultural life but also had much more scope for intellectual and professional development. Moreover, urban school superintendents, unlike many of their rural counterparts, had little interest in deliberately favoring poorly qualified teachers. They applied similar standards of selection and certification to black teachers and white teachers, and usually showed some interest in developing black teachers' skills. They often assembled their teachers for regular meetings—blacks and whites attending separately, of course—to discuss problems, methods, and discipline. In the 1900s, for example, black teachers in Houston were studying James's *Psychology* and Tompkins's *Philosophy of Teaching* in twice-monthly institutes.[12]

It was hardly surprising, then, that city schools recruited the best-educated black teachers. In Georgia, for example, 60 percent of black teachers in rural counties held third-grade certificates in 1910, but less than 1 percent of the city teachers sank that low. In North Carolina, at about the same time, 41 percent of black city teachers held college diplomas, while only 12 percent of rural teachers did. By 1930 only 10 percent of Memphis's 328 black teachers had not graduated from a high school, compared with 35 percent of black teachers in the rural South. Urban school boards now required of new teachers at least two years of "normal training," if not four years of college. In Houston the proportion of black teachers holding college degrees increased from 12 to 35 percent between 1924 and 1930. The proportion with less than a high school education declined from 13 percent to 5 percent.[13]

It was not a case of the cities drawing well-educated teachers away from rural districts. Despite the expansion of black city schools, especially after the First World War, the overall flow of better-educated teachers was from the city to the country, not in the other direction, due to the fact that there were far more city-born teachers than there were jobs in city schools. By 1940 about half of the black teachers in rural Georgia were city-born.

However, most of the best-educated teachers, the college graduates, came from the cities and stayed in them. Black high schools, colleges, and normal schools were concentrated in the cities and drew the bulk of their students from close by. In 1940, Georgia's six black colleges recruited 60 percent of their students from the counties in which they were situated, whereas less that a fifth of the state's black population lived in those counties. Fewer than one in ten college-educated teachers hailed from the countryside, and only one in five ended up teaching there.[14]

Because teaching became a stable profession far earlier in the cities, urban teachers taught for longer, and many made it a lifelong career. Almost every city school could boast a handful of dedicated teachers—usually women, often unmarried—who provided cohesion, continuity, and commitment. Lincoln School in Sumter, South Carolina, produced two such stalwarts: Martha A. Savage taught from 1882 until her death fifty years later; Mamie E. Glover served from 1889 to

1933. When the school board built a new school, it named it after these two teachers. In fact, it became a common practice for southern towns and cities to honor long-serving black teachers in this way.[15]

The remarkable longevity of many women teachers stemmed from their single-minded dedication and from the fact that they had no children. In the rural South, it was normal for black women teachers to carry on working after they married, and to return to teaching after bearing children. In the cities, however, school boards were less permissive. The rules varied, but up to the 1930s women teachers were normally expected to resign when they got married. The regulation was usually applied less stringently to blacks. Nevertheless, most black city teachers were unmarried. Many women teachers therefore focused on their careers rather than families. Unmarried or childless teachers also avoided one of the main causes of early death: pregnancy and childbirth.[16]

The narrow economic basis of the black middle class meant that many teachers married other teachers, and that their children became teachers as well. In every southern city one could find black families that produced two or more generations of schoolteachers. Houston had the Yates family; Petersburg, the Colsons; Durham, the Fitzgeralds. Yates High School in Houston, which opened in 1926, took its name from Rev. Jack Yates, a former slave who, with the assistance of white missionaries, organized Antioch Baptist Church (the oldest surviving brick building in downtown Houston). Yates and his wife, Harriet, ensured that all eleven of their children received the best education Baptist missionaries could provide. Seven Yates children became teachers—one of them, Pinkie Yates, taught for sixty-five years. Yates grandchildren were teaching in the civil rights era. In Petersburg, Virginia, the Colson family, which descended from free blacks, produced three generations of teachers. James Major Colson, whose mother taught a private school after the Civil War, taught at Virginia Normal and Collegiate Institute (VNCI) for almost thirty years. He married Kate Hill, one of the first black public school teachers in Petersburg. Two of the Colsons' children also taught at the school after its programs were slashed and the school was renamed Virginia Normal and Industrial Institute. One of them, the redoubtable Edna Meade Colson, who died in 1985 at the age of ninety-six, served the college for forty-four years. When she retired in 1953, it was estimated that half of Virginia's black schoolteachers had sat in one of her classes. In North Carolina, three daughters of Robert Fitzgerald, the Union veteran who taught freedmen's schools and public schools until he went blind, became fixtures in the public schools of Durham. One of them, Mary Pauline Fitzgerald, became a schoolteacher in 1885 at the age of fourteen and retired in 1946 at the age of seventy-six.[17]

In their quest for middle-class respectability, city teachers sometimes betrayed an aversion to the black poor that evoked the very stereotypes they were disputing. They were, in fact, deeply ambivalent about the black lower classes. On the one hand they regarded them as kinfolk and fellow victims of slavery and racism. On the other hand they believed, with whites, that slavery had debased the black family and made it hard for the freed people to establish moral habits. Middle-class blacks deplored gambling, drinking, smoking, and Sabbath breaking. They disapproved of the many common-law marriages, easily entered into and easily broken, among the poorer classes. The race needed a "higher standard of social purity," and teachers, the moral instructors of black children, were expected to lead the way.[18]

Moral oversight by black churches made it unlikely that teachers would stray very far from this higher moral standard. "While Nashville's black community revered its teachers," writes one historian, "it also held them accountable, placing heavy obligations and powerful pressures upon them." Baptist prohibitions against smoking, drinking, and gambling still constituted an informal code of conduct, even in the cities, well into the twentieth century. No teacher could afford to be spotted in a juke joint or saloon. Dancing also incurred censure. In 1894 some black teachers in Birmingham were reported to the school board by a group of ministers, who deplored their "sinful amusement." Some preachers even disapproved of teachers seeing plays, complaining that it set a bad example to children. Ida B. Wells received a "severe lecture on going to the theater" from a minister's son. She apparently took the rebuke to heart. "When I grow weary and despondent and think my life useless and unprofitable," the chastened teacher confided to her diary, "may I remember this episode, and may it strengthen me to the performance of my duty." When James Weldon Johnson staged an operetta, which ended with a dance routine, at his school's closing exercises, he incurred "the wrath of several of the colored clergy," who also condemned Johnson's own fondness for dancing and smoking. The worldly Johnson suffered no pangs of conscience, only irritation, and the school board took no notice. Nevertheless, teachers always had to look behind their backs.

The worst offense a teacher could commit was sexual impropriety. Even when blameless, teachers were vulnerable to malicious gossip and false accusations. In Raleigh, North Carolina, three teachers resigned in 1897 after being criticized, groundlessly it seems, for immoral behavior. In Memphis, Ida B. Wells—attractive, vivacious, and unmarried—constantly set tongues wagging. She once inspired an erroneous story that she and another teacher had been dismissed for "immoral conduct." Petersburg teacher William H. Johnson recounted how his act of patching some cracks in his classroom door excited the prurient fantasies of a woman colleague: "[She believed] I was trying to prevent her prying through the cracks on my possible, as she thought, unprincipled like actions."[19]

The lives of urban teachers were far from dour, however. As well as setting moral examples and "uplifting the race," they also enjoyed cultural pursuits and organized entertainment. The diary Ida B. Wells kept in the 1880s provides a revealing insight into the life of a young woman whose occupation placed her at the heart of a small and clearly defined black middle class. Religion—attending church, teaching Sunday school, seeing a Moody and Sankey revival meeting—was important to Wells, but so were intellectual, cultural, and social activities. She attended weekly meetings of the Lyceum Club for "recitations, essays, and debates interspersed with music." She organized theater parties, joined a drama club, and paid for elocution lessons. She attended tea parties and visited other teachers. When alone in her boardinghouse, she kept her diary, wrote letters, and read novels. Struggling to maintain middle-class appearances, she was continually in debt. "I need a parasol, fan, and I ought to have a hat and a pair of gloves," she noted, having just spent half a month's salary on one dress.

The social life of black teachers varied according to time and place, but every city could boast an array of middle-class clubs and societies. Jacksonville had the Oceala Club, which staged two or three dances each winter. New Orleans had the Bunch Club, which focused on Carnival. "This social life was . . . a replica of the pettiness of 'society' in general," recalled James Weldon Johnson. "There were present the same snobberies, the same envies and jealousies, the same strivings and heartburns, the same expenditure of time and energy upon futilities. And, as in 'society' in general, it was the women who were the chief sticklers and arbiters."[20]

For some teachers, like Wells, the job ended when the school bell sounded at the end of the day. Judging by her diary entries, she found little satisfaction in teaching. The teacher that she once wrote about in a short story—one who dutifully visited the homes of pupils, and who "instilled elevated thoughts, race pride and ambition" with her daily lessons—was a fictionalized ideal. Teaching attracted men and women of great talent because the economic opportunities open to educated blacks were so limited. But many of those talented people would rather have been doing something else. Teaching was their second or third choice. Often this showed.[21]

Yᴇᴛ the commitment of many city teachers could not be doubted. Fannie C. Williams, the principal of Valena C. Jones School in New Orleans, provides an outstanding example. A unmarried woman who dedicated her long life and unflagging energy to education and racial uplift, she was, according to former pupil Andrew J. Young, "a handsome, dark-skinned woman with pressed, white hair, [who] believed in strict discipline and patrolled the halls of the three-story structure observing classes and seeing for herself that everything was in order. Miss Williams went about the task of uplifting the race with great gusto and an almost legendary determination, pacing the halls with her thick ruler ever at the ready." For thirty-three years, between 1921 and 1954, Williams ran an elementary school that enrolled as many as two thousand pupils in grades one through seven. During the 1930s she also headed a normal department that annually selected thirty students from the city's secondary schools and gave them two years of teacher training. She did all this with "a little cubbyhole for her office and no room anywhere for a secretary."[22]

Williams saw to it that education at Valena C. Jones embraced health, welfare, Negro history, and current affairs. She established a nursery and a kindergarten. She organized a health program and persuaded two dentists to donate their services. She lobbied the Girl Scouts to allow the city's first black troop to be organized at her school. She gave pupils a taste of politics and democracy—and enlisted the children for school chores—by organizing "the whole school . . . into a Republic." Each classroom was designated a state, and each state elected a governor, secretary of state, judges, policemen, senators, health inspectors, and a cleanliness committee. A school magazine, *The Moving Finger,* chronicled the amazing variety of extracurricular activities in which pupils took part. It also reported the parade of stellar figures whom Williams persuaded to visit Valena C. Jones. In 1938–39, for example, the school hosted Olympic gold medalist Jesse Owens, self-help guru Dale Carnegie, and the Philadelphia preacher-politician Marshall Shepherd, who assured pupils that "the Negroes 'break' in southern politics is not far off." For years after her retirement Williams tutored slow-learning children, illiterate adults, and Spanish speakers. She died in 1980 at the venerable age of ninety-seven.[23]

The driving dedication of women like Fannie Williams exacted a price. Part of that price was paid by the teachers under them. Lucille Hutton, who taught at Valena C. Jones in the 1930s, recalled the pressures of working for such an exacting superior in difficult conditions. With chronic overcrowding and an acute lack of material and equipment, it was hard enough to carry out her regular classroom duties. But Williams's ambitions for the school created an enormous amount of extracurricular activity for her teachers, much of which fell upon Hutton, whose expertise in music was always in demand: "She had a class night, and one teacher had to teach a play, and practice that play . . . The next night was baccalaureate, a Sunday night, and I was the one to whom the music fell, of course, and I had to get the music, and have somebody play the processional march . . . And then there was the commencement exercise and, again, I had to teach the songs and that was extra work, but you didn't say a word about it, you just got to work and did it." When the National Education Association met in New Orleans in 1936, the head of the NEA's entertainment committee asked Williams to arrange for "some singing of spirituals by a colored group." It fell to Hutton to provide the choir (which, when it arrived at the Roosevelt Hotel, had to use the elevator marked "freight"). Determined to attend concerts in order to keep up with the latest music, Hutton found herself correcting papers and writing report cards at three in the morning. When she left the school in 1939 for a different teaching job, she breathed a sigh of relief. "It saved me from losing my mind."[24]

Black city schools were overcrowded and underequipped. In rural schools, the problem of excessively large enrollments was often mitigated by the fact that many children failed to attend regularly or show up at all. In the cities, on the other hand, even though compulsory attendance laws were rarely enforced with any stringency, a larger proportion of children attended school regularly. This meant that class sizes were often larger. The Great Depression, which eliminated much of the casual employment that had kept urban children out of school, swelled enrollments. New Orleans' black schools illustrated the problem in an extreme form. In the white elementary schools, only 14 percent of the classes had more than 40 pupils and only 0.4 percent had more than 50. In black elementary schools, 84 percent had more than 40 pupils and 42 percent more than 50. In New Orleans and other cities, school boards responded to overcrowding through a "platoon" system, dividing the school day into two shifts, half the children attending in the morning, half in the afternoon.

Comparisons between black and white schools also revealed large disparities in equipment. The white schools in New Orleans received textbooks, paper, pencils, art and construction supplies, drawing supplies, and library books. Black schools received only textbooks (usually discarded ones), paper, and pencils. While both white and black schools depended upon PTAs to buy extra supplies and equipment, black PTAs had to do more with less. Fannie Williams had a secretary only because the PTA paid a mother to help her. "There were no library books, there was no library at all," Lucille Hutton recalled, "and we raised money and bought books, but they were cheap books, they didn't have any colored pictures." And this was in the middle of the Great Depression. Veronica B. Hill, who taught at the same school, remembered buying paper and pencils out of her own salary when supplies promised by the school board failed to arrive. "But with all that," she added, "we were dedicated to seeing to it that our children received the best education that we were able to give them.[25]

By the 1930s the principals of black city schools—especially those who headed high schools—occupied positions of great significance. They managed large, complex organizations and were relatively well paid. Newspapers reported what they said and did. They had extensive contacts in the black community and direct access to the white power structure. They were leaders, mediators, and diplomats. "My position is an important one," James Weldon Johnson remembered thinking upon his appointment to the thousand-pupil, twenty-five-teacher Stanton School in Jacksonville. "Relatively, it is far more important than the principalship of the white . . . school. . . . I shall be scrutinized. I shall meet with envy and antagonism on the outside; and, perhaps, with disloyalty on the inside. . . . Through all these thoughts run alternating currents of confidence and doubt."[26]

The great majority of black principals were men. The proportion ranged from 95 percent in Mississippi to 72 percent in Texas. It was higher still in the cities. In the case of black public high schools, it was virtually unknown for a school board to appoint a woman. This gendered hierarchy reflected a clear policy of reserving the top positions in public education for men.[27]

The most important person in the professional life of the black principal was his white superintendent of schools. Everything—resources, appointments, his own job—depended upon this official. With the confidence and support of the superintendent, a black principal could build a successful school and establish himself as influential figure in the community. Without it, his life was miserable and insecure.

The relationships between black principals and white superintendents ran the gamut. In the small cities, where they were more likely to be amateur administrators, white superintendents could be capricious and oppressive. "She was a mean old something," K. B. Young recalled of his superior in Tuskegee, Alabama. "Her favorite expression was 'Well, Young, we don't even have that in the white schools.'. . . . She didn't want your school to have anything until every white school had some of it. You got the leavings." Young attributed some of the tension in their relationship to the fact that he was much better educated than his superintendent—a not uncommon situation in the small-town South. "I had to walk a tightrope," he remembered. "They watched the 'professor' to see if he was going to get smart." Other small-town superintendents adopted an easygoing, hands-off approach that betrayed a lack of interest. "That's your school and I want you to run it," C. C. Wills told Horace Tate in Greensboro, Georgia. Each month Tate went to Wills's office to turn in his attendance report and collect his teachers' paychecks. "That was the extent of my contact with Mr. Wills."[28]

In the larger cities, where they were more likely to be trained, experienced administrators, sometimes recruited from outside the state—even from outside the South—superintendents usually treated black principals with, by contemporary standards, professional courtesy. This was true even in the Deep South. In Columbia, South Carolina, for example, black principals usually commanded the respect of the school board and enjoyed a businesslike relationship with their superintendent. When J. E. Wallace, the principal of Howard school, was arrested for resisting an officer—he had refused to let the policeman arrest some children in the schoolhouse—the school board opposed the prosecution and criticized the police. C. A. Johnson, the first principal of Booker T. Washington High School, enjoyed a close relationship with A. C. Flora, the young teacher who became Columbia's superintendent in 1927. In 1931 Flora secured a General Education Board grant to employ Johnson as his deputy. Charged with improving the black schools, Johnson introduced achievement and intelligence tests. He collected figures on, and analyzed the reasons for, tardiness, absence, retardation, and withdrawals. He introduced a program of "character education" that included citizenship and sex education. He held weekly meetings with principals and monthly meetings with all teachers. "Topics for discussion grew out of problems as sensed by teachers themselves."[29]

Fruitful collaborations between black principals and white superintendents could be found throughout the South, in cities large and small. In Fort Myers, Florida, for example, James R. Dixon forged a friendship with J. Colin English, the principal of the white high school, that paid off handsomely when English became the superintendent of schools. In 1927 English appointed Dixon the first principal of Dunbar High School. "Their interaction is not discernible in Board minutes," writes the school's historian, but "some sort of enduring partnership was forged." In Jacksonville, James Weldon Johnson felt so confident about his relationship with his superintendent that he turned his elementary school into a high school by the simple expedient of adding a grade, on his own initiative, and then teaching the class himself. His confidence was entirely justified. The superintendent, when he learned what Johnson had done, backed him completely.[30]

A principal's relationship with his superintendent crucially affected his ability to run an effective school. Everywhere, male principals had to win the cooperation of their predominantly female teaching staff through leadership and persuasion. Teachers expected to be treated with respect and to be involved in decision making. On the other hand they were quick to exploit perceived weaknesses. Principals had to be very confident that they could rely upon their superintendent to buttress their authority. Without such backing, they were in trouble.

The experience of Charles N. Hunter illustrated how a principal could lose the respect of his teachers if he felt unsure about his superintendent. A former slave who became highly literate, Hunter was a Republican activist, prolific journalist, and well-known race leader. As the principal of Oberlin graded school in Raleigh, North Carolina, he had charge of four women teachers. By 1904, however, Hunter's relationship with three of them had deteriorated. Reporting to superintendent E. P. Moses, he excoriated the trio for being insubordinate, irresponsible, and woefully lacking in "that mental, moral, social, and physical discipline so essential to . . . the great responsibility of teaching." When he made suggestions, Hunter complained, these teachers questioned his authority. Thus challenged, and failing to make the teachers do what he wanted, Hunter quickly lost the battle. "I did not feel that there was within me sufficient authority to enforce compliance and I thought it best not to make such an attempt." Twelve years later, Hunter complained that "each teacher seems to be under the impression that she is conducting a distinct, separate school." Hunter found himself cleaning rooms, lighting fires, and cleaning toilets when three of the four "lady teachers" refused to carry out janitorial work. "They said they thought that my duty." Hunter believed that the source of his difficulty was an absence of support from the superintendent. Teachers believed that they answered to the white man who appointed them, not their black principal. "The frequency of the questions, 'Did Professor Moses order this?' 'Are the other schools doing this?' soon convinced me that unless every suggestion, direction, and scheme of work bore the stamp of your authority, teachers felt themselves under little or no obligation to follow it."[31]

Principals often dreaded visits by the superintendent and other whites. Such occasions could reinforce their authority but just as easily undermine it. It was all too easy for whites to criticize black teachers and to treat them with lack of respect. "There are . . . superintendents of schools who will enter a school room with such a degree of freedom and unostentation that for them to cross the threshold of the door creates a perfect sense of cooperation and good will," wrote William H. Johnson. "With others, their very shadow seems to charge the atmosphere with explosives." Perhaps the most common cause of resentment on the part of principals—and black teachers generally—was being criticized in front of their pupils. Johnson, who began teaching in the 1870s and retired in the 1920s, served under a handful of superintendents and experienced problems with only one. Like all experienced teachers, he had very individual methods of managing his children. One involved allowing the pupils brief periods between recesses when they could relax and talk. When the new superintendent entered the room during one of these periods, he berated Johnson for failing to quiet his class. "After the close of school I repaired to the office . . . and told him I thought it unfair to be thus spoken to in the presence of the pupils."[32]

Teachers resented, above all, whites' refusal to accord them courtesy titles. Even the most fair-minded superintendent hesitated to violate the white taboo on addressing a black person as "Mr." or "Mrs." It was profoundly humiliating for a teacher to be called by her first name in front of the pupils. "I feel like walking right out of that school and never going back," exploded Pauline Fitzgerald after one superintendent's visit. "I spend a lifetime trying to teach my children respect for themselves and respect for authority, and those dirty Rebs come right behind me and tear down everything I've built up." The lack of respect rubbed off on the children, reminding them that their teacher had no greater status in the eyes of whites than any other black person. "Don't call her Rosalee," one principal asked his superintendent, "just call her 'teacher.'" Whites sometimes compromised by calling the principal "professor" or, as Horace Tate remembered, "nothing at all." Like other black professionals, principals tried to avoid the first-name problem by using initials, encouraging whites to call them "K. B." or "R. C." rather than "Kenneth" or "Richard." But none of these subterfuges and circumlocutions could disguise the aura of white supremacy.[33]

Principals also had to worry about their school boards. Blacks in the cities were less fearful about petitioning school boards than blacks in the countryside, and they frequently requested improvements and expressed their support for this or that principal. City school boards usually listened to black delegations politely, and sometimes acceded to their requests. In 1927 the school board of Franklin, Tennessee, fired James K. Hughes after a delegation of colored citizens filed certain "charges" against him. On the other hand, city school boards felt free to hire and fire black principals at will. Twelve years after it had dismissed Hughes, Franklin's school board fired his successor, I. H. Hampton, for "lack of cooperation and inefficiency." In both cases, their wives also lost their jobs.[34]

In smaller cities, individual school board members sometimes carried more clout than superintendents. Poorly qualified principals whom superintendents wished to replace found protectors on the school board—people for whom they did small favors or cultivated in some other way. In other cases, ambitious teachers forged alliances with school board members that enabled them to oust long-standing principals. Henry Carroll of Monroe, Louisiana, for example, owed his ascent to James A. Noe, a politician and wealthy businessman whose wife, Anna, sat on the school board. In 1944 Carroll abruptly replaced M. J. Foster as principal of the Colored High School. Although the change caused much resentment in the black community—two teachers resigned in protest—Carroll's relationship with Noe enabled him to secure a new building, which the school board renamed "Carroll High School," and to run the school with absolute authority. "When I put you out of here," he told erring pupils, "you can go to the mayor, the school board or anybody else, but you are out." Noe gave Carroll a weekly program on his radio station. When blacks started voting again after 1948, the two men became close political allies. By the 1950s Noe's patronage had made Carroll the most influential African American in Monroe.[35]

Memoirs and oral histories depict black city schools as places where order prevailed, teachers commanded respect, and parents supported the teachers. "The teachers were very dedicated," said a former pupil of Booker T. Washington High School in Columbia, South Carolina. "They shared their lives with us, they made us feel like we were the most important people in the world, and they taught us pride and tradition." Former teachers emphasized the community loyalty that their schools inspired. "Parents believed in the teachers and cooperated," said Fannie Phelps Adams, a member of the last generation of teachers who served segregated schools. "They put their trust in us. What we felt was best for the children, they went along with us." Again and again in such recollections, former teachers and pupils described their school as an anchor of the black community and likened it to an extended family. Teachers continued to visit the homes of pupils. One Alabama school assisted bereaved families by arranging for its home economics department to clean and cook for them. Edmond Jefferson Oliver boasted that in his forty-three years as principal of Fairfield Industrial High School near Birmingham Alabama, he had occasion to expel only twenty pupils. Of the loyalty between the school and its pupils, Oliver said, "If necessary, I can get in touch with a thousand of the 3,162 graduates within ninety days."

The Great Depression made schools even more important to the black community. City teachers worked with welfare agencies to see that children were fed, clothed, and housed. In 1932–33, Columbia's black teachers distributed five thousand sacks of flour, provided by the Red Cross, to needy families. PTAs ran soup kitchens. Schools housed clinics, held night schools, and offered extension classes. Closer involvement with the poor had a profound effect upon city teachers. "This contact gave [them] an opportunity to see, understand, and appreciate conditions under which many children live," reported a black official, "and the almost insurmountable handicaps which pupils and parents must overcome." By the 1930s, too, black city schools were providing a plethora of voluntary activities for their pupils— debate teams, drama clubs, bands, choirs, and athletics teams, all of which encouraged institutional loyalty among pupils and parents. "We were loaded with extra-curricula activities," remembered someone who attended Columbia's black high school. The 1944 catalogue listed fifty-four of them. "It was so different then," recalled one former teacher. "So wonderful then."[36]

But was it really so wonderful? Were the bonds between teachers, pupils, and parents as close as these memories suggest? The oral histories upon which so many of the recent histories of segregated schools are based must be treated with caution. The retired teachers who served in these schools naturally praise their own efforts. The former pupils who volunteer glowing appraisals of them are usually successful adults who responded positively to education. These recollections tell an important part of the story. But there is another part of the story that is sometimes overlooked in the celebratory, and occasionally hagiographic, post-integration literature on the subject.

Teachers cemented their authority not only by evoking affection but also through physical coercion. Corporal punishment was just as common in city schools as it was in rural ones. Teachers who had received any kind of teacher training, whether at a college or a normal school, would have learned that educational theory frowned upon the practice. In the words of Petersburg's William H. Johnson, good teachers knew that "if you secure a child's respect and love, if you get a child's confidence, then there'll be no trouble in discipline." Yet although teachers often struggled with their consciences, most came to accept that some degree of corporal punishment was necessary. "The attitude of the teacher toward his pupils and the response he draws from them constitutes a delicate problem," wrote James Weldon Johnson of his days at Stanton School. "Shall he act the tyrant, and be feared as one? Or shall he just be one of the fellows, and loved as one?" Concluding that "no fixed policy could be laid down," Johnson tried to avoid corporal punishment if possible, but nevertheless "carried a slender rattan cane, which I sometimes used to flick the legs of unruly boys."

Other teachers resorted to corporal punishment with gusto. "I had one teacher who would whip us half to death, and she was an ordained preacher" recalled Rev. John Porter, who attended Birmingham's Parker High School. "We were very, very respectful of them, and almost afraid of them," agreed Emmett W. Bashful, who attended public schools in Baton Rouge in the 1920s and 1930s. "And at that time they didn't have any laws about corporal punishment—they would beat the living stew out of you."[37]

Edmond Jefferson Oliver, the long-serving principal of Fairfield Industrial High School, relished his reputation as a strong man. Some pupils could be appealed to with reason, he told his superintendent, "the remainder of the pupils had to be appealed to through their hides." Given carte blanche to implement his very physical approach to discipline, Oliver used corporal punishment consistently and liberally, the strap being his preferred mode of delivery. During one two-week period he punished half of his two hundred pupils for tardiness. Faced with overt insubordination from one boy, he dragged the offender to the cloakroom. "We had a short tussle and he hit the floor. . . . I grabbed a pick handle as if to strike him and told him quietly that I was going to beat his brains out. I raised the handle as if to strike him and he began to holler and plead."

When it came to selecting a black principal, therefore, communities placed a high value on physical prowess. J. K. Hughes, the principal of a school in Franklin, Tennessee, in the 1920s, was a "big, stout fellow with a big heavy voice." If his size failed to command respect, his paddle, with four holes in it, did. Blacks worried when the school board replaced him with I. H. Hampton, a Tuskegee graduate who stood only five feet six inches. They stopped worrying when Hampton, challenged by a burly football player, "pulled his belt off . . . wrapped it around the boy . . . and just threw him like a spinning top."[38]

Corporal punishment was part of the culture of American schools, and it was more deeply entrenched in the South than in other regions. There is evidence, too, that black schools practiced it more frequently than white schools. J. H. Phillips, Birmingham's superintendent of education, kept track of how often his schools suspended pupils and how often they recorded the use of corporal punishment. In the white schools, suspensions greatly exceeded instances of corporal punishment. Black schools recorded fewer suspensions but far more corporal punishments. In 1894–95, for example, the 78 punishments recorded by the white schools represented 0.04 punishments per pupil, and suspensions accounted for three-quarters of them. The black schools recorded 157 punishments, 0.2 per pupil, four-fifths of which were corporal punishments. Figures from Columbia, South Carolina, more than thirty years later, show a similar pattern. During a six-week period in 1928, twelve white schools recorded fourteen instances of corporal punishment. The city's five black schools inflicted corporal punishment sixty-one times.[39]

Why was corporal punishment more common in black schools? One reason was that school boards placed few, if any, restrictions upon its use in black schools. In Columbia, explained superintendent E. S. Dreher, "corporal punishment is not inflicted on pupils of the [white] high school or on girls in any of the grades of the white schools." No such exemptions applied to the black schools. The fact that black parents lacked any political influence also played a part. If white parents complained about how their child had been disciplined, the school board sometimes interceded on their behalf, reversing or modifying the punishment. Black parents might lodge similar complaints, but school boards rarely, if ever, heeded them. White officials approved of strong black principals, and they did not blanch if such men dished out corporal punishment liberally. "As long as you didn't go over budget, and you didn't rock the boat," explained one South Carolina principal, whites did not interfere. Black schools enjoyed more autonomy than white ones, but it was an autonomy defined by poverty and neglect. In the final analysis, the higher incidence of corporal punishment in black schools reflected time-honored white attitudes that sanctioned and encouraged a certain level of violence against blacks, including violence between blacks.[40]

Historians of black schools have neglected the subject of corporal punishment. Former pupils and teachers, on the other hand, mention it all the time. Neither group faults the practice: they agree that it made for effective discipline and claim that parents rarely objected to it. "[We] received total support," recalled a former teacher at Lincoln High School in Sumter, South Carolina. "Parents expected that corporal punishment would be used." Indeed, some research suggests that because corporal punishment was more widely used by black parents than by white parents, its cultural legacy made it an effective method of promoting positive behavior in black children.

It is questionable, however, that corporal punishment was as beneficial, or as universally approved, as this conventional wisdom asserts. Most studies of black schools are heavily dependent upon middle-class testimony. The memories of the men and women who taught there, and of the former pupils who enjoyed and benefited from education, portray black schools in an overwhelmingly positive light. These are the people who, in general, learned to avoid corporal punishment and gain their teachers' approval. In many cases such behavior patterns reflected what had already been learned at home. Middle-class and lower-middle-class parents tended to discipline their children by praising and rewarding them, rather than by physically chastising them.

In working-class families, on the other hand, many parents used physical violence against their children with great frequency, seldom rewarding or praising them. This was not an effective means of motivating children to behave well, especially if the physical punishment were delayed, arbitrary, or excessive. When these children encountered similar treatment at school—little praise, much punishment—

they were just as unlikely to respond positively. A study of black children in Natchez and New Orleans concluded that frequent corporal punishment rendered the average working-class pupil sullen, hostile, and more resistant to schooling. It also encouraged physically aggressive behavior, often directed against middle-class peers. "These poor . . . struck back at the only thing in the system they could hit: our heads," recalled Nathaniel Lacy, the son of a wealthy dentist, who attended a public school in Shreveport, Louisiana. Angela Davis, another middle-class child, recalled the fighting at Parker High School as verging on fratricide. "Hardly a day would pass without a fight—in class or outside." The children on the receiving end of most of the corporal punishment were the ones doing most of the fighting. They were also the ones most likely to leave school early.[41]

The question arises as to whether teachers discriminated against darker-skinned pupils within black schools. African Americans were highly conscious of, and very sensitive to, intragroup color differences. It could hardly be otherwise, given the fact that light complexion was a visible indicator of white (and Indian) ancestry, which in many cases conferred a distinct advantage upon the individual. Although color and social class did not coincide precisely, the black upper and middle classes, whose ancestral base rested upon the antebellum free Negroes, contained a disproportionate number of mulattoes. Teachers, the most substantial element of the black middle class, as a group had more white and Indian blood than the African American population as a whole.[42]

But white ancestry did not evoke a common response in those who bore it. It could evoke pride, shame, or confusion. For some families it was a source of cohesion, for others a cause of rancor and conflict. Cornelia Fitzgerald, the fair-skinned wife of North Carolina teacher Robert Fitzgerald, exulted in her white ancestry. "All her life," recorded Pauli Murray, her granddaughter, "she would strive to identify herself with the best of her [white] father's world and reject all associations which linked her to slavery." For decades—generations—Cornelia's emotional loyalty to her slave-owning Confederate forebears sparked family arguments. In the family of fair-skinned Jane Hunter, the daughter of South Carolina freed people, color caused a bitter division between father and mother. Hunter's father, the son of an overseer, favored his light-skinned daughter, but her dark-complexioned mother "disliked and feared the characteristics of the white race in me." In some mulatto families, color was an ever-present topic; in others all mention of color was forbidden. "I never knew exactly what connection we had with the white people in our grandmother's house," recalled Susie Williams Jones, the light-skinned daughter of a black teacher. "We talked a good deal at mealtime, but we were never allowed to describe anybody by the color of their skin. My father was adamant on things like that."[43]

Mulattoes acquired a reputation for caste exclusiveness, but the extent to which they merited that reputation is unclear. In the South as a whole, mulattoes did not form a distinct or exclusive social group, and the law did not accord them a higher status. In parts of the South, on the other hand, the light-skinned descendants of free people of color resisted mingling with darker-skinned blacks, forming endogamous groups. The Creoles of color in New Orleans were notoriously clannish and color conscious, holding themselves aloof from the darker-skinned "American blacks," whom they regarded as culturally inferior. The same was true of the mulatto elite in Charleston. In late nineteenth-century Georgia, color divided black teachers, pitting the mulattoes of Savannah and Augusta, led by William Jefferson White, against a group of dark-skinned former slaves led by Richard R. Wright. Some churches perpetuated color distinctions, as did some schools. Charleston's Avery Institute, for example, acquired a reputation for favoring light-complexioned mulattoes. Sometimes mulattoes attempted to monopolize certain public schools, preventing the appointment of dark-skinned teachers. At black colleges, some clubs and sororities reputedly used skin color as a criterion for admission.[44]

It was universally acknowledged among blacks that light color was an advantage in dealing with white people. Although some whites professed a distrust of mulattoes, most felt more comfortable dealing with African Americans who possessed fair complexions and European physiognomies. Moreover, miscegenation persisted well into the twentieth century, and white people sometimes acknowledged their black offspring. Black teacher Jacob L. Reddix recalled a scene in

Wilcox County, Alabama, in the 1900s: "I will never forget seeing a planter ride his horse to the school, dismount, and enter the principal's office to pay the year's expenses of a very light-skinned girl, said to be his daughter."[45]

Whites treated mulattoes—and the latter often considered themselves—as the natural mediators between the black and white communities. It is a striking fact that many of the men appointed to head black colleges, both public and private, were very light-skinned. Charles W. Chesnutt, John H. Burrus, Thomas E. Miller, James Hugo Johnston, John M. Gandy, Henry A. Hunt, John Hope, Mordecai Johnson, and David Dallas Jones could all have passed for white. Dark-skinned blacks suspected that whites favored mulattoes because they regarded them as dependable allies in their efforts to control the black masses. Few expressed the point as bluntly as Alabama teacher Kenneth B. Young, but many would have agreed with it. "The white folks respected [mulattoes] much more than the ordinary blacks. And we black folks who had that white blood, we were proud of it. Proud because it meant extra privileges for us." One superintendent of schools told Young, "K. B., you can handle them niggers. . . . You've got enough white blood in you to handle them."[46]

Color was so interwoven with class that it is impossible to assess how each factor affected teachers' attitudes. Nevertheless, if light color was an asset in dealing with whites, and in many cases coincided with middle-class status, it would not be surprising if it influenced teacher-pupil relationships. Hence, even if black teachers did not deliberately discriminate against darker-complexioned pupils, they might nevertheless have expressed color prejudice informally or subconsciously.

Certainly, many darker-skinned children convinced themselves that they were the victims of this kind of discrimination. "I hate her," one thirteen-year-old said of her teacher in 1939. "When she gives plays she only puts the real light ones in them with long pretty hair. She always lets them go on her errands, too. An' she don't never let no dark children do nothin'." More than fifty years later, a woman who attended a black high school in Wilmington, North Carolina, recalled that both class and color influenced teachers' preferences. "The doctor's children and the lawyer's children were treated differently. The very fair skinned were treated differently." Charlotte Moton, who attended Tuskegee Institute in the 1920s and 1930s, believed that she and her sister suffered because of their dark skin even though their father, Robert R. Moton, headed the school. "Most of the heads of the departments were rather fair-skinned Negroes, and we were not. . . . And my mother always told us that we didn't have 'bad' hair, that God made all of us, and that no hair was better than anyone else's."[47]

If darker-skinned pupils felt that mulattoes were the teachers' favorites, they got their revenge outside the classroom. "The fair skinned blacks, especially the fair skinned blacks with long hair, were very much disliked by the darker skinned," recalled Margaret Rogers of Wilmington. They ran a gauntlet of verbal and physical abuse. Christia Adair, who grew up in Victoria, Texas, recorded how her mother, who had a white father, suffered at school because of her color. "They pulled her hair and made fun of her and used vulgar language to her about her parentage." Fair-skinned Ella Earls Cotton endured similar taunts from her classmates in Nansemond County, Virginia. "They lambasted me and my ancestors in all ways—the color of my skin, texture of my hair and features." Some stories were heartrending. A fourteen-year-old girl in Smithfield, North Carolina, told a Fisk University researcher that "I used to cry all the time . . . because some of the children wouldn't let me play with them because I was the only light skin girl over at the school." Sarah Rice, who grew up in rural Alabama, confessed to throwing rocks at "two little mulatto girls" just to "let them know."[48]

What one historian called "black-skinned chauvinism" was far more blatant than mulatto prejudice against "pure blacks." Mulattoes rarely expressed open bias against dark-complexioned people. Booker T. Washington, himself the son of a white man, downplayed the idea that light-skinned blacks looked down upon dark-skinned brethren. "Among individuals there is somewhat of that disposition," he wrote Lord Bryce, "but it does not take any organized shape and I question whether any light person . . . would permit it to be known if he could prevent it that he did not care for dark colored people." Mulattoes, on the other hand, endured a "barrage of criticism," much of it published in black newspapers, for their alleged snobbism and exclusiveness. This criticism reflected a concern to promote racial solidarity, but it also betrayed class resentment, folk superstition, and simple prejudice. For example, mulatto society was reputed to employ "brown bag tests" to screen out blacks with dark skins and apply "fine-tooth comb tests" to exclude those with kinky hair. But there is no evidence that such tests were ever used. Occasionally, in private, even educated blacks admitted to a dislike of mulattoes. As the journalist J. Max Barber told the very dark-skinned William Pickens, "I never warmed up to—never quite trusted—a half white or near white Negro. He is under a diversity of complexes which do not help his soul." In the 1920s, Jamaican-born Marcus Garvey became one of the few black leaders openly to attack mulattoes, and to extol racial purity, in his effort to build a black nationalist movement. However, Garvey's anti-mulatto rhetoric, which he pushed to demagogic excesses, ultimately backfired. In the American context, where mulattoes did not form a separate caste, and where "pure blacks" were in the minority, it proved too divisive.[49]

The color issue was so potentially explosive that few teachers openly expressed color preferences. Indeed, city schools made an enormous contribution to the erosion of color distinctions within the African American community. They acted as a kind of melting pot for blacks of different racial ancestries. In a few rural communities, where the persistence of one-teacher schools made it relatively easy for a community to get the teacher it wanted, "mulatto schools" could still be identified in the civil rights era. But these were rare exceptions. In city schools, teachers of all colors taught children of all colors. In Wilmington, for example, the appointment of dark-skinned teachers to every black public school marked an important step in breaking down mulatto exclusiveness. Of course many other factors helped bridge the social division between mulattoes and other blacks. The decline of miscegenation, intermarriage between people of dark and light appearance, the force of racial segregation, and the crushing impact of the Great Depression all played their part. Over the long term, however, the work of teachers—despite their occasional lapses—may have been the most important single factor in breaking down intragroup segregation based upon color.[50]

In the 1930s most of the South's black children were still living in the country, and many attended schools that, in appearance, had barely changed since emancipation. County school boards in the rural South still resisted building schoolhouses for black children. Many of the school buildings owned by the counties had been constructed by blacks themselves and then deeded to the board of education. In Wilcox County, Alabama, churches owned seventeen black schoolhouses, the state owned three, and the county owned "perhaps" one. The remaining twenty-two were owned by "communities, lodges and private individuals." Occasionally a white planter would give an unused building, or a school board would allow blacks to use an old schoolhouse formerly occupied by whites.[51]

The biggest physical improvement in black rural schools came in the shape of five thousand "Rosenwald schools," new buildings erected between 1917 and 1931 according to standard designs. Gifts of $5 million from the Julius Rosenwald Fund—established by the businessman who headed the Sears, Roebuck mail-order empire—sparked a massive fundraising campaign by black southerners, whose voluntary donations eventually exceeded those of the Fund itself. Rosenwald philanthropy also stimulated increased spending by states and counties, with tax funds contributing 64 percent of the schools' total cost. The Rosenwald schools eventually accounted for about one-fifth of the South's black schoolhouses, employing over a third of all black teachers.[52]

Of the other twenty thousand school buildings, however, few passed muster as schoolhouses. Erected by voluntary, often unskilled, labor, and built from donated lumber that consisted of odds and ends, these wooden constructions were often jerry-built affairs. They usually consisted of unplaned, ill-fitting clapboards that bristled with splinters. Walls leaned and bulged, meeting at irregular angles. "Of all the oddly shaped and oddly placed steeples in Christendom," wrote one observer, "the oddest are on the rural Negro churches in the Black Belt." Roofs often lacked ceilings; walls lacked plaster and paint. Potbellied iron stoves provided heating, but the absence of insulation and the numerous chinks and gaps made them ineffective beyond a couple of feet. Although most schoolhouses now had glass windows, broken or missing panes were common. Some still used wooden shutters; when these were closed on winter days, they plunged classrooms into gloom. Less than one school in ten had electricity. Half the schools did not even possess oil lamps. Many schools had no toilets: the woods and fields sufficed. Drawing their water from springs or wells, most lacked any facilities for pupils to wash their hands. When black teachers in Louisiana were asked, "What is wrong with your building?" most of them replied, "Everything."[53]

Furniture and equipment were almost as scarce in the 1930s as in the 1880s. Church pews, homemade benches, or even wooden boxes still substituted for desks, compelling children to write on their laps. Most teachers had a chair, but many did not. Some did not even have a table. Most blackboards were of the homemade variety, perhaps a rough pine board that was stained and restained, and many were too small to be effective. Virtually all school equipment had to be supplied by teachers and parents. Often the only supplies a teacher received from the school board were an attendance register and, if she were lucky, a box of chalk. In Georgia, where black pupils accounted for a third of public school enrollment, black schools received 1 percent of the spending on teaching equipment. If teachers did not spend part of their meager salaries on maps, globes, and paper, the children went without. A survey of small black schools in Louisiana revealed that none contained a radio, a musical instrument, or a newspaper.[54]

Teachers often had to teach children who had no books or only tattered and mismatched volumes that had been handed down from one family member to the next. For a class to possess a complete set of textbooks, let alone up-do-date ones, was all but unknown in rural schools. Even when, in the 1930s, states began supplying free textbooks, black schools usually received the worn-out tomes discarded by white schools. One teacher was told by the county superintendent to take a pickup truck to the storage warehouse and "get all the books you want." He found a mound, literally, of dog-eared textbooks mixed together promiscuously. Extracting a complete set, and finding books with all their pages intact, was well-nigh impossible. The books were sometimes so filthy and grease-stained that they would be covered with cockroaches the next morning.

Teachers also faced the same problems connected with sharecropping that had plagued rural schools since emancipation. The decline of the cotton economy in the 1930s, and the enactment of state laws extending the school year, led to a large increase in school enrollments in the 1930s. Yet no matter how carefully the schools adjusted their terms to the agricultural seasons—many operated split sessions—the demands of sowing, hoeing, and harvesting, and the seemingly endless tasks to be done around the farm, still promoted widespread absenteeism. "The average rural Negro youth is doing well," thought Charles S. Johnson, "when he can attend school 'when the crop is in' and when the 'weather isn't too bad' for him to walk his five to fifteen miles daily."[55]

The annual migration encouraged by sharecropping, when black farmers exchanged one landlord for another, further disrupted attendance. Outside the Black Belt, where landowners were more common, black rural communities tended to be more stable. In plantation areas, however, teachers still found it hard to keep track of who lived where. "In September we tried every available means to locate every child of school age and have each child enrolled in the nearest school," reported a frustrated teacher from Pittsylvania County, Virginia. "We had scarcely completed that survey when scores of families moved away to other communities."[56]

Many teachers never knew from one year to the next where they would be teaching, nor when the school year would start and finish. By the 1930s, county school boards were consolidating white rural schools, closing many of the one- and two-teacher schoolhouses, and transporting children by bus to larger schools. But notwithstanding a sharp decline in the need for black agricultural labor, they resisted consolidating black schools. They did not wish to pay for bus transportation, and white planters still wanted black workers readily available as and when required. Instead of consolidating the small black schools, therefore, school boards opened and closed them according to population movements. By the same token, they varied the school year according to the economic requirements of the plantations. The school year began only when the harvest was gathered. And it ended when the school board decided that the money had "run out." In

Bulloch County, Georgia, black schools operated for 160 days in 1942 but only 120 days in 1944. Ironically, a good cotton crop often meant a shorter school year.[57]

Inside the single room of the typical rural schoolhouse, the female teacher faced a fluctuating number of children of all ages and sizes. Attendance was so still so erratic in the 1930s that teachers considered it pointless to keep a record of it. Written records of any description—grades, test scores, report cards—were rare. Teachers classified students by rule of thumb and guesswork, sorting them into three or four groups based largely on reading ability. The youngest children were grouped in a "primer" grade (always pronounced "primma") in which they learned the alphabet, basic numbers, and how to write their names. "I would go to the next group for spelling," recalled Emma Gresham. This group, the largest one, approximated grades one to three, and in the 1930s it still provided most of the education that black children absorbed. Children as old as nineteen sometimes sat alongside toddlers in the first grade. Teachers placed the more advanced children in one or two further grades, giving them such instruction as they could. These pupils—usually only a handful—helped the younger ones. By the time a child reached the equivalent of seventh grade, at the average age of fourteen, she had usually learned all the teacher had to offer.[58]

Such conditions taxed even the most skilled teachers. "A teacher must conduct approximately thirty classes a day," wrote one education official, with each lesson or "recitation" lasting twelve minutes. In practice, children's attention wandered whenever the teacher addressed a different group, for every word could be heard by everyone else. The fact that children were often cold, hungry, and sick made it still more difficult for them to concentrate. In a one-room school in Northampton County, Virginia, where at least a quarter of the eighty-seven children on the books failed to attend on any given day, a quarter of those who did show up had not eaten any breakfast. Sixty years after Booker T. Washington had extolled the merits of the toothbrush, virtually all the children had decayed teeth.[59]

Teachers could not afford a lack of discipline. While they accorded children a good deal of latitude for chatting and fidgeting, they did not tolerate serious misbehavior. Former pupils and former teachers agree that discipline was rarely a problem. "It is a practice in the rural schools for the teachers to use a switch," reported a practice teacher from Tuskegee Institute. Black gum trees provided a ready supply of homemade whips. "All the teachers had them long whips," recalled Ruth Johnson of North Carolina. Teachers could usually resort to corporal punishment in the confidence that parents would support them. Indeed, the close relationship between teachers and parents perpetuated a kind of "double jeopardy" rule whereby a pupil punished for misbehaving in school could expect further chastisement at home. Some teachers still employed the dunce's cap and other ritualized forms of humiliation. "Lazy blockhead, why can't you learn something?" the other children would chant at the unfortunate dunce. "Four or five biscuits in your belly and no sense in your head. Ho, ho, ho!"[60]

The curriculum of the one- and two-teacher schools was basic. "The whole morning would be writing, spelling, and reading. And then we would have math." A little history and geography, taught on alternate days, some health education, and occasionally some rudimentary handicrafts, fleshed out the curriculum. Fridays saw a relaxation of the normal routine, with much of the day devoted to games, stories, spelling bees, and, during the spring, preparing the elaborate "school closing" exercises that children and parents expected.

Georgia's agent of Negro schools, Robert L. Cousins, marveled at the courage and dedication of the ill-prepared teachers who labored under such handicaps. With little equipment and no supplies, they became masters of improvisation. Virtually every scrap of paper was pressed into service. Teachers cut out pictures from old magazines. They made their own flash cards. Lacking exercise books, they brought in wrapping paper. "Any piece of paper, like a handbill, that had a clean back, I saved," remembered Sarah Webb. Sears mail-order catalogues—ubiquitous in the rural South—were endlessly recycled, eventually ending up as toilet paper. Dorothy Robinson recalled using "nuts, sticks, grains of corn, and creative games." Another teacher collected old baking powder cans, painted a child's name on each one, and used them to cover individual drinking glasses. A third described conducting an "elementary science" class in 1945 "with nothing but tin cans and going getting tadpoles."[61]

We do not have to trust teachers' memoirs for examples of dedicated and resourceful teaching. In 1941 and 1942 a team of researchers under the direction of Fisk University sociologist Charles S. Johnson observed teachers in the one- and two-teacher schools of rural Louisiana. In a small, whitewashed schoolhouse in East Feliciana Parish, immaculately clean inside and out, a middle-aged teacher, a widow, prepared her children for the Christmas season. A manger stood on the table. Children worked in groups, using scissors, paper, and paste to make party gifts and "favors." The teacher then utilized the "unit method"—all the rage in progressive educational circles— to teach about cotton, approaching the subject from various angles, through reading, math, art, and so on. She carefully tailored her teaching methods to the different age groups in the classroom. With the younger ones she used flash cards; the middle children constructed sentences; the seventh-graders wrote short stories. "Despite handicaps," the observer concluded, "the children learn, and reflect this in their speech, manner, and general alertness."[62]

Unfortunately, no amount of dedication and resourcefulness could compensate for deficient education and training. Examples of ineffective teaching abounded. Social scientists and other observers described ill-organized classrooms and transcribed lessons that were exercises in confusion. Having received no education beyond high school, many teachers were ignorant of all teaching methods other than the "recitations" and memory drills to which they themselves had been subjected. They neither made lesson plans nor understood the need for them. Excessive reliance upon corporal punishment betrayed a lack of confidence and an ignorance of other classroom management techniques. Many made no effort to brighten up bare classrooms by putting pictures on walls and displaying pupils' work. Many did not think to mitigate the lack of supplies by collecting samples and specimens from the immediate environment. Many tolerated filth and grime. A wall of one school—to the horror of the observer, a nurse— displayed advertisements for snuff.[63]

Studies of rural schools in the 1930s plumbed the depths of teacher incompetence and pupil ignorance. Some educational horror stories would be too fantastic to believe, were it not for the credentials of the sober social scientists who penned them. This example from sociologist Arthur F. Raper can stand for many others: "When in a one-teacher school . . . in Macon County the writer asked a child by the name of Booker T. Washington Williams for whom he was named, he did not know. The teacher had heard the name, but he could not be certain whether he was a lawyer, preacher, farmer, doctor, or something else; whether he was living or dead; whether he was a native of America or Europe; whether he was a white man or a Negro." Many teachers, even in the presence of observers, betrayed a kind of weary defeatism. Having to teach when sick—there were no substitutes, and classes could not be canceled when a school had only one teacher—added to the burden. "I'll just keep the children busy today," stated one long-suffering teacher. "I don't feel like teaching." Another, acknowledging the chaos of her classroom, greeted an observer with a wry, "You'll have some pages to write up from this mess!"[64]

How to improve the one-teacher rural school vexed education experts. By the 1920s a kind of weary truce had ended the ideological war between supporters and opponents of industrial education. The death of Booker T. Washington in 1915 removed the main *casus belli,* and the industrial education idea lost much of its force. By the 1920s it was clear that white southerners, despite their verbal commitment to industrial education, would not spend money on equipping black schools and had no intention of training blacks to compete against white workers. Rising state standards for the certification of teachers also weakened the industrial education idea. Hampton and Tuskegee both had to introduce college courses to qualify their graduates for jobs in public high schools. Blacks themselves encouraged the gravitation of their schools toward the academic. They disliked the notion that racially segregated schools should offer different curricula. More than ever, they associated industrial education with enforced segregation and low academic standards.[65]

But the concept stubbornly refused to die. The sheer inadequacy of rural schools compelled black teachers to concentrate on the here and now. Few believed in "industrial education" in the sense that Washington had conceived it, but plenty worried that an overly academic curriculum failed to help rural children address the challenges and difficulties they faced in their daily lives. "Peons, small tenant farmers, and the great mass of people have not been served," complained one. Charles S. Johnson argued that education carried "no meaning" for most children because it bore so little relationship to their actual situation. Black teachers ought to, on the one hand, relate education to the "familiar and the real"—teaching practical subjects like health and hygiene—and, on the other hand, give black children an understanding of their own "marginality." Johnson wanted black children to learn about Negro history and culture, but he wanted them to "cultivate a stark objectivity about themselves," not racial chauvinism. Johnson denied that a less academic and more practical curriculum would perpetuate segregation and second-class citizenship. Good education, whatever its form, would challenge Jim Crow by raising and then frustrating black aspirations. It inevitably generated conflict and pressure.[66]

The philanthropic foundations—which constantly turned to Johnson for advice, although he may have been telling them what they wanted to hear—deplored the move toward "conventional book knowledge." The foundations kept the industrial education idea alive by repackaging it under different names: rural education, life-related teaching, functional education, rural adaptation. The Rosenwald Fund, for example, shifted its focus from building rural schools to developing a curriculum geared to rural life. It found an important instrument in Mabel Carney, the author of *Country Life and the Country School* (1912) and the head of the Department of Rural Education at Teachers College between 1918 and 1942. Developing a particular interest in the education of blacks, Carney taught and mentored hundreds of black students at a time when Teachers College of Columbia University was the most influential institution of its kind in the United States. Many of those students came from the South (sometimes on Rosenwald scholarships) and a few gained master's degrees and even doctorates. Most returned South to teach.[67]

Jane E. McAllister, a Carney protégé who in 1928 became the first black student to gain a Ph.D. at Teachers College, perhaps did most to implement Carney's ideas about "rural adaptation." As head of teacher training at Grambling State College in Louisiana between 1937 and

1942, she created a program that prepared teachers for rural schools by pairing them with specific communities, pooling ideas and experiences in a "curriculum laboratory," and providing in-service training through a traveling "field service unit." Ignoring ideological debates about curriculum differentiation, McAllister focused on the same kind of practical goals that the Jeanes teachers—with whom she cooperated closely—had long pursued. "We wanted a school that could carry a heavy load of social welfare work along with its regular work and adult education," wrote McAllister, "a school in which unwise use of textbooks, teacher-centered methods and rote memory were eliminated." Foundation officials praised McAllister's work to the skies.[68]

But McAllister's approach was not widely emulated. With a few exceptions, black state colleges made little effort to prepare teachers for rural life or adapt the curriculum to rural schools. State and county education officials largely abandoned the idea of giving black schools a different curriculum. Negro high schools in Alabama had the same course as the white high schools, explained state agent J. S. Lambert, "and this is what the colored people wanted." As John C. Dixon of the Rosenwald Fund concluded: "Rural education? It just isn't being done."[69]

The notion that black teachers could spearhead rural improvement was always unrealistic, and the urbanization of the black population now made it increasingly redundant. The Great Depression ended Booker T. Washington's vision of turning black sharecroppers into yeoman farmers. King Cotton was in his death throes; the plantation economy that had underpinned black rural life since slavery was in terminal decline. Agriculture represented the past, not the future. The shrinking acreage devoted to cotton and other staples, plus the replacement of men by machines—the tractor and the mechanical cotton picker—were drastically reducing the need for sharecroppers and day laborers. Black farmers struggled to survive. In the 1940s and 1950s, blacks left the countryside in droves. Before long most black children would be enrolled in city schools

The reality was that blacks saw education as an escape route from a dying way of life that they associated with poverty, cultural isolation, and political repression. When Charles S. Johnson's researchers asked a sample of two thousand children in four Black Belt counties about their ambitions, only 7 percent of the boys and 1 percent of the girls said they wanted to be farmers. Even among the sons of farmers, 91 percent aspired to do something else. The preferences of high school students were even more emphatic. Boys said they wanted to be teachers, doctors, aviators, ministers, mail clerks, carpenters, lawyers, and musicians; girls wanted to be teachers, nurses, beauticians, seamstresses, musicians, and clerical workers. Nobody mentioned farming. At least 80 percent of the students graduating from state colleges chose teaching—the one easily accessible occupation that could take them away from farming and manual labor. In 1934 the president of Salisbury College, a school sponsored by the AMEZ Church, reported that of 250 students responding to a questionnaire, "not a single student chose agriculture." At one of the few colleges that took agriculture seriously, Prairie View in Texas, only 7 percent of those graduating from the agricultural department "actually go back into farming."[70]

By the 1930s, city schools had become beacons of hope for black southerners. But they were embedded in a system of white supremacy that seemed unyielding. Although black teachers pressed the intellectual and moral case for equality, and even made material gains, the Great Depression underlined all too clearly the political powerlessness of black southerners. Black teachers had pushed Booker T. Washington's accommodationist strategy as far as they could, and relative inequalities were as blatant in 1935 as they had been in 1895. The moment had not yet come when teachers had to decide whether or not to reject racially segregated schools. But they could not escape the logic of their own language. They had to decide whether, collectively, they should openly challenge white supremacy.

CHAPTER EIGHT

Teachers Organize

Boy, these southern teachers have
acquired brand new backbones.

Thurgood Marshall, 1941

Thurgood Marshall speaking to NAACP supporters in South Carolina.

Cecil Williams Photography.

In October 1938 Aline Black, an African American high school teacher, sued her employer, the school board of Norfolk, Virginia, in a state court. Thurgood Marshall, the NAACP's top attorney, filed her petition, which asked for a salary increase that would bring her wages into line with what similarly qualified white teachers earned. A state judge denied Black's petition, and before she could appeal, the school board fired her. The Norfolk NAACP organized a mass meeting and demonstration to protest Black's dismissal. Schoolchildren paraded through the streets bearing placards that read, "We Want Our Teachers to Be Equally Prepared and Equally Paid," "The Right of Petition Must Not Be Denied to American Citizens," and "Qualify to Vote: School Board Must Go!" Addressing a jam-packed church, Thurgood Marshall and Walter White, the NAACP's national leaders, lambasted the school board and urged blacks to support their teachers. In September 1939 Marshall filed suit on behalf of Melvin Alston, another Norfolk teacher, this time in federal court. After losing in the district court, Alston won on appeal. Norfolk's school board stood guilty of "unconstitutional discrimination."[1]

Between 1938 and 1948, black teachers in every southern state except North Carolina—which equalized teachers' salaries voluntarily—sued local school boards. Their actions formed part of a legal campaign, coordinated by the NAACP, against racial inequalities in public education. The equal-salaries campaign seems rather mild compared to the militant civil rights protests of the 1960s. However, in the context of the 1930s and 1940s it was a bold strike against white supremacy. In taking their employers to court, black teachers broke with their traditional tactics of conciliation and accommodation, and instead launched a direct confrontation, albeit a legal one, with the South's white leaders. Although the salaries campaign did not attack racial segregation per se, it did seek substantive equality under the Fourteenth Amendment, not merely concessions that might lessen inequality. Moreover, in aligning with the NAACP, black teachers rejected the leadership of the South's white liberals—men who considered themselves best qualified to steer Negro education in the right direction—in favor of independent black leadership that was based in the North, in New York City to be precise. For the NAACP, the salaries campaign was critically important. By persuading the federal courts to take the Fourteenth Amendment seriously in the field of public education, it established a crucial precedent. The black teachers of the South helped the NAACP weaken the legal foundations of white supremacy, helping clear the way for the civil rights movement of the 1950s and 1960s.

COLLECTIVE action among teachers provided the key to the equal-salaries campaign. The women and men who stuck out their necks by agreeing to become plaintiffs did not act in isolation. They enjoyed the support of fellow teachers throughout their respective states. The various state associations of black teachers entered into alliances with the NAACP: black teachers collected defense funds; the NAACP represented the plaintiffs in court. The state associations also arranged alternative employment for plaintiffs who lost their jobs—as most of them did—for suing their employers. For the first time, black teachers associations took on the roles of unions and civil rights organizations.

Growing professional confidence, and the political militancy of the 1930s, fostered the will to collective action. In the 1920s and 1930s, black teachers increased both in number and in competence. Teaching stabilized as an occupation and teachers became better trained. The state associations of black teachers gained members. Although the onset of the Great Depression temporarily halted their expansion, the state associations quickly resumed their growth. By the end of the 1930s, some represented most black teachers—a few nearly all—and enjoyed sufficient income to maintain permanent headquarters and employ full-time officials. The growth of these associations formed part of the dynamic expansion of organized labor during the 1930s. The teachers associations were not labor unions, but they reflected union consciousness. Against a background of strikes, boycotts, and sit-downs in American industry, black teachers could not help but be affected by labor's determination to improve its conditions and assert its rights. In some southern cities, including New Orleans—still the largest city in the South—black teachers joined the American Federation of Teachers (AFT), which was indisputably a labor union.

In backing the NAACP's equalization campaign, black teachers took a momentous step. Public school teachers were at the mercy of school boards; they had no job security. Moreover, the state associations had long cultivated friendly relations with white officials. Indeed, although they had struggled hard to establish themselves as independent organizations, they to some extent depended upon white officials for their existence. A glance at their history shows why.

THE black teachers associations came into being between 1877 and 1906; Kentucky was the first to be organized, Mississippi the last. Outwardly, these organizations were similar in appearance. They all existed to facilitate the professional development of teachers in black schools and to lobby for better public funding of black education. Meeting once a year, their members listened to speeches, debated resolutions, and elected officers. Although some published newspapers or journals, their early history is sketchy: few records were produced, fewer survived. However, the published proceedings of the Alabama State Teachers Association (ASTA) for 1888 and 1889 were probably typical. Speakers addressed such topics as "Arnold of Rugby," "The Need of Educated Labor in the South," and "The Proper Grading of Schools." Others discoursed on the protection of female virtue, inveighed against "tobacco or intoxicants," and denounced "Romanism" as a "crafty, treacherous and perilous" threat to public schools. A conviction that teachers should above all instruct pupils in morality—a missionary spirit imbued with the values of evangelical Protestantism—pervaded the meetings.[2]

The early associations had been staunchly independent and robustly political. The North Carolina Colored Teachers Association opposed the adoption of pro-Confederate textbooks. Alabama's association condemned the "inhuman and barbarous treatment" of state prisoners. The Colored Teachers Association of Texas structured its annual meetings "to accommodate candidates seeking offices, leaders of political factions, and sponsors of legislation." They all lobbied state legislatures and endorsed political candidates.[3]

The state associations had had their share of internal divisions, however. Some teachers saw themselves as missionaries competing against rival churches; others wanted to free schools from sectarianism. Public school teachers resented the dominance of private school teachers. The prominence of white teachers in the associations—few in number but influential by virtue of their position—caused jealousy among black teachers. Republican Party factionalism spilled over into association affairs. In 1894 Georgia's association almost tore itself apart debating a resolution to endorse Ida B. Wells's anti-lynching campaign. Twenty years later the issue of industrial education divided Alabama's association into two opposing wings, one led by Booker T. Washington, the other by William L. Pickens, a Yale-educated teacher at Talladega College.[4]

A second group of associations, founded later, had been less overtly political. In three majority-black Deep South states—South Carolina, Louisiana, and Mississippi—teachers formed associations only after new state constitutions had disenfranchised black voters. From the outset, therefore, they exercised extreme restraint in their public pronouncements and generally abstained from political comment. Other associations suffered from a lack of autonomy because they were closely identified with white sponsorship. In Virginia, for example, the association was first organized at a state summer school for public school teachers in 1887. Most teachers "were suspicious of the movement," explained John M. Gandy, and their suspicions "were greatly intensified" when the association continued to meet at the annual summer school held at Virginia Normal and Collegiate Institute. Many teachers viewed the man who headed the state college and served as the association's president, James H. Johnston, as subservient to the Democratic Party. White sponsorship also tainted the South Carolina State Teachers Association. This group emerged at the 1900 summer school for colored teachers, which, at the insistence of the state superintendent of education, had an all-white faculty. As a result, many black teachers had boycotted the school. In both Virginia and South Carolina, the associations never expanded beyond the relatively small number of black teachers who attended these annual summer schools.[5]

All the state associations struggled to recruit members. While white associations embraced a majority of the white teachers in their respective states, no black association represented more than a fraction of its state's black teachers. In Virginia, only about two hundred of the state's three thousand black teachers belonged to the association in 1916. North Carolina had about the same number of black teachers, of whom only a hundred had joined their state association. The bulk of public school teachers knew little about their state association, were too poor to attend its annual meetings, or had no interest in it. Short school terms, low qualifications, and abysmal pay encouraged constant movement in and out of teaching. Most teachers had little sense of themselves as full-time professionals. The career of the average teacher lasted only a few years.

Before the First World War, therefore, the state associations consisted mainly of teachers from private schools, mission schools, and state colleges—the only teachers with the education, the time, the money, and the interest. This well-educated minority had little idea how to appeal to the badly educated majority. "Appeals for cooperation were of the platitudinous type," recalled Virginia's John M. Gandy. "Teachers were told that they should cooperate . . . because it was their duty to do so. Very little help was offered to the teachers as an incentive." Most associations did little more than hold an annual meeting.[6]

Their ardent desire to improve standards discouraged the associations from expanding their membership. They believed that the mass of rural public school teachers were not fit to teach and disparaged them in contemptuous terms. "Worn-out politicians, broken-down preachers, sickly youth, the lame, halt and crippled all find an asylum behind the teacher's desk," complained a speaker at the Alabama association's 1889 meeting. Over twenty years later, Nathan B. Young, head of the Florida State Colored Normal School, characterized a large proportion of the public school teachers as "intellectual incompetents and moral derelicts." Average teachers were rightly distrustful of professional organizations, explained W. J. Hale, another state college president, because they feared that higher standards would put them out of a job.[7]

Efforts to create a *national* organization for black teachers foundered on similar problems. The National Education Association, a highly influential organization, represented America's white teachers. It did not specifically exclude blacks, but it effectively shut them out by according exclusive recognition to the South's white teachers associations. Blacks could attend NEA meetings as individuals, but the black teachers associations of the southern and border states were denied representation. In 1889 a group of black teachers, mostly from private colleges, formed the American Association of Educators of Colored Youth. It had little life beyond its annual meetings and expired after a few years. The National Association of Teachers in Colored Schools (NATCS) proved more durable. Founded in 1904, renamed the American Teachers Association in 1937, it lasted for sixty-four years, eventually merging with the NEA in 1966. The NATCS aspired to do for black teachers what the NEA did for white teachers. But ordinary public school teachers saw little point in joining a separate national organization that had so little influence. Top-heavy with college teachers, the NATCS had fewer than 250 members in 1916.[8]

Dᴜʀɪɴɢ the 1920s, however, the membership of the black teachers associations exploded. South Carolina's association grew from 393 to 2,385, North Carolina's from 97 to 3,500. Even the NATCS enjoyed an upsurge of support. Its membership grew to 5,000; its 1927 meeting, held in Nashville, drew 1,500 people.[9]

What caused such spectacular growth? The expansion of public education brought about some of it. Elementary school enrollment leaped forward in the 1920s. The number of black high schools and "county training schools" multiplied. The faculties of black state colleges grew as student enrollments increased. More teachers were in the system, and they were better trained. A second factor—more difficult to quantify—was the joining culture of the 1920s. If ever the phrase "a nation of joiners" had meaning, it applied to that decade. Joining something became a mark of social status. Relative prosperity, better communications, and the growth of car ownership made it easier for people to join organizations and attend meetings.

The leaders of the state associations made a determined effort to recruit among the mass of public school teachers. They met with success because the waning of religious sectarianism, and the decline of black private schools, had eroded the associations' elitism and weakened divisions among public school teachers. By the 1920s more of the teachers' leaders were coming from public high schools and state colleges. The state colleges played a key role in strengthening the associations. In earlier decades, institutions like Southern University and South Carolina State College had suffered because of their origins. Many black teachers had once derided them as "Jim Crow" schools— products of white supremacist schemes to downgrade black higher education. However, as these state-funded institutions developed into de facto teacher-training colleges, and then began to grant degrees, they largely overcame that opposition. The state colleges trained an increasing proportion of black public school teachers, among whom they built a loyal constituency.

The state associations made themselves more attractive to ordinary teachers by publishing regular journals, rotating the venues of their annual meetings, and organizing local units that enjoyed voting power. They also established specialized sections for different types of teachers. South Carolina's association gave a rebate to county associations that achieved 100 percent membership. Members attending the annual meeting in North Carolina received free board at Slater Normal School (Winston-Salem State College). In South Carolina, Louisiana, and elsewhere, association leaders made a concerted effort to win the cooperation of local superintendents. The Virginia Teachers Association (VTA) asked superintendents to distribute membership forms, which many did gladly. Once teachers realized they would not suffer reprisals, they were more willing to join. Many superintendents encouraged—sometimes virtually required—their teachers to become members.[10]

Of all the state associations, Virginia's probably experienced the most spectacular growth. It owed much its newfound dynamism to John M. Gandy, who was elected leader of the VTA in 1924. Although a native of Mississippi, Gandy knew Virginia's black organizations inside out. He had served for eight years as the field agent of the Negro Organization Society (NOS), an umbrella group founded in 1909 that included "practically every kind of Negro organization in the State." Espousing a traditional brand of racial uplift ("Better Schools, Better Health, Better Homes, Better Farms"), the NOS developed into a quasi civil rights group—protesting against segregation in public transportation, for example. Gandy also had a hand in organizing a statewide School Improvement League, which in 1909 joined forces with the teachers association. In fact, by the First World War the three organizations were practically indistinguishable, and Gandy, a faculty member and then president of Virginia Normal and Industrial Institute (VNII), served as the key member of an interlocking directorate.

As president of the VTA, Gandy established two priorities. The first was to strengthen the Association's identity as an independent body that represented black teachers. Its four-year confederation with the Negro Organization Society had not been a success. Teachers felt that their particular concerns were swallowed in wider causes, and they complained that the NOS leaders—a charge that perhaps reflected tensions between teachers and ministers—were "overbearing and dictatorial." In 1921 the teachers association ended the union. The experience taught Gandy the importance of keeping the professional interests of teachers distinct from wider programs of racial uplift.

Gandy made it his second goal to expand the Association's membership by giving ordinary public school teachers stronger incentives for joining. Although a graduate of Fisk University, Gandy was completely committed to public education, and he believed that the best way to improve black public schools was to give black teachers a college education. When he became president of VNII in 1914, the institution was basically a high school. In 1920 Gandy persuaded the state legislature to make his institution, not Hampton, Virginia's black land-grant college. Three years later he won back the power to grant degrees, abolished in 1902. In 1930 he had the legislature rename his school Virginia State College. "We had to fight to re-establish the belief in education for Negroes," Gandy recalled. "It was a long fight—and a hard one." His leadership of the state teachers association reflected the same determination. During his presidency the VTA set up district associations, organized a speakers bureau, published a quarterly bulletin, created an employment service, sponsored a parent-teacher organization, and undertook educational surveys. Teachers flocked to join. Beginning the 1920s with fewer than two hundred members, the VTA ended the decade with three thousand.[11]

It seems something of a paradox, but the cooperation of certain white officials proved enormously beneficial to the black teachers organizations. In the 1890s and 1900s, the overbearing sponsorship of white officials had damaged some of the teachers associations. By the 1920s, however, the relationship between black teachers and state education officials was changing for the better. Black teachers welcomed the expansion of state education departments because they laid down minimum standards and diminished, albeit very gradually, the arbitrary local power of county school superintendents and school boards. States began to accredit high schools, standardize the curriculum, and assume control of teacher certification. They took greater responsibility for teacher training by expanding state colleges and encouraging teachers—sometimes requiring them—to attend regular summer schools.

The state agents for Negro education became black teachers' most effective allies within the state education bureaucracies. These officials lacked power but wielded influence. They could persuade other white officials, including local superintendents, to take a greater interest in the education of blacks. They used their close links with the General Education Board, the Rosenwald Fund, and other foundations to channel philanthropic money into black schools. Some took a personal interest in helping superintendents recruit better-trained teachers. The state agents also encouraged the black teachers associations. In North Carolina, N. C. Newbold persuaded local superintendents to allow teachers paid leave to attend the annual meeting of the North Carolina State Teachers Association (NCSTA). This allowed the NCSTA to move its meeting from June to November, boosting attendance tenfold. When the Great Depression practically bankrupted many associations, the state agents rode to the rescue. In Georgia, John C. Dixon persuaded the white teachers association to bail out the Georgia Teachers and Education Association. At Dixon's request, superintendents urged black teachers to join the association, some even instituting a "check-off" system whereby they deducted membership dues from their teachers' salaries and forwarded the money, via Dixon, to the GTEA.[12]

White state officials became unofficial advisers to the associations. In 1922 the Louisiana Colored Teachers Association (LCTA) found itself bitterly split by internal politics, and its president, O. L. Coleman, clearly out of his depth, tried to enlist the state superintendent of education, T. H. Harris, against the "dangerous character" who led an opposition faction. Harris declined to take sides but told Coleman that "future trouble would be avoided and past sores would soon be healed" if the LCTA amended its constitution to provide for the election of officers by secret ballot. Twenty years later Robert L. Cousins, Georgia's state agent of Negro education, found himself counseling James L. Grant, the president of Georgia's association, who ran into similar difficulties. Dixon's analysis was the same as Harris's: the GTEA needed a more democratic structure.[13]

The black teachers associations received further encouragement from the philanthropic foundations. The foundations' financial support, although limited, helped to keep the associations alive when the Great Depression drove them to the brink of collapse. Equally important, foundation money gave the associations an imprimatur of respectability. Indirectly, practically everything the foundations did helped the associations grow. The foundations strengthened the infrastructure of black education by paying for state agents and Jeanes teachers, building schoolhouses, awarding graduate scholarships to black teachers, and giving large grants to black colleges. All this made it easier for teachers to organize.

The foundations' biggest contribution to the growth of the black teachers organizations was the sponsorship of the summer school movement. In the 1890s and 1900s, state-run summer schools had been small affairs. Most in-service training had been done at the county level, in weeklong "institutes" conducted by black instructors. Even these had struggled to enroll teachers. By the First World War, as state education departments began to take certification seriously and applied an element of compulsion, these "institutes" were attracting much larger enrollments. In Alabama, for example, 84 percent of Alabama's twenty-five hundred black teachers attended five-day institutes in the summer of 1914.[14]

By 1920, weeklong institutes were being superseded by longer summer schools, at the end of which teachers and would-be teachers sat the state teachers examination. In Louisiana, for example, such was the shortage of teachers after the First World War that the state enrolled 1,777 people in thirty-two summer schools that ran for twelve weeks. About half of those enrolled passed the exam. "In no other way could the necessary teachers with licenses be secured." Many teachers faithfully attended summer schools year after year. Those with the lowest grade of certificate, which expired after a year, were virtually compelled to attend in order to retake the exam. Others were motivated by a desire to improve their grade of certificate so that they could qualify for a higher salary or obtain a better job. As states insisted on higher qualifications for teachers, summer schools offered a means of gaining college credits and even earning degrees. With the help of subsidies from the General Education Board between 1915 and 1931, attendance at summer schools ballooned. In 1916, summer schools enrolled about five thousand black teachers. By 1928 more than twenty-three thousand teachers—54 percent of all the teachers in black public schools—attended.[15]

The summer schools were, in essence, a means of training teachers cheaply—a very inadequate alternative to the college education that states ought to have provided. They constantly disappointed the GEB. Leo M. Favrot, the Board's southern field agent, persistently ques-

tioned whether summer school attendance helped teachers to improve their teaching skills. He complained that many of the instructors were "dull and unimaginative" and simply lectured to their
classes. But the biggest problem, Favrot believed, was that most teachers attending summer schools were so poorly educated that they were
incapable of mastering the material they were presented with. "[They]
go back to summer school year after year and study algebra and geometry, textbook biology or French in the effort to acquire the higher
rating upon which the state insists. It is a pathetic sight." Instead of
helping teachers develop their classroom skills, the summer schools
functioned as "cramming schools for a teachers' exam . . . [where] the
instructors are doing little more than going through the process of distributing, in daily doses for six weeks, the state adopted textbooks."
Mississippi's summer schools, which had the largest attendance, were
the worst. Teachers could extend their certificates by paying $5 and
attending a four-week summer school, where instructors were appointed because they were "political adherents . . . or family favorites."[16]

Nevertheless, summer schools were powerful instruments for the
forging of a collective consciousness among black teachers. Men and
women who worked in one-teacher schools found them a blessed relief from rural isolation. Summer schools offered teachers intellectual
challenge, exposed them to new ideas, and encouraged them to regard
themselves as professionals who shared common interests. For the
teachers associations, they were ideal recruiting grounds. Indeed, the
instructors who ran the summer schools were often the very people
who ran the state associations. In this way the state colleges charged
with organizing summer schools powered the associations' expansion.
Institutions that specialized in summer school work even spawned
identifiable groupings or factions within the state associations. In the
GTEA, for example, teachers associated with Fort Valley State College
in southwest Georgia—the "Fort Valley group"—became a force to be
reckoned with.[17]

Summer schools became a vehicle for the Negro history movement.
Founded in 1915 by Harvard-trained historian Carter G. Woodson, the
Association for the Study of Negro Life and History (ASNLH) spon-

sored the *Journal of Negro History,* published pioneering books on black history, and inaugurated Negro History Week. Teachers were the movement's largest natural constituency, and—especially after Woodson fell out with the philanthropic foundations—provided most of its financial support. With the cooperation of state college presidents like John M. Gandy, Woodson coordinated book-selling drives and membership campaigns with the teachers associations. In Virginia, for example, the ASNLH sold memberships and subscriptions through Luther Porter Jackson, a professor of history at Virginia State College, prominent VTA member, and dedicated civil rights activist. "My best and about the only approach to this matter of raising money," he explained to Woodson, "will be through the school teachers of the State." He asked every teacher to give at least fifteen cents. The fact that half of Virginia's black teachers, about two thousand people, attended four summer schools enabled Jackson to collect these donations simply and "with a minimum of cost." When a sales team headed by Lorenzo J. Greene reached Alabama State College in August 1930, it found eleven hundred black teachers assembled in summer school, a captive audience if ever there was one. "Speak in classes," Greene recorded in his diary. "Sell books in hall."[18]

THE Great Depression hit the black teachers organizations hard. The Arkansas association lost half its members; Florida's association suffered a "sharp decline"; Georgia's "almost collapsed." The National Association of Teachers in Colored Schools, which had always found it hard to attract ordinary public school teachers, was struggling to survive even before the 1929 crash. The onset of the Depression almost killed the NATCS. Unable to afford clerical assistance, it became unable to communicate with the state associations. In 1932 it devised a rescue plan whereby state associations could become affiliates if they paid the NATCS fifty cents per member. By 1935, however, not one southern association had signed on to the scheme. Black teachers in the northern and border states kept the NATCS going. In the South, the NATCS found solid support only in Alabama, thanks to the leadership of its longtime executive secretary, H. C. Trenholm, the president of Alabama State College.[19]

Put simply, in the early 1930s teachers had no spare cash. In some cases they had, literally, no money at all. Teachers saw their salaries shrink by an average of 13 percent between 1930 and 1934. In Alabama, Louisiana, Mississippi, Tennessee, and South Carolina, their pay fell by between a fifth and a quarter. In Arkansas and North Carolina they suffered an average loss of one third. The teachers who were already the South's poorest—those who taught in the one-room schools—suffered the most. They saw their pay decline by 34 percent. These raw percentages fail to reveal the full extent of economic hardship teachers endured. They often went unpaid for months. Some school boards returned to the nineteenth-century system of paying teachers in scrip, which the recipient then had to sell at a discount to turn it into hard cash. Teachers stopped receiving annual increments. In some districts, they actually returned a portion of their salaries—5 or 10 percent—to help keep schools open. Black teachers suffered disproportionately severe pay cuts. In Louisiana, the average salary of black teachers declined from 40 percent of the white average in 1930 to 32 percent in 1935. The arrival of federal funds from New Deal programs gave white officials further scope for discrimination. Two typical Black Belt counties in Georgia, for example, had by 1935 received thirty-two thousand dollars in federal funds for improving school properties, but spent "not one cent" of that money on black rural schools.[20]

Yet the Depression ultimately helped black teachers organize more effectively. In contrast to employees in nearly every other sector of the economy, teachers did not lose their jobs on a massive scale. Across the country the number of teaching positions declined by less than 1 percent during the early 1930s. Only South Carolina and Mississippi experienced higher than average job losses. In every other southern state, the number of teachers remained steady or increased. This was partly because so many teachers worked without pay, and partly because governments viewed the public school system as one of the last lines of defense against a collapse of the social order. Mass unemployment and the decline of agriculture caused school enrollments to grow, and the increases in attendance were especially large in the South. Even conservative whites recognized that it would be folly to force jobless teenagers and the children of unemployed workers to roam the streets by closing public schools. In 1934–35 the federal government gave the states twenty million dollars to help keep schools open by paying teachers' salaries. Although school boards sometimes opened schools late and closed them early, the average school year decreased by an average of only 1.1 days during the first five years of the Depression.[21]

The Great Depression therefore made teaching a relatively more attractive occupation. In a time of mass unemployment, teachers clung to their jobs. The turnover of teachers in Columbia, South Carolina, had become "exceptionally small," noted superintendent A. C. Flora in 1931. Moreover, the growth of state and federal funding in proportion to the total spending on public schools diminished one of the most glaring disparities between black and white schools, the length of their respective school terms. North Carolina established a standard school term of eight months, South Carolina one of seven months. Alabama set up a Minimum Program Fund, financed by a state sales tax, in an effort to eliminate the gross inequalities between the Black Belt counties and the rest of the state. By 1940 only a handful of Alabama counties operated black schools for less than seven months. Longer school terms made an enormous difference in how teachers approached their jobs. New entrants—most of them better educated—were more likely to regard teaching as a career. "Teaching is rapidly becoming a stabilized profession," reported N. C. Newbold, North Carolina's state agent of Negro schools.[22]

So the teachers associations recovered quickly. In every state, they recouped lost members and soon exceeded their pre-1929 strength. By the end of the 1930s, at least half of the South's black teachers belonged to state associations. In North Carolina, South Carolina, and Virginia, virtually all black teachers were members.[23]

In campaigning for a more equitable distribution of educational funds, black teachers began to change their approach. The missionary era of education was over: statistics had replaced sentiment as the main units of educational currency. The methods of the social sciences and business management had invaded the world of education, and black teachers learned the new language. As Dwight O. W. Holmes of Howard University put it, "Profound sincerity, appealing eloquence and a sob in the voice without substantial statistics failed to bring in the returns in cash of former years." The teachers associations did not possess the resources to undertake systematic research. But they did utilize the data—a torrent of graphs, maps, tables, pie charts, and other statistics—produced by the many school surveys commissioned by cities, states, foundations, and the federal government.

The work of black researchers, meanwhile, became more influential. The social science department of Fisk University, under the leadership of Charles S. Johnson, attracted a string of foundation grants to carry out studies of race relations, the plantation economy, black youth, black college graduates, and black schools. Atlanta University and Howard University also developed graduate programs that produced statistically oriented research on black education. Black students holding scholarships from the General Education Board and the Rosenwald Fund attended northern universities where they wrote master's theses and doctoral dissertations. In the U.S. Office of Education, Ambrose R. Caliver, appointed as a specialist in Negro education, produced a series of reports on secondary schools, school finances, and teacher training. All this provided the teachers associations with ammunition.[24]

Gradually, the state associations established a customary right to be consulted by state officials. In 1938 South Carolina's state agent of Negro schools reported that members of the Palmetto State Teachers Association were invited to appear before legislative committees, something that never happened in the 1920s. When Governor John B. Ehringhaus of North Carolina appointed a committee to study "the state's program for Negro education," five of its fourteen members came from the black teachers association. In Georgia, Louisiana, Virginia, and elsewhere, state education authorities included black teachers in the process of curriculum revision.[25]

Before black teachers could openly challenge racial discrimination, however, they had to move out of the orbit of the philanthropic foundations and squarely align themselves with the NAACP. The foundations were sympathetic to many of the goals of the black teachers associations. They encouraged black leadership by supporting black higher education and strengthening teacher training. Yet the foundations were uncomfortable with independent black leadership. Moreover, they gave black teachers little encouragement or guidance in the matter of bringing about substantive equality. Although everything the foundations did was "political," they scrupulously abstained from criticizing racial segregation or commenting on the South's undemocratic political structure.

This is not to say that the philanthropic foundations were uncritical supporters of Jim Crow. Their influence on race relations was more benign than malign. After the First World War, the General Education Board retracted its previous endorsement of white supremacy, downplayed efforts to promote industrial education in the public schools, and overcame its hostility to black higher education. A tour of the South in 1919 persuaded Wallace Buttrick, president and secretary of the GEB, that his earlier racist thinking had been in error. Buttrick compared test results in black and white schools, and the results astonished him. Not only were the results uniformly bad, but also, more to the point, "one would find it practically impossible to tell whether they came from white or colored high schools, from white or colored colleges." The best results, in fact, came from the girls of Hartshorn Memorial College in Richmond, an institution supported by the American Baptist Home Missionary Society that the GEB had formerly regarded as overly bookish and not worthy of its financial support. Buttrick decided that blacks did after all possess the same intellectual potential as whites. And he proposed that the GEB should spend "larger sums" on black colleges and universities. In 1922 the General Education Board confirmed its change of policy. "Once started," it affirmed, "Negro education cannot be stopped at any arbitrarily determined level. The Negro cannot be educated 'for his place,' any more than the average white man could be educated for his place, for in this modern world no men and no race will accept the place which some other man or some other race selects for him." The Board condemned "discrimination between races" as "futile."[26]

The GEB's policy shift did not stem merely from Wallace Buttrick's Damascene conversion upon comparing white and black test scores.

That was a convenient way of justifying a change of direction dictated by economic and political conditions. The Great Migration of black southerners from the plantations of the South to the factories of the North had unsettled race relations and depleted the South's labor force. The race riot in East St. Louis shocked black Americans and turned Marcus Garvey from a moderate follower of Booker T. Washington into a black nationalist firebrand. Wartime mobilization further heightened racial tensions. Blacks burned with resentment over the army's treatment of black soldiers in France. Southern whites were determined to crack down on any challenge to Jim Crow when the black veterans returned.

The foundations were well aware that the mood of black America had changed. James H. Dillard, president of the Jeanes Fund and one of the most influential foundation officials, listened to a litany of black grievances when he met a group of teachers from Fisk University in April 1919. Said one:

> You ask me for an honest statement of the way the Negro feels toward the white man, and I will tell you. There is a strong feeling that the white men of the South militantly took their prejudice against the Negro to France . . . trying to spread it among the French people. . . . The Negro feel[s] that he is permanently to be regarded as inferior, second-rate, endured for his service but not respected for his humanity. There is small hope that the white people of the South will know from the Negroes what their real grievances are. The reason is, in plain words, the Negroes no longer trust the white people to give them a square deal.

The group presented a list of demands: the right to vote, an end to lynching, protection for black women, the abandonment of segregation "in every one of its forms," and "no discrimination as between Negro and white schools." The fact that the blacks selected the most conservative member of their group—Isaac Fisher, a protégé of Booker T. Washington— to read out these demands underlined the message.[27]

The crisis-laden atmosphere of the immediate postwar years abated, but the mood of black America remained volatile. The rise of the Garvey movement, and the string of student strikes that rocked the campuses of Fisk, Hampton, and other black colleges, gave substance to the idea that a "New Negro"—race proud, militant, and fiercely independent—had appeared on the scene. "Resistance to all forms of enforced segregation is almost as outspoken in the South as in the North," noted the GEB's Jackson Davis in 1927. "In the South, the Negro is more impatient, more aggressive, less inclined to conciliate prejudice and opposition." The ability of whites directly to influence blacks was fading. Black students resented paternalistic white teachers; black teachers resented white foundation officials. When Davis visited black state universities, he often felt unwelcome, encountering "brusque-mannered teachers with an air of condescension and reserve." W. E. B. Du Bois and Carter G. Woodson launched bitter attacks on the activities of the foundations, singling out the director of the Phelps-Stokes Fund, Thomas Jesse Jones—"the evil genius of the Negro race"—for especially harsh criticism. The GEB's 1922 policy document "Negro Education" stated the obvious and the unavoidable: "More and more the Negro Race is led by Negroes." In funding black universities like Atlanta and Fisk, the GEB committed itself to "training those leaders as well as possible."[28]

According to historian James D. Anderson, the foundations tried to create "a conservative black leadership that would cooperate with instead of challenge the Jim Crow system." There is some truth in this judgment. The General Education Board, the Rosenwald Fund, and the Phelps-Stokes Fund favored black leaders who conciliated rather than confronted. They wished to achieve progress without conflict. Alarmed by swelling black discontent after the First World War, and distressed by an upsurge of white violence—much of it directed against returning black soldiers—they helped create the Commission on Interracial Cooperation (CIC) to avert further violence. In 1920 the white members of the CIC invited a handful of black southerners to join their project. Significantly, three of the first four blacks to support the CIC—Robert R. Moton, John Hope, and John M. Gandy—were college presidents. One of its architects, Thomas Jesse Jones, viewed the CIC as a counterbalance to the confrontational NAACP. "This overemphasis on *conflict* . . . should be entirely reversed," he believed.[29]

The foundations strongly discouraged black teachers from employing assertive or confrontational tactics. "Any indication of a radical tendency on the part of a trusted Negro leader, or a bold and outspoken insistence upon equal rights and privileges in public education or in anything else, would temporarily check, in many communities, the advance of Negro public education," warned Leo M. Favrot. GEB officials also worried that northern-born teachers, who were being appointed to secondary schools and state colleges because of the paucity of qualified southerners, were an unsettling influence—"prone to interpret everything on racial lines, to foster a spirit of bitterness and to preach the Sinn Fein, go-it-alone, doctrine of non-cooperation." It was partly to check the influence of northerners that the GEB made such a strong effort to improve the training of black teachers in the South.

The foundations' insistence upon extreme caution stemmed from that old bugbear: fear of a white racist backlash. Leo M. Favrot had personally experienced that backlash. In 1919, as an idealistic state agent of Negro education in Louisiana, he had addressed the NAACP's annual convention in Atlanta. The following year he gave a series of talks at the summer school of Southern University on the subject of "the Negro question." His actions set off a storm of criticism, and state superintendent T. H. Harris told him in no uncertain terms, "The time [is] not right for public utterances of this kind." At the same time, Favrot's efforts to promote county training schools ran into opposition from "the ignorant, irresponsible and racially prejudiced element of the white race." In Jackson Parish, a fire "of incendiary origin" razed the training school. Shocked and shaken, Favrot learned how readily opponents of black education would exploit anything that might be characterized as extreme or radical. Having learned his lesson, he never forgot it. "I think we should avoid antagonizing [white] southerners," he told James H. Dillard, advising him to decline an invitation to join the NAACP's board of directors.[30]

The foundations' incessant message of caution also reflected their lack of genuine commitment to fostering independent black leadership. They could never create the black leaders they wanted because, by the 1920s, no black leader could advocate acceptance of white supremacy and expect to retain any influence. Hence even the leaders whom the foundations considered most reliable, such as Robert Moton, displayed an independence that made them difficult to control. In 1919 Du Bois had excoriated Moton for doing the government's bidding in traveling to France to tamp down the anger of black soldiers in France. Shaken by the attack, Moton retrieved his reputation by effecting a rapprochement with the NAACP—Washington's bête noire—and opposing racial discrimination in forthright terms. Moton's finest hour came in 1923, when he stood up to Alabama's white politicians, and faced down a threat from the Ku Klux Klan, in a campaign to have the Veterans Hospital in Tuskegee staffed by black doctors and nurses. In 1929 the NAACP awarded its coveted Spingarn Medal to Moton. His position of moderate militancy frequently placed Moton in opposition to his white friends in the foundations. He rejected George Foster Peabody's arguments against a federal anti-lynching bill, insisting that because the states had failed to stop "this American crime of crimes," the federal government should suppress it. He added a college course at Tuskegee Institute over the objections of the Rosenwald Fund trustees. Moton used the foundations more than they used him. He remained his own man.[31]

The reality was that the foundations did not wish to share power with black leaders. All the General Education Board's top officials were whites. Most GEB meetings were all-white affairs. The Board could argue, of course, that political conditions in the South made it essential to employ whites in the most influential and sensitive posts. But there was more to it than that. In the voluminous records of the GEB, the views of black teachers were rarely recorded. As Leo M. Favrot argued in 1930, "White leadership is needed on account of money, initiative, and influence." The Rosenwald Fund was more inclusive—it allowed Charles S. Johnson and other black educators to influence its policies. Nevertheless, the Fund's executive director, Edwin Embree, agreed that "white leadership was more necessary at this time than Negro leadership." Thomas Jesse Jones of the Phelps-Stokes Fund was even more disdainful of black leaders—privately spluttering, "Leaders for what?" when he contemplated the expansion of black colleges. White philanthropy, which employed money as a way to extend its influence, was leery of autonomous black institutions. "The niggery kind" of church schools, complained one GEB official—the kind "taught and controlled entirely by negroes"—were inward-looking, uncooperative, and hostile to contact with white people. The foundations and their bureaucratic agents looked upon black teachers as objects of educational policy rather than partners. "Negro teachers must be made to feel that they are human beings and that they must be dealt with and recognized as persons," Nathan Newbold reminded his fellow state agents in 1930.[32]

The General Education Board's attitude toward the National Association of Teachers in Colored Schools underlined the tentative nature of its support for black leadership as well as its reluctance to tackle the inequalities of segregated education. A major aim of the NATCS was to join the system of regional accreditation then being devised by white educators in collaboration with the foundations. State accreditation procedures were haphazard and, when applied to black schools, notoriously lax. Blacks teachers like William A. Robinson argued that a more rigorous and uniform system of regional accreditation not only would raise standards but—if the same criteria were applied to black schools as white schools—also would legitimize the principle of equality of educational opportunity. The NATCS also viewed accreditation as a means of cooperating with, and ultimately integrating, the virtually all-white NEA. However, the regional accreditation body, the Southern Association of Colleges and Secondary Schools (SACSS), was reluctant to rate black institutions, and the NEA still refused to recognize the black teachers associations.[33]

The General Education Board encouraged NATCS ambitions by persuading the NEA to create a "Committee to Cooperate with the National Association of Teachers in Colored Schools." When, at the committee's suggestion, the NEA included a Negro speaker in its 1929 convention program, Robert R. Moton used the occasion to gently chide the Association for its Jim Crow character. "I am somewhat embarrassed this morning, but I don't want to embarrass you," said the dark-skinned Moton, peering into a sea of white faces. "This platform and this auditorium are not lacking in character and dignity. I think they are somewhat lacking in color. I shall not attempt to add anything in the way of dignity or character . . . but I am perfectly sure that I will bring more color than any other speaker." However, beyond providing NEA conventions with "color"—usually in the form of musical entertainment from Negro choirs—the committee meetings achieved little.

Favrot of the GEB complained that the black members wasted too much time trying to "avoid any commitment to segregated schools for the Negroes." But the NEA's own lack of enthusiasm for the project could be gauged by the fact most of the committee members were foundation executives, state agents of Negro education, and black teachers.[34]

The committee did, however, enable the NATCS to raise the issue of accreditation. At the suggestion of Leo M. Favrot, who promised GEB funding for the project, the SACSS considered extending its purview to black schools. Progress was glacial, but by 1933 the SACSS had devised a ratings system that could be applied to all schools. To the disgust of black teachers, however, the two ratings, A and B, turned out to be virtually synonymous with white and black. White institutions received A ratings; nearly all black schools were "berated." The NATCS formed a parallel organization, the Association of Colleges and Secondary Schools for Negroes (ACSSN), in order to drive the accreditation process forward and eliminate the differential ratings. But accreditation turned out to be of limited usefulness. For one thing, many local superintendents refused to consider black high schools for regional accreditation. By 1942, black schools accounted for only 7 percent of the schools accredited by the SACSS. Moreover, even when the SACSS accorded its coveted A rating to black schools, the suspicion lingered that the Association covertly applied a lower set of standards. As ACSSN stalwart W. A. Robinson concluded in 1945, striving to meet, and even meeting, accreditation requirements did not eliminate "the traditional pattern of limited support from public funds for all segregated public facilities for Negroes."[35]

Robinson was typical of many black teachers of his generation. He took advantage of every opportunity to improve black schools, but he ached to destroy the entire structure of segregated education. In many ways, he was a quintessential "insider." As North Carolina's first supervisor of Negro high schools, Robinson worked as an assistant to Nathan C. Newbold, probably the most liberal of all the state agents. When Atlanta University Laboratory School became one of the first black schools to win accreditation, he was its principal. A favorite of the General Education Board, he won a large grant to direct a study of seventeen black secondary schools in eleven southern states, an ambitious three-year project that produced a stream of reports and bulletins. Yet Robinson was ever conscious of the fact that the entire system of black education was run by white men who, however well intentioned, could not adequately represent the people they purported to serve. "There has been so little recognition of the need of participation by Negroes in the educational leadership set up by the philanthropic foundations." Robinson heartily supported a resolution by the NATCS, adopted in 1934, that "schools for Negro youth be under the immediate control and supervision of members of the Negro race." But he knew that this could never happen under a regime of white supremacy. Accreditation, and philanthropic efforts, could affect only the margins of racial inequality. The basic issue was whether blacks could achieve equality of educational opportunity within a segregated school system. And to that question, Robinson answered a decisive no. Without political power, he argued, blacks would never induce southern whites to share public funds equitably. Segregated schools were "essentially un-American and undemocratic."[36]

THE time was ripe for a searching debate among black teachers about the fundamental orientation of Negro education. In the early 1930s the segregation issue, hitherto largely dormant—or, as far as southern schools were concerned, largely abstract—once again became contentious. The National Association for the Advancement of Colored People, founded in 1910, opposed all segregation by law, a position that proved popular with northern critics of Booker T. Washington. In 1930, however, Carter G. Woodson's *Mis-Education of the Negro* criticized the cultural influence of the mission schools and argued that blacks needed an Afrocentric education. Four years later, in an editorial calculated to stir up controversy, W. E. B. Du Bois attacked the NAACP's commitment to integration as dogmatic and unrealistic, contending that black children did better when taught by black teachers who cared about them, rather than by whites who looked down upon them. Meanwhile, the National Advisory Committee on Education, appointed by President Hoover in 1929, resurrected the issue of federal aid to education within the context of the South's segregated school system. The Committee recommended that any federal aid to education should be allocated to individual states without any specific conditions with regard to race—ignoring the South's history of racial discrimination and assuming that segregation presented no difficulty. The three black members, Robert R. Moton, John W. Davis, and Mordecai Johnson, politely but vigorously dissented. "It is a fact that the Federal Government is committed practically . . . to a policy of segregation," Moton pointed out. The government had a moral responsibility to allocate some grants specifically for Negro education "so that the Negro child could have a more nearly equal chance with other children, not because of but in spite of segregation." The minority report proposed that such grants should be administered by federal-state committees that included black representatives.[37]

Segregation remained a vexing issue for black teachers. Most of them agreed that legally mandated segregation was both morally indefensible and a primary cause of inferior black schools. Two powerful factors, however, militated against attacking segregation head-on. The first was a feeling that Jim Crow was so solidly entrenched that open opposition would be futile. In the opinion of D. O. W. Holmes, Howard University's dean of education, segregation would never collapse "without some form of social upheaval, which none can foresee at the present time." The second restraining factor was a widespread fear that many black teachers would lose their jobs if segregated schools disappeared. A large cohort of southern black teachers therefore persisted in the institution-building strategy of Booker T. Washington. They acted on the assumption that, in the words of college administrator R. O'Hara Lanier, "some sort of segregation is inevitable for generations to come." Grounded in expediency, this strategy cultivated white paternalism and also, by the 1930s, exploited whites' fear of integration. The presidents of the black state colleges—institution builders par excellence—became outstanding exponents of these methods, becoming in the process de facto allies of white politicians in their defense of segregation. As the president of North Carolina State College for Negroes once told the legislature when he pleaded for increased funding, "Gentleman, segregation comes high."[38]

A new generation of black intellectuals, however, deplored segregation and the tactics of expediency it encouraged. The most influential were three scholar-activists who in the early 1930s taught at Howard University: sociologist E. Franklin Frazier, economist Abram L. Harris, and political scientist Ralph J. Bunche. Irreverent and iconoclastic, they criticized in equal measure the romantic racialism of Du Bois, the economic separatism of the Garveyites, and the bourgeois integrationism of the NAACP. Absorbed with Marxist ideas, they regarded capitalism as the root of racial oppression, arguing that the path to equality lay in an interracial working-class movement that would fundamentally change the structure of economic power. As for segregation, they detested it. Frazier, who had taught at Tuskegee and Atlanta universities, was so outspoken that he had quit the South before—as he feared would happen—a lynch mob came after him. All three believed that segregated schools were tainted at the source. The notion of achieving equality within segregation was a chimera, insisted Bunche, because Jim Crow "segregates a racial group in order to maintain it in subservience." The philanthropic programs for making black schools better actually ensured that "the masses of Negroes remain what they are now—a handy and docile labor supply from which additional profits can be wrung, some minute portion of which will in turn find its way to the support of 'Negro Education.'"[39]

These intellectual firebrands challenged other beloved shibboleths of the South's black teachers. They had no use for Christian idealism, regarded interracial cooperation as largely irrelevant, and derided the idea that education could "solve" the race problem. When J. R. E. Lee, the veteran educator who headed Florida A&M College, argued that black students needed to develop "Christian character," E. Franklin Frazier dismissed him as an aging relic of the Victorian era. Black colleges could no longer control their students' thinking and behavior, he pointed out. "Consequently when the Negro college announces that it is developing Christian character . . . it does not have the machinery to develop such character, and it indicates a lack of knowledge of the trends in the outside world." Doxey A. Wilkerson, a teacher at Virginia State University, scorned black teachers' cultivation of white "good will," and their participation in interracial groups, as a means of improving race relations. Organizations like the Commission on Interracial Cooperation "[are] not only impotent to aid the Negro . . . but they are also positively vicious. They would lull the Negro into the idealistic belief that real progress is possible without sharp disturbance." Ralph Bunche flatly stated that whites would never permit black teachers to "remodel the social order" or "revolutionize the position of the Negro group." Horace Mann Bond, a young scholar then establishing himself as the foremost authority on black education, underlined the "unsoundness of relying upon the school as a cure-all for all our ills." The Depression gave these critiques particular resonance, and the growth of teachers organizations guaranteed them wide circulation at conferences and meetings.[40]

The *Journal of Negro Education,* founded in 1932, fostered these debates. Edited by Charles H. Thompson, who headed Howard University's department of education, the *Journal* maintained rigorous scholarly standards and functioned as the foremost source of up-to-date research. By sponsoring conferences and commissioning special editions, the *Journal* also provided a forum for intellectuals, civil rights leaders, and teachers to address all the major issues affecting black education. The *Journal* helped break down divisions between northern and southern teachers, and between teachers in public and private institutions. Thompson believed that the vulnerability of public school teachers made journals like the *Bulletin,* the organ of the NATCS, insufficiently forthright, especially when it came to criticizing segregation. Thompson kept the *Journal* open to all comers, but he was keen to promote criticism of Jim Crow.[41]

To young black radicals—and Thompson was one—the time-honored strategy of institution building merely entrenched an oppressive caste system. How could teachers work within segregation but at the same time work against it? To what extent could teachers—should teachers—influence what their students thought about race, politics, and social change? Should they be political activists or merely strive to be good teachers? Doxey Wilkerson, a Marxist and later a Communist, believed the answer was clear: black teachers should foster conflict, not accommodation. "The price of 'peace' is permanent inferiority." Teachers should be advocates of social change, not "colorless dispensers of facts." College teachers, in particular, had a duty to encourage their students to think critically about various "minority group strategies" for the "abolition of caste." If they lacked serviceable textbooks, then they could look at their own local communities and analyze race relations "in the raw." To the charge that he advocated "indoctrination," Wilkerson pleaded guilty. "There are no Hamlets among the proponents of caste," he pointed out, "they *know*, and *act*, with alarming success." Black teachers should strive to "partially counteract the deliberate indoctrination of the forces of reaction." Bunche put the point more bluntly: "The teacher who says he does not believe in indoctrination is unconsciously doing it by his pacifism." Both of these young radicals argued that blacks were proletarians, that the source of their exploitation was capitalism, and that their ultimate salvation lay in union with "the masses of all workers."[42]

Black teachers were wary of embracing the kind of nakedly political indoctrination advocated by Wilkerson and Bunche. In the rural South, admitted Walter Chivers, professor of sociology at Morehouse College, "the Negro school principal who survives . . . most often does so because he has accommodated himself to the white education board's definition of the 'Negro's place' in the local scheme of things." Any teaching that challenged the status quo had to be smuggled in covertly. Even in the colleges, teachers faced practical restraints. One Mississippi college teacher, asked if he taught the social sciences by having students go into his local community, stated the obvious. This was Mississippi: "attempts to use the community as a laboratory were extremely hazardous." The private colleges were less vulnerable to political interference, but activist-inclined teachers still complained about lack of academic freedom. "The quickest way I know to become *persona non grata* in a college community is to . . . question the existing order," asserted a teacher from Bennett College in Greensboro, North Carolina. Black colleges were doing little to improve the lot of ordinary blacks, this teacher added. "Too often, they are little islands of smugness and safety in a sea of hate."[43]

Teachers had more positive reasons for being cautious. Although Bunche and Wilkerson became stars of the conference circuit, few southern educators shared their uncompromising rejection of race-based strategies, their dogmatic condemnation of interracial movements, and their blind faith in the labor movement. Hard history had taught the South's black teachers flexibility and pragmatism—pursuing a multilayered approach to social change—rather than trust in the latest radical fad.

Black teachers felt a duty to protect their students. They wanted black youth to be dissatisfied with discrimination, but they did not wish to use them, or see them used by others, as cannon fodder. "We do not want to stagger the rising tide of racial consciousness," explained one college teacher, "[but] we want to be very, very sure that we do not say anything that is going to produce ultra-radical action on the part of the students." Teachers had to walk a fine line between encouraging righteous indignation over an unjust system and enabling their students to cope with that system. Brailsford R. Brazeal, the dean of students at Morehouse College, explained how, in weekly chapel, he taught students about race. "I ask them to think with me when I talk about 'Segregation and the Negro Student.' An attempt is made to have them realize what segregation is designed to do; what our reaction to it should be and how we as Negroes can rise above the mental limitations of segregation while at the same time being forced to submit to its physical limitations." Making blacks *too* conscious of race, some believed, constituted a danger. As one college administrator explained, many black students entered college bearing emotional and psychological scars that fostered "warped attitudes." Lacking in "healthy race consciousness" because of white racism, prone to "mixed loyalties and confused thinking" because of racial stereotypes among their own group, some were "overly aggressive, deceitful, lazy, unscholarly, and resentful of discipline."[44]

Nevertheless, teachers did what they could to provide their students with some kind of political education. In the colleges, the burgeoning number of classes in social sciences—history, politics, sociology, economics—provided opportunities to study race. In 1944 Luther Porter Jackson estimated that over the previous twenty years about four thousand students had taken his course in American government at Virginia State University. Jackson took his students on field trips to observe the police court in Petersburg, the Virginia state legislature, the U.S. Congress, and the U.S. Supreme Court. A survey of black colleges' social science offerings provided the broader picture. "Current problems are discussed; courses in race relations are organized; prominent colored and white persons are invited to give addresses and lectures indicating the unfairness and injustices of such practices. Studies are made of the social origins, the psychological aspects, [and] the laws . . . bearing upon the subject. Students are urged to patronize Negro businesses and boycott places where they are not treated fairly. . . . The basic principles underlying segregation, discrimination and race hatred are discussed." Virtually all black colleges offered classes in Negro history. Only Atlanta University offered one on "Karl Marx and the Negro."[45]

Teachers in the public schools were more circumscribed, but they, too, trained their children's eyes on the past and the future, not just the present. In New Orleans, Birmingham, and other cities, black teachers incorporated Negro History Week into the curriculum. Many used poetry and literature to combat racist stereotypes and challenge feelings of inferiority. If they found textbooks that contained derogatory depictions of Negroes, black teachers complained to school boards. Science teachers used biology lessons to discuss genetics and refute white supremacist theories. Although the ballot remained a sensitive issue, many teachers expounded upon citizenship, democracy, and the right to vote. W. A. Robinson wrote about a small-town high school principal who had his pupils pledge, after reciting the oath of allegiance to the flag, "I promise God and my teacher that when I am twenty-one I will register and vote." In Newport News, Virginia, teachers instructed pupils to "go home and harass and harangue their parents into paying their poll taxes."

Even in rural schools of the Deep South, teachers introduced politics. In 1940 the principal of an elementary school in St. Charles Parish, Louisiana, could be found reading to her class from Richard Wright's *Native Son*. Over in Coahoma County, Mississippi, English teacher Thelma K. Shelby asked her students to give an oral report on the same book, then being serialized in black newspapers. The youngsters were gripped by Wright's shocking tale of a black youth from Chicago's South Side ghetto, a native of Mississippi, who murdered twice and was executed. "We got the message that the white South and the white North . . . did not consider a Negro equal to a white," recalled one. They also got a dose of the party line, but Shelby, a loyal NAACP member, warned her impressionable charges not to trust Wright's glowing account of Communist lawyers defending helpless Negroes.[46]

If black teachers were attracted to radicalism in the 1930s, it was mostly the radicalism of John Dewey, the New Deal, and the NAACP. They had no intention of abandoning the political mainstream when it was finally flowing in the right direction. Using the ideas of the progressive education movement, and borrowing the language of the New Deal, they used every opportunity to strengthen the association between education and democracy. Not that they were especially starry-eyed about either FDR or the gurus of progressive education. FDR was well known for resisting Eleanor Roosevelt's racial liberalism. He declined to support a federal anti-lynching bill and failed to challenge white supremacy; the New Deal operated within the framework of racial segregation. The leading lights of "progressive education" were similarly disinclined to confront America's race problem, believing that racial prejudice would yield before modernization, economic planning, and education itself. Yet black teachers had always been adept at exploiting egalitarian tendencies in programs that contained both conservative and liberal characteristics—"industrial education" was the classic example. Now they realized that the New Deal, despite Roosevelt's deference to the southern wing of the Democratic Party, was weakening the political system that sustained Jim Crow through its drastic extension of federal power. Similarly, they recognized the radical possibilities of the progressive education movement, especially its ideas about the role of schools in "social reconstruction."

Institutionalized in the Progressive Education Association, founded in 1919, "progressive education" had stressed the need for reform of the curriculum in order to facilitate the self-expression and self-development of children as individuals. In the 1930s, however, educational theorists like John Dewey, William H. Kilpatrick, and George S. Counts moved away from "child-centered learning" in favor of collectivism. The Wall Street crash had killed laissez-faire capitalism, they believed, and a new social order, characterized "by close integration of social life and by collective planning and control," should replace it. They wanted teachers to play a key role in shaping this order by making schools incubators of democracy, cooperation, and "social intelligence." These thinkers were more interested in class and economics than in race and constitutional rights. But the "social reconstructionists" implicitly challenged racial discrimination and economic exploitation. Their combination of missionary fervor and social engineering appealed to black teachers. As W. A. Robinson put it, "We in the Negro schools must be courageous enough to arouse social unrest and a lively dissatisfaction with things as they are; we must be intelligent enough to help our children to become socially wise."[47]

The South's white education officials had their own interpretation of progressive education. In drafting standardized curricula in the 1930s, they tailored the latest educational thinking to the South's dual labor market and strict segregation. When they spoke of the pupil's "adjustment to life," they emphasized that they meant "existing social life." Louisiana, for example, recommended that blacks should have better schools, but affirmed that they should still be educated for lives "as a plantation worker, as a tenant farmer, as a domestic servant, as a laborer . . . and as a professional man or woman rendering service to his own race."[48]

Yet black teachers were able to influence the process of curriculum revision. Capitalizing on the popularity of progressive ideas, they enshrined the language of democracy and opportunity in the new curricula. In ringing statements of democratic idealism, state education officials proclaimed a commitment to equal opportunity that, at least in writing, embraced blacks. "Every child . . . is entitled to an equal educational opportunity," stated Tennessee's department of education. Even in the Deep South, black teachers could use the concept of education as "adjustment to life" to bootleg antiracist ideas into the curriculum. In Georgia, for example, the state supervisor of rural Negro schools, Helen A. Whiting, drafted a "teacher's guide" for use in rural schools. "The democratic society," her 1937 document stated, "is a society in which people are working together . . . to secure a genuine and full opportunity for the best development of which each person in the group is capable; [and] to remove as rapidly as possible the handicaps that prevent this achievement. . . . The broad task of education is fixed upon this conception of democracy." Although the language was anodyne, the message would have been crystal clear to black teachers who read it.[49]

POLITICAL action and even political expression could still be dangerous. Indeed, white elites often expected black teachers to condemn radicalism in all its forms. Many were happy to oblige, insisting that blacks were loyal, cheerful workers who eschewed alien influences and rarely went on strike. In Birmingham, where the Communist Party made its first open appearance in the South, and where industrialists responded to CIO organizing drives with "something like a reign of terror," Arthur Harold Parker, principal of Industrial High School, remained a faithful ally of the employers. In North Carolina, Jack Atkins, who in 1934 succeeded his father as president of Winston-Salem State College, opposed the unionization of the R. J. Reynolds tobacco factory. Condemning CIO organizers as "foreign agents" motivated by greed, Atkins praised the company's welfare policies and extolled "mutual respect and co-operation between the races."[50]

State college presidents tried to insulate their own campuses from radical influences. When faced with serious student dissidence, they cracked down hard. In 1934, for example, John M. Gandy faced a student strike at Virginia State College over the web of rules that restricted student conduct. No hidebound reactionary, Gandy wanted to adjust student grievances amicably but feared fatally damaging the college's authority—and feared his own dismissal—if he yielded to a student strike. He reformed student regulations, but not until he had broken the strike by expelling two dozen young militants. The letters of support Gandy received revealed the deep conservatism of some black educators. W. R. Banks, the president of Prairie View State College, suspected that Marxist faculty member Doxey A. Wilkerson was the real troublemaker, and urged Gandy to clean house. "I do not believe that a teacher should be continued . . . five minutes who attempts to influence the minds of irresponsible youths."[51]

Yet the one national organization that represented black teachers, the American Teachers Association (ATA; formerly the NATCS) reflected a growing radicalism among African American educators. The ATA, dominated by college presidents and high school principals, was not known for militancy. Yet in the mid-1930s it endorsed the federal anti-lynching bill, condemned Italian aggression in Abyssinia, and supported the unionization of the "laboring masses." The ATA also rejected a policy of political self-abnegation. Condemning "any and all efforts to limit the elective franchise to persons of a certain race or color," it "urgently recommend[ed] the teaching of the value of the ballot in all schools for Negroes." Writing in the ATA's *Bulletin,* Catherine J. Duncan, a supervisor of rural schools at Fort Valley College in central Georgia, reinforced the point in words that would have made Booker T. Washington spin in his grave. "The franchise is the one thing we need to help us as a race right now. . . . A definite campaign in all the elementary schools of the country with an adopted slogan concerning the ballot will bear fruit in the generation to come."[52]

The scope of teachers to implement such proposals was limited. In much of the South, especially in the vast rural stretches of the Deep South, attempting to register to vote was so dangerous that few blacks tried it. Yet teachers not only took part in the "Right to Vote" movement that stirred in the mid-1930s but also in some places led it. Faculty members at Virginia State College, encouraged by president John M. Gandy, organized a League of Negro Voters that encouraged blacks in Petersburg to pay the poll tax and become registered voters. The League's chief instigator, history professor Luther Porter Jackson, enlisted his class on government to find out "what the people think about voting." Sixty students interviewed two thousand people, and the results were a revelation. "Why boy, don't you know that votin' is fo' the white folks?" one respondent chastised his young interviewer. As an exercise in political education, Jackson's exercise could hardly be bettered. Appalled by the ignorance, indifference, and suspicion they encountered, the students resolved to obtain the ballot for themselves and others. The Petersburg League was so successful in boosting the black electorate that in 1941 Jackson helped form a statewide organization, the Virginia Voters League. Members of the Virginia Teachers Association provided its backbone.[53]

A growing number of teachers began to see themselves as workers and identified with the resurgent labor movement. Until the 1930s, teachers had regarded labor unions as irrelevant to them. The South was notoriously inhospitable to organized labor, and the associations that represented teachers, both black and white, defined themselves as professional bodies, not labor unions. However, the American Federation of Teachers, founded in 1916 and affiliated to the AFL, challenged the National Education Association by mounting organizing drives in the nation's big-city school systems. The NEA maintained its dominance among teachers, but the AFT scored some successes. In the South, black teachers in Washington, Atlanta, Birmingham, Chattanooga, and New Orleans organized AFT locals. Although these locals were segregated by race, the AFT had something to offer black teachers. Professional associations may have given teachers "the prerogatives and dignity of professional life," but they still left them "at the mercy of school superintendents and boards of education." The AFT held out the prospect of security, autonomy, and material advancement. In addition, while the NEA for all practical purposes excluded black teachers, the AFT included them at every level of the organization. Indeed, the AFT did more than most other AFL unions to recruit black members and discourage racial discrimination.[54]

"We had to educate the teachers, who knew very little about collective bargaining," recalled Veronica B. Hill, a founder and stalwart of AFT Local 527 in New Orleans. The defense of teachers' living standards, however, provided an ideal issue. White teachers formed AFT Local 353 in 1935 to oppose the salary cuts and loss of fringe benefits that the Orleans Parish School Board imposed as a Depression austerity measure. After a two-year campaign, they won their demand. Black teachers were outraged to find that salaries were restored to former levels only for the white teachers. Encouraged by Sarah Towles Reed, the leader of Local 353, a group of black teachers formed a separate local, and, accompanied by some white union members, petitioned the school board to make the restoration apply to all teachers. The delegation found the office building locked, whereupon the teachers climbed up a fire escape, entered through a window opened by a friendly janitor, and slipped their petition under a relevant door. The school board quickly relented and approved the restoration. It was a testament to the success of Local 527 that in 1938 the AFT decided to move its national convention from New Orleans because the hotel would have required black delegates to use the elevators marked "freight."[55]

The state teachers associations still dwarfed the AFT in terms of membership. Nevertheless, the labor militancy of the 1930s rubbed off on them. They never gave up on the tactics of conciliation and persuasion. By the late 1930s, however, the NAACP offered them a very different method of effecting change: the filing of lawsuits against white education officials to directly challenge racial discrimination. Less drastic and risky than strikes, litigation of this kind nonetheless challenged black teachers to behave like workers. They had to recognize their economic interests, act collectively, and maintain solidarity under intense pressure.

THE campaign for equal salaries kicked off in Maryland in 1936, when Thurgood Marshall filed a suit in state court on behalf of William Gibbs, the principal of a small elementary school in Montgomery County. In 1937 the school board agreed to equalize salaries over two years. When faced with similar legal action, other counties quickly settled without going to trial. Although gratifying, these easy victories did not give the NAACP what it needed to give its campaign regional momentum: a clear legal ruling that paying black teachers less than white teachers violated the Fourteenth Amendment. In 1939, however, federal district judge W. Calvin Chesnut, in a case affecting Arundel County, handed down just such a decision.[56]

Despite this crucial precedent, it took the NAACP more than ten years to win in the South. Maryland was a border state where blacks voted and wielded considerable political influence. It had a sympathetic governor, Harry Nice, who supported equalization. It had a strong teacher tenure law that made it relatively easy to find teachers who were willing to act as plaintiffs. None of these favorable conditions obtained in the South proper. From Virginia to Louisiana, school boards fought the NAACP tenaciously, drawing upon a battery of tactics, some nakedly aggressive, others cunningly subtle. They brought pressure to bear on potential plaintiffs. They dismissed and black-listed teachers who filed suits. They used legal delaying tactics to wear down teachers' morale. They used spies and informers to manipulate divisions within the teachers' ranks. They enlisted the support of white teachers, warning them that higher salaries for blacks would mean lower pay for whites. They threatened to implement equalization by cutting salaries across the board. And they devised complicated "merit systems" to mask the discrimination involved in paying black teachers less.

The NAACP based its legal strategy on a kind of "domino theory." It calculated that one key victory in each state would cause all the other school boards to anticipate certain defeat in the courts and quickly fall into line. But this did not happen. In a foretaste of the problems it would encounter after its victory in *Brown v. Board of Education* (1954), the NAACP found itself fighting the same battle over and over again, as individual school boards—each a separate legal entity—acted as if previous decisions did not apply to them, taking their chances that the law's delay, weak opposition, or a sympathetic judge would defeat the black plaintiffs.[57]

In Virginia, for example, Judge John J. Parker gave Norfolk's black teachers a clear victory when, in a 1940 decision, he branded the school board's pay policy "as clear a discrimination on the ground of race as could be well be imagined." Yet when black teachers in Newport News initiated an equalization suit in 1941, they met unexpected resistance. They had regarded the local superintendent of schools, Joseph H. Saunders, as a progressive and fair-minded official. But when Dorothy Roles sued the school board, Saunders reacted angrily. He threatened to demote and even dismiss black teachers if they insisted on immediate equalization. And he warned Roles's lawyer: "Your clients may, like Sampson, pull down the pillars of the temple but they will crush themselves under the weight of the falling stones. I am also afraid that animosities will be built upon the ruins that will not disappear in the life time of any of us who are concerned in this matter."

In 1943, after a federal court ruled in favor of the plaintiff, the Newport News school board weakened the teachers' ability to negotiate terms by dismissing six leaders of the Newport News Teachers Association, including Lutrelle F. Palmer, the executive secretary of the Virginia Teachers Association and the highly respected principal of Huntington High School. The plaintiff, Dorothy Roles, also lost her job. Palmer and Roles sued the school board for reinstatement, but the board's legal delaying tactics eroded the teachers' fighting spirit. "Although they have tried valiantly to rally, the odds have been too great, their morale has been broken, and they are completely without funds," Palmer reported in 1945. Luther Porter Jackson noted that teachers were winning equalization suits but failing to eliminate unequal pay. He blamed divisions among teachers, and the failure of blacks to vote, for encouraging the white resisters. The state chairman of the NAACP complained, "The teachers' fight over the state is at a complete standstill."[58]

Louisiana followed a similar pattern: after a relatively easy victory in New Orleans in 1942, teachers encountered intransigent resistance elsewhere. In Jefferson Parish, an area adjoining New Orleans that was home to some of the state's most powerful politicians, the school board made it clear that any teacher who took court action would suffer. The first two would-be plaintiffs were drafted into the army; the next two withdrew under pressure. Eula Mae Lee, the fifth in line, whose name appeared on the suit, was dismissed on the grounds of persistent tardiness. "My superintendent told me his best nigra teacher wasn't as good as his poorest white, and as long as he was superintendent no Negro teacher was going to get the same salary as a white teacher." Lee's fellow teachers paid her seventy-five dollars a month until she found work in Washington D.C.[59]

Iberville Parish became the main symbol of white resistance to Louisiana's equalization campaign. Superintendent Linus P. Terrebonne was a prominent leader of Louisiana's white teachers association and wielded considerable influence over the state board of education. The outcome of his effort to prevent equalization would set the pattern for much of the state. Terrebonne used both bludgeon and stiletto. He dismissed the original plaintiff, Wiley B. McMillon, on the grounds of "incompetence, dishonesty, and willful neglect of duty." When the teachers came up with more plaintiffs, he dismissed those as well. Instructed by federal judge Adrian Caillouet to file stipulations for a consent decree, Terrebonne devised a system for paying teachers according to "merit" as well as responsibility, education, and experience. Apparently objective, his system for rating teachers was anything but. He had teachers fill out a sixty-item form and then deducted points for "each error, inaccuracy, and omission." He then looked at any letters that teachers had written to the school board and assessed them for "errors of spelling, punctuation, sentence structure, neatness, indentation, rules of letter writing, accuracy of statements, mathematical computations, and promptness in following directions." Teachers were also assessed on their "personal and social qualities." Terrebonne got the result he wanted. Of the parish's eighty-five white teachers, all but one rated an A or B. Forty of the forty-four black teachers rated D and E. Only the presence a lone white teacher in grade C, alongside four black teachers, prevented the system from being a perfect reflection of Jim Crow. Even so, Terrebonne did not place a single white teacher below a black teacher.[60]

The teachers associations tried to cushion plaintiffs from the financial consequences of dismissal by providing them with at least a year's salary. Black-owned businesses, insurance companies in particular, sometimes undertook to employ them. However, multiple dismissals, and long delays in the legal process—some cases took four or five years to resolve—played havoc with teachers' morale. Unity between teachers, local NAACP branches, and local citizens committees proved difficult to maintain.

Most disheartening to teachers who backed litigation, however, was lack of support from other black teachers. Advocates of court action tried to swing the state associations behind the NAACP's strategy. In some states, like Virginia, that support was easy to secure. In others, opposition to litigation caused bitter divisions that hindered the campaign. "There are plenty of Negro appeasers and those who will be bought off or intimidated by fears of all sorts," the president of the Alabama State Teachers Association told Thurgood Marshall. "Many Negro teachers are yet hesitant and must be won over." Poorly educated teachers were the most hesitant. "These teachers are old and inefficient," a confidante of Marshall's reported from Savannah, Georgia; they feared that higher salaries would pit them in competition against better-qualified teachers. Teachers in rural schools, who were well aware of their low qualifications, felt especially vulnerable. Hence many teachers preferred the devil they knew to the one they did not. A fairer but more rigorous system might disqualify them from employment altogether.

Fear alone, however, did not fuel the opposition to court action. Many teachers did not wish to jeopardize the alliances with white officials that they had laboriously constructed over the years. Much of what black teachers had gained under Jim Crow stemmed from the personal relationships they had forged with school superintendents, state officials, and other whites. Court action was by nature adversarial; putting white officials in the dock threatened to turn friends into enemies. Many believed that litigation should be held in reserve as a kind of ultimate deterrent, a threat that would strengthen the hand of those who pursued more conciliatory methods. "Only when all reasonable peaceable measures have failed should we resort to more drastic expedients," argued James E. Shepard, president of a black state college in Durham. As president of the North Carolina State Teachers Association, Shepard preempted the NAACP by negotiating an equalization agreement with the state. Between 1937 and 1941 the average salary of black teachers in North Carolina increased from 70 percent of the white level to 83 percent. In 1944 the legislature voted to equalize salaries completely in the following year.[61]

The success of Shepard's strategy in North Carolina heartened advocates of conciliation elsewhere. In Georgia, for example, where the state had already reduced the gap between white and black salaries, the leaders of the Georgia Teachers Education Association promised to "exhaust all resources to get what we want within the school system of the state . . . before appealing to outsiders for aid." The GTEA negotiated a three-year equalization plan and attempted to keep the deal quiet lest a white backlash scupper it. As the president of Albany State College, Joseph W. Holley, put it, "It is not a good idea to take a man to court to collect a bill until the bill has been presented and the debtor refuses to pay." In South Carolina, year after year, opponents of equalization prevented the Palmetto State Teachers Association from backing the NAACP's litigation strategy. Thurgood Marshall had to rely upon the South Carolina NAACP, and its strong branches in Columbia and Charleston, to give local teachers the backing they needed.[62]

These divisions caused immense ill will. Proponents of litigation were frustrated and then angered by the advocates of caution and conciliation. Teachers in New Orleans complained that "a tight little Uncle Tom clique of . . . out-of-town principals who are 'in good' with the school board bigwigs" stopped the state association from backing the NAACP. In Georgia, complained Walter Chivers, a professor of sociology at Morehouse College, the leaders of the GTEA were trying to isolate the more militant Atlanta teachers in an effort to head off litigation. "Do the Georgia public school teachers mean to continue teaching in inadequate school buildings, working for starvation wages, because misleadership continues to tell them that the time is not ripe to exercise their legal rights?" When Walter White, the head of the NAACP—of all people—suggested delaying an equalization suit in Georgia lest it inadvertently help Governor Eugene Talmadge get reelected, a backer of court action sent him an incredulous rejoinder saying that the only people who wanted delay were "week-kneed and spineless friends of the Negroes" and "a few school heads here and there who are willing to sacrifice the good of the Race for the sake of their own pocketbooks." Even when plaintiffs had the support of their state associations, they sometimes felt betrayed. Vernon McDaniel, a high school principal in Pensacola, Florida, won his case against the Escambia County school board in 1941. Three years later, when the board dismissed him, he was distressed by the absence of sympathy or financial support from his fellow teachers. "I could give you the names of many . . . Negroes who helped the [school] board fire my husband," Mrs. McDaniel wrote Walter White. She called them pimps, Uncle Toms, and "'yes, yes,' white folks" men.[63]

Teachers who initiated equalization suits were dangerously exposed and gathered support wherever they could get it. Sometimes, as in Columbia, South Carolina, they were backed by strong NAACP branches. Elsewhere, they concentrated on building support at the state level. In Louisiana and Georgia, proponents of litigation eventually gained control of the state teachers associations. In Texas, the state association established the Texas Commission for Democracy in

Education, chaired by Joseph J. Rhoads, the president of Bishop College. Everywhere, teachers formed local citizens committees to widen community support. In New Orleans, where teachers could not rely upon the local branch of the NAACP, the group of principals who planned the equalization suit turned to Local 527 of the American Federation of Teachers, which asked every teacher to contribute ten dollars to the defense fund. The money came in dribs and drabs—sometimes under assumed names—but most teachers coughed up. The AFT's involvement in the case had the additional advantage of minimizing opposition from the city's white AFT members, whose leader, Sarah Towles Reed, supported equalization.[64]

Thurgood Marshall considered the American Federation of Teachers a key ally in the equalization fight. The union rallied national support and helped prevent splits between black and white teachers in the South. If school boards succeeded in setting black and white teachers "at each other's throats," Marshall feared, the result could be disastrous to the NAACP's campaign. Left-right divisions within the AFT, however, threatened to undermine the union's support. Marshall knew that some of the AFT's strongest locals were controlled by Communists, but the fact did not bother him. Indeed, he was keenly aware that Communist Party influence invariably pushed organizations to oppose racial discrimination. He was therefore alarmed by a move within the AFT to exclude three New York locals on the grounds that they were Communist-controlled. These were precisely the locals, Marshall contended, that did most to combat racism, whereas those who proposed the purge had a "longstanding record of opposition to Negroes." The AFT's weakness in the South limited its ability to influence the equalization struggle. The bulk of white teachers belonged to affiliates of the National Education Association, not the American Federation of Teachers. Still, the opposition of white teachers to equalization was on the whole relatively restrained. In Virginia, Lutrelle F. Palmer reported, white teachers had been neutral—"neither for us nor against us."[65]

Marshall quickly realized that, having knocked a small hole in the wall of legalized discrimination, he needed to file a battery of additional lawsuits in order to widen that hole into a breach. Ultimately, although it took longer than expected, his courtroom victories did set up a kind of domino effect. As one federal judge after another ruled in favor of black plaintiffs, the equalization campaign developed an unstoppable momentum. Many school boards decided to equalize salaries voluntarily, and by the late 1940s state legislatures had laid down uniform salary scales that eliminated overt racial differences.

To be sure, it was not an unqualified victory. Although the NAACP knocked down blatantly unfair "merit" systems in Little Rock and Iberville Parish, federal courts upheld more ostensibly objective merit systems in Miami and Charleston. Worse, in 1945 South Carolina required all its teachers to take the National Teacher Examination (NTE), a series of tests devised by Ben D. Wood, a native of Texas and a "central figure in the spread of standardized testing." Wood predicted that most black teachers would achieve lower scores than most whites, but assured South Carolina that the tests were thoroughly objective—they were graded by machines—and therefore legally foolproof. By 1947, 44 percent of the state's white teachers had scored A grades, compared to only 6 percent of South Carolina's black teachers. Black teachers so resented the test that many resorted to cheating. In 1951 hundreds had their certificates revoked when they were found to have obtained answer keys. Although the relationship between performance on the NTE and competence as a teacher was not clear, other southern systems followed South Carolina's lead.[66]

Still, if it was a partial victory, the equalization campaign was a victory nonetheless, and it transformed the black state teachers associations. They had taken on the white power structure and beaten it. They had asserted their independence from local superintendents, state education officials, and the big foundations. Under the leadership of men like Charles Lincoln Harper in Georgia and John Kermit Haynes in Louisiana, they aligned themselves with the NAACP. Even in Mississippi, widely regarded as the most repressive state in the South, the black teachers association eventually backed an equalization suit. The firing of plaintiffs was a trial by fire from which the associations emerged stronger. Buoyed by growing membership rolls, they hired full-time executive secretaries—some of whom were dismissed plaintiffs—and acquired permanent headquarters. Above all, they helped put equalization, in all aspects of public education, on the political agenda.[67]

They could not have done so without the *Gaines* decision. In 1938 the Supreme Court decided that the state of Missouri should afford Lloyd Gaines, a black would-be law student who was rejected by the University of Missouri Law School, facilities for a legal education "substantially equal" to those it afforded white students. Missouri faced the alternatives of integrating the University of Missouri Law School or creating a separate law school at the black state university. The decision alerted white southerners to the possibility—hitherto unthinkable—that the Supreme Court might overrule segregation. At the very least, it put the southern and border states on notice that the federal judiciary would no longer turn a blind eye to egregious discrimination. They had to take "separate but equal" seriously. In the 1940s and early 1950s every southern state reformed its public education system to reduce inequalities and lay down minimum standards. However, the NAACP made no secret of the fact that the intent of its equalization strategy was to soften up Jim Crow before a direct attack upon the principle of segregation itself. Equality within segregation, it believed, was a political and practical impossibility.[68]

Black teachers would soon face an agonizing choice. Should they continue to push for "separate but equal" or risk everything by advocating integration? The progress they had made in the short space of ten years made them want to believe that whites would reform the system to make it fair; and yet at the same time they did not believe they would. H. Councill Trenholm, the ATA stalwart and president of Alabama State College, realized the awful truth when, in 1949, he sat on a committee appointed by Governor Jim Folsom to study the higher education of Negroes. When Trenholm insisted that the state should provide blacks with an equal education, the committee's white members demurred. "I would not say equal," replied one. "There is no way to get your complete equality," said another. The difference between the words *adequate* and *equal* was the gap between hope and despair. "Being in the field of education and also being a Negro," Trenholm confessed, "seems to me to be tragic."[69]

Convinced that equalization had both run its course and revealed the bankruptcy of "separate but equal," the NAACP made up its mind to overturn *Plessy v. Ferguson* (1896), the Supreme Court ruling that provided a constitutional justification for segregated schools. The NAACP's decision challenged the South's black educators to abandon their time-honored strategy of institution building. "Now is the time to attack," proclaimed Mordecai Johnson, the president of Howard University. "Now is the time to proceed. Now is the time to precipitate the decisive combat."[70]

CHAPTER NINE

Black Teachers and the Civil Rights Movement

Men like President Reddix stood between us and the raw nakedness of our educational plight. They went before hard-core segregationist school boards and pleaded for money to buy us a library, a chemistry lab, or a football stadium. I do not envy men like President Reddix. Only with reluctance do I sing their praise. Yet praiseworthy they are. They fashioned us into the rebels we are.

Hermel Johnson, student government president,
Jackson State College, 1967

Students from Claflin University, Orangeburg, South Carolina, protesting against segregation.

Cecil Williams Photography.

In October 1954, six months after the Supreme Court ruled that segregated public education was unconstitutional, the South's leading black educators gathered in Hot Springs, Arkansas. After deliberating for two days, they issued a ringing endorsement of the *Brown* decision. "It was the right and moral thing to do," the group stated. "We urge that immediate steps be taken to implement the decision." For good measure, the statement urged black teachers to shun "any plan designed to nullify the Court's decision." It was an impressive display of unity. This group could claim to represent the vast majority of black teachers employed in segregated public schools and colleges. The black state teachers associations sent their top officers, and a bevy of state college presidents—including two from Mississippi—attended. The South's black educators, at all levels, appeared to be foursquare in favor of integrated schools.[1]

That impression was misleading, however. Black teachers' support for integration may have been widespread, but it was shallow. The NAACP had not decided to attack the principle of segregated schools until 1950, which did not allow sufficient time to build up grassroots support for this change of tactics. Many teachers endorsed the general principle of *Brown* but harbored deep misgivings about the prospect of abandoning segregated schools. They felt vulnerable.

A 1953 poll provided some clues about what the rank-and-file black public school teachers thought about integration. Two Howard University professors questioned 150 teachers who attended a summer school at South Carolina State College. The poll disclosed no clear consensus either for or against integration. Only two-fifths of the teachers believed that "Negro teachers will be worse off in a desegregated school system." But asked if they preferred to work in the present system or in a desegregated one, the group divided almost evenly. And when asked how they thought black teachers would vote in a secret ballot on the question, three-quarters believed that most black teachers would oppose integration. Almost three-quarters of the respondents anticipated a "great amount of job displacement" in the event of integration. Four-fifths predicted that white officials would become more hostile to black teachers and would devise "new ways . . . to evade granting equality in employment." Almost three-fifths believed that white students would refuse to accord proper respect to black teachers. This poll confirmed what many black educators instinctively knew. If the Supreme Court were to rule against segregated public education, warned Frederick D. Patterson, the president of Tuskegee Institute, the NAACP should not expect a "wave of enthusiasm" from black teachers.[2]

The NAACP's national leaders were well aware that the attitude of black teachers could make or break its campaign to end segregated public education. In crucial states like North Carolina and Louisiana, its legal strategy hinged upon a close alliance between the NAACP Legal Defense and Educational Fund (the LDF or "Inc. Fund") and the state teachers associations. The state associations, moreover, had been a critical element in the growth of the NAACP's southern membership from about fifty thousand in 1939 to almost half a million in 1946. They organized branches and instigated voting rights lawsuits. They gave money directly to the national NAACP. It would be difficult to rally community support for integration if black teachers were against it.[3]

The NAACP tried to convince black teachers that they would not suffer large-scale job losses as a consequence of integration. Lawyer Oliver Hill pointed out that the equalization of salaries had not resulted in fewer black teachers, despite warnings by white school superintendents that that would happen. Still, the NAACP recognized that teachers who worked openly for integration would be exposed to retaliation and that the process of implementing *Brown* carried enormous potential for racial discrimination. In 1955, therefore, the Inc. Fund created a Department of Teacher Information and Security, under the veteran black educator John W. Davis, in order to dispel fear among teachers and prevent unfair dismissals. Most of its funds came from the state teachers associations.[4]

Ultimately, however, the NAACP expected black teachers to embrace integration as a noble cause that would advance the interests of the entire race. Certainly, for about twenty years the tide of opinion had been swinging against segregation. After 1930 black teachers organizations made a point of refusing to endorse the principle of segregation even when forced to accept the practice. In 1934 one thousand delegates at the National Conference on Fundamental Problems in the Education of Negroes, organized by Ambrose Caliver and sponsored by the U.S. Office of Education, voted to oppose "the extension of segregated schools." In the late 1930s nearly all of the black teachers organizations changed their names—eliminating the word *colored* or *Negro*—to emphasize their opposition to segregation. In 1944, when a group of black leaders met in Durham, North Carolina, to plan a new alliance with southern white liberals to replace the moribund Commission on Interracial Cooperation, they made a point of declaring their fundamental opposition "to the principle and practice of compulsory segregation in our American society." Indeed, these black moderates—most of them college presidents or college teachers—regarded opposition to Jim Crow as the only real basis for interracial action. As Charles S. Johnson of Fisk University explained to Alfred K. Stern, a fellow trustee of the Rosenwald Fund but a staunch segregationist, "I go right on living in a segregated system instead of trying to leave it; but not believing in the principle of segregation as the ultimate of American democracy, and willing to help dissolve it as rapidly as it can be dissolved."[5]

In 1945 racial segregation in the South was substantially intact and few predicted its imminent demise. Yet within the space of a mere five years, political developments transformed the prospects for integration. In 1946 President Truman appointed a committee on civil rights, whose report, issued the following year, echoed the platform of the NAACP. In 1947 Truman addressed the NAACP's annual convention—the first president to do so—and in 1948 he proposed sweeping civil rights legislation. Truman also set in motion the desegregation of the armed forces. In 1950 the Supreme Court ordered the admission of a black applicant, Heman Sweatt, to the University of Texas Law School and on the same day ordered the University of Oklahoma to cease imposing internal segregation upon George McLaurin, a black graduate student in the school of education. With two branches of the federal government withdrawing their support from legalized racial segregation, the NAACP sensed that it was being offered, almost on a plate, an historic opportunity. Thurgood Marshall seized that opportunity with both hands. In July 1950, at a conference of lawyers and top NAACP officers, the Inc. Fund decided that instead of seeking to equalize segregated education it would sue for the admission of blacks to white institutions. "We attack segregation head on," Marshall proclaimed.[6]

At a conference at Howard University organized by the *Journal of Negro Education,* speaker after speaker urged blacks to meet the challenges posed by integration, and, if necessary, accept institutional and personal losses for the greater good. Oliver Hill advocated "religious zeal" in crusading for the "utter elimination of all racial designations and racial concepts." Acknowledging that integration would expose both pupils and teachers to stiff interracial competition, others argued that there could be no progress without pain. The situation of black pupils, pitched into competition with better-educated whites, gave cause for concern, but for the moment—partly because nobody had studied this problem, let alone hit upon a solution to it—the NAACP shrugged it off, simply pointing out that all social change produced casualties. The NAACP recognized, too, that blacks would incur cultural losses when segregated institutions, especially the black state colleges, closed. But perpetuating Jim Crow schools and colleges meant perpetuating inequality. The benefits of integration—better facilities, better opportunities—outweighed the career interests of black teachers and administrators. The NAACP expected teachers with a vested interest in segregation to yield. Black colleges should "work themselves out of a job as segregated institutions." In the wake of the *Brown* decision, advocates of integration ordered teachers to fall into line. "Any leadership that prepares today's Negro to live in yesterday's world of inferiority," declared R. C. Ragland of Alabama A&M, "is not only a shortsighted leadership but is a leadership reeking in treachery."[7]

Talk of "treachery" reflected the passion of the integrationists. It also betrayed the NAACP's anxiety that its strategy could be derailed by the conservatism of southern black educators. The NAACP was especially worried that the presidents of black state colleges might encourage opposition to *Brown*. True, the *Brown* decision concerned public schools, not colleges. If the courts extended the principle of *Brown*, however, higher education would surely be affected. Although few black college presidents openly opposed *Brown*, the NAACP feared that some of them would subtly encourage resistance to it. They might collaborate with white officials to evade its implementation. They might exploit white fear of integration to leverage increased funding for their segregated colleges. And because state college presidents often dominated the leadership of the state teachers associations, they might exert a negative influence over the vast body of ordinary public school teachers.

Among the South's black teachers, the presidents of state colleges had long stood out as the most egregious exponents of accommodationism. Dutch observer Otto Schrieke, a former colonial official, wrote in 1936 that their "servility and . . . wily skill in handling politicians" caused many northern blacks to despise them as "the personification of insincerity and intrigue." Certainly, such men were past masters at the arts of flattery and manipulation. "You should resort to the technique of persuasion," advised John M. Gandy, one of the longest-serving members of this admired and reviled group. "I am thinking about the reaction of the white race to the music ability of the Negro. Each of you know how great an appeal can be made through music. . . . Now every year at this college we have an Annual Sacred Concert for the Governor and his staff, and it undoubtedly has a good effect. . . . We cannot persuade people who we do not know; they must know us, and we must know them." As well as being serenaded with tear-inducing spirituals, influential whites were stuffed with mouth-watering food and treated to little perks that were tantamount to bribes. One state college president, William J. Hale, the founder of Tennessee Agricultural and Industrial Normal School, presented members of the state board of education with tailored suits made by his students.[8]

In the shark-infested waters of southern politics, black state college presidents needed robust survival skills, and they regarded friendly dealings with white politicians as part of the job. Even a sophisticated intellectual like Horace Mann Bond—University of Chicago Ph.D., protégé of renowned sociologist Robert E. Park, and leading authority on Negro education—quickly learned the ropes. When Bond was appointed head of Fort Valley State College in 1939, he arrived in the middle of a political firestorm. Governor Eugene Talmadge, an archetypal southern demagogue, beloved of rural whites but despised by blacks, was wreaking havoc on Georgia's state college system. Talmadge charged that "foreigners" in the University of Georgia, aided and abetted by the Rosenwald Fund—which he called "Jew money for niggers"—were plotting to bring about race mixing. He had the board of regents dismiss the dean of the University of Georgia's school of education, the president of a white state college, and five other white professors. Bond felt threatened because of his close relationship with the Rosenwald Fund, which had selected him for the post and liquidated Fort Valley's indebtedness. Determined to neutralize Talmadge, he invited the governor to speak at Fort Valley and, on the advice of a white friend, had a faculty member photograph the governor smiling, laughing, and generally enjoying himself. Afterward, "Bond quietly passed the word that he had pictures of Talmadge cozying up to black folks but would forget about them if Talmadge forgot about the Rosenwald Fund." Talmadge decided to drop the issue.[9]

State college presidents also knew where the bodies were buried. We shall never know the secrets that they kept to themselves, buying political friendships by their silence. However, the revelation after his death that, as a young man, Senator Strom Thurmond had fathered a mixed-race daughter affords a glimpse into this murky world of political *omerta*. When his daughter was a student, Thurmond—the most powerful politician in South Carolina—paid regular visits to South

Carolina State College to see her. President M. F. Whitaker let the pair meet in his office, colluding in the pretense that the girl was a friend of the Thurmond family. His knowledge of the true nature of the relationship was money in the political bank.[10]

State college presidents argued that their dealings with white politicians, although distasteful and demeaning, were necessary. They were protecting and strengthening black higher education at a time when there was no alternative to segregation. However, as the NAACP fought for the admission of black graduate students to white state universities, segregationist politicians sought to thwart the NAACP by expanding the black state colleges. And some college presidents cooperated. James E. Shepard, the president of North Carolina College for Negroes, stymied the NAACP's plan to integrate the graduate school of the University of North Carolina by refusing to release the transcript of the would-be applicant and plaintiff, Thomas R. Hocutt. Not coincidentally—an explicit quid pro quo was not necessary—Shepard saw the state appropriation for his college increase from $23,000 in 1933–34 to $128,000 in 1939–40. After the *Gaines* decision, in which the Supreme Court told segregating states that they must either provide blacks with the same opportunities for graduate study as they afforded whites or else integrate their universities, the presidents of black state college almost fell over themselves to avail themselves of this NAACP-sent opportunity. They pressed the states to fund graduate programs. They won the coveted title, so long denied them, of "university." They "seem finally to have realized what a helluva chance they had of doing anything really big and constructive," admitted Horace Mann Bond, "and that everybody else was getting his, so they . . . get theirs while the getting is good."[11]

In the eyes of the NAACP, however, these college presidents were no longer pragmatic accommodationists making the best of a bad situation: they were directly assisting efforts to prevent integration. "Each time the NAACP wins a court victory against a southern state," Walter White lamented, "new buildings spring up on the campuses of the colored land-grant colleges. We must make the public conscious of the fact that this is a waste of the tax payers' money." Others were more forthright. State college presidents were heedless of black opinion, charged Lewis K. McMillan, a South Carolina–born history professor. "Indeed the president stands a surer chance of keeping his job to the extent that he is hostile to the interests of his own people."[12]

By 1950, when zeal for integration reflected a conviction that the Second World War had discredited race-based societies, ushering in a new conception of universal human rights, black intellectuals were depicting the black college president as the symbol of a corrupt, oppressive, and undemocratic past. Black state colleges were bywords for nepotism and authoritarianism. It was not uncommon for presidencies to pass from father to son, or from father to son-in-law. Within the campus, the president was often a capricious tyrant. Faculty members—whose tenure at some state colleges averaged a mere eighteen months—lived in perpetual insecurity. Above all, state college presidents answered to whites, not blacks, and they cynically exploited that relationship. In his novel *Stranger and Alone,* J. Saunders Redding wrote of "President Winbush," the devious, malicious, and unprincipled head of a black state college (rumored to be the mulatto son of a white politician) who reveled in his power to betray the militant teachers who were campaigning for equal salaries. His treachery operated in secret—Winbush belonged to the NAACP and made all the right speeches—but it was all the more effective for that. "Boy, I beat them out of bed," he crowed, upon learning that all the NAACP militants had lost their jobs. "I beat 'em!. . . . Son, they don't know I was behind it. They don't know what happened. They don't know that you keep your power hidden if you want to keep it strong." Redding, a native of Delaware who taught at Southern University in the late 1930s, claimed that he did not stray far from fact. The South's real-life Winbushes, he charged, perpetuated a kind of "fascism in reverse."[13]

After the NAACP's shift from equalization to integration, every time a black college added a graduate program its president, ipso facto, ranged himself against the NAACP. What Charles H. Thompson described as a "sort of obsequious but effective educational blackmail" threatened to "block the march of progress." In Texas, the site of the *Sweatt* case, Thurgood Marshall engaged in a bitter war of words with Carter Wesley, an influential Houston newspaper publisher who contended that lawsuits demanding the admission of black applicants to white institutions should not preclude efforts to equalize segregated institutions. Marshall retorted that blacks like Wesley, who supported the establishment of a new segregated college, Texas State University for Negroes, were "selling the race down the river." Jim Crow "de luxe" was still Jim Crow—"It is impossible to have equality in a segregated system." Marshall complained that every time the South's white politicians found an honest and influential black who endorsed so-called "equalization," they won a propaganda victory over the NAACP that was as valuable as a victory in the courts. The saga of the law school for blacks that the Texas legislature created in order to avert the integration of the University of Texas Law School reinforced Marshall's point. The law school of Texas State University for Negroes was so lacking in resources that its dean, Ozie H. Johnson, resigned in frustration, concluding that "the apathy of governing officials . . . will forever doom such schools to mediocrity."[14]

Even after *Brown,* however, the presidents of black state colleges refused to abandon their institution-building strategy. As the southern states lavished money on black colleges to maintain segregation in higher education, they gladly accepted new buildings, larger faculties, and branch campuses. They may have supported *Brown* in theory, but these men were nothing if not political realists. Their personal experience and knowledge of the South cried out caution. They regarded it as folly to crusade openly for integration.

The position of J. W. Seabrook, the longtime president of Fayetteville State College, was typical. The son of former slaves who became teachers and Presbyterian missionaries, Seabrook spent his formative years in South Carolina when Benjamin R. Tillman was defending lynching and branding the education of blacks a danger to white supremacy. He had attended Harbison College, the Presbyterian school whose principal was run out of town and that eventually closed its doors because of white hostility. As the president of a state college, Seabrook championed the cause of equal educational opportunity, and he decried the policy of confining blacks to certain occupations. His upbringing, however, made him painfully conscious of black vulnerability. It taught him that white power was overwhelming and that blacks in the South had no dependable friends. They could not expect protection from the North: Tillman's South Carolina had demonstrated the futility of looking to the federal government to enforce black rights.[15]

The fact that national policy had shifted in favor of integration did not reassure Seabrook. The change was too sudden to be convincing; he perceived it as a consequence of international circumstances rather than internal pressure. Leading black educators knew full well that the cold war had been the decisive factor in the federal government's change of heart. The United States found itself suddenly pitched into an ideological struggle for the allegiance of the nonwhite peoples who were emerging from colonial rule. "The world situation made [*Brown*] inevitable," he argued. "The white man is no fool, he knows the Communists are after Asia and Africa. He is not going to take the stand that he will continue to discriminate *legally* on race and color alone." But Seabrook did not detect a national consensus in favor of abandoning Jim Crow, and white opinion in the South was dead set against integration. He warned blacks not to place too much faith in the Supreme Court: it was difficult to enforce any law with which a majority of the people strongly disagreed.[16]

When he received the governor's invitation to serve on an "advisory committee on education," Seabrook knew he was being handed a poisoned chalice. But as the president of a state college controlled by white politicians, he could hardly refuse it. Governor Luther Hodges appointed the committee to consider North Carolina's official response to *Brown*. At the committee's behest, the state legislature enacted a "pupil placement law" that enabled local school boards to allocate pupils to schools on grounds other than race. Everybody knew, however, that race would still be the determining factor behind the assignment of pupils. The law was a clear attempt to preserve segregated schools, and it proved so successful that other states copied it. That Seabrook and two other black educators—also state employees—should acquiesce in such schemes angered opponents of segregation. Whatever they may have said in private, their public subservience, the NAACP believed, disqualified such men from any claim to leadership.[17]

Yet Seabrook never opposed integration. In the closing years of his long career he exhorted his students to prepare themselves for the cold winds of interracial competition. His message was brutally frank. Blacks would fail to win the legal struggle for integration unless they convinced public opinion that they were ready for it. After the Civil War, he reminded his students, white southerners had won the propaganda battle: their novelists, journalists, and polemicists had convinced the white North of black inferiority. Integration would force black youth to compete against anyone, "not just with members of our own race." Blacks would have to "talk like educated Americans, think like educated and intelligent Americans, read like college students in Europe." But at the moment, he warned, they were woefully unprepared for that challenge. "Most of you are working beneath your capacity and achieving below your ability." Worse, if students belittled academic achievement and shirked excellence, they perpetuated the myth that blacks were inferior—they betrayed the race. Referring to recent events in the civil rights movement, Seabrook held up the examples of Martin Luther King Jr. and Elizabeth Eckford, the girl who braved a white mob on the way to Little Rock Central High School. "Follow their example—walk in pride, dignity, with head held high . . . win the public opinion of the world to your side."[18]

For the mass of black public school teachers, *Brown* brought as much fear as hope. They were hardly comforted by the NAACP's contradictory statements: on the one hand downplaying the likelihood of job losses, on the other hand telling teachers they should be prepared to sacrifice their jobs in a worthy cause. And they found it difficult to believe that integration, if and when it happened, would be implemented evenhandedly. The example of integrated schools in the North was not reassuring. In Pittsburgh, mixed schools meant the exclusion of black teachers. In Philadelphia and Chicago, blacks had only secured teaching positions by acquiescing in schools that were de facto segregated. If northern whites resisted having black teachers in mixed schools, why would whites in the South accept them? Deeply attached to segregation as an all-embracing "way of life," white southerners regarded separate schools as the foundation of their social system. Convinced that "social equality" would bring interracial marriage in its train, they regarded with horror the prospect of black men teaching white girls. Whites still controlled the entire system of state and local government. It seemed a fair bet that, if forced to adopt unitary school systems, they would take advantage of the resulting efficiency savings to reduce the number of black teachers. School boards would safeguard the jobs of white teachers at the expense of blacks.[19]

Even if hiring procedures were to be outwardly fair, many black teachers were fearful of being thrown into competition with white teachers. True, by 1954 the educational gap between white and black teachers had been greatly reduced. According to one study, "there was only 0.3 of a year's difference" in the training of each group. In five southern states—Virginia, North Carolina, Tennessee, Georgia, and Texas—black teachers averaged *more* years of education. However, regional averages masked sharp disparities in states such as Mississippi, where only a quarter of the black teachers, but half of the white teachers, had four years or more of college education. Moreover, some black teachers had little faith in the quality of their paper qualifications. Degrees obtained through years of attendance at state college summer schools—where a desire to collect fees often trumped rigorous assessment—were of dubious value. Whenever states raised their certification requirements, complained one black college teacher, "we have a mad rush on the part of . . . old incompetents to get into extension classes and summer schools in order to get more credits," which were usually liberally awarded. Hence even college graduates often dreaded being at the mercy of the National Teacher Examination.[20]

Black teachers were acutely aware that their employment was insecure. In 1944 Myrdal noted that they enjoyed virtually no job security. Ten years later, despite being in a more stable, better organized, and more highly paid profession, teachers still held their positions at the grace and favor of local school boards. Black teachers could, and did, join the NAACP. They could, and did, become voters. But the salary equalization campaign, although moderately successful, underlined the ease with which school boards could oust politically offensive teachers. True, a few of the victims were reinstated. In 1948, for example, Judge Herbert W. Christenberry ordered the school board of Jefferson Parish, Louisiana, to restore Eula Mae Lee to her former position. But it had taken Lee five years to get her job back. Effective legal action against unfair dismissal remained lengthy, difficult, and costly. Teacher tenure laws were weak. Even principals depended upon yearly contracts that were renewed or canceled at the whim of their employer. The absence of alternative employment heightened black teachers' sense of insecurity. As the NAACP acknowledged, white teachers could "move easily into business or a variety of other white collar occupations without loss of economic or social status." Black teachers had far fewer options.[21]

The *Brown* cases themselves had provided a foretaste of what black teachers could expect if they participated in integration lawsuits. Rev. Joseph A. DeLaine was a preacher-teacher who led the fight for better schools in Clarendon County, South Carolina, a struggle that generated the pivotal case of *Briggs v. Elliott*. When the school board realized that DeLaine would not back down, it fired him, and for good measure fired his wife as well. A black principal, whom the school board had dismissed at the insistence of angry parents and pupils, sued DeLaine for slander, and a state court awarded damages of twenty-seven hundred dollars. DeLaine's house burned down, then his church burned down. DeLaine was shot at, and when he returned fire the state charged him with assault. He escaped from South Carolina on the floor of a car, hidden under blankets. Another of the *Brown* cases, *Davis v. County School Board,* had its genesis in a strike by the black students of Robert R. Moton High School in Prince Edward County, Virginia. Although the school's principal, M. Boyd Jones, did nothing to encourage the protest, the school board dismissed him for not doing enough to suppress it. These examples sent a clear message to black teachers in the South: support the NAACP's assault on Jim Crow at your peril.[22]

By 1955 the initially muted reaction of white southerners to the *Brown* decision, an attitude of "wait and see," gave way to vehement opposition led by ultra-segregationists. And when these ultra-segregationists launched an aggressive legal and political campaign—dubbed "Massive Resistance"—to prevent school integration they ruthlessly exploited black teachers' vulnerability in an effort to destroy the NAACP. School superintendents ordered black principals to circulate pro-segregation petitions; teachers who refused to sign were fired. School boards warned teachers that their schools would be closed, and their retirement benefits lost, if integration came to pass. State officials branded the NAACP a subversive organization, subjected its members to legislative investigations, and prosecuted NAACP lawyers for unlawful practices. They required the NAACP to hand over its membership lists, and when branches refused to do so, state courts banned the NAACP from operating. Some states weakened or abolished their teacher tenure laws.

If this were not enough to scare teachers away from the NAACP, new state laws explicitly prohibited public employees from advocating integration and belonging to any organization that did so. Some school boards required teachers to fill out questionnaires that asked if they supported integration and belonged to the NAACP. Affirmative answers triggered dismissal. Covert intimidation, orchestrated by the Citizens Councils movement, which included white politicians, businessmen, and education officials, accompanied this overt repression. Some states created special agencies to identify, spy on, and harass civil rights activists. Recommending that two schoolteachers, the wives of NAACP members, should be dismissed, a staff member of the Mississippi State Sovereignty Commission explained the obvious. "If examples of these two women are made, word will get around quickly enough through our negro friends and will have a decided impact on other negroes who might be tempted to agitate in behalf of the NAACP."[23]

John W. Davis, the NAACP official whose job it was to protect them, grimly noted that "the degree of fear among Negro teachers is alarming." In time, the NAACP would challenge and overturn many of the punitive laws passed to stifle freedom of association and expression. Meanwhile, however, damage was being done. Teachers began to quit the NAACP. In Georgia, many teachers allowed their NAACP memberships to lapse—or even sent letters of resignation—after the state attorney general, Eugene Cook, ordered the board of education to dismiss anyone who "contributes to or is affiliated with" the organization. A few teachers defied pressure to renounce the NAACP. In South

Carolina, twenty-one teachers at Elloree Training School chose to quit their jobs rather than disclose their NAACP membership. Eleven teachers in Charleston also refused to toe the segregationist line. But these cases were exceptional. After losing her job upon declaring her NAACP membership, veteran teacher Septima P. Clark urged South Carolina's black teachers to show solidarity with the NAACP. Few responded. Across the South, teachers dropped out of the NAACP or kept their membership hidden. Given the fact that teachers were a substantial portion of its membership, the NAACP suffered a crippling blow.[24]

The ban on public advocacy of integration also muzzled the state teachers associations. Many stopped inviting speakers from the NAACP and ceased campaigning for school integration. Indeed, for several years—well into the 1960s—their meetings and publications barely mentioned integration. Six years after *Brown,* Lucius H. Pitts, head of the Georgia Teachers and Education Association (GTEA), assured the state superintendent of schools that his organization "has not made any effort now nor will it in the foreseeable future make any effort to press for desegregation."[25]

The lack of national commitment to enforcing *Brown* further discouraged the South's black teachers. President Eisenhower made plain his distaste for the decision. Congress did nothing. Even the Supreme Court made no effort to bring about widespread and immediate compliance. Although the federal courts eventually struck down most of the state laws designed to harass the NAACP and silence black teachers, the federal government remained passive while the NAACP struggled for its life.

Black teachers could not even count on the support of their profession. The National Education Association was moving away from racial segregation, but its progress toward integration was glacial. In 1943 the NEA voted to avoid holding its conventions in cities that refused to treat delegates "without discrimination" with regard to "race, color, or creed." But when it discovered that few cities completely met that standard, it watered down the motion, requiring only a "maximum degree of equality" rather than no discrimination at all. In 1951 the NEA finally accorded recognition to the black state teachers associations, permitting dual affiliates to represent the southern and border states. However, proposals to integrate the segregated associations were regularly voted down.[26]

Faced with the *Brown* decision, the NEA's national leadership tried to prevent the explosive integration issue from ripping the organization apart. It also feared that any split over *Brown* would doom the NEA's long-held goal of federal aid to education. The Association passed an anodyne motion blandly noting that integration "of all groups" was "an evolving process which concerns every state and territory." Instead of support for, obedience to, and enforcement of *Brown,* the NEA meekly stated that "all problems of desegregation . . . are capable of solution at the state and local levels by citizens of intelligence, saneness, and reasonableness." In his speech to the 1956 convention, President William Carr—formerly the superintendent of schools in Columbia, South Carolina—did not mention integration. In 1959, New York delegate Walter Ludwig ridiculed the NEA's silence. "I have examined the latest list of NEA publications," he told the convention, "over 1,000 books, pamphlets, periodicals, research reports. . . . There is a report on hogs, ax handles, and woodpeckers, which turns out to be a comparison of American and Russian education. And pamphlet 1034—brace yourself—'What Policies Should Guide the Handling of Controversial Issues?' But in this list there is not one report on integration."[27]

The NEA's policy of "calculated silence" encouraged southern white resistance to *Brown* by adding to the impression of northern irresolution. Indeed, the NEA not only failed to take a strong stand in favor of integration but also did virtually nothing to assist black teachers who faced threats, harassment, and dismissal. Most of the help for teachers who lost their jobs came from the black community itself—the NAACP, black businesses, other black teachers—and from northern human rights organizations such as the American Friends Service Committee.[28]

In 1956 NAACP official Dan Byrd reported that black teachers in Louisiana were so disgusted with the NEA that it was futile to ask them to join. "Is the NEA selling out to the Citizens Councils or meeting with Senator Eastland?" asked one. "What do we get for our money but a magazine and a sellout to the South?" The fact that they felt inhibited from contributing to NEA debates on integration—because of repressive state laws—compounded their frustration. Even full-time officials of the state associations feared that open support for *Brown* would imperil the jobs of their members back home. Thus Lucius Pitts, the executive secretary of the Georgia Teachers and Education Association, bit his tongue as southern white delegates battled against a motion before the 1960 convention to strengthen the NEA's commitment to integration. Unable to hold his peace any longer, Pitts pointed out that it was nonsense for NEA leaders, including President Carr, to claim that they understood the southern situation when "90 per cent of the Negro members who are present in this Association . . . could not speak." Moreover, when these NEA officers traveled about the South, "they don't get a chance really to know what we live under. They get off of a white train and live in a white hotel . . . [and] are ushered around by the [white] officials of the South." Picott called the 1954 resolution on *Brown* weak and insignificant. "It does not say that NEA *believes.*"[29]

By 1960, when the NEA finally made "continued support" for *Brown* a "pledge," the civil rights movement was gathering so much strength that black southerners were able to force the pace of integration. The success of the Montgomery bus boycott in 1956 made Martin Luther King Jr. a national figure and inspired the organization of the Southern Christian Leadership Conference (SCLC). In 1957 Congress passed the first Civil Rights Act since Reconstruction. In the same year, President Eisenhower sent troops to enforce the integration of Little Rock's Central High School after the governor of Arkansas, defying a federal court order, encouraged white mobs to keep black children out. Three years later, black college students in Greensboro, North Carolina, organized "sit-ins" in order to gain service at "whites only" lunch counters. The sit-in movement took the South by storm and prompted the formation of another new civil rights organization, the Student Nonviolent Coordinating Committee (SNCC).

Slowly but surely, the National Education Association responded to these changes. During the New Orleans school integration crisis of 1960–61, when the Louisiana legislature imposed a financial blockade on the Orleans Parish School Board to prevent it from paying teachers, the NEA offered its members interest-free loans. When the school board of Prince Edward County shut down its entire public school system, the NEA worked with the NAACP and other organizations to open free schools. In 1963 the NEA endorsed President Kennedy's Civil Rights Bill. The following year, it voted to desegregate its own ranks. Segregated state associations were instructed to open their membership to all and submit merger plans by 1966. Associations that failed to comply risked expulsion from the NEA. Also at this time, the NEA finally started to defend black teachers who suffered unfair dismissals.[30]

The NEA's rival, the American Federation of Teachers, was consistent and resolute in its support for integration. In *amicus curiae* briefs to the Supreme Court, the AFT supported the NAACP's legal attack on segregation, declaring that "segregated and discriminatory schooling . . . prevents the interplay of ideas, personalities, information, and attitudes, impedes a democratic education and ultimately prevents a working democracy." In 1953 the AFT encouraged its segregated locals to integrate. Two years later it threatened to suspend any locals that continued to practice racial discrimination. By 1958 the AFT had revoked the charters of offending white locals in New Orleans, Atlanta, Fulton County, and Chattanooga. The black locals endorsed the AFT's policy, opened their membership to white teachers, and remained part of the union.[31]

Throughout these years of white backlash against *Brown,* many black teachers maintained their support for integration. Always acutely aware of their vulnerability, they were accustomed to working indirectly, advancing behind the collective strength of organizations. The 1950s were no exception. Although banned from joining the NAACP, the South's black teachers continued to send regular contributions to the Inc. Fund at the rate of one thousand dollars for each one thousand members. To disguise the fact they were supporting the NAACP, they used the National Conference of State Teachers Associations (NCOSTA) as a conduit. NCOSTA was a loose body, with no constitution, bylaws, or membership lists—a difficult target for the kind of state repression that had so damaged the NAACP in the South.

To make these New York–bound contributions even more difficult to trace, NCOSTA used a complicated set of banking arrangements to "launder" the money. Moreover, although teachers could not act as plaintiffs in desegregation suits, state associations like the Louisiana Education Association "played a significant—although often behind the scenes—role in instituting the important suits the NAACP filed."[32]

The NAACP liked to believe that in pressing for integrated schools it was articulating the aspirations of a majority of black southerners. In this way it could attribute the reluctance of black teachers to crusade openly for integration to intimidation and repression. It could also depict black opponents of integration as a self-interested and unrepresentative group.[33]

In reality, black teachers' doubts about integration reflected widespread ambivalence among black southerners. In private, the NAACP's lawyers and state officers acknowledged that the organization's southern members were unprepared for the abrupt switch from equalization to integration. In 1947 Marshall had expressed his "doubt that our branch officers are fully indoctrinated on the policy of the NAACP in being opposed to segregation." Three years later, when the NAACP took its unequivocal stand in favor of directly attacking segregation, these doubts resurfaced. "Some of the lawyers are ready to fight through the college level," Marshall told the board of the Inc. Fund, "but are not ready through the high school and elementary level. They will accept a Jim Crow school. Many desire to leave it up to the local community." Daniel E. Byrd, a field secretary for the Inc. Fund in Louisiana, told Marshall that the branches needed to be educated about the shift in policy. "This is something entirely new and the branches are uninformed." The notion of integration as a strategy bubbling up from the grass-roots is therefore imprecise. In the two *Brown* cases that emanated from the South—the Prince Edward County, Virginia, case, and the Clarendon County, South Carolina, case—black plaintiffs initially pressed for better school facilities. They changed their goal to integration because the NAACP made them conform to its new all-or-nothing legal strategy.[34]

Looking back on the 1950s, veterans of the Inc. Fund conceded that the NAACP had miscalculated the level of black support for school integration. "We were, in our aggressive program, out in front of many members of the black community," concluded Jack Greenberg. "Among the reasons was that school integration would create problems for black teachers . . . [W]e didn't fully appreciate how serious this problem would become."[35]

Constance Baker Motley, Greenberg's colleague, pointed to a second reason for limited black support: the importance of black schools as community institutions. Neither fear nor apathy accounted for the fact that "we didn't really get any grass roots activity around school desegregation." The Montgomery bus boycott, on the other hand, mobilized an entire black community in a courageous, disciplined, and determined protest that lasted for more than a year. Motley attributed the contrast, at least in part, to the different issues involved. Segregated buses generated burning resentment among all blacks; it was a humiliating public expression of white supremacy. Many blacks viewed segregated schools, on the other hand, as community institutions in which they took great pride. Although schools were public institutions, black communities often felt a sense of ownership toward them. Individual teachers had harnessed community support to create them, and for many years blacks had heavily subsidized them. In arguing the case for integration, Marshall had insisted that separate-but-equal was a chimera. He may well have been right. But to many blacks in the 1950s, the building of new black high schools and the expansion of black state colleges indicated that the equalization strategy was at last paying off. Other blacks were ready to make the leap of faith demanded by the NAACP's integration strategy. However, as integration proceeded at a snail's pace—often not at all—the NAACP's argument that integration was the *only* way to secure better schools lost its force. Motley recalled, "More blacks would be saying in effect 'look, we want our kids in first-class education. You're not doing anything about it. It's moving too slowly.'"[36]

THE Montgomery bus boycott, which began on December 5, 1955, signaled a seismic shift in the black struggle for equality. Harnessing the enthusiastic support of a virtually unanimous black population, it revealed the tremendous potential of mass nonviolent direct action.

The boycott—and similar protests in Tallahassee, Florida, and else-where—brought ministers, especially Baptist ministers, to the fore-front of a new civil rights movement. As a perceptive white newspa-per editor recalled, "The preachers took over from the teachers."[37]

Teachers in fact played an important role in the opening phase of this new movement. A group of teachers at Alabama State College, led by Jo Ann Robinson, a member of the English department, organized the Montgomery bus boycott after the arrest of Mrs. Rosa Parks. In Tallahassee, Dr. James H. Hudson, chairman of Florida A&M's philos-ophy department and an ordained minister, enlisted the support of the city's black clergymen after the twenty-seven-hundred-strong student body voted to boycott segregated buses following the arrest of two fel-low students. In both Montgomery and Tallahassee, faculty members gave steady and important support to the protests, but their economic vulnerability prevented them from assuming key leadership positions. They worked in the background.

The participation of faculty members in these protests nonetheless placed the presidents of those black colleges in an awkward position. To publicly identify with the protests could damage their institutions and would almost certainly trigger their own dismissal. Yet in discreet ways, they also supported the bus boycotts. H. Councill Trenholm, the long-serving president of Alabama State College, exerted no pressure on faculty members not to take part in the Montgomery bus boycott. He retrospectively endorsed Jo Ann Robinson's actions in organiz-ing the boycott, and, according to Robinson, contributed behind-the-scenes support and advice for the duration of the protest. The position of George W. Gore, president of Florida A&M, seemed less sympa-thetic. At a faculty meeting he warned staff members not to take an "active part" in the Tallahassee bus boycott, "lest such participation would embarrass them and the university." He repeated this message in private conversations, reminding activists "that they would be on their own if they continued, because [he] wouldn't be able to defend them or protect them." But none of the faculty members believed that Gore was instructing them not to participate in the boycott, and Gore took no actions to impede their activities.[38]

The rise of student activism, however, placed black state college presidents in a much more difficult position. When college campuses became centers of civil rights militancy, white politicians expected the men who ran these institutions to prevent challenges to segregation. The Orangeburg student movement, which blossomed in the spring of 1956, presented the first clear example. Led by Fred H. Moore, the president of the student council, about fifteen hundred students at South Carolina State College mounted a boycott of white-owned businesses—in fact it was a counter-boycott, responding to pressure from the white Citizens Council. Students marched in the streets and organized protests on campus. At the behest of the board of trustees, Benner C. Turner, the president of South Carolina State College, expelled Fred Moore and fourteen other activists. His actions left a bitterly resentful student body and a deeply alienated faculty. The arrival of a legislative committee bent on ferreting out NAACP supporters rubbed salt into the wounds. Benner Turner kept his job, but students branded him "Uncle Tom" and burned him in effigy.[39]

The following year J. R. Otis, the president of Alcorn State College in Mississippi, became a casualty of student activism when the state board of education fired him. Students at Alcorn had boycotted classes to protest against anti-integration statements by Clennon W. King, a minister and history teacher who had written a series of articles, published in a segregationist newspaper, attacking the NAACP. Otis allegedly sympathized with the students. After closing the campus and expelling most of the students, Governor J. P. Coleman appointed J. D. Boyd, a reliably pliant administrator, as Otis's successor.[40]

T HE sit-in movement of 1960 placed black college presidents on the firing line all over the South. At the private colleges, students usually received praise and protection. At the state colleges, however, presidents faced strong pressure—and sometimes direct orders—to expel dissident students and any faculty members who supported them. Some of them, including H. Councill Trenholm and George W. Gore, did so. Their actions attracted widespread condemnation from civil rights activists. Even Thurgood Marshall, who was skeptical of nonviolent direct action, castigated college heads who obeyed segregationist dictates. In one of his last actions as head of the Inc. Fund before joining the federal bench, Marshall committed the NAACP to the students' legal defense.

The response of the state college presidents was not all of a piece, however. In North Carolina, which had evolved a somewhat less repressive system of race relations, and whose proportionately small black population boasted a relatively high level of voting, state college presidents had more room for maneuver. Warmoth T. Gibbs, the president of North Carolina A&T College in Greensboro, whose students launched the first sit-in movement, resisted pressure from the mayor and governor to discipline or expel the demonstrators. State college presidents in the Deep South, on the other hand, had virtually no leeway. When students at Alabama State College organized sit-ins in Montgomery, state authorities unleashed what one historian called "intense official coercion." The governor of Alabama ordered H. Councill Trenholm to dismiss history professor Lawrence D. Reddick "before sundown." Trenholm balked—refusing to hand over Reddick's personnel file—but eventually complied. Twenty other faculty members lost their jobs. The state board of education also told Trenholm to suspend thirty-nine students. Although he whittled the number down to nine, the leaders of the sit-in movement had to leave. Despite allowing himself to be an instrument of this segregationist crackdown, Trenholm had to retire early. He died soon afterward.[41]

A reserved, enigmatic man, Trenholm suffered his public humiliation in silence. A file of incoming letters, however, documented the excruciating pressure he endured. On the one hand, white segregationists damned him for allowing the sit-ins to happen in the first place. "YOU could have controlled your students," wrote a Chattanooga man. "YOU and your faculty evidently approves of what they do and even encourage them. You deserve and will have the ill will and even the hatred of the white people." On the other hand, blacks rebuked Trenholm for betraying his race. "The Uncle Toms are supposed to be dead," wrote a man from Philadelphia, "and those that are leaders are supposed to be out front carrying the banner of freedom, dignity and justice for all. . . . How will you face tomorrow?" One of his own cousins sent him a telegram with the terse message, "You should have resigned yourself."[42]

Men like Trenholm believed that they were shielding their institutions from possible destruction at the hands of segregationist politicians. But their feelings went beyond institutional loyalty. Trenholm had run Alabama State College since 1925; before that, his father had been president. His identification with the college was so complete that he found it difficult to distinguish between his own personal interests and those of the institution he served. In the case of Felton G. Clark, who "inherited" Southern University from J. S. Clark, his father, the institution's founder, the confusion of interests was complete. Clark interpreted criticism of his actions as nothing more than an attempt by outside agitators to attack Southern University. NAACP leaders in New Orleans had opposed the creation of a satellite campus—Southern University in New Orleans (SUNO)—in the 1950s. Now, Clark believed, these leaders, many of them graduates of rival colleges, were using the sit-ins to hit back at Southern. "*Somebody* got to the students. Somebody . . . who was just plain mean, viscious [sic] and out to destroy the president of Southern University, or . . . destroy his nearest symbol, that is, the University itself."[43]

The sit-in movement sparked a spirited debate among black teachers about educational values. When leading black educators refused to support the civil rights movement, they believed that they were protecting black schools and colleges by insulating them from politics. Education, they argued, was an end in itself. "I have never personally participated in an organized protest," reflected Jacob L. Reddix, the former president of Jackson State College. But he believed that his fifty years "devoted . . . to the education and enlightenment of young people" was "as important as participating in organized protests."[44]

To those imbued with the democratic and religious idealism of the civil rights movement, however, such arguments revealed a tragic narrowness of vision. "Can 'education' exist in the abstract? Can there be 'education' that exists apart from people and issues?," Adolph L. Reed, a member of Southern University's history and political science department, asked Felton G. Clark. In a blistering ten-page letter of resignation, Reed compared Clark's moral stance—that he was only obeying orders—with that of Nazi war criminal Adolph Eichmann, then on trial in Jerusalem. George R. Woolfolk, a professor of history at Prairie View State College, argued that the obsession of black college presidents with institutional survival resulted in "intellectual and spiritual sterility." For Samuel L. Gandy, a professor at Dillard University, the sit-in movement was a moment of truth that exposed the high-sounding educational ideals of the black college as hollow rhetoric. It was easy to advocate "liberty and justice and equality" in the abstract, "when words were not required at the moment of their utterance to have legs attached to them." Even in private colleges like Dillard, Gandy added, "teachers who teach the goals of democracy with an urge toward personal involvement may . . . find themselves subject to displacement."[45]

A conference of black college presidents held in Washington in November 1960 revealed the extent to which the men who headed state institutions felt intimidated by segregationist pressures. The Phelps-Stokes Fund organized the conference, and invited officials from the NAACP to attend, for the purpose of considering how best to respond to the sit-in movement. The presidents insisted that no minutes be taken. Many wanted no record of their participation. Some failed to attend.[46]

As the civil rights movement unfolded across the South, promoting an open and broad-ranging revolt against racial segregation, some teachers joined it. In Richmond, Virginia, in 1963, teachers took part in demonstrations and suffered no reprisals. In Orangeburg, South Carolina, several teachers suddenly "fell ill" when one of their number, a woman who had been arrested eight times, was dismissed. Louisiana's civil rights movement boasted W. W. Harleaux, the principal of a small elementary school in Plaquemine; Frederick Douglass Kirkpatrick, a physical education teacher at Jackson High School in Jonesboro; and Hazel Matthews, a young teacher in East Feliciana Parish. All three became involved with the voter registration and direct action campaigns of the Congress of Racial Equality (CORE). Matthews joined CORE over the warnings of her principal. "I tell him if getting me fired will add another star to his Crown do so."

But most teachers abstained from militant activism. "As a group black teachers in the 1950s refused to take a stand," writes John

Dittmer, the historian of the civil rights movement in Mississippi, "and the movement of the early 1960s passed them by." When teachers marched to the courthouse in Selma, Alabama, in support of King's campaign for voting rights, the impact was all the greater because it was so rare for teachers to engage in public protest. By and large, civil rights workers neither expected nor received strong support from public school teachers. Indeed, they routinely—if unfairly—dismissed teachers as "the most Uncle Tom group around." They were especially contemptuous of black principals, whom they dubbed "pseudo-leaders" who were either corrupt or complacent.[47]

Teachers heard the "Uncle Tom" jibe and resented it. Black principals believed that they played a valuable role as racial diplomats, even if, because they dealt with white officials behind the scenes, most blacks remained unaware and unappreciative of what they achieved. Moreover, many teachers disliked and felt threatened by the confrontational tactics of nonviolent direct action. "The sit-in demonstrations . . . may be the undoing of black teachers," warned W. E. Solomon, the longtime executive secretary of the Palmetto Education Association. "The demonstrators have proved that they are adults." It was an unusually frank admission. Solomon added that at one recent PTA meeting, teachers had angrily rejected parents' suggestions that they should assume leadership roles in the sit-in movement. "A near riot broke out."[48]

The disruption of school routine and discipline violated the professional instincts of many black educators. It threatened both their own authority and the process of education itself. Moreover, teachers often distrusted the motives and questioned the legitimacy of intruding civil rights workers. They charged these activists with deliberately fomenting class divisions within the black community, undermining respect for traditional leaders, and using gullible students as cannon fodder in their confrontations with the police. Civil rights workers used black schools as a political weapon, they believed, but had no real interest in them. In Wilcox County, Alabama, for example, many teachers strongly disliked the SNCC and SCLC workers who, in 1965, encouraged pupils at Camden Academy to boycott classes and take part in civil rights demonstrations, some of which entailed ugly confrontations with heavily armed police and state troopers. "They weren't concerned about your feelings," complained one, "they wanted to make you angry." Others lamented the way that the rebelliousness encouraged by the civil rights movement also eroded politeness, manners, and deference to elders. "When the outside civil rights workers came in, it was us against them," recalled one former teacher. "It became so ugly." But as historian Cynthia G. Fleming shows, nonviolent direct action also pitted some teachers against other teachers, the children of teachers against their parents, and married teachers against each other. The divisions were deep and often enduring.[49]

The civil rights movement made it difficult for black principals to continue their traditional role as community leaders. The men who headed black high schools, in particular, faced strong pressure from school boards to stop pupils and faculty members from engaging in protests. The pressure increased when civil rights groups such as CORE, SNCC, and the SCLC recruited high school students for demonstrations. In the spring of 1963, as Martin Luther King's campaign of nonviolent direct action in Birmingham, Alabama, tottered on the verge of defeat, SCLC organizers turned the tide by persuading schoolchildren to join the demonstrations. The principal of Parker High School, R. C. Johnson, locked the school gates in a futile effort to stop the exodus. At nearby Fairfield School, principal Edmond Jefferson Oliver suspended a dozen pupils who left school to participate in the demonstrations. "Two or three self-styled leaders of the community called a meeting at the school for the purpose of getting the students back in school without any kind of punishment," Oliver recalled. He resolved this angry confrontation by persuading parents to let the faculty decide the appropriate punishment and not appeal over his head to the superintendent. Reasoning that the students ought to have stayed at home if they wished to march with the SCLC, the faculty allowed them back but placed them on probation.[50]

Some black principals connived with school boards to engineer the dismissal of teachers who became involved with the civil rights movement. The head of a school in Taylorsville, Mississippi, for example, regularly supplied the State Sovereignty Commission with the names of teachers who were "NAACP agitators." Straightforward opportunism often motivated such actions. Soliciting a "personal donation" from the governor toward his school's football field, this man assured the state's chief executive, "We stand for separate schools for our race." Other black principals assisted the Mississippi State Sovereignty Commission. In 1959 B. L. Bell, a graduate of Morehouse College who headed a school in Cleveland, Bolivar County, volunteered his services as an informant. After receiving a positive reference from the county's superintendent of education, A. H. Ramsey, who described him as a "'white man's Negro' . . . worthy of confidence and trust," the Commission employed Bell to spy on the NAACP. J. C. Dunbar performed a similar service in Claiborne County, where he served as the Negro county agricultural agent. "[He] is a good Negro and one that can be depended upon for reliable information," advised Superintendent of Education R. A. Segrest, after Dunbar handed him the names of eighteen suspected NAACP members. In 1964 the school board appointed Dunbar principal of Addison High School in Port Gibson, from which position he continued to work against the NAACP. Elsewhere, school superintendents made it clear that they expected black principals to report any "outside agitation" and "subversive activity."[51]

The numbers of black informants, and the damage their activities inflicted upon the civil rights movement, are difficult to assess. Men like Bell and Dunbar not only provided the segregationists with information about the NAACP but also tried to impede the NAACP in other ways. In practice, however, informants often betrayed themselves through their actions. Addressing a civil rights meeting in 1960, for example, NAACP state president Aaron Henry publicly denounced B. L. Bell as an informant for the State Sovereignty Commission. Bell hotly denied the charge, but the mere fact that he attended NAACP meetings gave him away. No other black schoolteachers attended civil rights meetings, Henry pointed out, because they feared dismissal. Why wasn't Bell afraid of losing his job? And J. C. Dunbar, in Port Gibson, found himself evicted from his office in the Negro Masonic Building when the other members of the lodge, over his opposition, voted to allow their building to be used for civil rights meetings. Civil rights activists took it for granted that whites employed black spies and informants; this was part and parcel of Jim Crow culture. They could do little to prevent such infiltration, and could only attempt to identify and isolate the infiltrators.[52]

Their dependent relationship with white superintendents and school boards made black principals automatically suspect in the eyes of many civil rights activists. Medgar Evers, the NAACP's field secretary in Mississippi, charged black principals with collaborating with white segregationists in order to maintain their privileged position within the segregated status quo. Whites gave them payoffs and unmerited promotions, and even named schools in their honor in order to bolster their prestige. In return, black principals "assumed the role of community dictator" and tried to suppress black dissent. In later years, when black principals looked to the civil rights movement to protect their jobs in the wake of integration, they received precious little sympathy from NAACP officials.

Yet it was all too easy to confuse suspicion and fact, especially in situations where principals were caught in the middle of divided communities. In Wilcox County, Alabama, for example, one teacher believed for decades that his dismissal during the civil rights movement had been instigated by his principal. In reality, the school board had fired the activist over the principal's head.[53]

Teachers' fears about openly identifying with the civil rights movement were slow to dissipate. Some refused to rejoin the NAACP unless their school board explicitly permitted them to do so. By the mid-1960s, though, lawsuits had knocked out many of the state laws that banned public employees from advocating integration and otherwise harassed the NAACP. In addition, a 1966 decision of the Fourth Circuit Court of Appeals made it more difficult for school boards to arbitrarily dismiss teachers who happened to be civil rights activists. North Carolina teacher Willa Johnson, who was secretary of her local NAACP branch, won twenty thousand dollars in compensation from the Halifax County School Board after the court decided that civil rights, not incompetence, had prompted her dismissal.[54]

When North Carolina governor Terry Sanford sought the help of J. W. Seabrook in getting students off the streets of Fayetteville during the tumultuous summer of 1963, Seabrook politely declined. This venerable black educator explained to the governor the historical significance of what the students were doing: "They are driven by a religious and emotional fervor which reminds me of the Children's Crusade to deliver the Holy Land from the Moslems. This fervor is in part mass psychology, the effect of occurrences elsewhere in the nation, and may in part be tinged with exhibitionism. Fundamentally, however, it is the manifestation of a determination to bring to an end all vestiges of slavery . . . and by the groundsweep all over the world for the elimination of exploitation, discrimination, and oppression." Now retired, Seabrook acknowledged that black students probably regarded him as "old-fashioned and conservative, to put it mildly." In any case, he added, the "current crop of Negro youth" could not be controlled by their elders.[55]

As teachers gradually returned to the NAACP, their state associations abandoned the self-denying ordinance that had kept them quiet over the integration issue. In 1964, for example, for the first time in many years, the Louisiana Education Association invited a prominent NAACP leader, Constance Baker Motley, to address its annual convention. At the same time, many white leaders quietly revised their attitude toward the NAACP. The rise of nonviolent direct action, the emergence of Black Power, and the eruption of urban riots created a fear of black radicalism that made them doubt the wisdom of destroying the NAACP. They saw the advantage of bolstering moderate black leadership, and isolating "radicals" and "extremists," by recognizing the NAACP as a legitimate representative of the black community. When cities, counties, and states created biracial committees to foster dialogue over race relations, they turned to the NAACP to supply teachers, preachers, and businessmen—the blacks with whom white leaders felt most comfortable. The passage of the 1965 Voting Rights Act, which drastically increased the black electorate, especially in the Deep South, gave white politicians another incentive to cultivate black leaders. Trimming their segregationist sails, men like John J. McKeithen, the governor of Louisiana, used the state teachers associations as bridges to black voters. The leaders of those associations often became powerful political players. Some of them—Alphonse Jackson (Louisiana), Joe Reed (Alabama), Horace Tate (Georgia)—went on to hold elective office.[56]

Aᴄᴄᴏʀᴅɪɴɢ to liberal teleology, education was automatically liberating; it inevitably eroded the spirit of caste and undermined the legitimacy of racial discrimination. This belief received classic expression in Gunnar Myrdal's *American Dilemma,* published in 1944, a book that swiftly became the all-but-official bible of the movement for racial integration. Regardless of curriculum and control, Myrdal wrote, "the long-range effect of the rising level of education in the Negro people goes in the direction of nourishing and strengthening the Negro protest." Others have echoed this claim. According to Henry Allen Bullock's *History of Negro Education in the South* (1967), black schools and colleges provided the "main leverage . . . pushing the movement toward the complete emancipation of the Negro American." The product of segregated schools himself, Bullock contended that black colleges like Virginia Union University, his alma mater, had deliberately prepared its students to become leaders of this movement. In his study of campus protests during the 1920s, Raymond Wolters agreed: students and alumni turned black colleges into "institutional bastions for the assault on segregation and white supremacy." Even the dilapidated schools of the rural South, James Leloudis asserts, contributed to the denouement of the civil rights movement. The schools that black teachers built were "vital bridges between the freedom struggles of the late nineteenth century and those of the mid-twentieth."[57]

Most civil rights veterans can recall at least one teacher who, in the 1940s and 1950s, encouraged them to question the South's racial order. Aaron Henry, a leader of the civil rights movement in Mississippi, was inspired by his English teacher Thelma K. Shelby, a graduate of Dillard University and a member of the NAACP, who "talked with us inside and outside the classroom about the struggle for human dignity." Three of the four students who kick-started the sit-in movement in 1960 were influenced by a pair of teachers at Greensboro's Dudley High School: Vance Chavis, who taught physics, and Nell Coley, their English teacher. NAACP members both, Chavis and Coley questioned segregation, stressed the importance of voting, and urged their students to strive for the highest values of decency, fairness, and individual fulfillment.[58]

Inspiring as these examples are, there was no simple cause-and-effect relationship between black schools and the civil rights movement. Most black teachers did not impart lessons in protest and activism. Some were afraid to; others had ethical qualms about using the classroom as a political pulpit. Their dominant message was largely a restatement of the old "uplift" philosophy of racial progress. And that credo betrayed the same limitations that it had always suffered—excessive individualism, class bias, and blind faith in education. To Angela Davis, the ethos of Birmingham's Parker High School—"Work hard and you will be rewarded"—appeared oblivious to the reality of racial discrimination. In New Orleans, recalled Andrew Young, black teachers "seemed to believe that the path to freedom was to be found in manners and diction as much as intelligence and morality. It was an illusion." Tom Dent never once heard his teachers discuss the possibility of ending segregation, let alone openly challenge it. Even when he reached Howard University, that training ground of civil rights lawyers, Dent heard nobody—neither teachers nor students—discuss the feasibility of direct action against Jim Crow. Examining the civil rights struggle in South Carolina, one historian concluded, "The colleges did not produce the activism and protest. Rather, they were invaded by activist, protesting students."[59]

Recalling their own school days, however, veterans of the civil rights movement are wont to temper the harsh judgments that many activists leveled against black teachers during the 1960s. Over and again, they remember people who challenged them to stretch their minds and thereby demonstrate, through their own achievements, that racism was a myth. Teachers had no need to engage in political didactics to demonstrate that white supremacy was an ideological fantasy, not an immutable law of nature. They simply had to teach French, English literature, and science. At Gilbert Academy—an elite private school whose very presence on St. Charles Avenue, the millionaires row of New Orleans, proclaimed black ambition—Tom Dent received little instruction in black history and culture, but lessons aplenty in scholarship, imagination, and confidence. His science teacher, Dent recalled, simply assumed that "anyone could understand the basic laws of the physical world . . . [and] we strove to prove we were not hopelessly stupid." At McDonogh 35, the black public high school in New Orleans, students received the same bracing challenge. As one remembered, "There was no acceptance by our teachers that we were in any way limited to learn. We were expected to destroy the stereotype of black inferiority."[60]

Black teachers had also encouraged a more general sense of racial pride that played an important role—so pervasive that it was often taken for granted—in motivating the civil rights movement. For teachers who feared the personal consequences of activism or disliked introducing politics into the classroom, the Negro history movement provided a safe vehicle for conveying lessons about oppression, resistance, and black identity. The pantheon of heroes regularly presented during Negro History Week was hardly calculated to incite revolution. The usual suspects included Crispus Attucks, Benjamin Banneker, Booker T. Washington, and George Washington Carver. Nat Turner rarely made an appearance, and by the 1950s Du Bois and Paul Robeson had become too "un-American" to be safely praised. Nevertheless, inside a dominant culture that either ignored or denigrated black contributions outside sport and entertainment, Negro History week made the essential point. "By the time I was in third grade," recalled SNCC veteran, now congressman, John Lewis, who had attended a one-teacher school in Pike County, Alabama, "I had learned that there were actually black people who had made their mark on the world." Miles away, in Birmingham's Carrie A. Tuggle Elementary School, Angela Davis discovered that Frederick Douglass, Sojourner Truth, and Harriet Tubman had helped to destroy slavery; every morning, at assembly, she thrilled to the words of James Weldon Johnson's "Lift Every Voice and Sing," the Negro national anthem. "I always sang the last phrases full blast: 'Facing the rising sun, till a new day is born, let us march on till victory is won!'"[61]

This sense of racial solidarity helps explain a familiar paradox: the civil rights movement, which pressed for the integration of blacks into white-controlled sectors that excluded them, rested upon a bedrock of segregated schools, colleges, and churches. The NAACP's brief in *Brown* argued that black schools, being creatures of white-made law, nurtured feelings of inferiority in the children who attended them.

Given the central role of white racism in creating black schools and colleges and stunting their growth, that assertion made logical sense and had some empirical basis. On the other hand, those same segregated schools and colleges gave black southerners the security and confidence—including the social networks and organizational skills—to assert their rights. As Angela Davis recalled, "Black identity was thrust upon us."[62]

Like religion, education gave black southerners faith in themselves and faith in the future. Each force, depending on the time and the place, fostered quietism and activism, accommodation and protest. Both contributed to the growth of black insurgency in the 1950s and 1960s, but the black church was better able to capitalize on it. Because of their dependency, black teachers organized no equivalent of the Southern Christian Leadership Conference to encourage protest against Jim Crow. If we take a longer view of the black struggle for equality, however, we can see that during the classic age of segregation black teachers did far more than black ministers to breed dissatisfaction with, and opposition to, racial discrimination. Ultimately, the record of black teachers over the best part of a century overshadows their limited role in the civil rights movement. As a group, black teachers never submitted to white supremacist ideology. Their dogged pursuit of better schools reflected a conviction of their own worth and the worth of their pupils. Aaron Henry never forgot what he learned from his own teachers: "You are as good as anybody. You must believe . . . that you are equal to any other man. Racial superiority is a myth."[63]

CHAPTER TEN

Integration: Loss and Profit

Whether we gained more than we lost, I still don't know.
But it was something that had to happen.

Lovie Smith, 1999

Teacher, Suffolk County, Virginia, 1979.

Hamblin Collection, Library of Virginia

School integration turned the lives of black teachers, and white teachers, upside down. For the first time in their lives, they found themselves working alongside colleagues of a different race. For the first time in their lives, they taught children of another race. Teachers had to adapt to this novel situation at a time of continuing turmoil. Desegregated schools never had time to stabilize. Continuing white opposition, and rapidly changing residential patterns, ensured that school populations were in constant flux. Many schools that were once all-white enjoyed only a few years—sometimes only a few months—of "racial balance" before resegregating as virtually all-black institutions. In some rural areas, white children quit the public schools overnight, en masse, taking their white teachers with them.[1]

Cultural change exacerbated this instability. Teachers were accustomed to having their authority respected by both children and parents. By 1970, however, years of student activism, civil unrest, urban riots, antiwar protests, and racial militancy had weakened the prestige of traditional institutions, including schools. At the same time, the late 1960s and early 1970s spawned an anarchic youth "counterculture" that extolled the use of drugs, encouraged sexual freedom, spread contempt for middle-class values, and challenged adult authority. Control and discipline became a massive problem in many integrated schools. Small wonder that one black teacher, Dorothy Robinson of Texas, called school integration "the greatest social trauma the South has known since the Emancipation Proclamation."[2]

In much of the South, the integration of school faculties had a disproportionate effect upon black teachers. Desegregation plans tried to create majority-white/minority-black ratios in individual schools. Nashville, for example, established a target of 80:20; Baton Rouge set the ratio at 65:35; Greensboro aimed for 70:30. Hence more black schools were closed, more black teachers transferred. The impact on black teachers was also greater in the sense that they were moving from all-black institutions, always headed by a black principal, to schools where most of the other teachers were white and whose principal was also white. For virtually all black teachers, the period immediately before integration was a time of uncertainty and apprehension. The basic premise of integration, that white schools were better than black schools, encouraged an implicit assumption that the white teachers were also better. Some black teachers worried about their inferior qualifications and doubted their ability to measure up against white colleagues. They felt trepidation, too, over the prospect of dealing with whites—teachers, pupils, and parents—who had for so long tried to keep them out of their schools. Would they be treated with equality and respect? Even teachers who welcomed integration felt a degree of anxiety. Freddie Millican of Baton Rouge recalled, "We didn't know where we were going or . . . whether you were going to some hostile environment where you would probably face firing in six weeks."

Some city school boards, taking advantage of federal funds and foundation grants, made a serious effort to prepare teachers for desegregation. In Nashville, teachers were required to attend twenty hours of workshops, spread over five weeks, taught by staff from the Peabody School of Education of Vanderbilt University. The course included "multiracial history and culture, communication, [and] sensitivity training." The preparations in Greensboro, North Carolina, were even more thorough. Hundreds of teachers, administrators, students, and parents attended weekend retreats. Over two thousand citizens participated in one-off "human-relation workshops." A smaller group of influentials formed "cell groups" that met regularly. School principals attended an eight-day workshop. Committees were formed and task forces created. Hundreds of community meetings were organized. The school board, chamber of commerce, and citizens groups inundated Greensboro with pamphlets, billboards, and bumper stickers. Television, radio, and newspapers carried the message that desegregation would benefit everyone. Ministers preached to that effect on "Public School Sunday."[3]

In the Atlanta suburb of DeKalb County, on the other hand, teachers received absolutely no preparation or training. School boards in the South's small towns and rural counties betrayed the same carelessness. Teachers were pitched into integrated schools—often learning about their transfers only days beforehand—and expected to fend for themselves. They had to sink or swim. The result was that many teachers, both black and white, felt isolated and vulnerable.[4]

The reception that black teachers received from white colleagues and pupils ran the gamut. "There were teachers who were open and accepting and there were those who would prefer that you not be there," remembered Iola Taylor of Austin, Texas. "Then, there were some who were independently aloof." Some complained of being humiliated by principals who addressed them by their first names or criticized them in front of parents. Others referred to students who imported the racist attitudes of parents who told them "not to listen to no nigger." One black woman, transferred to a school in a wealthy white area of a large southern city, recalled her difficulty in getting along with white colleagues who were still hostile to integration. "I remember a time in a faculty meeting when a man was talking about the 'Nigras' and how the standards had been lowered because the 'Nigras' had come." Many black teachers believed that they were deliberately assigned to remedial classes or vocational classes in an effort to minimize their contact with white children. Some elementary schools even "departmentalized" instruction so as to prevent white children from being with a black teacher for the entire day.

But examples like this seem to have been exceptional. Many black teachers "were overwhelmed with kind words and gestures," writes one historian about integration in Nashville. "I never encountered a case of overt racism," recalled Dorothy Robinson, who spent the last four years of her career as the principal of an integrated primary school in Palestine, Texas. Because schools integrated at a time of great racial tension, black and white teachers were hypersensitive to any references, open or implied, to race. There was vast scope for misunderstanding and misplaced resentment. One black teacher, the only black faculty member in her school, felt slighted by being designated a "roving teacher." She later discovered that the school was merely following its standard policy in deploying new staff. In most schools, it seems, black and white teachers quickly learned to respect each other. Indeed, the challenges of integration fostered an esprit de corps. "In education the common ground is the student," explained one black teacher. "During the day . . . we could get together because we had something to talk about. . . . Everything was very professional." Outside school, on the other hand, black and white teachers usually went their separate ways.[5]

Black teachers in predominantly white schools were painfully conscious of the fact that they were on trial. They had to demonstrate their competence in a way that was not expected of the white teachers. "I felt like I had to prove myself," recalled one. Many took special care over their elocution, aware that any grammatical slips in their spoken English, or lapses into black "dialect," would be held against them. Black teachers also had to be on their mettle in front of white pupils who delighted in catching them out. "You had to be doubly prepared," remembered one teacher, "because . . . the white students felt that they wanted to test your knowledge." By and large, black teachers adjusted more easily to white pupils than white teachers adapted to black students. However, although they soon overcame any lingering fear that they might not be as competent as their white colleagues, black teachers sometimes faced unexpected challenges in predominantly white schools. Black schools tended to be very traditional. Many of their teachers were unfamiliar with innovations such as team-teaching and open-plan classrooms. Black teachers also sensed a different organizational ethos in white schools—less authoritarian but more highly organized.[6]

If black teachers adapted to integrated schools relatively easily, the same could not be said of black children. Indeed, black teachers watched in frustration as many, alienated from their new environments, underperformed and misbehaved. Discipline had rarely been a problem in segregated black schools. In many integrated schools, however, lack of discipline reached crisis proportions. When control broke down—often resulting in "free-for-alls" between white and black students—school authorities reacted by suspending or expelling the offenders. In Charlotte, North Carolina, the number of suspensions skyrocketed from fifteen hundred in 1968–69 to sixty-five hundred—90 percent of them African American children—in 1970–71. In Louisiana, an estimated hundred thousand schoolchildren were suspended or expelled in 1971–72 alone. The high incidence of suspensions shocked black parents. Segregated black schools had seldom employed suspension or expulsion as punishments. Now, not only were black students being disciplined in this way in large numbers, but in absolute numbers they were receiving most of the punishments. Students and parents alleged that systematic bias—white offenders being treated more leniently than blacks—tainted the administration of school discipline. "Black students have been harassed, insulted, nagged, and discouraged as a device to have them drop out or transfer," complained a petition to one school board.[7]

Many black teachers blamed the failure of black students to thrive in newly integrated schools on the one-sided manner in which courts and school boards implemented desegregation. Black students entered majority-white schools feeling resentful that their old schools had been closed to facilitate integration. Their new schools offered nothing to inspire them, nothing with which they could identify, nothing to evoke loyalty, affection, and pride. They had lost their school mascots, trophies, teams, magazines, and songs—all their school traditions, in fact. Moreover, many of the traditions of their new schools offended them. They could not warm to schools named after Confederate generals and school mascots called "Rebel." And they felt deliberately excluded from the prestigious social positions—cheerleader, homecoming court—that high school students prized. Black students experienced "terrific adjustment problems," recalled one black principal.

Black teachers faulted white colleagues for failing to adapt their teaching methods to black students, complaining that their approach was too didactic, that they tended to lecture too much. They criticized white teachers, too, for giving up on black children too readily. They declined to push, challenge, or inspire them. They allowed them to "act dumb" and shirk work. "Black students were not expected to perform," alleged a teacher who was reassigned from a segregated black high school to an integrated, majority-white school. "Expectations of black children were lower. . . . If you're not expected to do anything, you won't do anything." Black teachers also complained that white colleagues exacerbated discipline problems among black students. Whether through fear of black students, fear of being labeled racist, or lack of familiarity with the behavior patterns of black and lower-class children, too many white teachers allowed black students to ignore, defy, and even insult them. Some, having lost all semblance of control, lived in a permanent state of fear. "The black teachers . . . said that we were allowing the black students to get away with murder," recalled one white teacher, "which they never did when the schools were all black."[8]

Within integrated schools, however, black students often comported themselves very differently from the way they had behaved in their old segregated schools. The rebellious currents of the 1960s—the civil rights movement, Black Power, antiwar protests, the counterculture—had left their mark on the high school students of 1970. Many were defiant, cynical, hostile to whites, and distrustful of adult authority. High school students petitioned school boards to institute programs in Black Studies and to sanction the formation of black student unions. In one Louisiana Parish, they demanded "the renaming of Jeff Davis High School to either DuBois High School or Frantz Fanon High School or Malcolm X High School or Martin Luther King High School." Seemingly trivial issues were pregnant with racial overtones. At a time when long hair and work clothes had become youth's alternative uniform, many black students resisted attempts by schools to enforce dress codes. They demanded the right to wear jeans, bell-bottoms, dashikis, and "Afro" hairstyles. "Some students like to style their hair downward toward their shoulders while other students like to style their hair upward toward heaven," explained a group of "Concerned Citizens for Equal Education" in Shreveport. Assertive and politically aware, black students responded to the loss of their old schools by insisting upon their racial identity and demanding respect from white teachers. They regarded themselves as "educational freedom fighters," noted one NAACP official, "[and] often enter desegregated schools with a view of disciplining the instructor."[9]

Although black students directed most of their animus toward white teachers, black teachers discovered that their own ability to enforce discipline and teach effectively also suffered. In segregated schools, teachers had relied upon a structure of black authority, usually reinforced by a stern principal, to back them up. Desegregation not only removed black principals but also displaced other symbols of black authority such as counselors, coaches, and band directors. Even the Jeanes teachers were phased out at the end of the 1960s. Often a minority within the faculties of integrated schools, black teachers sensed that their status had been diminished and their authority weakened. Many felt less confident.

Teachers could no longer rely upon corporal punishment to enforce control. Corporal punishment had usually been less common in white schools, and the period of desegregation—the late 1960s and early 1970s—coincided with a general decline in the practice. It was still used, but instead of the informal brutality of former years, "teachers had to go through channels and procedures to discipline a child." Moreover, desegregation—often achieved by busing black students into white neighborhoods—weakened the link between black teachers and black communities. Teachers used to assume that if they punished a child, parents would not only back them up but also reinforce the punishment at home. They could no longer count on this kind of parental support. Racial tensions within integrated schools further discouraged corporal punishment. Teachers were afraid to inflict corporal punishment upon students of the other race. The contrast between the authoritarian parenting styles in many black homes, where corporal punishment persisted, and the "permissive" approach to discipline employed by young white teachers, created a cultural dissonance that exacerbated student rebelliousness, especially among African American boys.[10]

Black teachers found that an increasing number of their black students openly scorned the model of middle-class respectability that they personified and promoted. "Students desperate to embrace and define black culture in a sea of whiteness sometimes accused teachers who insisted that they speak properly . . . of not acting 'black,'" writes an historian of Nashville's integration experience. Teachers' efforts to encourage academic achievement encountered more resistance than in the past. Their ideas of what constituted appropriate behavior and deportment were often greeted with derision. NAACP official Daniel Byrd watched in dismay as black students displayed belligerent attitudes, segregated themselves, and used vulgar and profane language in the presence of adults. In one school, he noted sadly, "if one of them makes the honor roll he is called a 'hunky' lover by other sisters and brothers."[11]

THE process of school integration brought the festering tensions between black teachers and the NAACP to the surface, where they sometimes boiled over. Between 1954 and 1964 the South's public school systems had remained overwhelmingly, and often completely, segregated. The implicit threat to black teachers' jobs had not materialized on a large scale. However, the passage of the 1964 Civil Rights Act, and stronger federal court decisions implementing *Brown,* dramatically accelerated the pace of integration. Unfortunately for black teachers, the federal government was slow to recognize their interests in the implementation process. Despite strong federal involvement, the actual implementation of integration plans and court orders remained largely in the hands of white school boards. The dismissal and demotion of black teachers, and the closure or downgrading of black schools, now became a widespread reality. Black teachers turned to their state associations, the NEA, and the NAACP for help. However, the confusion, conflicts, and anxieties surrounding integration stretched the alliance between black teachers and the NAACP to the breaking point. By the early 1970s large numbers of black teachers were disenchanted with integration and angry at the NAACP for failing to protect them. To the NAACP, on the other hand, the interests of black teachers were secondary to those of black children. Integration came first.

Black teachers, through their state associations, supported school integration in principle. The North Carolina State Teachers Association, for example, backed the 1965 NAACP suit, filed on behalf of the Swann family, against the Charlotte-Mecklenburg school board. But teachers remained reluctant to lend their names to litigation against segregated schools. In Louisiana, no teacher acted as a plaintiff in a desegregation suit until 1967. In other states, too, teachers were disinclined to stick out their necks. The prevalence of "freedom-of-choice" plans between 1964 and 1969 did not help. In theory, "freedom of choice" abolished race-based pupil assignments and allowed children to enroll in the school of their choice. In practice, virtually all whites, and the vast majority of blacks, chose to enroll in their old schools, with only a small number of blacks transferring to previously all-white schools. Integration was thus a one-way process that threatened to gradually reduce the pupil population of black schools. Moreover, before 1967 the courts failed to address the question of faculty integration, allowing integrated but largely white schools to retain all-white faculties. At a regional meeting in 1965, black educators and civil rights leaders drew the obvious conclusion. "Negro teachers . . . could hardly be expected to push hard for integration knowing that they would be depriving a colleague of a position for every 30 students who could be persuaded to transfer."[12]

Some black teachers positively discouraged their students from transferring to white schools. They told them that the black schools were just as good, that black teachers were more highly qualified than whites, and that to request transfer reflected badly upon the entire black community. "They concentrated their fire most heavily upon the best Negro students," complained an American Friends Service Committee official in Baton Rouge, "and told them it was extremely unfair of them to transfer as they were needed most of all."[13]

Declining black populations in many parts of the rural South compounded the sense of insecurity felt by many black teachers: school boards could take advantage of integration to close black schools. In one of the first legal skirmishes over job losses, seven black teachers, dismissed after the closure of two black schools, sued the school board of Giles County, Virginia. "It is necessary to abolish your jobs," the board had informed the teachers. "Please accept this letter as notification that your services will not be needed after the close of this school session." A federal judge, however, declared that "the burden of integration must not be shifted to their backs alone." The plaintiffs won the right to be notified of vacancies on a preferential basis. This 1965 case, pressed by the Virginia Teachers Association and the National Education Association, established that integration plans should consider the interests of teachers as well as pupils. It also furnished an impressive example of the NEA's newfound commitment to the defense of black teachers. But it applied to only one county.[14]

When the Supreme Court in October 1969 finally ordered school districts to "terminate dual systems at once," the Giles County situation was repeated all over the South. School boards, which still had virtually no black representatives, implemented desegregation in the spirit that black teachers had always feared. They minimized the exposure of white children to black teachers and safeguarded the interests of white teachers at the expense of black ones. Surveying the chaos of school integration in 1970, an NEA investigating committee described the "near total disintegration of black authority in every area of the system of public education." School boards closed black schools rather than white ones. If they retained black high schools, they reclassified them as junior highs. They transferred the best black teachers to formerly all-white schools, while placing the least qualified whites in previously all-black schools. They dismissed black teachers on the grounds of falling enrollments and—often employing the National Teachers Examination as a basis—for incompetence. Some school boards simply offered integration itself as grounds for dismissal. "In compliance with the most recent court order . . . this is to advise you that your services as a teacher . . . will no longer be needed."[15]

The most visible casualties of school integration were the men who had headed the hundreds of black schools that were closed. Across the South, school boards operated on the covert principle that integrated schools, especially if white pupils were in the majority, should be headed by white principals. As black schools shut, their principals were induced to retire early, accept reassignment to classroom teaching, move to paper-shuffling jobs in the central office, or take subordinate administrative positions in the integrated schools. The result was a precipitous decline in the number of black high school principals. In South Carolina, their number fell from 142 in 1963 to 48 in 1972. Before integration, black high school principals constituted 39 percent of the total; after integration, they made up 20 percent of South Carolina's principals. In states with smaller black populations, the decline were even sharper: North Carolina, 226 to 15; Arkansas, 134 to 14; Florida, 102 to 14; Tennessee, 73 to 17; Virginia, 107 to 16.[16]

To many black southerners, the closure of black high schools represented the symbolic decapitation of their communities at the hands of white officials who were hostile to integration and contemptuous of blacks. "They were very vindictive," claimed Cyrus Jackson, the former principal of A. B. Simon School in New Iberia, Louisiana. "All I can say is that the powers-that-be said . . . 'The niggers want integration, but they're going to have integration on our terms.'" The Iberia Parish School Board closed two of New Iberia's three black high schools. The third became a junior high school and had its name changed. The name change added insult to injury. Iberia's black schools had been named after black teachers: all those names vanished. At a stroke, decades of community effort, school spirit, and family tradition disappeared. The one black high school building that was retained by the school board was renamed "Freshman High School." It had formerly been named Jonas Henderson School, after the Baptist minister who had headed Howe Institute, a private school that had served New Iberia's black population from the 1880s to the 1930s. Under Henderson's tutelage, Howe Institute had produced a rich crop of black teachers and principals, many of whom went on to Leland University before finding jobs in the public school system. Jonas Henderson's son, J. B. Henderson, was principal of Jonas Henderson High School at the time when integration erased its identity. The only remaining clue as to the school's history was a large "H" embedded in a concrete floor, which the school board decided would be too costly to remove. Integration produced an "obliteration of black identity," the NEA reported. Pictures, plaques, and trophies vanished into storage or disappeared. "In one formerly all-black school, a large wall mural depicting the school's history had been painted over."[17]

The NAACP now found itself wracked with conflict over the fate of black teachers. The fact that it was in reality two separate organizations made that conflict worse. While the legal strategists of the NAACP's Legal Defense Fund (LDF) single-mindedly pursued their goal of destroying Jim Crow schools, many black southerners, including members of local NAACP branches, recoiled against the closure of black schools and loss of black principals. In 1970 Harvey Britton, the NAACP's Louisiana field secretary, reported that "the safeguarding of students, faculty, and administrative personnel" was now a greater priority than desegregation. In Iberville Parish, the local NAACP organized a school boycott, accompanied by marches and demonstrations, to protest the dismissal of one black principal and the reassignment of two others as "coordinating principals." The protests were anything but peaceful. Black youngsters hurled bricks and bottles at the police. Police and sheriff's deputies fired tear gas. During a fracas at the school board office, a white board member drew a gun. In Hyde County, North Carolina, the Southern Christian Leadership Conference supported a similar protest that, after more than a year, succeeded in saving two black high schools from closure. As full-scale school integration finally occurred in the South, black enthusiasm for it ebbed. From Louisiana, Dan Byrd gloomily reported that in one parish "the Negro elementary and secondary students are petitioning to get their own schools back." In another parish, where the NAACP had previously enjoyed strong support, "you won't find a dozen [black] people who will speak in favor of integrated schools."[18]

But many NAACP leaders, both full-time and voluntary officers, were not about to be deflected by the complaints of black teachers, the demotion of black principals, or sentimental ties to black high schools. They regarded the closure of black schools as a legitimate, indeed essential, means of achieving integration. The federal government—the courts, the Department of Justice, the Department of Health, Education and Welfare—agreed. The NAACP had always known that school integration would entail some job losses, especially in rural areas that were losing population. But it calculated that urban school systems, whose black enrollments were fast expanding, would be employing more black teachers, not fewer. Many in the NAACP also believed that a shakeout of black teachers would be no bad thing, because it would weed out the incompetents. As for black principals, the NAACP expressed skepticism that such men were community leaders and role models, and showed little interest in saving their jobs. Black high school principals had mostly shunned the civil rights movement. As one branch leader put it, 99 percent of them "wouldn't be seen dead inside the NAACP." Many civil rights activists therefore scorned black principals as willing collaborators in white supremacy. "He was what a lot of superintendents referred to as one of the good ole boys," recalled a North Carolina woman of the man who had headed her town's black high school. "You know, he's a good ole nigger over there. He doesn't give us any problems." Such men were false leaders, agreed NAACP field secretary Harvey Britton, "because they had already sold out the black community." Because high school principals had failed to stand up for black rights—including their own—some saw a certain poetic justice in their demise.[19]

As for the NAACP's commitment to defend black teachers against unfair dismissals, it was hardly surprising that the teachers suspected it was less than wholehearted. In 1955 the LDF had promised to protect black teachers. When it made that commitment, however, it possessed neither the resources nor the legal strategy to implement it. Moreover, as Jack Greenberg later admitted, the LDF "had not anticipated how seriously black teachers would be at risk during desegregation." By 1967, to make matters worse, the demands upon the LDF were skyrocketing. "The riots, demonstrations etc. . . . have doubled our work load here on many fronts," explained John W. Davis. "The Negro teachers situation in your State is not inviting." The LDF did not ignore the issue. By 1970 it was representing black teachers in more than twenty-five dismissal cases, winning many. But the organization faced the perennial problem of the South's decentralized school system. Each case applied to only one school district, of which the South had well over a thousand. In addition, it took so much time to settle such cases that many dismissed teachers found alternative employment, reducing the deterrent value of favorable court rulings. Thus when black teachers looked to LDF to make good its pledge to defend them, they criticized the organization's response as inadequate. "I have defended our failure . . . explaining that the shortage of funds and staff has plagued the LDF and curtailed our activities," Louisiana field secretary Dan Byrd told Greenberg in 1972. But black teachers replied that the LDF had given them an unqualified commitment that it was now seeking to evade.[20]

In private, of course, black teachers conceded that the training of some colleagues left much to be desired. Pointing to the academic lag between white and black schoolchildren, J. Rupert Picott, executive secretary of the Virginia Teachers Association, argued that many black teachers were poorly qualified and lacked motivation. Desegregation might displace some of them, he believed, but "the 'best teachers' will be kept." Basile Miller, a black principal in Church Point, Louisiana, and a future president of the LEA, agreed that parents who pushed for integration often had cause to be dissatisfied with black teachers. "They only wanted honest teaching in the classroom, which they had *not* been having." One way to improve standards, Miller argued, was to "brutally remove, or at least censure, teachers known by everybody not to be willing or able to teach."[21]

"We were lax about the quality of our black teachers before desegregation," one Georgia education official claimed. "Now we are paying the price and having to clean house, which is why more blacks have been fired in the last twelve months." But black teachers rejected the suggestion that incompetence explained the disproportionate job losses they suffered. White administrators, many of them admitted segregationists who worked in a system where whites wielded overwhelming political power, were deciding which teachers were incompetent. Black teachers found it hard to believe—and historians have no reason to suppose—that whites had now abandoned the racial bias which they had, until recently, openly expressed. Even Omer Carmichael, the highly praised superintendent of schools in Louisville, Kentucky, who had overseen peaceful integration in 1956, contended that black teachers were invariably inferior. "Whatever group of children a Negro teacher teaches, that group of children will in my judgement suffer a little."

Even when teachers were measured against ostensibly objective criteria such as the National Teachers Examination, blacks cried foul. Black teachers—and some white teachers—criticized the NTE on the grounds that the test bore little relevance to competence in the classroom. "There are hundreds of items on that test that have nothing to do with a teacher's ability to teach," claimed Harold Trigg, a black member of North Carolina's board of education. A few school boards were restrained from using the NTE after black teachers, backed by the NEA, sued in federal court. In Florida, which introduced the test in 1961, political pressure from both white and black teachers induced the legislature to repeal it in 1968.[22]

The number of black teachers whom integration displaced has never been accurately established. A study of 108 school districts that implemented desegregation between 1968 and 1970 showed a net loss of 923 black teachers, about 10 percent of the total. Moreover, of the 5,196 new teachers who were hired, 86 percent of them were whites. A survey of Louisiana showed that although the proportion of black children in the public schools increased from 39 percent in 1964 to 41 percent in 1971, the proportion of black teachers declined from 36 percent to 33 percent. In Mississippi, the number of black teachers fell by about 12 per between 1970 and 1973, while the number of white teachers increased by about 9 percent. Definitive regional figures are difficult to come by, because while the proportion of white teachers increased, the absolute number of black teachers increased. By one estimate, based on the assumption that if schools had remained segregated the black teaching force would have continued to grow at pre-Brown rates, thirty-one thousand teaching posts were lost between 1954 and 1972.[23]

The job losses were not as severe as they might have been. The state teachers associations, with vigorous support from the NEA, helped teachers facing dismissal to sue their school boards in federal court. Scores of cases were filed and a large percentage won. In North Carolina, for example, the North Carolina Association of Educators sponsored nineteen law suits on behalf of black teachers dismissed for alleged incompetence. It won eighteen of them. This high success rate reflected the fact that federal judges, in overseeing the desegregation process, were paying more attention to discrimination against black teachers. In an important 1969 decision concerning faculty integration, the Fifth Circuit Court of Appeals laid down the principle that the proportion of black and white teachers in a school should broadly reflect the racial composition of the school district as a whole. By the 1970s, moreover, it became increasingly common for federal judges to appoint biracial committees in the hope that integration plans would have more chance of success if community representatives, not just lawyers, helped to draft them. These committees usually included black teachers, and they provided a check against unfair dismissals. In some cities, including Shreveport and Atlanta, black negotiators agreed to limit the scope of integration in order to preserve an agreed percentage of black teachers and administrators.[24]

IF school integration proved painful for black teachers, so did the process of integrating the black and white teachers' associations. In 1966, after two years of negotiations, the American Teachers Association voted by 172 to 3 to merge with the National Education Association. Although the ATA surrendered its identity as a black organization, the union proved successful. In 1964 the NEA employed only two black personnel, less than 1 percent of its total professional staff. Ten years later, blacks comprised more than a third of the NEA's total staff, and about 15 percent of its managerial and professional employees. Moreover, black participation ensured that the NEA now paid close attention to issues of race and civil rights. It monitored school integration, developed materials for teaching black history, encouraged black voter registration, and took legal action—in cooperation with the LDF—in defense of black teachers.[25]

The merger of the state teachers associations, on the other hand, proved more difficult and took much longer. In 1964—almost ten years after its rival, the AFT—the NEA voted to integrate its southern affiliates. By 1968 the black teachers associations in all of the border states, as well as Texas, Florida, Tennessee, Virginia, and South Carolina, had merged with their white counterparts. However, this first wave of mergers masked serious problems. In joining organizations in which whites enjoyed large numerical majorities, the black associations failed to negotiate any kind of guarantees that the interests of black teachers would be recognized and protected. Everything depended upon good will. Moreover, the black associations simply surrendered their identities. The black education journals ceased publication; the white journals continued to appear. The merged organization kept the name of the white association. No head of a black association became the executive secretary of a merged association. This failure to drive a hard bargain reflected, in part, an idealistic faith in integration. It also stemmed from the relative weakness of these black associations. In Florida and Texas, for example, the black organizations steadily lost members after the white associations opened their membership to all. In all of these states, with the exception of South Carolina, black teachers were far outnumbered by white teachers. In South Carolina, the Palmetto Education Association (PEA) tried to win concessions, but found itself out-maneuvered. The South Carolina Education Association "took over the PEA's bank account . . . [and] sold the PEA building." It gave a job to Solomon E. Walker, the PEA's long-serving executive secretary, but the position was subordinate and vaguely defined.[26]

By the time the second round of merger negotiations took place, the leaders of the black associations in Arkansas, Louisiana, Mississippi, Georgia, Alabama, and North Carolina were determined to prevent their members from being swamped by white majorities. As Charles Lyons of North Carolina put it, merger should entail "the combination of two associations into a new association," not the "absorption of the Negro association and the complete loss of its identity and influence." The remaining black associations therefore presented a list of demands that included guaranteed representation for black members, the rotation of leadership positions between blacks and whites, the retention of black staff members, the proper disposition of black-held assets, and the adoption of new names. "Each time a merger was approved," one NEA official recalled, "the price went up for the next one in terms of protection demanded by the black associations." The white associations were in no mood to capitulate to black demands: the negotiations were therefore hard-fought. But the NEA, which in 1968 adopted more stringent criteria for mergers, drove the process forward and used the threat of disaffiliation to promote compromise.[27]

The sticking points varied from state to state. In Alabama, the paramount concern of the black association was that a unified organization should continue the court cases that had already been filed on behalf of black teachers. The white association, on the other hand, placed a high priority in retaining the name "Alabama Education Association." In every state, black representation proved an important bone of contention, whites typically preferring "one man, on vote," blacks pressing for 50:50 representation on boards and committees. The black executive secretaries also strongly influenced the tenor of the negotiations. In Georgia, for example, Horace Tate harbored ambitions to head the merged association. When he felt cheated of that ambition, Tate, "a naturally aggressive person, became more aggressive." In Louisiana, J. K. Haynes harbored no such ambition, and he fought merger tooth and nail. The leaders of Louisiana's white association were just as hostile to merger, and they used whatever delaying tactics and procedural devices they could devise—including taking the NEA to court—in order to thwart it. In 1969 the NEA suspended both the white Louisiana Teachers Association and the black Louisiana Education Association. In Mississippi, on the other hand, merger was approved by the black Mississippi Teachers Association but overwhelmingly rejected by the white Mississippi Education Association. Compromise proved possible in Alabama, Arkansas, Georgia, and North Carolina, where the two sides agreed on merger in 1969. Not until 1977, however, after ten years of mediation, arbitration, negotiation, diplomacy, and legal action did the associations in Louisiana and Mississippi finally come together.[28]

The fact that the white and black associations had quite different cultures complicated the merger negotiations. The white organizations were often dominated by school superintendents, and were loath to defend teachers' rights by taking school boards to court. The black associations, by contrast, had cut their teeth on suing their employers, and behaved more like unions. Moreover, the black groups had a much wider membership—often including bus drivers, custodians, and PTA members—and were more closely involved in politics. One NEA official was amazed at the amount of influence the Louisiana Education Association (LEA) wielded in Louisiana politics. It nominated state officials; it operated Head Start programs; it swayed crucial elections. LEA leaders traveled to out-of-state meetings in the governor's private plane. "That kind of power is difficult to give up."[29]

Some former leaders of the black associations were never reconciled to the new organizations. "Black educators no longer existed in any viable and visible leadership roles in those merged associations," grumbled Volover Williams, onetime president of the LEA. Merger "removed a power base for black teachers that has not been replaced," agreed J. Rupert Picott, the former executive secretary of the Virginia Teachers Association. Rank-and-file public school teachers, on the other hand, strongly favored merger. They realized the advantages of having access to the services of the National Education Association, which was becoming more militant and effective—partly under pressure of competition from the American Federation of Teachers—in the way it represented its members. They could also see that a united teaching profession would be better placed to negotiate with government over pay, conditions, and job security. Some also welcomed the prospect of replacing the authoritarian style of the old black associations—the dominant role of J. K. Haynes in the LEA was a good example—with a more inclusive and democratic structure. Women teachers felt they would have a better chance of attaining leadership positions in the merged associations. If ordinary teachers regarded merger with mixed feelings, quiet satisfaction predominated. They recognized that the abolition of this racial barrier was a major civil rights victory. After a century of exclusion, black teachers finally joined the mainstream of their profession.[30]

By the end of the 1970s, as the initial novelty and shock of integration wore off, racial tensions within schools abated. However, many blacks now questioned whether the benefits of integration outweighed the costs. Many schools had resegregated, and subsequent decades saw the further unraveling of integration. By 2000, more than half of the South's black students attended public schools that had few or no white students. Even when integration achieved numerical stability, a certain bleakness of spirit persisted. "Physical desegregation . . . occurred without any spiritual or emotional desegregation," noted Dorothy Robinson. Moreover, the academic benefits of integration seemed elusive. School facilities were usually better, but the overall educational environment seemed worse. Whether black students performed less well in integrated schools is unclear, but there was a widespread perception that they did. There is an almost universal conviction that the closure of so many black high schools damaged the fabric of black communities.[31]

Almost every black teacher complained that students were more difficult to motivate, that parents had less involvement in schools, and that their own influence as mentors and community leaders had declined. Moreover, after integration there were relatively fewer black teachers to act as role models for black youngsters. As the proportion of black students in the nation's public schools increased from 14 percent in 1970 to 16 percent in 2000, the proportion of black teachers stayed the same. Even in the South, where the proportion of black teachers was far higher than the national average of 8 percent, the percentage of white teachers greatly exceeded the percentage of white students. The gap was greatest in South Carolina, where blacks made up 42 percent of the students but only 19 percent of the teachers. It was least in Louisiana, where the proportions were 39 percent and 26 percent. Talk of the "disappearing black teacher" has become commonplace in educational circles. Commentators lament, in particular, the paucity of black male teachers who, according to one estimate, constitute a mere 1 percent of the nation's teaching force.[32]

Small wonder that many elderly black teachers look back to the Jim Crow era with a touch of nostalgia. They bristle at the idea that they were unable to teach effectively, or that black children were unable to learn, in the pre-*Brown* schools. Indeed, some segregated black high schools, despite poorly paid teachers, crowded classrooms, hand-me-down textbooks, and inadequate facilities, achieved miracles of academic achievement. Institutions like Atlanta's Booker T. Washington High School and New Orleans' McDonough 35 High School refuted the notion that all-black environments—denigrated by integrationists as "racial isolation"—necessarily impaired the ability of black children to excel. "Leaving us alone to teach our children . . . may not have been such a bad idea," thought Horace Tate of Georgia. Others felt that their early doubts about *Brown* had been vindicated. "I was never convinced that our children would be better off in an integrated school if we would have had separate but equal," stated Fannie P. Adams of Columbia, South Carolina. Some even insisted that "separate but equal" was already a reality by the time of *Brown*. In Iberia Parish, Louisiana, claimed one retired principal, the school board had done a "magnificent job" of equalization, building black high schools that were "top rank."[33]

It was certainly true that in the decade or so before *Brown* the southern states greatly reduced disparities in expenditure between white and black schools. In 1939–40, for example, a white teacher earned almost twice as much as a black teacher. By 1951–52 black teachers were making 86 percent of what white teachers earned. The states also inaugurated school-building programs of unprecedented scale in a deliberate effort to equalize facilities. In 1940 white pupils received three to ten times more capital expenditure than black pupils did. By 1951–52 black pupils were receiving, per capita, about two-thirds of state expenditure on buildings and equipment. Progress continued during the fifteen years after *Brown* when the South's public schools remained overwhelmingly segregated.[34]

Black teachers had a right to feel proud of what they had achieved under segregation. Between 1950 and 1970, the educational attainment of black Americans had skyrocketed. In 1947, 35 percent of whites 25 years and older had completed high school or college. Only 13 percent of blacks had done so. In 1970, when the figures included the last cohort of students to pass through segregated schools, the figures stood at 57 percent of whites and 33 percent of blacks.[35]

Yet the NAACP was right to contend that "separate but equal" was a will-o'-the-wisp. Black educational attainment may have dramatically increased during the last two decades of segregation, but the wide gap between white and black remained. At the time of *Brown,* moreover, no southern state had achieved "separate but equal" as measured by per capita expenditure. Even genuine state efforts to reduce racial discrimination were often hampered by local school boards that allowed gross disparities to persist. In Mississippi, for example, the state government decided to divide capital outlays equally between the races. But between 1946 and 1953 local school districts spent almost three times as much on building white schools as on building black ones. Similarly, when the state appropriated money to improve the pay of black teachers, many school boards refused to spend it all. Mississippi's efforts to improve black education were feeble, concludes historian Charles Bolton. "Educational equalization was never a viable alternative."[36]

Perhaps the most revealing indictment of equalization came from a white official charged with preserving segregation. In 1958 T. A. Carmichael was appointed to the position of Georgia's state agent of Negro education. Like many whites, he had assumed that new school buildings had largely eliminated educational disparities. But he discovered that many school boards had failed to complete their building programs. Others stinted on equipping and maintaining new black schools. Most white schools had gymnasiums, auditoriums, lighted athletic fields, and custodial staff. Many black schools had none of these. "I am amazed and dumbfounded at how little they have," he told a white audience in 1959. Carmichael also identified the principal weakness of the equalization strategy. Whites continued to control the expenditure because they still enjoyed a near-total monopoly of political power. Only three of Georgia's two hundred or so school boards included black members. Blacks were taxed but not represented. Moreover, blacks who dared to oppose discrimination exposed themselves to retaliation. Carmichael cited the example of twelve blacks who sent a letter to their school board: all but one of the signatories "had been arrested on one pretext or another."[37]

Some attribute a persisting "achievement gap" between white and black students in test scores—the average 17-year-old black student is still about four years behind the average white student in reading and math—to the consequences of integration. Integrated schools, the argument goes, lack the sense of community that segregated schools promoted; black students in integrated settings cannot derive the same inspiration from white teachers that their predecessors had taken from committed and concerned black mentors. Male students, in particular, find few, if any, black male role models who might offset the anti-intellectual influences pervading popular culture—entertainers, athletes, rappers, gang members—and promote commitment to schooling and academic achievement. Some even assert that lingering racism helps explain why so many states have adopted competency tests that would-be black teachers fail in disproportionate numbers.[38]

Complaints about the paucity of positive role models for black students are so widespread that they should not be lightly dismissed. Yet talk of the "disappearing black teacher" is exaggerated. Black teachers constitute about the same proportion of the nation's teaching force today as they did in 1960, about 8 percent. Historically, too, the relatively small number of black male teachers is an old phenomenon—women dominated the teaching profession, especially at the elementary level, throughout the twentieth century. What changed is that the number of black teachers did not increase in proportion to the growing black student population.[39]

Without a doubt, the spread of teacher competency tests—now practiced by nearly all states—has made entry into the profession more difficult. Blacks, moreover, are more likely to fail these tests. According to one study, "typical first-time passing rates . . . range from 15% to 50% for black candidates . . . compared to 71% to 96% for white candidates." The relationship between competency tests and effectiveness in the classroom is a hotly debated topic. Some believe that these tests discriminate against black candidates. Yet the example of Southern University shows that it is quite possible for black candidates to pass at the same rate as whites. In 2001 only a third of the trainee teachers at Southern's Baton Rouge campus passed the Praxis exam. Threatened with closure, the education department halved its number of admissions and three years later achieved a pass rate of 90 percent.[40]

Integration, far from fostering an "achievement gap," merely revealed long-standing problems that remained largely concealed during the Jim Crow era. Memories of good black schools in the pre-integration South are not false, notes Gary Orfield, director of the Harvard Civil Rights Project, but they tell only part of the story. Segregated schools served a minority well, but they failed—through no fault of their own—the many. Although the students who graduated from segregated high schools often received a sound educational foundation, most black children never completed high school. "The leading black middle-class school in an urban area thus had a far more selective student body than central city high schools have today," writes Orfield. "The most troubled and disruptive students were often not in school at all." Anti-intellectualism and hostility to schooling among some students, especially black males, is therefore not a new phenomenon. From the late nineteenth century on, teachers and sociologists noted widespread cynicism about education and alienation from school.[41]

School integration, despite all its difficulties and failings, ushered in an era of spectacular academic achievement. By 1990, when the first cohort of students had graduated from desegregated schools, 66 percent of blacks 25 years and older had completed high school or college. This was double the 1970 figure. True, the attainment of whites had also increased. But it exceeded that of blacks by only 13 percent, down from 24 percent in 1970. The gap was closing. Test scores, too, showed that blacks were catching up. According to the National Assessment of Educational Progress, the scores of black students taking math and reading tests increased dramatically. Between 1971 and 1988, the gap between black and white scores narrowed by more than 20 points, the equivalent of two age grades. By 2004, 85 percent of white and 80 percent of black seniors finished high school. Clearly, a variety of factors were at play here, and it is impossible to separate them. Yet it would be foolish to dismiss the impact of integration.[42]

The NAACP was also correct to assume that the primary reason the southern states maintained segregated schools was whites' perception that blacks were inferior. Segregated schools were part and parcel of white supremacy. Even if white lawmakers and officials had redirected spending to the point where "separate but equal" schools became a reality, blacks would still have faced systematic discrimination in the job market.

Here was the basic contradiction between the concept of equalization and political reality. White southerners remained committed to the idea of excluding blacks from entire sectors of the economy. Even in North Carolina, probably the most progressive southern state with regard to education, many school superintendents were expressing the same views about black education in 1940 that their predecessors had held fifty years earlier: It was pointless to train blacks to be machinists, stenographers, or secretaries because only whites could find employment in those fields. Blacks were demanding French and other "impractical and useless courses" simply because the white high schools offered them. Blacks wanted school buses "not for educational reasons, but as a means of getting away from the farms." Education was making blacks averse to manual labor.[43]

White attitudes were malleable, of course, and the views of these county superintendents were not necessarily typical. Nevertheless, a belief in black inferiority was widespread and persistent. So was the conviction that the products of black schools should slot into distinct occupational niches. The men in charge of upgrading black education still viewed the future in terms of the past. Louisiana's director of higher education deplored the "unrealistic outlook . . . that [blacks] want to get as far away as possible from anything that smacks of labor or work." The vast majority of blacks were employed as laborers "and the vast majority of their children will follow similar occupations." It was, of course, a self-fulfilling prophecy. From the 1941 to 1964 white southerners vehemently resisted black efforts to break into skilled, white-collar, and professional occupations. When President Roosevelt appointed a Fair Employment Practices Committee (FEPC), they fought it tooth and nail and prevented significant change. The FEPC expired in 1946, and employment discrimination continued to flourish. Most Negroes "lacked native ability," stated the manager of a large industrial plant in 1955. "From the mentality standpoint," a CIO official agreed, "the Negro is a somewhat inferior race."[44]

The issue of school integration, therefore, concerned much more than schools. It could not be separated from the political and economic dimensions of white supremacy. Not only could blacks never establish equal educational opportunity in the Jim Crow South, but also education, by itself, could never produce equality. Most black teachers knew these realities, but there was always a temptation to oversell education. This was part pure Americanism, part sheer opportunism. When blacks had no political power and little room to maneuver, education was the one avenue of progress that was not entirely blocked. With their talents and energies confined to this channel, black teachers promoted education with evangelical fervor and invested it with exaggerated power. Moreover, the strategy of institution building that segregation forced upon black southerners could prove seductive. "You southern educators are all bound up with some special cause or other, devotion to which sometimes warps your judgment as to what is best for the general welfare of the race," Charles Chesnutt complained to his friend Booker T. Washington in 1903. "Your institution, your system of education . . . is apt to dwarf everything else and become the sole remedy for social and political evils which have a much wider basis."[45]

The current nostalgia among some blacks for the schools of the pre-integration era has been likened to the nostalgia among citizens of Russia and the countries of eastern Europe for life under Communism. The parallel is suggestive. When a bad system breaks down, the consequences are often hugely disappointing to those who labored for its abolition. The exhilaration that accompanies the collapse of an oppressive system often gives way to confusion and insecurity. And the people who did relatively well under the old regime often suffer a loss of status. In each case, however, there is a tendency to gloss over the evils of the old order and attribute the difficulties of today, wrongly, to its passing. Although many mistakes were made during the process of school integration—some of them unavoidable due to America's cumbersome and fragmented political system—integration was the only avenue by which black southerners could gain access to the higher level of funding that whites enjoyed. "They had better schools," insisted one teacher. "They had better books. They had more paper. They had just better everything in the white schools." School integration was also essential to breaking down the wider system of racial discrimination.[46]

The loss of community and leadership was real. Yet the pains and the gains of political and economic change are hard to disentangle. The agricultural and industrial revolutions disrupted the tightly knit villages of rural Europe. The Welsh mining communities, famed for their solidarity and culture, are no more. Likewise, the boll weevil, the Great Depression, the New Deal, and the mechanical cotton picker uprooted rural southerners and sent them to towns and cities, emptying their country churches and rendering obsolete their one-teacher schools. The closure of so many black high schools, on the other hand, was cruel and unnecessary. The malice of white southerners, the insensitivity of the federal government, and the fixation of liberal integrationists on percentages and quotas all conspired, inadvertently, to destroy something valuable. Denied even symbolic recognition of their worth, the black high schools disappeared leaving scarcely any physical trace, their existence preserved only in the memories and reunions of former students and teachers. Fortunately, black colleges and universities survive. By the time the NAACP attacked segregated public higher education, the South's black communities had no desire to see their beloved colleges swallowed up or merged. The HBCUs struggled to define their educational mission in the post–civil rights era. They are chronically underfunded. Nevertheless, they stand as proud monuments to black achievement in adversity—institutional links to emancipation and all its liberating potential. Not only are they important to African Americans' sense of community, they are also one of America's richest cultural assets.

For about a hundred years, black teachers helped black southerners adapt to emancipation, the loss of political rights, and the imposition of Jim Crow laws. But they did much more than that. They shaped and guided communities. They inspired and empowered individuals. They created schools and colleges. By and large eschewing revolutionary or left-wing doctrines, they espoused Christian values, middle-class virtues, and American ideals. In that sense, they were a conservative force. Yet they resisted white efforts to place a ceiling upon black achievement and refused to indoctrinate black children into white supremacy. Instead, they inculcated ambition, confidence, self-respect, and racial pride. Trapped in a system designed to insult black people, they insisted upon dignity and decorum. They made it difficult, nay impossible, for whites to turn racial segregation into a full-fledged caste system. Indeed, the educational infrastructure they painstakingly constructed helped to discredit and undermine Jim Crow. In this other sense, therefore, black teachers were far from conservative. Their work embodied, in the words of Horace Mann Bond, the "radical acceptance of the principle of human equality."[47]

Notes · Acknowledgments · Index

Notes

Abbreviations

AMA Papers	American Missionary Association Papers, ARC
ARC	Amistad Research Center, Tulane University, New Orleans
AUA	Atlanta University Archives, Archives and Special Collections, Robert R. Woodruff Library, Atlanta University
Bond Papers	*Horace Mann Bond Papers,* ed. John H. Bracey Jr., microfilm (LexisNexis), Perkins Library, Duke University, Durham, North Carolina
BRFAL (Ga.)	Records of the Superintendent of Education for the State of Georgia, Bureau of Refugees, Freedmen, and Abandoned Lands, National Archives, RG M799, (Washington: National Archives), Georgia Department of Archives and History, Atlanta
BRFAL (La.)	Records of the Superintendent of Education for the State of Louisiana, Bureau of Refugees, Freedmen, and Abandoned Lands, RG M1026, microfilm (Washington: National Archives), University of East Anglia, Norwich, UK
BRFAL (Tenn.)	Records of the Superintendent of Education for the State of Tennessee, Bureau of Refugees, Freedmen, and Abandoned Lands, M1000, microfilm, Tennessee State Archives, Nashville
BRFAL (Tex.)	Records of the Superintendent of Education for the State of Texas, Bureau of Refugees, Freedmen, and Abandoned Lands, RG M822, microfilm (Washington: National Archives), Texas State Archives, Austin
BTV	Behind the Veil Oral History Collection, Rare Book, Manuscript, and Special Collections Library, Duke University, Durham, North Carolina
DNE (Ga.)	Division of Negro Education, Department of Education Records, Georgia Department of Archives and History, Atlanta
DNE (N.C.)	Division of Negro Education, Department of Public Instruction Records, North Carolina State Archives, Raleigh

DNE (La.)	Division of Negro Education, Department of Education Records, Louisiana State Archives, Baton Rouge
DocSouth	Documenting the American South, electronic texts, University Library, University of North Carolina at Chapel Hill, *http://docsouth.unc.edu*
FAS	Freedmen's Aid and Southern Educational Society of the Methodist Episcopal Church Records, microfilm, AUA
FSU	Fayetteville State University
GEB Papers	General Education Board Papers, Rockefeller Archive Center, Sleepy Hollow, N.Y.
GEB Archives	*General Education Board Archives,* Series 1, *Appropriations,* Subseries 1, *The Early Southern Programs,* microfilm, 159 reels (New York: Rockefeller University; Wilmington, Del.: Scholarly Resources, 1993); *(La.)* reel 72, Perkins Library, Duke University; *(Tex.)* reels 140–156, Texas State Archives, Austin; *(Va.)* reels 157–159, State Library of Virginia, Richmond
HEQ	*History of Education Quarterly*
JNE	*Journal of Negro Education*
JNH	*Journal of Negro History*
JRF Papers	Julius Rosenwald Fund Papers, Fisk University, Nashville, Tenn.
LC	Manuscripts Reading Room, Library of Congress
MSRC	Moorland-Spingarn Research Center, Howard University, Washington
MSSCR	Mississippi State Sovereignty Commission Records, Mississippi Department of Archives and History, Jackson, *http://mdah.state.ms.us/arlib/*
NAACP Papers	Papers of the National Association for the Advancement of Colored People, LC
NAACP Papers (La.)	Papers of the NAACP Field Director for Louisiana, ARC
Papers of the NAACP	*Papers of the NAACP,* Part 3: *The Campaign for Educational Equality,* Series B: *Legal Department and Central Office Records, 1940–1950,* microfilm, 19 reels, ed. August Meier (Frederick, Md.: University Publications of America, 1986)
PSF Papers	Phelps-Stokes Fund Papers, SCRBC
SCRBC	Schomburg Center for Research in Black Culture, New York Public Library
SEF Papers	Southern Education Foundation Papers, AUA
SW	*Southern Workman and Hampton School Record,* Special Collections, Main Library, Edinburgh University
TU	Tuskegee University
USC	South Caroliniana Library, University of South Carolina, Columbia
VSU	Special Collections, James H. Johnston Library, Virginia State University, Petersburg
VTA Papers	Virginia Teachers Association Papers, VSU
WSSU	Winston-Salem State University

Prologue: The Odyssey of Black Teachers

1. Hortense Powdermaker, *Stranger and Friend: The Way of an Anthropologist* (New York: Norton, 1966), 144, 149. Powdermaker gave Lillian Rogers the pseudonym "Annie Wilson."
2. Carter J. Savage, "From Claiborne's Institute to Natchez High School: The History of African American Education in Williamson County, Tennessee, 1890–1967" (Ed.D. diss., Peabody College of Vanderbilt University, 1998), 145–146.
3. Anthony L. Edwards, "Booker T. Washington High School (1916–1974): Voices of Remembrance" (Ph.D. diss., University of South Carolina, 1998), 124.
4. Robert H. Jackson, "Memorandum on the School Segregation Cases," 15 Mar. 1954, copy courtesy of Professor Michael J. Klarman.
5. A. St. George Richardson, "What Is the Negro Teacher Doing in the Matter of Uplifting His Race?" in *Twentieth Century Negro Literature,* ed. D. W. Culp (1902; New York: Arno, 1969), 332. Although many of the children who attended black schools looked white, black teachers did not teach children whom the law defined as white.
6. Minutes of Seventh Annual Session of the Alabama State Teachers Association, Selma, 11–13 Apr. 1888, box 30A, H. C. Trenholm Papers, MSRC.
7. The "South" of this book consists of the eleven ex-Confederate states— those states with the largest relative black populations, the states that shared a common experience of defeat, occupation, and Reconstruction. It does not attempt to include all the states that had legally mandated school segregation before 1954. The border states of Kentucky, Maryland, and Missouri receive relatively little attention. Washington, D.C., which had a unique system of government, does not figure in this book at all.
8. Ambrose Caliver, "Some Problems in the Education and Placement of Negro Teachers," *JNE* 4 (Jan. 1935): 99.
9. Robert C. Morris, *Reading, 'Riting, and Reconstruction: The Education of Freedmen in the South, 1861–1870* (Chicago: University of Chicago Press, 1982), 103–108; Edward L. Wheeler, *Uplifting the Race: The Black Minister in the New South, 1865–1902* (Lanham, Md.: University Press of America, 1986), 68–74, 108–109.
10. Howard N. Rabinowitz, "'Half a Loaf': The Shift from White Teachers to Black Teachers in the Negro Schools of the Urban South, 1865–1890," *Journal of Southern History* 40 (Nov. 1974): 565–594; James M. McPherson, *The Abolitionist Legacy: From Reconstruction to the NAACP* (Princeton: Princeton University Press, 1975), 271–293; August Meier, *Negro Thought in America, 1880–1915: Racial Ideologies in the Age of Booker T. Washington* (1963; Ann Arbor: University of Michigan Press, 1988), 35.

11. Minutes of the Eighth Annual Session of the Alabama State Teachers Association, Selma, 10–12 Apr. 1889, box 30A, Trenholm Papers, MSRC.

12. Ronald E. Butchart, "Race and Education in the Twentieth Century," *HEQ* 26 (Spring 1986): 144.

13. Thomas Jesse Jones, *Negro Education: A Study of the Private and Higher Schools for Colored People in the United States,* 2 vols. (Washington: GPO, 1917), 2:12–16.

14. J. Saunders Redding, *Stranger and Alone* (New York: Harcourt, Brace, 1950); Ralph Ellison, *Invisible Man* (1952; New York: Vintage, 1972); Horace Mann Bond to Ralph Ellison, 29 June 1967, *Bond Papers.*

15. *SW,* Feb. 1875; Richard Brodhead, ed., *The Journals of Charles W. Chesnutt* (Durham, N.C.: Duke University Press, 1993), entry for 11 Aug. 1875, p. 82.

16. Jacqueline Jones, *Soldiers of Light and Love: Northern Teachers and Georgia Blacks, 1865–1873* (1980; Athens: University of Georgia Press, 1992), 133; Ronald E. Butchart, *Northern Schools, Southern Blacks, and Reconstruction, 1862–1875* (Westport, Conn.: Greenwood, 1980), 177–179.

17. Charles S. Johnson, *The Negro Public Schools: A Social and Educational Survey* (Baton Rouge: Louisiana Educational Survey Commission, 1942), 123–124, 148–151; Charles S. Johnson, *Growing Up in the Black Belt: Negro Youth in the Rural South* (1941; New York: Schocken, 1967), 125–134; *SW,* June 1876.

18. Richard R. Wright Jr., *87 Years behind the Black Curtain: An Autobiography* (Philadelphia: Rare Book Co., 1965), 31; Bertram Wyatt-Brown, "Black Schooling during Reconstruction," in *The Web of Southern Social Relations,* ed. Walter B. Fraser et al. (Athens: University of Georgia Press, 1985), 159–160.

19. Carter G. Woodson, *The Mis-Education of the Negro* (1933; Trenton, N.J.: Africa World Press, 1990), 17.

20. Ibid., 1, 17, 145.

21. August Meier and Elliott Rudwick, *Black History and the Historical Profession, 1915–1980* (Urbana: University of Illinois Press, 1986), 55; Jacqueline Goggin, *Carter G. Woodson: A Life in Black History* (Baton Rouge: Louisiana State University Press, 1993), 161, 204; Woodson, *Mis-Education of the Negro,* 29, 68–70; Woodson, *The History of the Negro Church* (Washington: Associated Publishers, 1921).

22. Wheeler, *Uplifting the Race,* 1–5; Goggin, *Carter G. Woodson,* 9–13.

23. Woodson, *Mis-Education of the Negro,* 13; Robert G. Newby and David B. Tyack, "Victims without 'Crimes': Some Historical Perspectives on Black Education," *JNE* 40 (Summer 1971): 193.

24. Michael Fultz, "African American Teachers in the South, 1890–1940: Pow-

erlessness and the Ironies of Expectations and Protest," *HEQ* 35 (Winter 1995), 406–413.

1. Freedom's First Generation

1. Booker T. Washington, *Up from Slavery* (1901; New York: Norton, 1996), 19.
2. 39th Cong., 1st sess., Exec. Doc. 70, *Freedmen's Bureau, 1865–66* (Washington: GPO, 1866), 334; Elijah P. Marrs, *Life and History of Elijah P. Marrs* (1885), DocSouth, 2004, http://docsouth.unc.edu/neh/marrs/menu.html; Charles O. Boothe, *The Cyclopedia of the Colored Baptists of Alabama: Their Leaders and Their Work* (1895), p. 10, DocSouth, 2004, http://docsouth.unc.edu/church/boothe/menu.html.
3. Washington, *Up from Slavery,* 19; Louis R. Harlan, *Booker T. Washington: The Making of a Black Leader, 1856–1901* (New York: Oxford University Press, 1972), 34–35; Exec. Doc. 70, *Freedmen's Bureau, 1865–66,* 342.
4. Orville Vernon Burton, *In My Father's House Are Many Mansions: Family and Community in Edgefield, South Carolina* (Chapel Hill: University of North Carolina Press, 1985), 251–253; Eli Kimble to G. L. Eberhart, 18 Oct. 1865, reel 8, BRFAL (Ga.); Joseph P. Reidy, *From Slavery to Agrarian Capitalism in the Cotton Plantation South: Central Georgia, 1800–1880* (Chapel Hill: University of North Carolina Press, 1992), 145, 171–172; Gloria T. Williams-May, "Lucy Craft Laney—The Mother of the Children of the People, Educator, Reformer, Social Activist" (Ph.D. diss., University of South Carolina, 1998), 110–114; Lewis Smith, James H. Taylor, Lewis Williams, and Ella Watson to Freedmen's Bureau, 18 Oct. 1865, reel 8, BRFAL (Ga.); 39th Cong., 2d sess., Exec. Doc. 6, *Freedmen's Affairs, 1866* (Washington: GPO, 1867), 65, 149, 255; Exec. Doc. 70, *Freedmen's Bureau, 1865–66,* 255, 342; Exec. Doc. 6, *Freedmen's Affairs, 1866,* 65; Jones, *Soldiers of Light and Love,* 91; Christopher M. Span, "'I Must Learn Now or Not At All': Social and Cultural Capital in the Educational Initiatives of Formerly Enslaved African Americans in Mississippi, 1862–1869," *Journal of African American History* (Mar. 2002): 200–203.
5. Sally G. McMillen, *To Raise Up the South: Sunday Schools in Black and White Churches, 1865–1915* (Baton Rouge: Louisiana State University Press, 2001), 21, 165–166; 46th Cong., 2d sess., Senate Report 693, *Causes of the Removal of the Negroes from the Southern States to the Northern States,* 3 vols. (Washington: GPO, 1880), 2:437; *SW,* Feb. 1873; Burton, *In My Father's House,* 245–246; W. T. Walker to E. A. Ware, 14 Sept. 1868, folder 1, box 10, Edmund Asa Ware Papers, AUA.
6. Jones, *Negro Education,* 1:3; Janet Duitsman Cornelius, *When I Can Read*

My Title Clear: Literacy, Slavery, and Religion in the Antebellum South (Columbia: University of South Carolina Press, 1991), 7–10. The extent of black literacy is notoriously hard to gauge, and historians have since come up with varying estimates. Taken together, however, these estimates suggest that Jones's figure of 10 percent may not have been far wrong.

7. William J. Simmons, ed., *Men of Mark: Progressive and Rising* (1887; Chicago: Johnson Pub. Co., 1970) 145–146; Susie King Taylor, *A Black Woman's Civil War Memoirs: Reminiscences of My Life in Camp with the 33rd U.S. Colored Troops, Late 1st South Carolina Volunteers,* ed. Patricia W. Romero and Willie Lee Rose (1902; New York: Markus Wiener, 1988), 29–30; Richard R. Wright, *A Brief Historical Sketch of Negro Education in Georgia* (Savannah: Robinson Printing House, 1894), 20, African American Pamphlet Collection, http://memory.loc.gov/ammem/aapchtml/aapchome.html. After the war, Taylor opened a school in Savannah.

8. Wright, *Brief Historical Sketch,* 21; James D. Anderson, *The Education of Blacks in the South, 1860–1935* (Chapel Hill: University of North Carolina Press, 1988), 17; Cornelius, *When I Can Read My Title Clear,* 7, 84. Anderson claims that most slaves acquired literacy from other slaves, but the evidence for this assertion is far from conclusive.

9. Marrs, *Life and History,* 11–12; William H. Hughes and Frederick D. Patterson, eds., *Robert Russa Moton of Hampton and Tuskegee* (Chapel Hill: University of North Carolina Press, 1956), 8.

10. Cornelius, *When I Can Read My Title Clear,* 61; Rev. Henry B. Delaney, "Notes of My Life," *The Augustinian,* 8 Jan. 1909, Henry B. Delaney and Non J. Delaney Correspondence, St. Augustine's College, Raleigh, N.C.

11. Cornelius, *When I Can Read My Title Clear,* 54–57; Eugene D. Genovese, *A Consuming Fire: The Fall of the Confederacy in the Mind of the White Christian South* (Athens: University of Georgia Press, 1998), 24–25, 140 n. 34.

12. Vernon Lane Wharton, *The Negro in Mississippi, 1865–1890* (New York: Harper and Row, 1965), 160–161; Brooks Dickens, "Negro Education in North Carolina During Reconstruction," *Quarterly Journal of Higher Education among Negroes* 7 (Jan. 1939), 6; Janet Sharp Hermann, *The Pursuit of a Dream* (New York: Vintage, 1983), 3–20; Whittington B. Johnson, *Black Savannah, 1788–1864* (Fayetteville: University of Arkansas Press, 1996), 129. Joseph C. Davis was an admirer of British industrialist and utopian reformer Robert Owen, and placed the business affairs of his plantation in the hands of Benjamin Montgomery. Accorded wide latitude to govern themselves, the Davis slaves furnished numerous teachers, politicians, and businessmen after the Civil War. Davis Bend, an inverted Owenite experiment, was hardly a typical plantation, but it showed that slaveholders violated the laws against slave literacy with impunity.

13. Marrs, *Life and History,* 15; Berry Mansfield, "That Fateful Class: Black

Teachers of Virginia's Freedmen, 1861–1882" (Ph.D. diss., Catholic University of America, 1980), 15–23; Cornelius, *When I Can Read My Title Clear,* 54, 86, 107; M. F. Armstrong and Helen W. Ludlow, *Hampton and Its Students* (1874; Freeport, N.Y.: Books for Libraries Press, 1971), 102–103.

14. Edmund L. Drago, *Initiative, Paternalism, and Race Relations: Charleston's Avery Normal Institute* (Athens: University of Georgia Press, 1990), 30; Mansfield, "That Fateful Class," 6, 46–48; John Boles, *Black Southerners, 1619–1869* (Lexington: University of Kentucky Press, 1984), 135, 163; Woodson, *History of the Negro Church,* 41–49, 77–78, 85–86, 110–118; Joseph Logsdon and Caryn Cossé Bell, "The Americanization of Black New Orleans, 1850–1900," in *Creole New Orleans: Race and Americanization,* ed. Arnold R. Hirsch and Joseph Logsdon (Baton Rouge: Louisiana State University Press, 1992), 211–214. The AME's church in Charleston was suppressed in 1822, its church in New Orleans banned, after years of harassment, in 1858.

15. Woodson, *History of the Negro Church,* 58–59; Wharton, *The Negro in Mississippi,* 159; Dickens, "Negro Education," 2–3.

16. Caryn Cossé Bell, *Revolution, Romanticism, and the Afro-Creole Protest Tradition in Louisiana, 1718–1868* (Baton Rouge: Louisiana State University Press, 1997), 123–126; Stephen J. Ochs, *A Black Patriot and a White Priest: André Cailloux and Claude Paschal Maistre in Civil War New Orleans* (Baton Rouge: Louisiana State University Press, 2000), 40; Nathan Wiley, "Education of the Colored Population of Louisiana," *Harper's,* July 1866, 246–248; Victor B. Howard, *Black Liberation in Kentucky: Emancipation and Freedom, 1862–1884* (Lexington: University Press of Kentucky, 1983), 166; Simmons, *Men of Mark,* 369; Woodson, *History of the Negro Church,* 104; Lorenzo J. Greene, Gary R. Kremer, and Antonio F. Holland, *Missouri's Black Heritage* (Columbia: University of Missouri Press, 1993), 67–68; John Hope Franklin, *The Free Negroes of North Carolina, 1790–1860* (Chapel Hill: University of North Carolina Press, 1995), 165–169. In Mobile, Alabama, the mostly Creole population of free Negroes, although much smaller, enjoyed similar latitude, and the city provided public schools for them. Most of the free Negroes were literate by 1860. See Peter Kolchin, *First Freedom: The Responses of Alabama's Blacks to Emancipation and Reconstruction* (Westport, Conn.: Greenwood, 1972), 140.

17. C. W. Birnie, "Education of the Negro in Charleston, South Carolina, Prior to the Civil War," *JNH* 12 (Jan. 1927): 18; Drago, *Initiative, Paternalism, and Race Relations,* 38–39; Johnson, *Black Savannah,* 21, 41–42, 127–128. For evidence of secret schools in Virginia and Georgia, see Lewis C. Lockwood, *Mary S. Peake: The Colored Teacher at Fortress Monroe* (1863; New York: Arno, 1969), 6–15; Alrutheus Ambush Taylor, *The Negro in the Reconstruction of Virginia* (Washington: Association for the Study of Negro

Life and History, 1926), 138; Simmons, *Men of Mark,* 269; Ridgely Torrence, *The Story of John Hope* (New York: Macmillan, 1948), 54–55; Morris, *Reading, 'Riting, and Reconstruction,* 124. In 1835, South Carolina forbade free blacks to keep schools "or any other place of instruction" for teaching "free people of color" to read and write. Five schools in Charleston had to close. Mob action then forced Bishop John England to shut down his Catholic school for free blacks. Virginia prohibited free blacks from sending their children out of state to be educated. South Carolina exiled any free person of color who traveled outside the slave states.

18. Wheeler, *Uplifting the Race,* 61–62; Stephen W. Angell, *Bishop Henry Mc-Neal Turner and African-American Religion in the South* (Knoxville: University of Tennessee Press, 1992), 9–10, 28–29.

19. Reidy, *From Slavery to Agrarian Capitalism,* 114–120; Genovese, *A Consuming Fire,* 58; Simmons, *Men of Mark,* 145–146, 255–256, 269, 277–278; Morris, *Reading, 'Riting, and Reconstruction,* 14–16; Jacquelyn Slaughter Haywood, "The American Missionary Association in Louisiana during Reconstruction" (Ph.D. diss., University of California, Los Angeles, 1974), 39–40, 66–67, 93; C. Peter Ripley, *Slaves and Freedmen in Civil War Louisiana* (Baton Rouge: Louisiana State University Press, 1976), 143–145; Jones, *Negro Education,* 1:251; Taylor, *Civil War Memoirs,* 52; Joe M. Richardson, "The American Missionary Association and Black Education in Louisiana, 1862–1878," in *Louisiana's Black Heritage,* ed. Robert R. MacDonald, John R. Kemp, and Edward F. Haas (New Orleans: Louisiana State Museum, 1976), 149; Armstrong and Ludlow, *Hampton and Its Students,* 121; *SW,* June 1893. By the end of the war, 121 government schools in Louisiana enrolled 13,462 children and employed 216 teachers, 85 of whom were blacks

20. William H. Heard, *From Slavery to the Bishopric in the AME Church* (1924; New York: Arno Press, 1969), 31–36.

21. J. W. Sprague, Arkansas, Missouri and Indian Territory, 18 Oct. 1866, in Exec. Doc. 6, *Freedmen's Affairs, 1866,* 29; W. H. Early to Eberhart (20 Mar. 1867), and E. A. Cooley to G. L. Eberhart (22 Dec. 1866), reel 8, BRFAL (Ga.); untitled report, n.d. [1866], reel 6, AMA Papers (Tenn.); J. P. Bardwell to M. E. Strieby, 24 Oct. 1865, box 9, AMA Papers (Miss.).

22. Exec. Doc. 70, *Freedmen's Bureau, 1865–66,* 255, 337, 342, 392; Exec. Doc. 6, *Freedmen's Affairs, 1866,* 65; E. C. Morris, *Sermons, Addresses and Reminiscences and Important Correspondence* (Nashville: National Baptist Publishing Board, 1901), 17, DocSouth, 2004; Boothe, *Cyclopedia of the Colored Baptists,* 34; Charles A. Meyers, report, 21 May 1866, reel 3, BRFAL (La.); A. H. Mayer to Charles Gaveston, 1 Oct. 1867, reel 4, BRFAL (Tex.). For

complaints about preacher-teachers, see also Leonard R. Morton to Edwin A. Wheelock, 25 Oct. 1866, reel 4, BRFAL (Tex.); B. Randolph, report, 14 Apr. 1866, reel 3, BRFAL (La.); Burton, *In My Father's House,* 251–253. White public schools, Burton notes, were rarely linked to churches.

23. Exec. Doc. 70, *Freedmen's Bureau, 1865–66,* 336; Jennifer Carol Lund Smith, "'Twill Take Some Time to Study When I Get Over': Varieties of African American Education in Reconstruction Georgia" (Ph.D. diss., University of Georgia, 1997), 14–25; Morris, *Reading, 'Riting, and Reconstruction,* 120–124; Butchart, *Northern Schools, Southern Blacks,* 133; Heather Williams, *Self-Taught: African American Education in Slavery and Freedom* (Chapel Hill: University of North Carolina Press, 2005), 87–90; Whitelaw Reid, *After the War: A Tour of the Southern States, 1865–1866,* ed. C. Vann Woodward (1866; New York: Harper and Row, 1965), 142; A. P. Ketchum to R. Saxton, 1 Sept. 1865, reel 34, M869, BRFAL, http://www. freedmensbureau.com/southcarolina/scoperations4.htm; E. A. Cooley to G. L. Eberhart, 22 Dec. 1866, reel 8, BRFAL (Ga.).

24. Jones, *Soldiers of Light and Love,* 113–115; Clara M. DeBoer, "The Role of Afro-Americans in the Origins and Work of the American Missionary Association, 1839–1872" (Ph.D. diss., Rutgers University, 1973), 470–473, 482; Horace Mann Bond, *Negro Education in Alabama: A Study in Cotton and Steel* (1939; New York: Atheneum, 1969), 16–18.

25. Butchart, *Northern Schools, Southern Blacks,* 115.

26. School report, Perry County, Mar. 1868, reel 17, BRFAL (Ga.); James Davison to G. L. Eberhart, 6 Mar. 1867, reel 8, BRFAL (Ga.); Roberta S. Alexander, "Hostility and Hope: Black Education in North Carolina during Presidential Reconstruction, 1865–1867," *North Carolina Historical Review* 53 (Apr. 1976): 128; Edward Miller to Edwin A. Wheelock, 30 Mar. 1867, reel 4, BRFAL (Tex.).

27. John W. De Forest, *A Union Officer in the Reconstruction* (Hamden, Conn.: Archon Books, 1968), 118–121; R. W. Mitchell to G. L. Eberhart, 28 Oct. 1865, reel 8, BRFAL (Ga.); Marcia Elaine Turner-Jones, "A Political Analysis of Black Educational History: Atlanta, 1865–1943" (Ph.D. diss., University of Chicago, 1982), 36.

28. Lawrence H. Williams, *Black Higher Education in Kentucky, 1879–1930: A History of Simmons University* (Lewiston: Edwin Mellin Press, 1987), 189; Smith, "'Twill Take Some Time to Study,'" 143.

29. Simmons, *Men of Mark,* 636–637, 433; Morris, *Reading, 'Riting, and Reconstruction,* 114; Earle H. West, "The Harris Brothers: Black Northern Teachers in the Reconstruction South," *JNE* 48 (1979), 126–128.

30. Clara M. DeBoer, *His Truth Is Marching On: African Americans Who Taught the Freedmen for the American Missionary Association, 1861–1877* (New

York: Garland, 1995), 279; "Letters to the American Colonization Society," *JNH* 10 (Apr. 1925): 298–299; Simmons, *Men of Mark*, 505–506.

31. Barry A. Crouch, "Black Education in Civil War and Reconstruction Louisiana: George T. Ruby, the Army, and the Freedmen's Bureau," *Louisiana History* 38 (Summer 1997): 287–296; Mortimer A. Warren to H. R. Pease, 31 Dec. 1865, and 31 Jan. 1866, reel 4, BRFAL (La.).

32. Pauli Murray, *Proud Shoes: The Story of an American Family* (New York: Harper, 1956), 102–228.

33. Ronald E. Butchart, "'We Can Best Instruct Our Own People': New York African Americans in the Freedmen's Schools, 1861–1875," in *African Americans and Education in the South, 1865–1900*, ed. Donald G. Nieman (New York: Garland, 1994), 27–49.

34. Butchart, "'We Can Best Instruct Our Own People,'" 40–41; DeBoer, "Role of Afro-Americans," 236, 264–277, 295; Morris, *Reading, 'Riting, and Reconstruction*, 110–111; Mansfield, "That Fateful Class," 102; Linda M. Perkins, "Black Female American Missionary Teacher in the South, 1861–1870," in *Black Women in American History from Colonial Times through the Nineteenth Century*, 3 vols. (Brooklyn: Carlson, 1990), 3:126–127; DeBoer, *His Truth Is Marching On*, 213; Ronald E. Butchart, "Mission Matters: Mount Holyoke, Oberlin, and the Schooling of Southern Blacks, 1861–1917," *HEQ* 42 (Spring 2002): 7–8.

35. Mansfield, "That Fateful Class," 89; B. Randolph, "Supplementary Report," 17 Mar. 1866, reel 3, BRFAL (La.).

36. Sarah G. Stanley to Sam L. Hunt, [?] Mar. 1866; 4 May 1866, reel 4, AMA Papers (Ky.); Mary J. R. Richards to G. L. Eberhart, 16 Mar. 1867, reel 8, BRFAL (Ga.).

37. Leon Litwack, *Been in the Storm So Long: The Aftermath of Slavery* (New York: Random House, 1979), 468; Peter R. Hines to G. L. Eberhart, 1865, reel 8, BRFAL (Ga.); Geo. F. Bowles to D. Burt, 22 Nov. 1866, reel 47, BRFAL (Tenn.); Exec. Doc. 6, *Freedmen's Affairs, 1866*, 149; Exec. Doc. 70, *Freedmen's Bureau, 1865–66*, 354–355.

38. Exec. Doc. 6, *Freedmen's Affairs, 1866*, 149; J. R. S. Van Fleet to Rev. Samuel Hunt, 29 Jan. 1866, AMA Papers (Tex.); Taylor, *The Negro in the Reconstruction*, 142; Paul A. Cimbala, *Under the Guardianship of the Nation: The Freedmen's Bureau and the Reconstruction of Georgia, 1865–1870* (Athens: University of Georgia Press, 1997), 110; B. Randolph, supplementary report, 17 Mar. 1866, and George T. Ruby, monthly report, 16 May 1866, both reel 3, BRFAL (La.); Reidy, *From Slavery to Agrarian Capitalism*, 147–149. It should be noted that because large parts of Louisiana had been occupied by Union forces early in the war, blacks there—unlike those in other southern states—had enjoyed the luxury of government-sponsored

free schools. When these schools were suspended and blacks were asked to pay tuition fees, the decline in attendance was especially marked.

39. George R. Bentley, *A History of the Freedmen's Bureau* (New York: Octagon, 1955, 1970), 173; William Preston Vaughan, *Schools for All: The Blacks and Public Education in the South, 1865–1877* (Lexington: University Press of Kentucky, 1974), 11–12; Cimbala, *Guardianship of the Nation,* 107; Mansfield, "That Fateful Class," 198–201.

40. Noah Russell to G. L. Eberhart, 29 Oct. 1865, reel 8, BRFAL (Ga.); Cimbala, *Guardianship of the Nation,* 51–57, 107–108; George T. Ruby, monthly report, 16 May 1866, reel 3, BRFAL (La.); Barry A. Crouch, "Freedmen's Bureau Records: A Case Study," in *Afro-American History: Sources for Research,* ed. Robert L. Clare (Washington: Howard University Press, 1981), 89–90. For examples of blacks being afraid to organize schools, see Richard Simpson to J. R. Lewis, 1 Sept. 1866, reel 5, BRFAL (Tenn.); John H. Burrus, "Educational Progress of the Colored People in the South," in National Education Association, *Journal of Proceedings and Addresses* (Topeka, Kans.: NEA, 1889): 202–203; Hughes and Patterson, *Robert Russa Moton,* 11. It would be a mistake to suppose that all Freedmen's Bureau agents were evangelists for black education. Some showed little interest in black schools, and their sympathies often lay with the former slaveholders rather than the freedmen.

41. Greene, Kremer, and Holland, *Missouri's Black Heritage,* 97; Lawrence O. Christensen, "Schools for Blacks: J. Milton Turner in Reconstruction Missouri," in Nieman, *African Americans and Education,* 66–67; Cimbala, *Guardianship of the Nation,* 108; William J. White to G. L. Eberhart, 29 Mar. 1867, reel 8, BRFAL (Ga.); Heard, *From Slavery to the Bishopric,* 89, DocSouth, 2004, docsouth.unc.edu/neh/heard/heard.html.

42. Crouch, "Black Education," 296–305; G. T. Ruby, reports, 12 Apr., 1 May, 16 May 1866, reel 3, BRFAL (La.).

43. Marrs, *Life and History,* 89–90; Eric Foner, *Freedom's Lawmakers: A Dictionary of Black Officeholders during Reconstruction* (Baton Rouge: Louisiana State University Press, 1996), 26, 32; Kolchin, *First Freedom,* 121; 43rd Cong., 2d sess., House Report 262, *Affairs in Alabama, 1875,* 73, 292.

44. Eric Foner, *Reconstruction: America's Unfinished Revolution, 1863–1877* (New York: Harper and Row, 1988), 278; DeBoer, "Role of Afro-Americans," 286–287.

45. Foner, *Freedom's Lawmakers,* 20, 29–32, 185; Senate Report 693, *Causes of the Removal of the Negroes,* 2:37–38, 214; 44th Cong., 2d sess., House Misc. Doc. 34, *Recent Election in Louisiana,* 4:122.

46. Susan E. Dollar, *The Freedmen's Bureau Schools of Natchitoches Parish, Louisiana, 1863–1868* (Natchitoches: Northwestern Louisiana State University

Press, 1998), 90; Murray, *Proud Shoes,* 191; Foner, *Freedom's Lawmakers,* xviii, 29, 96–97, 140, 164; Frenise A. Logan, *The Negro in North Carolina, 1876–1896* (Chapel Hill: University of North Carolina Press, 1964), 26–29; Morris, *Reading, 'Riting, and Reconstruction,* 103–108; Wharton, *The Negro in Mississippi,* 160–161, 164; Thomas Rothrock, "Joseph Carter Corbin and Negro Education in the University of Arkansas," *Arkansas Historical Quarterly* 30 (Winter 1971): 277–279. The state superintendents were Jonathan C. Gibbs in Florida, Thomas W. Cardozo in Mississippi, J. C. Corbin in Arkansas, James Walker Hood in North Carolina, and William G. Brown in Louisiana.

47. For examples of actual, rather than merely rhetorical, southern white support for black schools in 1865–67, see T. G. Steward, *Fifty Years in the Gospel Ministry, 1864 to 1914* (Philadelphia: AME Book Concern, 1921), 44, DocSouth, http://docsouth.unc.edu/church/steward/menu.html; Bond, *Negro Education in Alabama,* 79–81; Joel Williamson, *After Slavery: The Negro in South Carolina during Reconstruction, 1861–1877* (New York: Norton, 1963), 214–215; Vaughan, *Schools for All,* 40–42; monthly school report, Taylor County, n.d., reel 16, BRFAL (Ga.); James R. Smith to G. L. Eberhart, 6 Mar. 1867, and Mrs. Sellmer to Eberhart, 11 Mar. 1867, reel 8, BRFAL (Ga.).

48. For arson and violence against black schools and teachers, see Steward, *Fifty Years in the Gospel Ministry,* 67–68; Cimbala, *Guardianship of the Nation,* 113; E. Garrison Jackson to W. G. Whiting, 29 Mar. 1866, reel 1, AMA Papers (Maryland); Litwack, *Been in the Storm So Long,* 487; Foner, *Freedom's Lawmakers,* 217; Senate Report 693, *Causes of the Removal of the Negroes,* 2:53; DeBoer, "Role of Afro-Americans," 328.

49. Walter L. Fleming, *Civil War and Reconstruction in Alabama* (1905; Spartanburg, S.C.: Reprint Co., 1978), 626–629; Exec. Doc. 70, *Freedmen's Bureau, 1865–66,* 273, 328; Exec. Doc. 6, *Freedmen's Affairs, 1866,* 66, 75.

50. Thomas J. Burney to G. L. Eberhart, 18 Mar. 1867, reel 8, BRFAL (Ga.). Relatively few teachers, black or white, lost their lives because of political violence. The Ku Klux Klan and other terrorist groups generally refrained from killing northern white teachers. Women suffered social ostracism, verbal abuse, threats, and other forms of harassment. Male teachers were sometimes whipped, but rarely killed. The murder of the Canadian-born teacher William Luke by Alabama Klansmen in 1870 was a notorious exception to this calculated policy. See Jones, *Soldiers of Light and Love,* 82; Gene L. Howard, *Death at Cross Plains: An Alabama Reconstruction Tragedy* (Tuscaloosa: University of Alabama Press, 1994), 90–92.

51. The following examples represent a random sampling of white attitudes as reported by Freedmen's Bureau officials in Georgia, Louisiana, and

Texas. For favorable attitudes, see monthly school reports, Americus (Dec. 1867), Cuthbert (Dec. 1867), Stockton (Dec. 1867), and Rome (Jan. 1868), reel 16, BRFAL (Ga.); H. M. Roberts to H. R. Pease (26 Sept. 1865), and Jno. S. Chapman to Pease (5 Oct. 1865), reel 3, BRFAL (La.); A. J. Manning to E. A. Wheelock (1 Jan. 1867), A. N. Mayer to J. F. Kirkman (19 Apr. 1867), Albert A. Metzner to Kirkman (31 May 1867), E. Miller to Kirkman (30 June 1867), Bryan Porter to Wheelock (23 Jan. 1867), George T. Ruby to Kirkman (17 Aug. 1867), A. H. Mayer to C. Gaveston (1 Oct. 1867), and D. L. Montgomery to Gaveston (30 Sept. 1867), reel 4, BRFAL (Tex.). For unfavorable attitudes, see monthly school reports, Lincoln Free School, Macon (Jan. 1868), and Gainesville (Dec. 1867), reel 16, BRFAL (Ga.); H. M. Roberts to H. R. Pease (22 Nov. 1865), E. N. Larkin to Pease (7 Oct. 1865), Aaron Walker to Pease (31 Oct. 1865), B. Randolph (supplementary report, 17 Mar. 1866), Randolph (report, 12 Apr. 1866), George T. Ruby (16 May 1866), and monthly school report, Ascension Parish (June 1866), reel 3, BRFAL (La.).

52. Wharton, *The Negro in Mississippi,* 243–244; Alexander, "Hostility and Hope," 122; Ward M. McAfee, *Religion, Race, and Reconstruction: The Public School in the Politics of the 1870s* (Albany: State University of New York Press, 1998), 102–103.

53. *Proceedings of the South Carolina Constitutional Convention,* 3 vols. (Charleston: Denny and Perry, 1868), 2:685–725, 3:389–394; McAfee, *Religion, Race, and Reconstruction,* 94, 106–109. Interestingly, the most centralized public school system in the South, that of Texas, was directed by a former Union officer who was also a Prussian immigrant. It is also significant that the border states of Kentucky and Maryland, which were not subjected to Radical Reconstruction, failed to establish black public schools until the mid-1870s.

54. McAfee, *Religion, Race, and Reconstruction,* 169–171; Vaughan, *Schools for All,* 89–90; Louis R. Harlan, "Desegregation in New Orleans Public Schools during Reconstruction," *American Historical Review* 67 (Apr. 1962): 663–675; Roger A. Fischer, *The Segregation Struggle in Louisiana, 1862–1877* (Urbana: University of Illinois Press, 1974), 93–97, 101–105, 113–119, 131. Only Louisiana attempted to promote integration, but the policy proved self-defeating because whites shunned the public schools. In New Orleans, the integration policy worked after a fashion, but whites—many of whom transferred their children to private and Catholic parochial schools—were never reconciled to it.

55. Maxine D. Jones, "'A Glorious Work': The American Missionary Association and Black North Carolinians, 1863–1880" (Ph.D. diss., Florida State University, 1982), 300; Alton Hornsby Jr., "The Freedmen's Bureau

Schools in Texas, 1865–1870," *Southwestern Historical Quarterly* 76 (1972–73): 413; Kolchin, *First Freedom,* 93; W. S. Sutton, "The Education of the Southern Negro," *Bulletin of the University of Texas* 221 (Mar. 1912): 9–10.

56. Diary of Archelaus M. Hughes, entries for 15 Dec. 1868, 31 May 1869, and 4 Sept. 1869, Tennessee State Library and Archives, Nashville; Cynthia G. Fleming, "Development of Black Education in Tennessee, 1865–1920," (Ph.D. diss., Duke University, 1977), 26.

57. Wharton, *The Negro in Mississippi,* 245; James W. Garner, *Reconstruction in Mississippi* (1901; Baton Rouge: Louisiana State University Press, 1968), 359–363; 42d Cong., 2d sess., House Report 22, *Condition of Affairs in the Late Insurrectionary States: Mississippi,* 11:82–83, 277, 283, 325–329, 420–421, 493, 513, 570–574; 12:622–663; 777–779, 849, 1151. Mississippi's public school law levied a property tax of 1.5 percent and a poll tax of two dollars.

58. [Albion W. Tourgee], *A Fool's Errand, by One of the Fools* (New York: Fords, Howard, and Hulbert, 1880), 119

59. Foner, *Freedom's Lawmakers,* 20; William Hicks, *History of Louisiana Negro Baptists and Early American Beginnings, from 1804 to 1914,* ed. Sue Eakins (Lafayette: Center for Louisiana Studies, 1998), 53, 98; 43rd Cong., 2d sess., House Report 261, *The Condition of the South: Louisiana Affairs* (Washington: GPO, 1875), 3:292, 550; House Misc. Doc. 34, *Recent Election in Louisiana* (Washington: GPO, 1877), 1:190, 2:144, 4:122. Records also spell Blunt's name "Blount," and his middle name (which he used in preference to "Alfred") "Rayford" and even "Buford."

60. Senate Report 693, *Causes of the Removal of the Negroes,* 3:251–256; House Misc. Doc. 34, *Recent Election in Louisiana,* 4:1877, 160; Dollar, *Freedmen's Bureau Schools,* 92–93. Faulkner did not vote in the election, and in subsequent contests he advertised himself as a colored Democrat. The vice president of the Fifth Ward Republican Club, Alfred Hazen (or Hayson), was shot dead by masked white men. Dollar points out that at Town School no. 3, for example, the number of pupils over the age of sixteen shot up from four to fifty-one in the run-up to the November 1868 election, suggesting that the teacher, Lucius Taylor, was priming black voters.

61. 43rd Cong., 2d sess., House Report 101, *Condition of the South,* 23; House Report 261, *Condition of the South,* 3:140–142, 550; 42d Cong., 3d sess., House, *Condition of Affairs in Louisiana* (Washington: GPO, 1873), 115–118, 125. Ironically, in 1874 E. L. Pierson joined the Republican Party. In 1875 he was shot and mortally wounded on the streets of Natchitoches by a band of white men. See House Misc. Doc. 34, *Recent Election in Louisiana,* 4:157.

62. Ted Tunnell, *Edge of the Sword: The Ordeal of Carpetbagger Marshall H. Twitchell in the Civil War and Reconstruction* (Baton Rouge: Louisiana State

University Press, 2001), 171–173; House Report 261, *Condition of the South*, 3:227, 551. The truce in Natchitoches accorded with the conciliatory policy of Republican governor William P. Kellogg, who offered local appointments to Democratic opponents. See Foner, *Reconstruction*, 550.

63. House Report 261, *Condition of the South*, 3:224, 280–290, 550, 924.

64. 44th Cong., 2d Sess., Exec. Doc. 30, *Use of the Army in Certain of the Southern States* (Washington: GPO, 1877), 199; House Report 261, *Condition of the South*, 3:789, 927.

65. Tunnell, *Edge of the Sword*, 173–174, 203–206, 242–243; House Report 261, *Condition of the South*, 3:214–224, 282–292, 550, 921–929; House Misc. Doc. 34, *Recent Election in Louisiana*, 1:122–125; 3:87–166; 45th Cong., 3d sess., Senate Report 855, *Louisiana in 1878* (Washington: GPO, 1879), 143; 44th Cong., 2d sess., House Report 156, *Recent Election in Louisiana* (Washington: GPO, 1877), 1:122; House Misc. Doc. 34, *Recent Election in Louisiana*, 4:92, 100; Senate Report 855, *Louisiana in 1878*, 115–127, 132–147, 154–159, 485–514; Senate Report 693, *Causes of the Removal of the Negroes*, 2:45–47, 429–431, 3:219–220.

66. House Report 22, *Condition of Affairs in the Late Insurrectionary States*, 9:1341–44, 1352; 11:590.

67. Charles W. Dabney, *Universal Education in the South*, vol. 2: *The Southern Education Movement* (Chapel Hill: University of North Carolina Press, 1936).

68. Fleming, *Civil War and Reconstruction*, 457–468, 626–629. For evidence of corruption in Louisiana, for example, see House Report 261, *Condition of the South*, 3:934–938; House Misc. Doc. 34, *Recent Election in Louisiana*, 1877, 1:143, 3:256–262; Tunnell, *Edge of the Sword*, 148; Litwack, *Been in the Storm So Long*, 489. Raford Blunt's practice of paying an assistant thirty dollars a month to do his teaching for him—thereby pocketing a profit of seventy dollars—illustrated the fine line between sharp practice and outright corruption.

69. Fleming, "Black Education in Tennessee," 26–27; Edgar W. Knight, *Public School Education in North Carolina* (1916; New York: Negro Universities Press, 1969), 249–253; Frederick Eby, *The Development of Education in Texas* (New York: Macmillan, 1925), 169–171; Stuart G. Noble, *Forty Years of the Public Schools in Mississippi: With Special Reference to the Education of the Negro* (1918; New York: Negro Universities Press, 1969), 48–54; Bond, *Negro Education in Alabama*, 135–136, 148–150; William Ivy Hair, *Bourbonism and Agrarian Protest: Louisiana Politics, 1877–190* (Baton Rouge: Louisiana State University Press, 1975), 60–62; *Report of the Superintendent of Public Instruction of North Carolina for the Year 1873* (Raleigh, 1873). In Tennessee, a conservative legislature in 1869 got rid of the post of state superintendent of education and made the organization of public

schools a matter of county option. Most of the counties outside Knoxville, Nashville, and Memphis opted out. In 1871 more than two-thirds of the state's 96 counties still had no public schools. North Carolina's Democrats, who gained control of the state legislature in 1870, slashed the salary of the state superintendent, denying him a clerical staff and giving him no travel expenses. The new school law made no effective provision for local school districts to levy taxes. Three years after "redemption," North Carolina reported that fewer than half of the white children were enrolled in schools, and only about a third of the black children. Texas abolished the post of state superintendent altogether and reduced a child's entitlement to free schooling to six years. Mississippi cut teachers' salaries and prohibited counties from levying taxes to subsidize schoolhouses.

2. Black Teachers for Black Children

1. Foner, *Reconstruction,* 322; Marcus C. S. Noble, *A History of the Public Schools of North Carolina* (Chapel Hill: University of North Carolina Press, 1930), 291. Hood presided over the constitutional convention of 1868–69. He subsequently served as North Carolina's superintendent of education.
2. Exec. Doc. 70, *Freedmen's Bureau, 1865–66,* 345–346.
3. E. M. Wheelock to George Whipple (10 Mar. 1866), Rev. George R. Hovey to W. B. Stickney (2 Feb. 1866), both in AMA Papers (Tex.); Jones, *Soldiers of Light and Love,* 89–90; Exec. Doc. 6, *Freedmen's Affairs, 1866,* 149. In Georgia, 70 percent of the white freedmen's teachers taught in the five largest cities. However, only 15 percent of the state's black population lived in those cities.
4. George F. Bowles to D. Burt (22 Nov. 1866), William Lowery to Burt (26 Nov. 1866), reel 47, BRFAL (Tenn.); Jack Heard to G. L. Eberhart, 8 May 1867, reel 8, BRFAL (Ga.). Sometimes freedmen asked for a black teacher without citing any reason.
5. G. L. Eberhart to Edward P. Smith, 8 Apr. 1867, roll 4, AMA Papers (Ga.); Willard Range, *The Rise and Progress of Negro Colleges in Georgia, 1865–1949* (Athens: University of Georgia Press, 1951), 15; William C. Harris, *The Day of the Carpetbagger: Republican Reconstruction in Mississippi* (Baton Rouge: Louisiana State University Press, 1979), 319; House Report 22, *Conditions of Affairs in the Late Insurrectionary States,* 2:443, 448; Wharton, *The Negro in Mississippi,* 246; Garner, *Reconstruction in Mississippi,* 364; Howard A. White, *The Freedmen's Bureau in Louisiana* (Baton Rouge: Louisiana State University Press, 1970), 171; Martin Abbot, *The Freedmen's Bureau in South Carolina, 1865–1872* (Chapel Hill: University of North Carolina Press, 1967), 95; Corinne L. Saucier, *History of Avoyelles Parish,*

Louisiana (New Orleans: Pelican Pub. Co., 1943), 96; Luther Porter Jackson, *A History of the Virginia Teachers Association* (Norfolk, Va.: Guide Pub. Co., 1937), 30–31; Rabinowitz, "'Half a Loaf,'" 557. In 1867 there were 147 whites teaching in Georgia's black schools; of these, 83 were native Georgians. When Mississippi started its public school system in 1871, the 860 black schools included only 339 black teachers. In Lowndes County, for example, whites taught 16 of the 25 black schools. In Louisiana, too, native whites provided most of the teachers in the freedmen's schools between 1865 and 1868. In Avoyelles Parish, the school board went out of its way to employ native whites, "good Democrats," in order to soften opposition to black schools. In eight counties of western South Carolina, 15 of the 26 teachers were white southerners. In Virginia, whites provided most of the first teachers in black public schools, and in 1880 still accounted for 38 percent of them.

6. B. Randolph, supplementary report, 17 Mar. 1866, reel 3, BRFAL (La.)

7. Fleming, "Black Education in Tennessee," 22; D. Burt to Lewis Botton, 31 Jan. 1867, reel 5, BRFAL (Tenn.); Crouch, "Black Education," 298–301.

8. Christensen, "Schools for Blacks," 59, 68.

9. Williams, *Self-Taught,* 99.

10. *Proceedings of the Second Conference for Christian Education in the South, 1899* (Washington, n.d), 25; Wharton, *The Negro in Mississippi,* 244.

11. "An Address to the Colored Citizens of the City of Petersburg, to the Public and To Whom It May Concern," n.d., folder 16, box 1, Henry Williams Papers, Virginia State University.

12. House Misc. Doc. 34, *Recent Election in Louisiana,* 1:628; *SW,* Nov. 1875, Mar. 1876; Rabinowitz, "'Half a Loaf,'" 579.

13. Hughes and Patterson, *Robert Russa Moton,* 14; Antonio Frederick Holland, "Nathan B. Young and the Development of Black Higher Education" (Ph.D. diss., University of Missouri–Columbia, 1984), 7–8; Boothe, *Cyclopedia of the Colored Baptists,* 227–229.

14. *SW,* Jan. 1872; Martha Short Dance, *Peabody High School: A History of the First Negro Public High School in Virginia* (New York: Coulton Press, 1976), 21–26; George F. Bragg, *History of the Afro-American Group of the Episcopal Church* (1922), 132–134, DocSouth, 2000, http://docsouth.unc.edu/church/bragg/bragg.html.

15. "An Address to the Colored Citizens of the City of Petersburg," Henry Williams Papers.

16. Bragg, *Afro-American Group of the Episcopal Church,* 128.

17. *Protestant Episcopal Church, Ninth Annual Report of the Commission of Home Missions to Colored People, 1874–74,* 7–8, Daniel A. P. Murray Pamphlet Collection, online text, LC.

18. House Report 22, *Conditions of Affairs in the Late Insurrectionary States,* vol.

2, *North Carolina,* 214–224; Cecil D. Halliburton, *A History of St. Augustine's College, 1865–1937* (Raleigh, N.C.: St. Augustine's College, 1937), 6–7.

19. Bragg, *History of the Afro-American Group of the Episcopal Church,* 150–155; Henry B. Delaney, *Memorial of the Convocation of the Colored People in the Diocese of North Carolina Presented to the Diocesan Convention of 1916,* 2–3, DocSouth, 2001, http://docsouth.unc.edu/church/convocation/convocation.html.

20. Wilmoth A. Carter, *Shaw's Universe: A Monument to Educational Innovation* (Rockville, Md.: O. C. National, 1973), 9–15; Perry v. Tupper, 71 NC 387 (1874), 74 NC 722 (1876), 77 NC 413 (1877), case files, North Carolina Department of Archives; Perry v. Shepherd (1878), *North Carolina Reports,* 83–84.

21. DeBoer, "Role of Afro-Americans," 390; Butchart, *Northern Schools, Southern Blacks,* 77–94; Ralph Luker, *The Social Gospel in Black and White: American Racial Reform, 1885–1912* (Chapel Hill: University of North Carolina Press, 1991), 10–16; McMillen, *To Raise Up the South,* 26–35; *First Mohonk Conference on the Negro Question, Held at Lake Mohonk, Ulster County, New York, June 4, 5, 6, 1890* (1890; New York: Negro Universities Press, 1969), 127; H. M. Tupper, *A Narrative of Twenty-Five Years' Work in the South, 1865–1890* (New York: American Baptist Home Missionary Society, 1890), 21–23.

22. Steward, *Fifty Years in the Gospel Ministry,* 44; J. W. Hood, *One Hundred Years of the African Methodist Episcopal Zion Church; or, the Centennial of African Methodism* (1895), 16, DocSouth, 2001, http://docsouth.unc.edu/church/hood/hood.html; James T. Campbell, *Songs of Zion: The African Methodist Episcopal Church in the United States and South Africa* (Chapel Hill: University of North Carolina Press, 1998), 55.

23. Clarence E. Walker, *A Rock in a Weary Land: The African Methodist Episcopal Church during the Civil War and Reconstruction* (Baton Rouge: Louisiana State University Press, 1982) 51–55, 75–77; Campbell, *Songs of Zion,* 51.

24. Steward, *Fifty Years in the Gospel Ministry,* 65–69, 97–99.

25. Boothe, *Cyclopedia of the Colored Baptists,* 9–11.

26. Walker, *Rock in a Weary Land,* 86–93; Sandy Dwayne Martin, *For God and Race: The Religious and Political Leadership of AMEZ Bishop James Walker Hood* (Columbia: University of South Carolina Press, 1999), 51; Wilbert L. Jenkins, *Seizing the Day: African Americans in Post–Civil War Charleston* (Bloomington: Indiana University Press, 1998), 124–125; Litwack, *Been in the Storm So Long,* 468; A. H. Caldwell to G. L. Eberhart, 16 Apr. 1867, reel 8, BRFAL (Ga.).

27. Steward, *Fifty Years in the Gospel Ministry,* 116–122; Othal H. Lakey, *The*

History of the CME Church (Memphis: CME Pub. House, 1985), 140–141, 239.

28. Charles Stearns, *The Black Man of the South, and the Rebels* (1872; New York: Negro Universities Press, 1969), 345; Jones, "A Glorious Work," 139–140; Katherine L. Dvorak, *An African-American Exodus: The Segregation of the Southern Churches* (Brooklyn: Carlson, 1991), 94–95.

29. Jones, "'A Glorious Work,'" 140; *First Mohonk Conference,* 65, 96.

30. Mansfield, "That Fateful Class," 255–256; John Scott to Edward P. Smith, 28 Nov. 1869, 7 Dec. 1868, 12 Dec. 1868, 14 Jan. 1869, 20 Jan. 1869, 25 Jan. 1869, 13 Feb. 1869, 26 Feb. 1869, rolls 10–11, AMA Papers (Va.).

31. Sarah W. Stansbury to Edward P. Smith, 17 Apr. 1869, 3 July 1869, 19 Nov. 1869, roll 5, AMA Papers (Ga.); Stansbury to Smith, 1 Aug. 1871, box 31, AMA Papers (Ga.).

32. Titus Brown, *Faithful, Firm, and True: African-American Education in the South* (Macon: Mercer University Press, 2002), 44; John Scott to Edward P. Smith, 28 Nov. 1868, roll 10, AMA Papers (Va.); Sarah Stansbury to Smith, 28 Mar. 1870, box 30, AMA Papers (Ga.).

33. Palmer Litts to George Whipple, 3 Apr. 1866, box 91, AMA Papers (Miss.); Jones, "A Glorious Work," 157.

34. DeBoer, "Role of Afro-Americans," 359–362.

35. Campbell, *Songs of Zion,* 55, 60–63.

36. Jones, "'A Glorious Work,'" 153–159; Walker, *Rock in a Weary Land,* 91; Brown, *Faithful, Firm, and True,* 61; Paul Harvey, *Redeeming the South: Religious Cultures and Racial Identities among Southern Baptists, 1865–1925* (Chapel Hill: University of North Carolina Press, 1997), 46.

37. Turner-Jones, "Black Educational History," 67; Allison Dorsey, *To Build Our Lives Together: Community Formation in Black Atlanta, 1875–1916* (Athens: University of Georgia Press, 2004), 86–92; McPherson, *Abolitionist Legacy,* 272; Rabinowitz, "'Half a Loaf,'" 581–583.

38. Foner, *Freedom's Lawmakers,* 230; DeBoer, "Role of Afro-Americans," 426; Turner-Jones, "Black Educational History," 64–66; Jones, *Soldiers of Light and Love,* 191; Sarah W. Stansbury to E. M. Cravath, 20 Feb. 1871, 2 Mar. 1871, box 30, AMA Papers (Ga.); Rabinowitz, "'Half a Loaf,'" 580–581; Joe M. Richardson, "Christian Abolitionism: The American Missionary Association and the Florida Negro," *JNE* 40 (Winter 1971): 40.

39. McPherson, *Abolitionist Legacy,* 185–186; DeBoer, "Role of Afro-Americans," 554.

40. Jones, "'A Glorious Work,'" 206–211, 249–250; Mansfield, "That Fateful Class," 106, 130.

41. Mansfield, "That Fateful Class," 188–189, 344; Taylor, *Negro in the Reconstruction,* 157–159.

42. DeBoer, "Role of Afro-Americans," 553; McPherson, *Abolitionist Legacy,* 187; T. Thomas Fortune, *Black and White: Land, Labor and Politics in the South* (1884; New York: Arno, 1968), 67–70.

43. Jones, *Soldiers of Light and Love,* 65–70; Jones, "'A Glorious Work,'" 229–232; Dorothy Sterling, ed., *We Are Your Sisters: Black Women of the Nineteenth Century* (New York: Norton, 1984), 364–365.

44. McPherson, *Abolitionist Legacy,* 269; "An Address to the Colored Citizens of the City of Petersburg," Henry Williams Papers, VSU.

45. Bond, *Negro Education in Alabama,* 204; Harlan, *Washington: The Making of a Black Leader,* 113–114; Turner-Jones, "Black Educational History," 54–57; Dorsey, *To Build Our Lives Together,* 196 n. 37; J. Morgan Kousser, "Making Separate Equal: Integration of Black and White School Funds in Kentucky," *Journal of Interdisciplinary History* 10 (Winter 1980): 399–428.

46. "Alfred William Harris," n.d., folder 35, box 1, John M. Gandy Papers, VSU; Jane Dailey, *Before Jim Crow: The Politics of Race in Postemancipation Virginia* (Chapel Hill: University of North Carolina Press, 2000), 69–76.

47. Hardy Mobley to AMA, 29 Aug. 1873; Laura F. Mobley to E. M. Cravath, 8 Dec. 1874; Samuel Keller and Trustees of St. Paul's Church to Cravath, 1 Mar. 1875; all in box 59, AMA Papers (La.).

48. Laura F. Mobley to Cravath, 3 Dec. 1874, 8 Dec. 1874, 11 Dec. 1874, box 59, AMA Papers (La.).

49. Laura F. Mobley to Cravath, 8 Dec. 1874, 10 Mar. 1875; *American Missionary,* July 1874, 153; *American Missionary,* Oct. 1874; Samuel Keller and L. J. McGaffy to Cravath, 12 Feb. 1875; Keller to Cravath, 1 Mar. 1875; all in box 59, AMA Papers (La.).

50. Hardy Mobley to Cravath, 22 Feb. 1875, 15 Mar. 1875; Keller and McGaffy to Cravath, 12 Feb. 1875, 2 May 1875; all in box 59, AMA Papers (La.).

51. West, "The Harris Brothers," 126–138.

52. Ibid., 134; Jones, "'A Glorious Work,'" 195; Robert Harris to Edward P. Smith, 13 May 1867, roll 3, AMA Papers (N.C.); Harris to Smith, ? Dec. 1868, 2 Aug. 1869, roll 4, AMA Papers (N.C.).

53. Harris to Smith, 24 Oct. 1867, roll 3, AMA Papers (N.C.); Harris to Smith, n.d. [1867], roll 4, AMA Papers (N.C.); Jones, "'A Glorious Work,'" 486.

54. Harris to Smith, 1 Jan. 1868, roll 4, AMA Papers (N.C.); Brodhead, *Journals of Charles W. Chesnutt,* 9; Viola Collier, "The Historical Development of Fayetteville State University," 1974, folder 3, box 8, James Ward Seabrook Papers, University Archives, Charles W. Chesnutt Library, Fayetteville State University. Cicero Harris went on to head the Peabody School in Charlotte, taught at Livingstone College (which he helped found), and served as a bishop in the AMEZ Church.

55. June Odessa Patton, "Major Richard Robert Wright, Sr. and Black Higher

Education in Georgia, 1880–1920" (Ph.D. diss., University of Chicago, 1980), 102; minutes of the Southwestern Georgia Teachers Association, Howard Normal School (1 Dec. 1877), and Richard R. Wright to M. E. Strieby (15 Apr. 1878), both in roll 12, AMA Papers (Ga.).

56. Patton, "Richard Robert Wright," 274.

57. Culp, *Twentieth Century Negro Literature,* 131; Louis R. Harlan, ed., *The Booker T. Washington Papers* (Urbana: University of Illinois Press, 1974) 3:227, 242–243.

58. Culp, *Twentieth Century Negro Literature,* 134–135; "Minutes of the American Association of Educators of Colored Youth: Session of 1894, Held at Baltimore, Maryland, July 24–27, 1894," 75, Daniel A. P. Murray Pamphlet Collection, online text, LC; McPherson, *Abolitionist Legacy,* 272; Dorsey, *To Build Our Lives Together,* 90–91.

59. Lura Beam, *He Called Them by the Lightning: A Teacher's Odyssey in the Negro South, 1908–1919* (Indianapolis: Bobbs-Merrill, 1967), 23; Culp, *Twentieth Century Negro Literature,* 127, 130.

60. McPherson, *Abolitionist Legacy,* 280–281, 286–288; Eugene TeSelle, "The Nashville Institute and Roger Williams University: Benevolence, White Paternalism, and Black Consciousness, 1867–1910," *Tennessee Historical Quarterly* 41 (Winter 1982): 368–374.

61. *Catalogue of St. Augustine's Normal School and Collegiate Institute, 1885–86;* Inez Moore Parker, *The Biddle-Johnson C. Smith University Story* (Charlotte: Charlotte Pub., 1975), 12; McPherson, *Abolitionist Legacy,* append. B; Beam, *He Called Them by the Lightning,* 153–154.

62. "Minutes of the American Association of Educators of Colored Youth: Session of 1894," 75.

63. Walker, *Rock in a Weary Land,* 129–130; John Dittmer, "The Education of Henry McNeal Turner," in *Black Leaders of the Nineteenth Century,* ed. L. Litwack and A. Meier (Urbana: University of Illinois Press, 1988), 259–260; Hood, *One Hundred Years,* 11–12.

64. Paul Yandle, "Joseph Charles Price and His 'Peculiar Work,'" pt. 1, *North Carolina Historical Review* 1 (Jan. 1993): 46–47: Josephine Price Sherrill, "A Negro School-Master of the 1870s," *JNE* 30 (Spring 1961): 168.

65. Harvey, *Redeeming the South,* 64–73; E. C. Morris, *Sermons, Addresses and Reminiscences,* 75; McPherson, *Abolitionist Legacy,* 284–285.

66. J. A. Whitted, *A History of the Negro Baptists of North Carolina* (1908), 23, DocSouth, 2001, http://docsouth.unc.edu/church/whitted/whitted.html; McPherson, *Abolitionist Legacy,* 290–291; Harvey, *Redeeming the South,* 66–74; Arthur Ben Chitty, *A Brief History of St. Augustine's College* (Raleigh: St. Augustine's College, n.d.), n.p.

67. E. K. Love, *Annual Address to the Missionary Baptist Association of Georgia, May 24, 1899* (1899), 19–23, Daniel A. P. Murray Pamphlet Collection, on-

line text; Range, *Rise and Progress of Negro Colleges,* 108–111; McPherson, *Abolitionist Legacy,* 288–290; Lester F. Russell, *Black Baptist Secondary Schools in Virginia, 1887–1957* (Metuchen, N.J.: Scarecrow, 1981), 49–56.

3. Missionaries to the Dark South

1. Laura Mason to Thomas N. Chase, 1 Mar. 1876, folder 1, box 10, Ware Papers, AUA; Brodhead, *Journals of Charles W. Chesnutt,* 70.
2. *SW,* Mar. 1876.
3. Wright, *87 Years behind the Black Curtain,* 28; Harlan, *Washington: The Making of a Black Leader,* 35; Patton, "Richard Robert Wright," 70–71; Simmons, *Men of Mark,* 279; Senate Report 695, *Removal of the Negroes from the Southern States,* 2:580, 585; Sherrill, "Negro School-Master," 165–166.
4. Brodhead, *Journals of Charles W. Chesnutt,* 42–43; "Autobiography of William Henry Johnson," 2, box 7, William Henry Johnson Papers, VSU; Litwack, *Been in the Storm So Long,* 487. Although blacks often enjoyed representation on the district school committees, whites usually controlled the county school boards and the distribution of funds. See James L. Leloudis, *Schooling the New South: Pedagogy, Self, and Society in North Carolina, 1880–1920* (Chapel Hill: University of North Carolina Press, 1996), 7.
5. Johnson, "Autobiography," 35; James S. Russell, *Adventures in Faith: An Autobiographic Story of St. Paul Normal and Industrial School, Lawrenceville, Virginia* (New York: Morehouse Pub. Co., 1936), 12–13; Charles N. Hunter, *Review of Negro Life in North Carolina with My Recollections* (Raleigh, N.C.: privately pub., n.d.), 24–25, Hunter Papers, Duke University; Brodhead, *Journals of Charles W. Chesnutt,* 67; *SW,* Nov. 1874.
6. Leloudis, *Schooling the New South,* 9–10; *Biennial Report of the Department of Education of the State of Alabama, 1899 and 1900* (Montgomery, 1900), xii; *Report of the Superintendent of Public Instruction of North Carolina for the Year 1890* (Raleigh, 1890), xxix–xxxiv; Jackson Davis, "State Normal Schools and A&M Colleges for Negroes, 1912–13 to 1921–22," Sept. 1924, folder 3267, box 313, GEB Papers, 30.
7. J. W. May to Thomas N. Chase (3 Sept. 1875); Edward P. Johnson to Chase (18 Aug. 1875, 1 Aug. 1875), folder 1, box 10, Ware Papers, AUA; Smith, "'Twill Take Some Time to Study,'" 46; Senate Report 695, *Removal of the Negroes from the Southern States,* 2:217; 48th Cong., 1st sess., Senate Report 512, *Mississippi in 1883* (Washington: GPO, 1884), 663.
8. *SW,* June 1876.
9. W. E. B. Du Bois, "Atlanta University," in *From Servitude to Service: Being the Old South Lectures on the History and Education of Southern Institutions*

for the Education of the Negro, ed. Robert C. Ogden (1905; New York: Negro Universities Press, 1969), 181.

10. Hughes and Patterson, *Robert Russa Moton,* 19; Jacob L. Reddix, *A Voice Crying in the Wilderness: The Memories of Jacob L. Reddix* (Jackson: University Press of Mississippi, 1974), 56; *SW,* Apr. 1876. Sectarian rivalry was not an invariable rule: in the rural community of Promised Land, South Carolina, for example, the relationship between Baptists and Methodists was characterized by "mutual respect and interdenominational support" (Elizabeth R. Bethel, *Promiseland: A Century of Life in a Negro Community* [Philadelphia: Temple University Press, 1981], 79).

11. Senate Report 695, *Removal of the Negroes from the Southern States,* 1:111.

12. Jas. A. Whitted to Charles N. Hunter, box 2, Hunter Papers.

13. Wallace Buttrick to Frederick T. Gates, 21 Dec. 1903, folder 2689, box 260, GEB Papers; *SW,* Jan. 1901.

14. Mamie Garvin Fields with Karen Fields, *Lemon Swamp and Other Places: A Carolina Memoir* (New York: Free Press, 1983), 115, 135–136; Wright, *87 Years behind the Black Curtain,* 78; *First Mohonk Conference,* 23–24; Harvey, *Redeeming the South,* 124.

15. *SW,* Feb. 1873; Senate Report 695, *Removal of the Negroes from the Southern States,* 1:143; D. E. Williams, *A Brief Review of the Growth and Improvement of Education for Negroes in Florida, 1927–1962* (Atlanta: Southern Education Foundation, 1963), 15; Brodhead, *Journals of Charles W. Chesnutt,* 70; Thomas L. Sheppard to Thomas N. Chase, folder 1, box 10, Ware Papers; Jones, *Soldiers of Light and Love,* 131; John Wilson, interviewed by Horace Mann Bond, *Bond Papers.*

16. Gavin Wright, *Old South, New South: Revolutions in the Southern Economy since the Civil War* (Baton Rouge: Louisiana State University Press, 1996), 93; John M. Gandy, autobiography, folder 6, box 1, Gandy Papers; William Pickens, *Bursting Bonds: The Heir of Slaves,* ed. William L. Andrews (1923; Bloomington: Indiana University Press, 1991), 4–5.

17. Virginia L. Adams to Booker T. Washington, 15 May 1888, in Harlan, *Booker T. Washington Papers,* 2:453.

18. William H. Johnson, "Autobiography," pp. 2–3, unpublished typescript, William Henry Johnson Papers, VSU; Hunter, *Review of Negro Life,* 30–31; Charles N. Hunter, "East Raleigh School, Second Session, 1879–1880," p. 1, unpublished typescript, n.d., Hunter Papers, Duke University; Pickens, *Bursting Bonds,* 5; Wright, *87 Years behind the Black Curtain,* 28, 85; Gandy, autobiography; *SW,* June 1876.

19. *SW,* May 1875, Mar. 1876, June 1876; Johnson, "Autobiography," 2.

20. Williams, *Education for Negroes in Florida,* 15; Eugenia M. Fulcher, "Dreams Do Come True: How Rural One- and Two-Room Schools Influenced the Lives of African-Americans in Burke County, Georgia, 1930–1955" (Ed.D.

diss., Georgia Southern University, 1999), 33, 47. Although these studies deal with a later period, much of their description of one-teacher schools is applicable to the late nineteenth century.

21. Gandy, autobiography; Pickens, *Bursting Bonds,* 10; Russell, *Adventures in Faith,* 14; *SW,* June 1873. On the pedagogy of the period, especially as practiced in the rural South, see also Leloudis, *Schooling the New South,* 13–16.

22. *SW,* Feb. 1873; Johnson, "Autobiography," 5; *The Twenty-Ninth Annual Report from the Department of Education* (Atlanta, 1901), 89.

23. Gandy, autobiography, n.p.; Hunter, *Review of Negro Life,* 30; Brodhead, *Journals of Charles W. Chesnutt,* 60; *SW,* May 1875; Johnson, "Autobiography," 9.

24. Murray, *Proud Shoes,* 235–236; Hunter, *Review of Negro Life,* 30.

25. Brodhead, *Journals of Charles W. Chesnutt,* 61–62; James Weldon Johnson, *Along This Way: The Autobiography of James Weldon Johnson* (1933; New York: Penguin, 1990), 108–109; Hunter, *Review of Negro Life,* 23; Sterling, *We Are Your Sisters,* 379.

26. *SW,* Mar. 1872, Nov. 1872, Dec. 1872, Feb. 1873, Nov. 1874.

27. *SW,* Feb. 1873; Hunter, "East Raleigh School"; John H. Haley, *Charles N. Hunter and Race Relations in North Carolina* (Chapel Hill: University of North Carolina Press, 1987), 180–181; Dorothy Redus Robinson, *The Bell Rings at Four: A Black Teacher's Chronicle of Change* (Austin: Madrona Press, 1978), 122–123.

28. Senate Report 695, *Removal of the Negroes from the Southern States,* 1:142–143, 464–465, 538–539; Jeffrey R. Kerr-Ritchie, *Freedpeople in the Tobacco South, 1860–1900* (Chapel Hill: University of North Carolina Press, 1999), 171–173; *SW,* Aug. 1872; Brodhead, *Journals of Charles W. Chesnutt,* 61–62.

29. Brodhead, *Journals of Charles W. Chesnutt,* 74; Sherrill, "Negro School-Master," 166–169; Gandy, autobiography, folder 11, box 1, Gandy Papers.

30. Senate Report 512, *Mississippi in 1883,* 399, 547–548; *SW,* July 1875; Johnson, "Autobiography," 7; Louis R. Harlan, *Separate and Unequal: Public School Campaigns and Racism in the Southern Seaboard States, 1901–1915* (Chapel Hill: University of North Carolina Press, 1958), 214.

31. *SW,* Dec. 1874.

32. I. H. Tazewell, letter, *SW,* May 1875; unsigned letter, *SW,* May 1876; Julia A. Rutledge, letter, *SW,* Dec. 1872.

33. Augustus Prater to Thomas N. Chase, 18 Aug. 1875, folder 6, box 11, AUA; L., letter, *SW,* Nov. 1875.

34. James Weldon Johnson, *Along This Way: The Autobiography of James Weldon Johnson* (1933; New York: Penguin, 1990), 122.

35. Editorial, *SW,* Mar. 1876; Booker T. Washington, "The Colored Ministry:

Its Defects and Needs," 14 Aug. 1890, in Harlan, *Booker T. Washington Papers,* 3:72–73; unsigned letter, *SW,* June 1876.

36. Sherrill, "Negro School-Master," 167; Brodhead, *Journals of Charles W. Chesnutt,* 71; Wright, *87 Years behind the Black Curtain,* 31.

37. Brodhead, *Journals of Charles W. Chesnutt,* 72, 81; Johnson, *Along This Way,* 112, 118–119.

38. Edward T. Ware to Wickliffe Rose, 10 Dec. 1909, folder 6, box 28, Ware Papers. A partial exception to this generalization was South Carolina, where whites taught in the black public schools of Charleston, restricting the number of urban jobs available to black teachers.

39. Robert F. Engs, *Educating the Disfranchised and Disinherited: Samuel Chapman Armstrong and Hampton Institute, 1839–1893* (Knoxville: University of Tennessee Press, 1999), 80, 102–105; Anderson, *Education of Blacks,* 36–37, 55.

40. Anderson, *Education of Blacks,* 33–34, 67–78.

41. *SW,* Dec. 1874, Apr. 1875.

42. Ibid., Aug. 1872, June 1893; Engs, *Educating the Disfranchised,* 134–138.

43. *SW,* 1872–1876; Kerr-Ritchie, *Freedpeople in the Tobacco South,* 119–122.

44. Booker T. Washington to Edgar Gardner Murphy, 19 Oct. 1904, in Harlan, *Booker T. Washington Papers,* 8:103; Roscoe Conkling Bruce, "Tuskegee Institute," in Ogden, *From Servitude to Service,* 113; Washington, "A Speech before the New York Congregational Club," 16 Jan. 1893, in Harlan, *Booker T. Washington Papers,* 3:279.

45. "Twenty-Fifth Annual Report of the Principal," *SW,* June 1893; U.S. Commissioner of Education, *Report for 1891* (Washington: GPO, 1891), 961; Harlan, *Washington: The Making of a Black Leader,* 151; Booker T. Washington to William Leroy Broun, 15 Oct. 1890, and Washington to Wilson H. Reynolds, in Harlan, *Booker T. Washington Papers,* 3:87, 358–360; Mary Francis Albrier, interviewed by Malca Chall, 11 Nov. 1977, in *The Black Women Oral History Project: From the Arthur and Elizabeth Schlesinger Library on the History of Women in America, Radcliffe College,* ed. Ruth Edmond Hill (Westport, Conn.: Meckler, 1991), 1:207.

46. Washington to Broun, 15 Oct. 1890, and Washington to Wilson H. Reynolds, in Harlan, *Booker T. Washington Papers,* 3:87, 358–360; Richard D. Ralston, "American Episodes in the Making of an African Leader: A Case Study of Alfred B. Xuma," *International Journal of African Historical Studies* 6:1 (1973): 76–77.

47. Albrier interview, in Hill, *Black Women Oral History Project,* 1:214; Louis Harlan, *Booker T. Washington: The Wizard of Tuskegee, 1901–1915* (New York: Oxford University Press, 1983), 149; Holland, "Nathan B. Young," 64.

48. "Proceedings of the Triennial Reunion of the Hampton Alumni Association," 28 May 1893, and Washington, "The Progress of the Negro," 16 Jan. 1893, both in Harlan, *Booker T. Washington Papers,* 3:324–325, 284–285.

49. Washington, "The Work to be Done by Tuskegee Graduates," 28 Apr. 1895, in Harlan, *Booker T. Washington Papers,* 3:549–553.

50. House Report 261, *Condition of the South,* 224; Senate Report 695, *Removal of the Negroes from the Southern States,* 3:355; Bond, *Negro Education in Alabama,* 104; Horace Mann Bond, *Education of the Negro in the American Social Order* (New York: Prentice-Hall, 1934), 80–81, 108, 152–158; Noble, *Public Schools in Mississippi,* 141–142; *Report of John M. McKelroy, Superintendent of Public Instruction of the State of Alabama, for the Scholastic Year Ending September 30th, 1875* (Montgomery, 1875); *Thirty-First Annual Report of the Superintendent of Education of the State of Alabama* (Montgomery, 1886), 9–10; *Biennial Report of the Department of Education of the State of Alabama, 1899 and 1900* (Montgomery, 1900), x. The Alabama anomaly arose in part because low school enrollments often enabled state funds—which were allocated according to the school-age population rather than actual attendance—to be distributed among fewer teachers, a formula of particular benefit to African American teachers in the Black Belt counties.

51. Senate Report 695, *Removal of the Negroes from the Southern States,* 3:189; David Sanderson to Booker T. Washington, 11 Dec. 1889, in Harlan, *Booker T. Washington Papers,* 3:20–21.

52. Senate Report 695, *Removal of the Negroes from the Southern States,* 3:508; *Biennial Report of the State Superintendent of Public Instruction of Public Education [Louisiana], 1896–97* (Baton Rouge: The Advocate, 1898), 81–82; Noble, *Public Schools in Mississippi,* 81–82.

53. *Biennial Report of the Superintendent of Public Instruction of North Carolina for the Scholastic Years 1910 and 1911* (Raleigh, 1912), 70,76; *Biennial Report of the Superintendent of Public Instruction of North Carolina for the Scholastic Years 1919 and 1920* (Raleigh, 1920), 9. The comparison between 1911 and 1918–19 is inexact, but this does not affect the argument.

54. House Report 22, *Conditions of Affairs in the Late Insurrectionary States,* 11:448; Bond, *Education of the Negro,* 270–271; *Biennial Report of the Superintendent of Public Instruction for North Carolina, 1898–1900* (Raleigh, 1900), 117, 236.

55. Albert G. Davis to Booker T. Washington, 1 Nov. 1889, in Harlan, *Booker T. Washington Papers,* 3:14–15; Bond, *Education of the Negro,* 268; Edward L. Blackshear, *Future of the Negro: The Race Problem Discussed* (n.p., 1898), n.p.; Robinson, *Bell Rings at Four,* 40–42.

56. "History and Development of Negro Education in South Carolina" (Columbia: State Department of Education, 1949), 9–10, folder 1206, box 131, GEB Papers; "Conference of County Superintendents, Tennessee, Nash-

ville, April 8–9, 103," folder 2011, box 209, GEB Papers; *Annual Report of the Department of Education for the State of Alabama for the Scholastic Year Ending September 30, 1911* (Montgomery, 1911), 20–21.

57. Anderson, *Education of Blacks*, 111; Harvey, *Redeeming the South*, 168; Senate Report 695, *Removal of the Negroes from the Southern States*, 1:143, 538–539; Kelly Miller, "The Education of the Negro," in U.S. Commissioner of Education, *Education Report, 1900–1901* (Washington: GPO, 1902), 779–780; Johnson, "Autobiography," 10–11.

58. Harlan, *Booker T. Washington Papers*, 3:445; Kenneth B. Young, interviewed by Paul Ortiz, 12 July 1994, BTV; Lewis K. McMillan, *Negro Higher Education in the State of South Carolina* (Orangeburg, S.C.: Lewis K. McMillan, 1952), vii.

59. "Proceedings of the Triennial Reunion of the Hampton Alumni Association," 28 May 1893, in Harlan, *Booker T. Washington Papers*, 3:329–330, 332.

4. White Supremacy and Black Teachers

1. Frances Butler Simkins, *Pitchfork Ben Tillman, South Carolinian* (Gloucester, Mass.: P. Smith, 1964), 399; Stephen D. Kantrowitz, *Ben Tillman and the Reconstruction of White Supremacy* (Chapel Hill: University of North Carolina Press, 2000), 216; John Hope Franklin and Isodore Starr, eds., *The Negro in the Twentieth Century* (New York: Vintage, 1967), 67–69.

2. F. D. Jones and W. H. Mills, eds., *History of the Presbyterian Church in South Carolina since 1850* (Columbia: Synod of South Carolina, 1926), 269, 372; *Thirty-Fifth Annual Report of the Board of Missions for Freedmen* (Pittsburgh, 1905), *Thirty-Seventh Annual Report of the Board of Missions for Freedmen* (Pittsburgh, 1907), *Harbison College, Abbeville, South Carolina, 1908–1909*, all in folder 10, box 7, Seabrook Papers; "Thomas H. Amos," *Who's Who in Colored America*, n.p., n.d., 13–14; Inez M. Parker, *The Rise and Decline of the Program of Education for Black Presbyterians of the United Presbyterian Church, USA, 1865–1970* (San Antonio: Trinity University Press), 167–168.

3. *Abbeville Press and Banner*, 12 Sept. 1906, 23 Jan. 1907, 23 Mar. 1910; *College Catalogue* (Abbeville, S.C.: Harbison College, n.d.), 10; *Forty-Second Annual Report of the Board of Homeland Missions for Freedmen* (Pittsburgh, 1907); *Forty-Fifth Annual Report of the Board of Homeland Missions for Freedmen* (Pittsburgh, 1910); Fannie Amos Stewart to Thomas L. Jackson, 21 Nov. 1980, box 6, South Carolina Colleges/Universities Vertical File, USC; George B. Tindall, *South Carolina Negroes, 1877–1900* (Columbia: University of South Carolina Press, 1952), 225–226; McMillan, *Negro Higher Education*, 57; Harlan, *Separate and Unequal*, 201. The rival school of Rev. Williams—which Amos believed had schemed against him—

limped on for a few more years and finally closed in 1920. It was the only black school in the state sponsored by South Carolina's white Presbyterians.

4. Jones, *Negro Education,* 1:17; 2:12–13; Albert Salisbury, "The Supplementing of the War," *Journal of Proceedings and Addresses of the National Education Association, Session of the Year 1884* (Boston: NEA, 1885): 99–101.

5. Joseph E. Brown et al. to R. B. Bullock, "Report Board of Visitors on Examinations," 28 June 1871, folder 1, box 10, AUA; Range, *Rise and Progress of Negro Colleges,* 45; R. T. Hooker, "Avery Institute," *American Missionary* 36 (July 1882): 206; Ella A. Hamilton, "Teachers' Institute at Memphis," *American Missionary* 36 (Sept. 1882), 269; Leo M. Favrot, "School Provision for Negro Children," address at Teachers College, Columbia University, 2 Mar. 1932, typescript, p. 6, folder 3049, box 292, GEB Papers; *Atlanta University Bulletin,* Apr. 1911.

6. Henry M. Tupper, *Annual Report, 1883,* in idem, *Narrative,* 2–3; Horace Bumstead to J. L. M. Curry, 25 Sept. 1897, folder 2, box 21, AU; U.S. Commissioner of Education, *Education Report, 1890–91* (Washington: GPO, 1891), 966–967.

7. Maxine D. Jones and Joe M. Richardson, *Talladega College: The First Century* (Tuscaloosa: University of Alabama Press, 1990), 40–42; Range, *Rise and Progress of Negro Colleges,* 44–45, 60–61.

8. Du Bois, "Atlanta University," in Ogden, *From Servitude to Service,* 122; McMillan, *Negro Higher Education,* 136; Drago, *Initiative, Paternalism, and Race Relations,* 103.

9. C. Vann Woodward, *The Strange Career of Jim Crow* (New York: Oxford University Press, 1966), 31–65.

10. Clarice T. Campbell and Oscar A. Rogers, *Mississippi: The View from Tougaloo* (Jackson: University Press of Mississippi, 1979), 103; McPherson, *Abolitionist Legacy,* 177; Robert G. Sherer, *Subordination or Liberation: The Development of Conflicting Theories of Education in Nineteenth Century Alabama* (Tuscaloosa: University of Alabama Press, 1977), 24, 33–34; Bond, *Negro Education in Alabama,* 108–111; Leloudis, *Schooling the New South,* 74; Bond, *Negro Education in Alabama,* 108, 139–140; Logan, *The Negro in North Carolina,* 143–144; George R. Woolfolk, *Prairie View: A Study in Public Conscience, 1878–1946* (New York: Pageant Press, 1962), 40–46; Charles Vincent, "Laying the Cornerstone at Southern University," *Louisiana History* 17 (Summer 1976): 337; John A. Hardin, *Fifty Years of Segregation: Black Higher Education in Kentucky, 1904–1954* (Lexington: University of Kentucky Press, 1997), 4–5; Leadell W. Neyland and John W. Riley, *History of Florida Agricultural and Mechanical University* (Gainesville: University of Florida Press, 1963), 8–10; Chester Wilbert

Wright, "A History of the Black Land-Grant Colleges, 1890–1916" (Ph.D. diss., American University, 1981), 78, 83–86; J. L. M. Curry, *A Brief Sketch of George Peabody and a History of the Peabody Education Fund through Thirty Years* (Cambridge: Cambridge University Press, 1898), 61–65; McAfee, *Religion, Race, and Reconstruction,* 16. The Republican state government in Mississippi had created Alcorn University and Holly Springs State Normal; it also gave an annual subsidy to Tougaloo College, a private institution founded by the AMA. South Carolina gave a subsidy to Claflin University, run by the northern Methodists. Atlanta University and Hampton Institute, also AMA institutions, received state aid from, respectively, Georgia and Virginia. In Arkansas, the Republicans established Agricultural, Mechanical, and Normal College at Pine Bluff. Alabama's Republicans funded the State Normal School and University for Colored Teachers and Students in Marion. The Peabody Education Fund subsidized selected black and white schools, and also defrayed the cost of "summer normal schools" for white and black teachers. But it made no effort to promote racially mixed schools, and it allocated proportionately more money to white institutions.

11. Frenise A. Logan, "The Movement in North Carolina to Establish a State Supported College for Negroes," *North Carolina Historical Review* 35 (Apr. 1958): 167–180; Woolfolk, *Prairie View,* 73–84; Edgar Toppin, *Loyal Sons and Daughters: Virginia State University, 1882 to 1992* (Norfolk, Va.: Pictorial Heritage Pub. Co., 1992), 14, 51–52; Frederick Rudolph, *The American College and University: A History* (1962; Athens: University of Georgia Press, 1990), 252; Wright, "Black Land-Grant Colleges," 78, 83–86; Jones, *Negro Education,* 1:310. The Morrill Act of 1862 had offered substantial federal subsidies to the states, in the form of land, for the support of colleges that emphasized "agriculture and the mechanic arts." With this inducement, four states established schools for blacks or used Morrill money to subsidize black private schools. The Morrill Act of 1890 provided annual appropriations for state "Agricultural and Mechanical" colleges, but stipulated that funds must be "equitably divided" between "white and colored students." The southern states swallowed this condition. It presented no threat to racial segregation. Moreover, the Democrats could use the federal money to stint on state appropriations.

12. Davis, "State Normal Schools and A&M Colleges for Negroes, 1912–13 to 1921–22," Sept. 1924, p. 3, folder 3267, box 313, GEB Papers; *Annual Report of the Superintendent of Public Instruction of North Carolina, 1880,* and Charles W. Chesnutt, "Report for 1879–80" (27 Dec. 1880), both in folder 8, box 7, Seabrook Papers; *State Colored Normal School, Catalogue, 1883–84,* folder 8, box 8, Seabrook Papers, FSU; Logan, *Negro in North Carolina,* 144–145.

13. J. E. Schiele, "Concordia Parish," 11 May 1898, in *Biennial Report of the State Superintendent of Public Instruction, 1896–97* (Baton Rouge: The Advocate, 1898), 81–82.

14. J. Y. Joyner, *Biennial Report of the Superintendent of Public Instruction, 1904–1906* (Raleigh: E. M. Uzzell, 1907), 36.

15. Harlan, *Separate and Unequal*, 222, 255; Anderson, *Education of Blacks*, 97.

16. W. D. Weatherford, *Negro Life in the South: Present Conditions and Needs* (New York: Exposition Press, 1910, 1918), 36–38; Charles H. Smith, "Have Negroes Too Much Liberty?" *Forum* 16 (1893–94): 179; R. D. Rickoff, "Discussion," *Journal of Proceedings and Addresses of the National Education Association, Session of the Year 1890* (Topeka, Kans.: NEA, 1890): 520; Glenn quoted in Charles Francis Meserve, "Results of Attempts at the Higher Education of the Negro of the South," *Journal of the Proceedings and Addresses of the Southern Education Association, Atlanta, Georgia, December 29–31, 1908* (Chattanooga: SEA, 1909): 141; John Dittmer, *Black Georgia in the Progressive Era, 1900–1920* (Urbana: University of Illinois Press, 1977, 1980), 142.

17. Carl V. Harris, *Political Power in Birmingham, 1871–1921* (Knoxville: University of Tennessee Press, 1977), 173; Josephus Daniels, "The Progress of Southern Education," *Annals of the American Academy of Political and Social Sciences* 22 (1903): 311.

18. Daniels, "Progress of Southern Education," 310; T. H. W. McIntire to Charles A. Mebane, 7 Aug. 1900, in *Biennial Report of the Superintendent of Public Instruction of North Carolina, 1899–1900,* 117; *Twenty-Ninth Annual Report from the Department of Education* (Atlanta, 1901), 100.

19. John Hope Franklin, *Racial Equality in America* (Columbia: University of Missouri Press, 1976), 81.

20. Dittmer, *Black Georgia in the Progressive Era,* 99; letter to editor by Mark Johnson, and editorial "Shall We Blaze the Trail," both in *Atlanta Constitution,* 9 Oct. 1906, in folder 2, box 21, AUA; Hoke Smith, "Address of Welcome," *Proceedings of the Twelfth Conference for Education in the South* (Nashville, 1909), 17.

21. G. R. Glenn, "What the Negro Gets from the Common-School Education, and What He Gives to It," *Journal of the Proceedings of the National Education Association, Session of the Year 1898* (1898): 332; John W. Abercrombie, "Southern Education," *Journal of Proceedings and Addresses of the Southern Educational Association, 22nd Annual Meeting, Houston, Nov. 30–Dec. 2, 1911* (SEA, 1912): 46–47; W. H. Drane, "A Plea for Practical Education," *Journal of Proceedings and Addresses of the Southern Educational Association* (1906): 166.

22. C. N. Ousley, "Education of the Southern Negro," *Journal of Proceedings and Addresses of the Southern Educational Association, 22nd Annual Meeting,*

Houston, Nov. 30–Dec. 2, 1911 (SEA, 1912): 152; J. H. Phillips, "Essential Requirements of Negro Education," *Journal of Proceedings and Addresses of the Southern Educational Association* (1908): 125; George T. Winston, "Industrial Education for White and Black in the South," *SW,* Feb. 1901; J. L. M. Curry, "Education in the Southern States," *Proceedings of the First, Second, and Third Conferences for Christian Education in the South, 1898–1900* (1900), 25.

23. Abercrombie, "Southern Education," 47; J. H. Phillips, "Education of the Southern Negro," *Journal of Proceedings and Addresses of the Southern Educational Association, 22nd Annual Meeting, Houston, Nov. 30–Dec. 2, 1911* (SEA, 1912): 165; Joyner, *Biennial Report,* 37.

24. Winston, "Industrial Education"; Anderson, *Education of Blacks,* 85; Walter B. Hill, "Negro Education in the South," *Annals of the American Academy of Social and Political Sciences* 23 (1903): 322–323.

25. Phillips, "Education of the Southern Negro," 166; Phillips, "Essential Requirements of Negro Education," 127; Guy quoted in *Journal of Proceedings and Addresses of the Southern Educational Association, 24th Annual Meeting, Nashville, Oct. 30–Nov. 1, 1913* (SEA, 1914): 158; Hill, "Negro Education in the South," 326; Bishop T. D. Bratton, "The Christian South and Negro Education," *Proceedings of the Eleventh Conference for Education in the South* (Nashville: Committee on Publication, 1908), 89.

26. S. C. Mitchell, "The South and the School," *Proceedings of the Eighth Conference for Education in the South* (New York: Committee on Publication, 1905), 151–152; Harlan, *Separate and Unequal,* 138–139; Wallace Buttrick, "Conference of County Superintendents, Richmond, Virginia, January 14–16, 1903," n.p., folder 2011, box 209; idem, "Report of Conference with County School Commissioners, Athens, Georgia, September 10–12, 1902," 31, folder 3176, box 304; idem, "Conference of County Superintendents, New Orleans, Louisiana, Nov. 25–27, 1903," n.p., folder 2010, box 209, all in GEB Papers.

27. Alfred B. Hart, *The Southern South* (1910; New York: Negro Universities Press, 1969), 331; "Minutes of the Association of Educators of Colored Youth, 1894," p. 13, Internet text, Daniel A. P. Murray Pamphlet Collection, LC; Range, *Rise and Progress of Negro Colleges,* 68.

28. Michael R. Heintze, *Private Black Colleges in Texas, 1865–1954* (College Station: Texas A&M University Press, 1985), 47–48, 58–61; Anderson, *Education of Blacks,* 243; *Catalogue of St. Augustine's Normal School, 1889–90,* 11–14, *Catalogue of Shaw University, 1876–77,* 12–13; Miller, "Education of the Negro," 834–835; Drago, *Initiative, Paternalism, and Race Relations,* 82.

29. Edwin R. Embree, "Some Recent Developments in the Programs of the Julius Rosenwald Fund," 11 May 1937, folder 1, box 141, JRF Papers; W. E. B. Du Bois, "The College-Bred Negro," in U.S. Commissioner of Edu-

cation, *Education Report, 1901–1902* (Washington: GPO, 1902), 192; Miller, "Education of the Negro," 815–816, 832–833; W. T. B. Williams to Wallace Buttrick, 22 May 1907, box 4, W. T. B. Williams Papers, Tuskegee University; *Second Mohonk Conference on the Negro Question,* (1891; New York: Negro Universities Press, 1969), 52–53; *Atlanta University Bulletin,* Nov. 1885; Edward T. Ware, "Higher Education of Negroes in the United States," *Annals of the American Academy of Political and Social Sciences* 49 (Sept. 1913): 213–224; "General Survey for the Year Ending Sept. 30th, 1900," *American Missionary* 55 (Jan. 1901): 23; Anderson, *Education of Blacks,* 190–191, 249.

30. Kenneth R. Warlick, "Practical Education and the Negro College in North Carolina, 1880–1939" (Ph.D. diss., University of North Carolina, 1980), 178.

31. Herbert M. Kliebard, *The Struggle for the American Curriculum, 1893–1958* (New York: Routledge, 1995), 7–15; *Second Mohonk Conference,* 78–79; William T. Harris, "The Education of the Negro," in U.S. Commissioner of Education, *Education Report, 1890–91,* 975; Clarence A. Bacote, *The Story of Atlanta University: A Century of Service, 1865–1965* (Atlanta, Ga.: Atlanta University, 1969), 248.

32. Dittmer, *Black Georgia in the Progressive Era,* 142.

33. C. W. Bennett, "Third Report of Inspector of Schools in the South," 14 Jan. 1908, reel 1, FAS; Harlan, *Separate and Unequal,* 105.

34. Buttrick, "Conference of County Superintendents, Richmond"; Buttrick, "Conference of County Superintendents, New Orleans."

35. E. A. Ware, "Higher Education," *American Missionary* 35 (Dec. 1881): 392; "General Survey for the Year Ending Sept. 30th, 1900," *American Missionary* 55 (Jan. 1901): 23.

36. James G. Merrill, "Fisk University," in Ogden, *From Servitude to Service,* 217; Audrey Thomas McCluskey and Elaine M. Smith, eds., *Mary McLeod Bethune: Building a Better World* (Bloomington: Indiana University Press, 1999), 43; Horace Bumstead, "The Kind of University Most Needed in the South," *American Missionary* 36 (June 1882): 165.

37. Clarence A. Bacote, *The Story of Atlanta University: A Century of Service, 1865–1965* (Atlanta: Atlanta University, 1969), 24–25; Miller, "Education of the Negro," 833; Horace Bumstead, *President's Report, 1895,* folder 6, box 14, AUA; Anderson, *Education of Blacks,* 249; E. Horace Fitchett, "The Role of Claflin College in Negro Life in South Carolina," *JNH* 12 (Winter 1943): 54.

38. Drago, *Initiative, Paternalism, and Race Relations,* 82–83; Harold B. Dunkel, "Herbartianism Comes to America, Part I," *HEQ* 9 (Summer 1969): 202, 222–223; idem, "Herbartianism Comes to America, Part II," *HEQ* 9 (Au-

tumn 1969]: 376–387; Leloudis, *Schooling the New South,* 27–34; Ronald E. Butchart, "Punishments, Penalties, Prizes, and Procedures: A History of Discipline in U.S. Schools," in *Classroom Discipline in American Schools: Problems and Possibilities for Democratic Education,* ed. Ronald E. Butchart and Barbara McEwan (Albany: State University of New York Press, 1998), 25–27; *SW,* May 1874.

39. Bacote, *Story of Atlanta University,* 39; Fields, *Lemon Swamp,* 98–100.
40. McPherson, *Abolitionist Legacy,* 184–189; C. H. Richards, "The Future of the Negro in Our Country," *American Missionary* 44 (Mar. 1890): 93; C. W. Francis, "Atlanta University: Its Work," *American Missionary* 32 (Mar. 1878): 76.
41. Fields, *Lemon Swamp,* 97; *Shaw University, Catalogue* (1874–75, 1876–77, 1878–79); *Catalogue of St. Augustine's School, 1905–1906,* 10; Campbell and Rogers, *Mississippi,* 85–86; Heintze, *Private Black Colleges in Texas,* 161.
42. McPherson, *Abolitionist Legacy,* 189–193; Range, *Rise and Progress of Negro Colleges,* 126–141; Joe M. Richardson, *A History of Fisk University, 1865–1946* (Tuscaloosa: University of Alabama Press, 1980), 10, 17; *An Act to Incorporate Shaw University, 1870,* 7, in Tupper, *Narrative,* 31; *Catalogue of St. Augustine Normal School, 1892–93,* 18–19; Heintze, *Private Black Colleges in Texas,* 160–161; Fields, *Lemon Swamp,* 87.
43. Charles Francis Meserve, "Results of Attempts at the Higher Education of the Negro of the South," *Journal of the Proceedings and Addresses of the Southern Education Association, Houston, Nov. 30–Dec. 2, 1911* (1911): 136; E. A. Ware, "Atlanta University," *American Missionary* 32 (Mar. 1878): 75–76; Johnson, *Along This Way,* 68–69, 80; "Revival at Straight University," *American Missionary* 44 (Feb. 1890): 37; Clarkie M. Hughes, diary entry, 5 Jan. 1893, folder 17, box 1, Jones-Young Family Papers, USC; Gandy, "Experiences at Fisk," folder 13, box 1, Gandy Papers, VSU.
44. C. W. Bennett, "Fourth Annual Report," 10 Feb. 1908, reel 1, FAS; M. C. S. Noble to T. F. Toon, 18 Feb. 1901, box 16, Special Subject File, DNE (N.C.); Chesnutt, "Report for 1879–80."
45. George W. Henderson, "Straight University," *American Missionary* 53 (July 1899): 54–55.
46. Chesnutt, "Report for 1879–80"; E. E. Smith to John Duckett, 26 Oct. 1908, box 4, General Correspondence of the Director, Department of Public Instruction, Division of Negro Education, North Carolina State Archives, Raleigh; Benjamin E. Mays, *Born to Rebel: An Autobiography* (1971; Athens: University of Georgia Press, 1987), 38.
47. Tupper, "President's Annual Report, 1886," in *Narrative,* 3; Bennett, "Third Report of Inspector of Schools," n.p.
48. Elizabeth L. Wheeler, "Isaac Fisher: The Frustrations of a Negro Educator

at Branch Normal College, 1902–1911," *Arkansas Historical Quarterly* 41 (Spring 1982): 5; Brown, *Faithful, Firm, and True,* 93; catalogues of St. Augustine's Normal School for 1893–94 and 1905–06; *Atlanta University Bulletin,* Apr. 1911.

49. Chesnutt, "Report for 1878–80"; Chitty, "Brief History," n.p.; George C. Burrage, "Ballard Normal School," *American Missionary* 55 (Jan. 1901): 59.
50. Woodson, *Mis-Education of the Negro,* 1; Butchart, *Northern Schools, Southern Blacks,* 9, 53–57, 166–167, 200–207; Idus A. Newby, *Black Carolinians: A History of Blacks in South Carolina from 1895 to 1968* (Columbia: University of South Carolina Press, 1973), 111.
51. Jones, *Soldiers of Light and Love,* 140, 166; Butchart, *Northern Schools, Southern Blacks,* 153–154; Samuel T. Dutton, "Report of the Committee on Southern Educational Work," *American Missionary,* 55 (Jan. 1901): 44.
52. Cynthia G. Fleming, "The Effects of Higher Education on Black Tennesseeans after the Civil War," *Phylon* 44 (3rd Quarter 1983): 216; Kevin K. Gaines, *Uplifting the Race: Black Leadership, Politics, and Culture in the Twentieth Century* (Chapel Hill: University of North Carolina Press, 1996), 4; Butchart, *Northern Schools, Southern Blacks,* 166–167.
53. Campbell, *Songs of Zion,* 50–55.
54. Edith Starkey—To Whom it May Concern, n.d., box 3; John M. Gandy, "Horace and May Gandy—My Parents," n.d., 1–4, folder 5, box 1; "Entering School," n.d., 1–5, folder 6, box 1; untitled chapter, 1–5, folder 7, box 1; untitled fragment, n.p., folder 10, box 1; untitled fragments, n.p., folders 11 and 12, box 1; all in Gandy Papers, VSU.
55. Johnson, *Along This Way,* 81; W. E. B. Du Bois, *The Autobiography of W. E. B. Du Bois: A Soliloquy on Viewing My Life from the Last Decade of Its First Century* (New York: International, 1968), 109–111; Tupper, *Narrative,* 7–8; Harlan, *Washington: The Making of a Black Leader,* 73.
56. Arthur M. Cochran, "The Negro at the Beginning of the Twentieth Century," *American Missionary* 55 (Feb. 1901): 99; Johnson, *Along This Way,* 122.
57. Bumstead, "Kind of University Most Needed," 165; Janette T. Greenwood, *Bittersweet Legacy: The Black and White "Better Classes" in Charlotte, 1850–1919* (Chapel Hill: University of North Carolina Press, 1996), 83; Du Bois, *Autobiography,* 112; William H. Councill, *Synopsis of Three Addresses* (Normal, Ala., 1900), n.p., SCRBC; McPherson, *Abolitionist Legacy,* 201; Henry Allen Bullock, *A History of Negro Education in the South: From 1619 to the Present* (Cambridge, Mass.: Harvard University Press, 1967), vii.
58. C. C. Panter, "The Negro for His Place," *American Missionary* 35 (June 1881): 165; Richards, "Future of the Negro," 42–43; E. M. Cravath, "The Higher Education of the Negro," *American Missionary* 36 (Dec. 1882): 370–371; Dutton, "Committee on Southern Educational Work," ibid. 55 (Jan.

1901): 41–42; Augustus F. Beard, "Concerning Human Rights," *American Missionary* 52 (Dec. 1898): 202; Ware, "Higher Education of Negroes," 218.

59. Du Bois, "College-Bred Negro," 207; G. S. Dickerman to Edward T. Ware, 30 Nov. 1910, folder 9, box 28, AUA; Arthur F. Raper, *Preface to Peasantry: A Tale of Two Black Belt Counties* (1936; New York: Atheneum, 1968), 333.

60. Anderson, *Education of Blacks,* 111; Sutton, "Education of the Southern Negro"; Jones, *Negro Education,* 1:3, 12.

61. John M. Gandy, "Virginia State College: A History, 1882–1943," folders 33–34, box 1, Gandy Papers; James Hugo Johnston, "Industrial Training," 1901, folder 41, box 1, Gandy Papers; Conference of County Superintendents, Virginia, 14–16 Jan., 1903, folder 2011, box 209, GEB Papers.

62. Patton, "Richard Robert Wright," 573–574, 589, 611–613; Elizabeth Ross Haynes, *The Black Boy of Atlanta* (1952; New York: G. K. Hall, 1997), 380; Joyner, *Biennial Report,* 35; Wright, *87 Years behind the Black Curtain,* 36; Arthur J. Klein, *Survey of Negro Colleges and Universities* (1929; New York: Negro Universities Press, 1969), 330. Wright gave the college-level students private tutoring in the classics so that they could complete their courses.

63. Rothrock, "Joseph Carter Corbin"; Woolfolk, *Prairie View,* 108–109, 158, 208.

64. Woolfolk, *Prairie View,* 128–129, 197.

65. Charles Vincent, *A Centennial History of Southern University and A&M College, 1880–1980* (Baton Rouge: Southern University, 1981), 23–65, 101–102.

66. Melerson Guy Dunham, *The Centennial History of Alcorn A&M College* (Hattiesburg: University and College Press of Mississippi, 1971), 42–42; *Jackson Morning,* 21 June 1916, newspaper clipping, folder 871, box 97, GEB Papers; Hardin, *Fifty Years of Segregation,* 30; Holland, "Nathan B. Young," 127–139.

67. Noble, *Public Schools in Mississippi,* 88–89, 110–111; Leo M. Favrot, "Report on Conference with State Superintendents of Education and State Agents of Schools for Negroes," 3 Jan. 1928, folder 2002, box 208, GEB Papers.

68. Wharton, *The Negro in Mississippi,* 252–253; Harlan, *Separate and Unequal,* 134, 166; Patton, "Richard Robert Wright," 591–592; Davis, "Normal Schools and A&M Colleges," 8–11, 17–23, 27, 32, 42.

69. Anderson, *Education of Blacks,* 190–191, 194–195; W. T. B. Williams, "The Outlook in Negro Education," *SW,* Nov. 1911; Williams-May, "Lucy Craft Laney," 225–232; Donald F. DeVore and Joseph Logsdon, *Crescent City Schools: Public Education in New Orleans, 1841–1991* (Lafayette: Center for Louisiana Studies, University of Southwestern Louisiana, 1991), 117–118; "The New Orleans School System Takes Another Tumble," *Southwestern*

Christian Advocate, 13 Oct. 1904, clipping in folder 1, box 4, Robert E. Jones Papers, ARC.

70. Blackshear, *Future of the Negro;* Charles N. Hunter to D. G. Fowle (14 Nov. 1889), B. A. Johnson to Hunter (12 Jan. 1900), both in box 2, Hunter Papers; Simon G. Atkins to P. Claxton (31 Jan. 1899), Atkins to J. S. Carr (2 May 1899), Atkins to Julius D. Dreher (23 Mar. 1899), all in box 1, Simon Green Atkins Papers, University Archives, C. G. O'Kelly Library, Winston-Salem State University.

71. James B. Dudley to Booker T. Washington, 23 Aug. 1903, in Harlan, *Booker T. Washington Papers,* 7:271–272; Atkins to [?], n.d., box 1, Atkins Papers, WSSU.

72. T. Thomas Fortune to Charles N. Hunter, 21 Mar. 1899, box 2, Hunter Papers, Duke University.

73. Gunnar Myrdal, *An American Dilemma: The Negro Problem and Modern Democracy,* 2 vols. (New York: Harper, 1944), 2:896.

5. The Founders

1. Washington, *Up from Slavery,* 69–71.

2. Many private schools were actually public-private hybrids. Although Tuskegee Institute received a subsidy from the state of Alabama, most of its funds soon came from private sources.

3. Culp, "Prof. S. G. Atkins," in *Twentieth Century Negro Literature,* n.p.; Nathan C. Newbold, *Five North Carolina Negro Educators* (Chapel Hill: University of North Carolina Press, 1939), 4–6; Glenda E. Gilmore, *Gender and Jim Crow: Women and the Politics of White Supremacy in North Carolina, 1896–1920* (Chapel Hill: University of North Carolina Press, 1996), 35; Haley, *Charles N. Hunter,* 59–61; Yandle, "Joseph Charles Price," pt. 2, 145; S. G. Arkins to Charles N. Hunter (30 Sept. 1886), Atkins to D. G. Fowle (14 Nov. 1889), box 2, Hunter Papers, Duke University.

4. Atkins to C. H. Mebane (25 Oct. 1899), Atkins to Robert R. Moton (27 July 1900), box 1; faculty minutes, 30 Sept. ledger, box 9; *Industrial Education in the South: The Negro Problem Being Solved: Hampton, Tuskegee, Slater* [1900]; all in Atkins Papers, WSSU.

5. Leloudis, *Schooling the New South,* 146; Henry E. Fries to J. Y. Joyner (11 June 1903), D. B. Eaton et al. to Joyner (1 June 1903), box 16, DNE (N.C.); Newbold, *Five North Carolina Negro Educators,* 9; Knight, *Public School Education in North Carolina,* 325; Atkins to E. P. Graham, 31 Aug. 1928, folder 9, box 2, Atkins Papers, WSSU.

6. Atkins to Dear Sir, 23 Nov. 1903, folder 8, box 2; *Normal/Academic Curriculum* (Winston-Salem: Slater Industrial and Normal School, 1907), folder

46, box 4; Board of Trustees, minutes, 4 Feb. 1899, box 7, all in Atkins Papers; S. G. Atkins, "Should the Negro Be Given an Education Different from That Given to Whites?" in Culp, *Twentieth-Century Negro Literature,* 81; Newbold, *Five North Carolina Negro Educators,* 31.

7. Mary McLeod Bethune, "Spiritual Autobiography" (1946), in McCluskey and Smith, *Mary McLeod Bethune,* 54.

8. Audrey Thomas McCluskey, "Mary McLeod Bethune and the Education of Black Girls in the South, 1904–1923" (Ph.D. diss., Indiana University, 1991), 50–60; "Charles S. Johnson, Interview with Bethune," in McCluskey and Smith, *Mary McLeod Bethune,* 44.

9. McCluskey and Smith, *Mary McLeod Bethune,* 42; McCluskey, "Mary McLeod Bethune," 61, 67.

10. McCluskey and Smith, *Mary McLeod Bethune,* 50–51.

11. McCluskey, "Mary McLeod Bethune," 136–139; McCluskey and Smith, *Mary McLeod Bethune,* 48–49.

12. McCluskey and Smith, *Mary McLeod Bethune,* 5, 47, 51, 57.

13. Ibid., 47–48

14. Ibid., 53–54; Audrey Thomas McCluskey, "Ringing Up a School: Mary McLeod Bethune's Impact on Daytona," *Florida Historical Quarterly* 73 (Oct. 1994): 201–204.

15. McCluskey and Smith, *Mary McLeod Bethune,* 67–68, 76–79; McCluskey, "Ringing Up a School," 210–212; McCluskey, "Mary McLeod Bethune," 195–196; Helen Ludlow, "The Bethune School," *SW,* Mar. 1912; "A Press Release of Washington's Tour of Florida," 8 Mar. 1912, in Harlan, *Booker T. Washington Papers,* 11:486.

16. Cheryl Gilkes, Lucy Mitchell Miller interview, in Hill, *Black Women Oral History Project,* 8:17–20.

17. McCluskey and Smith, *Mary McLeod Bethune,* 68–69, 81. Mrs. Ferris L. Meigs to Bethune (28 Nov. 1934), Bethune to Myrtle Dean (25 Jan. 1934), both in reel 1, Bethune to Gerald E. Allen (14 May 1937), reel 3, in Randolph H. Boehm, ed., *Mary McLeod Bethune Papers: The Bethune-Cookman College Collection, 1922–1955,* microfilm, 13 reels (Bethesda, Md.: University Publications of America, 1995).

18. McCluskey and Smith, *Mary McLeod Bethune,* 68, 92–94; McCluskey, "Mary McLeod Bethune," 220; A. Fiot to Bethune, 12 Apr. 1935, in Boehm, *Bethune Papers,* reel 2.

19. A. W. Pegues, *Our Baptist Ministers and Schools* (1892; New York: Johnson Reprint Corp., 1970), 53–54.

20. Morris, *Sermons, Addresses and Reminiscences,* 17.

21. Sherer, *Subordination or Liberation,* 4, 176 n. 1; McMillan, *Negro Higher Education,* 35; Russell, *Black Baptist Secondary Schools,* 49–103; Whitted, *Ne-*

gro Baptists of North Carolina, 167, 183, 186; Lawrence H. Williams, *Black Higher Education in Kentucky, 1879–1930: A History of Simmons University* (Lewiston/Queenston: Edwin Mellen Press, 1987), 27, 181–191.

22. W. T. B. Williams, "The Outlook in Negro Education," *SW,* Nov. 1911.

23. Whitted, *Negro Baptists of North Carolina,* 183–185; W. T. B. Williams, "Colored Training and Industrial School, Faison, N.C.," 26 Feb. 1910, box 5, W. T. B. Williams Papers, TU.

24. David E. Cloyd to Wallace Buttrick, 17 Dec. 1902; John Marks and Jonas Henderson, "Leland University," 16 Dec. 1902; W. H. Heck, "Leland University, New Orleans, Louisiana," 6 Apr. 1904; all in box 79, GEB Papers.

25. Mary C. Reynolds to Wallace Buttrick, 27 Dec. 1905, folder 741, box 84, GEB Papers.

26. Ibid.; David E. Cloyd to Wallace Buttrick, "Coleman College," 22 Dec. 1902, folder 741, box 84, and Jackson Davis, "Coleman College," 6 Mar. 1918, folder 742, box 84, both in GEB Papers; Sue Eakins, "The Black Struggle for Education in Louisiana, 1877–1930s" (Ph.D. diss., University of Southwestern Louisiana, 1980), 82–91; O. L. Coleman to Leo M. Favrot, 3 Apr. 1920, Superintendent Records, 1904–1923, Department of Education, Louisiana State Archives, Baton Rouge.

27. Coleman to Favrot, 3 Apr. 1920; Vincent, *Centennial History of Southern University,* 74–76; John B. Cade, "The Education of Negroes in Louisiana," in *The African American Experience in Louisiana: Part C: From Jim Crow to Civil Rights,* ed. Charles Vincent (Lafayette: Center for Louisiana Studies, University of Louisiana, 2002), 232; Eula Lee Brown, interviewed by Felix Armfield, 16 July 1994, audio recording, tape 1, BTV. During the 1920s, J. S. Jones worked as the Rosenwald Fund's building agent for Louisiana.

28. Eakins, "Black Struggle for Education," 93–97; Hicks, *History of Louisiana Negro Baptists,* 103–104, 133–134; Leo M. Favrot, "Inspection of Public Schools, Sabine Parish," Oct. 1916, and Favrot, "Monthly Report," Mar. 1917, both in roll 69, "Early Southern Programs: Louisiana," *GEB Archives* (La.).

29. Alfred W. Nicholson, *Brief Sketch of the Life and Labors of Rev. Alexander Bettis* (Trenton, S.C.: author, 1913; electronic ed., Public Affairs Library, University of North Carolina, Chapel Hill, 2001), 8–13, 23–38, 56–58.

30. McMillan, *Negro Higher Education,* 22–35, 119–120, 139–140, 152–155; Raymond Gavins, *The Perils and Prospects of Southern Black Leadership: Gordon Blaine Hancock, 1884–1970* (Durham, N.C.: Duke University Press, 1977), 14–15.

31. Edward C. Mitchell, "Higher Education and the Negro," in *Report of the Commissioner of Education, 1894–95* (Washington: GPO, 1896), 1365–66.

32. McMillan, *Negro Higher Education,* 67; Six students to Warren Logan and Washington, July 26, 1890, in Harlan, *Booker T. Washington Papers,* 3:70–

71; J. Kenneth Morris, *Elizabeth Evelyn Wright, 1872–1906: Founder of Voorhees College* (Sewanee, Tenn.: University of the South, 1983), 22–37.

33. Morris, *Elizabeth Evelyn Wright*, 45–71.
34. Ibid., 82–100, 160–161.
35. McMillan, *Negro Higher Education*, 65–67; Morris, *Elizabeth Evelyn Wright*, 101–104; Elizabeth E. Wright to Washington, June 6, 1898, in Harlan, *Booker T. Washington Papers*, 4:431–433.
36. McMillan, *Negro Higher Education*, 69–72; Jones, *Negro Education*, 2: 479; Morris, *Elizabeth Evelyn Wright*, 105–154; Wright to Washington, 6 June 1898.
37. Washington to William Howard Taft, 16 May 1911, in Harlan, *Booker T. Washington Papers*, 11:158–159.
38. Robert E. Park to Washington, 1 Mar. 1912, in Harlan, *Booker T. Washington Papers*, 12:129–130; Kantrowitz, *Ben Tillman*, 176. Mayfield, a political ally of Ben Tillman, advocated black disenfranchisement, and, according to Kantrowitz, "arranged a lynching" in 1893.
39. Williams, "Colored Training and Industrial School," 26 Feb. 1910, box 5, Williams Papers, TU; Morris, *Elizabeth Evelyn Wright*, 100, 206; McMillan, *Negro Higher Education*, 258.
40. McMillan, *Negro Higher Education*, 60.
41. William James Edwards, *Twenty-Five Years in the Black Belt* (Boston: Cornhill Co., 1918; electronic ed., Academic Affairs Library, University of North Carolina, Chapel Hill, 1997), 2–20, 35; Donald P. Stone, *Fallen Prince: William James Edwards, Black Education, and the Quest for Afro-American Nationality* (Snow Hill, Ala.: Snow Hill Press, 1990), 44–69.
42. Stone, *Fallen Prince*, 71–72, 101–102; "An Account of the Tuskegee Negro Conference, Feb. 20–21, 1895," in Harlan, *Booker T. Washington Papers*, 3:526–527; Washington to Jacob Henry Schiff, 18 Sept. 1909, in Harlan, *Booker T. Washington Papers*, 10:175.
43. Edwards, *Twenty-Five Years*, 37; Stone, *Fallen Prince*, 79–80.
44. Edwards, *Twenty-Five Years*, 30, 36; Stone, *Fallen Prince*, 85, 270.
45. Edwards, *Twenty-Five Years*, 42–55; Stone, *Fallen Prince*, 125–127, 156, 166–170; Cynthia Griggs Fleming, *In the Shadow of Selma: The Continuing Struggle for Civil Rights in the Rural South* (Lanham, Md.: Rowman and Littlefield, 2004), 42–43; State Department of Education, Alabama, "Report of a Survey of Wilcox County Schools, 1929–1930," folder 12-6-14, box 1, Georgia Division of Negro Education, Georgia Department of Archives and History, Atlanta.
46. Eakins, "Black Struggle for Education," 229–241; Mildred D. G. Gallot, *A History of Grambling State University* (Lanham, Md.: University Publications of America, 1985), xiii–xiv, 2–23; Fidelia Adams Johnson, interviewed by Lucy Brown Franklin, in Hill, *Black Women Oral History Pro-*

ject, 6:248–249; Thomas Jesse Jones to Booker T. Washington for Mr. Schiff, 23 July 1914, folder 2, box 44, PSF Papers; Leo M. Favrot, report, Oct. 1916, folder 772, box 87, GEB Papers; Professor Hill to Thomas Jesse Jones, 17 Apr. 1916, folder 47, box 8, Robert R. Moton Papers, Hollis Burke Frissell Library, Tuskegee University, Tuskegee, Alabama. The Allen Greene school was named after the white carpetbagger who had sold the land.

47. Henry S. Enck, "Black Self-Help in the Progressive Era: The 'Northern Campaigns' of Smaller Black Industrial Schools," *JNH* 61 (Jan. 1976): 73–87; Professor Hill to Thomas Jesse Jones, 6 Feb. 1916, folder 47, box 8, Moton Papers, TU.

48. Anderson, *Education of Blacks,* 258; Thomas Jesse Jones to Rossa B. Cooley, 15 Mar. 1929, folder 1014a, box 133, Moton Papers; Eric Anderson and Alfred A. Moss, *Dangerous Donations: Northern Philanthropy and Southern Black Education, 1902–1931* (Columbia: University of Missouri Press, 1999), 212–213.

49. Anderson and Moss, *Dangerous Donations,* 85; William H. Baldwin to Robert R. Moton, 3 Sept. 1928, and Baldwin to Harry Simms, 15 Aug. 1927, folder 882, box 120; Thomas Jesse Jones to Moton, 3 Aug. 1926, folder 936, box 125; Jackson Davis to Jones, n.d., folder 1035, box 133; Susie N. Edwards to Mrs. Phelps Stokes, 7 Aug. 1928, and Jones to Phelps Stokes, 21 Aug. 1928, folder 1041b, box 133; all in Moton Papers, TU.

50. Jones, *Negro Education,* 2:614–615; Russell, *Adventures in Faith;* Anderson and Moss, *Dangerous Donations,* 30–31, 142–146; www.saintpauls.edu (16 May 2006). St. Pauls was spelled without an apostrophe until 1941.

51. Emmanuel M. McDuffie, "Sketch of My Life," in Edwards, *Twenty-Five Years,* 68–70.

52. Ibid., 71; W. A. Robinson, "Report on School Situation for Negroes in Laurinburg, N.C." (8 July 1926), Maxcy L. John to N. C. Newbold (19 Aug. 1927), Newbold to John (24 Aug. 1927), all in box 4, DNE (N.C.); www.scotlandcounty.org/History.htm (16 May 2006); Jones, *Negro Education,* 2:437–448; Jackson Davis to Alex H. Sands, folder 5, box 75, SEF Papers.

53. Charles W. Wadelington and Richard F. Knapp, *Charlotte Hawkins Brown and Palmer Memorial Institute: What One Young African American Woman Could Do* (Chapel Hill: University of North Carolina Press, 1999), 228 n. 1; www.laurinburginstitute.com (accessed 23 Nov. 2004); Ronald Roach, "A Rich, but Disappearing Legacy: Remembering Black Boarding Schools: A Tradition Obscured by Desegregation's Impact," *Black Issues in Higher Education,* 14 Aug. 2003, in Find Articles, www.findarticles.com (17 May 2006).

54. Charlotte Hawkins Brown, "Autobiography," n.d., 17, folder 1, reel 1; Brown, "Some Incidents in the Life and Career of Charlotte Hawkins

Brown Growing out of Racial Situations, at the Request of Dr. Ralph Bunche," (1939–1940), 1–3, folder 2, reel 1, both in Charlotte Hawkins Brown Papers (microfilm), Schlesinger Library, Radcliffe College; Wadelington and Knapp, *Charlotte Hawkins Brown,* 14–17.

55. Brown, "Autobiography," 16–19; Brown, "Some Incidents," 5; Wadelington and Knapp, *Charlotte Hawkins Brown,* 20–35.

56. Brown, "Some Incidents," 3, 9; Cecie Jenkins, "The Twigbender of Sedalia," [1946], folder 7, reel 1, Charlotte Hawkins Brown Papers.

57. Wadelington and Knapp, *Charlotte Hawkins Brown,* 38–45; Brown, "Some Incidents," 5.

58. Wadelington and Knapp, *Charlotte Hawkins Brown,* 45–51, 58–59, 78–80; Gilmore, *Gender and Jim Crow,* 183–189; Sandra N. Smith, "Charlotte Hawkins Brown," *JNE* 51 (Summer 1982): 193–195.

59. Wadelington and Knapp, *Charlotte Hawkins Brown,* 77–78; Gilmore, *Gender and Jim Crow,* 184.

60. Brown, "Some Incidents," 8; Jenkins, "Twigbender of Sedalia"; Wadelington and Knapp, *Charlotte Hawkins Brown,* 173–174; Constance Hill Marteena, *The Lengthening Shadow of a Woman* (Hicksville, N.Y.: Exposition Press, 1977), 73; Smith, "Charlotte Hawkins Brown," 196–201.

61. Wadelington and Knapp, *Charlotte Hawkins Brown,* 68, 73, 110–163; Jones, *Negro Education,* 2:419; "Report of Graduates of Palmer Institute," 20 Feb. 1917, reel 4, Charlotte Hawkins Brown Papers; *Palmer Memorial Institute Bulletin, 1935–36,* folder 58, reel 4, Charlotte Hawkins Brown Papers; Leslie Alexander Lacy, *The Rise and Fall of a Proper Negro* (New York: Macmillan, 1970), 52.

62. Jones, *Negro Education,* 1:8–9, 14–17, 49; "Conference of the GEB [General Education Board] of the Rockefeller Fund on 'Negro Education,'" 29 Nov. 1915, report 17, series 7, GEB Papers.

63. McMillan, *Negro Higher Education,* 8–9. The situation in Laurinburg, N.C., was exceptional only in how long the private school monopolized black education.

64. J. Silsby to M. E. Strieby, 3 Aug. 1880, roll 6, AMA Papers (Tenn.); Wallace Buttrick, untitled report on Negro education, 12 June 1903, folder 3176, box 304, GEB Papers.

65. Eric Anderson, *Race and Politics in North Carolina, 1872–1901: The Black Second* (Baton Rouge: Louisiana State University Press, 1981), 327–329.

6. The Faith of Women

1. Sarah Rice, *He Included Me: The Autobiography of Sarah Rice,* transcribed and ed. Louise Westling (Athens: University of Georgia Press, 1989), 1–4, 52–57, 68–75.

2. N. C. Newbold, "Outline of Some Activities of the State Agent of Negro

Schools and His Associates," 18 Nov. 1938, folder 1045, box 115, GEB Papers; Jackson Davis, "Negro Colleges," 1932, folder 3195, box 692, GEB Papers; Mississippi Department of Education, "Program for Improvement of Instruction," paper submitted to Conference of State Superintendents of Education in the South with Officers of the GEB, 16 Dec. 1938, folder 4288, box 408, GEB Papers; P. Easom to Directors of Negro Summer Schools, "Third Follow-Up," 10 July 1950, folder 4, box 76, SEF Papers; Caliver, "Education and Placement of Negro Teachers," 99; Carroll L. Miller and Howard D. Gregg, "The Teaching Staff," *JNE* 1 (July 1932): 205–207; Fred McCuiston, *The South's Negro Teaching Force* (Nashville: Julius Rosenwald Fund, 1931), 7–8, 19; Ambrose Caliver, *Education of Negro Teachers* (Washington: GPO, 1933), 10–14, 96–97. The number of students enrolled in college-level courses at black colleges and universities increased from 5,231 in 1921–22 to 22,769 ten years later.

3. U.S. Commissioner of Education, *Education Report, 1917* (Washington, 1917), 76.

4. *Atlanta University Bulletin,* Apr. 1911. More than half of the normal graduates of Atlanta University became teachers, compared with 39 percent of the college graduates.

5. Charles S. Johnson, *The Negro College Graduate* (Chapel Hill: University of North Carolina Press, 1938), 108–109; "Work, Watch, Wait, Work: Facts, Ideas, and Suggestions Developed in Conference Concerning the Education of Negro Children in Small High Schools," [1938], 16, 19–20, folder 1471, box 158, GEB Papers.

6. U.S. Commissioner of Education, *Education Report, 1917,* 76; *Report of John M. McKelroy, Superintendent of Public Instruction of the State of Alabama, for the Scholastic Year Ending Sep. 30, 1875* (Montgomery, 1875); *Annual Report of the Department of Education of the State of Alabama for the Scholastic Year Ending Sep. 30, 1911* (Montgomery, 1911); *Report of the State School Commissioner of Georgia for 1892* (Atlanta, 1893); *Thirty-Ninth Annual Report of the Department of Education* (Atlanta, 1911), 443; U.S. Commissioner of Education, *Education Report, 1928* (Washington, 1928), table 35; Michael Fultz, "African-American Teachers in the South, 1890–1940: Growth, Feminization, and Salary Discrimination," *Teachers College Record* 96 (1995): 544–568, http://www.tcrecord.org (8 Feb. 2006).

7. Leander L. Boykin, "The Status and Trends of Differentials between White and Negro Teacher' Salaries in the Southern States, 1900–1946," *JNE* 18 (Winter 1949): 41–42. Individual counties disclosed even more extreme inequalities. In the Georgia counties of Macon and Greene in 1930, for example, black teachers earned a quarter of what white teachers earned. Four years later the Great Depression had lowered that proportion to 14 percent. See Raper, *Preface to Peasantry,* 331.

8. *Annual Report of the State Superintendent of Education of Louisiana for the Session, 1924–1925* (Baton Rouge, 1926); *Fifty-First Annual Report of the State Superintendent of Education, 1919* (Columbia, S.C.: Gonzales and Bryan, 1920), 43–44, 167; W. T. B. Williams to T. E. Rivers, July 8, 1920, box 6, W. T. B. Williams Papers, TU.

9. Charlotte Hawkins Brown, "The Role of the Negro Woman in the Fight for Freedom," June 1943, 5, folder 14, reel 1, Charlotte Hawkins Brown Papers.

10. Robinson, *Bell Rings at Four,* 45.

11. Hortense Powdermaker, *After Freedom: A Cultural Study in the Deep South* (1937; New York: Atheneum, 1969), 211, 299, 309.

12. Russell, *Adventures in Faith,* 1–4. See also the similar testimony of Robert R. Moton in Hughes and Patterson, *Robert Russa Moton,* 8, 11.

13. McCluskey and Smith, *Mary McLeod Bethune,* 36, 53; Charlotte Hawkins Brown, "Autobiography," 14–15, folder 1, reel 1, Charlotte Hawkins Brown Papers.

14. Jacqueline Jones, *Labor of Love, Labor of Sorrow: Black Women, Work and the Family from Slavery to the Present* (New York: Vintage, 1986), 96–97, 222; Johnson, *Along This Way,* 11; biography, n.d., folder 2, box 1, Robert E. Jones Papers, ARC.

15. Edith Polk, interviewed by Kate Ellis, 2 Aug. 1994, BTV; Pickens, *Bursting Bonds,* 7.

16. Haynes, *Black Boy of Atlanta,* 301–313; Patton, "Richard Robert Wright" 53–60; Harlan, *Washington: The Making of a Black Leader,* 3–10; Ann P. Malone, *Sweet Chariot: Slave Family and Household Structure in Nineteenth-Century Louisiana* (Chapel Hill: University of North Carolina Press, 1992), 14–18, 254–263.

17. Jones, *Labor of Love, Labor Sorrow,* 62–65; Amy Dru Stanley, *From Bondage to Contract: Wage Labor, Marriage, and the Market in the Age of Slave Emancipation* (Cambridge: Cambridge University Press, 1998), 47–55.

18. Ambrose Caliver, *A Background Study of Negro College Students* (1933; Westport, Conn.: New Universities Press, 1970), 44; McCluskey and Smith, *Mary McLeod Bethune,* 37; Stewart E. Tolnay, *The Bottom Rung: African American Family Life on Southern Farms* (Urbana: University of Illinois Press, 1999), 106–119.

19. Johnson, *Growing Up in the Black Belt,* 58–59; family histories of Agnes Hardie (n.d), Malcolm B. Harwood (20 Jan. 1936), Alma S. Hastie (Aug. 1943), Gracie L. Hawkins (14 Mar. 1944), Lula Mae Haynsworth (n.d.), Geraldine B. Herndon (July 1944), Edna M. Henry (n.d.), Daisy T. Hicks (n.d.), Ann M. Hines (n.d.), Esther D. Holloway (n.d.), Gerha L. Howell (n.d.), John L. Hubbard (n.d.), Davis L. Hughes (27 Jan. 1936), Katherine Irving (n.d.), Mildred F. Jackson (n.d.), Alice May James (n.d.), Juanita C.

James (5 June 1946), Betsy R. Johnson (15 May 1942), Edith Johnson (n.d.), Elaine E. Johnson (n.d.), Gwendolyn Z. Johnson (n.d.), Lois P. Johnson (4 June 1946), Mignon P. Johnson (n.d.), William A. Johnson (27 Jan. 1936), Eloise F. Anderson (n.d.), all in E. Franklin Frazier Papers, MSRC.

20. Fulcher, "Dreams Do Come True," 165; Tolnay, *The Bottom Rung,* 39–42; Conference of State Agents of Rural Schools for Negroes, 5–6 June 1930, Atlantic City, 145, folder 2002, box 208, GEB Papers.

21. Mays, *Born to Rebel,* 20, 36. J. J. Starks also recalled encouragement from his mother rather than his father; John Jacob Starks, *Lo These Many Years: An Autobiographical Sketch* (Columbia S.C.: State Co., 1941), 20–22. There were exceptions, of course; see, for example, Jane Edna Hunter, *A Nickel and a Prayer* (Cleveland: Elli Kani Pub., 1940), 11–12.

22. Harlan, *Washington: The Making of a Black Leader,* 35; Patton, "Richard Robert Wright," 70–71; Simmons, *Men of Mark,* 279.

23. Lula Mae Haynesworth, student essay (n.d.), and Edith Johnson, student essay [1942], box 87, both in Frazier Papers; Jones, *Labor of Love, Labor of Sorrow,* 91; Tolnay, *The Bottom Rung,* 45–47; Raper, *Preface to Peasantry,* 340–341; *Report of the State School Commissioner of Georgia for 1892* (Atlanta, 1893), n.p.; *Ninth Annual Report of the City Schools of Columbia, South Carolina, 1891–92* (Columbia, 1892), 10.

24. U.S. Commissioner of Education, *Biennial Survey of Education, 1920–1922* (Washington: GPO, 1922), 70; Charles S. Johnson, *The Negro Public Schools: A Social and Educational Survey* (Baton Rouge: Louisiana Educational Survey, 1942), 18; *Commonwealth of Kentucky Educational Bulletin: Negro Education in Kentucky* (May 1943), box 1, series 12-6-4, Georgia Division of Negro Education.

25. Anderson, *Education of Blacks,* 275; Caliver, *Background Study,* 21–26; Ambrose Caliver, *A Personnel Study of Negro College Students* (1931; Wesport, Conn.: Negro Universities Press, 1970), 118; Ann Short Chirhart, *Torches of Light: Georgia Teachers and the Coming of the Modern South* (Athens: University of Georgia Press, 2005), 48–49.

26. A. C. Griggs et al., "Lucy Craft Laney," *JNH* 19 (Jan. 1934): 97–98; Jones, *Negro Education,* 2:236–237; Williams-May, "Lucy Craft Laney," 181; Oswald Garrison Villard to Wallace Buttrick, 17 Apr. 1905, folder 1937, box 203, GEB Papers.

27. Wright, *87 Years behind the Black Curtain,* 32; Torrence, *Story of John Hope,* 60.

28. Williams-May, "Lucy Craft Laney," 311–312, 363–365.

29. Anna Julia Cooper, *A Voice from the South* (Xenia, Ohio: Aldine, 1892; electronic ed., Academic Affairs Library, University of North Carolina, Chapel Hill), 28, 70, 76–77; *SW,* Aug. 1893.

30. Fannie Barrier Williams, "The Club Movement among Colored Women of

America," in *A New Negro for a New Century*, ed. John E. Brady (1900; Miami: Mnemosyne, 1969), 382; Anne Firor Scott, "Most Invisible of All: Black Women's Voluntary Associations," *Journal of Southern History* 56 (Feb. 1990): 12; Paula Giddings, *When and Where I Enter: The Impact of Black Women on Race and Sex in America* (New York: Morrow, 1984), 96–98; Debra Gray White, *Too Heavy a Load: Black Women in Defense of Themselves, 1894–1994* (New York: W. W. Norton, 1999), 27–39; Kathleen C. Berkeley, "'Black Women Also Contributed': Black Women's Activities from Benevolence to Social Welfare, 1866–1896," in *The Web of Southern Social Relations: Women, Family, and Education*, ed. Walter J. Fraser Jr., R. Frank Saunders Jr., and Jon C. Wakelyn (Athens: University of Georgia Press, 1985), 181–196. Williams-May, "Lucy Craft Laney," 262.

31. White, *Too Heavy a Load,* 27–33, 59, 73; Stephanie J. Shaw, "Black Club Women and the Creation of the National Association of Colored Women," in *"We Specialize in the Wholly Impossible": A Reader in Black Women's History*, ed. Darlene Clark Hine, Wilma King, and Linda Reed (Brooklyn, N.Y.: Carlson, 1995), 436–442.

32. Philip A. Bruce, *The Plantation Negro as a Freeman* (1889; Williamstown, Mass.: Corner House, 1970), 19; Cooper, *Voice from the South,* 204; Arthur W. Calhoun, *A Social History of the American Family,* 3 vols. (New York: Barnes and Noble, 1919, 1945, 1960), 2:291–292; 3:294; W. E. B. Du Bois, ed., *The Negro American Family* (Atlanta: Atlanta University Press, 1908), 41; Linda O. McMurry, *To Keep the Waters Troubled: The Life of Ida B. Wells* (New York: Oxford University Press, 1998), 13–14.

33. Brown to Galen S. Stone, [1921], folder 43, reel 1; Brown, "What the Negro Woman asks of the White Women of North Carolina," May 1928, folder 14, reel 1; both in Charlotte Hawkins Brown Papers.

34. Wadelington and Knapp, *Charlotte Hawkins Brown,* 64–65; Gilmore, *Gender and Jim Crow,* 195–202; Brown, scrapbook, 1937–1938, folder 8, reel 1, Charlotte Hawkins Brown Papers.

35. Brown, speech on Negro woman, fragment, [1944?], folder 43, reel 1; "Where We Are in Race Relations," 22 Oct. 1926, folder 14, reel 1; both in Charlotte Hawkins Brown Papers.

36. "President Negro State Teachers Association Carry Cause of Teachers before State School Commission," 1935; Brown, "Role of the Negro Woman," June 1943; "Where We Are in Race Relations," all in folder 14, reel 1, Charlotte Hawkins Brown Papers.

37. Unidentified correspondent to Mrs. C. B. McMahon, 20 Oct. 1921, folder 43, reel 3; Ceci Jenkins, "Twig Bender of Sedalia," draft chapter, [1946?], p. D, folder 7, reel 1; both in Charlotte Hawkins Brown Papers.

38. Rosa J. Young, Paul Ortiz interview, 12 July 1994, transcript, 38, BTV; George E. Cunningham, "Reasons for Belated Education: A Study of the

Plight of Older Teachers," *JNE* 27 (Spring 1958): 199; Robinson, *Bell Rings at Four,* 14.

39. Fulcher, "Dreams Do Come True," 68; Irene Monroe, Tywanna Wharley, and Mansiki Searles interview, 11 July 1994, transcript, 5, BTV.

40. "Report of Two or More Teacher Group," 15 Jan. 1938, reel 279, microfilm, Department of Education, Record Group 92, Tennessee State Archives, Nashville; J. L. Whiting, *Shop and Class at Tuskegee: A Definitive Story of the Tuskegee Correlation Technique, 1910–1930* (Boston: Chapman and Grimes, 1940), 32; "Report of the Workshop for Rural School Leaders, Grambling, Summer 1942," folder 4680, box 443, GEB Papers; "Ecological Surveys: Ascension Parish," folder 3, box 225, Charles S. Johnson Papers.

41. Bond, *Education of the Negro in the American Social Order,* 392; Alphonso Owens, Warren G. Palmer interview, [1977], transcript, n.p., Warren G. Palmer Oral History Collection, Ina Dillard Russell Library, Georgia College and State University, Milledgeville, Ga.; Whiting, *Shop and Class at Tuskegee,* 34–35.

42. Julia Taylor, Paul Ortiz interview, [1994], transcript, 212, BTV; Tate, Palmer interview; Owens, Palmer interview; Maenelle D. Dempsey, Palmer interview, 1977, recording; all in Palmer Collection.

43. "Ecological Surveys: Claiborne Parish," [1941–42], folder 3, box 225, Charles S. Johnson Papers; unsigned, "Special Report of Jeanes Teacher for School Year 1939–1940: Goochland County, Virginia," folder 6, box 145, SEF Papers.

44. "Ecological Surveys: Jefferson Davis Parish," [1941–42], folder 3, box 225, Charles S. Johnson Papers; Estelle Massey Riddle, "The Mineral Springs Community," [1934], folder 4, box 335, JRF Papers; Hitch, "Report on Negro Schools in Region III of Eastern Kentucky," 10–21 Nov. 1952, folder 3, box 75, SEF Papers.

45. Miller and Gregg, "The Teaching Staff," 209; W. Wallace Stewart, "Factors Affecting the Education of Negroes in Rural Communities in Louisiana," *JNE* 8 (Jan. 1939): 47; Ambrose Caliver, *Rural Elementary Education among Negroes under Jeanes Supervising Teachers* (Washington: GPO, 1933), 29.

46. W. T. B. Williams, "An Inviting Opportunity for the Negro Teacher," 5 Mar. 1919, box 6, Williams Papers, TU; John Hope, "Negro School and Community," [1932], folder 621, box 70, GEB Papers; William J. Reese, "The Origins of Progressive Education," *HEQ* 41 (Spring 2001): 23.

47. Virginia E. Randolph to James H. Dillard, folder 8, box 29, SEF Papers; Jackson Davis, "The Jeanes Visiting Teacher in the Southern States," n.d., folder 8, box 37, SEF Papers; Lance G. E. Jones, *The Jeanes Teacher in the United States, 1908–1933* (Chapel Hill: University of North Carolina Press, 1937), 22–30; Kliebard, *Struggle for the American Curriculum,* 11–14;

Booker T. Washington to James H. Dillard, 14 June 1909, folder 20, box 29, SEF Papers.

48. Harlan, *Washington: The Wizard of Tuskegee,* 194–196; Jones, *Jeanes Teacher,* 15–18, 41–43.

49. Wallace Buttrick to M. L. Brittain, 10 June 1913, and Brittain to George W. Godard, 23 Dec. 1913, folder 585, box 67, GEB Papers; Anderson, *Education of Blacks,* 66; John E. Fisher, *The John F. Slater Fund: A Nineteenth Century Affirmative Action for Negro Education* (Lanham, Md.: University Press of America, 1986), 139–147; S. L. Smith, *Builders of Goodwill: The Story of the State Agents of Negro Education in the South, 1910 to 1950* (Nashville: Tennessee Book Co., 1950), 3–31. Jackson Davis's position as state agent for Virginia was initially subsidized by the Peabody Fund; the GEB assumed the cost a year later. The work of two additional foundations, the Phelps-Stokes Fund (1911) and the Julius Rosenwald Fund (1917) meshed with that of the GEB and the Jeanes Fund in their support for industrial education. The fact that the men who administered these foundations constituted an interlocking directorate, sitting on each other's boards, magnified their influence.

50. Nathan C. Newbold, "First Biennial Report of the State Agent of Negro Schools, 1915," folder 1045, box 115; Jas. L. Sibley to H. J. Willingham, 27 Sept. 1913, folder 142, box 17; Stanley L. Smith, "Report for July 1915," folder 1466, box 158; Leo M. Favrot, "Report on Negro Summer Schools in the South in 1926," folder 3160, box 302; all in GEB Papers.

51. Leo M. Favrot, "Monthly Report for March 1917," folder 774, box 87, GEB Papers.

52. Samuel L. Smith, "Report for Oct. 1914," "Report for Oct. 1915," folder 1466, box 158, GEB Papers.

53. W. E. B. Du Bois and Augustus Granville Dill, eds., *The Common School and the Negro American* (Atlanta: Atlanta University Press, 1911), 105–106, reprinted in W. E. B. Du Bois, ed., *The Atlanta University Publications* (New York: Arno, 1968).

54. Jackson Davis, 1911 diary, 27 July 1911, www.lib.virginia.edu/speccol/jdavis/; Leo M. Favrot, "Monthly Report for February 1916," "Monthly Report for September 1914," Monthly Report for January 1916," all in folder 219, box 25, GEB Papers. The absence of school boards and county superintendents in Arkansas made it doubly difficult to influence the public school teachers. Schools in the rural areas fell under the authority of two sets of district boards, with black directors responsible for the black schools.

55. Anderson and Moss, *Dangerous Donations,* 87, 95, 220; William A. Link, *A Hard Country and a Lonely Place: Schooling, Society, and Reform in Virginia, 1870–1920* (Chapel Hill: University of North Carolina Press, 1986), 180.

56. Jones, *Jeanes Teacher,* append., "Virginia—Summary of Work of 23 Supervising Industrial Teachers, Session 1912–1913, n.p.

57. Virginia E. Randolph to James H. Dillard, 24 Jan. 1911; "Quilt Contest: Henrico County Schools," 10 Mar. 1911, 28 Nov. 1911, 12 Mar. 1911, all in folder 7, box 29, SEF Papers.

58. Randolph to Dillard, 14 Jan. 1914, 30 Jan. 1920, 4 Dec. 1924, 17 Oct. 1925, 27 June 1927, 27 July 1930, 14 Apr. 1931, all in folder 7, box 29, SEF Papers.

59. Randolph to Dillard, 13 Apr. 1926, 18 June 1927, 21 June 1927, 2 Jan. 1929, all in folder 7, box 29, SEF Papers.

60. Randolph to Dillard, 15 Jan. 1914, 30 Oct. 1920, 31 Aug. 1928, 2 Jan. 1929, all in folder 7, box 29, SEF Papers.

61. Booker T. Washington to James H. Dillard (30 Sept. 1907), and "J. H. Dillard's Address before the Workers' Conference," Tuskegee Institute (20 Jan. 1910), both in folder 20, box 29, SEF Papers.

62. Leloudis, *Schooling the New South,* 187–189; Marion Vera Carter, *Education and Marginality: A Study of the Negro Woman College Graduate* (New York: privately published, 1942), 3. See also Gilmore, *Gender and Jim Crow,* 147–148: "In a nonpolitical guise, black women became the black community's diplomats to the white community."

63. J. S. Lambert to J. C. Dixon, 4 Jan. 1932, box 1, DNE (Ga.).

64. Virginia L. Miller, report for school year 1939–40, folder 5, box 145, SEF Papers.

65. Lily F. R. Dale, "The Jeanes Supervisors in Alabama, 1909–1963" (Ph.D. diss., Auburn University, 1998), 1, 53–54, 62.

66. "Notes Made at the Conference of State Agents for Negro Rural Schools, Asheville, North Carolina, Nov. 26–28, 1921," folder 2000, box 208, GEB Papers; "Ecological Surveys: East Feliciana Parish," [1941], folder 3, box 225; Cattrell Collier, "Special Report, 1939–40," folder 1, box 145, SEF Papers; Dale, "Jeanes Supervisors in Alabama," 80–81, 91–92.

67. Irene Monroe, Tywanna Wharley and Mansiki Scales interview, 11 July 1994, 10–11, BTV; Blanche Parker, "Special Report, 1939–40," folder 1, box 145, SEF Papers

68. George D. Godard to Wallace Buttrick, 30 Apr. 1914, folder 591, box 67, GEB Papers; N. C. Newbold, reports, Apr. 1915, Mar. 1916, Apr. 1917, folder 1043, box 115, GEB Papers; Leo M. Favrot, "Negro Public Education in the South: A Confidential Report for the Officers of the General Education Board," 1927, 10, folder 1, box 33, SEF Papers; Eva Myers Lee, "Special Report, 1939–40," folder 2, box 145, SEF Papers; Leloudis, *Schooling the New South,* 204–206.

69. Dennis Hargrove Cooke, *The White Superintendent and the Negro Schools in North Carolina* (Nashville: George Peabody College for Teachers,

1930), 95–97; Johnson, *Negro Public Schools,* 39–40; "Ecological Surveys: Avoyelles Parish," [1941], box 3, folder 225, Charles S. Johnson Papers.

70. Johnson, *Negro Public Schools,* 36.

71. "Ecological Surveys: Ascension Parish" [1941]; Georgia Cash-Frierson, "Special Report, 1939–40," folder 1, box 145, SEF Papers; Johnson, *Negro Public Schools,* 30; Maenelle D. Dempsey, Narvie J. Harris, and Susie W. Wheeler, interview by Warren G. Palmer, 1977, recording, Palmer Collection.

72. Estelle Massey Riddle, "Political Structure," 1934, folder 1, box 334, JRF Papers; "Mrs. E. M. Riddle's Report," 1934, folder 1, box 335, JRF Papers; "Gertrude Ammons," monroefreepress.com/history/blkhist1.htm (28 Mar. 2002). The author has found no other references to superintendents making sexual advances to Jeanes teachers.

73. Josie B. Sessoms et al., *Jeanes Supervision in Georgia Schools: A Guiding Light in Education; a History of the Program from 1908–1975* (Atlanta: Georgia Association of Jeanes Curriculum Directors and Southern Education Foundation, 1975), 136–138.

74. Jones, *Jeanes Teacher,* 93–94; Dale, "Jeanes Supervisors in Alabama," 16–17; Courtney S. Woodfaulk, "The Jeanes Teachers of South Carolina: The Emergence, Existence, and Significance of Their Work" (Ed.D. diss., University of South Carolina, 1992), 103–108, 118–119, 132–135; Robinson, *Bell Rings at Four,* 40–42; Bond, *Education of the Negro,* 278.

75. Sessoms et al., *Jeanes Supervision in Georgia Schools,* 131–135.

76. "Ecological Surveys: Avoyelles Parish" [1941]; "Ecological Surveys: Claiborne Parish" [1941–42].

77. Woodfaulk, "Jeanes Teachers of South Carolina," 106; Fulcher, "Dreams Do Come True," 90–96; Alphonso Owens, interview by Warren G. Palmer, 1977, transcript, n.p., Palmer Collection, GCSU.

78. W. T. B. Williams to Arthur D. Wright, 16 Oct. 1935, folder 14, box 23, PSF Papers; *Report and Recommendations of the Commission to Study Public Schools and Colleges for Colored People in North Carolina* (Raleigh, 1938), 21.

79. Myrdal, *An American Dilemma,* 2:1417 n. 22. On the growth of educational disparities in the interwar years, see Bond, *Education of the Negro,* 166–171; John C. Dixon to William Crowe, 16 Aug. 1939, folder 16, box 103, JRF Papers.

7. The City and the Country

1. A. H. Parker, *A Dream That Came True: Autobiography of Arthur Harold Parker* (Birmingham, Ala.: Birmingham Industrial High School, 1932–

1933), 12; Ambrose Caliver, "The Largest Negro High School," *School Life* 18 (Dec. 1931): 73–74.

2. Parker, *Dream That Came True,* 26–27, 34–35; Carl V. Harris, "Stability and Change in Discrimination against Black Public Schools: Birmingham, Alabama, 1871–1931," *Journal of Southern History* 51 (Aug. 1985): 403.

3. Parker, *Dream That Came True,* 45, 63–65; W. K. Tate, "Negro Schools: Birmingham, Alabama," [1916], folder 1, box 16, PSF Papers.

4. Harris, "Stability and Change in Discrimination," 393–396, 409; Parker, *Dream That Came True,* 38–39, 58; Marshall Fred Phillips, "A History of the Public Schools in Birmingham, Alabama" (M.A. thesis, University of Alabama, 1939), 111–113.

5. Parker, *Dream That Came True,* 19–21, 59–60; Lynne B. Feldman, *A Sense of Place: Birmingham's Black Middle-Class Community, 1890–1930* (Tuscaloosa: University of Alabama Press, 1999), 133; "Howard W. McElrath: An Interview," May 1940, box 1, Edward E. Strong Papers, MSRC.

6. Charles S. Johnson, "Report to the Julius Rosenwald Fund on Survey in Birmingham, Alabama, to Determine Vocational Opportunities for Negro Youth," Jan. 1930, folder 17, box 546, JRF Papers; Harris, "Stability and Change in Discrimination," 409.

7. Caliver, "Largest Negro High School," 73–74; Feldman, *Sense of Place,* 127; Parker, *Dream That Came True,* 61; A. H. Parker, "Negro Pupils Plan Programs," *Nation's Schools* 23 (Apr. 1939): 45.

8. Don H. Doyle, *New Men, New Cities, New South: Atlanta, Nashville, Charleston, Mobile, 1860–1910* (Chapel Hill: University of North Carolina Press, 1990), 260–269; Harlan, *Separate and Unequal,* 263.

9. Doyle, *New Men, New Cities, New South,* 273–277.

10. Williams, "Outlook in Negro Education"; George A. Works et al., *Texas Educational Survey Report,* vol. 1: *Organization and Administration* (Austin, 1925), 249–271; Elizabeth H. Turner, *Women, Culture, and Community: Religion and Reform in Galveston, 1880–1920* (New York: Oxford University Press, 1997), 244. The provision of black high schools, however, was not an infallible guide to the overall quality of black schools. For example, the schools sponsored by the Tennessee Coal and Iron Company in Jefferson County, Alabama, were reckoned among the best in the South, yet the TCI system did not provide a high school education.

11. "Report of Dr. J. M. Mason, County Health Officer," 26 Mar. 1903; J. H. Phillips, monthly report, Nov. 1907, Board of Education; James L. Sibley to William F. Feagin, 11 Dec. 1914, folder 145, box 17, GEB Papers.

12. John F. Potts Sr., *A History of the Palmetto Education Association* (Washington: NEA, 1978), 49; *Thirty-Ninth Annual Report of the [Georgia] Department of Education* (Atlanta, 1911), 444; *Biennial Report of the Superintendent of Public Instruction of North Carolina for the Scholastic Years 1918–19 and*

1919–20 (Raleigh, 1920), 202; Ira D. Bryant, *The Development of the Houston Negro Public Schools* (Houston: privately published, 1935), 13, 41.

13. *Thirty-Ninth Annual Report of the [Georgia] Department of Education,* 443; *Biennial Report of the Superintendent of Public Instruction of North Carolina for the Scholastic Years 1910–11 and 1911–12* (Raleigh, 1912), 76; Miller and Gregg, "The Teaching Staff," 205; Caliver, *Education of Negro Teachers,* 10; Bryant, *Houston Negro Public Schools,* 94.

14. John W. Morgan, *The Origin and Distribution of the Negro Colleges of Georgia* (Milledgeville, Ga.: privately published, 1940), 113–114.

15. Joseph M. Hathaway, "The Class of 1944 at Lincoln High School: Finding Excellence in a Black Segregated School" (Ed.D. thesis, University of South Carolina, 1997), 98–99.

16. In New Orleans, for example, a third of black teachers, but only 14 percent of white teachers, were married in 1939; see Citizens' Planning Committee for Public Education in New Orleans, *Summary Report on the New Orleans Study and Program of Public Education* (New Orleans, 1940), 98, 142. A sample of rural elementary school teachers in Louisiana showed that only 28 percent were single; see Johnson, *Negro Public Schools,* 52. A much broader survey of black teachers in Texas yielded information that a third of the female teachers and 23 percent of the male teachers were single; see Henry A. Bullock, "Availability of Public Education for Negroes in Texas," *Proceedings of the Eighth Annual Conference: Prairie View Bulletin* 29 (Nov. 1937): 52.

17. Miscellaneous material, folders 1–16, box 1, Rev. Jack Yates Family and Antioch Baptist Church Collection, MSS 281, Metropolitan Research Center, Houston; *Historical Highlights of Antioch Baptist Church* (1976), folder 2, box 2, Metropolitan Research Center, Houston; "John Henry Yates," http://www.tsha.utexas.edu/handbook/online/articles (accessed 21 Mar. 2005); Luther P. Jackson, "Free Negroes of Petersburg, Virginia," *JNH* 12 (July 1927): 327–378; Horace Mann Bond, *Black American Scholars: A Study of Their Beginnings* (Detroit: Balamp, 1972), 167–169; Myles N. McLaughlin, "One of Virginia State University's Finest Educators: Edna Meade Colson" (M.A. thesis, Virginia State University, 1995), 1–11; Murray, *Proud Shoes,* 238–240, 244.

18. Miriam DeCosta-Willis, ed., *The Memphis Diary of Ida B. Wells* (Boston: Beacon, 1995), 188; Valinda W. Littlefield, "A Yearly Contract with Everybody and His Brother: Durham County, North Carolina Black Female Public School Teachers, 1885–1927," *JNH* 79 (Winter 1994): 41; Willard B. Gatewood, *Aristocrats of Color: The Black Elite, 1880–1920* (Bloomington: Indiana University Press, 1990), 245–246; White, *Too Heavy a Load,* 70–76; Williams, "Club Movement among Colored Women," 400, 417.

19. Sonya Yvette Ramsey, "More Than the Three R's: The Educational, Eco-

nomic, and Cultural Experiences of African American Teachers in Nashville, Tennessee, 1869 to 1983" (Ph.D. diss., University of North Carolina at Chapel Hill, 2000), 30, 51–55; Feldman, *Sense of Place,* 131; DeCosta-Willis, *Memphis Diary of Ida B. Wells,* 113, 134; Johnson, *Along This Way,* 148; Dorothy A. Gay, "Crisis of Identity: The Negro Community in Raleigh, 1890–1900," *North Carolina Historical Review* 50 (Apr. 1973): 130; Johnson, "Autobiography," 18–19.

20. DeCosta-Willis, *Memphis Diary of Ida B. Wells,* 33, 58–60, 110; 148; Gatewood, *Aristocrats of Color,* 211–241; Johnson, *Along This Way,* 133–134; Maurice Prevost, interviewed by Michelle Mitchell, 13 July 1994, audiotape, BTV.

21. DeCosta-Willis, *Memphis Diary of Ida B. Wells,* 184–184.

22. Andrew Young, *An Easy Burden: The Civil Rights Movement and the Transformation of America* (New York: HarperCollins, 1996), 18–19; Lucille L. Hutton, "Interview for 'Lessons Learned,'" WYES-TV, 1991, 3, folder 10, box 3, Lucille Ley Hutton Papers, ARC.

23. Biography, folder 2, box 1, Fannie C. Williams Papers, ARC; *American Missionary* 35 (2 Feb. 1933), clipping, ARC; *The Moving Finger* 5 (1939), ARC; *Valena C. Jones Normal and Practice School: Class of 1933 Fifty-Year Reunion, June 17–19, 1983,* box 24, Orleans Parish School Board Papers, Earl K. Long Library, University of New Orleans; Fannie C. Williams, "Introduction to Civic Project," *The Bulletin* 10 (June–July 1930): 6, SCRBC.

24. Hutton, "Interview for 'Lessons Learned,'" 2–8; Florence E. Dixon to Fannie C. Williams, 23 Oct. 1936, folder 1, box 6, Hutton Papers.

25. A. C. Flora, "Statement to the County Delegation," 9 Feb. 1937, folder 16, box 1, A. C. Flora Papers, USC; Citizens' Planning Committee for Public Education in New Orleans, *Summary Report,* 44, 100–102, 114, 143–144; Juliette L. Landphair, "'For the Good of the Community': Reform Activism and Public Schools in New Orleans, 1920–1960" (Ph.D. diss., University of Virginia, 1999), 105; Hutton, "Interview for 'Lessons Learned,'" 3–4; Veronica B. Hill, interview by Leatrice R. Roberts, 7 Oct. 1983, audiotape, United Teachers of New Orleans Collection, Earl K. Long Library, University of New Orleans; W. A. Robinson, "The Present Status of Negro High School Education among Negroes—A Factual and Critical Survey," *The Bulletin* 11 (Nov. 1930): 3–4, 20–22.

26. Johnson, *Along This Way,* 125–126.

27. "Mississippi, Summary of Information on Negro Principals, 1952–53," folder 4, box 76, SEF Papers; "The Status of Negro Principals in Virginia," 1956, 105, folder 27, box 160, SEF Papers; Bullock, "Availability of Public Education," 47.

28. Young, Ortiz interview, 54–55; Tate, Palmer interview, Palmer Collection.

29. Potts, *Palmetto Education Association,* 35–36; C. A. Johnson to A. C. Flora,

9 Feb. 1931; Johnson to Flora, "Report for 1931–1932," 17 June 1932; Annual Report, 1932–1933," 14 June 1933; "Report for 1933–1934," 6 June 1934; all in folder 1219, box 132, GEB Papers.

30. Janet S. Matthews, "The African American Experience in Southwest Florida and the Origins of Dunbar High School in Fort Myers, 1841 to 1927" (Ph.D. diss., Florida State University, 1999), 223, 232; Johnson, *Along This Way,* 129–130.

31. Charles N. Hunter to E. P. Moses, 28 May 1904, box 2, Hunter Papers; Hunter to D. F. Giles, 25 Dec. 1916, box 4, Hunter Papers. Hunter also had a drinking problem that contributed to his difficulties.

32. Johnson, "Autobiography," 23–25.

33. Murray, *Proud Shoes,* 156–157; Harriet Tabor, Houser Miller, and Sylvia Bryant, interview by Warren Palmer, 1977, audiotape; and Tate, Palmer interview, both in Palmer Collection.

34. Savage, "Claiborne's Institute to Natchez High School," 73–78.

35. "Morris Henry Carroll," monroefreeprress.com/history/ (28 Mar. 2002).

36. Edwards, "Booker T. Washington High School," 108, 112–113, 123; C. A. Johnson to A. C. Flora, "Annual Report, 1932–33," 14 June 1933, folder 1219, box 132, GEB Papers; Edmond Jefferson Oliver, *The End of an Era: Fairfield Industrial High School, 1924–1968* (Fairfield, Ala.: privately published, 1968), 9.

37. William H. Johnson, "Discipline," 1911, box 4, William Henry Johnson Papers; Johnson, *Along This Way,* 128; Joe N. Dickson, "Rev. John Porter Remembers Teachers at Parker," *Birmingham World,* 4 Mar. 1998; Emmett W. Bashful, interview by Felix Armfield, 28 June 1994, audiotape 1, BTV.

38. Oliver, *End of an Era,* 7–8, 44–45; Savage, "Claiborne's Institute to Natchez High School," 59–60, 78.

39. J. H. Phillips, "Annual Report, 1894–95," Board of Education Minutes, Birmingham Public Library; A. C. Flora, "Report to the Columbia School Board," 8 Jan. 1929, Flora Papers, USC.

40. *Fifteenth Annual Report of the City Schools of Columbia, South Carolina, 1897–98* (Columbia, 1898), 21–23; Hathaway, "Class of 1944," 116.

41. Hathaway, "Class of 1944," 122; Jelani Mandara, "The Impact of Family Functioning on African American Males' Academic Achievement: A Review and Clarification of the Empirical Literature," *Teachers College Record* 108 (Feb. 2006): 209–217; Allison Davis and John Dollard, *Children of Bondage: The Personality Development of Negro Youth in the Urban South* (Washington: American Council on Education, 1940), 252–253, 266–272, 281; Lacy, *Rise and Fall of a Proper Negro,* 35; Angela Davis, *An Autobiography* (1974; New York: International Pub., 1988), 100. Vanessa Siddle Walker, *Their Highest Potential: An African American School Community in the Segregated South* (Chapel Hill: University of North Carolina Press,

1996), makes no mention of corporal punishment. On violence and corporal punishment in rural lower-class families, see Fleming, *In the Shadow of Selma*, 147–148.

42. Berlin, *Slaves without Masters*, 178; Joel Williamson, *New People: Miscegenation and Mulattoes in the United States* (New York: New York University Press, 1984), 130–131. A 1932 study reported that 22 percent of mulattoes whose occupations were known worked as teachers.

43. Murray, *Proud Shoes*, 50; Hunter, *Nickel and a Prayer*, 21–22; Susie W. Jones, interviewed by Merze Tate, 14 Aug. 1977, in Hill, *Black Women Oral History Project*, 6:330.

44. Adam Fairclough, *Race and Democracy: The Civil Rights Struggle in Louisiana, 1915–1972* (Athens: University of Georgia Press, 1995), 4–5, 14–18; Gatewood, *Aristocrats of Color*, 158, 254–255, 281–282; Jenkins, *Seizing the Day*, 86–87; Drago, *Initiative, Paternalism, and Race Relations*, 67–70, 130–133; Fields, *Lemon Swamp*, 12–13, 24; McMillan, *Negro Higher Education*, 4; Patton, "Richard Robert Wright," 184–185; Ramsey, "More Than the Three R's," 95–96.

45. Reddix, *Voice Crying in the Wilderness*, 61.

46. Gatewood, *Aristocrats of Color*, 173; Young, Ortiz interview, 4–5. Chesnutt was the second principal of Fayetteville Normal School (N.C.). Burrus was the second president of Alcorn A&M College (Miss.). Miller was the first president of South Carolina State College. Johnston and Gandy were the second and third presidents of Virginia State College. Hunt was the first president of Fort Valley State College (Ga.). Hope was the first black president of Morehouse College and the first president of Atlanta University. Johnson was the first black president of Howard University. Jones was the president of Bennett College.

47. E. Franklin Frazier, *Negro Youth at the Crossways: Their Personality Development in the Middle States* (1940; New York: Schocken, 1967), 97–99, 111; Margaret Rogers, interview by Kara Miles, n.d., 42, BTV; Charlotte Moton Hubbard, interview by Helene K. Sargent, 3–5 Nov. 1982, 9–10, Women in the Federal Government Project, Schlesinger Library, Radcliffe College.

48. Rogers, Miles interview, 41; Christia Adair, Dorothy R. Robinson interview, 25 Apr. 1977, in Hill, *Black Women Oral History Project*, 1:48; Ella Earls Cotton, *A Spark for My People: The Sociological Autobiography of a Negro Teacher* (New York: Exposition Press, 1954), 114; J. Masuoka and Charles S. Johnson, eds., *The Social World of Negro Youth* (Nashville: Social Science Institute of Fisk University, 1946), 78; Rice, *He Included Me*, 7–8.

49. Gatewood, *Aristocrats of Color*, 153; Drago, *Initiative, Paternalism, and Race Relations*, 68, 130–131; Washington to James Bryce, 29 July 1910, in

Harlan, *Booker T. Washington Papers,* 10:358; J. Max Barber to William Pickens, 17 June 1930, reel 1, William Pickens Papers, SCRBC.

50. Williamson, *New People,* 89–130; Thomas R. Webber, "New Hanover County and Its Negroes," 14 July 1941, box 3, Correspondence of the Director, Division of Cooperation in Education and Race Relations, DNE (N.C.).

51. "Report of the Survey of Wilcox County Schools, 1929–1930."

52. Edwin R. Embree, *Julius Rosenwald Fund: Review of Two Decades, 1917–1936* (Chicago: Julius Rosenwald Fund, 1936).

53. Ibid.; Raper, *Preface to Peasantry,* 324–326, 361–362; "Report of W. F. Credle," Feb. 1929, box 8, Special Subject File, DNE (N.C.); Robinson, *Bell Rings at Four,* 4–5; Fulcher, "Dreams Do Come True," 104–108, 111–126; Johnson, *Negro Public Schools,* 45–46.

54. George E. Cunningham, "Reasons for Belated Education: A Study of the Plight of Older Negro Teachers," *JNE* 27 (Spring 1958): 198; Johnson, *Negro Public Schools,* 46.

55. Fulcher, "Dreams Do Come True," 146–147; Johnson, *Growing Up in the Black Belt,* 109–114.

56. Susie A. Shepperson, Report, 1939–40, folder 5, box 145, SEF Papers.

57. Leo M. Favrot, "Report on Negro Summer Schools in the South in 1926," 8, folder 3160, box 302, GEB Papers; Fulcher, "Dreams Do Come True," 24–25; 71, 89–91, 146–147; Anderson, *Education of Blacks,* 180–181; Robinson, *Bell Rings at Four,* 43; Enola Gay Smith Mosley, "Rediscovering Educational Giants: African-American Schools in Bulloch County, Georgia, 1920–1949" (Ph.D. diss., Georgia Southern University, 1999), 76–79.

58. Fulcher, "Dreams Do Come True," 134–135; Caliver, *Rural Elementary Education among Negroes,* 14–15, 20; Whiting, *Shop and Class at Tuskegee,* 38–39.

59. McCuistion, *South's Negro Teaching Force,* 23–24; Fulcher, "Dreams Do Come True," 137; L. F. Palmer, "The Hampton Institute Experiment in Community Experience Education: First Annual Report, 1944–45," 19 Mar. 1946, folder 4575, box 436, GEB Papers.

60. Mosley, "Rediscovering Educational Giants," 111, 118; Ruth Johnson, interviewed by Rhonda Mawhood, n.d. [1993?], 9–10, BTV; Fulcher, "Dreams Do Come True," 137–138, 174–175.

61. Rice, *He Included Me,* 69; Robinson, *Bell Rings at Four,* 5; Fulcher, "Dreams Do Come True," 142; Mosley, "Rediscovering Educational Giants," 109–110; M. J. Hitch, "A Report on Negro Schools in the Region III of Eastern Kentucky, Nov. 10–21, 1952," folder 3, box 75, SEF Papers; Mrs. Dempsey, Mrs. N. J. Harris, and Susie W. Wheeler, interviewed by Warren G. Palmer, recording 1977, GCSU.

62. Johnson, *Negro Public Schools,* 164–165.
63. D. E. Williams, *Education for Negroes in Florida,* 16; Johnson, *Negro Public Schools,* 48–51, 90, 107–109; Estelle Riddle, "The Mineral Springs School," [1934], folder 1, box 335, JRF Papers.
64. Raper, *Preface to Peasantry,* 334; Johnson, *Growing Up in the Black Belt,* 106; Johnson, *Negro Public Schools,* 57.
65. N. C. Newbold to James E. Gregg, 28 June 1921, folder 1074, box 118, GEB Papers; J. B. Moore et al. to Robert R. Moton, 25 July 1925, box 1, Williams Papers, TU; A. S. Brower to Moton, 23 Aug. 1922, folder 563, box 85; Moton to Trevor Arnett, 9 Mar. 1929, folder 1423, box 170, both in Moton Papers, TU; W. T. B. Williams, "Is Tuskegee Just Another College?" *Journal of Educational Sociology* 7:3 (1933): 172–174; Edward K. Graham, "The Hampton Institute Strike of 1927: A Case Study in Student Protest," *American Scholar* 38 (1969): 681.
66. R. O'Hara Lanier, "The Reorganization and Redirection of Negro Education in Terms of Articulation and Integration," *JNE* 5 (July 1936): 371; Charles S. Johnson, "On the Need for Realism in Negro Education," *JNE* 5 (July 1936): 375–382.
67. Thomas Jesse Jones, "Universality of Educational Objectives," *JNE* 5 (July 1936): 407–411; Thomas J. Jones to Rossa B. Cooley, 13 Mar. 1929, folder 1014a, box 133, Moton Papers; Walter G. Daniel, "Negro Welfare and Mabel Carney at Teachers College, Columbia University," *JNE* 11 (Oct. 1942): 560–562; Kathleen Weiler, "Mabel Carney at Teachers College: From Home Missionary to White Ally," *Teachers College Record* 107 (Dec. 2005): 2599–2633.
68. Mabel Carney, "Desirable Rural Adaptation in the Education of Negroes," *JNE* 5 (July 1936): 132–143; Jane E. McAllister, "A Venture in Rural-Teacher Adaptation among Negroes in Louisiana," *JNE* 7 (Apr. 1938): 132–143; Winona Williams-Burns, "Jane Ellen McAllister: Pioneer in Excellence in Teacher Education," *JNE* 51 (Summer 1982): 342–357.
69. Jackson Davis, "Recent Developments in Negro Schools and Colleges," 25 May 1927, 5–6, folder 6, box 30, SEF Papers; W. T. B. Williams to James E. Gregg, 24 Jan. 1919, box 6, Williams Papers, TU; John Simon, "Negro Trade Schools and State Colleges" [1936], folder 11, box 127, JRF Papers; "Conference of State Agents of Rural Schools for Negroes, June 5–6, 1930," 27, folder 2002, box 208, GEB Papers; John C. Dixon to Edwin Embree, 2 May 1938, folder 11, box 103, GEB Papers.
70. Johnson, *Growing Up in the Black Belt,* 194–201; Johnson, *Negro Public Schools,* 154; R. Clyde Minor to N. C. Newbold, 16 Apr. 1934, box 1, special subject file, DNE (N.C.); *Proceedings of the Thirteenth Annual Conference of Presidents of Negro Land Grant Colleges, Nov. 18–20, 1935* (Washington, 1935), 15–16; "Interviews, RJH, Visit to Prairie View State College,

Feb. 17, 1940," reel 132, "Early Southern Programs: Texas," *GEB Archives* (Tex.).

8. Teachers Organize

1. Mark V. Tushnet, *The NAACP's Legal Strategy against Segregated Education, 1925–1950* (Chapel Hill: University of North Carolina Press, 1987), 78–80; J. Douglas Smith, *Managing White Supremacy: Race, Politics, and Citizenship in Jim Crow Virginia* (Chapel Hill: University of North Carolina Press, 2002), 256–257.

2. *Minutes of the Seventh Annual Session of the Alabama State Teachers Association, Selma, Alabama, April 11–13, 1888; Minutes of the Eighth Annual Session of the Alabama State Teachers Association, Selma, Alabama, April 10–12, 1889,* both in box 30A, Trenholm Papers, MSRC.

3. Percy E. Murray, *History of the North Carolina Teachers Association* (Washington: NEA, 1984), 15–16; Vernon McDaniel, *History of the State Teachers Association of Texas* (Washington: NEA, 1977), 21; Eby, *Education in Texas,* 268.

4. Patton, "Richard Robert Wright," 473–478; Sheldon Avery, *Up from Washington: William Pickens and the Negro Struggle for Equality, 1900–1934* (Newark: University of Delaware Press, 1989), 33–34; J. L. Sibley to William F. Feagin, 30 Apr. 1914, folder 145, box 17, GEB Papers.

5. Luther P. Jackson, *A History of the Virginia Teachers Association* (Norfolk: Guide Pub. Co., 1937), 2, 11–15, 32; Gandy, autobiography, 133, Gandy Papers; Potts, *Palmetto Education Association,* 26–27, 42.

6. Jackson, *Virginia Teachers Association,* 36; Gandy, autobiography, 135.

7. J. G. Clayton, "The Educational Scylla and Charybdis," *Minutes of the Eighth Annual Session of the Alabama State Teachers Association,* 46; Nathan B. Young, "An Imminent Innovation in Southern Education" [1910], 2, folder 2689, box 260, GEB Papers; W. J. Hale, "Purpose and Program of the National Association of Teachers in Colored Schools," *The Bulletin* 1 (Nov. 1928): 6, SCRBC.

8. Michael J. Schultz, *National Education Association and the Black Teacher: The Integration of a Professional Organization* (Coral Gables, Fla.: University of Miami Press, 1970), 47–52; Patton, "Richard Robert Wright," 478–479; Thelma D. Perry, *History of the American Teachers Association* (Washington: NEA, 1975), 42–49; Hale, "National Association of Teachers in Colored Schools," 7.

9. Potts, *Palmetto Education Association,* 54–55; Murray, *North Carolina Teachers Association,* 151; Gandy, autobiography, 137; Hale, "National Association of Teachers in Colored Schools," 7.

10. *Minutes of the Forty-Fifth Annual Session of the North Carolina Negro*

Teachers Association, Greensboro, November 25–27, 1925, folder 1, box 3; Simon G. Atkins, *President's Address, Goldsboro, November 23, 1927,* both in Atkins Papers, WSSU; Ernest J. Middleton, *History of the Louisiana Education Association* (Washington: NEA, 1984), 56; Potts, *Palmetto Education Association,* 47; Executive Board, minutes, 26 Nov. 1929; 28 Nov. 1935, minute book 1, box 1, VTA Papers, VSU.

11. "Committee on Common Carriers, Negro Organization Society of Virginia," 17 Nov. 1913; Negro Organization Society, minutes of executive committee, 26 Dec. 1913, box 5, Williams Papers, TU; Gandy, autobiography, 133–141; "chapter 56," folder 46, box 2; Gandy, "Land Grant College Program," 19 July 1939, transcript of radio talk, both in Gandy Papers, VSU; J. Rupert Picott, *History of the Virginia Teachers Association* (Washington: NEA, 1975), 54–58, 75–76. On the growth of the VTA, see also Michael Dennis, *Luther P. Jackson and a Life for Civil Rights* (Gainesville: University Press of Florida, 2004), 108–112.

12. Murray, *North Carolina Teachers Association,* 33; Ann Short Chirhart, *Torches of Light: Georgia Teachers and the Coming of the Modern South* (Athens: University of Georgia Press, 2005), 169–170; J. C. Dixon to Dear Superintendent, 20 Sept. 1932, box 1, series 12-6-2, Guy Wells to Dixon, 19 Oct. 1932, and T. J. Dempsey Jr. to Dixon, 10 Nov. 1932, all in DNE (Ga.).

13. O. L. Coleman to T. H. Harris, 9 May 1922; Harris to Coleman, 18 May 1922, DNE (La.); Robert L. Cousins to James L. Grant, 26 Feb. 1941, box 3, series 12-6-71, DNE (Ga.).

14. James L. Sibley to H. J. Willingham, 27 Sept. 1913, folder 142, box 17, GEB Papers; "Program for Institutes for Colored Teachers, 1913," GEB Papers; Sibley to William F. Feagin, 1 Dec. 1914, 26 May 1915, folder 145, box 17, GEB Papers. This increase in attendance coincided with the appointment of the first GEB-funded state agents of Negro education, who saw summer schools as a means of instructing teachers in manual training, domestic science, and community organization.

15. "Summary of Reports from Summer Schools for Negro Teachers" [1922], folder 3160, box 302, GEB Papers; Leo M. Favrot, "Report on Negro Summer Schools in the South in 1926," 15, GEB Papers. Attendance rates varied from 29 percent in Georgia (1924) to 77 percent in Mississippi (1921–22).

16. Favrot, "Report on Negro Summer Schools in the South in 1926," 5–8, 12–13; Favrot, "Interview with Supt. W. F. Bond," 24 Sept. 1934, folder 895, box 99, GEB Papers; Favrot to Jackson Davis, 18 Dec. 1934, GEB Papers; Jackson Davis, "Summer Schools for Colored Teachers," *The Bulletin* 9 (Feb. 1929): 7, 21; Leo M. Favrot, "How the Small Rural School Can Most Adequately Serve Its Community," *JNE* 5:3 (July 1936): 434.

17. W. Blanchet, interview by Warren G. Palmer, 1977, audiotape, Palmer

Collection; J. S. Wilkerson, interview by Warren G. Palmer, 1977, audio-tape, Palmer Collection.

18. August Meier and Elliott Rudwick, *Black History and the Historical Profession, 1915–1980* (Urbana: University of Illinois Press, 1986), 61–62; Dennis, *Luther P. Jackson,* 50–58; Luther P. Jackson to Carter G. Woodson (20 Feb. 1935, 4 Apr. 1935), Woodson to John M. Gandy (20 Mar. 1935),both in folder 973, box 35, Luther Porter Jackson Sr. Papers, VSU; Lorenzo J. Greene, *Selling Black History for Carter G. Woodson: A Diary, 1930–1933* (Columbia: University of Missouri Press, 1996), 89–90.

19. Thomas E. Patterson, *History of the Arkansas Teachers Association* (Washington: NEA, 1981), 53–54; Gilbert L. Porter and Leedell W. Neyland, *History of the Florida State Teachers Association* (Washington: NEA, 1977), 3; Chirhart, *Torches of Light,* 169; Leo M. Favrot to James H. Dillard, 18 Apr. 1928, folder 19, box 27, SEF Papers; William W. Saunders, "Annual Report of the Executive Secretary," *The Bulletin* 14 (Nov. 1935): 61–62; Perry, *American Teachers Association,* 237–238; *ATA Newsletter* [1944], folder 1264, box 82, VTA Papers; "Report of the Executive Secretary," 23–25 July 1946, box 82, VTA Papers. Members of the Alabama State Teachers Association made up about a third of the ATA's total membership.

20. W. S. Deffenbaugh, "Effects of the Depression upon Public Elementary and Secondary Schools and upon Colleges and Universities," in U.S. Commissioner of Education, *Biennial Survey of Education, 1934–36* (Washington: GPO, 1938), 10–15; Chirhart, *Torches of Light,* 173–177; Fairclough, *Race and Democracy,* 23; Raper, *Preface to Peasantry,* 329. Per capita expenditure decreased by 22 percent between 1930 and 1934. North Carolina—previously the most generous southern state—inflicted a reduction of 43 percent, the highest in the country. School-building programs all but ground to a halt. Capital outlays shriveled by 84 percent.

21. Bond, *Education of the Negro,* 233; Deffenbaugh, "Effects of the Depression," 1, 15, 22–23.

22. Columbia School Board Meeting, minutes, 28 Apr. 1931, 1, folder 8, box 1, Flora Papers; Michael C. Scandaville, *A Brief History of South Carolina Schools, from 1895 to 1945* (Columbia: South Carolina Department of Archives and History, 1989), 13; R. L. Johnson to Horace Mann Bond, 5 Dec. 1940, reel 5, part 1, series 2, *Bond Papers;* H. C. Newbold, "Some Achievements in the Equalization of Educational Opportunities in North Carolina" [1944], box 1, special subject file, DNE (N.C.); "Study of Institutions of Higher Learning for Negroes in North Carolina, 1929–1931," minutes of conference, Raleigh, 3 June 1931, folder 1043, box 115, GEB Papers.

23. Murray, *North Carolina Teachers Association,* 41; Potts, *Palmetto Education Association,* 56; Picott, *Virginia Teachers Association,* 48–49.

24. Dwight O. W. Holmes, "The Present Status of College Education among Negroes," *The Bulletin* 11 (Jan. 1931): 5; Patrick J. Gilpin, "Charles S. Johnson: An Intellectual Biography" (Ph.D. diss., Vanderbilt University, 1973), 631; Richard Robbins, *Sidelines Activist: Charles S. Johnson and the Struggle for Civil Rights* (Jackson: University Press of Mississippi, 1996), 78–96; John H. Stanfield, *Philanthropy and Jim Crow in American Social Science* (Westport, Conn.: Greenwood, 1985), 119–123; Perry, *American Teachers Association,* 247–249.

25. J. B. Felton to Leo M. Favrot, 17 Jan. 1938, folder 1201, box 131, GEB Papers; Murray, *North Carolina Teachers Association,* 46.

26. Wallace Buttrick, "Memorandum on a Trip to Southern Schools," Oct. 1919, 5–7, folder 3194, box 306, GEB Papers; minutes of the General Education Board, "Negro Education," 13 Oct. 1922, 31–32, folder 2689, box 260, GEB Papers.

27. "Ninth Meeting, University Commission on Southern Race Questions, Nashville, Tennessee, April 25–26, 1919," PSF Papers.

28. Jackson Davis, "Recent Developments in Negro Schools and Colleges," 25 May 1927, 5–6, folder 6, box 30, SEF Papers; Davis, "Normal Schools and A&M Colleges," 30; "Robert Moton in France," *The Crisis* 18:1 (May 1919); Meier and Rudwick, *Black History and the Historical Profession,* 37–43; Kenneth J. King, *Pan Africanism and Education: A Study of Race Philanthropy and Education in the Southern States of America and East Africa* (Oxford: Oxford University Press, 1971), 144–145, 184–185; General Education Board, "Negro Education," 32–33.

29. Wilma Dykeman and James Stokely, *Seeds of Southern Change: The Life of Will Alexander* (New York: Norton, 1962), 52–76; Thomas J. Jones to James H. Dillard, 28 Mar. 1927, folder 10, box 17, PSF Papers; Anderson, *Education of Blacks,* 276.

30. Leo M. Favrot, "Negro Public Education in the South: A Confidential Report for the Officers of the General Education Board," [1926], p. 11, folder 1, box 33, SEF Papers; Favrot, "Report," Apr. 1917, folder 772, box 87, GEB Papers; Favrot to E. C. Sage, 16 July 1920, and Favrot to Wallace Buttrick, 6 Sept. 1921, both reel 69, *GEB Archives* (La.); Favrot to James H. Dillard, 23 Jan. 1929, folder 19, box 27, SEF Papers.

31. Adam Fairclough, *Teaching Equality: Black Schools in the Age of Jim Crow* (Athens: University of Georgia Press, 2001), 20–33.

32. "Conference of State Agents of Rural Schools for Negroes, June 5–6, 1930," pp. 3, 20, folder 2002, box 208, GEB Papers; "Conference of State Agents of Rural Schools for Negroes, Nov. 26–28, 1921," 2–4, folder 1998, box 208, GEB Papers; Jones to Rossa B. Cooley, 13 Mar. 1929, folder 1014a, box 133, Moton Papers, TU.

33. H. Councill Trenholm, "Accreditation of Negro High Schools," *JNE* (Apr. 1932): 37.

34. Perry, *American Teachers Association*, 165–169, 174–184; *Proceedings of the 67th Annual Meeting, Atlanta, June 28–July 4, 1929* (Washington, D.C: NEA, 1929), 107; Leo M. Favrot, "Minutes Bearing on Negro Education at the Department of Superintendents Meeting at Cleveland, Ohio, Feb. 26–27, 1934," folder 2688, box 260, GEB Papers.

35. Melanie Carter, "From Jim Crow to Inclusion: An Historical Analysis of the Association of Colleges and Secondary Schools for Negroes, 1934–1965" (Ph.D. diss., Ohio State University, 1996), 63–75, 92–105; Leland Stanford Cozart, *A History of the Association of Colleges and Secondary Schools* (Charlotte, N.C.: Association of Colleges and Secondary Schools, 1965), 2–16; W. A. Robinson to Robert L. Cousins, 2 Nov. 1939, box 1, series 12-6-71, DNE (Ga.); *Progress and Plans of Negro High Schools toward Regional Accreditment* [1945], folder 5, box 411, series RG92, Department of Education, Tennessee State Archives, Nashville, Tennessee.

36. Cozart, *Association of Colleges and Secondary Schools*, 34–38; W. A. Robinson, "Some Problems in the Administration, Support, and Accreditation of Negro Secondary Schools," *JNE* 9 (July 1940): 478; W. A. Robinson, "What Peculiar Organization and Direction Should Characterize the Education of Negroes?" *JNE* 5 (July 1936): 396–398; "Resolutions Adopted at the Baltimore Meeting of the National Association of Teachers in Colored Schools," *The Bulletin* 13:1 (Oct. 1934): 9.

37. Woodson, *Mis-Education of the Negro*, 1; Meier and Rudwick, *Black History and the Historical Profession*, 55–57; David Levering Lewis, *W. E. B. Du Bois and the Fight for the American Century, 1919–1963* (New York: Henry Holt, 2000), 335–340; Robert R. Moton to C. R. Mann, 8 Dec. 1931, folder 1219, box 152, Moton Papers, TU; David A. Lane Jr., "The Report of the National Advisory Committee on Education and the Problem of Negro Education," *JNE* 1 (Apr. 1932): 6–8.

38. D. O. W. Holmes, "Does Negro Education Need Reorganization and Redirection? A Statement of the Problem," *JNE* 5 (July 1936): 319; Lanier, "Reorganization and Redirection of Negro Education," 370; Roger M. Williams, *The Bonds: An American Family* (New York: Atheneum, 1972), 132.

39. Jonathan Scott Holloway, *Confronting the Veil: Abram Harris Jr., E. Franklin Frazier, and Ralph Bunche, 1919–1941* (Chapel Hill: University of North Carolina Press, 2002), 104–119, 137–144, 164–177; Ralph J. Bunche, "Education in Black and White," *JNE* 5 (July 1946): 356.

40. *Proceedings of the Fifteenth Annual Conference of the Presidents of Negro Land Grant Colleges, November 15–17, 1937* (Washington, 1937), 41–42; Doxey A. Wilkerson, "American Caste and the Social Studies Curricu-

lum," *Quarterly Review of Higher Education among Negroes* 5 (Apr. 1937): 71; Bunche, "Education in Black and White," 358; Bond, *Education of the Negro,* 12–13.

41. [Charles H. Thompson], "Editorial Comment: Why a Journal of Negro Education?" *JNE* 1 (Apr. 1932): 1–4.

42. Wilkerson, "American Caste," 69–74; T. E. McKinney, "A Discussion of Mr. Bunche's Paper on 'Social Attitudes and the Constitution,'" *Quarterly Review of Higher Education among Negroes* 7 (July 1939): 197–199.

43. Wendell G. Morgan, "A Survey of the Social Science Offerings in Negro Colleges, 1935–36," *Quarterly Review of Higher Education among Negroes* 3 (1935): 175; Walter R. Chivers, "The Negro Social Science Teacher in the Southern Rural Community," *Negro College Quarterly* 1 (Mar. 1943): 11; Ivan E. Taylor, "An Appraisal of the Symposium," *Negro College Quarterly* 2 (June 1944): 104–112.

44. McKinney, "Discussion of Dr. Bunche's Paper," 201; B. R. Brazeal, "The Function of the Dean in the Development of Attitudes," *Quarterly Review of Higher Education among Negroes* (Jan. 1943): 4; Velma B. Hamilton, "The Function of the Registrar in the Development of Attitudes," *Quarterly Review of Higher Education among Negroes,* ibid., 6–9.

45. Luther P. Jackson, "Teaching American Government at Virginia State College," 11 Aug. 1944, folder 1620, box 64, Jackson Papers, VSU; Morgan, "Survey of the Social Science Offerings," 175–179; John Hope Franklin, "Courses Concerning the Negro in Negro Colleges," *Quarterly Review of Higher Education among Negroes* 8 (July 1940): 138–144.

46. "Negro History Week," n.d., folder 7, box 1, George S. Longe Papers, ARC; Alfred Farrell, "Teaching Race Pride through Poetry," *Quarterly Review of Higher Education among Negroes* 9 (1941–42): 20–23; Division of Negro Education, "The Open Road: A Teacher's Guide to Child and Community Development," 1937, box 2, series 12-6-71, DNE (Ga.); Robinson, "What Peculiar Organization," 400; minutes of meeting of Newport News Teachers Association, 1 Nov. 1943, folder 533, box 38, VTA Papers; "Enola E. Thompson, Killona Elementary School, St. Charles Parish," folder 1, box 226, Charles S. Johnson Papers, Special Collections, Fisk University, Nashville; Aaron Henry with Constance Curry, *Aaron Henry: The Fire Ever Burning* (Jackson: University Press of Mississippi, 2000), 40–43. Many black newspapers at the time serialized *Native Son.*

47. C. A. Bowers, "The Ideologies of Progressive Education," *HEQ* 7 (Winter 1967): 456, 461–465; Ronald K. Goodenow, "Paradox in Progressive Educational Reform: The South and the Education of Blacks in the Depression Years," *Phylon* 39 (1978): 54–65; Robinson, "What Peculiar Organization," 400.

48. Goodenow, "Paradox," 50–53; Carleton Washburne, *A Summary Report of the Louisiana Educational Survey Commission* (Baton Rouge, 1942), 105.

49. "Program for Public Education in Tennessee," 1936, reel 411, Record Group 92, Tennessee State Archives; Bowers, "Ideologies of Progressive Education," 470; "The Open Road: A Teacher's Guide to Child and Community Development," 1937, box 2, series 12-6-71, DNE (Ga.).

50. J. Mills Thornton, *Dividing Lines: Municipal Politics and the Struggle for Civil Rights in Montgomery, Birmingham, and Selma* (Tuscaloosa: University of Alabama Press, 2002), 147; Jack Atkins et al. to *Winston-Salem Journal and Sentinel,* 18 July, 24 July 1943, clippings, folder 73, box 4, Atkins Papers. Given the fact that the R. J. Reynolds Company had been an important contributor to the college, Atkins's anti-union stance was understandable.

51. "Students' Platform," 24 May 1934; Gandy to Student Body, 24 May 1934; the Student Body to Gandy, 28 May 1934, folder 106, box 3; letters of dismissal, 29 May 1934, folder 117, box 3; T. S. Inborden to Gandy, 1 June 1934; W. R. Banks to Gandy, 4 June 1934, folder 122, box 3; all in Gandy Papers. "Any student who tried to bar the entrance to a class room should be sent to the chain gang at once," wrote T. S. Inborden, the principal of Bricks Junior College in North Carolina. See T. S. Inborden to Gandy, 1 June 1934, folder 122, box 3, Gandy Papers, VSU.

52. *The Bulletin* 13 (Oct. 1934): 9, and 14 (Nov. 1935): 58; Catherine J. Duncan, "What Should Be Done in the Elementary Schools about the Present Situation as Regards the Negro?" ibid., 71. It should be pointed out that the southern states were relatively underrepresented in the ATA at this time.

53. Voters' Central Committee, minutes, 3 Feb. 1934, folder 517, box 18; Luther P. Jackson to Dear Friend, 23 Feb. 1935; Jackson and Doxey A. Wilkerson to Dear Fellow Citizen, 22 Mar. 1935, folder 509, box 18; "What the People Think about Voting in Petersburg, Virginia" [1939], 1, folder 524, box 18,; Jackson to Local Chairmen, 16 Dec. 1941, folder 512, box 18; all in Jackson Papers, VSU; Dennis, *Luther P. Jackson,* 72–84.

54. Melvyn Dubofsky, review of Marjorie Murphy, *Blackboard Unions: The AFT and the NEA, 1900–1980* (Ithaca: Cornell University Press, 1990), in *HEQ* 31 (Winter 1991): 552; H. A. Callis, "The Negro Teacher and the AFT," *JNE* 6 (Apr. 1937): 188–190; Rolland Bewing, "The American Federation of Teachers and Desegregation," *JNE* 42 (Winter 1973): 79.

55. Edith R. Ambrose, "Sarah Towles Reed and the Origins of Teacher Unions in New Orleans" (M.A. thesis, University of New Orleans, 1991), 16–22; Veronica B. Hill, interview by Leatrice R. Roberts, 7 Oct. 1983, audiotape, United Teachers of New Orleans Collection, Earl K. Long Library, University of New Orleans; Hill, interview by Edith Ambrose, 7 Nov. 1990, audiotape, Earl K. Long Library.

56. Tushnet, *NAACP's Legal Strategy,* 62–64.
57. Ibid., 82.
58. Ibid., 78–80; Picott, *Virginia Teachers Association,* 119–120; Joseph H. Saunders to Oliver Hill, 27 Dec. 1941, box 38, VTA Papers; L. F. Palmer to J. M. Tinsley, 14 May 1945, folder 531, box 37, VTA Papers; Tinsley to Irma B. Thompson, 9 May 1945, ibid.; Luther Porter Jackson, "Winning Victories but Standing Still," 19 June 1944, box 1618, Jackson Papers, VSU; Dennis, *Luther P. Jackson,* 123–131. Saunders had supported the VTA by giving teachers paid leave to attend Delegate Assembly meetings, and providing Lutrelle F. Palmer with free office space.
59. Eula Mae Lee Brown, Felix Armfield interview, 16 July 1994, audiotape 2, BTV; A. P. Tureaud to Thurgood Marshall, 10 May 1943, part 3, series B, box II-B-178, in *Papers of the NAACP,* reel 8.
60. "Present Status of Twenty-Four Plaintiffs," 28 Mar. 1946, folder 7, box 35; "Procedure Used for Rating Teachers in Iberville Parish, 1945–1946," folder 10, box 35; A. P. Tureaud to Thurgood Marshall, 17 Nov. 1945, folder 25, box 34; Tureaud to Marshall, 30 Aug. 1946; W. W. Harleaux to Daniel E. Byrd, 15 Oct. 1946, folder 28, box 34; all in A. P. Tureaud Papers, ARC.
61. Murray, *North Carolina State Teachers Association,* 48–50.
62. "Meeting of Joint Committee of State Teachers Association and Georgia Association of Colleges and Secondary Schools," 10 Mar. 1941, Macon, box 3, series 12-6-71, DNE (Ga.); James W. Holley, *You Can't Build a Chimney from the Top* (1949; Lanham, Md.: University Press of America, 1992), 168–169; Potts, *Palmetto Education Association,* 62–66; Drago, *Initiative, Paternalism, and Race Relations,* 240–242.
63. Donald Jones to Thurgood Marshall, 16 Nov. 1940, box II-B-178, reel 8; Walter White to Eugene Martin, 9 Dec. 1941; Martin to White, 13 Dec., 29 Dec. 1941, box II-B-177, reel 7; B. D. McDaniel to Walter White, 29 Sept. 1944, box II-B-175, reel 6; all in *Papers of the NAACP;* "Walter Chivers Says—Attention Again Georgia Teachers," *Atlanta World,* 12 Mar. 1941.
64. Joseph J. Rhoads, *Texas Commission on Democracy in Education: Abridged Annual Report* (Texas Colored State Teachers Association, 1942), 3, 5–6; Chirhart, *Torches of Light,* 199–200; Hill, Roberts interview. Teachers in Texas could count upon the Texas Council of Negro Organizations, a wide-ranging coalition put together by black leaders in Dallas and Houston.
65. Mark V. Tushnet, *Making Civil Rights Law: Thurgood Marshall and the Supreme Court, 1936–1961* (New York: Oxford University Press, 1994), 44–46; Marshall to Walter White, 17 Jan. 1942, part 3, series B, II; Marshall to Layla Lane, 11 Aug. 1941; Marshall to John Haynes Holmes, 9 Sept. 1941; H. W. Wright-LTA Members, 14 May 1943; Marshall, "Memo: Conference re Louisiana Teachers Salary Case," 23 Jan. 1945; all in *Papers of*

the NAACP; Porter and Neyland, *Florida State Teachers Association,* 67; Rhoads, *Texas Commission,* 15. In Louisiana, the white teachers association opposed equalization and supported "merit" systems—having previously opposed them—in an effort to preserve the racial differential. In Florida, white teachers intervened against the plaintiffs in one of the cases.

66. Tushnet, *NAACP's Legal Strategy,* 90–97; Scott Baker, "Testing Equality: The National Teacher Examination and the NAACP's Legal Campaign to Equalize Teachers' Salaries in the South, 1936–63," *HEQ* 25 (Spring 1995): 49–64; "Report on Negro Education in South Carolina," 26 July 1951, folder 4294, box 409, GEB Papers.

67. Chirhart, *Torches of Light,* 199–200; Constance Baker Motley, *Equal Justice under Law: An Autobiography* (New York: Farrar, Straus and Giroux, 1998), 71–79; Middleton, *Louisiana Education Association,* 71–84; Potts, *Palmetto Education Association,* 71–84; Picott, *Virginia Teachers Association,* 101; Porter and Neyland, *Florida State Teachers Association,* 76–77, 107–112; Murray, *North Carolina Teachers Association,* 34, 43. North Carolina's association appointed a full-time executive secretary as early as 1934. Florida's did not appoint one until 1954.

68. Tushnet, *NAACP's Legal Strategy,* 70–75; Walter White to Anson Phelps Stokes, 2 Nov. 1936, folder 11, box 31, PSF Papers.

69. "Transcript of Meeting of the Sub-Committee of the Governor's Committee on Higher Education for Negroes in Alabama," 1949, Trenholm Papers, MSRC.

70. Jack Greenberg, *Crusaders in the Courts: How a Dedicated Band of Lawyers Fought for the Civil Rights Revolution* (New York: Basic Books, 1994), 115.

9. Black Teachers and the Civil Rights Movement

1. Official Statement Adopted at the Conference of Negro Educators in Hot Springs, Arkansas, 26–27 Oct. 1954, pp. 8–9, folder 19, box 112, PSF Papers.

2. Hurley H. Doddy and G. Franklin Edwards, "Apprehensions of Negro Teachers concerning Desegregation in South Carolina," *JNE* 24 (Winter 1955): 30–31, 35; F. D. Patterson, "The Private Negro College in a Racially-Integrated System of Higher Education," *JNE* 21 (Summer 1952): 376.

3. Tushnet, *NAACP's Legal Strategy,* 113; J. K. Haynes to Thurgood Marshall, 26 Apr. 1974, folder 10, box 3, Daniel E. Byrd Papers, ARC; Middleton, *Louisiana Education Association,* 85.

4. Ira De A. Reid et al., "Court Action and Other Means of Achieving Racial Integration in Education," discussion, *JNE* 21 (Summer 1952): 396; Thurgood Marshall, "Report on Department of Teacher Information and

Security, January 1–June 30, 1955," folder 13, box 9, John W. Davis Papers, MSRC.

5. Ambrose Caliver, *National Conference on Fundamental Problems in the Education of Negroes: Fundamentals in the Education of Negroes* (Washington: GPO, 1934); Gavins, *Perils and Prospects of Southern Black Leadership,* 123–126; Gilpin, "Charles S. Johnson," 155.

6. Marshall to A. P. Tureaud, 11 Oct. 1950; Tushnet, *NAACP's Legal Strategy,* 136.

7. Chas. H. Thompson, "Editorial Comment: Negro Teachers and the Elimination of Segregated Schools," *JNE* 20 (Spring 1951): 135–139; Reid et al., "Court Action and Other Means," 386, 396; Martin D. Jenkins, "Problems Related to Racial Integration and Some Suggested Approaches to these Problems—A Critical Summary," *JNE* 21 (Summer 1952): 411–421; Virgil A. Clift, "Discussion of Papers," *JNE* 21 (Winter 1952): 302; "Report of Institute on Educational Leadership, July 12–16, 1954, Alabama A&M, Normal, Alabama," folder 22, box 160, SEF Papers.

8. B. Schrieke, *Alien Americans: A Study in Race Relations* (New York: Viking, 1936), 152; *Proceedings of the Fourteenth Annual Conference of the Presidents of Negro Land-Grant Colleges, November 10–11, 1936* (Washington, 1936), 37; Dennis, *Luther P. Jackson,* 18–19; Gerald L. Smith, *A Black Educator in the Segregated South: Kentucky's Rufus B. Atwood* (Lexington: University Press of Kentucky, 1994), 101; Lester C. Lamon, *Black Tennesseans, 1900–1930* (Knoxville: University of Tennessee Press, 1977), 103. Hale once faced a hostile board of examiners that, at an open meeting in the college chapel, threatened to close Tennessee A&I on the basis that it was no longer filling its function, as a land-grant college, of teaching agriculture. Hale thereupon addressed the assembled students "and called upon everyone who was taking agriculture to stand." The ploy worked: "Everyone stood, male and female, old and young, visitors and students. Even his gray-haired mother who was visiting him stood." See Greene, *Selling Black History,* 80.

9. Williams, *The Bonds,* 133–142; B. Carlyle Ramsey, "The Public Black College in Georgia: A History of Albany State College, 1903–1965" (Ph.D. diss., Florida State University, 1973), 146–164; Horace Mann Bond, "Proposed Statement, Negro Education" [1941], reel 5, part 3, series 4, *Bond Papers;* Edwin Embree to Bond, 7 Mar. 1941, *Bond Papers.* Bond also felt threatened because one of Talmadge's few black allies was Joseph W. Holley, head of a rival state school in Albany.

10. Essie Mae Washington-Williams and William Stadiem, *Dear Senator: A Memoir by the Daughter of Strom Thurmond* (New York: Regan Books, 2004), 115–118.

11. Augustus M. Burns III, "Graduate Education for Blacks in North Carolina,

1930–1951," *Journal of Southern History* 46 (May 1980): 195–205; White, "Some Tactics," 342; Bond to L. M. Lester, 27 Feb. 1941, reel 5, part 3, series 4, *Bond Papers.*

12. White, "Some Tactics," 342; Lewis K. McMillan, "Negro Higher Education as I Have Known It," *JNE* 8 (Jan. 1939): 14.

13. McMillan, "Negro Higher Education as I Have Known It," 18; Walter D. Cocking, "Outline for the Discussion of Higher Education for Negroes in Georgia," May 1938, folder 6, box 546, JRF Papers; J. Saunders Redding, *On Being Negro in America* (1951; New York: Bantam, 1964), 66–67; Redding, *Stranger and Alone,* 188; Lamona N. Evans, "The Administrative Styles of Presidents of Black Colleges in the Academic Novel" (Ph.D. diss., University of Oklahoma, 1987), 4–5, 162–194. Ralph Ellison's *Invisible Man* (1952) contains the best-known portrait of a black college president, "Dr. Bledsoe," but the novel made no attempt at realism and is less valuable as a historical source than Redding's novel. Colleges passing from fathers to sons or sons-in-law: Alabama State College (William B. Patterson to John W. Beverly, George W. Trenholm to H. Councill Trenholm); Southern University (J. S. Clark to Felton G. Clark); Winston-Salem State College (Simon G. Atkins to Fred L. Atkins); Tuskegee Institute (Robert R. Moton to Frederick D. Patterson).

14. Chas. H. Thompson, "Editorial Comment: Administrators of Negro Colleges and the Color Line in Higher Education in the South," *JNE* 17 (Fall 1948): 441, 445; Carl T. Rowan, *Dream Makers, Dream Breakers: The World of Justice Thurgood Marshall* (Boston: Little, Brown, 1993), 151–153; Tushnet, *NAACP's Legal Strategy,* 107–108; Ozie H. Johnson, *Price of Freedom* (Self-published, 1954), 28, 176.

15. Bessie V. Sampson and Rosa S. Riley, "A Brief History of Ebenezer School, Dalzett, South Carolina," 1976, folder 3, box 8; *Minutes of the General Assembly of the Presbyterian Church* (New York, 1877); *Ninety-Eighth Annual Report of the Board of Home Missions of the Presbyterian Church* (New York, 1900); clipping, *Durham Herald,* 25 May 1961, all in folder 1, box 7; all in Seabrook Papers, FSU.

16. Charles S. Johnson, "Remarks at Opening of the Institute," 2 July 1951, folder 16, box 160, Charles S. Johnson Papers; Charles H. Thompson et al., "Discussion of Papers," *JNE* 21 (Summer 1952): 263–264. J. W. Seabrook, speech for workshop of the North Carolina Division of the American Association of University Women, 21 Mar. 1955, folder 2, box 4, Seabrook Papers; speech, Lincoln Academy, King's Mountain, 19 Apr. 1940, folder 8, box 4, Seabrook Papers; speech to Wilson American Legion, St. John AME Church, 12 Nov. 1950, folder 2, box 4, Seabrook Papers.

17. William H. Chafe, *Civilities and Civil Rights: Greensboro, North Carolina, and the Black Struggle for Freedom* (New York: Oxford University Press,

1980), 66–68; Ella Louise Murphy, "J. W. Seabrook's Role as an Educator in North Carolina," n.d., folder 16, box 3, Seabrook Papers, FSU. Like many black professionals, Seabrook used initials to discourage whites from addressing him by his first name.

18. Seabrook, "Speech to Chapel Assembly, Fayetteville State Training College," 30 Sept. 1957, folder 3, box 4, Seabrook Papers, FSU.

19. Judy J. Mohraz, *The Separate Problem: Case Studies of Black Education in the North, 1900–1930* (Westport, Conn.: Greenwood, 1979); Vincent P. Franklin, *The Education of Black Philadelphia: The Social and Educational History of a Minority Community* (Philadelphia: University of Pennsylvania Press, 1979).

20. Truman M. Pierce et al., *White and Negro Schools in the South: An Analysis of Bi-racial Education* (Englewood Cliffs, N.J.: Prentice-Hall, 1955), 200; Albert L. Turner, "Higher Education in Alabama," *Quarterly Review of Higher Education among Negroes* 5:4 (Oct. 1937): 156–157. On barely literate teachers acquiring college degrees, see also William Couch Jr., "Rural Education in Mississippi," *JNE* 21 (Spring 1952): 228.

21. A. P. Tureaud to Thurgood Marshall, 30 July 1948, box III-B-178, reel 8, part 3, series B, *Papers of the NAACP;* Myrdal, *American Dilemma,* 2:880; "Statement of John W. Davis," 20 June 1955, folder 1, box 5, Byrd Papers; "North Carolina Workshop for Principals, North Carolina College, Durham, June 21–31, 1954," folder 11, box 160, SEF Papers; NAACP Legal Defense and Educational Fund to Foundations, "Program to Protect Negro Teachers from Dismissal as a Result of Integration of Public Schools" [1955], folder 13, box 9, Davis Papers, MSRC.

22. Richard Kluger, *Simple Justice: The History of Brown v. Board of Education and Black America's Struggle for Equality* (New York: Knopf, 1976), 4–26, 451–479; Julie M. Lochbaum, "The Word Made Flesh: The Desegregation Leadership of the Rev. J. A. DeLaine" (Ph.D. diss., University of South Carolina, 1993), 127–149; Sonny DuBose, *The Road to Brown: The Leadership of a Soldier of the Cross, Rev. J. A. DeLaine* (Orangeburg, S.C.: Williams Pub., 2002), 30–53.

23. Numan V. Bartley, *The Rise of Massive Resistance* (Baton Rouge: Louisiana State University Press, 1969), 212–222; Tushnet, *Making Civil Rights Law,* 272–300; statement of Clara Jackson [1961]; statement of Gloria S. Prescott; Daniel E. Byrd to A. P. Tureaud, 30 Aug. 1961; *Lake Charles American,* 21 Dec. 1960, all in folder 10, box 62, Tureaud Papers; Daniel E. Byrd to Thurgood Marshall, "Intimidation of Plaintiffs in Louisiana," 23 Aug. 1955, folder 26, box 10, Tureaud Papers, ARC; Hal D. DeCell to Ney M. Gove, "Negro School Teachers," 7 Aug. 1957, MSSCR.

24. John W. Davis, "Statement to Members of the Board of Directors," 11 May 1955, folder 5, box 23, Davis Papers; Stephen G. N. Tuck, *Beyond Atlanta:*

The Struggle for Racial Equality in Georgia, 1940–1980 (Athens: University of Georgia Press, 2001), 99–100; notes of meeting of Georgia NAACP, 16 July 1955, folder 19, box 33, Davis Papers; Cecil J. Williams, *Freedom and Justice: Four Decades of the Civil Rights Struggle as Seen by a Black Photographer of the Deep South* (Macon, Ga.: Mercer University Press, 1995), 123–126; Septima Clark, Jacquelyn Hall interview, 25 July 1976, 69, Southern Oral History Project, University of North Carolina, Chapel Hill; Janice B. Modjeski, "The Whittemore School: An African-American School in Horry County, South Carolina, 1870–1970" (Ph.D. diss., University of South Carolina, 1999), 24. The dismissal of Septima Clark benefited the civil rights movement. Clark joined the staff of the Highlander Folk School, and, in 1960, the staff of the Southern Christian Leadership Conference.

25. Lucius H. Pitts to Claude Purrell, 19 July 1960, box 87, VTA Papers.

26. Schultz, *National Education Association and the Black Teacher,* 58–64; *Addresses and Proceedings of the Eighty-first Annual Meeting of the National Education Association* (Washington: NEA, 1943), 189–197.

27. Schultz, *National Education Association and the Black Teacher,* 70–80, 103–105; *Addresses and Proceedings of the Ninety-Seventh Annual Meeting of the National Education Association* (Washington: NEA, 1959), 191.

28. Schultz, *National Education Association and the Black Teacher,* 83; Williams, *Freedom and Justice,* 124. *Addresses and Proceedings of the Ninety-Eighth Annual Meeting of the National Education Association* (Washington: NEA, 1960), 179.

29. Daniel E. Byrd to John W. Davis, 8 Feb. 1956, box 89, VTA Papers.

30. Schultz, *National Education Association and the Black Teacher,* 124–160.

31. Rolland Dewing, "The American Federation of Teachers and Desegregation," *JNE* 42 (Winter 1973): 81–90.

32. Byrd to J. Rupert Picott, 9 Jan. 1957, box 87, VTA Papers; NCOSTA, minutes of special meeting, Richmond, Va., 19 Jan. 1957, VTA Papers; John W. Davis to Picott, 31 Oct. 1957, VTA Papers; Picott to Lucius H. Pitts, 15 Dec. 1959; Davis, "NCOSTA: Review and Report," 8 Feb. 1963, folder 21, box 2, Byrd Papers, ARC; Middleton, *Louisiana Education Association,* 90.

33. Tushnet, *NAACP's Legal Strategy,* 115, 151.

34. Amilcar Shabazz, "The Opening of the Southern Mind: The Desegregation of Higher Education in Texas, 1865–1965" (Ph.D. diss., University of Houston, 1996), 120–130; Jack Greenberg, *Crusaders in the Courts: How a Dedicated Band of Lawyers Fought for the Civil Rights Revolution* (New York: Basic Books, 1994), 86; Byrd to Marshall, 12 Sept. 1951, folder 1, box 1, Byrd Papers, ARC.

35. Greenberg, *Crusaders in the Courts,* 85.

36. Motley, *Equal Justice under Law,* 107; Constance Baker Motley, interview

by Jack Bass, 21 June 1979, 72, Jack Bass Collection, Tulane University Law Library.

37. Malcolm Johnson, interview by Jackson Lee Ice, 7–12, part of "An Oral History of the Civil Rights Movement in Tallahassee, Florida," Special Collections, Strozier Library, Florida State University.

38. Jo Ann Gibson Robinson, *The Montgomery Bus Boycott and the Women Who Started It: The Memoir of Jo Ann Gibson Robinson* (Knoxville: University of Tennessee Press, 1897), 47–52; Florida Legislative Investigation Committee, "Florida Bar Association: NAACP Investigation Files, 1957–1960," transcripts of testimony, 336–337, 716–728, 741, 761–768, M81–O17, Florida State Archives, Tallahassee; Glenda Alice Rabby, *The Pain and the Promise: The Struggle for Civil Rights in Tallahassee, Florida* (Athens: University of Georgia Press, 1999), 38–40.

39. Williams, *Freedom and Justice,* 97–113.

40. *Pittsburgh Courier,* 16 Mar. 1957; West Point, Mississippi *Daily Times Leader,* 3 May 1958, both in Clennon King file, MSSCR.

41. Chafe, *Civilities and Civil Rights,* 95; Thomas Dent, *Southern Journey: A Return to the Civil Rights Movement* (New York: William Morrow, 1979), 28–33; Smith, *Black Educator in the Segregated South,* 157. At Kentucky State College, located in a border state, Rufus B. Atwood expelled twelve student activists and fired two faculty members.

42. K. H. Steele to Trenholm, 11 Mar. 1960; B. Hudson to Trenholm, n.d.; T. J. Austin to Trenholm, 3 Mar. 1960; all in box 26, Trenholm Papers, MSRC.

43. Felton G. Clark to Chicago alumni of Southern University, 29 Apr. 1960, sit-in file, Felton G. Clark Papers, Southern University, Baton Rouge.

44. Reddix, *Voice Crying in the Wilderness,* 222.

45. Adolph R. Reed to Felton G. Clark, 24 Jan. 1962, folder 349, series 5, *Papers of the Congress of Racial Equality, 1941–1967,* microfilm, 49 reels (Sanford, N.C.: Microfilming Corp. of America, 1980); Woolfolk, *Prairie View,* 330; Samuel L. Gandy, "Education and Responsibility," n.d. [1960], box 33, Davis Papers, MSRC.

46. James A. Colston to Frederick D. Patterson, 13 Oct. 1960, folder 18, box 118; Patterson to Robert Van Wares, 1 Dec. 1960; both in PSF Papers.

47. W. E. Solomon to NCOSTA, 18 Oct. 1963, box 87, VTA Papers; J. Rupert Picott to Solomon, 23 Oct. 1963, VTA Papers; W. W. Harleaux to Wiley Branton, 16 Oct. 1962, series F, folder 134, addendum, *Papers of the Congress of Racial Equality;* Miriam Feingold to Family, 31 July, 5 Aug., 19 Aug. 1963, reel 1, and Hazel P. Matthews to Miriam Feingold, 6 Oct. 1963, in Feingold Papers, State Historical Society of Wisconsin; Lance Hill, *The Deacons for Defense: Armed Resistance and the Civil Rights Movement* (Chapel Hill: University of North Carolina Press, 2004), 62; John Dittmer, *Lo-*

cal People: The Struggle for Civil Rights in Mississippi (Urbana: University of Illinois Press, 1994), 75. Jack Minnis to Wiley A. Branton, 20 Aug. 1963, folder 153; Jack Brady, report from Lake Charles, 18 Oct. 1963; Lavert Taylor, report from Iberia, La., 30 Oct. 1963; all in Southern Regional Council Papers (microfilm), Alderman Library, University of Virginia. See also Charles M. Payne, *I've Got the Light of Freedom: The Organizing Tradition and the Mississippi Freedom Struggle* (Berkeley: University of California Press, 1995), 138, 177.

48. David Matthews, Paul Ortiz interview, n.d., 20, BTV; Edran Auguster, Michele Mitchell interview, audiotape 3, 21 July 1994, BTV; Cyrus Jackson, Michele Mitchell interview, audiotape 1, 10 Aug. 1994, BTV; "Conference of Executive Secretaries of State Teachers Associations and Phelps-Stokes Fund, July 25–27, 1960," 4–5, box 87, VTA Papers.

49. Fleming, *In the Shadow of Selma,* 154, 189–193.

50. Glenn T. Eskew, *But for Birmingham: The Local and National Movements in the Civil Rights Struggle* (Chapel Hill: University of North Carolina Press, 1997); Oliver, *End of an Era,* 44–45.

51. Zack J. Van Landingham to Director, "NAACP, Taylorsville, Mississippi," 14 Nov. 1958, and Rev. J. H. Harvey to James P. Coleman, 20 Oct. 1958, both in file 9-7-7, MSSRC; B. L. Bell to Governor J. P. Coleman, 13 Nov. 1958, ID 9-9-0-1-2-11; Zack L. Van Landingham to Coleman, "B. L. Bell," 12 Jan. 1959, ID 2-10-0-6-1-1-1; Van Landingham to Director, State Sovereignty Commission, "NAACP, Claiborne County," 18 Mar. 1959, ID 2-109-0-1-1-1-1; Tom Scarborough, "Attala County," 2 Sept. 1960, ID 2-78-0-11-1-1-1, all in MSSCR; Emilye Crosbye, *A Little Taste of Freedom: The Black Freedom Struggle in Claiborne County, Mississippi* (Chapel Hill: University of North Carolina Press, 2005), 72–73, 104–105.

52. Zack J. Van Landingham, "B. L. Bell," 26 Jan. 1960, ID 2-2-0-56-1-1-1, and Andy Hopkins to Director, "NAACP Activities, Claiborne County," 27 June 1960, ID 2-109-0-7-1-1-1, both in MSSCR.

53. Zack J. Van Landingham, "Medgar Evers," 24 July 1959, ID 1-23-0-48-1-1-1, MSSRC; Fleming, *In the Shadow of Selma,* 243.

54. Michael J. Klarman, *From Jim Crow to Civil Rights: The Supreme Court and the Struggle for Racial Equality* (New York: Oxford University Press, 2004), 335–339; Anthony G. Pierre to Mary Jamieson, 27 Apr. 1966, folder 3, box 1, NAACP Papers (La.); Linton J. Carmouche to Harvey R. H. Britton, 22 Oct. 1968, NAACP Papers; Murray, *North Carolina Teachers Association,* 94.

55. Seabrook to Sanford, 16 June 1963, folder 8, box 1, Seabrook Papers, FSU.

56. *LEA Journal* (Feb. 1965): 3, 24; J. Rupert Picott to J. K. Haynes, 15 Aug. 1960, box 87, VTA Papers.

57. Ronald E. Butchart, "'Outthinking and Outflanking the Owners of the World': A Historiography of the African American Struggle for Education," *HEQ* 28 (Fall 1988), 341–351; Myrdal, *American Dilemma,* 1:881; Bullock, *History of Negro Education in the South,* vii–ix; Raymond Wolters, *The New Negro on Campus: Black College Rebellions of the 1920s* (Princeton: Princeton University Press, 1975), 341; Leloudis, *Schooling the New South,* 223.

58. Henry, *The Fire Ever Burning,* 40–42; Chafe, *Civilities and Civil Rights,* 23–24.

59. Davis, *Angela Davis,* 92–93; Young, *An Easy Burden,* 30–33; Newby, *Black Carolinians,* 273.

60. Dent, *Southern Journey,* 304, 329–330.

61. Henry, *The Fire Ever Burning,* 44; John Lewis, with Michael D'Orso, *Walking with the Wind: A Memoir of the Movement* (New York: Simon and Schuster, 1998), 45–46; Davis, *Angela Davis,* 90–91.

62. Davis, *Angela Davis,* 91.

63. Henry, *Fire Ever Burning,* 44.

10. Integration: Loss and Profit

1. There may gave been a small number of teachers, mostly black teachers, who had previously taught in racially integrated schools in the North.

2. Robinson, *Bell Rings at Four,* 128.

3. Ramsey, "More Than the Three R's," 271–272; Douglas R. Davis, "Crossing Over: An Oral History of the Desegregation Experience of Public School Personnel in East Baton Rouge Parish, Louisiana" (Ph.D. diss., Louisiana State University, 1999), 98; Chafe, *Civilities and Civil Rights,* 222–233.

4. Jane C. McKinzey, "In the Crossfire: A Case Study of Teachers and Racial Transition" (Ph.D. diss., Georgia State University, 1999), 171–174.

5. Dana V. Wilson and William E. Segall, *Oh, Do I Remember! Experiences of Teachers during the Desegregation of Austin's Schools, 1964–1971* (Albany: SUNY Press, 2001), 92; Edith Polk, interview; NEA, "School Desegregation in Louisiana," 10–12; Ramsey, "More Than the Three R's," 275, 278, 288; Robinson, *The Bell Rings at Four,* 114; McKinzey, "In the Crossfire," 288–290; Davis, "Crossing Over," 104, 120.

6. Michele Foster, *Black Teachers on Teaching* (New York: New Press, 1997), 60–61; McKinzey, "In the Crossfire," 182, 225; Davis, "Crossing Over," 102–103; Ramsey, "More Than the 3 R's," 279–283.

7. Davison, *Reading, Writing, and Race,* 226; J. K. Haynes to Jack Greenberg, 26 Apr. 1975, folder 10, box 3; Daniel E. Byrd to Margrett Ford, 16 Dec. 1972, folder 8, box 3; Vermilion Parish Citizens for a Democratic Society

to Vermilion Parish School Board [1972], folder 9, box 4; all in Byrd Papers, ARC.

8. Robinson, *Bell Rings at Four,* 130; Daniel E. Byrd to Michael H. Cohen, 30 Apr. 1971, folder 6, box 3, Byrd Papers; Winfred E. Pitts, "E. E. Butler High School, Desegregation, and the Gainesville City-Hall County, Georgia, Schools, 1821–1973: A Victory of Sorts" (Ph.D. diss., Georgia State University, 1999), 210–212; Wilson and Segall, *Oh, Do I Remember!* 87; McKinzey, "In the Crossfire," 271; Auguster, Mitchell interview, tape 1.

9. Harvey Britton, "Chronological Summary of Events of Student Demonstrations at Alcee Fortier High School," 17–28 Jan., folder 6, box 5; "Report of the Special Committee by the Orleans Parish School Board and Superintendent Carl Dolce on the Fortier High School Crisis," 17 Mar. 1969, folder 1, box 6; Harvey Britton, Summary Report, 14 Sept. 1970, folder 5, box 25; Students of Jefferson Davis High School to Britton, 17 Dec. 1969, box 6, folder 7; all in NAACP Papers (La.); Concerned Citizens for Equal Education to Caddo Parish School Board, Aug. 1972, folder 5, box 5, Byrd Papers.

10. Pitts, "E. E. Butler High School," 145; W. Blanchett, Warren G. Palmer interview, 1977, audiotape, Palmer Collection; Ramsey, "More Than the Three R's," 293; Jodi B. Petit, "A Community That Cared: The Study of an All-Black School: E. E. Smith High, Fayetteville, North Carolina, 1955–1969" (Ph.D. diss., University of Kansas, 1997), 147–152; McKinzey, "In the Crossfire," 270–272; Gerald A. Foster and Vonita W. Foster, *Silent Trumpets of Justice: Integration's Failure in Prince Edward County* (Hampton, Va.: UB&US Communication System, 1993), 19; Janice B. Modjeski, "The Whittemore School: An African American School in Horry County, South Carolina, 1870–1978" (Ph.D. diss., University of South Carolina, 1999), 219–220; Mandara, "Impact of Family Functioning," 216–219.

11. Ramsey, "More Than the 3 R's," 292–293, 309; Daniel Byrd, "Special Report: Vermilion Parish," 14 Jan. 1972, folder 9, box 4; Byrd, "Special Report: St. John Parish," 2 Mar. 1973; Byrd to Norman Chachkin, 31 Mar. 1973; Byrd, "Special Report: Lafourche Parish," 7 Apr. 1973; all in Byrd Papers, ARC.

12. Davison M. Douglas, *Reading, Writing, and Race: The Desegregation of Charlotte Schools* (Chapel Hill: University of North Carolina Press, 1995), 111–112; A. P. Tureaud to J. K. Haynes, 6 Dec. 1967, folder 3, box 3, Byrd Papers; Samuel B. Ethridge to Richard E. Kennan, "Regional Meeting of Educators and Civil Rights Leaders," 14 June 1965, folder 1227, box 78, VTA Papers; Rabby, *The Pain and the Promise,* 235.

13. Wade Mackie to Garnett Guild, "Fourth Month, 12–18 Days, 1964," 24 Apr. 1964, South Central Regional Office files, AFSC Papers, Philadelphia.

14. E. Ahalt to Dear [Teacher], 15 May 1964, folder 1218; S. W. Tucker to

Judge Thomas J. Michie, 15 June 1965; Rupert E. Picott to Oscar E. Thompson, 26 Jan. 1965; Robert L. Cousins to Executive Secretaries, 24 Sept. 1965, all in box 78, VTA Papers.

15. Report of NEA Task Force III, "School Desegregation in Louisiana and Mississippi," Oct. 1970, 9, 14, 23–25, UTNO Collection.

16. Ibid., 4–7; Jeremiah Floyd, "A Study of Displaced Black High School Principals in the State of South Carolina," 1963–1973" (Ph.D. thesis, Northwestern University, 1973), 14–18, 33–34, 72–101.

17. Cyrus Jackson, Mitchell interview, audiotape 1, BTV; J. B. Henderson, Michele Wallace interview, 20 July 1994, audiotape 1, BTV; Edran Auguster, Michele Mitchell interview, 19 July 1994, audiotape 1, BTV; NEA, "School Desegregation in Louisiana and Mississippi," 17.

18. Harvey Britton, "Annual Report," 18 Nov. 1970, folder 8, box 9, NAACP Papers (La.); *Baton Rouge Morning Advocate,* 2 Apr. 1970; Fairclough, *Race and Democracy,* 451; David S. Cecelski, *Along Freedom Road: Hyde County, North Carolina, and the Fate of Black Schools in the South* (Chapel Hill: University of North Carolina Press, 1994), 161–162; Daniel E. Byrd, "Activity Report," Dec. 1972, 1, folder 3, box 4, Byrd Papers.

19. Margaret Rogers, Kara Miles interview, Wilmington, N.C. [1994], 12, BTV; Marion O. White, Patricia Rickels interview, 1979, recording, University of Southwestern Louisiana, Lafayette; Harvey R. H. Britton, Adam Fairclough interview, 4 Nov. 1987, 5, ARC; Britton to Johnnie Mae Walton, 2 Nov. 1970, folder 7, box 9, NAACP Papers (La.).

20. Greenberg, *Crusaders in the Courts,* 85, 391; John W. Davis to J. K. Haynes, 31 Oct. 1967, folder 3, box 3, Byrd Papers; Daniel E. Byrd to Jack Greenberg, 29 Nov. 1972, folder 8, box 3, Byrd Papers, ARC.

21. "Conference of Executive Secretaries of State Teachers Associations," 4; Basile Miller to Daniel E. Byrd [1967], folder 2, box 3, Byrd Papers, ARC.

22. Michael Fultz, "The Displacement of Black Educators Post-*Brown:* An Overview and Analysis," *HEQ* 44 (Spring 2004), 84; Robert W. Hooker, *Displacement of Black Teachers in the Eleven Southern States* (Nashville: Race Relations Information Center, 1970), 13–14; Porter and Neyland, *Florida State Teachers Association,* 147.

23. Fultz, "Displacement of Black Educators," 46–48; Hooker, *Displacement of Black Teachers,* 6–7; Daniel E. Byrd to Norman Chachkin, 16 Dec. 1972, folder 8, box 3, Byrd Papers; Charles C. Bolton, "The Last Stand of Massive Resistance: Mississippi Public School Integration, 1970," *Journal of Southern History* 61 (Winter 1999): 349.

24. Fultz, "Displacement of Black Educators," 38–45; Cecelski, *Along Freedom Road,* 8; Perry, *American Teachers Association,* 362–365; Murray, *North Carolina Teachers Association,* 93–96; Patterson, *Arkansas Teachers Association,* 156–157; McDaniel, *State Teachers Association of Texas,* 64–74, 116–

120; Hooker, *Displacement of Black Teachers*, 14; Tuck, *Beyond Atlanta*, 212; Ronald H. Bayor, *Race and the Shaping of Twentieth-Century Atlanta* (Chapel Hill: University of North Carolina Press, 1996), 249; Fairclough, *Race and Democracy*, 456–457.

25. Perry, *American Teachers Association*, 357–362, 371–372; Allan M. West, *The National Education Association: The Power Base for Education* (New York: Free Press, 1980), 117–121.

26. Schultz, *National Education Association and the Black Teacher*, 150–154, 169–197; West, *National Education Association*, 128–133; Potts, *Palmetto Education Association*, 203–209.

27. Murray, *North Carolina Teachers Association*, 114.

28. West, *National Education Association*, 116–161; Don Eddins, *AEA: Head of the Class in Alabama Politics* (Montgomery: Alabama Education Association, 1997), 95–116; Fairclough, *Race and Democracy*, 457–458.

29. Eddins, *AEA*, 111; Middleton, *Louisiana Education Association*, 149.

30. Middleton, *Louisiana Education Association*, 132, 138, 148; Picott, *Virginia Teachers Association*, 222.

31. Robinson, *Bell Rings at Four*, 131; John T. Yun and Sean F. Reardon, "Trends in Public School Desegregation in the South, 1987–2000," paper presented at the Resegregation of Southern Schools Conference, University of North Carolina at Chapel Hill, 30 Aug. 2002, 10, accessed at www.civilrightsproject.harvard.edu.

32. "JBHE Ranks the States in the Employment of Black Teachers," *Journal of Blacks in Higher Education* (Autumn 1998): 25–27; Mildred J. Hudson and Barbara J. Holmes, "Missing Teachers, Impaired Communities: The Unanticipated Consequences of *Brown v. Board of Education* on the African American Teaching Force at the Precollegiate Level," *JNE* 63 (Summer 1994): 388–389; Chance W. Lewis, "African American Male Teachers in Public Schools: An Examination of Three Urban School Districts," *Teachers College Record* 108 (Feb. 2006): 224.

33. Catherine Ellis, "The Legacy of Jim Crow in Rural Louisiana" (Ph.D. diss., Columbia University, 2000), 379–393; Thomas Sowell, *Education: Assumption versus History; Collected Papers* (Stanford: Hoover Institution Press, 1986), 7–37; Tate, Palmer interview; Edwards, "Booker T. Washington High School," 126; Auguster, Mitchell interview, tape 1.

34. Pierce, *White and Negro Schools in the South*, 165–177, 206, 289.

35. U.S. Bureau of the Census, "Percent of People 25 Years and Over Who Have Completed High School or College, by Race, Hispanic Origin and Sex: Selected Years 1940 to 2004," www.census.gov (accessed 26 Jan. 2006). These figures do not distinguish between regions, so part of this improvement may reflect migration from southern to northern states.

36. Charles C. Bolton, "Mississippi's School Equalization Program, 1945–

1954: 'A Last Gasp to Try to Maintain a Segregated Educational System,'"
Journal of Southern History 4 (Nov. 2000): 781–814. This discussion of
equalization does not include border states like Kentucky and Maryland.
In three southern states, Virginia, North Carolina, and Tennessee, the average pay of black teachers slightly exceeded that of whites.

37. T. A. Carmichael, speech to Greenville Kiwanis Club, 28 Apr. 1959, box
10, series 12-7-71, DNE (Ga.).

38. Lewis, "African American Male Teachers in Public Schools," 224–226;
Wilson and Segall, *Oh, Do I Remember!* 117–129; James D. Anderson, "The
Historical Context for Understanding the Test Score Gap," *Journal of Pub-
lic Management and Social Policy* 10 (Summer, 2004): 2–22.

39. Bureau of the Census, *Social and Economic Characteristics of the Black Population,* 76; Bureau of the Census, *1970 Census of Population, Supplementary
Report,* table 236, "Detailed Industries of Employed Persons by Race and
Sex: 1970," http://www2.census.gov; Bureau of the Census, *Household
Data, Annual Averages, 2005,* table 11, "Employed Persons by Detailed Occupation, Sex, Race, and Hispanic or Latin Ethnicity," ftp://ftp.bls.gov/
pub/special.requests/lf/aat11.txt.

40. G. Pritchy Smith, "Tomorrow's White Teachers: A Response to the
Holmes Group," *JNE* 57 (Spring 1988): 180; Abigail Thernstrom and
Stephan Thernstrom, *No Excuses: Closing the Racial Gap in Learning* (New
York: Simon and Schuster, 2003), 202–205; "Southern University Regains
Teacher Training Accreditation," *Black Issues in Higher Education,* 2 Dec.
2004, http://www.findarticles.com.

41. Gary Orfield, "Unexpected Costs and Uncertain Gains of Dismantling De-
segregation," in *Dismantling Desegregation: The Quiet Reversal of Brown v.
Board of Education,* ed. Gary Orfield and Susan E. Eaton (New York: New
Press, 1996), 84.

42. U.S. Bureau of the Census, *Educational Attainment, Historical Tables,* table
A-2, "Percent of People 25 Years and Over Who Have Completed High
School or College," http://www.census.gov/43population/socdemo/educa-
tion/tabA-2.pdf (30 May 2006); "Closing the Achievement Gap," North
Central Regional Educational Laboratory, 2002, http://www.ncrel.org/gap/
library/racetrends.htm (30 May 2006).

43. Minutes of group superintendents meetings, Winston-Salem, 28 May
1940; Washington, 31 May 1940; Carthage, 5 June 1940; Wilmington, 25
June 1940; Asheville, 12 July 1940; all in box 11, Special Subject File, DNE
(N.C.).

44. Joseph E. Gibson, "An Approach to the Problem of Vocational Education
for Negroes," 18 Apr. 1942, reel 67, "Early Southern Programs: Louisiana,"
GEB Archives; Gene Sutherland, "H. J. Voorhies, vice-president and general manager, Esso," 2 May 1955; Sutherland to Thelma Babbit, "James L.

Mehaffy, international representative, Communication Workers of America, Local 3403, CIO," 12 Mar. 1955; all in South Central Regional Office Files, AFSC Papers, Philadelphia.

45. Chesnutt to Washington, 11 Aug. 1903, in Harlan, *Booker T. Washington Papers*, 9:265.

46. James C. Cobb, *The Brown Decision, Jim Crow, and Southern Identity* (Athens: University of Georgia Press, 2005), 65–66. Savage, "Claiborne's Institute to Natchez High School," 152; Davis, "Crossing Over," 106.

47. Horace Mann Bond, "The Present Status of Racial Integration in the United States with Special Reference to Education," *JNE* 21 (summer 1952): 250.

Acknowledgments

During the eleven years it has taken me to research and write *A Class of Their Own,* I have accumulated innumerable debts—so many that I am in danger of overlooking more than a few. To those whom I have inadvertently omitted, my apologies and thanks. Impossible to overlook, and a pleasure to place first, is my gratitude to Joyce Seltzer, my editor at Harvard University Press. Joyce's confidence in my ability to write this book has buoyed me during the last five years. Her enthusiasm for the project and her constructive criticism enabled me to complete it. Joyce kept me going during the slack times and spurred me on to the finishing post. Other members of the Harvard University Press team, including Camille Smith and Gwen Frankfeldt, were also a pleasure to work with. They, too, left a mark on this book.

If this book is at all readable, it owes a great deal to Wendy Nelson, my manuscript editor. Wendy's unobtrusive but meticulous editing has spared readers from innumerable stylistic infelicities, incomprehensible anglicisms, and puzzling non sequiturs. Whatever weaknesses survive the editorial process are of course my responsibility alone.

Institutional support, and the individuals who helped me to secure it, also come high on my list of debts. A year-long fellowship at the National Humanities Center in Research Triangle Park, North Carolina, in 1994–1995 enabled me to lay the groundwork for this book. The staff of the NHC—librarians, secretaries, and administrators, some now retired—all contributed to making that year enjoyable and productive. The NHC fellowship launched my research into black teachers and also contributed to three other books, each of which rehearsed some of the arguments presented here. I hope that *A Class of Their Own,* although a long time coming, vindicates the NHC's endorsement of this project so many years ago. Thanks to the NHC, I also established scholarly contacts that affected this book in intangible but very positive ways. Vernon Burton, David Carlton, Ellen Schrecker, Rhonda Cobham-Sander, and many others furnished friendship and intellectual stimulation during a marvelous year.

The first four chapters of this book were drafted during a semester's leave made possible by a research grant from the Spencer Foundation. This generous support kick-started the book at a time when I had begun to doubt that my research would ever cohere or appear between the covers of a book. I completed the writing during a year of leave jointly financed by the University of East Anglia and the Arts and Humanities Research Council. The University of East Anglia supported my research in many other ways during my eight years there, enabling me to obtain microfilm, attend conferences, and visit archives. That admirable institution, the British Academy—efficient, flexible, red-tape free—financed three research trips to the United States, enabling me to visit Nashville, Atlanta, Tuskegee, Petersburg, Richmond, and several cities in North Carolina. The Gilder-Lehrman Institute financed a visit to New York to work at the Schomburg Center for Research in Black Culture. A generous grant from the Rockefeller Archive Center enabled me to study the massive collection of the General Education Board.

Many eminent scholars took the time and trouble to respond to my incessant requests for letters of recommendation. They include Steven Lawson, David Garrow, Bill Chafe, John Dittmer, Jeff Norrell, Glenda Gilmore, and Tony Badger. I thank them all—but make no promise that I will not bombard them with many similar requests in the future. For encouragement and help along the way I am also indebted to Richard Crockatt, Michael Cass, Jack Doherty, David Carlton, Shearer D. Bowman, Ray Gavins, David Thelen, Glenda Gilmore, Jacquelyn

Dowd Hall, Connie Curry, Cita Cook, and several anonymous readers. Ronald Butchart's incisive review of a first effort, *Teaching Equality,* proved bracing and useful. Brian Kelley's equally trenchant review of *Better Day Coming* challenged me to reconsider my view of Booker T. Washington. In breach of an old habit of never sending draft chapters to other scholars, I asked two historians, Eric Foner and Ann Short Chirhart, to comment on portions of the manuscript. Their suggestions were invaluable; and I am deeply grateful to them both. Pat Haggler generously shared with me her research on Laurinburg Institute, whose fascinating history features in Chapter 5. My new colleagues at Leiden University, especially Eduard van de Bilt, Joke Kardux, and Chris Quispel, do not realize how they helped me to finish this book. But their friendly welcome, and patience with my atrocious Dutch, made everything that much easier as I came down to the wire.

The librarians and archivists I encountered during eleven years of research were consistently helpful and accommodating. We historians could not function without them. I wish to thank them all. Lucius Edwards of the Special Collections at Virginia State University and Carter Cue of the University Archives at Winston-Salem State University deserve a special word of appreciation in that they both went out of their way to make me feel welcome.

Several people have helped me in ways that went above and beyond the call of duty. Tony Badger, the Mellon Professor of American History at Cambridge University and now also Master of Clare College, has supported and helped me over many years. Tony continues to provide me, and other British Americanists, with an inspiring example of scholarly generosity and academic leadership. Over the last ten years Ellen Schrecker and Marvin Gettelmann have given me hospitality, friendship, and intellectual companionship. Undertaking research in New York, while staying with Ellen and Marv, has always been a pleasure. My wife, Mary Ellen Curtin, has contributed to this book not merely through patience and love, but also through our ongoing after-dinner debates about the South, Reconstruction, Barbara Jordan, and African American history. I think Mary Ellen knows how much this book owes to her. Words of thanks are inadequate. They are offered here nonetheless.

A study as broad as this one rests upon the work of many other scholars. My footnotes attest to the many Ph.D. dissertations that I have consulted. They also show the extent to which I have relied upon the research of Horace Mann Bond, Henry Allen Bullock, George Woolfolk, Louis Harlan, James D. Anderson, Robert Engs, Ronald Butchart, Michael Fultz, and many other historians of African American education. Although I have often differed with the conclusions of these scholars, their work has influenced and inspired me.

In writing a book about teachers I became acutely aware of how much my interest in history depended upon the encouragement and enthusiasm of my own teachers. Mr. Johnston (I never knew his first name) encouraged me, as an eight-year-old boy, to write stories about the American Civil War. Two teachers at Hampton Grammar School, Ernest Badman and Simon Williams, employed very different styles to show their students how, by analyzing the past, we make the study of history more compelling. At Oxford I had the privilege of being taught by, among others, Maurice Keen, John Prest, Richard Cobb, Raymond Carr, Angus Walker, and Duncan McLeod. Carl Degler, the Harmsworth professor in 1973–74, also made a profound impression upon me. Mary Ellison at Keele University and Charles Crowe at the University of Georgia guided my graduate research while allowing me the freedom that I needed. To these teachers—and to all my teachers—I give thanks.

Index

Disenfranchisement *(continued)*
schools, 219; mass, 137; as measure of
control, 272; proposals of Democratic
Party for, 172; race relations and, 183;
in state constitutions, 312
Dittmer, John, 381–382
Dixon, John C., 305, 318
Douglass, Frederick, 82, 389
Du Bois, W. E. B., 20, 82, 105, 162, 328–
329, 389; attack on NAACP, 332; at-
tacks on philanthropic foundations,
327; on black college graduates, 167; at
Fisk University, 165–166; opposition to
industrial education, 249–250; racial-
ism of, 334; religious skepticism of,
165; on sexual exploitation of black
women, 238
Dudley, James B., 172
Duke Endowment Fund, 212
Dunbar, J. C., 384
Duncan, Catherine J., 342
Dunton, L. M., 91

East St. Louis, Missouri, race riot, 326
Eberhart, G. L., 64
Edwards, Susie, 208
Edwards, William J., 189, 199, 202–204,
207–208, 209, 210, 246
Eisenhower, Dwight D., 371, 373
Elections: of 1868, 53; of 1872, 53, 71; of
1874, 54, 86; of 1876, 54–55; of 1878,
55; of 1883, 104; blacks prevented from
voting, 53
Elliott, Charles W., 215
Elliott, Rev. G. M., 8, 10
Ellison, Ralph, 16, 489n13
Embree, Edwin, 329
Engs, Robert, 122
Episcopal church, 69, 70, 92, 106, 209.
See also African Methodist Episcopal
(AME) denomination; Colored Method-
ist Episcopal Church (CME); Methodist
Episcopal Church (MEC)
Equal salaries campaign, 343, 344–345,
368; black teachers and, 346; black
teachers associations and, 347, 351;
conciliation versus litigation debates,
347–349; lack of black support for,
347–348; lawsuits, 309–311, 345–346,
348–349, 350–351; Marshall and, 344;

of NAACP, 309–310, 311; white opposi-
tion to, 346, 350
Evans, Walter P., 209, 210, 211
Evers, Medgar, 385

Facen, Anthony C., 244, 259
Fair Employment Practices Committee
(FEPC), 417
Farmer-teachers, 129–130
Faulkner, R. L., 52–53, 436n60
Favrot, Leo M., 249, 250, 319–320, 328,
329, 331
Fayetteville Normal School, North
Carolina, 476n46
Fayetteville State University, North
Carolina, 86
Ferguson, Washington, 233
Fields, Mamie Garvin, 156
First World War, 207; black discontent
following, 327; black veterans of, 326,
327; effect on teachers' salaries, 226;
teacher shortage following, 226; treat-
ment of black soldiers in France, 326,
329
Fisk University, Tennessee, 7, 51, 63, 120,
153, 165–166, 326; entry standards,
153; GEB funding for, 327; Jubilee
Singers, 206; research on black education at, 302–303, 324; student strikes
at, 326
Fitzgerald, Cornelia, 292
Fitzgerald, Mary Pauline, 277
Fitzgerald, Robert, 41–42, 112, 129, 277,
292
Fleming, Cynthia G., 383
Fleming, Walter L., 49, 57
Flora, A. C., 283, 323
Florida, 81, 186, 188; black teachers associations in, 321; decline in number of
black principals, 403; equal salaries
campaign, 349; lack of normal schools
in, 168; levels of black teacher education in, 224; merger of teachers associations in, 408, 409; merit system in, 351,
487n65; normal schools in, 141; Republican Party in, 55; segregation protests,
377; universities, 12
Florida A&M (State Colored Normal
School), 170, 314, 377
Fortune, T. Thomas, 82–83, 173

and white teachers, 309; equal salaries campaign in, 348; itinerant teachers, 112; lack of normal schools, 168; land grant colleges, 182; length of school terms, 323; level of education of black teachers, 368; merger of teachers associations, 409, 410; normal schools in, 86, 141, 171, 182; opposition to black education, 143, 144; preference of blacks for black teachers, 61; preparations for integration, 394–395; public schools, 38, 50, 210, 216; race relations, 379; Republican Party in, 61; research on black education, 324; response to *Brown* decision, 366; salaries of black teachers, 128, 322, 498n36; school closing exercises in, 114; school protests in, 404; "secret schools," 31; segregation in, 81; sit-ins in, 373; standard of certification, 127–128; standards for teaching candidates, 103–104; state agent of Negro schools, 318, 323; state funding of schools, 89; subscription schools, 116; superintendents of education, 438n69; suspensions of students, 397; tax revenues for black schools, 144; teacher certification in, 275; white teachers from the South, 64; white teachers replaced by black teachers, 81
North Carolina Association of Educators, 407–408
North Carolina A&T College, 379
North Carolina College for Negroes, 363
North Carolina Federation of Colored Women's Clubs, 239
North Carolina State College for Negroes, 333
North Carolina State Teachers Association (NCSTA; formerly North Carolina Colored Teachers Association), 180, 239, 312, 318, 401
Northern aid societies, 35, 39–40, 72; control over employment of black teachers, 83; employment of blacks by, 82; establishment and support of schools by, 101, 138; funding for black schools, 45; training of black leaders, 81
North Louisiana Agricultural and Industrial Institute, 205

Oliver, Edmond Jefferson, 287–288, 289, 383
Oliver, John, 43
Orangeburg, South Carolina, student movement, 378
Orfield, Gary, 416
Orr, Gustavus, 56
Oswego Normal School, New York, 154
Otey, Charles N., 105–107
Otis, J. R., 378
Owen, Robert, 428n12

Palmer, Alice Freeman, 213, 214, 215
Palmer, Lutrelle F., 346, 486n58
Palmer Memorial Institute, 212–213, 215–217, 220, 228
Palmetto Education Association (PEA), 382, 409
Palmetto State Teachers Association, South Carolina, 324, 348
Parent-teacher associations. *See* Black schools: PTAs; PTAs
Park, Robert E., 362
Parker, Arthur Harold, 267, 268–272, 341
Parker, Judge John J., 345
Parker High School, Alabama, 267, 292, 388
Parks, Rosa, 377
Paterson, William B., 90, 489n13
Patterson, Frederick D., 358, 489n13
Peabody, George Foster, 329
Peabody Education Fund, 451n10, 469n49
Pestalozzi, Johann Heinrich, 154
Pettiford, Rev. W. R., 268
Phelps Stokes, Mrs. Anson, 208
Phelps-Stokes Fund, 14, 205, 208, 327, 381, 469n49
Philanthropic foundations, 14, 23, 121–122, 173, 174, 181, 194, 324–325, 330; black leadership and, 328–329, 332; black public schools and, 254; black teachers associations and, 317, 318–319; decline in contributions, 206–207; failure to criticize segregation, 325; funding for black schools, 250; goal of progress without conflict, 327–328; industrial education and, 304; scholarships granted by, 318–319; support of